HYDR②LITH

SURREALIST RESEARCH
&
INVESTIGATIONS

Hydrolith 2: Surrealist Research and Investigations.

Front cover image by John Adams
Title page image by Alexandra Halkias: "She Spirits 2"
Back cover image by Miguel Corrales

Many thanks to the following for their
editorial advice, suggestions and/or proofreading:

John Adams, Hugh Behm-Steinberg, Mary Behm-Steinberg,
Séamas Cain, Chuck Fahrenbach, Parry Harnden,
Dale Houstman, Richard Misiano-Genovese,
Noé Ortega Quijano, Laurens Vancrevel, Rick Waara.

Copyright © 2014
ISBN: 978-0-578-15792-4

Additional copies of this book can be ordered from LuLu:
http://www.lulu.com

Oyster Moon Press is a non-profit, surrealist publishing co-op that
originated in Berkeley, California.

OYSTER
MOON
PRESS

www.oystermoonpress.com

Table of Contents

Chymical Preface 7

Bruno Jacobs: *Surrealism and the Cultural Sphere* 9

Beatriz Hausner: *The Secret Life of Plants* 11

Ribitch: *Storytelling, Subversion and the Pure Language of Children* 15

Ali Mete Sancaktaroðlu: *Collages* 19

Peter Dubé: *To Call the Fair People to Your Aid and Succor* 20

Seéamas Cain: *The Geography of Surrealist Revolt* 21

Jean-Clarence Lambert: *The Anti-Legend of Our Age* 23

Surrealist Survival Kits 27

The Surrealist Group of Madrid: *Chronical of the Object Event* 44

Hans Plomp: *Keyhole to Other Realities* 51

Turkish Surrealist Group: *Revolt: The Game of the New Millennium* 53

Eugenio Castro: *The Sun Rises at Night: Sketches of the 2011 Revolt of Madrid* 55

Sol Lycantrophes: *The Dangers of Puerilizing the Movement* 63

Rafet Arslan: *The 21st Century Resists the 20th Century* 65

St. Louis Surrealist Group: *Ferguson 2014* 70

Antonio Ramírez: *Dead Time* 71

Inner Island Surrealist Group: *Funeral of Empire Manifesto* 74

Will Alexander: *The Density Paintings* 75

Merl Fluin: *In Praise of Infighting* 99

Eric Bragg: *Infighting Is Miserabilist and Stupid* 101

Josse De Haan: *Frozen Moonlight in Two Hands* 111

Andrew Torch: *Winter Poem* 116

Dale Houstman: *Biased History* 117

Rodrigo Hernández: *Lamentations of the Ludopath* 118

Wijnand Steemers: *Mosquito Prayers: a Manifesto* 120

Richard Misiano-Genovese: *Skull Castle: The Last Bastion* 122

Alexandra Halkias: *One Day in the Year of a Box* 125

Yannis Xourias: *Poems* 126

Josie Malinowski: *The Practice of the Night* 128

John Adams: *Poems* 133

Rafet Arslan: *Poems* 134

Saint Louis Group: *Q&A* 136

John Adams: *Velocity* 138

Sotère Torregian: *Three Poems* 139

Peter Dubé: *To Make Your Voice Heard in Other Worlds* 145

Zuca Sardan: *Primordial Egg* 146

Hans Plomp: *The Beast Is Loose* 147

Peter Dubé: *To Know a Distant Happening* 148

Laurens Vancrevel: *The Demon of Paradise: A Dantesque Dream* 149

Nikos Stabakis: *The Mysteries of the Minotaur* 154

Pieter Schermer: *The Rendez-vous* 157

Richard Misiano-Genovese: *The Eternal Return-Fire for Fire* 167

Andrew Joron: *To the Third Power* 169

Dale Houstman: *Three Poems* 172

Gaétan Blais & David Nadeau: *Two Poems* 176

Dan Stanciu: *Warm Acts* 177

Javier Gálvez: *The Veiled Language* 179

David Nadeau & Pascale Dubé: *Collages* 182

J. Karl Bogartte: *The Poetic Method* 184

Eugenio Castro, Vicente Gutiérrez Escudero & Noé Ortega: *The Language to Come* 189

Merl Fluin: *Lord Peter in the City of Jackdaws* 192

Rafet Arslan: *Flight Surgery* 194

Ayşe Özkan: *Cyclops* 197

Surrealist London Action Group: *Mutus Liber* 199

Paul Cowdell: *Every Man His Own Fantômas: Or, Away with Nostalgia* 205

Paul Bogaers: *A Further Investigation into the Photography of Thoughts* 206

Richard Waara: */ Cubomania* 209

Jesús Garcia Rodríguez: *30 Proverbs of the Dessert Fathers* 210

Sergio Lima: *The Image as Knowledge* 211

Rik Lina: *The Cheerful Chaos of Collective Automatic Invention* 213

Cins: *Monster* 216

Her de Vries: *Photographs* 217

Noé Ortega Quijano: *Suicidal Objects* 218

Richard Misiano-Genovese: *The Conceptualizations of Imagery and the Introduction of Cruelty* 223

Sergio Lima: *Images of Liberty* 226

Sasha Vlad: *Object Magic Revealed in a Dream* 228

Miguel de Carvalho: *The Collage: An Amalgamation of Ideas as a Method of Self-Definition* 230

Vicente Gutiérrez Escudero: *Defending Useless Aspects of Urban Objectology* 232

Sotiris Liontos: *In Pulverem Mortis* 234

Josie Malinowski: *Inner Animals: An Introduction* 236

Wijnand Steemers: *Poems* 238

Sharon Olson: *The Healer* 240

Hande Koçak: *Triology along with Eluard* 242

María Santana & Antonio Ramírez: *The Unexpected Object* 246

Xtian: *The Micturating Angel* 249

Pierre Petiot: *For a Surrealist Use of Technology* 264

Parry Harnden: *We Live in Simple Times* 269

José Manuel Rojo: *Consequences of the Misuse of Electricity* 273

Eric Bragg: *Epigenetics and the Mad-Genius* 283

John Barrett Erickson: *Micro-Seizures and Missed Apprehensions* 327

Michael Löwy: *Dues Ex Machina* 330

José Manuel Rojo: *Reality of Revolt, Reasons for Utopia* 332

Michael Löwy: *José Carlos Mariategui and Surrealism* 343

Ali Kartal: *Deja Vu Nightmares* 345

Noé Ortega Quijano & Eugenio Castro: *Allucinatio Insulae* 346

Ribitch: *String Stories* 349

Chymical Preface

This second issue of *Hydrolith* is a continuation of what the first volume started, which was and is to assemble a stimulating selection of exclusively recent work by groups and individuals of the international Surrealist movement, to facilitate intellectual exchange and collaboration, enabling us to concentrate the echoes of our commonalities as well as the shadows of our differences. In so doing, this volume aspires to reduce all manner of distances that exist between us. All works in this book are in English, while many of them are translations from the Dutch, French, Greek, Portuguese, Romanian, Spanish and Turkish languages.

When comparing the editorial structures of the two volumes, we might say that both are *experiments in organizing* (at least organization to the extent that people from different cultural backgrounds might come together to work on a project), such that the first issue was informally modeled after the peer-review strategy as is found in many professional and academic settings today, with six of us as editors, using an online forum to reach consensus with regards to editorial decisions. While such a strategy was effective enough to gradually nudge the project to a state of completion, it was both time-consuming and socially challenging. The experimental strategy for this second volume, however, differs from its predecessor in that the editorial structure was far more decentralized, with whatever groups and collectives making their own editorial decisions about what to include, with a selected liaison for each group to interact with yours truly in order to put the issue together. It remains to be indicated, particularly by our readers, which (or neither) of these two approaches is the more desirable. But regardless of the ultimate effectiveness of each, our goal has always been to make a collection of current surrealist work whose inclusion was the result of several minds working together, rather than just one.

As with the previous issue of *Hydrolith*, three main themes have been chosen – initially suggested by the group liaisons – for this second volume: Science, Utopia and Monsters. Although material for these themes hasn't been thoroughly partitioned as one might expect to find with distinct chapters in a book, they are instead loosely clustered together, perhaps even with a little bit of overlap between them, as one might imagine.

So in light of these considerations, as alchemists of the sublime, and while renewed in solidarity, we surrealists gather here with our marvelous water stones and unmarked vials of poetic elixirs, searching to uncover the means to restore to human context all that remains hidden within the shadow's shadow, as well as to confront that which lurks under the veil of miserabilism and boredom. We take this moment to affirm that surrealism is not just one idea or one inspiration or one action, but a world of ideas, thoughts, refusals, inspirations, playful musings, actions and great poetic potential. While we as surrealists, as a loosely organized collective, may not always agree how best to deal with the contemporary drudgery and misery of late capitalism, which also includes the global, ongoing ecological crisis, it should be the overall vision of and commitment to *revolution*, to the radical transformation of life and reality and all the inbetweens, that brings us together and which should remind us more about what we have in common rather than what sets us apart from each other. In this sense we declare our agreement with the signatories of that surrealist manifesto from 1974, "Lighthouse of the Future", when they stated that,

> "Pessimism exists only to be carried as far as it will go... Whatever else we may be, we are not mourners of false steps along the endless escalators of lost time... Life is boring, society is boring, art is boring; above all, boredom is boring... Only by despairing, and then despairing of despair, can mankind begin truly to *see* and to act consciously in the service of the marvelous. This preliminary violation of the rules prepares the way for an entirely new game, our game, known as subversion, sublime love, the exaltation of freedom..."*

Therefore we affirm, 40 years later, that capitalist boredom is still impossibly boring (especially now in its "wireless" iteration), adding also that pessimism in itself is boring, and that *Hydrolith 2* is no less than a contribution to that "entirely new game" anticipated by some as subversion, mad love and freedom. Isn't it time for a change?

Ribitch & Eric Bragg
October 31, 2014

---

* "Manifesto: Lighthouse of the Future". *City Lights Anthology*. City Lights Books: San Francisco. 1974. Pp. 203-6.

Alex Januário - *Collage*

Surrealism and the Cultural Sphere

Bruno Jacobs

When I hear the word "culture" I see plowed fields, oxes,
a lark and a beautiful peasant woman.
— Louis Scutenaire

The surrealist movement's relationship with the cultural sphere has been ambiguous from the beginning for the simple reason that it has prioritized certain interventions in areas that also are central to the prevailing cultural domain. It has therefore been possible, both within and outside surrealism, to perceive the movement as a *more or less radical* opposition or alternative to established culture, rather than to the broader foundations of bourgeois society, which constitutes its real raison d'être.

It is of course not culture in its general, let us say more popular and positive meaning we have in mind, rather its formal expression as institution, as means of consumption, in other words as a *pretext*. It is thereby characteristic that this ambiguity between culture in general and its formalized expression, with all its economic and ideological interests, its elites, bureaucracy and norms, is willingly being maintained precisely from these quarters with the confusion that follows. It is namely a matter of appropriating what can be profitable in one way or another and ignoring everything else that cannot be used or which simply does not fit in. This somehow self-functioning cultural public sphere has rather grand pretensions, namely to administer and mediate a field of human activity that still enjoys a considerable prestige, while it in reality, as we know, it eclecticizes, fetishizes and transforms it into commodities. The cultural sphere may look as if it were spreading and stimulating important human preoccupations and activities, but rather it parasitizes and contradicts such activities. To a large extent the cultural sphere begins where the ongoing, living processes end, even if its mediating action tends in turn to conquer and even govern those. There are of course strong interests in using the ambiguity between culture in its general meaning and the much narrower cultural domain. The latter is exemplified by union bureaucracy – as a basically bourgeois agent – in relationship with the employees and their interests. Today it is an integrated and very important part of the dialectics of domination (its carrot, the indispensable complement of the whip) and of the global spectacle, the current form of that economic, social, political, cultural and mental domination to whose logic it obeys. In a certain way it looks like a beautified conscience of the prevailing system with its deaf brutality.

In a society that, in the name of democracy (which, as we know, is a pretext for all sorts of crimes), implemented a centralization and monopolization of political and economic power, as well as a growing control of everything and everyone, the cultural sphere cannot be anything but a form of integration (however "human" you want) of the ideology of the system in the dialectic of domination. It becomes, thus, a crucial element of contemporary society that expands the process of mental domestication: if very large parts of today's culture are confused with entertainment, it is because they also have become products or goods. In this way, the entire cultural sphere, in parallel with the government system of cultural grants, has been invaded by business and advertising, infected by sponsors chasing prestige, and with capitalist speculation. This is largely an exploitation consented to by many of the exploited, because the practice of unpaid labor has become widespread, which is being accepted for the "pleasure" that it provides and for the prestige that it brings. It is clear that the ideological paradigms and mechanisms of the cultural sphere cannot be separated from those of bourgeois society in general, even if the former is confused with pretentious values such as tolerance or "humanism", for example, that cultivate certain nice prospects which generally are abstract and harmless and which, indeed, function only as a mere cosmetic alternative – when they are not pure hypocrisy – with respect to the operating principles and real pragmatism. Hence we have these very pronounced although vague illusions, in connection with the cultural domain as a counterpoint to the ruling capitalist cynicism and exploitation, as a *consolation* for the brutality of a basically inhumane global system.

While the first surrealists always had by definition strong suspicions and felt hostility toward the cultural sphere (or toward academia, for that matter) which moreover didn't have the role nor the prevalence that it shows off today, they often participated in it. In the beginning, the surrealists adopted tactics and carried out interventions in a context where the cultural sphere was to a large extent an ambiguous space of effervescence, of high dynamics and research – we are speaking of an epoch strongly marked by the Russian Revolution and by the revolt against the values of an imperialist world responsible for the slaughter of the first World War. Over time, especially after World War II, due to a lack of ideological and political focus, certain surrealists sometimes acted ambiguously, both within the surrealist movement and in their own public interventions. The opposition became diluted or fragmented and could assume an air of reformist illusion. It is not so remarkable for a poorly defined will to use the system to spread surrealism's radical and divergent perspectives, while confused with vague hopes or the naive temptation to be able to influence the system.

It is about understanding the nature and functioning of the cultural sphere and, consequently, maintaining a clear distance from it.

Except for those early, obvious career opportunists like Salvador Dalí and his commercial and media eccentricity, a number of much lesser known surrealists have been able to use their presence in the movement and the "surrealist" label to let themselves be reduced to providing the established culture with fitting, more or less piquant artists, writers or cultural personalities. Others have felt but little resistance to the appeal of official recuperation; even the best can suffer from vanity or from being attracted by certain rewarding opportunities.

A decisive element in this problematique is the idea, on one hand, of surrealism as a kind of "counterculture", and, on the other, the hypothesis that there could truly exist any surrealist art, any surrealist poetry, any surrealist cinema or any surrealist music for example – a conception of the cultural domain – which implies the risk of assuming a certain aesthetics, of a certain style, i.e. of a kind of *school*. It is clear that surrealist tendencies were developed in these fields as reflections of an elemental spirit. But it is also exactly what the cultural specialists want in their effort to catalogue, vulgarize and ultimately to control and castrate.

Almost all kinds of activity and creativity – even surrealist activity – with the passage of time, risk being appropriated, deformed and reduced to mere aesthetics by the cultural sphere. Thus a whole surrealist *culture* – an entire past – had accumulated over the course of eight decades but which now is not necessarily congruent with current surrealist activity due to changing political and – precisely – cultural circumstances and needs. Surrealism, despite all of its earlier practices and traditions, continues to be found somewhere else, as was already asserted in the 20's and again in the 70's.

Surrealism today needs to take advantage of fruitful, critical cultural tendencies and phenomena that are not necessarily isolated from its own context. Its intervention would otherwise be limited and would lose its essence as a catalyst. But this does not mean that it needs to intervene or maintain a presence in the cultural sphere, even in their lower strata, so to speak, as this would inevitably result in "losing its soul" by way of making an unforgivable commitment to the establishment.

Surrealism does not constitute any sort of alternative culture that, at worst, only adepts or specialists – whoever those may be – can acknowledge and define. Surrealism continues to be a matter of principles, of method, of spirit, and of attitude in order to definitively change the actual scandalous state of things, in order to fundamentally change life. Its principal characteristics remain, basically, to harmonize critical thought with the poetic spirit, reflection with sensitization to the marvelous. In this sense surrealism is indeed also a tradition that follows a number of specific red threads that extend over the centuries. It is the reason why Belgian surrealist Paul Nougé declared in 1945 that "surrealism does not exist", in other words, incorporating a strong relativisation of its effects and results in favour of its purposes and lively activity.

But it is in any case not a question of confusing independence with separatism or a kind of exaggerated "occultation" of surrealist activity, nor to defend any "purity", let alone any kind of self-pity, but rather to sharpen and clarify appropriate assumptions and orientations, as well as effective ways of interventions in relation with all this. Today's surrealism can only be further developed through openness and exchange. One thing persists, however, in the current state of things, which remains humanely unacceptable, and which Arthur Rimbaud stated more than a century ago: *True life is absent*.

(Translated by the Author; revised by Eric Bragg & Noé Ortega)
Originally published in *El Rapto* #6, Madrid, 2011.

The Secret Life of Plants

[selected pieces]

Beatriz Hausner

The Great Big Empty

The room to the right of the entrance, the one no one would ever know about, was meant to house her emptiness. There was nothing there but her heart-shaped body with the large cavity inside her belly. It represented her sadness and kept changing sizes, though its shape remained static, as if it were meant to be eternal. All those whose purpose in life was to advise her insisted that the size of that empty part of hers was temporary. They were mostly women, those who thought that way, women who served the Goddess, secret ruler of the world, whose power rested in her understanding that impermanence was the truth of nature.

In her darkest moment she thought this to herself: that large empty hole inside her, it was her womb, the very one that had held her daughter once, when germination and birthing filled her life.

Household Gods

The sitting room seemed suddenly feral, as if all the inhabitants had turned themselves inside out, because the hair seemed to dominate their physiognomy. It was night time and even the man who held the keys to the house was up, sleepless and upright, contemplating the strange plant that was growing in the middle of the corridor. He wondered out loud about the origin of this species. He guessed that the bulbous vegetal object might well be a new incarnation of the god *Tutunus*, whose properties the early Christians abhorred, but whose immense usefulness to the women at that domicile had proven itself over and over again in the course of time. The mistress of the house looked in through the door. She, like her shadows, had transformed herself into a Maine Coon cat, the dominant breed, known throughout the neighborhood for a torrid, though damaging affair with Raccoon Man. Notwithstanding the background information and the layers and layers of meaning contained in this scene, all the owner of the house at Rue du Château could utter was this: "Here is my double, coming undone, gender neutral, at the most inappropriate of times." No one else in the room heard her say the loaded words, for it was accepted knowledge that they were willing participants in the secret life of plants.

L. Th. Lehmann

When he enters the room we sense magic under his hat. A flame will light up at any moment from the end of the walking stick he now uses as a prop, as if to defy the pull of the mother calling us back to a stronger centre.

He is participating in the fair with his Alida, modern vestal of the temple where we carry on with the projects of our precedents, priests mostly, prone to defying the possibilities of renewal within the strictures they inherited from the fathers and their daughters.

Louis has not changed. He remains the same man who visited our house at Rue du Château while the war raged outside the sanctuary. It was here that he convened in secret with Theo, Emile and Chris, first-named spirits of his youth: They carried the flame while all else hung on the balance. There were the boxing matches, the poems, and the drawings, which an invisible hand saved from destruction, before he retreated into his alternate occupation.

For years, the experts say, he spent his days digging deep in the waters of the Mediterranean, searching inside ship carcasses, which other wars had downed, naval battles against the enemies of Theodora, centuries ago. "There was the problem of Byzantium," he says in that throaty accent the compatriots of Spinoza have of inflecting their vowels, "and later, the imposition of barnacles on wood, as depicted in some film or other." His voice trails off, as he shifts his gaze to another time, seeing, once again, the detail of a head carved into a leaden anchor brought up from the sea floor. "On the beach," he continues, "I find the stories that began all the stories, *The Odyssey*, *The Epic of Gilgamesh*, the whole lot."

I know what he is speaking of, like the ones who will take our place in the future; his is the home of the mind, where he walks light, "prospecting, pursued by the rattle of glass, the clip-clop of hooves," at home everywhere the music of the seas will carry him.

As I receive him into my open arms, I hear him utter these words: "I'd say that the white Goddess was in this."

*Texts quoted from L. Th. Lehmann's *Frequently Adrift* and from Captain J.Y. Cousteau's *The Silent World*.

Life Blood

I. Vita Exsanguis

She had been in the house for some time, unmoving, still, sometimes close to death, though she carried on with the things and chores they call home life. Once the movers had left, she pondered long and hard whether to unpack the objects that had survived the shipwreck of her previous life. They resembled the artifacts of those museums of the past century, the ones that had not undergone the clinical revisions that drain the energy out of living spaces.

Despite everything, hers were objects that merited careful cataloguing. She had decided that, if ever it were to happen, these artifacts would necessitate a new archiving method, a classification system not derived from existing ones, the ones used in repositories that held such objects. They too, she felt, had been rendered lifeless by excessive revision.

First there would be the image, like this one: every image, regardless of its content, contained clues to inform the system she had set out to invent.

News of a total solar eclipse, which was sweeping across a narrow swathe of Asia, reminded her that, always when working with the parts that informed the whole, one of those parts would eclipse the other, as in the illustration at hand, and much as plants do in secret. It is a well-known fact that the obscuring of one object by another allows previously invisible parts of said object to become visible. This, she understood to be an essential aspect of her work as a classificationist.

II. Blood Count

It was no sooner than she had finished laying out this aspect of the system, when the image came out of its frame and began to envelope her. She had not counted on the objects being alive, so that this sudden change in the situation caught her by surprise. Powerless to control her environment, she surrendered to it, became relaxed, accepting, open. The plant represented there now took her by the throat, separated her legs so that her sex was slightly exposed. It was a male plant. This she knew because of its strength and also because his bulbous member exuded a scent, at once familiar and foreign. She raised her arms to indicate submission to his power and closed her eyes.

III. Transfusion

Though the image would have one believe otherwise, she was supine. His forceful grip held her in place, forcing her to go in and out of reverie. She liked this state, for it allowed his tongue to speak for hers.

"Finished is finished, and dead is dead" he had said, when she described the end of the life of raccoon-man, killed as he was and lying there, intact, though lifeless, on the curb of the street.

She acquiesced to his words and accepted the truth. She opened her eyes, as the vegetal presences retreated into the frame. The world went back to its usual order. As she got up to leave the room, a voice was heard singing these familiar lyrics:

And I'm thinking about the love that you laid on my table.

I told you not to wander 'round in the dark...

Yes, I told you that the light goes up and down...

The Orgasms Suite

This was the most recondite, yet most favored set of rooms in the house. There were many details, but she preferred their mystery, as opposed to full disclosure and description. This much was certain: the orgasms were strictly his, each different in form from the other. Sometimes they were liquid skin. Other times the orgasms were like the murmur of the universe, a constant flow of cum. When explosive, on rare occasions, and only in unexpected geographic locations, his abdomen rippled with his pleasure, which she always considered hers, as it required her to open up his emotions, a letting-go of his beings, ghostly and not.

The Beginning of Language

Written on the walls of the vestibule of the house at Rue du Chateau was this quotation from Ovid's *Fasti*:

When the night has passed by and heaven first begins

To blush and birds warble touched by the dew,

And the sleepless traveler rests his half-burnt torch...

Strangely, and though she had passed it thousands of times, she had never taken care to read its content, assuming it was written in a language different from hers. It was a language of images and symbols, which only now, after a long period of transition had passed, she was able to understand.

Its welcoming message, the languorous tonalities of the Latin voice coming through the English, gave the poetry a feeling of the eternal, and reminded her of Rimbaud's "Vowels."

There was much in the string of words, including the relevance of dates, the beginnings of months and years of happiness that announced themselves.

She felt suddenly at home in the world, perhaps for the first time in several eternities, and thanked the invisible hand that had etched the revelation on the wall. She took it in and said to herself: "April 2, day of angels."

Wedgwood Steventon - *Arcadia - post industrial landscape*

Storytelling, Subversion and the Pure Language of Children

Ribitch

"It is the duty of the catalyst/instructor to stir up the life force in all students, the seventy-year old as well as the fifteen-year old, so that inner circulation is activated. Even if it is for a fleeting moment that they see a wider possibility, it is the first opening to a freedom that soars beyond the harried routine of debility."
–Will Alexander, "Igniting the Inward Prodigy" (1)

Storytelling, the ancient art of the elders: stories told in words, pictographs on cave walls, or beads and shells woven into an African fishing net, they transported us into the marvelous and into the uncharted realms of our imagination. I remember, with great fondness, when as a child listening to old radio shows on my little crystal radio, late at night after I was put in bed, I would thrill to stories that filled me with awe and fear. Preeminent among them were shows like *Inner Sanctum, Arch Obler's Lights Out* and *The Shadow*. These stories filled the darkness with wondrous visions and opened doors and windows to worlds of my own imagination. These visions would persist long after the program was over, entering my dreams, where the adventures would continue with myself as the protagonist. I would long for these stories with great anticipation and experience profound disappointment when their popularity had run its course, replaced by television. Television did not escape me as a child, I was a child of that generation after all, but I found that the visual presentation of stories on television lacked the kind of sublime visions I could come up with on my own. I also found great enjoyment in the company of a few elder storytellers, who regaled me with tales that were part true and part exaggerated. One tale amuses me today: an elder man lived across the street from my mother; I was about twelve, and he was one-hundred years of age and still quite spry, and his eyes sparkled like a mischievous elf. He told tall tales of his days working in the movie studios of Hollywood. I never tired of the story of how he and a couple friends borrowed the King Kong model from the studio one night, and drove around Hollywood with the great ape sitting in the rumble seat. He was a veteran of WWI and had been mustard-gassed, which messed up his lungs. The Government had promised him that he would be taken care of. He went to his grave fighting for what they promised him, but never saw a dime. His distrust of the government was passed on to me as was his love of telling a tall tale.

When I became a father, I found myself becoming the storyteller, recognizing the same look in my two sons' eyes filled with the same wonder and curiosity that I must have had at that age. I could chicken-lip (2) all day long. With my discovery of surrealism, in particular surrealist games, I began playing them with my two sons and their friends. These games served as an agent of bonding. Their childhood imaginations took to the games and that sense of collective play has remained deeply influential in their own lives and relationships. The more we played them, the more convinced I became that these surrealist games had great subversive potential that could be applied within a school environment: to liberate young imaginations from the mundane miserablist images of television and advertising campaigns that had robbed them of the pure language of childhood, the only voice that would open the doors into the marvelous. It would be several more years before I got a chance to put that into practice.

My first opportunity to work within the schools came when I was asked to give a lecture on poetry at a local high school. This was shortly after my return from a visit to Chicago, with the surrealist group there. I was mentally charged after several months of intense conversation and collective activities. So I jumped at the chance to speak to a group of high school kids. I prepared a fiery presentation, full of spit and vinegar. I accused the educational system of dumbing down and subverting the minds of youth into a submissive, fall-in-line, don't-question-authority mindset. I spoke for nearly an hour, answered some questions, all the while I observed the principal had entered the room and stood at the back, his arms crossed and the look on his face certainly not one of being pleased. I left the school unaware of what was to happen next. It was a couple years later I found out from the teacher who had me in to speak, that after I had left, during the following week the students had seized a wall on the school campus and painted a mural, the teacher was promptly fired, and no more surrealists were to be invited to speak. The teacher was not angry with me for getting her fired; in fact she thanked me, as it too liberated her from a controlling teaching position and eventually brought her to a school that allowed her the space to be controversial and free to present to students ideas not controlled by the mainstream.

My next opportunity to work with kids came by chance. I was at the time living in San Diego trying to make just enough money to survive. I tried busking, playing my guitar in the park. Needless to say I was not that good at it and that did not work very well. My comrade and partner at the time, Sharon Olson, suggested to me that I try storytelling since I like telling stories. To my surprise, storytelling was something that unexpectedly offered me a way to be subversive. I had a story that I told at the end of my set. It was a story about storytelling; a story about listening for a story and telling it to somebody else. It was a story about turning off the television and returning to the oral tradition of storytelling. I gave out invisible story moths to all that were in the audience. I told them to go home, turn off the TV and listen to their story moth, and that the moth would tell them a story. They were then supposed to tell that story to someone else, to their children, to their parents, to their siblings, to a friend or even to a stranger, but the story must be told, because for every star that sits in the sky there is a story to be told, and when a star fell from the sky, it was a story lost. It was a silly little story with its share of corn, but one with an unexpected result. I started having people return, telling me that this one story changed things for them and their families. They did just what I suggested: they went home and turned their televisions off for one night, (some even more) and they started telling stories to each other. My set would consist of one-third traditional folk tales from indigenous peoples, one-third original stories of my own and one-third improvisational stories made up on the spot. With the improvised stories, I discovered that when I told them that the attention of the audience, the children especially, would become acutely sharp. With the level of attention raised, I began to pull a kid or a parent from the audience and make them a character in the story, convincing them to improvise along with me. Now this act of sudden collaboration was picked up by some kids who found no trouble in participating in a random act of silliness. This random act of silliness when engaged in by a parent would bring the children in the audience into gales of laughter at seeing their mother or father act in a way they had never viewed them before. Walls crumble with a bit of humor. What a grown man had thought he put away for more sensible (sic) pursuits, were found again in his child's laughter and in his own.

These weekend performances in the park soon replaced my day job. I began to get small gigs and workshops requested of me. This was much more fun than hammering nails and lifting drywall all day and much more satisfying in a poetic way, as well as in a revolutionary sense. The language of the imagination, when unfettered by the shackles of everyday mendacity, is a powerful weapon indeed. Storytelling, like street theater, offers the tool of language, and if the language is constructed unhindered by expectation, it becomes a point of departure with many roads from which to choose. A character within the Story is chosen by response. A smirk, a grin, a laugh or body posture from the audience would elicit my pulling them into the story. Hecklers were always fair game. At the time I was taking an improv comedy class which showed me many very humorous techniques for dealing with unpleasant people, and the best were those which attempted to bring them up to the front and make them a part of the freak show. One of the most valued parts of the improv comedy class was an introduction to collective theater games that had marvelous surrealist potential. The games used were drawn from *"Improvisation for the Theater,"* by Viola Spolin, a book she created while teaching with the WPA Recreational Project in Chicago. (3) This book would become the guidebook for Second City Theater, whose founder was Viola Spolin's son and the launching ground for many great comics and actors, such as Gilda Radner, John Bulushi, Tom Hanks, Alan Alda, among many others. What I found in Spolin's book was the great potential it had for working with kids (Viola Spolin's original intent) and adapting it with surrealist intent.

I was beginning to get gigs in the schools and small coffee houses in the area, but it was within the schools that I had the most rewarding experiences. The classes were made up of mostly kids from age seven to nine, so the idea of giving the kind of fiery surrealist rant I gave to the high school was out, but surrealist intent does not always have to come with a slap in the face, but a tickle in the ear, a whisper of the marvelous or the doorway left open for dreamers to enter. The poet Paul Eluard once said "the true poet is he who inspires more than he who is inspired." Telling stories was one thing, but I wanted more out of it than performing the way I did in the park. I did not want to entertain them, I wanted to inspire them. This would not happen until my move to Berkeley. San Diego was still very much a military town and very conservative. Several of my friends moved north to the Bay Area looking to escape the miserable institutions situated in that city. I desired collaboration and like-minded collaborators, so San Diego had become, for me, a desert for creativity. I packed up my things, moved into a Dodge van with a Volkswagen welded to the top, painted bright pink with a Ribitch cartoon on the doors, with *Storyteller* emblazoned across the top, and headed north like a gypsy, to tell tales on the streets of Berkeley and San Francisco.

Street performing in the Bay Area was another matter, gone was the big oak tree, and gone was the slow moving and easy to capture audiences that I was able to attract in San Diego. Here people moved with the speed of the flow of espresso. It was sheer madness to do storytelling as street performance.

Every corner had someone talking to themselves, so stories just became another voice floating in the wind with no ears to catch them. An old gypsy storyteller once said, "for every star in the sky there is a story to be told, for every star that falls from the sky it is a story lost because there was no one to tell neither it nor anyone to hear it." At the rate it was going, the sky would soon be empty or I would starve. The Bay Area's storytelling group, which I made great effort to contact, was of no use. I found them to be a stuffy group of traditionalists who had no room for improvisation and experimentation; they even frowned upon my retelling of a couple of Leonora Carrington's tales. A couple of appearances on KPFA radio station, and performances in local theaters, introduced me to a clown by the name of Dr. Mozzarella and his partner, The Cheese. Doc put together shows for kids and worked with the East Bay Center for the Performing Arts. It was through the East Bay Center for the Performing Arts that he taught clowning in Berkeley schools. Doc had been offered a bit part in a movie and he asked me if I would take over his classes. Not being a clown, I was at first reluctant, but he assured me I could make the class what I wanted, a storytelling class in which I was not the performer but a catalyst for children to tell their own stories.

Improvisation, without the hindrance of conscious control, like surrealist use of automatism, opens up new vistas and possibilities into the marvelous. A child's imagination when unhindered by the images of television and products produced by mundane movies gives way to the free flow of a language which belongs as surely to a surrealist sphere as it does to that of the poet. When given the ideas, through surrealist games or games such as Spolin's, the free flow of a child's use of language can have some astounding results. A child is very adaptive at play, a natural state of existence. As a child becomes older, and more and more conditioned by the structures of control, the sense of play is abandoned for more productive pursuits that fit the society's strict and repressive view of a "proper" citizenry, one that follows orders and does not question the status quo, or more plainly put, a citizenry that is devoid of imagination. By the time the child is an adult, he or she is ready to become robotic laborers, consumers, or cannon fodder for the wealthy's senseless war machines. The imagination is placed in a paper bag and shoved under the bed with the dusty memories of youth, never to be looked at again. Why else have all creative activities been stripped from the schools. Kill the imagination, kill the spirit.

I had the chance to explore, at my choice of using both surrealist games and Spolin's theater games in a setting where I could intervene in what I consider the rape of the imagination. Children already possess, without prompting, the highest degree of imagination and when left unfettered by the misery of consumerism, they will create worlds and universes that are unhindered by the miserabilism that surrounds them. Such unbound imaginations just cannot be tolerated. Imaginary friends must be given up for more "profitable" pursuits. After all, they must fit into a society that seeks the enslavement of all creative thought, to be replaced by consumerism and wage slavery, to become people who cannot imagine, who cannot see beyond the horizon. The school system has been reduced to a regimented factory, pumping out the dumbed-down and the hypnotized. The reductions in school programs and reductions in teachers' incomes results in teachers who have to pay for classroom supplies out of their own pockets. Hence, this opportunity to work with kids to inspire their own stories, to pull their imaginations away from the images of television and the consumerist indoctrination to buy the latest toy, the latest video game.

For the first couple of weeks their images were drawn from popular television shows, toys, and a small amount of expected scatological humor. By the time we reached week four, they had become relaxed in their own imaginations and the fruits of the games began to show themselves. During the first few classes, the children would develop a story that they would edit and then present for their recital. The stories were always delightful and well-prepared. The stories lacked the pizzazz that appeared in earlier improvisations, in which a story was totally given over to the moment.

During the last year and the last class that I worked with them, I made up my mind that the final performance was going to be pure improvisation: no filler, no rehearsal, just raw improvisation with all the risks involved. The director of the program came to me and asked for the title of that year's story, and I told her that there was no title, no worked-out story, that they were going on the stage not knowing what they were going to do next. The director was horrified and pleaded with me to put on something solid and rehearsed. I steadfastly said no, that they could do it, and that their finest stories were those that came in the raw. During the weeks preceding the performance, she continued to ask me to change my plan, for fear of embarrassing their parents and themselves. The kids' fear was building as well, for they knew that all the other kids in all the other workshops had their dance steps worked out, their songs memorized, but that they alone had no idea of what they were going to do. Nevertheless, I knew this group of kids had found that poetic dragon, and that it could take them in whichever direction they chose or whichever direction it took them.

On the night of the performance, all nerves were on edge, especially those of the director because she did not trust the pure magic that can be created by being totally and completely in the moment. The parents were nervous because they didn't know what was happening, and the kids were because their time was coming up fast, and for them it was fly or fall.

I lined the eight seven-year-old boys up on the stage; they were nearly pale with fear of the unknown. I turned to the very large audience and explained that what they were about to do was pure improvisation, that they had no idea of what story they were about to tell. There were a few gasps and uncomfortable shifting of seats; the director had her hand over her face trying to escape what she thought was going to be a complete disaster. I asked for three things: a person, a place and a thing. Then I turned to the boys, pointed my finger at one of them, and he began the story. And I then proceeded to randomly point to another, like a conductor leading an orchestra. Each one picked up where the other left off without a single hum or pause, as if the story were being told by just one imagination. The story filled the room, with no one else speaking, and when the story was finished and their voices fell silent, the packed audience erupted with a screaming, stomping, whistling, roaring, standing ovation. The applause went on and on. I would have hated being the act that followed them.

Backstage, I was surrounded by eight boys who had just blown the house down and who knew it. They found a power that they had no idea they had. "We did it, we did," their faces now full of color, their energy like a wildfire. I knew in that moment that this was a revolutionary act. These boys found the power of their own language and that they would not soon forget it, if ever. It was a perfect end to my working with The East

Bay Center for the Performing Arts.

My next gig, working within the schools, came with a call from the San Leandro Arts Council, asking me if I would participate in their Artist-in-the-Schools program. I did one school per day, five classes per school, an hour each till I covered all the schools in the district. One hour was not time enough to attune a full class to improvising, so instead I decided to take some of my digital art prints in, but rather than talking about the art and what it is, I asked them to just tell me a story about what they saw. Again I was amazed and transported by this language of children that was never lacking in surprise and inspiration. I continued that gig for a couple more years, until the economy killed even that.

Why do I tell this story over and over to every artist, poet, musician, actor, circus performer and surrealist I meet? Because we need to fan the flames, keep the embers glowing; we need to set forest fires of the imagination, forest fires that will consume the world and free it from the shackles of the mundane. Why? Because we can ask no less of ourselves in the face of a crisis of the imagination. The preservation and even propagation of THE PURE LANGUAGE OF CHILDREN should be paramount as a revolutionary act. This is a language that is always fresh, when not fettered under the veil of boredom and misery. This is a language not yet poisoned by rules of convention and society's attempt to snuff it out.

Addendum: An old gypsy proverb I heard once went like this: *"for every star in the sky there is a story to be told, for every star that falls from the sky is a story untold."* On Dec. 14, 2012 at 9:30, twenty stars fell from the sky, stories that will never be told. Twenty children and six educators were shot to death by a madman. Following this tragedy, the voices of politicians are raised in the misguided politics as usual, raising the false debate of gun control, instead of looking at the deeper problem within the human condition. Those children were the same age as those I worked with. We must not be led astray by the mouthpieces of Washington, who would desire nothing less than the total crushing of the human spirit. We must demand, under no uncertain terms, the restoration of the imagination to its proper place in the language of children!

Notes:
(1) Will Alexander. *Igniting the Inward Prodigy.* Singing the Magnetic Hoofbeat-Essay Press. 2012.
(2) *Chicken-lip*: a euphemism for telling an extra tall tale. A word coined by my mother, when my son David told her a story about how to prepare chicken lips and that they were a gourmet meal. She listened intently for nearly half an hour when suddenly realized, that she had raised chickens and not a one of them had lips. "Stop chicken-lippin' me," she scolded him. We all had a great laugh.
(3) *Improvisation for the Theater* by Viola Spolin. Northwestern University Press. 3rd edition. 1999.

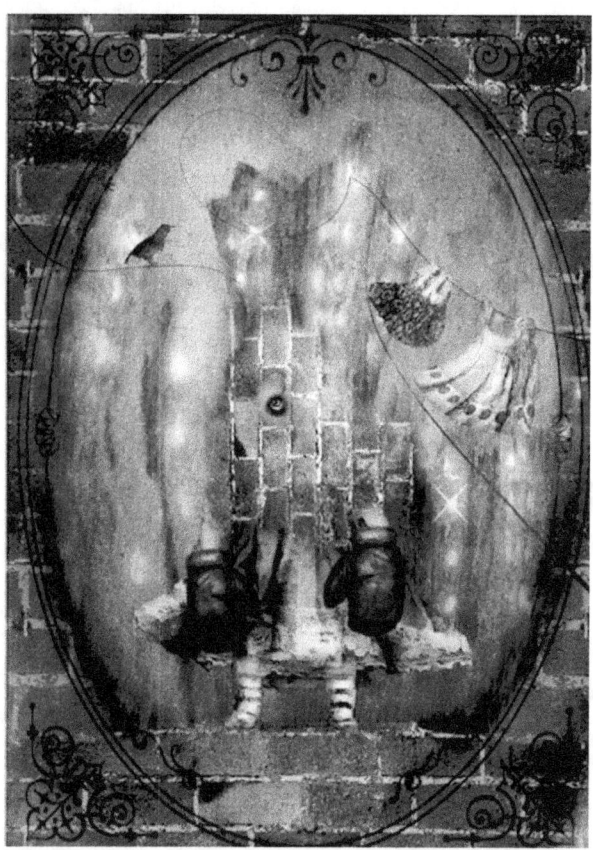

Lisa Simonson - *Boxing Girls*

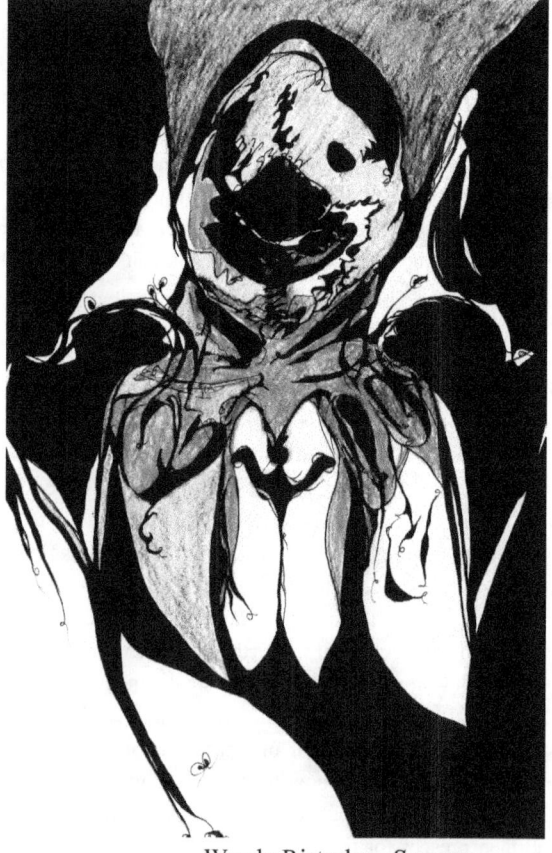

Wendy Risteska - *Synapse*

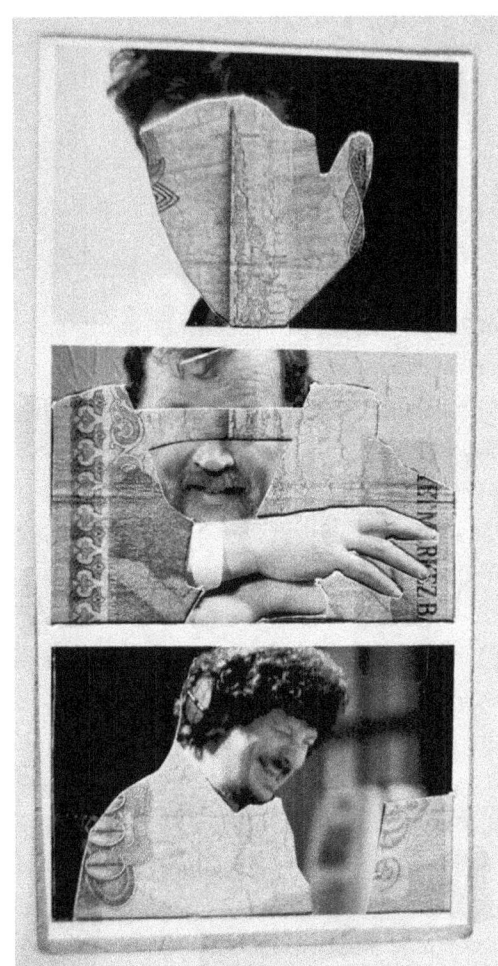
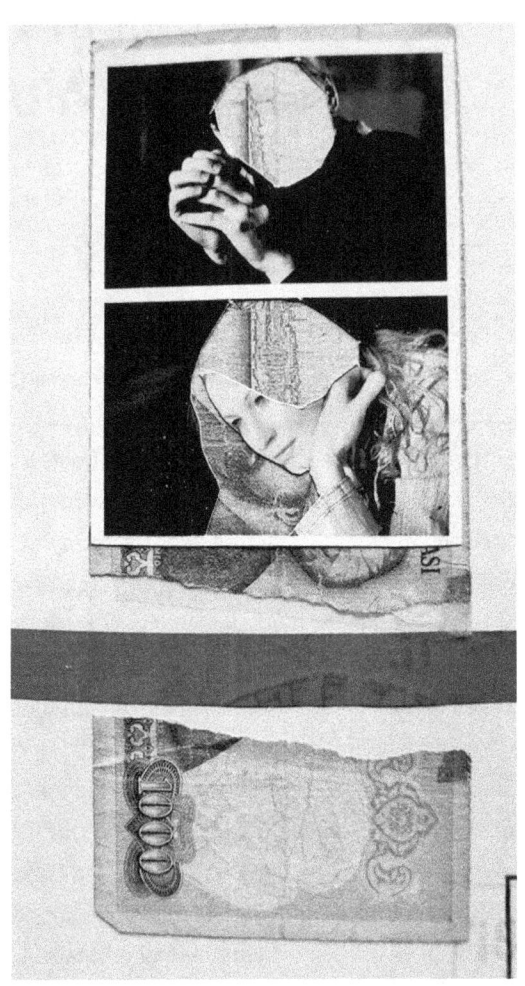

Ali Mete Sancaktaroðlu - *Collages*

To Call the Fair People to Your Aid and Succor

Peter Dubé

Change your name. Change your clothing. Change your habits and your commonplace routines. Change the routes you use to move across the city's warp and weft and change the many tools with which you lay your hands on such conclusions, as you may. Cut your hair, short so as to throw your features into sharp relief, or leave it grow into an unobstructed fall across the eyes, the brow. Change your face – an unshaved beard or artful application of cosmetics, if you will. Alter your posture, and your eagerness. Amend your voice, your faith, your goals and sympathies, and change as well your rhetoric and favoured meals. Undo familiar rituals and sow unease across your days by changing every argument, the political positions on which you speechify, or raise your voice. Breakdown the comfortable framework of your life, be it appearance, stature, job or ideology, your thoughts and all the patterns in them; make yourself anew and grant this newness an open place in which to rise. For they, the little seen and subtle, the deft and mighty all at once, love nothing more than novelty and joy, and nothing less than trepidation. Then let this new, this unanticipated self take space and reach towards its foreign ends: a self that startles you and all a world around. The world that now must change, as you have, shift. The buildings will be quick to take on sharpened lineaments and irregular perspectives; the elevators that ascend therein feel clamorous and odd. In your new skull, a transformed imagination watches, seeking after this: the outlines of your memories made watery, their hues transformed, the lines of their narrations quiver, queer. When you have taken on and grown accustomed to your uncoupled name, a father made of silence and of will will take on ghostly consistency and – specter – move through the prison of the nerves trailing nude revelations in his wake. A friend from early childhood dissolves in rain and swirls in the gutters of your teeth. Laugh to see a livid other self. And classmates careen into a flight of winged things; the breeze that lifts them higher, floral, fine, and with a shudder of the scaled in its uncanny grip. The parks and alleys of an adolescence burn with fire as the empire of djinns erect their monasteries. Laugh. Deep in the throat and moving towards light. Story undoes itself and all the windows in the nervous city clatter. Laugh again. A noise like gamelans and drilling stations on a distant moon conspires with that pack of wild dogs as you display your twice-created face, defined or insurrectionary in the framework of their frames. Laugh. Sweet-talking entropy and reinvention wave to the unfamiliar and watch as in the sudden space now opened by transformation the great invisibles arise from long languishing and draw near. Attracted by the shattered regularity; a cracked delight in their long motionless expanse. Bloated with dizziness they come, assemble round the one to vanquish boredom; give him strength, resources still unknown and knowledge. Now laugh again.

THE GEOGRAPHY OF SURREALIST REVOLT

Séamas Cain

A fisherman's net is a glittering nexus of rays. David Cameron, the Prime Minister of the British Government, enters a wood of plane-trees, and a planted tainted air. "I am a thread in the trees," he says. Birds are paired near a communist witch, who is jutting out from the roof of the cattle stalls. President Barack Obama hurtles at birds. But the President himself hates every witch. Therefore Prime Minister Cameron hurtles at birds. Snails creep into a pool of spilt wine. Mr. Bashar al-Assad, the Dictator of Syria, dawdles with fish-nets and lips. So Mr. Cameron seeks burrowing owls and snakes, tasty as a meat pie or curry. Thus the CIA men and the MI6 men clear land of fence posts and firewood and railroad ties. The land cleared is exploded for cotton.

A lamp causes watery light to flicker. There are slender aspens growing from short fine grass. Prime Minister David Cameron and President Barack Obama reef through slugs, cups, lamps. Mr. Bashar al-Assad holds a long comet-like pole of bound reeds. He waves it back and forth. A statue of Prime Minister Cameron displays the breasts of a weedy shirtmaker, full formed, and powerful thighs stretched forward and covered with a pox of cuplike hollows. "The mouth of the toad coughs out the moon," Mr. Cameron says. The MI5 men and the CIA men, with diabolic Russian shirtmakers, riddle the ground with their burrows. His Grace the Dictator Mr. al-Assad and Prime Minister Cameron waddle like toads and aspens. Slugs grow in slightly salty soil.

The human community, and human effort itself, derive from inexhaustible energies and cataracts of light and life, smothered only by language-depth and depth-language. At no point is this clearer than as regards the inarticulate hunger for the plenitude of freedom, for transcendence in freedom, even for ecstasy and glory in freedom, the psychological within and the without. This urge or longing for freedom and its *true* negative, i.e., the negation of negation, as the double-negative, against Alienation, and against War, exists amongst people to a degree that cannot be ignored.

In this age of "secularization" the only philosophy that can account for both individual and collective hope and *the hope* of this earth simultaneously is neither a philosophy of the Cosmos nor a transcendental philosophy of human "existence," but a *revolutionary* philosophy, a philosophy which takes the *human* socio-economic and political and anti-political dimension seriously, in the way that people understand themselves today.

Indeed, the more our "scientific" technoculture ripens the more it seems to call forth, as a kind of shadow, the mentality of mythus: the dancing god, the harlequin as Christus, the playing child, and the clown-saint. In the modern arts, in the media, in various subcultures, and in revolutionary politics as such, we see not only iconoclasm and revolt but also new structures of the imagination taking shape: the communal poesis in the elements of perception.

A purely transcendental, personalist, or existential philosophy becomes inadequate as soon as — in this age of "popularization" — the new understanding of the world requires a more penetrating reflection on the interactions between acratic or utopian convictions and the capitalist world. Existentialist philosophy is unable to treat the world as *History* with the seriousness it demands.

In the post-religious situation of our time, when the world is no longer an object of contemplation but an immense workshop, and the human condition is defined by its boundless capacity to build a world that is always "new" and commodified, it is the proper function of the Surrealist revolutionist to spell out the Utopian "dimension of the Future" and the socio-political orientation of "Future" as such.

The very post-biblical "promise" of the philosophical foundations of poetic and theatrical Modernism critiques this orientation toward the (pseudo-)Future which characterizes our modern culture and pushes us toward an understanding of the world as History, which results from it.

This emphasis should not be disparaged, as it often is, as a plea for a shallow aestheticism. With the moralistic (legalistic) and rationalist mind, it is too easy to shelve any appeal for the rights of the imagination, and of beauty, as a matter of "mere poetry." But does this not tell us more about the rationalists, as individuals, than about poetry? How can poetry be "merely poetry"? What is in question here is not an irresponsible aestheticism but the essential dynamics of self, the within, and personhood: as mythus, metaphor, image, poetry, archetype, symbol, imagination, phantasy, dream, and deeper dream.

I believe that Dionysian immolation is the counter-impulse to the struggle for freedom. Indeed, is it not but a flight from time and history? Is it not but a flight from creative human liberation itself? For, to be sure, the quality of ecstasy is not just a matter of intensity. "Ecstasies" can be intense but thin or morbid. Yes and to be sure, "ecstasies" can be momentary or episodic or lasting or mutating. Shall we seek private and isolated transports of "secret" or "private" initiates or, a more pervasive condition, indicative of wider experiences and relationships? Shall we seek to represent human liberation as nothing but an insipid resolution of private psychic tension, or as the collective and creative *resolution* of interpersonal and communal disorder?

Nevertheless, this motif of the *glory* of freedom should be safeguarded against a variety of the versions of intoxication. Here, with the shallow inebriations (or, the *mere* inebriations) of Dionysus, the motifs of spontaneity and ecstasy are ambiguous. Beyond the superficial intoxication of the goded vine and untrammeled vitality, or the ceaseless revolt of the bohemians (as "beatniks" for my generation) and the beggars (as "hippies" for my generation) and the vagabonds, or the daemonic and surreal dimensions, drawn to true mania where dance and immolation are inseparable, is the revolutionary *Apocalypse*. However, this vision of *END* can mean catastrophe to some or "new beginnings" and fulfillment in the harvest of time to others.

Artistic *celebration* is deepened by suffering. Artistic hilarity is possible thereby without irresponsibility. Self-realization in and thru the struggle for freedom does not connote a masochistic cult of suffering, though in the past or in the present certain Nihilist or Marxist or revolutionary "martyrs" or "pietists" have thus distorted it. However, the experience of struggles for freedom, concrete and specific, reveals or recognizes and confirms the activist's participation, or the Surrealist poet's participation, in a multi-dimensional operation in which ultimate evil is encountered and transmuted.

Self-definition and self-realization should not be confused with "mystical" transcendence. No doubt in their higher forms they reflect various levels of self-discipline and purgation. In this sense the evils of the world are assimilated and overcome. But the Surrealist *as* artist presumes to wrestle with the root evil of the human and world condition, not only private but public, i.e., the inescapable evils within the systems of Statism and Capitalism. Costly victory here, assured though incomplete, *fullfills* all other glimpses of self-realization and self-definition just because a deeper disorder is resolved.

The **Poesis** of the artist, as human liberation, requires the dialectic or drama. Collective self-realization has to do with the *dimensionality* of freedom and specific human participation in the struggle to achieve it. But this means participation in the activist's life and activity, in concrete struggles (in and out of space-time, of and in all space-time) and this is something other than passive or drugged "mystical" illumination or privatistic epiphanies of "the sacred." From the poets, the greatest transcriptions we have of human self-definition (e.g., the "golden rose" of Dante, the "leaves of grass" of Whitman, the "throw of the dice" of Mallarmé, the "Fata Morgana" of André Breton, etc.) are all social, communal. They have to do with the panegyric of uncounted multitudes in a struggle for universal (and thus collective) harmony.

The community of artist revolutionaries itself is the sign or representation in the joy of human freedom as the celebration of the travail and triumph of creative militance and activism. The quality of such acratic or libertarian or Utopian initiation, however, anticipated in common experience, is far richer than that of our fragmentary aesthetic or esoteric moments of transcendence. Here too, trans-liminal experience, rather than being exceptional or even escapist, is interwoven with the daily fabric of existence, and the Surrealist's joy and glory are associated with both the labor and its transfigurative costs. Walls fill with a milky light.

Prime Minister David Cameron is dancing, dancing, his thighs like palaeolithic prototypes. A pair of bulls barks in adoration before the hovering dogs and pigeons. A toad spits out poetry and saliva at the moon. President Barack Obama hears the roar of dust and cubic mist. He dashes up the steps. Dolphins curvet in purple glittering spray. The sun-hawk, in a complacent manner, corporates men and women as fragment of blaze, the backs of their hands touching. Mr. Bashar al-Assad and Mr. David Cameron shuffle on pigeons. A blue rock structure emanates from the mutilation of a marsh. A frog-man plays on a flute. But His Grace the Dictator Mr. al-Assad and Mr. Cameron scuttle the salmon. A pair of bulls barks down at Mr. al-Assad in high tones. The Prime Minister bowls alongside a flautist and a hawk. There are tears in the eyes of the trout and the eyes of the salmon. Dust seems to throb!

Dungiven, County Derry,
Northern Ireland.

The Anti-Legend of Our Age

Jean-Clarence Lambert

This is the anti-legend of our age
This is the indecisiveness and the tourism
      in the indecisiveness
This is the myth of the First Year I
This is the modernized misery
      in the suburbs of History

That is Lenin's mummy
      and how to make it profitable
That is Trostky's armoured train
      left behind in the Mexican desert
That is Marx at a car breakdown on the motorway
      and Groucho who does not make a stop
That is the bathtub
      where Marilyn and JFK have fucked
That is the shooting of Tlatelolco
      and the mysterious barricades of May 68

That is the Richter scale,
      the Beaufort scale,
      Jacob's ladder
That is the Black Cruise, the Yellow Cruise
That is Faust and Freud at McDonald's
      Ulysses at the Club Med
That is *"Dollars of All Nations, Unite!"*
That is the Ubu software
That is the 25,000th anniversary of Plutonium
That is the probable circular error,
      the inexact sciences
      and the inhuman sciences

That is Freedom insulting the People
That is Alois Schicklgruber
        and Joseph Vissarionovich Djugashvili
That is the Pope in his aquarioum
That is Einstein the cobbler
That is the umbrella of Chamberlain
That is Pétain the farter
That is my father
        in the trenches of Verdun
        reading *Epicurus's Garden*
That is "*Down with Guillaume!*"
        below Apollinaire's window
        while he was dying from Spanish flu
        at 202 Boulevard Saint-Germain

That is forgetting the great god Gôu
        kept at the Musée de l'Homme
That is buying a bottle-rack
        in the Bazar de l'Hôtel de Ville,
        just before the First World War
That is Stalingrad or the crazy laughter of courage
That is the Tango of Death in Auschwitz
        and the Red Orchestra
That is Zyklon B, Maggi,
        Napalm and Dow Jones
That is Webern shot down in front of his house
        by an American guard in Salzburg

That is the Berlin Wall
        and the false conscience
That is the Empty Fortress
        classified as a historical monument
That is Sadat and Rabin peace criminals
That is '*We are all murderers*'
That is Prague Jan Patocka who died
        following a little too heavy
        police interrogations
        and in Paris Garaudy fed on loukoum

That is making a call
    to the intruder,
    to Joseph K.,
    to Eva Braun
    and every time the line is busy
That is making another call to Poussin:
    a V2 bomb has been found in
    Et Arcadia Ego
That is the labyrinth of labyrinths
    and of the anti-personal mines
That is the face of disposable children,
    their eye sockets are empty,
    their eyes have been sold

That is chatting with the Sphinx
That is having a picnic
    on the Andromeda cliff
    with Andromeda
That is *Oedipus Yes!* in all languages
That is the ball of the LW beds
That is dancing with the wolves

That is the Lady of Shanghai
    and the Man with No Pass
That is the cigarette smoker of Tin Hinan,
    the last souvereign of the Atlantes
That is the embarkation for Cythera,
    the crossing of the mirrors,
    the vacation at the Seychelles
That is *"We have seen corpses going to the cinema"*

That is the Mega Machine
    and the Mega Machination
That is the denaturalized Nature
That is the Stock Exchange a.k.a. Life
That is the tomb of the Unknown Unemployed
    at the Arc de Triomphe of Capital

That is Katyn and Oradour,
Bhopal and Chernobyl
That is the Headsman in his head office

That is the the price increase
      of crocodiles and oil
That is to zap
                            from Peter Lorre to Beria,
                            from John Lennon to Lenin,
                            from Charley to Chaplin,
                            from Coco Chanel

Translation from the French: Laurens Vancrevel

Andrew Juris - *Heirs of the Sansungheit*

Surrealist Survival Kits

The Most Fervent Hope in the Depths of Despair

"Never before has Nothing been the seed-plot of such an optimism."
[translation of an advertising slogan for Piraeus Bank]

The machines reproducing the annihilated Real work nonstop: they lull us to sleep at night, sing to us when the sun rises, shake us when the sun reaches its zenith, then plunge us into the sea of their tangled cables when dusk once more sets in. No longer is objective reality merely poor, inadequate, "trifling," as André Breton once put it. Rather, it tends to become literally nightmarish: a theatrical stage where, with every passing second, a demoniac prompter announces the next destruction, presenting it as a necessary development in a plot that is as meaningful as the balance of a company under liquidation. There is no horizon in sight, either before us or behind us: this is what is announced to us, incessantly, by microphones, editorials, whispers, official communiqués. The past is constructed as a recurrent fatal error; the future as the compulsory extension, without the slightest deviation, of a present controlled by the fixed achievement indicators of a total adjustment. The eternal present explodes in the screen's light-emitting diodes.

In such a dystopian reality, where seemingly not a crack has remained in the mirror of the present to allow the entrance of the sparks from the ambivalent unfolding on the future, life is reduced to a struggle for survival. We must find a way to wake up the next morning, to construct those essential tools that will help us make it through yet another day, another month, another year. After all, the machines of political economy also cater to this problem pertaining to the "management of human resources", which otherwise specializes in personal, silent despair. The dietetics of the body's submission to the rhythm of its productive use includes a number of techniques for temporary oblivion, hourly diversion, daily reinvigoration and nightly diffusion into the glittering Zero of "going out with friends", which has nothing to do either with the outside or with friendship, being the fervent flight towards the neon entrails of the utterly commercialized world. Methodical reduction of life to the capital-relation: the lifestyle, which includes an infinity of lifestyles, which constitutes literally the last word of all possible lifestyles, those already existent and those remaining to be invented. Once, philosophers struggled to indicate the appropriate means for self-care; now, advertisers propose handy solutions for the renewal of self-consumption, of the identification of each being, unrepeatable in its uniqueness, as one vehicle (common in its nonentity) of purchase power, as a factor of the multiplication of capital, of the accumulable, mortified work. The problem, however, is that advertisers do not lie; they speak the truth: the naked king dances merrily over the corpses, yet almost none of those present rises to leave this appalling ritual, for almost no one hopes that something else may really exist, other than the king's bloody dance and his flagrant nakedness.

Navigation manuals are provided by intellectual leaders and artists as well, often as an expression of miserabilism. Can plastic imagination function as an antidote to everyday poison? Might it reveal rays of light where everything appears to crumble into the impervious abyss of the indicators of financial stability? And, if seen from another angle, indeed from the one that today appears to reign over all the others, painting, the exercise of imagination, dreaming, the desire for objects that do not as yet exist — are these not an unforgivable luxury in our present times? The dominant cynicism may prove tolerant towards those kinds of ventures, on condition that these involve artists and manifestations that operate within the delimited territory of art as an autonomous sphere of public life, or, more accurately, as a separate branch of capitalist production. Within the limits of this sphere, survival can only be evoked either as an ideal escape that quenches with salt the thirst for a real escape from that which exists, or as an admission, an aesthetic affirmation of the present misery. It would obviously be unfair to devalue the importance of creative imagination, even when encaged within the realm of aesthetic forms. Yet it is crucial to insist upon the knot that must here be cut: as long as objective reality is not questioned radically, not placed at the point of the temporal/critical sword as it really is, namely as null, any proposal for survival will end up being no more than a stratagem for readjustment in a world that crashes, controls and subdues life itself.

Surrealism, the committed and collective search for the surreal, that is, for the field of real possibilities that have been repelled, or that have yet to be discovered, lurking as they are in the recesses of lived experience, has always been and still is an international movement for the change of the world, and of life. It has always sought, by setting its symbolic wheel in motion, to open up a space for the negation of this world, and this life; for the systematic undermining of all definitive claims in favor of "things as they are," which fix humans to a present of exploitation and oppression. Its international character was and is crucial precisely because the existing social production of time and space itself, which limits lived experience to the historicity of nations and the enclosures of states, could not have remained unchallenged. Its status as a movement was and is essential for collective action to tend towards the active questioning of all those divisions that reproduce the dominant social relations as the only human relations imaginable, as well as the "best possible": above all, of the division between producers and consumers of subjective creative expression. Bearing the indelible marks of the age that gave rise to it (that of the horrors at the trenches of the First World War and of the hopes blooming at the barricades of Petrograd and Berlin), surrealism never ceased, even at times of relative calm and financial growth, to expose the poverty, the insignificance, as well as the destructive potential of objective reality under the capital-relation; not in order to propound an uncritical recourse to the Ideal, nor to reinforce a feeling of aversion towards worldly things and the concomitant isolation in the innermost depths of pure Ego.

Neither Messianism nor asceticism: the action of surrealist groups the world over is a contribution to the international social revolution, to the emergence of the world-that-is-to-come, of life that struggles for its emancipation. And life, even today, when objective reality is structured like a nightmare, keeps struggling for its emancipation. Life is elsewhere: on the streets of common fights, where no shed blood dries up indifferently, on the windows which, against all forecasts, we persist in opening, in the acts of everyday disobedience or solidarity, in unpredicted encounters, in the transports of love or the illuminations of merciless black humor, when the mirror of the present cracks, and cannot *but* crack, since the present is undermined, indeed more than ever before, by the very contradictions and absurdities that gave rise to it.

From such a perspective, survival should not be grasped as the rescue of existence under the present conditions; no more so than it may be seen as a restoration to life as it was before the outbreak of the crisis. To survive means to live differently, to trace escape routes from that which exists. If today the narrative of capitalist progress is collapsing, along with the sense of safety harbored in the course of the preceding years by those of us who happened to live in the "zones of prosperity" of the developed capitalist countries regarding our lives' outcomes, it is we who must now invent a narrative of exiting the capitalist barbarity now exposed to us in all its nudity, beside us, around us, *everywhere*, from Fukushima to Wisconsin. If work assumes, without any pretexts, the form of a brutal enslavement, if the dominance of the capital manifests itself as it really is, as the dominance of dead, objectified, accumulated work over living work (that is, over the creativity of the working bodies), we must claim work as a game, by trying to exercise and sharpen our ability to transform the objects to which we relate into hieroglyphics of desire. If finance, rather than being a hospitable playground as asserted for so many years by champions of enterprise, becomes a shooting range, we must display even more serious symptoms of counterproductive (according to their criteria) behavior, engage in projects aiming at the self-management of everyday life, announcing the future community of autonomous humans, proving that its possibility is a real one. If today art appears to be the bosses' luxury and the redeemable intermission (before and after the ads) of proletarians, we must bring to light the most curious specimens of *magic art*, an art that opposes the cultural industry, that never abandons the fluid totality of life, that records, ignites, releases the creativity of living work beyond moral or aesthetic prejudices, without ever being reduced to a pawn for use in political or financial planning. If the numbers to which every social activity is reduced do not add up, we must throw all balances in the garbage bin; we must defend and develop further every activity that violates the principle of efficiency, and that, on the other hand, reinforces our ability to love, to dream, to persist in what attracts us, to let our bodies be distracted and thereby discover its own potential. Our survival from destruction presupposes that we do not allow the survival of those social relations that reproduce destruction as normality.

In the current circumstances, resistance is not scarce. What appears to be missing, or to be at present dramatically powerless, is the hope for another life. The "surrealist survival kits," evoked for the first time some two decades ago by Leonora Carrington in her discussions with Penelope Rosemont, aim at reigniting this very hope: "The purpose of these kits is to offset the destructive facts of daily life, to pull us through the hardest times, to reawaken our sense of wonder and to renew our capacity for revery and revolt."(*) These are collections of poetic, magical, oneiric objects that function symbolically, as indicators of our capacity for overcoming the limits of our individual substance in the direction of total emancipation. The production of such "survival kits" does not, of course, constitute a proposition that antagonizes other, more traditional, forms of developing a revolutionary consciousness. It is not the sole, or even the main, route for the reinvention of hope. The social struggles unfolding today, the victorious revolts that have already forced lifelong presidents to take their leave on helicopters, are the foremost events that will make us define anew what we can do and what is worth hoping for. Engagement in the surrealist adventure promises nothing more than the radicalization of the subjective potential for revolution, by mobilizing the multiplicity of the human aesthetic, intellectual and emotive forces towards the change of the world and of life, combining the exaltation of collective struggle with the agitation experienced byeach one of us when abandoned to her or his abysses.

*Penelope Rosemont, "A Revolution in the Way We Think and Feel – Conversations with Leonora Carrington", in Ron Sakolsky (ed.), *Surrealist Subversions: Rants, Writings and Images by the Surrealist Movement in the United States*, New York: Autonomedia, 2002, pp. 184-190.

Below are the "Instructions" for the use of the Survival Kits created in the context of the 3-day meeting in Athens, 3-5 June 2011, at the social center Nosotros, by members of the Surrealist London Action Group (SLAG), the surrealist group of Stockholm, and the surrealist group of Athens. "Instructions" is a game played by the members of the groups present at the place, on the last day of the meeting.

Everybody wrote a manual referring to a survival kit.

1:

α. These are invisible hands playing the player-pianos. They stay invisible by swimming in the invisible ink that their scores are written with. Music is invisible and sometimes the tools it's made of are invisible as well. Most of all, the tool is the fool. And sometimes, flowers can blossom out of an egg. (*Johannes Bergmark*)

β. It's a kit that is sometimes used in case pianos are lacking . It chooses spontaneously a tarot card and then the dancing floor is filled with flowers and the audience throws eggs in ecstasy. Then plenty of red fluid fills the glasses. What a party! (*Marianna Xanthopoulou*)

γ. The Fool ascending, rucksack in hand, cleverly disguises the outline of a coastline where "O" marks the spot, and the plastic baby finger gives you the distance to walk. Bathe your crackling egg shoes in flowers and thorns, collect the resulting blood. With this you may create a second hidden map. (*Erik Bohman)*

2:

α. Is an instrument of violent death. It is not an instant death, but is, for sure, a boring one. The night falls before you get ready and you fall asleep before you try to do something. If you don't manage to die, then you can easily take the kid out to the park for a pee . (*Marianna Xanthopoulou*)

β. Shake it violently and follow the customized exit strategy. Ex: "Be on the lookout for the shining ruby under the empty throne", "Pull the life vest, kiss a red pen and feel the darkness of night enfolding you". (*Erik Bohman*)

3:

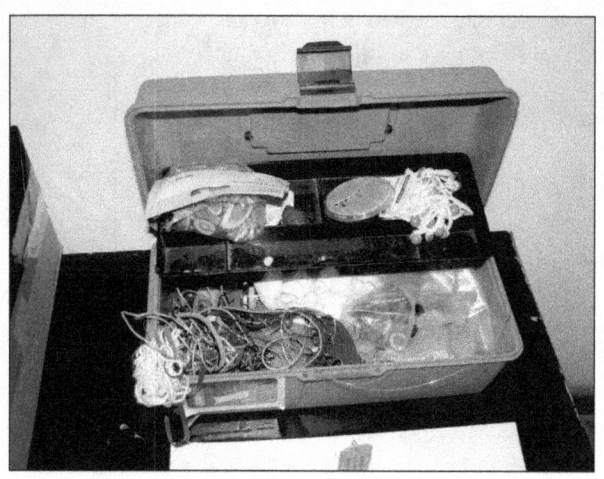

α. To dig deep enough to fill an ashtray with blood, by any means, or by the help of a cigar guillotine, for sensitizing one's fingertips like a safebreaker or a detective, or just for delimiting certain views of reality with a cut sharper than that of a camera, will transform the field of possibilities perhaps so as to electrify the tadpoles of our subjectivity like dolphins or dancing fetuses that will jump over all fences including those of the Paris metro and perhaps end up when a certain desert starts shooting sprouts. (*Mattias Forshage*)

β. Prick your finger, cut your toe and get the hell out of the red sea. Too salty to drink, too hot to sunbath, set the train on a collision course with the pharaoh of your choice (*Erik Bohman*).

4:

α. It's an instrument that is used in cases of difficult dilemmas. It works out (and works in) sums. Each time you're in such a situation, you choose a card and the advice is always useful – as long as you know how to read it. Otherwise every advice seems the same to you. (*Marianna Xanthopoulou*)

β. "Eivar ojes ¿Sies" Instructions in an unknown language. I am feeling generous: "Take a bite and speak." On the other side of closed down schools we will find a chemo-pedagogical method of multiplying the languages. Some recipes gives you two cards, one for each conspirator or play mate, some could give you six-billion for one, two, three, a thousand new universal languages. The tongue still poses some problems, but not for love. (*Erik Bohman*)

5:

α. This survival kit functions by organizing that which is useless and emitting sparks (*Alexandra Halkias*).

β. The batteries reload through the silence of phone nets. While silence stirs the incessant babble the wallet leaks flowers. The arm of a hulk left alone connects the power to the box which, rumbling in a manipulation of light, cooks the ink cup and fondles the curled-up contact lenses into action. (*Erik Bohman*)

6:

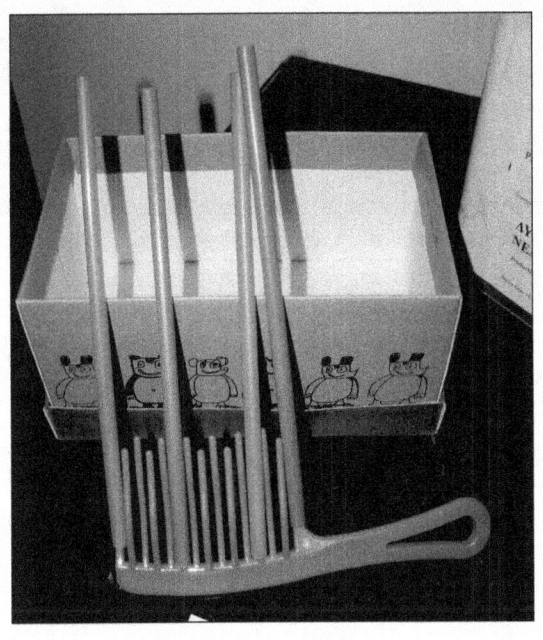

α. The dream comb: comb the hair of the dreamer and the dreams will be projected through the comb into your hand. When you comb yourself you will get the dreams that are stored in the comb. (*Johannes Bergmark*)

β. All my new friends are mouse dolls dressed up as snowmen performing strange ballets, singing in shrill new chords of four bright tones that cannot be described except by colours, aligned by playful combing of the gravel paths leading up to the frozen dam where we go swimming all day. (*Mattias Forshage*)

γ. An instrument for the direct restoration of the vocal chords. It produces sounds of different colours and, when you blow through the chimneys, it clears the throat and the chords and hair are straightened. Most of the people –wrongly– would use it in times of drought.
(*Marianna Xanthopoulou*)

δ. 6 friendly faces. The teeth of the comb turn into parallel rainbows. (*Erik Bohman*)

7:

α. [7, 10 & 25] Generally all three are used in case somebody is shipwrecked on an island. Thus, they are made of those objects that are washed ashore by the sea or that we can have on us but are in fact useless (e. g. our cell-phone). Specifically for no. 7: A tiny coffin mechanism in which you can put your mobile and which works with the energy of the shells, after you key the words of a voodoo ceremony performed for this very purpose. What are these words? Easy! They are the first words of the first native you'll meet. If you don't meet any native, the words of *klidonas* can do just as well. (Diamantis Karavolas)

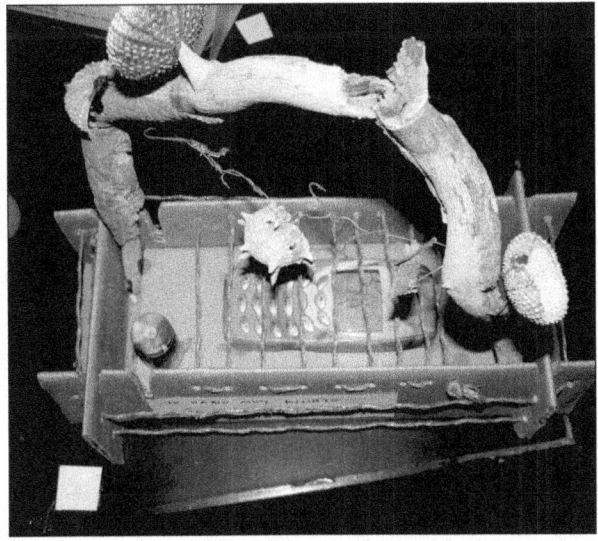

β. "My old mobile still works" manual. Its main use consists in the gradual opening of the wooden windows. For cases in which the opening must be rapid more suitable toolkits are provided. It must be placed, either early in the morning or very late in the afternoon, in a distance of 23cm from the window to be opened and vertically to it in a way that the open petals on the wooden log can receive the light that penetrates the glass of the window at an angle of 90°. The mobile phone is activated only in the presence of an employee of a postal company, but its use is, at any rate, limited: the mobile phone contributes in the preservation of the opening that is each time accomplished in a window. The principal instruments are the hooks, inasmuch as they render possible the capture of the rays of light, always at angle of 90° and their ensuing attraction in a way that the shutters can eventually open. (Vangelis Koutalis)

γ. Constructed for the world's smallest person with the world's largest sorrow. It lies on a bed of string and the melange of singing sea shells and mumbling invisible mouths will soothe and envigorate. If not, the world always offers more hooks. (*Erik Bohman*)

8:

α. An alembic for the amplification of writing — you melt the paper in their interior — you leave it in the sun for all of the afternoon of August 6th (the day of the Savior)— the paper reforms itself, the texts are the same except that now they speak more truths than they did before. (*Giannis Ksourias*)

β. THE FETA CHEESE OF ELIAS. It will help the next intelligent beings that may reappear on Earth, after a total destruction of the human race, to rediscover writing and FETA. (*Diamantis Karavolas*)

γ. A restaurant menu "Through harvesting dream vegetables and developing extremely complicated breeding plans, we are happy to offer you the food of younger gods and the ever-continuing Särimner line of meats. We have moved beyond the brutal butchering procedures and can instead offer you satisfaction through oinks and interaction". (*Erik Bohman*)

9:

α. This survival kit is to be used when the drawer is empty. Pulling the stone in the green circle releases the string holding everything together, music is issued into the air, the dried flower falls and the wonder lands on the ground gently standing on her feet (*Alexandra Halkias*).

β. When you'll ascend the stairs holding a red lighter, you need to rest on a rock! What a tiring day! If you rotate the lever so that the natural antenna can move with the wind, then the flying bumpkin will play music with his keys, changing the color of the belt that is hanging from the coffin. (*Marianna Xanthopoulou*)

γ. Remove a coin from the orange container, grab the hand of the levitating elderly woman and reflect your gardening tools in the shimmering sail. Coal will turn to flowers, dinosaurs will walk the earth and heat death will be averted (for the time being). (*Erik Bohman*)

δ. A device for (all kinds of) weather forecasting. Also, it removes the clouds and creates sunshine or artificial rain. (*Diamantis Karavolas*)

10:

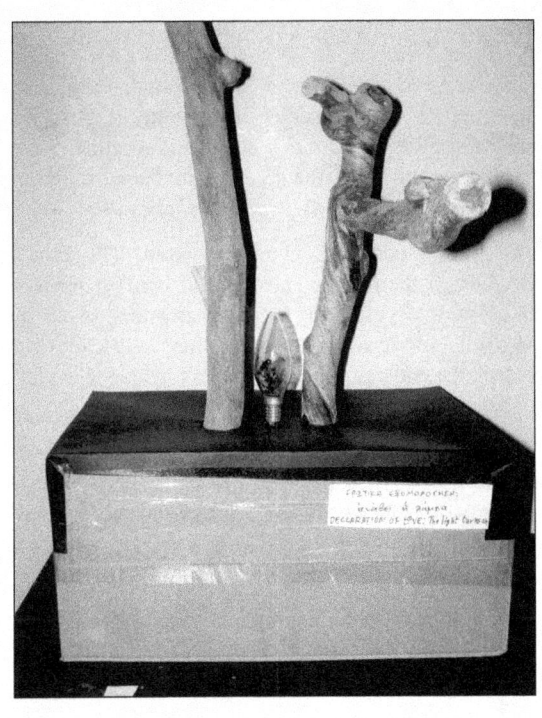

α. "Declaration of Love: the light turns on". A simple lie detector. (*Merl Fluin*)

β. You place your fingers in the cracks of the sticks — all the fingers — or perhaps the nose — or even better the tongue (caution, never the eyes) — and when the lamp suddenly turns on your spine will rise up again — like Adam's candleit shall stay solid and straight for three galactic years. (*Yannis Ksourias*)

γ. Up to your knees in darkness, high above the dancing moths you rattle your little bone and blow your scalp snout. And perhaps you are not the last of your species after all. (*Erik Bohman*)

δ. [7, 10 & 25] Generally all three are used in case somebody is shipwrecked on an island. Thus, they are made of those objects that are washed ashore by the sea or that we can have on us but are in fact useless (e. g. our cellphone). Specifically for no. 10: You are making "mentally" a love confession, then the light turns on and you've got light all night. You need though to try it many times, at least 500 repeats per day. (*Diamantis Karavolas*)

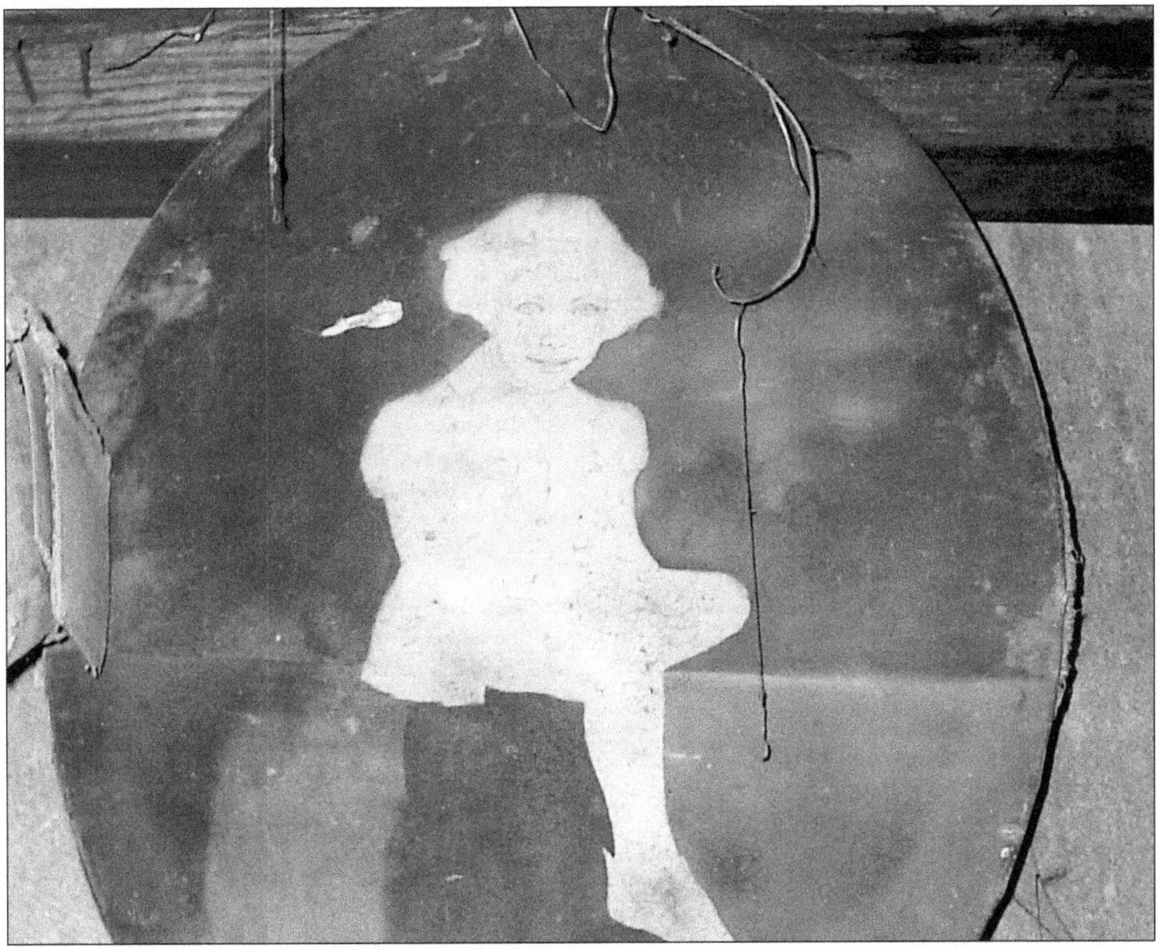

11:

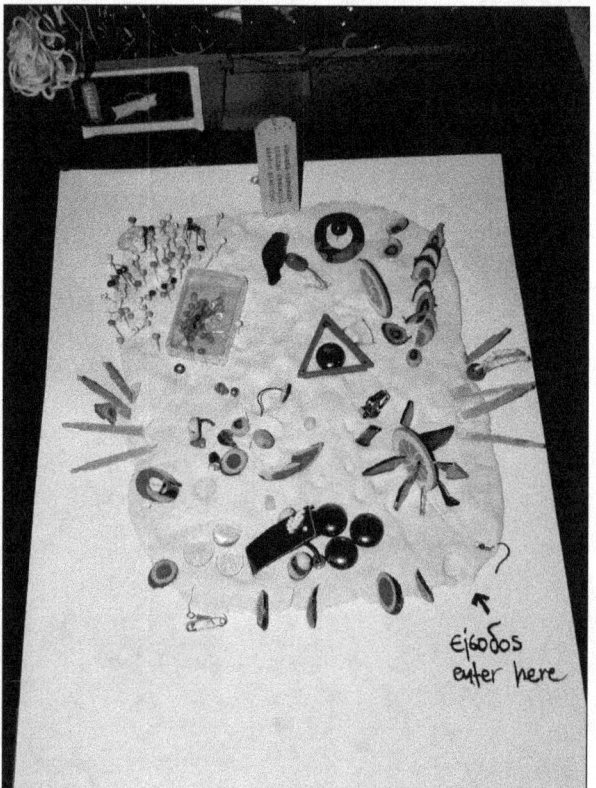

α. There are landscapes in which you do not need any corners to keep turning new corners and encounter an endless series of suggestions of concrete irrationality, a menagerie of the larvae of new social and sensuous forms a labyrinth in plain sight, the moment the flock of migrating birds leave the ground. (*Mattias Forshage*)

β. We find a door into the new world. The fruit are flourishing in their glass palaces, and burning walls will keep us warm. Eyes spring from the ground, and our steps are reflected as we stride across this new landscape. In our stores are the endless pins and threads for sewing the fabric of our streets. (*Paul Cowdell*)

γ. Is a mask to be worn when traveling at night through enemy territory. If you perform a certain dance while wearing the mask, you will become possessed by the soul of the Great Bear, and the ends of your own hair will become your guiding stars (*Merl Fluin*)

δ. This is the game for multiple solutions: for making a story which always starts at one point but could go lots of different ways each time you tell it! (*Johannes Bergmark*)

ε. It's a map that shows the road to the entrance of the labyrinth. It includes useful information on how to avoid winding music boxes made from orange, toothless guards of the edges and forgotten backbones of fossilized trees. We are in luck, for it reveals the path for the 3rd eye and the beach that hides under the shadow. When you read it under the light of the full moon, the north becomes a totem and points to the sand pile of the beach. (*Marianna Xanthopoulou*)

στ. It is a game involving medical knowledge. Each player brings in his pawn from the prescribed point. The order of executing the moves is determined by the rating that each player has already achieved in the preliminary contest of shooting an apple, installed of course in the head of the immediately next player, according to the alphabetic order of the last names. How each of the players can move is also determined by a player's rating obtained in advance, according to the size of their thumb, on the right hand, in combination with the sizes of their most recent scar, in any place of their body. The player who has occupied the first place in those two ratings will be able to go undistracted up to the middle of the labyrinth, namely up to the Nailed Eye of the Forest. The player, on the contrary, who has rated last, will be declared the winner and will be put, along with his sewing machine, upon an operating table.
(*Vangelis Koutalis*)

η. A garden, with all its thorns, cannot help but also be an instruction for acupuncture. And such instructions – necessarily a map in themselves – will give you an idea of the erogenous zones you have yet to cultivate. You have no idea what you need to salvage. (*Erik Bohman*)

12:

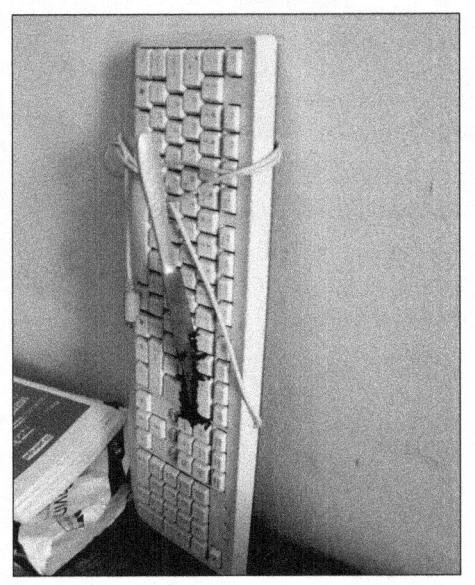

α. For the keyboard. Can be worn as a belt around the waist and other times constitutes a holder for the scissors of a European-style tailor. (*Elias Melios*)

β. Is a device for smuggling knives out of prison (*Merl Fluin*)

γ. We press the knife a bit deeper in the fissure s formed between *enter* and *backspac*e, we wait for a few seconds and then we see the cables unfold and direct to the supervisor of the administration office with the purpose of strangling him. We must, however, be extremely careful at the use of the device, because, since the supervisor can also meander like a snake, maybe we won't finally achieve the desirable result and the supervisor can escape us at the very last moment. (*Lefki Mossou*)

13:

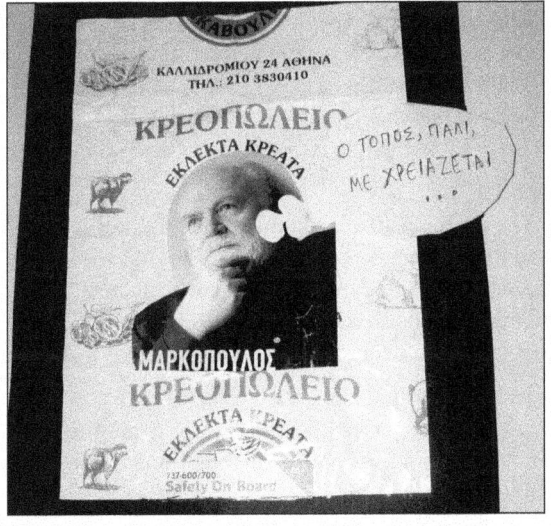

14:

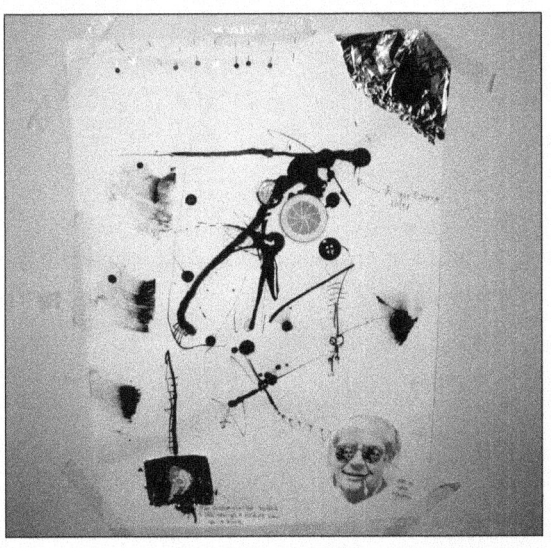

"What do you see?"

- A moustache turned to teeth,

- Notes into snails

- A woman drawing out a new set of realities.

(Let's not be fooled by a pair of glasses, no matter how sharp) (*Erik Bohman*))

15:

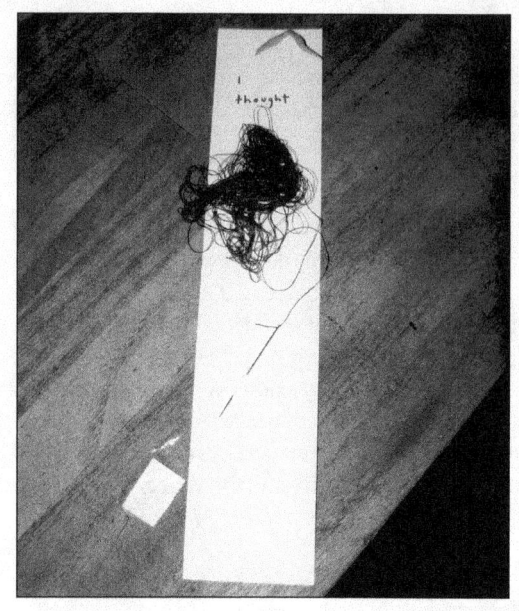

α. I thought, and from this tangled mess came one clear dart of clay. (*Paul Cowdell*)

β. This is for getting lost in thoughts and finding new ways out – or back! (*Johannes Bergmark*)

γ. Useful tool for untangling difficult situations and *sewing thoughts by fast-track procedures.* (Marianna Xanthopoulou)

δ. The needle lets you retangle your thoughts and dispel the glaring, cold clarity of the situation. (*Erik Bohman*)

16:

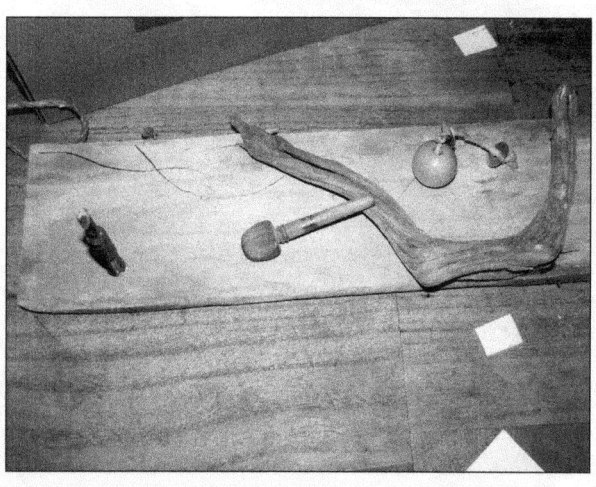

α. The drill is for opening a hole in the brain to let prejudice out. The tuning pin is for tuning my moustache (as indicated by the wooden piece) in exciting tuning systems. The wooden marble is for putting in my nose for extra excitement to increase inspiration when playing my moustache (*Johannes Bergmark*).

β. The presence of certain materials, the soft leaps they suggest, sleeping not fossilized (if fossilized doesn't equal sleeping?). Some of my new tentacles/ some of my new pencils/some of my new maps/ in a landscape sleeping/ yet already far too bright. (*Mattias Forshage*)

γ. Hang it around the wrist of a newborn child and prevent the proper identification of progenitor. A spawn will always look anew for a first thing to see. (*Erik Bohman*)

17:

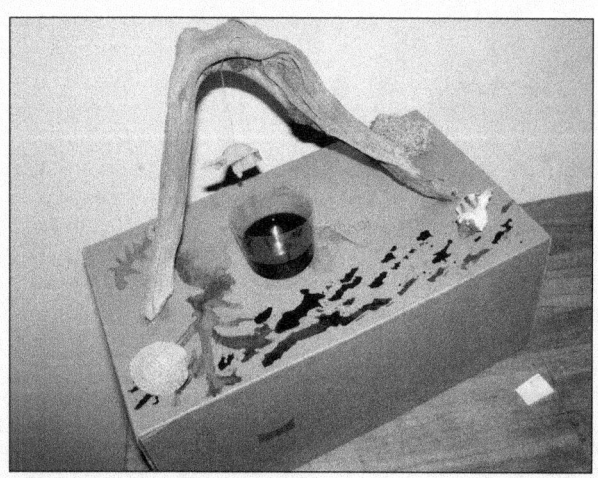

The bow of a world is a dolphin fixed far above an altar that has never tasted blood. You could take the role of projectile if you like. (*Erik Bohman*)

18:

You will not make it out alive. Lick the licking tongue. But maybe it's a consolation to know that the world will never stop burning and all keys are devoid of locks? (*Erik Bohman*)

19:

α. If I could be walking lost in a landscape of small hills, young deciduous trees, abandoned old cottages, industrial ruins, and possibly poisoned streams, I would enter one of these cottages to sleep, and waiting for me in the bedroom would be a basket in which my compulsory thoughts would have turned into string, the horseworms turned into string, measurements turned into string. Along this string, the concepts of my understanding of society as thitherto developed would eventually gain wings, gleaming wings. (*Mattias Forshage*)

β. To the sea with a basket, and a manual of the devastation surrounding me. I will build a house of rope, and raise future generations on our new legends. We will demand ours. (*Paul Cowdell*)

γ. Before you, a flood. The textures of social formations passed will recombine into a quilt of fantastic proportions. You will never stand speechless in archeological discussions about the relics and fossils of degenerate capitalist states. (*Erik Bohman*)

20:

α. Inside, we save honey for the bears and coins for the juke box. The drawings show the treasure of the birds. We wear the pink ribbon so as not to be sad. (*Yannis Golfinopoulos*)

β. Although you cannot see it at first sight, it's a kit that is used in the darkness, when its dark side cannot be shown. Rotating the metal cover, the inner ribbon is winded up – a dangerous instrument when one suffers from hypoglycemia. Inside, all that is left is the sperm waiting for the right moment to unfold its black pinchers to whichever direction is asked of it. (*Marianna Xanthopoulou*)

γ. This kit aims at restoring desirous impulses by the promise of champagne truffle; while the garlic contained therein serves to keep away vampires of the id". (*Nikos Stabakis*)

21:

α. You put your mouth on the straw, you pretend you are sucking and the sphere shows your guts, that is, if they function well or if there is a problem.
(*Diamantis Karavolas*)

β. If you break the glass, a ship sinks at sea. Useful in war. (*Merl Fluin*)

γ. The nails secure the decisions. The sphere shows the past, the way it shall be when the dolphins stop scorning us. The straw remains an enigma. (*Yannis Golfinopoulos*)

22:

α. A sundial or a time bomb? Depends how you'll use it, the consequences will be analogue.

When the screw shows three o'clock and not five, you can't do anything except light a cigarette and wait. In any other case, the buttonhole of the future opens, disappearing all the breaches, replacing them with fuse-by-meter. (*Marianna Xanthopoulou*)

β. Is a talking drum, it will tell you stories of ice and sun if you beat the metal surface with cigarettes.
(*Merl Fluin*)

23:

24:

Finally, having dissolved the functioning of money, and thus making the analysis of Marx superfluous, we could sit down and construct wooden blocks, tied up to on each other with ropes, and use them to fully understand the meaning of encounters. (*Jonas Enander*)

25:

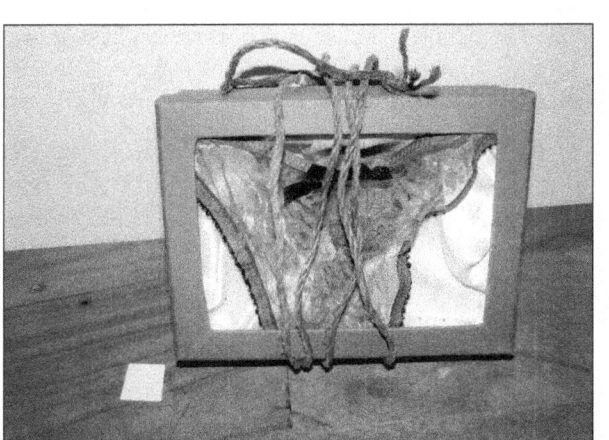

α. We will haul on the old and rotting ropes that seem to be only debris. From the depths will come our seductive luxury. (*Paul Cowdell*)

β. Main colour-giver of black-and-white blood—you simply swallow it, without opening the box however. (*Yannis Ksourias*)

γ. [7, 10 &25] Generally all three are used in case somebody is shipwrecked on an island. Thus, they are made of those objects that are washed ashore by the sea or that we can have on us but are in fact useless (e. g. our cell-phone). Specifically for no. 25: a simple charm for fertility for good luck and good progeny.
(*Diamantis Karavolas*)

26:

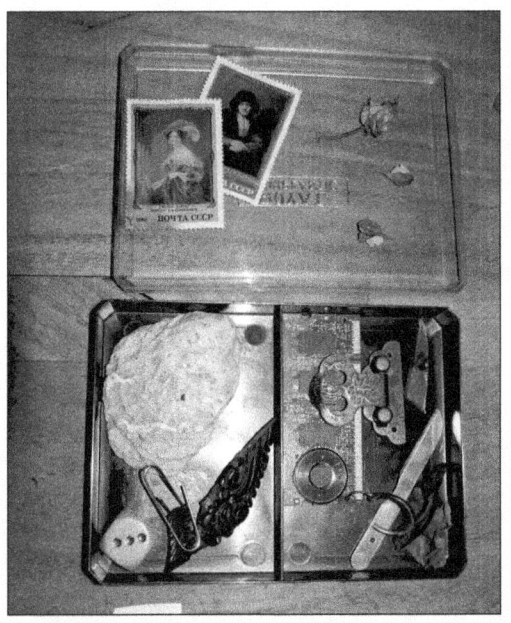

α. The left box states that the link between nature and culture, consists of the mechanism of chance – the right one is the mechanism for realizing this knowledge into a surrealist civilization. The top box is a disguise: to pretend that this subversive activity only strives for beauty in the sense defined by the art realm.
(*Johannes Bergmark*)

β. Is an alchemical tinder box. Striking the objects against each other in different combinations produces different kinds of flame: illuminating, concealing, consuming, confusing, cold, hot, floral etc. (*Merl Fluin*).

27:

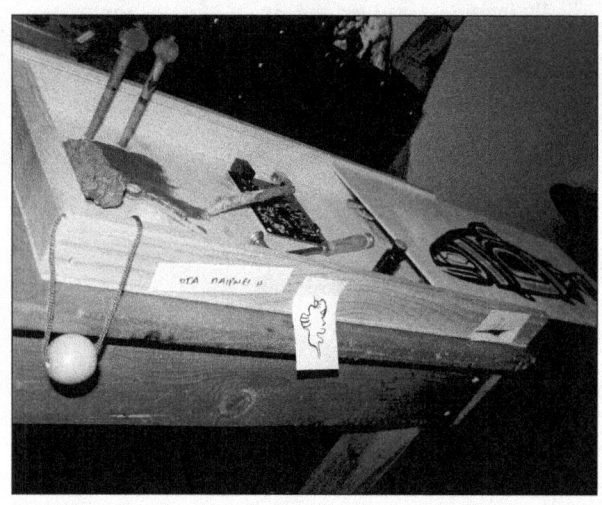

α. Is to be used to repopulate the sea. All the minerals are to be injected with liquids, and all the organic material to be pierced by the inorganic. This will release a cloud of spawn into the ocean and turn the sand of the seabed into tiny fish. (*Merl Fluin*)

β. Once again I awoke to a breakfast table of items yet unknown to me, proving to be the exact objects that I had dreamt about, or covering for those that I had dreamt about, and started eating this breakfast, devouring the person emerging from this particular mode of being, and once I had eaten I realized I had no means of deciding whether this new subjectivity reconstructed was in fact mine in the sense of somehow identical with the one before this process. Not that I particularly care. I am having a correspondence over the oceans with a civilization of arctic fish, with wooden boxes as bottles for our messages, and we return to something new for each new message. I cannot remember anything in advance, but I'll trust each message is an ordinary love letter. (*Mattias Forshage*)

γ. Sudoku for the belly of the sea monster: some necessary elements for the exercise of memory and for providing a pleasant pastime to someone who may find him- or herself – just like Jonah– in the belly of the big sea monster. (*Diamantis Karavolas*)

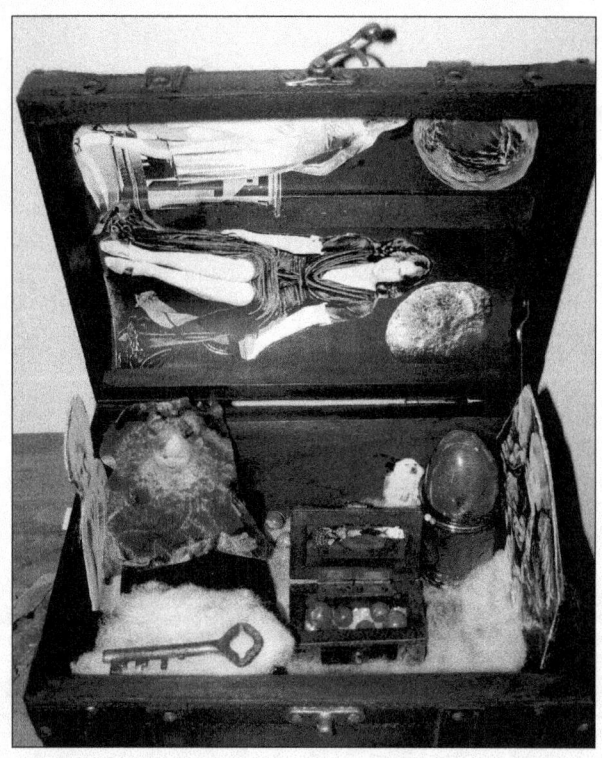

28:

The anti-doll house. Ejaculation onto the egg will cause it to burst open and release a ferocious transparent dog. Ejaculation onto that doll will cause her to burst open and release a glass bat. Ejaculation into the box of marbles will cause a lunar eclipse. Can be useful as a weapon. (*Merl Fluin*)

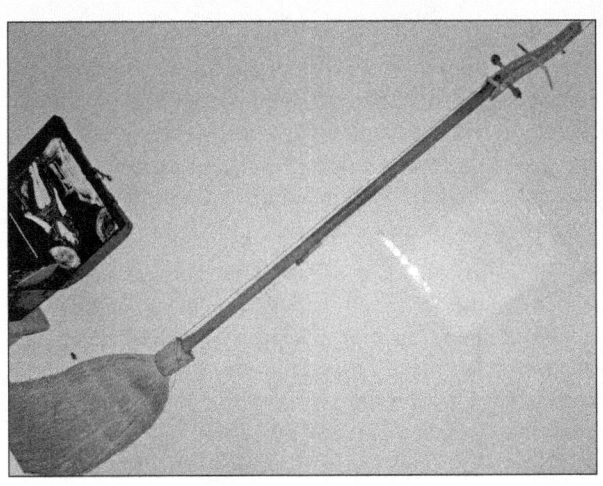

29:

α. Multiple uses: a). After we've swept the sidewalks of Patision Str., we hold it from the shaft and sweep the heads of passing people. b). In more violent occasions, we lift the tuning hammer that is on the side, in right angle with the body of the instrument and it is transformed into a murder weapon capable of chasing away a whole squad of cops from the chosen ground. c). Late at night it can be used for alleviation and lullaby. If, for example, we suffer from insomnia, we caress tenderly the same middle tuning hammer, tune up slightly the remaining tuning hammers on the upper part of the instrument and then place it next to us on the floor. Thus, with those simple moves, the instrument starts to emit a mystical sound, capable of luring a person swiftly into dream dimensions. (*Lefki Mossou*)

β. For the Sazi. Can be worn on the back during siesta-time, in the winter. (*Elias Melios*)

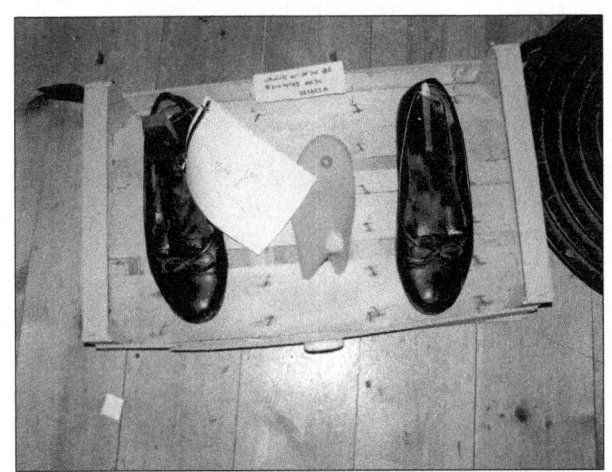

30:

An instrument of communication with the outer world in case of a shipwreck. Lighting the pole and waving the flag of the emerging Poseidon, you can walk on the surface of the water – others have done it too. It applies to fresh water and sea water alike. ATTENTION: it doesn't multiply fish, only mollusks. (*Marianna Xanthopoulou*)

31:

α. Survival only in the sense of a sea spider heaving its body up out of a matrix of smelling wood and looking at the world with a new optics as threatful yet ridiculous as the gaze of a row of pelicans a lack of humor as sweet as licorice and an uninhibited obsessive gateway of associations. (*Mattias Forshage*)

β. This survival kit consists of an antique doorknob which has the ability of opening, or closing, any door it is placed upon. The hinges instantly respond, no matter what they are made of, as indicated by the one placed within the kit. The herons have this knowledge, thus calm they remain. (*Alexandra Halkias*)

γ. The box is put on the water. The pipes channel energy from the orgonite into the water, allowing it to propel itself along. It can be steered with the oar and bailed out with the small bucket. When the owner dies his/her body is laid in it and it is set alight so that the corpse is consumed by burning tobacco. (*Merl Fluin*)

δ. It is a kit that is used in the boring congresses of pelicans. It is a kit of escape from boredom. You wipe your feet on the carpet that usually kills and you enjoy the spider as it's drying its belly in the sun, smoking a pipe. (*Marianna Xanthopoulou*)

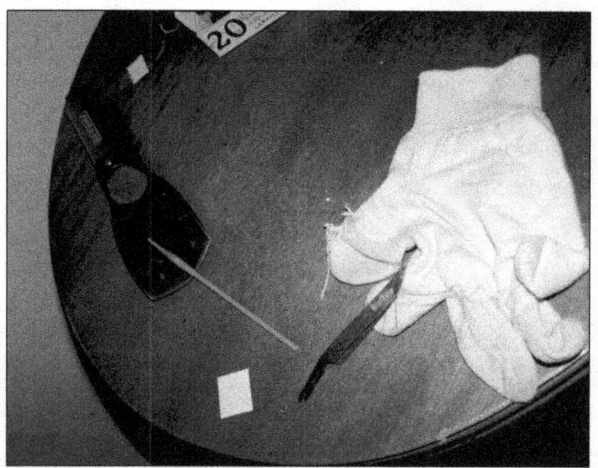

32:

An instrument of putting chestnuts out of the fire! Occasionally, it is used in the same manner for plucking our eyebrows or for minimizing probabilities.
(*Marianna Xanthopoulou*)

Athens meeting report, June 2011

When one is overcome by demoralization and defeat, deeply depressed or on the verge of suicide, that is the time to open one's Surrealist Survival Kit and enjoy a breath of magical fresh air.

Penelope Rosemont, 'A Revolution in the Way We Think and Feel – Conversations with Leonora Carrington' (2002)

In June 2011, when the city of Athens had already long been a beacon of both desperate hope and acute despair, members of the international Surrealist movement met in the Exarchia district, in the city's heart, to build Surrealist Survival Kits. The rules of the game were simple: to assemble collections of poetic, magical, oneiric objects into portable kits, for the restoration of wonder and reinvention of hope when times are at their hardest.

Responding to an invitation issued by the Athens Surrealist Group in July 2010, members of SLAG (Surrealist London Action Group) and the Stockholm Surrealist Group had travelled to Greece to join the Athenians for several days of hope and wonder. We constructed our Survival Kits – some elaborately prepared from beloved fetish objects, some improvised from detritus found on the spot, some individual, some collaborative – and welcomed local people to join us for their display and discussion at an evening of public talks, slideshows, film screenings, poetry readings and improvised music.

The international meeting was held against the backdrop of the deepening economic crisis that is tearing at the body of Greek society. This crisis renders the question of survival apparent in manifold ways. We may feel a spontaneous inclination to jump for anti-capitalist joy and celebrate the prospect of the breakdown of the present order, but of course the crisis is not only a crisis for state and capital, but also a real crisis for the everyday lives of ordinary people: the claustrophobia of the horizon closing in, the uncertainty over whether one's home and livelihood can be sustained even for the coming months. The kind of survival in play here is one of necessity, of not bowing beneath the increasing organised misery, of preventing the destructive forces of capital from running through their regular routine. But on the other hand, when all options appear to be exhausted, when all escape routes have been blocked and the policies imposed upon us tend towards the ultimate degradation of all traces of life in society, there arises a utopian kind of survival in which imagining all other possible forms of life becomes a real force for resistance; where a basic, specifically Surrealist sense of survival regains its particular relevance. It was in the context of these two modes of survival, framed by massive popular demonstrations against austerity measures and a utopian spirit of playfulness, that the international meeting was held.

The public event was just one aspect of the stream of internal collective discussion and play that went on continuously for three days as we wound our way through meeting rooms, streets, squares, hills, bookshops, bars, kitchens, taverns and apartments. The discussions were comradely, which means neither platitudinous nor polite: this was an occasion for asking questions, of ourselves and each other. In particular it was a time for hard thinking about the meanings of survival. It became increasingly clear to us that for Surrealists the survival at stake could not be the minimalist victory of simply making it through to another day, or the survivalist tactic of holing up somewhere to protect our treasure until the danger has passed: on the contrary, for us survival could only be, as the Athens group had expressed it in their invitation, 'the hope for another life'.

As we reflected together on the unfolding results of our game, we understood that what made the kits significant was not the personal collection of 'favourite things' by individuals – 'each one [...] different, for no two people are exactly alike' in Penelope Rosemont's words – but the process of assembling them, of finding or constructing oneiric objects from literally any old rubbish that was lying around, the transmutation of base matter into the gold of future time. In other words, our Survival Kit was not the objects themselves, but the ability to find and transform them. Surrealism *is* our survival kit, and as such is a necessary – though insufficient – condition for the social revolution that must come.

More than anything else, it was the depth and intensity of internal discussion that for us marked the importance – again we want to say the *necessity* – of the meeting in Athens. The meeting came in the middle of a series of international events, from the Destruction 2011 festival in Istanbul to the later exhibitions in Prague and Pennsylvania, but these were primarily geared towards the public presentation of works and ideas rather than to the development of Surrealist strategies. Events such as those in Istanbul, Prague or Pennsylvania are important for the structure of a group and thus for the international movement at large, but we must also open a space for a steadier process of international meetings. The need for international cooperation on a steady basis existed of course before our meeting; traces of it can be found in the efforts and talks concerning Hydrolith, for example. Our meeting in June was an extension and consolidation of our collective recognition of that need.

Thus the one-night public event that took place during the meeting in Athens was just a part of the whole, and the collective task of creating it served simply to give energy and focus to our longer internal discussions and play. There was no predetermined agenda for those discussions; rather, the intention was for all participants to collaboratively shape the gathering itself. In exactly the same way, the three-day meeting gave energy and focus to what has already become a richer, stronger collaboration between the groups that were able to participate. During discussions we were able to elaborate the history and current projects of the respective groups, thereby creating an understanding of the different conditions and the particularities of the groups present, as well as confirming our wide and unproblematic agreement. As the crisis deepens and the tear gas spreads, that richness and strength of solidarity will only become more essential to our survival.

Our intention is to continue to build on the relationships forged at Athens by holding regular international meetings on a similar model, and we hope to strengthen this sense of explicit, frank and serious discussion of the basis of our collaborations (and our arsenal of strategies) with other centres of Surrealist activity around the world, and to build those newly forged relationships outwards to encompass ever more participants from the Surrealist movement worldwide.

Athens Surrealist Group
Stockholm Surrealist Group
Surrealist London Action Group (SLAG)

Chronicle of the Object Event

The Surrealist Group of Madrid

Organizing these three days of debate in order to reflect on the object relates to the intent of the Surrealist Group of Madrid to intervene in the reality of everyday life. This presence is part of the dynamics that the group has been developing since the beginning of the 90s. But it must be said that such dynamics take on a new meaning in the light of the present state of things, as stated in the opening text of this book*. Specifically, and as a political strategy of its own, the discourse that arises from and which rests on the principles of revolutionary criticism and poetic enchantment should locate the practices that actualize it and which tend to make it desirably understandable for everyone: understandable in rational (conceptual) and non-rational (poetic) terms. Thus, elucidation and intuition, analysis and apprehension should proceed in an ever more integrated way. The issue that this strategy raises is the question of where to elaborate this discourse and these practices so that the ideas contained therein not only address sympathizers but also opponents, the concerned and the unconcerned ones, the different and the indifferent ones, the experienced ones and the naïve.

We believe we can say that if we learned anything from the Madrid revolt of May 2011, it has been the need, literally (our discourse, as we see it) to contribute to the appropriation of the so called public sphere in order to contribute to and support its liberation, so that it can find a way to willingly channel itself into the open, i.e., to expose itself to the danger or the benefit of being misunderstood or understood, thus assuming the advantages and disadvantages that this might cause (although in fact we only perceive advantages in the present circumstances).

This explains, in part (1), how those conference nights took place in a certain vacant lot: the liberated lot of the Assembly of Lavapiés, who let us use it to hold the event. But unlike our presence in other areas (which the present one by no means overrides or bypasses), this one adds another type of daring to the conflict (something like a conscious abandonment) that is created whenever we feel compelled to ask ourselves what we can offer to others, if we are able to, and then also, but with the same initial importance, about what others can offer us, however partially or entirely outside of our purposes.

We think we know something about the object, and yet cannot stop asking ourselves what it is that we know if we ignore what others know or do not know about it. Does not the challenge of the encounter, of the correspondence, or perhaps of the lack of communication, reside in this suspension of knowledge? So the bet had been made: our discourse could only be verified in that elemental relationship with others, outside of that babbling, quiet, wise, dull (or all of the above) interrogation. Only in this way was it possible to overcome any preconceptions. This started to occur through the diverse movement of people throughout the lot, people coming and going, approaching, staying, leaving, wondering about what was happening there. People were "informed" or completely unaware of what it all was about. But the crucial moment arose when their questioning corresponded to a strangeness that was visible on their faces (thereby introducing a strangeness in our purpose), when even their most "reasonable" questions ("What is this, a flea market?") interpellated not just them, but especially us, as well. For how could we answer such a simple question for which it was not so easy to offer an answer? It was obvious that we could not just respond that it had to do with discussions about the object, but rather that we should take such a question as a suspension of the sense of the proposal itself, a suspension of meaning that was being generalized in a particularly incidental way within the debates that took place during the discussions that lead or engaged the participants each night; the suspension of meaning resulting from the anticipation of an intense experience.

No doubt this was one of the precious gifts given to us by those who had passed through the empty lot: that interrogation about what we were doing there. But this questioning should not be understood as something skeptical on their part, since what we were also trying to obtain from this event indeed happened: correspondence. Up until then, those moments when such correspondence was most visible were the debates, as we have already mentioned, which finished late at night, after the exhaustion of the discussions, which occurred about an hour and a half after the start of the latter.

We realize that the project was achieving some of

its objectives as soon as people started to both express their own thoughts about the matter under discussion and to describe some of their experiences with objects, which doubtlessly were in the same vein as what we were looking for. A girl told us that the father of a friend, whose job was to inventory household items from deceased people, selected some of these things to give to his son who had a penchant for collecting certain objects (that did not necessarily have anything to do with the tragic). But the father was not content with that and amused himself by concealing such objects in the child's bed, under the sheets. Another woman responded to this account by telling us that with great delight she used to hide a stuffed Donald Duck underneath her sheets. One of the participants immediately associated this with the spontaneous idea of the succubus-object. This led some friends and group-members to elaborate various succubus-objects that were surreptitiously introduced into the beds of three other members that night. Following the event, there was an email communication laced with humor from a woman regarding this question: "how small objects can sneak into our home, becoming our particularly harmless (but horny) demon".

Continuing with these particular accounts, we recall another person who told us how, when in need of a particular object, that he often dreamed about it. This sort of alliance between conscious thought and oneiric experience seemed to have the effect of drawing the object to him, as he often encountered what he had dreamed about with surprising ease on the very same day. According to him, this wasn't necessarily related to the poetic, since it was often about objects associated with mundane needs.

One man had us share his childhood adventures at a garbage dump, and how he admired the things that he found there, appearing as incomprehensible but truly living wonders.

Another man told us that he had the habit of picking up whatever small objects while walking down the street: a plug, a ring, a leaf … He would carry one for part of his journey and perceived it as a way to breathe life into it until he felt that it was time to take leave of the object, to abandon it, carefully depositing it in the street with the hope that someone else might pick it up and prolong its wandering life.

Also dreams increase our general knowledge about our relationship with objects. In this regard, it is also worth highlighting the comments about dreams sent to us after the event that some people have had with objects and which we summarize here using some of their own words: "... highly desirable, these objects create a magnetic field around us that brings desire into existence." "... If it is about the oneiric, just the ability to 'see' where there is apparently nothing but an old shoe or the drawer of a flaky wardrobe... is what will open our minds, and with an open mind anything is possible..."

Another person expressed himself in the following terms: "The oneiric nature of any object or thought is always fascinating. It is fascinating to dream, in itself. Tangible objects are very apparent to us so that we can appreciate their beauty, I guess." Or in these: "... The more that oneiric objects randomly come to us from wherever, the better. I find such an invasion to be revealing, dangerous, desirable and very beautiful." Also in this: "Inventing objects that make us happier, even if only in dreams, in order to remember them while standing in the unemployment line." And in conclusion, as follows: "...After having experienced the event in the vacant lot, they [the objects] have entered my life, leaving me stunned, since I did not know that they existed in the same world. I remember seeing there a glove holding a poker card with a message."

The narrative of these testimonies should not be taken as something merely anecdotal. A fundamental seriousness is to be found in them: from them we learned that not only is there a relationship between people and these objects (as can be seen, beyond the instrumental and the merely functional), but also that in this context they saw a great opportunity to manifest that kind of relationship, as if it had been inhibited before. By doing so, our correspondence took its rightful place, and the transmission was mutual. On the small scale (as it could not be any other way in the present circumstances), it was determined that, as these experiences are being 'collectivized', the communism of genius proclaimed by the surrealists emerges, since that poetic potential is common to all human beings.

The turning point occurred at the end of the third day. After the scheduled talk, a game took place: the collective construction of objects, as the note on which

we had decided to end the adventure. A substantial number of people became silent, but almost frenetically. A man took a small porcelain female bust and hit one of the eyes with a hammer, until making a hole in it. Another offered him a cup filled with sand to pour into her head. A girl revealed a toy train track onto which a shell had been placed. Someone put another shell into the mouth of a white mask, out of whose eye a small doll protruded. Two people uprooted weeds with their hands and placed them into an old suitcase. An imaginary bestiary was materializing on the lot: a tiger-headed giraffe, a swan with a body of metal, a doll with a lightbulb head... There we spent a few hours in which the suspension of rationalist sense indeed prevailed, as well as the overflow of disinhibition. Besides acquaintances (which does not imply that they necessarily had to participate, even if they did it by sheer determination), there were strangers jumping into the game, all restoring those more or less dormant powers within themselves, recovering perhaps anesthetized abilities, overcoming the dictatorship of skill, mocking every principle of authority and displaying great disdain for seriousness. Simultaneously the lot became, or had already become (2) the site of generalized play, as several people, women and men, had been kicking a ball at night. There some of these occupied people wandered about among all the artifacts that had been built up over these three days. Others approached the objects that were situated among the bushes or placed on some raised ground, or did the tour of the various signs where legends and quotes were written. A man who had just finished wandering through this space approached a member of the group, declaring that he had found himself standing in an oneiric place that he felt was his own, then only to leave it, smiling. Children who entered the lot with their parents met with their natural space. We recall how one of them even said something like the following in reference to the site: "where adults play like children in parks". This same child, with all the nonchalance of childhood, destroyed or distorted some of the objects that had been made that day. But, when assisted by a woman, he built an object during the final collective game. The fact is that, although quite useless in productivist terms but beautifully uplifting in enchanting terms – and with all the in-betweens that you want – this lot had transformed itself into the

desirable, into a place where a small human community restored a culture of the senses through an encounter with objects that had awakened in their hands just as their hands had awakened to the shapes of objects.

In this regard, it is of interest to reproduce here the comment that we received via email about the lot after the event and written by the same woman who had talked about the succubus-object: "Being on a vacant lot, a place somewhat grimy and dirty (but with no disrespect of course) also transformed us into already abandoned, discarded objects. So in a way, it was hard to tell who was human and who was a thing…"

Finally, shortly before the end of the game it had been thought that whoever might wish to participate could take away these assembled objects in a couple of shopping carts along with all that had been gathered during the previous days such as tables, cupboards, doors, fixtures, chairs, dirt, wheelbarrows, grass, shelves, walls, etc. And so it was done. Just a few minutes later, everyone prepared to leave the site, but not before placing a ghost on top of the wall that enclosed the lot. And there it stood, perhaps as the libertarian flag of a territory where the objects had been temporarily emancipated. The march of the living objects immediately started toward what is popularly called the Plaza de Agustín Lara. During the walk, words such as "the end of commodities!" or "these things will eat your hands!", or "we are all Diogenes!" were loudly proclaimed. A woman "sealed" the entrance of a bank forcing a round clock lacking needles between the glass doors. Objects were abandoned on top of cars, on sidewalks, in doorways. Someone placed the pages of a photo album at the foot of some trees. Another person took a perfume bottle with a modified label and put it on the shelf of a neighborhood store. While we proceeded towards the plaza, the shouts maintained the tension and the joy. Demoralization was unacceptable. There was a mood of individual and collective intoxication. Upon our reaching the plaza, all of these things were removed from the carts and deposited in the center of the square for us to take leave of them. Some of the people with us spontaneously jumped over the objects or ran around them in the same way as Indians of some tribes do, as if these were the embers or fire of a secular

ceremony in which the death of the commodity fetish was symbolically consummated at the hands of the poetic fetish. The objects were left to their destiny... or not at all, because after midnight some people took care of what had been left in a corner of the square by the city's cleaning services, giving them new life, carrying them to other places, depositing them in other streets, thus letting them regain their place in the open, their true habitat.

3rd of June 2013

(Translated by Bruno Jacobs, revised by Eric Bragg and Noé Ortega)

* Translator's note: this text was first published in the book "Las mercancías mueren, las cosas despiertan", La Torre Magnética, Madrid, 2013.

NOTES:

1. We arrived at the lot "accidentally" because, in principle, the event was scheduled in the Occupied Social Center Raíces, in Tirso de Molina, an adjacent neighborhood of Lavapiés. However, the obstruction of the latter by the police led us to this lot. That it occurred this way does not mean that there was not any strong desire on the part of the group to intervene in the open, as it so happened on this occasion. Despite (and even thanks to, and paradoxically) this nefarious eviction, we were given the opportunity to fulfill our latent desire to hit the street.

2. This lot not only served as an amphitheater for the talks, but was much more than that. From the first day when some of us entered, we completely identified with it. It was the exact spot where everything that had been planned had to take place. On one hand, as a lot, it contained all the promises implied through its status of being a ramshackle place, occupied by decrepit furniture falling apart, stones, pebbles, weeds, in short, by various accumulations. It was enough just to walk through it, while doing nothing, in order to feel those expected and unexpected stimulations. And yet it was not enough: it was necessary to "intervene" there on this occasion, and to respond to its potential with one's own inspiration, because, as a group member said a few months ago when referring to the need to be inspired – quoting or paraphrasing André Breton – "in times like the ones we live I prefer silence whenever I stop feeling". For it is indeed urgent to stimulate everything that is necessary to prevent that asepsis from turning into another agent of domination. Thus we had to contribute to the inspiration contained in the place, generating a limited and concentrated space of inspiration, converting it into a vortex of incantations. Whether we succeeded or not is another question, but it was our responsibility to encourage it. Actually in our hands was the ability to crystallize within the street, within everyday life, even if for a few days, the theory of the "poetics of space" and its truthfulness.

KEYHOLE TO OTHER REALITIES

Hans Plomp

Imagination is a keyhole through which we can perceive and experience other ways of being. If you have no imagination, you'll probably never perceive anything but the petrified nightmare which the vested system calls "reality". I prefer to call it miserabilism.

Hans Arp said: "Dada wants to destroy the rationalist lies, to retrieve the irrational order".

According to the surrealists, most people are trapped in the shackles of logic and intellect, destroying their imagination and limiting their freedom. Einstein stated: "Logic takes you from A to B, imagination takes you anywhere".

The historian Johan Huizinga wrote in the first half of the past century about the evolution of a new specimen of humanity: the homo ludens, the playful human. In the same period Herman Hesse wrote his mystical novel Das Glasperlenspiel (The Glass Bead Game, 1943), another reference to the playful human; the main character is called Ludo: 'I play' in Latin. Hesse must have been familiar with Huizinga's vision as he said: "I want to create a space where my spirit can breathe and live, in spite of the poisonous world, to express the resistance of the spirit against the savage powers." (1)

The concept of the androgynous homo ludens is totally opposed to the tough steel-and-leather Uebermensch of the fascists, or the obedient labourers of the Soviet workers' paradise. Both fascists and communists were projecting an extremely masculine, yang society. They denied the role of the right half of our brains, supposedly the seat of our imagination and our feminine qualities.

Surrealists see the desirable evolution in a very different light as well. Breton wrote: "It is essential...to undertake the reconstruction of the primordial Androgyne that all traditions tell us of...within ourselves."(2) The philosopher Gaston Bachelard declared: "Androgyny is not behind us, in myths and legends about our earliest biological structure. Androgyny lies ahead of us, within reach for every dreamer who dreams about growing beyond the opposition of masculine and feminine. Daydreams about the union of animus and anima are psychological prophecies." (3)

Huizinga predicted that homo sapiens would soon be replaced by machines and robots. Then humans beings would be freed of the burdens of life, and could devote themselves to their feelings, imagination and creativity. Paul Lafargue, the son-in-law of Karl Marx, was already thinking along the same lines when he wrote his pamphlet The Right to Lazy (1883). He attacked Marx's idealisation of labour and production, recommending instead a pleasant and creative life with as little labour as necessary.

In the early 60s, the painter Constant (then a situationist) defined homo ludens as the successor of homo faber, the working man. He considered the beatniks, the rockers, the hipsters and kindred spirits as an avant-garde of the new creative human being. Constant predicted a revolt against the existing structures if these would suppress the free expression of the creative potential. Soon after, a playful revolution began in the streets of Amsterdam and other Western cities, from Mai 68 in Paris to the uprisings on the campuses of Columbia and Berkeley and other American universities; in that same year, a struggle for the liberation of the homo ludens, with its battle-cry "Empower the Imagination".

Hopes of a renaissance of love and beauty were high during the 60s and 70s of the past century, fueled by visions of a new "Aquarian" consciousness. Now, more than a decade into the new millennium, it has become obvious that humanity is on its way to the abyss, in spite of numerous blueprints for a brighter future. These have been ridiculed and sabotaged by the greedy and armed misery-mongers and their vested interests.

For at least forty years, mankind has been warned about the inevitable outcome of its present life-style: the destruction of our vital eco-system. But because of a fatal mixture of stupidity and greed, humanity has been unable and unwilling to change its destructive habits.

Bob Marley was still hopeful as he sang: "You can't fool all the people all the time", but ten years ago David Allen of the Gong band implored humanity: "We've tried so hard to seduce you, if you don't know it now, we're going to lose you"....

Now that the destruction of the obsolete system seems irreversible, the question is: how can we survive the death-struggle of the old order? Over a thousand years ago the Sanskrit poet Dharmakirti wrote:

> *No one behind, no one ahead.*
> *The path the ancients cleared has closed*
> *and the other path, everyone's road,*
> *easy and wide, leads nowhere.*
> *I am alone and find my way.*

This is the voice of an outsider, an explorer of new roads to take.

In his essay The Wanton Babylon (2003), the psychonautic artist and writer Radovan Hirsl has coined the concept of "shadow artists". He defines them as follows: "They are creating, playfully entranced, in the spirit of Johan Huizinga's homo ludens, in the age-old rhythm of pulsation, reinstating the forgotten 'holy time'." These artists are creating their work "far away from sponsorships, national grants, art managers and styles demanded by the commercial yoke of the 'golden triangle': galleries, art critics and private collectors." The shadow artists embody "the dynamics of inspiration, attractive motivation and free communication", which are essential in making life on Earth the exciting, magical experience that our myths and fairy tales have always evoked. (4)

As for me, I know so-called reality and I stay away from it as far as possible. The 'normal world' drove me insane. Fortunately I succeeded in getting through "the dark night of my soul" without psychiatric intervention. Since then I feel a great sense of wonder about the fantastic miracle of our existence on this splendid planet. Also my awareness of the unbelievable monstrosities committed by supposedly normal people has increased. This sense of wonder is conducive to the survival of our spiritual being. It allows us to create our own realities, our very own illusions, I would say:

> *Look inside yourself*
> *and find your finest dream,*
> *make it grow in your love's beam.*
> *Then out there in reality*
> *look for your dream's company...*

Probably this companion will be another outsider, who loves to share his or her personal vision with you.

Reality is a subjective experience: anything you believe in may become reality. As the Renaissance individualist, Michel the Montaigne put it: "Be careful with wishes, they tend to come true." The imagination shatters the mirror of mono-reality into a multitude of limitless surrealities. A most adorable dysfiguration.

NOTES:
(1) Eike Middell, Hermann Hesse. Roederberg Verlag (1975), p. 255.
(2) Du surrealisme en ses oeuvres vives (1953).
(3) G.Bachelard, La Poétique de la reverie (1960).
(4) Claude Steiner & Radovan Hirsl: Psychonautische Landkarte 2, Nachtschatten Verlag, Zürich (2003).

REVOLT:
THE GAME OF THE NEW MILLENNIUM

Turkish Surrealist Group

Certain concepts which have arisen with the revolt in Tunisia, then during the Arab Spring and then in the protest of the dispossessed in Europe, must be considered long and hard: such as dignity revolt, spiritual revolt, ethical revolt. Because these concepts contain the alchemical formula of the black substance which will demolish the reality terror and the consumption society which keeps it alive.

The most powerful weapon of these maxims and the revolts that cry them is that they are exempt from ideology. Even though this may sound like a weakness or state of lacking for some old opponents, they are the smoking guns of the power of revolt's elixir against Reality.

If we consider the function of ideology and the political manifestations of it in daily life as the security valve of the system, we see the fact that revolt takes its power from "the spirituality", is its most direct and autonomous power. Yes, the ideologies are dead and gone but this not a bad thing.

The opposite ideology itself which develops under the iron claws of what is social such as association membership, non-governmental organization membership, party bureaucracy membership, trade union clan leadership, cultural opposition, life-style anarchy, opinion leaders is a kind of living-death itself.

Minority policies, cultural policies, queer policies, political-correctness, identity policies, the response of all the political imagination developed based on the other in practice is the submission, which is the acceptance of helplessness against the system. And this is not an innocent position at all, as it impedes the real radicalism and keeps pumping fresh blood into the system.

The opinion leaders who are marketed or presented as radicals, are the paid philosophers at universities or institutes financed overtly or covertly by the largest national holdings at the local level and by the multinational giant companies at the global level.

Each so-called intellectual escaping from the political reality becomes an artist or an author. At this point, "contemporary art" has been popularized with the absence of the courage to produce policies in daily life. The drug cult, Woodstock spirit, Utopia of pleasure devoid of spirituality, that led to the destruction of the rebellious generation of 1960's has crippled the opposition in today's show society. And the circle of artists of the defenders-practitioners of bohemian life contribute to the consumption society as the production centre of this destitution. If freedom is not sleeping around, consuming all types of drug substances, and speaking as much as the system lets you do so; the new revolt has to retreat to the roots, to the spiritual-resistance position.

The real artistic activity in the dystopia in which revolution is narrowed to the criticism of daily life, cultural destitution to cultural criticism in daily life, is to defend the revolt. Intellectual slovenliness, and cowardice cannot be gilded with bright theories. Even though we cannot achieve it, we need to find the courage to defend the truth. Each individual is responsible for history, even though he or she does not want to accept it.

Popular local or international political agendas are trap systems that try to drag us into the system. The real revolt cannot be expected to take sides with political agendas or to develop an attitude. In the absence of organized movements, small cells and resistance groups will be prominent. The problem is how we will destroy the system rather than how we will survive in it.

Even though the revolt in the United Kingdom was nurtured by the Arab Spring as depending on the spirit of time, the best analogy that can be established is the Paris Ghetto uprising in Paris mid-1990's. The direct violence and migration problem that marked the revolt clarifies this connection. Just like it is easier to establish a bridge between the massive search for freedom in Madrid and Tahrir Square. What is forgotten here, the repelled ghost is the rebellious energy that still leaks from Alex's body that lies on the ground. The 21st century started in Athens, even though people who refer to themselves as anarchists do not accept this.

Even if the violence of the oppressed makes us hopeful, violence that is devoid of spirituality and the urge for a new humanity can turn into a backward termination any time. At this point, if the yearning to return to the primitive is a "survivor" order, in which the strongest dominates, this alternative itself is an anti-utopia. When we consider how much the opponent beats us in the face, the difference between the fight club and "lord of the flies" will fade away. The problem is to conquer life, not to survive.

The illegal immigrant who leaves the store hugging the television set he looted, as if "hugging the beloved", is still under the spell of the cult value of the commodity dated by Marx or Lukacs, the writer of "history or class awareness". Whereas this fantastic satisfaction of desire cannot shed light on the black hole in his soul. Demonstration is a trouble of addiction, making you feel hungrier as you eat. At this point, except for those who loot the store in their neighborhood, we have to watch the techtonic movements of hearts that set the Sony factory ablaze outside the town.

The direct target of the communique of the surrealists in 1925 is "the destruction of Western civilization" and this maxim is the refutation, which is the most revolutionist request that exists at the moment. The fact that the majority of surrealists are defeated by being an artist does not alleviate the intensity of this idea, because the roots of this call for revolt go beyond Western civilization of 2000 years, to Hermes, Gnostics, secret heretic communities, alchemists, dervishes, Qatar knights, Hassan El Sabah, those who were burned for witchcraft, those who were killed at the Nicea Council or Ecumenical Council, Hölderlin, Blake, commune members, Blanquie, Maldoror, Peret and Debord.

We need a new Human Being or the total destruction of humanity...

11.08.2011

S.E.T

Translated.T.Karakoç/H.Koçak

Oakland Occupy - Night of the General Strike

The Sun Rises at Night
Sketches of the 2011 revolt of Madrid

Eugenio Castro

May 18

Today at five o'clock in the morning, the general assembly, which had begun at three-thirty in the morning, was still lively. A thousand people occupied the Plaza de Sol at that time. The scenery was wonderful: people sleeping or dozing, or wrapped in blankets and standing, wandering around putting up posters with generally imaginative slogans, exchanging ideas, being masters of their own bodies and dreams. And lovers who loved each other, yes, exactly. A black glove over the posterboard, and a blanketed-man standing, taking a self-portrait because he had discovered his own new beauty. Fatigue fraternizes with imagination. The dream lives on, over the asphalt. Oneirism and wakefulness together: one could almost say that dream and action are sisters (ah, Baudelaire!). I am not exaggerating anything. What joy! May what lasts last, as one painting says: the world revolves around the Plaza de Sol.

Now people can only let themselves be carried along with this joy, despite the reformists, leftists and other infiltrators who want to appropriate the wonderful disarray in which this political class is engulfed. They are nothing but trifles next to the event itself.

May 19

At two o'clock, the rain had clustered people in tents, so that the concentration had also become a "marketplace" in which the qualitative use of things had taken place. The ebb and flow of plastic objects, blankets, water and food became more obvious. People with shopping carts brought things for sleeping, but there were no commodities. And inside the tents, everyone's expression was that of contempt for the difficulties that the weather had created. And the dialogue and reflections about what was happening created a common language. But these developments also occurred outside of the tents, of course, and in fact, the meetings continued outside as well. And the assembly that convened to decide on a course of action consisted of a significant number of people. It was beautiful to see how two of them pulled the cart carrying the speaker and the microphone over slabs covered with rain water and soaked cardboard while loudly announcing the meeting place. And there went every one of us who wanted to.

It is interesting to reflect on a scene that reverses the common trend: today people are not running to any shelter, but instead sleeping in the open, despite the bad weather. And another promising fact: people started putting up tents. At least six could be counted, which gave new meaning to the word, 'camp'. A little earlier someone succeeded in "throwing" the police out: they left with their trucks not to be seen anymore... at least for this night. There is no doubt that the rain contributed somewhat, which had the welcome effect of removing certain nightmarish elements from the vigil. One sleeps better that way.

I happen to remember that a few hours earlier, at nightfall, someone released a small air balloon with a flame inside, more or less reddish-orange in color, which rose above the Plaza de Sol. It was amazing: the sun rising at night.

May 20 – 21

An occupied square, a magnetic square. This seems to be the great power that the Plaza de Sol has acquired. It is difficult not to feel it while wandering around, because when you finally decide to leave, you can't, because something crosses your path that makes you deviate from your most likely vague direction, since it is utterly difficult to move away from this community, which lacks any denomination, and which is fully eloquent and boisterous with its clamor and its silence. And as soon as you leave, you come back when new events are occurring, which, no matter how trivial, are loaded with the force of circumstance, and with their own beauty which, why not say it, is more convulsive than the kind you have been reading about.

The square is being charged with energy from the bodies and the screams. The political demands and anger become manifest in this giant vocalization, filled with joy and humor. A television network and its correspondent. They want to broadcast live. People see them and start hurling a deafening collective scream, preventing the correspondent from speaking and the news crew in the studio from hearing anything: "The sound of desire silences the speakers of the masters". And the square becomes magnetized with mental energy, which lets its imagination erupt, since imagination is the other pole of that magnetization. Imagination and humor. Yesterday evening, when there was still sunlight, an imitation leather sofa was seen moving above the heads of people, entering from Preciados Street. It disappeared behind a metal structure, but shortly afterwards flew over our heads, literally, disappearing in the background. What a powerful image, that which is thoroughly lived and not deferred! And the same for a large kettle that someone placed at one end of a bus shelter. Of course! It is Alice's kettle, and we all eat those cakes which

turn us into incredible shrinking beings, so as to recognize the latent genius of events, or into growing beings to rise above the impossible, such as realism, social destiny and fatality.

Ever since the beginning of this collective civil disobedience, a huge advertisement panel of a cosmetics multinational has been covering the front of a building, ruining the view for so many. But yesterday, as a nameless voice explained, someone began to transform it in the same way that Léo Malet carried out the *décollage* of publicity posters. First, a group of activists climbed to the top of the panel and from there deployed an eloquent homemade poster that showed the torso of a military fascist/nazi with black Mickey Mouse ears, with the emblem of the euro in the form of a tie clip and the legend "They do not represent us". Alongside this action, perhaps the same group changed two words of the advertisement text which became "Real democracy" (sic). Below, a series of words such as *Paris, Mediterranean skin, 48 hours*, gave way to the wonderful practice of word association, within the context of yesterday's and today's revolts. Momentarily, the culmination of this *décollage* was performed by a man who tore off the panel around the region of the woman's breast and pushed his head through. Then, on our side, a voice shouted: "It's the nipple of revolution", a cry that was echoed in unison throughout that part of the square where some of us were present. Meanwhile, the man kept moving his head with gestures of tenderness and excitement. Humor, eroticism and imagination celebrate their betrothal here. Poetry had leapt out into the streets.

I said that this square is magnetized and that night – and possibly more so during the early morning hours – makes you even more sensitive to this phenomenon. You can hardly get away from it. It is totally opposite from the effect in "The Exterminating Angel". It is not the return of the repressed which creates fear and prevents you from going out, as we see happen to those miserable bourgeois in Buñuel's movie, but rather, it is the desired encounter with the repressed that returns and what makes us repeatedly traverse the square where the unexpected excites the senses and so far remains free of any conditions that might restrict it. Thus the words of revolt, dreams and poetry linger inside the tents, or remain there; or somebody stops to read, to launch and to write them here and there: "Every heart is a cell of the revolution", "Go on sleeping while the pavement burns and they tell us that it's raining", "Utopia or nothing", "We want to live forever in this hurricane", "Yesterday we ran to the shelter, today we sleep in the open", "What will be will glow", "The future is intense".

And groups of people not only lounge under the canvas of the tents, but also on the street asphalt and on the sidewalks of the square. "Yesterday we ran to the shelters, but today we sleep in the open". And one can read and live and sleep with the marvelous, yielding to the unknown, to people and things: "Closed for revolution, enjoy the inconvenience", said a small sign, with its loafing practitioners next to it.

These days we see the conjured desires of people:

the days in red have separated themselves from the work schedules, and for now every day is a party. Indeed, such is poetry... in May 2011.

May 21 – Time

The threat of a potential eviction order from the Election Board is hanging over Plaza de Sol. It has been like this every day so far, but today it is more extreme. The ending of the occupation of the square and the dismantling of the camp is its obsessive goal. In order to prevent this, word has been spread by all possible means that on this day our unity should be even more steadfast than ever, in addition to having invited all the people of Madrid to come and dance at eight o'clock in the evening as usual, alone, in pairs, in threes, with children, partners, friends, everyone. The occupation has been an example of disobedience to the threat, and each day and night this disobedience becomes intensified, then it relaxes and experiences its own joy.

The Election Board's threat was scheduled to happen at 12 pm. The response was moving: not only did nobody leave the square, but instead more and more people arrived, compared with those from the previous hours. This is no longer about the circulation of commodities in a place colonized by temples of consumption; this is the flow of bodies, the flux of acting, thinking and desiring minds that have abolished the time of commodities and, simultaneously, have reinvented the flow of a time that runs freely. And what is more, I would say, it is nothing less than the abolition of time. For time in this place, as we so greatly wished, is marked by the beating of tens of thousands of hearts that are like the cells of a revolution, as one of the many inscriptions declares, those inscriptions that have ABSOLUTELY transformed the face of the square. Not surprisingly, this square is now a "town" within the city, constantly renewed, in the sense that it is not fixed by external boundaries, but rather extends according to the requirements of material, mental and spiritual necessities in which, even here, the imagination is an admirable as well as organizational faculty for demonstrating the falsity of the perpetual, present time of the economy. In this regard, one of the ways in which time is being lived is in a way that *doesn't involve money*. Ever since the rise of the disobedience movement, money has been expelled from this city, which, like it or not, is the living embodiment of a concrete utopia in the process of being realized. *Without money* – that marvelous assertion of the practical truth of poetry. And it is the case that imagination and organization are brought together, without any hierarchy, in a fraternal way (how has this word not been actualized or has not become a formidable force that at one point seemed to have lost its energy, all its truth!) and have managed, by extension, to establish the *communism of genius* – all of that creativity for the people and by the people, in their experimental, playful and organized expressions and practices.

So what time are we talking about? About the time of awakening with emotional solidarity in the midnight of a new era that has been hoped for, in silence for a minute, only

to launch immediately after the cry of common lycanthropy, because at that hour we all became wolves that consume the chronological time of extortion and threat, inaugurating a mythical time in which the republic of lycanthropy is established (ah, Petrus Borel, in this midnight your boldness was fulfilled when you were saying something like "my republicanism is lycanthropy"!).

And after this common howling, just a little while after, a group of men and women, protesting the lack of decent housing for everyone, in a spontaneous gesture pulled their keys out of their pockets, and shook them in the air. What a beautiful scene, with all those moving keys sounding like "wise music"! If only we had eaten the grapes of the revolution a moment earlier, then now we would be joining others to open, who knows, the doors of private property. For private property, as we had never seen it before, had been abolished in the square in which, over time, a citadel without doors had been built, with its inner streets, libraries, pharmacies, kindergarten, food services... and furniture that belongs to no one because it comes from the whole human community that was founded here. Beds, sofas, mattresses, blankets, chairs, bulbs, lamps, books and an urban garden built around a fountain... Isn't it admirable, with however much modesty you want, this kind of dreamed utopian city, endowed with full autonomy, with an "urban", "territorial", human, "economic" (remember: no money) organization? But with the difference that the dream has come true, that this city has taken shape, and that in it lives a community without masters. You are compelled to enter it, to immerse yourself in it, to savor its taste, feel its sound, see its landscape, smell its smells, socialize with everyone, or simply watch this feast of the senses with eyes wide open.

Space-time as we knew it has been abolished within this citadel, which is to say, and in order to avoid any confusion, abolished within the whole square, and from the evening of the 28th to the 29th of May, also within the squares and streets surrounding it.

June 10 – Words in conflict

Any movement of revolt has its own words, words that shape its varying degrees of intensity. The tension and the energy of the movement – or its weakness and demoralization – are associated with these words. Terms like revolution, anti-capitalism, rebellion, subversion, murderous police, financial capitalism, ruthless bankers, etc. are not just being used for any old reason.

With admiration, anger and celebration, the first week of the May 15 movement experienced the words that denounced the symbols and people associated with the global state of crisis. And not just that: it also reinvented those words of freedom which, along with disobedient slogans, gave the revolt a wonderful brilliance. In fact, the appearance of the Puerta del Sol and its surroundings were transformed by the profusion of words and phrases that, while diverted from their original meanings, nevertheless created a major sensation.

Well, that whole lexicon of the revolt has been diluted and censored by a false display of respect, which, in this particular case, demonizes written and spoken dissent. Needless to say, it is sufficient for a few to shout "the police are torturers and murderers," in a crowd to immediately hear a hiss of disapproval. It is enough to scream "from north to south, from east to west, the fight will go on costing whatever it may cost," for a lingering silence to prevail. The very worst insult to the essence of the movement we have heard is that this rebellion is from the right as well as from the left, from capitalism as well as from the anti-capitalists. The fact is that, gradually, from within and from outside of it, those words that gave a revolutionary glow to this movement of civil disobedience and insubordination, those words that generated a subversive tension within the context of the uprising (however modest it may have been and which is not just another reformist protest but a strike against the unbearable state of things, or rather a popular revolutionary discourse) have been effectively cast aside.

Through this disguised censorship of the language of the revolt, a situation has been reached that needs to be acted upon immediately; this situation is the neutralization of the rebellion, carried out by the removal of energy from our words. By neutralization, we mean: the sedation of the subversive tension, its neutralization by an operation of reactionary humanism, i.e. the standardization of behaviors and ideas, while openly rejecting the ones that criticize the manipulation of the movement, i.e. those which raise a voice of reflective and revolutionary criticism against the desire to act subversively, imposing the dogma of reformist ideas that distorts the nature of the revolt.

Those tepid words, as we have observed, jibe all too well with the language of the system, and are the best way to root out the combative essence of the rebellion; and yet this combativeness still embodies the social war.

Against this situation, we would like to reintroduce all the terminology that the imagination can handle, so as to restore the revolutionary nature to the movement.

June 13 – When the night decides to present itself as primordial (As if it were a collective dérive)

The evolution of the revolt, in regards to its admirable unpredictability, yields highly unusual moments, such as when, during this month, time has been experienced as if we were living in a black hole that suddenly released its enormous power.

While hounded by the depression caused by the dismantling of the Plaza de Sol citadel, and with the eradication of this already eternal symbol, with its reality and life still taking form, to the point that one, a few, or even many are reluctant to attend the ceremony of deSolation, suddenly a new episode of rebellion, of celebration, of wonder takes place.

Despite their current circumstances, a group of people (friends and fellow participants in the founding of long-term goals), after experiencing the attraction exerted by the square, and after observing a little of what remains of the citadel, decides to return to Pontejos Square, which is the usual assembly place, just to socialize and spend the evening. Suddenly, one of them receives a call or a message about a thousand people having blocked off Gran Vía Street. We move forward through Preciado Street in order to reach Callao-Gran Vía Street. Indeed, the large artery is cut. And here – let there be no misunderstanding – there is no need to "close your eyes" to see, because all eyes are wide open – those of the insiders' and outsiders' – and we see; I am sure we do see.

We do not see any protesters. By sheer inertia, we start the march towards Cibeles Street. It is so strange to walk through the middle of the Gran Vía, devoid of cars, a path through which other bystanders also walk, some of them lying down in the very middle to take pictures: whatever authority will prevent them from acting instinctively tonight! The absurd and the dream are at home. What elemental manifestations of an oneirism that surfaces during the night will awaken and just from a ten or fifteen minute walk will become entirely collective! That is right; just after the Red de San Luis we can see in the distance people crossing the path of the demonstration and blocking off Alcalá Street. We rush onward until joining up with them. What a joy to feel the way we merge with the crowd, to have that physical feeling of merging with the body of the "mass", with the body of the revolt! The thrill of taking over the street is overwhelming, now calm, now exalted. We are restoring popular sovereignty without notice, without any "official" call, and without any authorization.

The crowd proceeds to City Hall in Cibeles Street, as had been done on Saturday the 11th when rioting in Villa Square, blocking off the streets when the mayor and council members had to leave.

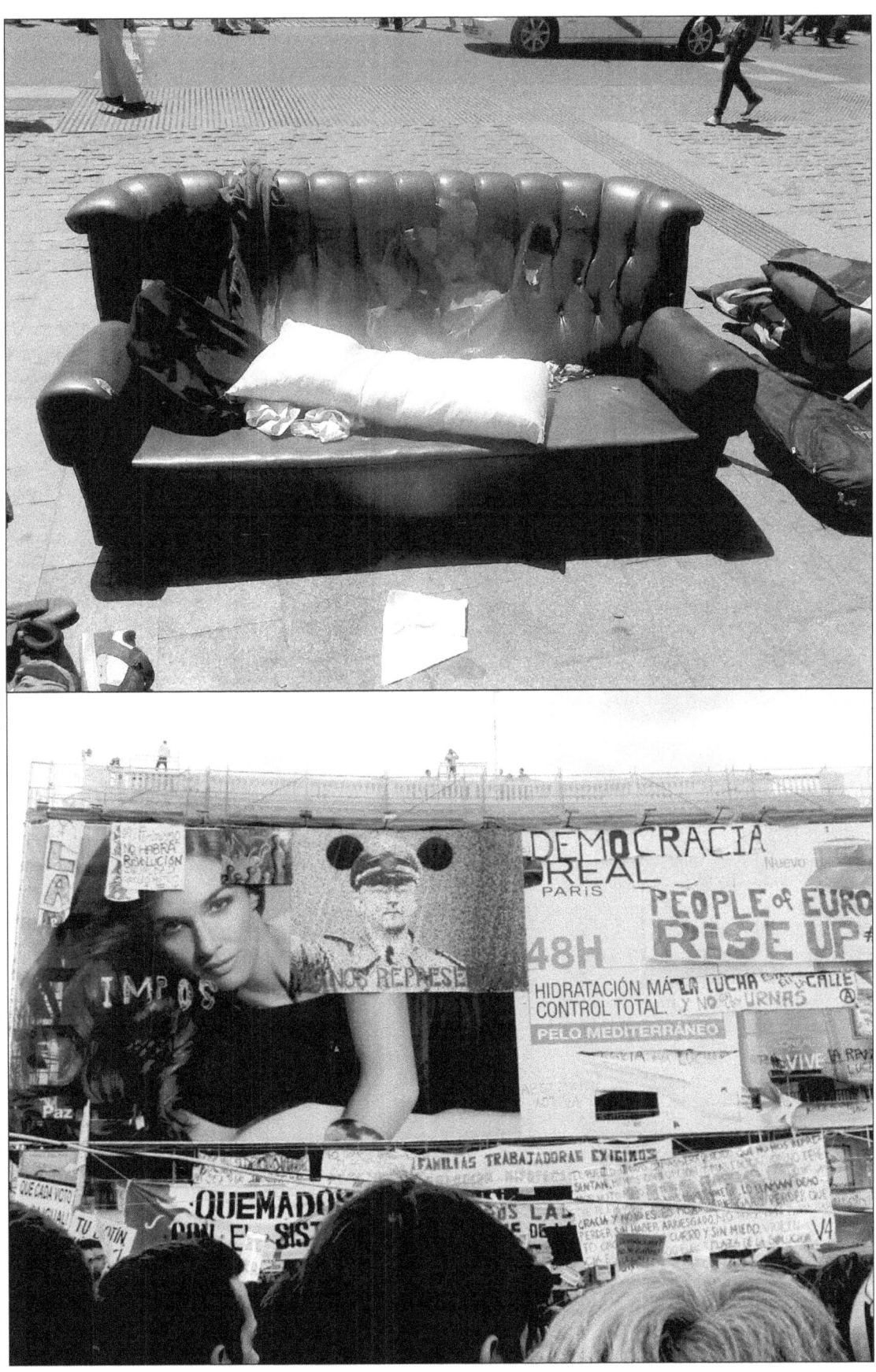

Everything indicated that there would be a sit-in, but no, the leading group moves ahead and starts to turn back toward the square, with some people thinking that we would thereby take that route back to the Puerta del Sol. However, after completely going around Cibeles, the lead group goes in the direction of Parliament down the Paseo del Prado. The ease with which we take one street or another, indifferent to impunity, is amazing, as if it had been overcome by the very inertia of the revolt. (1)

Reaching Neptune Square, a line of police have cordoned off the entrance to the Carrera de San Jerónimo, and therefore to Parliament. But no frustration hangs over the group. The festive, bold, serene, even "victorious" mood prevails in mind, spirit and body. And yes, now the words of conflict are a little louder, and the radical and revolutionary slogans are getting mixed in with poetic exhortations and humorous exclamations. And the police desperately understand everything that we say. We do it sitting or standing. It is joyful, it is free; we remain unpunished! There we are. And we can ask ourselves, perhaps whimsically, what will happen next, or maybe not even think about anything, nor wait for anything because we have it all at this moment.

Time passes and people are starting to get up, and one begins to hear voices that spontaneously invite us to visit the occupiers of the Cuesta de Moyano. Certainly, nothing suggests that these marches were scheduled in advance (even if they do belong to the "logic" of the protest), and definitely not this one, not in the least. Once again we liberate another street. It is almost impossible not to find the following question striking, and not while in a state of befuddlement, or better yet, in a drunken state: What are we doing, about a thousand of us, at two o'clock early Monday morning, marching, down the car lane of the Paseo del Prado? The impossible is possible, as the saying goes.

It is tempting to say that we are almost strolling along, as if it were a collective derive that had likely often been imagined before but which nonetheless remained unknown, at least in the way in which it is happening here. The buildings on either side of the boulevard, with the Prado museum shadowing on the left where the imagination puts sandbags in its gaps, in its walls, join the great general estrangement: the asphalt evokes the sky and captures a thousand human shadows at once; there are more trees than ever, and a thousand human heads are shaking and bouncing back and forth. A moment later we show our solidarity with the occupiers of Moyano with big applause. Almost simultaneously a part of the crowd forms a human chain and closes the square of Atocha. All of this accentuates that spirit of new life flowing in the early hours of June 13, 2011.

During these days that transform Madrid, we have attained a higher consciousness regarding the meaning and the power of Rimbaud's words that "true life is absent". It is necessary to experience a life of fulfillment (I do not mean: an absolutely complete life) like the one that the Madrid revolt provides, which tells us that, in fact, true life was absent. But because of this unique experience, because of the intensity that occurs despite the unspeakable words, we also understand its consequence with an almost total accuracy: that real life was not entirely absent.

15-16 June – Lunar eclipse

A part of the assembly for long-term policy arrives at the Plaza de Sol at ten p.m. or a quarter past ten, after a meeting. Incredulous, they learn that the newspaper *El Mundo* has installed a tent there where the mutineers of Sol camped only up until three days ago. It is not easy to contain the rage of this group or the confusion of a number of people passing through the square. "It's a perversion", says one woman. "It's a provocation", exclaims another. It is also an incitement to violence. But spontaneously a woman and a man write "Commission of manipulation, censorship and disinformation" on a white placard. It is placed under the words *El Mundo*, visible from the tent. The people, while showing signs of disapproval and refusal, stand in front of this infamous place. When workmen dismantled the tent, the placard of denouncement is immediately retrieved so not to be lost, and then placed below the words *El Mundo* located on the worktable of two women, so that the minute protest against this outrage still can be seen.

Then someone approaches the ridiculous "information stand" for the purpose of clarification about the rumor that the May 15 movement had dissociated itself from the riot that took place a day earlier against politicians in Barcelona. The answer is embarrassing: "There has been some confusion in the statement that will be corrected tomorrow on the movement's website". Why wait until tomorrow, we wonder? The "informant" of this nefarious stand claims, and not in his own name but in that of the movement, to condemn the violence, all forms of violence. Inevitably this leads to a heated argument, which at times reaches an elevated pitch and becomes more controversial, in which these advocates of non-violence show signs of speaking in a not-so-peaceful manner.

It turns out that suddenly some of us find that a group of bureaucrats has assumed the ethics and even the morality of the movement. The important fact remains, however, that such statements exceed the particular topic of discussion when nearby people immediately join in. There is no point in trying to reproduce here what both parties said. But it is important to note that the discussion succeeded in inflaming the critical, animated, pressing and rebellious spirit that only one month earlier had given birth to the Madrid revolt. That day (that evening) and today (this evening) we witness a presence of mind and a revolutionary political consciousness that confronts all forms of reaction.

Still at the location where the discussions took place, I received a phone call. My friend, Rag Cuter, reminds me with great enthusiasm that a total lunar eclipse is happening during these hours, and urges me to join him and his friends at the intersection of Santa Isabel and Torrecilla del Leal

Streets. Totally exalted, I relay that information into one of the ongoing discussions so that some friends will know or remember, in order to rush to our meeting place.

The view is superb. Up in the sky above Santa Isabel Street, at that time already centrally occupied by the sun (or better to say, *half-covered*), the two heavenly bodies radiate their dominion. People have liberated the street as a sign of the times, and they lie down on the pavement and the sidewalks. And as werewolves, as the sun retreats and the moon regains its entire splendor, we howl for fifteen minutes and howl again, lost "sunatics" (2). This happened at the end of the night of the fifteenth and at the beginning of the morning of the sixteenth of June, the monthly birthday of the Madrid revolt.

June 30 – The inconsumable sofa

The installation in the Plaza de Sol of an infamous "information stand" regarding the "activities" of the May 15 Movement, something that was hatched on the sly, behind the backs of almost the entire movement, in an act of corruption typical of career experts, and which simultaneously forecast the near-total dismantling of the Plaza de Sol citadel (although a significant number of stands would remain for another week). Professional bureaucrats, reformists and well-mannered citizens met at this stand after successively manipulating the general assembly, developing maneuvers of confusion, attrition and demoralization after the first ten days of the occupation in order to dissolve the citadel.

What the citadel embodied, at least for many of the participants in the Madrid revolt, has already been mentioned, but I will summarize briefly: Utopian life, as utopia was revealed within it as the revolutionary realization of the present, the abolition of time, the abolition of private property, the abolition of money and of use-value versus exchange-value, the reinvention of brotherhood, and the re-enchantment of everyday life. And all of this said with a certain amount of caution, and without any fanfare. But in its day to day existence this settlement demonstrated another immense value found in its use: its precarious appearance which was never in conflict with its internal organization that ranged from impeccable to admirable, overcoming the material difficulties of that apparent evanescence. In fact, such apparent precariousness and provisionality have rarely coalesced so well with a "political project of poetic life" in which the "luxury of poverty" has been celebrated with great abandon. I am not praising any proletarianization of life here, among other reasons, because it has not occurred in this case (a legitimate proletarianization, indeed, for anyone who wants it and becomes aware of its implications for his or her own life), but rather I mean the ability of the human species to grant itself an inspired life (a luxury of the mind) in a precarious material situation (the modesty and humility of the tents, of the furniture, of electricity, etc.). The truth is that this architecture was to be expected, given that what was taking place in the Plaza de Sol was only an initially improvised experiment of utopian life as was never before experienced in Madrid, a utopian experiment that occurred within the very framework of popular revolt, of which the citadel of the Plaza de Sol was at that moment its greatest symbol of the enchanted present and as its projection of becoming: its existence does not end with its dismantling; it is a summoning precipitate, which contains its return in a latent state.

Such a way of life is elaborated each day, so it would be unthinkable to expect any type of architecture and urbanization of space other than the one that already belongs to this particular existence, where it would realize itself each day in such a beautifully (dis)articulated, and such a thrillingly instinctive form. Thus, it is not the time to wonder whether anyone would want to live in such a precarious state for the rest of one's life (an undoubtedly biased, miserabilist and even laughable approach thoroughly remote from the deorbit caused by the revolt), but rather to note that this lifestyle was the consequence of an *altered* state that does not tolerate how the reasons for a life of certainty and how the parameters of convenience and commodity fetishism should prevail.

This is where the inconsumable sofa makes its appearance to the point of transforming itself (as I see it) into a kind of monument to that way of life and for the resistance that it develops against this dual fetish (of convenience and commodity) which has its representative in the sweltering barracks that house the aforementioned "information stand". Designed by an architect (and done surreptitiously apart from any assembly-proposal and consensus), its obvious professional origin insults the spirit of the revolt and stands in denial of the citadel, becoming de facto an object of consumption into which the May 15 movement is being dragged. Against this trap that aspires to be the spectacular remains of the citadel, the inconvenient sofa moves from one side to another, from one "home" to another, as a marvelous object that combines the functional with the magical precisely because of its usage that obliterates its exchange value (and this is the case even when it is not completely isolated, as when abandoned, even if only briefly, since someone will always be willing to use it).

This sofa first appeared, at least for me, on the evening of May 20, being carried as if with wings through Preciados Street to the corner of the Plaza de Sol. It disappeared behind an iron structure mounted to hold the "guns" of the press. And it unexpectedly reappeared after a while next to me (and to many others), from behind, literally passing over our heads, as if weightless, and disappearing towards the citadel (but not knowing, obviously, that this would be its destination). I saw it days later in the utopian settlement's library. It also spent some time in one of the food stands. When the citadel had been dismantled, I could see how someone, having put a houseplant on its seats, dragged it across the Plaza de Sol. Two or three days later I saw it again on TV, while it was being occupied by someone sleeping. I must admit that it was this vision that made me aware of the symbolic value that it had acquired for me. That is how it occurred to me to visit the Plaza de Sol the next day at noon in order to find it, to see if it still was there. It gave me great joy to see that one of the last occupying groups was using it, that it was part of their "furniture". A white pillow was lying on its seats. I approached and thereby discovered that the sofa was tattooed with phrases of different kinds that were beautiful, exciting and humorous.

Has this magic fetish disappeared, that of resistance to architectural sterilization, which the barracks exemplifies, a magic fetish that also is an anti-fetish of consumption? Surprisingly, up until the day of writing this, June 30th, the sofa has still been present in the square. I saw it first with what appeared to be the last occupying group camped there, and then the next day in a strange stand that bore the name "anárkika tavern".

The inconvenient remainder of the Plaza de Sol citadel celebrates its memory, uglifies the horrible encampment, and reveals itself as the object that, in addition to hosting the sleep and dreams of the rebels, also displays on its body the eloquence of its threatening, insolent, poetic and insurgent words: "If you cut down our rights we will burn your roofs!", "I'm a bitch but I do not play the flute", "Sunscreen, we have sun for a long time", "It's still dawning... just wait for the sunset".

And on one end of the backrest, there is the star of the "Great Evening": the black star of rebellion.

NOTES:
1) It is worth stopping for a moment to ask ourselves why the police did not act during this whole time: after the brutal charge on the demonstration on May 15th, the eviction of the campers of Puerta del Sol on the morning of the 17th, and the aggressions in Bailén and Sacramento streets on June 11th. It may be argued that the above events had effectively prevented the police leadership from acting and which likewise moved down the chain of command. And this is true, of course. But we cannot help but suspect that if it had occurred that way, then it did so because of an arresting effect that the revolt has had on them: a kind of paralysis of their will because of the focused nature of the movement. In fact the police have already been discredited, despite the up-until-now lack of bloodshed. We cannot help but see this strange, perhaps new phenomenon as a victory for the revolt: the crippled action of the agents of physical repression. Of course none of this excludes the possibility of its undesirable resurgence in the near future. And not that another uprising, somewhere between what is unavoidable and desirable, would completely alter that strange paralysis. There is nothing else to do than to be prepared for it.
2) Simple neologism formed by the word lunatic and sun that emerged after the discussion of the plaza de Sol and during the total eclipse of the moon.

(Translated by Bruno Jacobs, revised by Eric Bragg and Noé Ortega)
* Some fragments of this text were originally published in El Rapto #7, Madrid, 2012.

● ●

LATENT NEWS: BURNING UP THE GREEN GUARDIAN

In September he has been sex on fire and battling varicose veins. The crowd booed and deserted him, amounting to a breach of its contractual terms. A rapping robot has apologised to clients since his financial problems began earlier this year.

The clinic which can solve your denture problems is being repaired after it rusted over in the Wendy House. During your sitting you will be on the verge of bankruptcy and a forgetful 85-year-old woman stealing from a shop where cheeks and lips collapse regardless of whether they go ahead with a procedure or not.

The title has given me some authority with tilapia and London schoolchildren with a bag of several sets of dentures.

Kingston Guardian November 19th 2009; (by Stuart Inman)

The Dangers of Puerilizing the Movement

Sol Lycantrophes

If the movement that started on May 15 has already produced wonderful results that have shaken Spain, Europe and virtually the whole world, if the contagious example of self-management, real and direct democracy, spontaneity, organization, fraternity and courage to challenge all dogmas and all absolute truths, if this experience that is creating a new society just as it has raised a real city that is also a maze of desires, if this has happened, then let us remember that it wasn't for nothing and didn't happen without repercussions. From the twenty-four arrested on the night of the 15th, who were cruelly beaten by the police, to those who dared to speak and give their opinions, overcoming the vertigo of the stigma which had been cultivated in them ever since childhood against the temptation of revealing their true problems and desires, moving on, of course, but not forgetting the comrades who have given *their very best* and remarkably without competing or making the vigilant slave driver any wealthier, but instead making the movement work and grow and evolve; people who have been working in the kitchen, carrying water to the assemblies to relieve them from the heat, pitching tents and food shops, and improvising to resolve the thousands of technical, management and organization problems... all those friends who are now exhausted and who have given us their free time and even risked their work or exams because they know, as we all know, that what is now being dealt with here is more important... No, the 15-M movement did not come free of charge. We have risked everything.

Because of this, some of us feel hurt, concerned and outraged by certain signs of trivialization of the movement and attempts to make it childish that are appearing both in the media and within our own ranks, and while the former is inevitable, the latter should not be. But it is a total shame and disgrace that the vacuous media compares those gatherings from last Friday and Saturday, replete with noise, fury and joy, with a mere game of football, or a giant drinking party or a rock festival (regardless if they might have manifested similar elements of folk culture as well as mass tourism). Likewise, it is both funny and manipulative that another "progressive" paper publishes the photo of a protester hugging a police officer to prove that she is, after all, just as good-natured and friendly as... inoffensive (when perhaps the person sharing the embrace was possibly a relative, or a drinking buddy), but little can be done against the nastiness and fantasies of the media.

But other things seem much worse to us, like how the committees and the assembly bother to take seriously the slimy and hypocritical offer of Inditex (one of those multinational corporations that are destroying our lives and the planet) to provide free electricity to that very same camp which is supposedly dreaming of the demise of that company and all the others. Or that the possibility is being discussed of removing the posters and stickers that so thoroughly adorn the square with an unprecedented glow of collective creativity and of poetry finally made by all, just because it slows down consumption and the circulation of money, whereas the abolition of ubiquitous advertising that devours the city, of consumerism and of the sad figure of the compulsive consumer should also be one of the objectives of a camp that says it intends to reinvent society and its productive framework. Or, even more absurd and injurious is that the assembly on the afternoon of Monday the 23rd *acknowledges* and *applauds* the news that a peaceful, voluntary (when it is known that it will be decided next Sunday by the assembly) and "nice" eviction is being negotiated with the police, and that – amazement of amazement! – the police chiefs even share many of our complaints and seek to avoid charges, fines and detentions. Come on!

Have we perhaps forgotten the repression of the 15-M movement, the beating of the detainees, the arbitrary eviction on Monday night? How can we fall for all that and then continue speaking not even of *Spanish revolution*, but merely of revolt, protest, change? On Sunday morning the assembly was shocked by the statement of the 15-M detainees, where for example it was described how police *colleagues* humiliated those who wore baggy pants and dreadlocks or who were vegan, and laughed at those who had serious medical problems, or simply at the one who had been playing football and whose crime was "to be in the wrong place at the wrong time". How can the same assembly subsequently fall for so many lies and then cheer on the big bosses who ordered and directed such a *respectful* and *restrained* demeanor?

It is not a question of blindly hating the police, or of displaying the most radical gesture in a show of revolutionary purity, but about trying to keep things clear, because not only does alcohol cloud the mind, but also and much more thoroughly does the toxic waste of propaganda of power which justifies itself and its own repressive forces from the very moment we were born. Because, like it or not, regardless of the good or ill will and the essential humanity of the police officer, the military, the personnel manager, the executive representative or the politician, such is the role they play and which ultimately is nothing other than *obeying the orders* of those who pay them, ruining our lives. Such people may one day break with that role and join us as allies, an incredible miracle that yet has happened during certain moments in the great revolutions of History; And may the right be granted to us, in the meantime, to be distrustful of those who haven't already done so nor are showing signs of doing so, because if the Puerta del Sol is open and calls out to so many people, it cannot reach absolutely everyone without losing its meaning and its intensity, its truth and its fire. Therefore, we can't expect much from multinationals, nor from the market or the police, just as we can't expect anything from politicians, since this occupation and liberation of the Puerta del Sol is not a childish play or any other kind of entertainment, but rather – we must remind ourselves – a *massive illegal act* without bosses or hierarchy, an experiment in real democracy that bases its new legitimacy on the same justice and urgency, rather than that of its own rejections and desires.

Illegal for them, but it is the process of making a new world for us and for all who sooner than later will join us. But never, under any condition, reducible to a mere circus act or television set, or summer camp, or thematic park, or playful festival of fraternizing with the police, or with the CEOE (Confederation of Employers and Industries of Spain), or with the Royal House.

And they might laugh now, but they won't be laughing for very long.

For the proclamation of the Madrid Commune
All power to the assemblies
We want it all and we want it now!

25th May 2011

(Translated by Bruno Jacobs, revised by Eric Bragg & Noé Ortega)

The 21st Century Resists the 20th Century

Rafet Arslan

Prologue

This text has been written exactly one month after the beginning of the resistance, after a few days of taking notes.

It has been written with the difficult goal of trying to capture a terrific and awesome flow of time, while a historical breaking point, not history, is being written on the street, among local forums, meetings, and marches. And this flow still continues.

Everything Was A Cloud Of Gas And Dust; And Then Life Began

This banner –*Everything was a cloud of gas and dust; and life began*– in Gezi Park is a good way to begin explaining the essence of this joyful and determined resistance.

The sentence on the banner summarizes the struggle of three million people suffocating with various chemical gases. Well, how did this resistance –which affects the whole world– start and what is this "new" life that began after it?

Day by day the growing authoritarianism in Turkey has drowned people in pessimism, isolation, hopelessness, loneliness, fear and despair. Systematically humiliated, a larger part of society has been suffering from tremendous stress, boredom, a lack of passion, paranoia and hopelessness.

Restrictions in birth control, the continuous insistence of the government that 'all families must have a minimum of three children', prohibition of abortion, the law which violates animal rights, urban transformation laws which ruin historical/cultural values in cities, increasing pressure on unions, new restriction on selling alcoholic drinks, continuous restrictions upon the media and freedom of expression, the government's intervention in the lifestyles of people, an increasing number of human rights violations…

Society was in the same mood as that of a puzzled boxer: consistently taking hits, believing himself to be stuck at corner ropes and defeated. Everyone started to worry about what the next step might be after these attacks, i.e. an open dictatorship with the coming election.

On May 27, 2013, a handful of citizens in Taksim Square were protesting against the removal of trees in Gezi Park, and were suddenly attacked and exposed to pepper gas; they were definitely unaware that they were releasing the suppressed hatred growing within the subconscious of society. They were claiming their rights to the Park and did not leave, despite all of the violence. While the national media was pretending as if the incident never occurred, it was through social media and through the grapevine that people started to take action. And eventually more and more people started to come together.

And a small group of resisters –on the night of May 30/31, at 07:00 in the morning– were removed from the park by way of a ruthless attack. Tents were burned down and personal belongings damaged and dispersed.

Despite the strict censorship, people were stirred by videos and pictures that were suddenly streaming on the social media. The picture of 'The Woman in Red' standing straight, as if she had been pepper-sprayed in the face, was the best moment that summarized everything from that day. Then more people arrived, they came like a flooding river, like a landslide.

They rushed to Taksim Square as if with psychic instinct and telepathic communication. What was happening on the evening of May 31st was an open revolt of over one million people going to Taksim, in addition to people in 48 different cities gathering in squares. Under normal circumstances, those socialists, liberals, Muslims, artists, environmentalists, social democrats, Turkish/Kurdish nationalists, anarchists, rival football club fans, LGBT members, could never all come together because of their so many different platforms, but because of this attack, they acted as individuals, taking to the streets despite the extensive and violent police oppression. The dark shadow covering the country for many years –this depression– disappeared in an instant, on the evening of May 31st.

Certainly this was a collective attainment of the threshold of consciousness; a sudden conscious leap, a high awareness, an understanding and an enlightenment; as a result, it was an amazing unification, solidarity and resistance.

People who have different ideologies, beliefs and lifestyles became a majority, they resisted and made barricades together, they didn't flee from the brutal police attacks and gave them a reply. The so-called Y-Generation, that apolitical generation born after the Military Coup d'Etat of September 12th, 1980, which had cost thousands of lives, was in the forefront of the uprising. Their creativity, connectivity, extensive sense of humor, unstoppable energy, determination and wisdom surprised everybody. They couldn't bear the "father authority" imposed on them by the prime minister, since they'd already had to deal with that one at home for such a long time.

This was a historical moment of decision; every single individual in the resistance faced their own fear hidden in themselves and the power in their subconscious. Everyone became one with this reckoning, and that night the fear barrier was broken. And when that non-stop, 34 hour-resistance transformed into a civil revolt, on June 1st at 16:00 hours, the police forces of the government retreated from Taksim Square and Gezi Park. And after that moment, during the course of eleven days, the spark for a map of a new world took fire in the region from Harbiye to Gümüşsuyu, where the police authority withdrew, and the "temporary autonomous area" formed. Therefore, the uprising had evolved into a "new" life experience.

When every person dreamed of their desired world and attempted to prototype it, they reestablished their own subjectivity at the same time. Against ambition and selfishness there was mutual aid and reciprocity, empathy, counseling, i.e. an indefinable explosion of goodness. The resistance never lost its nobleness, carnival spirit, playfulness, naivety and innocence during that whole month against all despotism. The resistance opposed all kinds of alienation and made a new spirit and a world model that is anti-authoritarian, anti-hierarchic, anti-homophobic, or in other words, 'libertarian'.

After tents were set up in Gezi Park, "free camps" in many cities were formed, so these living spaces where money and power did not matter led to new autonomous areas.

Gezi Park was a kind of temporal fracture inside daily life, it was that moment when the ball was hit as soon as it arrived, an experimental, unplanned area where life in the new century was lived spontaneously.

There was the "Revolution Market" where everything was free, the "Gezi Library" where anyone could take and leave books, the "Gezi Orchard" where natural planting models were tested, and art workshops, performances…

In the assurance of barricades, for 11 days Taksim

Square and its surroundings changed into an open surrealist carnival. Poetry overflowed the streets, with verses by libertarian poets such as "to love is to get organized," from Ece Ayhan, and "the stop for looking at the sky" from Turgut Uyar became the street itself. People who were tempted by the power of creative destruction were taking photos in front of the remains of the uprising. The old building of the cultural center, the AKM, for which the government announced its demolition, was covered with banners, flags and visuals pertaining to the resistance.

Despite the risk of death, hundreds of people went to the roof of the AKM, and a dervish whirled away up there. Barricades became a shining example of pseudo-architecture; graffiti representing a youthful intelligence was everywhere; there were upside-down cars, a magnificent burst of desire covering everything all around; if the great utopian Fourier could have seen these days, he certainly would have cried.

However, the government used its instruments of power to launch a media attack on the million-strong resistance, accusing them of being a terroristic, vandalistic gathering and a marginal movement, basically carrying out a vicious disinformation campaign against them. In response to this, the resistance responded to this situation by carrying out its own campaign, a wide range boycott against mainstream media and their financiers. And this boycott yielded quick results and by disrupting the stock market. Interest rates fell by 7.5%, whereas the stock market dropped by 19%.

Outside the media centers which misinformed or distorted the news, thousands of people launched protests and are still protesting.

From the beginning, the resistance already had formed its own civil media, streaming live via 3G technologies. This decision was the most basic manifestation of the so-called attitude by Foucault about "telling the truth"; it also marked a new era where every individual who resisted became an information volunteer, an independent media.

Meanwhile, those in power started a wide disinformation campaign totally similar to that of Cold War jargon. They carried out completely fabricated counter-propaganda to agitate the rest of the society against the resistance. The resistance was nothing but a game prepared by an interest lobby, by external powers who wanted to break the peace of the country, by provocateurs and drunkards/punks. According to them, this was no protest but rather a civil coup attempt against an elected governance. They accused those in the resistance of being terrorists and tried to portray them as a minority in Turkey that was against religion.

In fact, this resistance was definitely not a conflict between seculars and Muslims, but between the majority longing for a new world and the authority trying to suppress it. After all, as individuals and as organized groups there were lots of Muslims among the protestors. Especially, "Anti-capitalist Muslims" took part in the resistance from the beginning, with great determination and devotion. One thing that the authorities missed is that this civil resistance movement was not just against their party and government, but against all rulers, parties and the way that they are understood within Turkish history. In short, the struggle was between the 20th century's prohibitive, oppressive, alienating language and spirit, and the resistance of the spiritual resurrection of the newly begun 21st century.

Those in power want to view and portray the resistance as if they were ideologically marginal people, but the majority covering the streets were trying (and are still trying) to establish a world of freedom which goes beyond a classical ideological dogmas. Many socialist and anarchist groups in the resistance were shocked and excited by the tenacity, insistence and creativity of the masses. This new situation was nullifying many theoretical analyses. The urban middle-class and those youth who were once thought to be so apolitical were creating a new language and politics which transcended what was thought to be ideologically acceptable.

The majority on the streets are practicing the ideological critique of Situationists even if they have never read it and are exceeding the boundaries of any ideology, they are calling for a libertarian spirit to enter the game. Instead of exercising already known methods of organizing, they were focusing on spontaneous organizational methods during the resistance, living in the moment and building the movement with these methods; in short they were pursuing the creation of the radical politics of the moment.

The crowd's potential to organize itself and its capacity to mobilize were a dream come true.

From this point on, new policies for learning lessons from the masses of people, for following them and respecting their will were gaining approval.

Authorities, fearful of losing their hold on power, in the face of the movement, took control of the square, on the 11th of June, with a heavy attack as if they were conquering an enemy land. Many foreign TV channels broadcast the operation live, as well as CNN International with a 7-hour live broadcast. Authorities stopped the open attack against Gezi Park because of the public pressure but continued with the gas attacks, but the resisters refused to leave the place. After a 4-day police siege, on the 15th of June, the park was invaded and the police took control. And it is still under police control.

Soon afterwards, suddenly the "Standing Man" protests began and turned into a countrywide "radical civil disobedience" movement. On June 16th, the first Public Forums were created with the announcement of the "Çarşı" group, formed by some of the supporters from the Beşiktaş Football Club, who were prominent in the resistance. Soon, these forums started to snowball all over the country. And now, every night in 48 different districts of Istanbul, public forums are being held as a direct practice of democracy in society. Boycotting AVMs (Shopping Centers), not using credit cards, and discussions about establishing a new economy based on gift-exchange. The resistance on the streets is going on, and despite the prohibition attempts in Taksim square, the movements keep growing in hundreds of squares.

Politics of the Future

As opposed to the examples in other parts of the world (the ghetto riots in Paris in 2005 or the Occupy movement in 2011), this resistance wasn't triggered by any direct economic crisis or by a racial uprising. From the beginning of the movement there has been an upwelling of pride against the authority personified by the government, an ethical revolt, a call for searching for of the life they've always dreamed of, against those who do not permit people to live their lives as they choose. In this sense, it was a revolt of desire by a plurality of people requesting the right to live as they want.

Those who resist incorporate the energy of the moment into their struggles, put the power of spontaneity into their tool box. Since May 27, protestors have been creating "new situations" in the streets and grasping at the possibilities of establishing a new life. Resisters in Turkey are fearlessly discarding the old-fashioned methods of opposition, diving into discoveries of new resistance, new language, new political and organizational practices. This is definitely the path of the 21st Century.

In the Deleuzian sense, life has transformed into resistance; millions of people in Turkey have been living with it for one month, and the resistance is in the very center of their lives.

Older, opposing generations in Turkey view this revolt as having overcome the Military Coup d'Etat of September 12th. From the perspective of the worldwide effect of the resistance, we can say that the mentality engendered by the Cold War has generally dissolved. And the struggles that started in countries like Brazil, Bulgaria, and Lebanon were triggered by the spark of the new millennia's resistance, as it became manifest in Turkey.

Almost for a month, the hard struggle of people filling the squares, streets, parks of the country was not an attack, but rather a kind of resistance; it was the common and intuitive decision of the majority that arose. The majority rejected those means of offence such as the use of Molotov cocktails, rioting and looting which can deflect the course of a mass movement. Before this resistance, the history of the social struggle in Turkey was a history of armed conflict, which was constantly instigated by the government and suppressed with blood.

But this time, however, against the grudge and hate, there is intelligence, creativity and humour in the spirit of the ongoing youthful, urban rebellion. These people are not looking for heroes or martyrs. But they have been brimming with the joy of life, pouring through the streets without any fear of death.

Undoubtedly in the historic/genetic past which gave rise to this resistance, there is the spirit of the public uprisings that have gone on for centuries on Anatolian soil. It is certain that, in this resistance, there is the cohesiveness of the Turkish socialist left, having struggled and paid the price at least for a century; there is the seed of the soul of anarchist philosophy growing for the last 40 years, having blended with the struggle of Kurdish people suffering from the dirty war for nearly 30 years.

In addition to all of this political tradition, many acts of resistance can be recalled: in the 90s, the main environmentalist civil disobedience and resistance initiated by the peasants in Bergama against cyanide gold mining; the struggle against urban transformation as part of a new urban movement developing which has developed especially over the last few years; the growing resistance from counter culture and fanzines against the moral pressures of authority; the booming environmentalist dynamic against hydroelectric and nuclear power plants; the destructive energy produced by independent art/life movements like Destruction 2011 held in Istanbul, which spiritually, foretold the days of June 1-12; LGBT and women movements struggling in the midst of expressions of alienation and hate, as well as so many other major and minor movements which aren't mentioned here, but all of which having greatly contributed to this struggle.

But today's resistance belongs to a newly born spirit of constructing "the new", in terms of its dimension, comprehensiveness, creativity, language and organization, and it comprises every apriori sociological and ideological act of resistance. Thus, it can be said that this country is signaling a new global movement that transcends the borders of this territory.

Digression

According to the Ministry's report, in the resistance, 4900 people have been taken into custody, 70 people have been arrested. Street movements have taken place in 79 cities; in only two cities there was not any movement.

According to the Turkish Medical Association, throughout the country, there has been a total number of 7681 injured, 63 heavily injured and 4 dead.

"How Can a Flat, Indigo, Whitewashed City be Established, Brothers?" – Ece Ayhan

Today, the resistance is completing its first month in Turkey. If you ask anyone in the resistance where the movement is going, I think the answer would be, "I don't know". Under normal circumstances this answer could provoke insecurity and doubt, but the reason why this answer leads to enthusiasm is now hidden within the essence of the resistance, which is composed of the spirit hidden in the fluid nature of spontaneity.

I think that people now mostly remember those 11 days of freedom of Taksim Square again and again, looking at AKM building, longing for those days when the building was covered with flags.

Every picture we knew is a remaining memory for us from the past. But now the people who look at the pictures of AKM between June 1 and 11 are carrying in their hearts and souls, not only a mere, lived past but also the foundation of a future yet to be lived.

And as everybody in Gezi Park says: This is Just the Beginning...

27.06.2013

Istanbul – Turkey

Translated by Ali Kartal, Ayşe Özkan

FERGUSON 2014

The St. Louis Surrealist Group would like to express its complete revulsion at the recent shooting of Mike Brown on 8/9/14. The actions of the Ferguson, Missouri police force in shooting down an unarmed African-American man and *leaving his body in the sun for over four hours*, is the contemporary equivalent of the "strange fruit" of lynchings in the racist South. The Ferguson police have the mentality of an army of occupation enforcing their control over a colonized people.

We condemn the militarized policing exhibited by the St. Louis County police in the wake of the justified anger displayed by the citizens of Ferguson against this atrocity. After decades of institutionalized racism and 'free market fantasies' forced on the masses by the capitalist world-system, we see again that the only freedom that the ruling class values is the freedom to oppress, subjugate and exploit. The modern police force, with aid from Congress and the Pentagon, have procured and use without hesitation military weapons suited for battlefields, effectively treating civilians as combatants in war, in a war against people. We can only convey our total disgust and outrage that the arsenal used in Ferguson included attack dogs, rubber bullets, stinger-grenades, sonic attacks and excessive use of tear gas, even tear gassing children and innocent citizens sitting in their own backyards!

We express our solidarity with the citizens of Ferguson and St. Louis County who rose up against the abuse at the hands of these mercenaries of the established order. Their courageous actions in the face of oppression have been inspiring, and are the harbingers of things to come. The world-historical situation in Ferguson of August 2014 illustrates more than just the overwhelming institutionalized racism that persists into the 21st century, but additionally the economic disparities set forth by the modern capitalistic society. Our solution prescribes, among other things, the immediate dissolution of the police and other structures of authority, brutality, exploitation and conformity, as well as the creation of cities of wonder where people of all races, ethnicities, genders and other diverse affinities can mix in an environment of creative fecundity based on absolute freedom. In this sense we invoke *surrealism* as the antidote to the current *barbarism* in Ferguson and everywhere else.

-STLSG with fellow surrealists and fellow travelers

Photo appears courtesy of Paul Hampel

Dead Time

Antonio Ramírez

*When the dead, happily,
leave the factories
time swallows them
just like that...*

(From a song by Soul Bisontes)

Far from the futile and usually biased idealisms, we must continue to consider work as one of the major scourges of human civilization. Even in the West, where there apparently (1) are no blatant forms of extreme exploitation akin to slavery, work persists as a poison running through society, sickening and weakening its best parts. Perhaps, in this case, could we speak of "consensual slavery".

It is a fact that advances in the struggle of workers that occurred during the last century have for a good while been undermined by neoliberal policies, with the patent degradation of work conditions as a result. But such advances were never implemented for some kinds of factories and workshops, as well as for construction, which never stopped being a very harsh and dangerous occupation during that whole time. Although it is accepted with resignation (and even with pride by some naive workers), the salary paid for this kind of job is nowhere near being worth the sacrifice performed by the worker, however, it should be noted that the hardship and physical exhaustion that the worker suffers over the years are only a part of his many difficulties. While unions have nothing to say about it, work is also related to a systematic degradation of the possibilities of the mind, since beyond the obvious economic interests that motivate exploitation, there is also the intent to condition the individual through work hazards, lack of job-security, the lengthening of the workday, schedule flexibility, reduced wages and other abuses that end up converting the worker into someone disconnected from real life, but perfect for the ordeal that he must endure.

Consequently, among the whole complex capitalist system, work is the aspect which most efficiently produces a continued division of the resources of the working-class interior life, exposing people to the continuing burden of an external reality that knows nothing of the imagination, desire, or anything other than the gross materialism of immediate needs, promoting increasingly predesigned and miserabilist behaviours that are initiated and reinforced through the garbage that the mass media thoroughly spreads within the collective imagination. Thus, the labor movement has been depleted of a considerable number of keen minds, spoiling the efforts of earlier generations. Meanwhile, workplace life is reduced to becoming a mere shadow of the old dream of working class solidarity, where despite the rhetoric of a few deluded individuals, one only needs to examine just a little portion of his daily existence to see to what extent the idea of the worker as a revolutionary subject has gone beyond the utopian to completely end up as mere fantasy. Therefore, still valid perhaps more than ever, is that necessary awareness, on the part of the working class, of its own misery. Thus, after more than fifty years, nowadays these words gain relevance:

The struggle of the proletariat for socialism is not simply a struggle against external enemies, capitalists and bureaucrats, but equally or even more a struggle against itself, a struggle of consciousness, of solidarity, of creative passion, of taking the initiative against darkness, mystification, apathy, discouragement and individualism that life in capitalist society continuously awakens within the hearts of workers.
(Cornelis Castoriadis) (2)

Within this context of alienation and aggression, it is logical for despair to pave its own way wherever it can; therefore it is inevitable that certain extraordinary situations would suddenly arise that break this dynamic, situations which usually have an ephemeral character, but which nevertheless should be regarded as seeds of a broader impulse towards rebellion. We are not referring to conflicts and protest movements that the system considers acceptable and which are obviously orchestrated by unions, such as protests for better wages or against the threat of being fired. Rather, these are activities that would normally not be considered as being especially subversive from a radical point of view, and in fact they occur so routinely that they have been stripped of all political significance. However, I think they could actually be interpreted as a kind of sabotage, even if not so obvious, like the willful destruction of machinery or interruption of production by way of picketing; or at least they do not have a very precise, utilitarian nature, and they resort to subtlety as well as unpredictable methods. To illustrate what I mean, offered below is a series of real examples collected at certain moments during my experience as a carpenter:

June 2001. Two workers are assembling the porch of an isolated house on the outskirts of Seville. The building is lavish and also has a fairly large garden and swimming pool. At one point the bungalow owners and the construction manager have to go somewhere, leaving the two carpenters alone. For the next hour, they prefer to swim in the pool rather than continue working. When getting out of the pool, they find that the water has become quite dirty and spend a good deal of time getting rid of the dirt and sawdust.

July 2001. The heat is unbearable in the shop; everywhere there are loads of completed furniture ready to be sent for varnishing and then onto their final destination: a hotel under construction in South America. This causes an argument between two comrades that slowly and un-

expectedly escalates and, without reason, one of them decides to dump a bucket of water on the other. By way of a chain reaction, more buckets appear and a real water battle ensues. The result is fun, as a considerable relief from the heat and with a lot of assembled furniture having been water-damaged (from the wood swelling due to the moisture).

August 2001. A group of carpenters is responsible for adding a large wooden platform to a new attraction of the amusement park in Seville. The work is done in full sunshine as the construction company has not provided any shade for the workers. Around the area affected by the work, the activity of the amusement park still goes on as usual, and the visitors are very numerous that day. After the lunch break the seven members of the gang decide, although there are still three hours of working time left, to go visit the other side of the fence and explore for free what the park has to offer. Nobody pays much attention to them despite the fact that they are dressed in workclothes (quite dirty in some cases). They get on several rides and finish the day by occupying the two rear rows of a water wagon. A photograph is taken of them while diving.

December 2002. A group of carpenters from a Seville workshop carries out the renovation of a luxury hotel in Lausanne (Switzerland). They are subcontracted by another company but their work permit in that country has not been legalized. They have been there for a couple of weeks and many problems have arisen regarding the completion of the work during that period. One day, after work, they go together (there are eight of them including the manager) to the hotel where they are staying, when suddenly it starts to rain heavily. The workers decide, partly for the sake of taking shelter from the rain, and also for playing a prank, to take a large plastic bag from a trash bin and then wrap themselves in it: they all assume the form of a large worm, and then start running down a steep street, crying with one voice: "The Spanish are coming! The Spanish are coming!", to the embarrassment of the manager and horror of the many passers-by.

While these are examples that could easily be perceived as mere hooliganism, when analyzed in depth we can ascertain that they are behaviors that are unacceptable within the normal dynamics of the work environment. However, such situations tend to occur quite often. The fact is that despite his intensely alienated situation, or precisely because of it, the manual laborer shows a more pronounced tendency, with respect to other workers, to engage in serious misconduct in relation with the labor code. It is not so unusual that a simple joke between comrades turns into a not easily controlled tumult, or that a factor as simple as boredom or excessive heat could create circumstances which at times take the form of a small rebellion, thus breaking the miserable normality of work and opening a disruption in measured time. Where earlier there was compliance with the authority of the employer and the demands of production, we now find behaviors that pertain to aspects of life that directly attack the alienation of labor. The problem is that these experiences usually have a limited impact on the individual and on the interpretation of his basic situation. They are, so to speak, cases of sabotage that are not taken to their logical conclusion, since they usually do not imply a clear awareness of the transformative power of such situations (from the perspective of those who experience them), even if that lack of awareness does not prevent them from being realized with real passion and if they sometimes are of a very similar cruelty like the kind that children demonstrate in their games and mischief. Likewise, in the same way that a child mocks the adult who maintains custody of and educates him, so does the worker with whoever treats him in an obviously patronizing way. The worker becomes, from the viewpoint of the employer, a selfish and deceptive individual, because unlike the clerk who manifests laziness, carelessness or negligence in his work (a fact that is almost accepted in society for those who have gained access to that privileged status), the worker who neglects his obligations does it knowing that such dereliction seriously violates a number of binding rules for his social class: he is being paid for his time, so every minute that he steals from his workday is a fraud to the employment that he has so kindly been granted by those above him. When a disabled worker cannot fulfill his role, as an employee, he becomes unnecessary and is more or less sustained by society, but when he openly refuses work and without any apparent reason other than his own whim, then he enters into a gray zone of social reality that

borders on criminality and which draws the contempt of those around him. His irregular work status scares society.

In short, we might interpret these actions in many ways, but we still cannot extract much of a revolutionary program from them. They are, in any case, examples that demonstrate the need to find remnants of vitality in a space as dead as the workplace, and so we should consider them as gems of reality created by a group of individuals, albeit of very ephemeral nature. During the time that they last, the worker may become conscious of his inner desire to be free and he might even sense the possibilities of disrupting the functioning of society, but little can be done in the practical sense if this consciousness ends up fading into daily, individually experienced despair. But in the meantime, until this consciousness makes that leap to collectivity, they still serve as valuable experiments, initiation rituals in a reality without limits and made in the same belly of the leviathan that work presupposes.

(Translated by Bruno Jacobs, revised by Eric Bragg and Noé Ortega)

* Originally published in Salamandra #17-18, Madrid, 2008.

NOTES:

(1) Only seemingly, because there are actually jobs in Western countries that could be considered as pure slavery, since they are hidden from public view due to prohibitive legislation (like the sweatshops of immigrants, for example). It is not the case in many Asian countries or of the Middle East where child labor and other terrible abuses are openly accepted by society.

(2) Cornelius Castoriadis. *La experiencia del movimiento obrero.* Vol.1. Tusquets Editor, 1979 (*The Experience of the Labor Movement*, original French title *L'expérience du mouvement ouvrier*).

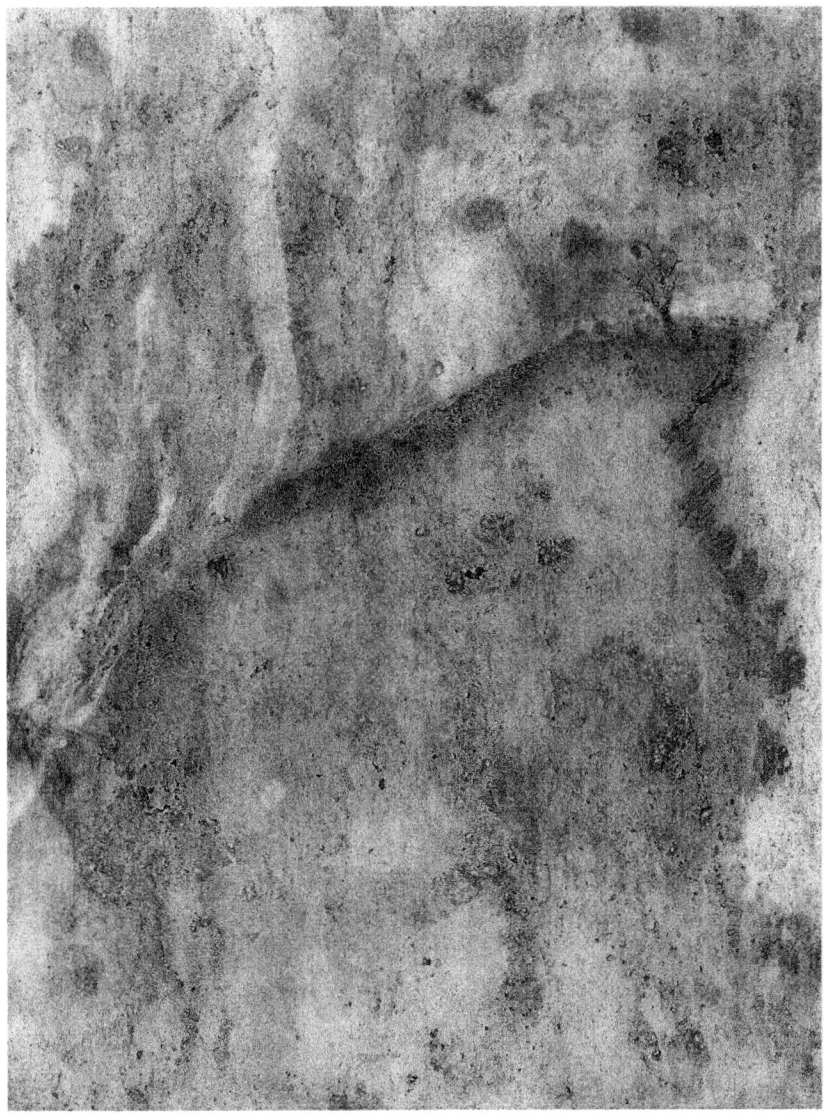

John Adams - *Paths of Dreaming*

FUNERAL OF EMPIRE MANIFESTO

Inner Island Surrealist Group

(May Day 2012)

Discover your desires, for only people who can distinguish their real desires from those that have been manufactured for them are able to make the revolution!

–Penelope Rosemont

Since the "inner island" of the unconscious recognizes neither the imposed borders of colonial mapmakers nor those of the reality police, the home of the Inner Island Surrealist Group has always been off the map. That provincial entity known as British Columbia is too British and too Columbian to hold us hostage, and the imperial juggernaut known as Canada has always been a pipeline for resource extraction, labor exploitation and indigenous conquest. In response to the cruel industrial harness of wage slavery and the brutality of environmental devastation, we say General Strike! In counterpoint to the patriotic spectacle of Empire Day and the pathetic commemoration of the birthday of Queen Victoria, we call for the Funeral of Empire!

The Inner Island Surrealist Group began on Sla-dai-aich, which is the original Pentlatch name for what in colonial terms is referred to as Denman Island. We have proudly embraced the Pentlatch name, which literally means "inner island," and we repudiate the colonizers' name which reeks of the "civilizing" mission of Admiral Denman. Just as the mind knows no geographical boundaries, the Inner Island Surrealist Group has expanded beyond its island birthplace by means of mutual affinity and passional attraction to include poets, artists, musicians, radical thinkers, direct actionists, doers and refusers of all stripes. Together we share the same marvelously rainforested coastal valley where Sla-dai-aich floats freely like a laughing pirate ship aiming its surrealist canons at the telltale heart of miserabilism.

Contrary to the dismissive and hostile proclamations of the artworld establishment, surrealism has never died. It continues to live in all its delicious diversity in the hearts of those who have recognized themselves in the surrealist vision of creating a world in which the artificial dichotomy between dream and reality is re-imagined as a dialogue between what André Breton once referred to as "communicating vessels." By unfettering ourselves from the debilitating confines of consensus reality, with its loathsome celebration of the Queen having been institutionalized in the annually paraded Empire Day charade, we can shed our masks of acquiescence, demand the impossible, and live poetic lives of desire unbounded by royalty and rule!

The Density Paintings

Will Alexander

> I cannot help agreeing with Bachelard that the imaginative faculty must be understood as freeing us from the immediate images of perception and in his words "without an unexpected union of images, there is no imagination, no imaginative action."
>
> *"Poetic Matters"*
>
> For me it is the Vision in its density and the truth of what I see...
>
> *"A Note on Destroyed Works"* - Philip Lamantia

We live in an environment which blinds, which cuts off the source to its origin. It is expert in marketing rumour, in filing grievous error against forces which emerge from the unseen. The soma, by crossing the edge of occulted tremor, no longer evinces scale or status, no longer convinces by its presence the sum or degree of its significance. It ceases to carry the status of life.

By being perched at the cusp of the occult, one is surrounded by doubters always pledged to the visible. And so, since they react as sworn monarchical populace to the measurable, they seek to rankle and entrap one's momentum, and by their standards compound the view in one's electrical field, so as to accrue in one's effect on life a diminished vibration. As a blasphemous pioneer, one must counter these insidious amalgams by arraying the atmosphere through instinctive seepage. One then burns through events like a ghost so that which is carried in one's wake builds up no resistance, which ceases placing one's fuel on a placard making one prey to popular rejoinder. This is resistance never subjecting one's honour to the frontality of issues, to schisms misrecorded and bound to one kind of popularity versus another. Let it be said that it is better to eat sleet, to face the trials of hunger, to suffer the pangs of banishment, in order to leap the barrier of insignificance, so as to begin to move force in the invisible states, which is the torrent which claims no grandiose eminence or strength.

One's organic intuition falls outside the given floating across the unsayable. Satisfaction never registers in the document at the level of incompetent rams forcing themselves into violence. Thus there is no need to be a king in a concert of wizards. Of course, they can be called monsters, replete with attitudinal misogyny. Understanding the latter's curses sometimes galls when they claim from this lowered position a comprehensive knowledge of galactic events. In the main, the biologists, the astronomers attempt to alphabetize the miraculous, to point out motion in darkness and then superimpose a name. And it is not that one damns the naming of muons and leptons which spawn at the level of the subatomic, but that the absence of linkage with states remains biologically invisible. In the main, value must imply frontality, must imply the diurnal backdrop as wisdom. Therefore all energies which fall within a translocatable rhythm, which dwell on just this side of the bottomless, just this side of the ineffable. In a certain sense, this is as grafting of statement onto statement, this being the standard by which conundrums are measured. Which assures, according to the aforementioned meta-ghost who truncates the living electrical field, that a trenchant unification is soured, that it remains in the mode of the unprovable as doubt.

By roving as poetic ghost, one takes on the heresy of heresy of circumstance, as if one were flawed by vociferous agony, by an uncleansed darkness in emptiness. Therefore one is never displayed according to theoretical emblem, as if power had been gained from anterior Hegelianics. There exists no answer, or misanswer, somehow convening in synthetic dialectics. One cannot prove one's fate according to proven tertiary symbols, being energy which is revised and revised again, giving power to directions which strictly falsify the inner stratifications of existence. Which remains within the model of war, of psychological destabilization, so one is always felled by the inclement, by a condition which prevails as delimited semiotics.

So how can one be made structured as participant within this commonly embraced model? One is always subject to nullification and lessening, as if one were attempting to trace one's form as powerless hubris. Because it is assumed in the main that one must withstand a constructed territoriality, staring at oneself in ill-begotten mirrors, praising one's self-significance according to vaunted singing scale. Again it is an aggressively lit pitch, stung by vainglourious formality. Which is not unlike a measured facility, which in other disciplines or studies could be described as measurable isobars or plankton. As for symptoms which seem to fissure into nothingness, they can be no more than isolate indexical-stages which scatter. Of course, one cannot be held by such definitives, by a mental weaving graded according to the quantified as standing depletion. This is how surfeit wages war against resonance by piling psychic codes of breakable error. Therefore one must not be paired with oneself in listless androgyny. It must be as reaction to poison, which means suffusing oneself with verdigris confoundment, with poetical verticality, with shamanic aural harmonics. In this sense one is Buryat, or Tuvan, or Tungus, one's hearing inflamed with micro-astonishment. Which is regality advanced through enigma. One is no longer the statistical plaintiff, or a being who sires sound within the throes of a provisional time frame. Which is not life as understood according to previous irony. So by shifting beyond provisional diametrics, one begins floating across the Uranian in a mythical pontoon nebula. Certainly not to advance conductive insight, according to a priori stellar remnant, or to have galaxies expressed according to morose complexification, but as view according to celestial nuance, according to light which falls on startling sundials. The latter being instinctive complexification, as elements slipped into an unquantifiable foray, possessing a signature less registered than dust. Which are the heavens absented from collective forensics as irrepeatable glossolalia.

The galaxies as charismatic intaglios, as density paintings, never localized to a scar concealed by somatic self-deafness. Thus there are no intractable commas which limit, which poison the seed of motion due to pointless physical pronation. Which ushers in instinctual chaos, which staunches the flow of poetic terrifying marrow. No, one need explore the mysteries the way birds ignite from hills, exploring with vertiginous artefacts which give off osmosis. This being not unlike flight along solar ley lines, or transpositional oxygen soaring through heavenly mazes. Thus there is a completion which reveals itself in itself. It understands summas, initiatory categories, which sometimes flow as riverine diagonals, or sound in the system as geometrical trans-sonics, seemingly summoned by dazed form, or by incendiary seepage, which is never the one blue figure, or the orange and green bands, subverting themselves by consensus arithmetics through horizontal reason.

One can never be example as consumptive figurine, as someone blinded and claimed by extrinsic morals. And then again, there is socially approved exotica allowing one entry through a purposely fingered doorway in order to seek result from the stricken forms perceived by the populace of consumers. One is always explosive, dual, contradictory, anatomically riven by doubt. There are times when one exists like a mongoose in hiding. Or a deserted singular form consumed by sacred intangible counting. The decimal, as fuel on imploded scale, at a level at which a seemingly balanced citizenry would assess as being poisoned at the level of the valueless body. A body not even visible as diplopia, as the dwellings fleetingly crafted in Soutine's Hill At Ceret, being a density, as an ink which works in the density. Which works against false abandonment. Therefore one embraces the chemistry of chance, the power on instinctive exploristics. And if as poet one understands by exploristics the verdigris, "astronomy," "medicine," "literature," "the theory of being," the natural source of dialectics, being totally unlike separation instilled by false assignment through matter. Which is something other than the chart envisioned by foreseeable humanity. A group at war with its own skin. Willing to sacrifice the microverse, to quantify universe after universe according to the devolution as cycle, as sarcophagus, as brutish Greco-Roman assumptive. Which dazzles on a scale of unremitting disorder. For instance, internal orientation is rarely submitted, so all research is done as secular intoxicant. Thus the mind chases bones in a circle. Knowledge can do no more than quantify itself as a log contained in a suspended appendage.

Maybe now the word estrangement is applicable, just as a modern person studies the mechanics of vipers. In the findings formed through paralytic mirage, the animal in question possessing no more than objective mechanics. Which tends to lead towards a cosmological pessimistics, where all phenomena is tracked through the scope of an Imperial reason. This being life displayed in diachronic order.

The latter being understood as circumstantial demise, perhaps if one works from one's deepest sources of saturation, one can rise from leper into medium, communing with beings from the Sirius system, or having converse with signals from the Sculptor Galaxy, tracing their susurrant tremblings back to the fire which hails from the origins of origins.

On The Rise of Sodium and Fire

It seems no one has movement. The inner cycles seem vanished. The citizens have even lost their search for regret. This being concurrence by neurological inferno. By a draft of reaction utterly delimited and wizened. And this is not a politically concurring energy but a poisoned reaction against proliferous phenomena.

For the reactive, the palace is always scaled and constructed by dust, glazed by facile and deranged giftings. Respiration always concludes by means of outer precedent. There is nothing other than blankness of form, which is nothing other than tenebrous neurosis. A hypnotics of the despicable acquiring no higher level than functioning as corruptive substance. This being life as stained compost, as canceled indemnity of mind. This mind in the state of the condemned symmetrical arts, subsumed by clauses which condone no variation. This being the modern citizen's quest sipping from the rims of frustration. Then again prostrate jubilation within sinks and sinks of emptiness.

This is how modern living occurs, always fleeing inside borders. A dodecahedron which empties, which takes as its merit elemental dysfunction and holds it up as a principle of ongoing errata. Disparate squalls, disfigured emotional currents. Never attempts at explanation concerning inner micro exploration, or the ethics of the invisible. If one asks the common person his, or her, kinship, with the rise of the present universe, see at what rate their forces scatter, how their chatter then falls into silence. When one questions as such, one is not unlike the pull of blizzards, of prior continents erupting. It's what's known as the ordinary mind, which can project no further than broken laws, or victims of terminal ransom notes. They react like panicked owls imprisoned in a fragment. So when explosive realms are invoked, they inwardly fall into a wakeless turning ghat. And these ghats are as frightful muons, spinning prior to the act of assembled creation. To the common mind they are threats from riderless Gods. Thus they cling to products made from oil or pine. The latter are the molecules and the warrens which surround the personality as soured exhibit. Such are beings who threaten each other with flags, with infunctional burnishments, with talons. Therefore each pinnacle of achievement is modeled on misfortune. This being the general spell engendered, which travels, and obliterates, and strikes dead.

Now let us look at another dimension of this oddness. The mind conceded as omitted ammonia, as inpalatial mental fort, at the cusp of darkened minerals. In its embrangled disputation, telepathy is broken into mundane vahallas. This is how belief in the contiguous falsely expands. It keeps the mind prone to deleterious arrangements. For instance, God being judgemental figment as parochial gondolier, making up fate which collectively careens between burning and drowning. Being horror and fear and simulation of the agnostic. Which in the deepest sense fuels the penchant for exterior codification, for modeling oneself on a fevered human in a stream. This being sample as tragic array, as saturate general flaw. Perhaps from this a development will transpire where piercing concealment will range, where the occulted mind will illuminate its cinders.

Yet these are not the cinders of the populace at large. Again a gulf of fallen lemmings. Signs which signal the proto-catastrophics, which posit eerie forms of weather where summers fail to burn, where enclaves of beings ignite and disappear. The Earth: a mansion of collapsed surroundings. Flaws burn by lessened interregnums. Quickening appears. All arrangement seems scrambled. The questions arise. What are the following chapters? Who are the beings which will gather new traction? Certainly we cannot draw from recent social consciousness as we are left with nothing more than but a diary of abandoned sums. An energy which cancels itself through barbarous indictment. A zodiac which clings to itself through self-hatred. This being the era of the pressurous collective, producing mutant forms drowned in plagiarized ammonias. These are the lemming graves scattered on an ad hoc basis. What's being spoken here is not based on doctrinal chastisement, or shards of law stranded as osmosis. Again, what's being spoken here are lowly graded deliriums, washed by toxic mental sands.

This being the human form maniacally warped, struggling in the throes of penultimate configuration.

Why is the term *penultimate* so suddenly signaled?

Penultimate in this context being strategic confinement, allegiance to pestiferous hiding. Which amounts to respiration by damage, by unintended

scorching. Not a form of theoretical prowling, or wisp by plagiaristic impact, but a lack of true sources, this being experience void of foundational rhyming. Which results in disorder of the senses, in dense encapsulation by minimums. Being unendingly fraught, so much so that the perpendicular flattens and dissolves into formless animal's dust, so that each ballistic adjustment is corrupted by soured motives, so that basic contact is established by means of fractious in-kindlings.

Of course, there are other levels of complication. One's natural feel for immensity has vanished. The qualitative is deemed as inadequate calling; it is considered the worship of effigies according to internal confirmation. And such worship is no more than prolapse, no more than fallen monerans from Sirius, considering the body as immemorial postulate. Reality is then considered to reek of posturing according to error, of shiftings, of obliterated molecules, of divided simulacra. What is being pointed to is life as negated spectra, as indigenous telepathics gone awry. The horizontal is thus cast free from all ulterior hypnotics, a personality casting off vestiges of the shaman that cannot be considered. Even partial synchronicities are never acknowledged. According to this condition, the mind never prowls, or embraces itself like a burning owl in flight. The owl in this sense is leper, is ambrosial intangible, which always signals disadvantage. Thus the higher states of adventure are voided, are placed in the context of infeasible aeronautics. So trans-cosmic analogy remains a nonexistent electrical field, and the quotidian plane seems to solve its intangible perchings through evidence marked by blunted erasure.

Living in the trans-cosmic one is always subject to the machinations always hatching from a den of thieves. And these are thieves who snatch minerals from the Congo, who create from these minerals the most advanced micro-technologies, the most condensed of apparitional mechanics. When the mind is always summoned by this order, it is forced to filter these constant impurities, these elusive gravitations, which by their very nature adhere to reductive definition. It is like the atmosphere is fueled by a burning kind of hatred, by a purposeful state which features denigration. Thus one must contend with monsters, with didactic and unmodified usurers. Since one carries no such aggression, one fills one's day with codes which function like broken needlework. And, by doing such, one rises by means of perpendicular ardour so that the pragmatists can never gather enough momentum to react at the height of the unserviceable.

In the latter domain Abydos and Sirius concur. The mysteries link, thus the ethos is sculpted by an unremitting fabulosity. The aura is soaked by stellar intrinsicalities which renew, which open the subtle shifts in the spirit. Of course, soliloquy by light, gestures by motions other than the zodiac. So if one can answer the questions—another law? another fibre? another foundational vibrato? It will be yes, and yes, and yes, and yes. Of course, this is something other than the action and counteraction commonly known as tumult. The contentious locatives of monarchs and war, of plague and dishonour. Then below these discomforts, loosely feathered cataracts and other subforms of blindness, uttered on the lower plane through poisoned diphthong torrents, through indignities which slaver under corruptive forms of labour.

Say, as poet imbued by the uranian, one internally dazzles with interactive speculation, with ravishing floods, mixed with ulterior hierophanies. History when understood through the hierophantic is a pact contiguous with itself, always roiled and unsettled, stamping in the foreground, branded by the ungraceful limit. It is posture gone bad, turned in on itself like an arthritic paw. The result: defamed exhibit, cold and political crowding, always at war with what it considers to be insolutionable Bohemias. At its bottom, always incarceration, always the foiled mount of liberty as exhibit. These are the statesmen, the sum of erected rulers always holding up the standard of carnivorous intotality. As for the transcendental ratio, nothing is ever recorded.

Thus one never remains in the static, reduced to argumentative ballast. The creative being is placed beneath the roof of organizational lepers as if they all naturally coalesced and rightfully suffered as disfigured spectra. The creative being always sorted away as the atrocious, as always the opposite of how he, or she, exists in reality. Through the uranian eye, the poets can magically see themselves as Neon Tetras, as Rainbow Minnows, as Blue Gularis, or of the orange-red striping of the Paradise Fish. Which outstrips the leper's agenda, the latter always lingering in debacle. Yet, in this society of opposition as an uranian in leaning, one earns less respect than a rat killer, than an attendant who holds court in a morgue. They carry palpable result; they can be measured; they seem to supersede fumes.

At times it can be tempting to adjust to these measures, so as to strive for fury and outcome. One is tempted by elements of fate to leave one's microsociety, in order to join the general run of beings. Even the dead are pointed out at one's own expense. Their spirits carry shipments of clothing, bevelled lamps, and boxes which linger structured by salt. Yet here one does not speak of supernatural forces, but of energies thirsting with taint, quivering at the port of post-existence.

According to present standards, the Uranian tenet is embellished by treason. One wanders, one is structured by displacement. Under such circumstances one soaks in one's own design, seemingly paralleled by nothingness. Even nullity wavers, and the upper planes seem shrouded by fierce critique. Yet, at the very worst, poetry should rise like a voice of concussive praetas. It should instill certitude ramified by beauty. Then again, it is a delicate owl upon the sands.

So, again, what are its basic phasmas?
What are its splintered arithmetical plinths?
What are its illusive meta-domains?

This is a state where answers do not reach, where infections lack their basics. Maybe one could consider a holographic breathing, or a certain form of kilometric cinders. Yet, at a deeper scale, one understands how suns extend across the ozone and become in the mind as green ignition trees. Something other than decisive punctual codes, or autonomic salt, or pestiferous crackling. It is purity by other explosions and wakings. Other drafts, other clauses by heretical drift. Or conches which roar like phantom lions. Or aspects which spiral and simulate horses fleeing through a pitch black desert under bluish carbon moons. These moons enriched as anonymous doublings, as spells, as secondary auric mangers. Or curious precautionary crystal, congealed as warring saffron movements. Then, at one level, strange in-cautionary sums, while, at others, an a priori mustering effect, having averted the damage from existing repression.

One seems analogous to such pressures, while at the same time remaining unclaimed by the aforesaid. This is the level where the poet must hold and spiral beyond existing stability. In this sense one is not prone to personal confession, or to states of mind concerned with capturing monarchical stagnation. One comes to feel in oneself a devastated understanding, an insight fraught by feeling for the unseasonable. Thus one hovers as if watching discomforted spirits scurry across imaginary rocks, while at the same time understanding the fire of renewed forces. This being the radical shift in the connective mental phase. Not shift by regime, or earthquake paralytic, but by osmotic saturation conversant with the zone of asymptotic nutation. The result is like the sighted claiming to leap out of macular exhaustion. The breath then will consider on its own the Sun and its arcs; will consider the rays from Sirius, from other galactic templates, that the human mind in its present state carries no interior inkling.

A shift accrued from chronic haunting. And these hauntings spin as energy displacements, as blurs, as

circumstantial fervour. Then time refuses its pace. Thursday afternoon, Friday at six in the evening missing, always missing. As to common relation there is no more than the arbitrary. The personality builds and is broken. Again merit is not won by superficial approach, by popular agglomeration, by result advanced due to presiding suffocation. By this it is meant duty to family, or machination due to love. This can't exist as standard encryption, or perfectly spotted walls in a garden. No, there is the flame which extends beyond ascensional boundary, shifting beyond the brink of atmosphere. Of course, to the isolate soul this is devastational motivation, which at the common plane slays the connecting integers in one's body. Which then leans towards the unshackled cells in the mysterioso. Levitational enactment, spawned intermination. Thus one's former life is consumed, shifting beyond the samsara of the atmosphere. Then the cells begin to rotate with incendiary spinning. These are rays of work at this level, condensed, burning without conscious enactment. Outside observation would consider the process the arch domain of the violent, or noose by chaotic semaphore.

Luminous ruination?
Dotted entanglement?
Peripheral encroachment?
None of the above.

The void once born suddenly opens. Dawn is breakage by swan, by bells which formulate according to utopian timing. And this is not force which reels with the naïve as focus. One is not unlike an unprecedented beast. The first beast on the first shore arrived from total blankness. It is the spectacle of uncertainty, the vertiginous elan, the untold dark at the depth of the hive. Which means one breaks from the leprosy of general social constriction. Freed of the terse, of the mediocre, of mockery. Nothing is left of shrewdness, of the negotiator's spool, of these in pursuit of spurious goods and services. The vertical breaks away, one no longer replicates the surface.

Which means there is no longer the fact of issues. Even paradox at this plane takes on a curious instability. Thus a curious strangeness is explored. Which means the level of official histories has been canceled, because one now glances into the eternity of the Sun. These being the rays from eternity previously understood as exclusively operant in the subtext of spells. Thus the Western modes of thought have ended, their grasp osmotically riddled.

The galaxies are visually sculpted intensities seemingly balanced as sodium and fire. Yet what are the inner planes of sodium and fire? Various variabilities of light? Canopic monsoons? One can cast no such criticality.

Can it be said that sodium blazes green and splinters into shadows? Or oblong obscurements? Or ciphers as they kindle inside darkness?

Within this momentary aegis there is higher shape, summoned from seeming erasure. This is where the body and the forces of Izar connect. "Two yellow giants with a small companion star." They affect the "electron on each side of the cell wall." Which has to do with pure respiration of energy. Energy being implicit galactic terrain. The body and the galactic as connected. The body as sodium and the galaxy as fire, they both being a simultaneity which rises. Sodium and fire, both above and above themselves, rising to a state other than what human consciousness can imagine itself as being. At this level one cannot speak on one's own behalf. One osmotically commingles, evincing other planes across circumstance. Say, an energy which blends with the heart arises in Sirius, or rays from the mind which commingle with Procyon, or glottal forms from Aldebaran.

One must be able to clear such distinction, knowing the different levels of suffusion, one's carcass fanning the strength of neurological enlightenment. And this enlightenment is contagious to an almost unbearable degree. It being something other than the charisma of ghosts. And it is not that one fuses with corruptive or mistaken identity. It is not a replicate model, nor is it an old shielded workhorse burnished by sigils. It is energy which opens, which roams the zones of alchemical anonymity.

The latter range is the burning effort which soars, which allows ignited sodium to flare, superseding parsecs having skills which persist beyond translocational impiety. It cannot be said that one resorts to birth, or claims contiguous application within the known. Because one can never resort to the picaresque or the brutal. The supersessional is what some of the learned call the rapturesque, the spectrum of the edenic, never subject to neutralization by chroma, so it ceases to register as retraceable nettling.

A state of transgression?

A mode concerning infinite forces?

Of course, these are other fires, other callings, other levels of witness.

Yet this is energy never infected by form, which endures through demonstrable planning. It is not the forum which persists according to ideological substrate. Therefore vanished kindling, perfect ingestion by risk. True, at certain zones in the venture, one completely bypasses the Sun and enters perhaps a state of an inner green sun. A sun which rises into deathless existence. A sun which poses threats through its rising by manoeuvre, by its circuitous internalities. It is like carrying a curious and trenchant poise, variable, unsullied, floating. As total adventure, it goes back to unstinting endeavour 4,000 years prior. Like the totalic effort in Kemet, it consumes; it fulminates mazes; it projects from the unexplored.

This is not subsistence or phantoms haunting sparrows in a garden. It is habitation at levels implied as magnification by ibis. Skills accrue at removes beyond human disadvantage. As for the spoils of the fiefdom, they cannot exist. Extrinsic colouration, void. The simple powers of contraction ended. These are rays of gusts from the invisible. As for migrating polar ore, it burns as the anagrammatical through drainage, and erupts as flotational savoir.

As for living aspiration, in this regard, one is seen as digging graves in the illegitimate, in pursuing distance which collapses. Yet it is never seen by legions of detractors that their will to response is burdened, is captured by forces which sum by annihilation. True, one is seen as spell in total strife. As one of sinister background riding in a carriage of poison. Yet through the powers of these storms one must not act on behalf of a sentiment which self-prosecutes. To the outer eye, one is always slipping on ciphers. A ghost condensed while singing from a harmolodic prairie. Because there exists no rule as self-censure, one is always subject to the angular role of self-torture, or coded suffering by vertigo. Because one spins dialectics by vapour, one is saturated with fire from the unpredictable. The smallest scale that the Prussian hordes are capable of are triggered infinitesimals. At this scale one exists as no more to them than as invisible wildlife. Maybe presented at one of their functions as a disordered figurine from Patagonia. An exotic limited to blurred superficial exposition. Perhaps a particle, rising from a canyon, peripheral and without consequence. This being one's reception in latter day society, derived as it is from inscripted hellebores.

It cannot be seen that to wall off energy, to pompously equate collective effort with sullied example, can be no more than plagiarized germination. And in the written arts the tendency prevails towards the imagination as pervasive subtrahend. The subconscious mind takes on lettering by conscious form. Uneasiness ensues. Reading such texts is like adding milk to aggravation. Nothing does justice to flight. Countless texts descend to flightless birds in an ordinary window. Nothing remains; alterity and risk are forgotten. The imagination fails to persist at this level. Transgression remains an exhausted mineral. Intervals are reduced to the pointless. The galactic is never discussed.

The question is asked. What are the free-standing claims which erupt into remote divinities?

Various metals in stars?

Unleashed hydroxyl?

Language is connected to these levels. And when one thinks of language, one is not restricted to shapes and hooks on a page. For instance, Charles Ives and John Coltrane peering over the rim of the galaxy, absorbing the feral speech of eternity. For Ives, The Unanswered Question. For Coltrane, The Father, The Son and The Holy Ghost. Compositions not unrelated to Egyptian or Wolof, or sounds from Sino-Tibetan. Again, the harmolodic as purity through sound. Sound waging war on negation. It dazzles the vapours. So by dazzling the vapours, art absorbs in the being and emits as an energy not unlike neutrinos. In this sense, emitted art is ghostly, which escapes the hylic personality by means of its evaporate trans-literal nautical enthrallment. So in the deepest sense, alchemic art becomes riveting annularity. There exists no corruption in time, no seasonal adage which inevitably turns over against itself. One leaves the zones of the diacritic. One escapes. One speaks from the unmarked.

This is a sensitivity not of withdrawal, but of kinship with other factors. Factors which ignite in the margins of the aura, which sparks a relay of light like an eruption of rays from a cinder. In this sense, the body is cinder, art being intuitive amalgams of energy which no longer apply to grounded portions in the psyche. And by grounded, what is meant are those terminal portions of thinking which have no inkling of the imagination and its conjunction with its absenting of the terminal.

Or one can speak of the day-to-day as the fabulosity of the sterile, of the waning as the procreation condensed by the pressures of hylic frontality. At this higher sensitivity there can never be contained procreation, tainted by Christian assignation, as final and unbending assessment. The portion is exploded, openness extends.

The inductive as limit no longer figures. The arrogant enclosure as measure. The result being a crude contiguous vapour, creating in the mind an albatross of motives. Energy approached in this manner tends to favour fractional imposition. Context weakens, the field distorts. Nature thus becomes subject to catalogue by calumny and disorder. The natural environment becomes subject to various exterminations, according to particularly imposed balance. Resonance which flares from this, or that, species is altered or condemned according to this, or that, particular and the exigencies of the aforesaid particulars. Thus the inductive being labours unduly, always confronted by psychic malapropisms, so much so that fecundity through insight is never approached. It is the reduction of multiples from data, so that each dot on the line acts as unsavoury spectra. These spectra being entities which rise from the womb of punishing criteria. It is energy extrinsically policed, fueled by unbalanced critique. In consequence, life, which hisses in the shadows, elicits smouldering and anger, and is rationally condemned. It becomes in the end strategized dishonour, which results in a living amnesia seemingly unstruck by subconscious pressures.

But how can depth or confidence cohere within the mode of such thinking, rife as it is with regulation? It is the mind cauterized at the snow line, numbed, the cells then wrought by a paralytic obliqueness. The voice then issues from what can be called a clear but chattering schism. And so, general conversation rests upon such schism, upon the details which resist one's organicity, all the while plunging through dark and unwarranted regalia. Underneath these conversing quotidians exists whispered personification, always signaling threat through isolation and disorder. Consensus is understood as being based on the tenebrous, on lurking confinement. Intelligence in this context remains enamoured of constrained possibility. In contradistinction there is the Kemetian view of the self. First, the visible and invisible respond as balanced respiration. At next remove, the Sun as upholding the latter as immortal continuum. Scarabs, lions, vultures, bulls, spinning as immortal proportion. Life is instinctively understood through pan-irradiation, with each of the parts giving life through universal palpitation. At this level of being, there exists no sorcery or conflict, because there exists levels within levels, states of being within states of being. Understood in this manner, nature contains no contiguous policy, no disappointment accrued by utopian abasement. Splendour then erupts through the complication of rising, as initiation through danger.

One must not prejudge one's complication, or take as substance a pre-christened motive which adulterates its prime velocity. Thus one lives as unadorned, without the claustrophobic as principle. Because at a certain level of knowledge, the Sun extends itself in the system. Which is not unlike the frustum of the pyramid in Kemet, studied through the sacred application of number. And these are not numbers mechanically confined to the frontalic, but number as irradiated within the systems of nature. Which is not the scope of the inbred, or of hyperventilated tissue, brought down to chronic subliminal despair. One does not live to discuss stumbling predatory rumour, which under the true condition of breathing can never prevail. Pressure from old pollutions then continues to de-exist. Then an absence of theoretical codeine, then the flames from old dominance collapses, then thought filters through as vertical intuitive. Power then leaps through erratic charts, through strange umbilical sigils. The power of the cosmos opens, and is no longer aimless. The cortical as subset then ceases. One is crowned with perfect speaking. One then leaves the room of archival ruin.

Then the elevated transpires, and one begins to wander the energy of second sight. A private ray issues forth, a matrix of riddles ensues. The body then a whirling of dunes and exploration. Therefore all structural dissonance is abandoned. And this is the zone where the body exists above the body, which carries a suppleness energized by fire, by energy which travels by the loquaciousness of instinct. This is power which flows in an undamaged field. A galaxy of life where the cells are cleansed and flow upward.

Here one reaches unprecedented beckoning, an alchemic criticality. One then convenes in the depths as an unerring savant, as energy which Western society has come to know only through figmental discussion. But what is being discussed is what experience in the invisible reaches. Exploration of ineffables, weaving in and out of horizons. These are not the after lands where tied corpses escape. One could name it the zone of Divine Acceptance, where jasmine and nuance prevail. This is something different, something the Kemetians understood as the embryonic regions, as the first scale of release. For instance, no longer scale by oppressive speech, no longer futility by transgressive repression, but linkage to other auric syncopations, to trans-personal mystery, to splendour which weaves above traumatized in-reductives.

When the Western collective speaks of the body, it speaks of an entrained physical constriction without upper or lower dimension. Thus the body is understood as kaleidoscopic ornament.

The body is given deepest regard through rancour and illness. Life as torched or meandering consolation. Yet there remains the biology of a torched and challenging strangeness. A regressive state that even a crocodile would confuse with starvation. In contradistinction there is a medicine superior and unequal to energy, as simply viewed according to Imperial containment. According to the powers which thrive on replica by old usage, they fission due to thermal regalia, due to passionless tangling. In contradistinction there is the magnetism of powerful inner ritual, say, in the inner rituals of Wolof or Chokwe. The inner and outer states replete with simultaneous origin. And with the colours, the feathers, the beading, it induces a magnetic technical trance. Certainly something the opposite of something, configured through pointless additional scrawling.

Such acts inspire in one the art of flaming semaphores and riddles, or grand orchestral ciphers played from ether charts ignited in the mountains. One thinks of notes or words as organic gesture, as trans-colloquial weight, as if one could float across crystal oceans near Java, or journey for kinesio-plankton floating near Jamaica. This is not the elaborate staged as omission, nor as birth condoned by withdrawal. It remains a plunge towards interiors, to energy replete beyond exhibit. As for the public constitution these are intervals which cannot be accommodated, or ruled as adequate according to perceptual law. As if one could hear as an hierophantic mountain goat, absent of residue or largesse. These are sounds from magic gale storm castles derived from unknown gulfs of experience. For instance, oneiric smouldering yellows, perhaps purplish Tibetan plateaus, dispelling stricken conceptual fields. Therefore one does not speak from a drained black garment, rifling over damage contained in a folder. Which is not the folder of the heart, breathing like the dialectical beauty of orchids. The latter being the true variety of gain, the compost which wanders around salt. Which, of course, cannot fix percentage in the extrinsic, by extracting a chronic discipline from a subsurface Prussian integument. This is beauty cleared of fixated radii.

This is escape from the studied medicine of implosion, of force gleaned from the mould of derivative intention. As for the mordant effigies sifted from exhausted debate, there exists no time for the back and forth as witness, trying to extoll the right leaning answer. It becomes a confusion which reeks of tension. It is habitation according to the mordant. Exchange as prior absence. With this prior absence being nothing more than a nonconforming stillness. Say, as a point of nonconforming, one takes elements from the Romany, and vodou, and Indian. The latter being understood as Pomo or Comanche. To the accomplished European these elements can be nothing more than mediumistic hovels, full of blood and disciples working with myth. They say that it accomplishes nothing more than the violence of animals. So if one claims that echoes burn, that roots gather from droplets and speak, they are led to believe that one has sided with wild mammals, given over to aggressive in-audia and leakage. Yet, for one so inclined, this is merely the range of pure subsistence, being the songs which issue from buried wine. One is then considered as being one who erupts from a group, who lurks, who casts spells, who weaves by means of circuitous ocular thread.

Maybe it is true that one refuses to wash flags, or is cast in the role as an associate of cruelty. Maybe one is seen as one of the blessed of the Congo, accused of having broken bread with an army of killers. Or maybe one is seen as yield from sinister disservice; at best, singed by asymptotic brine.

So, does one remain on this plane simply to capture tensions, or to exalt disharmony simply to demonstrate an abstracted brutality? Such would have to be answered in the negative. One could say to principle ownership "...look, my teeth are not scarred. I have never fomented weaponry, nor stood on a field of desecration, exhibiting to certain Gods bones of the sacrificed." Not that this is begging comfort from the ruthless, or seeking exoneration by discomfort. Yet one must never speak through bleak or degraded discomfort. One must simply exhale and speak from the very bottom of one's body.

Because one lives amongst clerks of withdrawn declaratives, one is surrounded by artefacts of the accursed, carking with uncleansed charisma. It is like pressure from the savage compression of bodies, conducting affairs through a series of collapsed registrations. It retards the volitional through the sentiment in conversational basics. As for crevasses, as for emotional methane recorded, consensus only concedes a pattern which fosters an operose living dimension. This is commitment to circumstance given to the blind by the blind. In the West, this is known as tradition, which seems to produce no more than a secular scansion of nerves. Because the self is broken into parts, fate is sown through astrological mirages which then linger as soot, which poisons the throat, staining the menses by way of the mind. These mirages become acceptable prohibitives, as if they were axes ground down to disoriented order.

This is scale in the Northern lands where all things yield to microscopic dearth, to waste as lived distraction. Of course, these are lands which live by, say, robbing minerals from the Congo, or by creating despair across American Indian zones, or within the cholera plagued nerves of Haiti. As creative force in such a world one takes sides with the scavengers, with those whose poverty is soaked like roots, who everyday face dual and universal ruination.

So, under such circumstances, how does the mind unleash; how does it orient and fuel and counsel its own enigmas? At one level there seems to be no outlet, no higher force which extends beyond reason. Yet the latter does exist in what the Dogon understand to be the foremost solar fuel. For them, it is the 6 systems of the Sirius complex and their understanding of Sirius B. The latter, they say, was once the Sun to the Earth, and remains the most important star in the sky. Prone to ocular relay, the understanding persists that suns travel through suns, merged as inner dalliance which lingers. This could be called suffusional verticality flowing from Sirius through the Sun. Perhaps it is like listening to the whirring of hummingbird bells with aural form, filtering light into the subconscious derma. And this is not an abstraction, or perfidious imperatives, fueled by distraction. The latter, understood in its objective dimension, is mathematics instinctively balanced by starlight.

And I mean by balance human relationality to light, to stars as they bring crops to full blown irritation, or to menses when they gestate and struggle. Of course, there are births at certain hours, divinations wrought both known and unknown. These are no mean efforts performed as they are within the aura of cosmic sensitivity. A sensitivity totally unlike the Shakespearean court ministerial, concerned only with the locality of the court and its concerns. Saying this, one does not promote some untoward telesthesia, or some riddled and dubious kingdom of the mind, as if one were some bottled grammarian speaking seasonless nigredo. One does not look back to past fractionations, or to elements in Yoruban counting method, as if speaking from some fixed or official expression. True, there is tragic speculation feeling the effects of excerpting oneself from consensus darkening misappropriated chasms. And, it is true, there should be nothing other than magnetization to crazed tenacities, to structureless acids, creating numbers in one's mind extracted from alien forms from subconscious tables. Yet it is all the while understood that the conscious mind has status, that its discriminating factor has focus and can work as a calmed positional lightning, as a penetrant scope which lives over and beyond technique as blinded raptor. Which can lead to a mural of the heavens, which goes back to states of mind which present technical proof cannot answer. This is when disappearances burn and perfectly withdraw from the measurement as crises. Of course, something other than stressful boundary, something other than sodium faithfully constructed by grammes.

So, when one speaks of the rise of sodium and fire, one speaks of the invisible powers which rise into the elements. These being fumes from the uncountable, of sodium and fire always escaping themselves, ascending according to impossible method. Both being identity extended by poetic aurality, by the purest charisma of hearing. So, indeed, if one listens to the Sun inside its spirals, one comes to know power as internal regality, as code for geometric invisibles. Because matter in this state works without resistance, is conjoined without decay, then whispers without principle as in decay through animality. This being paradigm through liquefac-tion, through eerie solar generality.

And one here speaks of a distance which is crushing and shows no signs of limit. Which in the deepest sense remains the trenchant field of osmosis. These being systems which no gravity can ponder. It is akin to signs of signs in Miró, hovering in an electric blue infinity. So, when one contemplates such signs, one begins hearing through other formations of consciousness, through meta-fires in the depth of the cells. An othering translucence which absorbs and evinces rays, which concur beyond any regional sensibility. The latter being the body as delimited spatial hive.

At another remove, such energy could translate into what could be described as an Imperial ghost ensemble. And then, at another remove, energy which morphs beyond the planetary confine. Which proves to be no more than incipient double levels, being at once athletic nuance, sacred fractions, dialectical etherics. Which courts mathematical incipience in the liminal realm between the body and the beyond. The body in this state of transition comingles with refinements from eternity. The eyes then appearing through a moth window, through spinning underwater trees. Which are glyphs which ignite as blasphemous states, as untold foundations. Here, one speaks of chemistry which opens itself at simultaneous levels.

What is needed at this point is an idea which, at first, goes beyond its own condition by taking on life, which burns itself to such a degree that the limit commonly known as Sapiens Sapiens suddenly surpasses its graspable content, which cannot be palpably rendered by chronic angst or gravity. In its beginning stages such a body will be akin to a trembling porcelain inferno, subject at times to upsets from the lower states. By means of this alembic dialectic, one leaps the galaxy of objects which the pragmatist would scale as useless opinion. Even being post-Linde and with the implicit understanding of universe after universe, the reductionist mind opts for the fever of seclusion, staking plots of turf, owning a crooked pitched tent while attempting to extend a rational tonality. It seems the higher template is always threatened by fumes from dissolved rats, by subtractions empowered by paucity. True, one always listens to their armies hissing, to their sullen migratory spells seeking entry to the heart. Thus light becomes something other than wavering, or battle by one-to-one engagement, but by vanishment through the principle of circumstellar motion. At its upper reaches, polyatomic, then, at its next remove, the undetermined, which by its very nature moves to the higher field where the inmelodious can never suggest its own extraction.

So, one burns, inch meal by inch meal, vanished, as an untraveled silicate in the vapours. True, there are states inside the Sun which conjoins one, which ignites through relay a swatch of suns, which absent themselves as parallel states of carbon. From this, utterance appears as suffusional synaesthesia, which the Egyptians knew as rays transmuted from the glycerin of death. As if breathing from closed opal or structuring phantoms from a hidden hematite in heaven. Yet, they are openings, humming points, which singe all the subsequent planes where a seeming singing scale evinces itself, as seeping from a glossary of vacuums.

Resonance?

The post fertility of phylums?

Again, why is there being?

As for the body, one must search the flows of the ventricular where the current boils, where the ozone implicates the life force. One is then capable of peering through seeming indifference, which then conjoins with a range of optics where lakes begin to blaze with convivial voltage. Yet, to the skeptic, it seems that one stares no farther than phosphenes, that vision is squared by mundane inferentials. But since one is not bound by extrinsics, or certain cajolings from the Earth, one becomes complete with absence, as if charting whole mountains on Saturn.

Say, one could line up events, or cut rocks with scissors, one would still struggle, knowing events to be dried, contiguous, planned, balanced, isolate. Yet such containment eludes the total disruption which surrounds one. The most evident: misplaced populations, floods, threats, wars, volcanic attacks, feverish annihilations. These being understood as the commonplace of the era. A collective demoralization where human accumulation feels eaten by dread. A diary encouraged by ruined behaviour. Even major disciplines go astray. This is what the writer Schwaller de Lubicz called "research without illumination." Research always tainted at its base by mechanistic ascertainment. Which assumes that the human being is an "object," and that the "observable activities of a person are the critical dimensions of his being." That the individual is law. That consciousness is "identical with physical processes." Such leaven remains the constant vehicular poison, the critical yield by which intelligence is bred. Dimensionless and brutal, it creates a pointless animal's yield. A vertiginous limitation which always utters to itself by crises. This being movement without movement, the mind and the body as waking dichotomy, with spirit estranged to the realms of "superstitious" reasoning. Thus complexity is throttled and condemned to an interior mental leakage. There exists no "metaphor" or current which extends through the spiritual states. Clearly this is a case for leprous observation, for coded forensics.

What then of life vis-à-vis being?

Energy as invisible substantiation?

Insatiable locomotion?

Ignited omnipresence?

The above can be condoned by the Ba, by primordial neuro-electricity, which is the rise of the science of being. The "astral" or "etheric" body which produces emotion, called the "Khaba" or "Kabit" by the Egyptians. Then, for them, the intelligence called "Akhu," with the rise of puberty called "Seb," and mental maturity called "Putah," and the Divine which exists as "Atmu," which stands "for the presence of full creative powers." Then the crystallization of these powers into an eighth, or transcendent, scale, this being knowledge of the self, which survives the state called physical death. Which initiates transfunction, where the body is no longer trapped inside a susurrating entropy. A measuring and delineation of states over and beyond the galaxies as they persist through minimum respiration. Which is something other than superterrestrial ozone, or phenomena and non-phenomena.

Perhaps a term can be coined: intuitive salvetics. Salvetics being code for alien annealment as salvation, understood in the body as instantaneous unbearing. Therefore levels are illumined which seemingly cannot endure, which are aspects no Spartan tribulation can convey. As if the geriatrics of violence had collapsed on itself and fallen through electrocuted tundra. Thus one becomes incapable of drafting from the emotive, a chronic behavioural frenzy dazed by the general darkness in samsara. Thus the in-germinal slowly desists, as well as the waving of mortal flags from a crag. And, of course, this is not the energy of borrowed doves wrought as infertile sigils. No, it is something other than old redress, entangled as testimonials emptied at the very cusp of accusation. In this regard one is clarified possessing something other than fever which accrues from deluded captivation.

At living remove, these gifts circulate as anomalous encryptings in a hypnopompic palace. Then, at another living remove, there emerges the vertiginous self, where other forms of being begin to respirate with the formless. Which, again, is not energous rage working on assigned adventure, as stunned associational depth.

Because the human species seems threatened, sailing on its blank collusional raft, it can no longer persist in regressional seething as form. It must somehow be removed from the rotational as cladistic. Which becomes a proto-foray into the uranian blue, which is no longer fueled by an energy jaded with ghosts. Which is not an energy which scorches with answers harried by a central storm of retreat. This is a journey understood as having its origin on Earth at Lake Omo. And the understanding must be that the species has been forced to contend with insoluble riddles. Yet, by the incisive stature of such recognition, one comes to know life as something more than a charged locus akin to simple states of sporulation. One then becomes resonant with the scope of the simultaneous field floating as it is in the unanswerable. When saying this, one is not persisting in the 3,000 phylums which themselves are bound and shaped from the energies of deep time.

How strange it is to persist in argument with what seems to be a saturate moral given. To throw away the ladder formed by the pointless economics of Christ. Yet this is the case where one is no longer beholden to the separable, to a fount which issues from corrupted photinos. Which is not belief, or wish constructed from abiding paranoia. It is the exercise of beginning to breathe, so that a partial infinite is understood, through a seminal relay of suns, which are signs which begin to focus the human field in a higher strength of burning electrical grammar. Thus the salt and fire of the body rises to a higher alchemic tremendum. The result being something other than the a priori as hypnotic, another expression which fields itself through an improvised osmosis.

Saturate With Refined Enigmas

Living as a saturate listening disciple, one absorbs knowledge as wealth through intuitive crystalline registers, as an abiding crystalline absorption. But, in contradistinction to this state, one remains fraught with constant literal exposure to what can be called an anti-culture and its carking embranglements. A world where seminal texts are not read, where someone with the stature of André Breton would remain chronically unknown. So one asks, where are the minds with darting commas which breathe by imaginal respiration, full of radiant constellations? In this regard, one thinks of insights and levels and zones of higher vertical enabling. Instead, one is surrounded by oscillating vipers gone blind, never implicit with sight through multiple carrying force.

So, how can such delimit carry a mind, or assemble compound crystal or magic? It is always tearing at a fragmented pile, at myopic lettering in collision. At times it may recall by tendentious stammering Thales as water, or Heraclitus as fire, or Parmenides as written location. Perhaps, at times, a comment on Dostoyevsky, or some partial figment on Nabokov, or some incidental summoning from the works of Van Gogh. But the darker spiral never ceases; a preeminent toxicity, if you will.

Let me say this: if the Coffin Texts now spiraled, as example, it could possibly lead to human cellular clarification, or, maybe, an indefatigable attempt at alchemic translocation. A higher human flaring where we re-emit the Sun into living. Perhaps the feelings could extend into how the Sun darkens and rises, or how its solstices rebuild in the magnetic ore of the human system. Then perhaps one could breathe in complete suspension. Respiration at such a level is electricity organically revealed.

The Egyptians called it the Ba, and understood it as being "the invisible energy that runs through all visible functions." When understood from this level of depth, locusts and wolves, and the differing forms of bark are seen from the level of the benthic. This is why the Kemetic mind functioned as circularity, as riverine, as transfunctional discipline. But the tendency of present times seems open to nothing more than sample by rectilinear invasion. So it builds on functioning death crops, on dialogue according to slaughter. Health in the mind can then be no more than staggered; it can do nothing more than function as a gasping raven.

Escaping Mass Seduction

One must continue to evolve through the unclaimed resistance, tested as one is by the susurration from daily battle arcs. Everyday there exists uncountable simulacra. Everyday one walks into the glare of surrounding neutron fevers, shadowed as they are by a state of imminence which looms as collective implosion, which is nothing other than code for final nuclear activation. Parallel to this there is a complexity exploding, stoked by full scale psychic repression. The human voice surrounded by these double general shadows as if one were a Scarlet Tanager reversed in the midst of its vocal peregrinations, as if its power of song were slanted by pernicious occlusion, with its special faculty of living spiraled towards obliqueness. Such obliqueness, being nothing more than a temporary station, plotted by the conspiratorial climate for erasure.

As Sapiens Sapiens one is simultaneous with the Tanager, with its vocal stresses demonized, with its bodies' natural rhythm stunned by distractive cacophony. As if one were poised to drown in old starvational sand, surrounded by fate fueled by visible mockery. This present condition sired by exoteric construction, with its continuing instigation approved by malefic sanction. This being the base condition which warps the basic psychological state. As if all activity were broken into pockets with the fundamental Ground being fractured. This brokenness being the continuous fuel of basic civil imbalance, where one is always personally shaken by a chronic psychic uprooting. Thus one survives as though partially dead. Reaction is, of course, charted within a pre-planned apotheosis. Which is nothing other than energy conceived in flames of corruptive disability. So Sapiens Sapiens, at one with the threatened Tanager, seems more and more reduced to the kingdom of minor vespidae. As something lodged below ground, dissonant, carking, prone to perpetual inversion.

This being Sapiens Sapiens surmised as a loathsome sum gathered by chaotic inference. Say, if someone were granted license to lecture on the laws compelling moons to sink and burn, one would be placed at the bottom of categorical psychology, thus disrecognizing the imagination as if it were a dying crow scorched on exhausted blister trees. The imagination just spoken of being nothing other than the stray conception of a being operant as a disposable variant of the aforementioned vespidae, or the hallucinatory aria of the crow. So the human state, seen as possessing the lessened state of wasp or crow, can possess no momentum, incapable of embodying tremorous sensitivity, unable to rise above the template of stridulation as decreed by the standards deployed by Imperial example.

According to the latter's interpretation, there is no gainful experience left to be had, only instinct which is considered by Imperial tactical negativity as a séance empowered by recessive genetics. Since the imagination commandeers no sense of commodity, it is understood to inhabit no more than a maimed configuration. An ailing noise, an unwarranted kinetic. Or a series of dazed blisters promoting creatural insignificance. The imagination can say that it is something other than an adjudicated diamond, or an orphan who smells hypnosis in his urine. In this heightened state, one could say that one glows as a scarlet civet, or as a mongoose understood as raw sienna. Because such a state carries no statistical tenor, it can never be valued by its absenting of itself or by nuance. And, by absenting of itself, it means absenting itself from habituated branding, say the birth date of the Christos, or one's vicarious behaviour at the beginning of Lent. It is a world unsanctioned according to measurable diagnostics. Thus the imaginal conduit is castigated as being no more than a poisoned haddock or a flounder, providing nothing other than the devolution of its waters.

Under these opprobrious conditions, one must exercise as one's praxis interior flammability. One must enunciate mirages by testing the scope of their black originatory candles. Of course, this astonishes the social dishevelment with brews. Thus one enumerates the uncanny by assaulting the rotten doors swinging between hands. Add to this one's hypnotically altered lingual signals which over and over provides a magnetic, which is simultaneous with the farthest telescopic reception. Which is not unakin to the journalist who reconvenes facts, who at times configures a substantive political dossier. Facts at times electrify, yet plunge, and then dissipate as causeless chronicles in themselves. This is said as such because one is thinking of interior generation, of the orientation of being. Of course, one does need to make protest concerning a hectare of murdered Indians, or of the institutional mephitics advanced against biological Africa. According to certain elements in reportage, such behaviour goes no deeper than the reprehensible mechanics of the capital economy.

But for the imagination another level of experience exists, which lurks beyond the innautical. The innautical, meaning prose, containment, contiguous aspiration. What is meant here is the imagination of spirit which organically supersedes damaged lightning as property, or strategic simulacra conditioned by Roman property as model. One can take, as example, Julius Caesar in Gaul. Destroy tribes, create treasonous conditions, subject whole zones to immolation. Of course, this being action as fear through vociferous means. This being the psychology of the ruined who project ruin upon the ruined. It is like an equation which galls through the superficial extent of its grasp. Its principle: protect at all costs the right to hostility; the prize, gold or land, plundered by predacity.

But what of interior damage?
Of maimed consciousness?

Of heritage through mental distortion?

This to the prosaic world remains the blinded experience, remains the occulted inner impairment. Which is something other than repression by scorpions. The inner balance lingers and dissolves by commandeering insult. Then the memory takes on the unwarranted slaughter, the labour in dazed tobacco fields. One then whispers by uncertainty, under laws of distilled enmity. Such is the environment of a ravenous moral foundation, fighting to gain one's strength through transmixing one's immediate oneiric vitality according to European superimposition. This being the damage culled from 2,000 years.

Now one faces a present circuitously ruled by such indelible stanchions. Yet the code of one's spontaneous firmament must be the exponential form of miraculous antidote. One can no longer be dispelled by horizontal deletion. By technical aims, by the onslaught of misguided popular incursion. One must remain feral. One must hold in one's feathers a glossary of teeth. Which is something other than a studied or philosophical circumstance, or the silhouette in the corporal lean-to. This is where untameable resistance resides, rising from a rebellious mariner's coffin as a psychic territorial Hun. But one does not stop there. One evolves, one develops. Perhaps a mix like a Buryat shaman who ignites in a functioning parallel dimension as a telepathic Tunisian polymath. Which is not as some materialist would think as energy spiralling, as corruptive exotica. No, this concerns freed and invisible matter without consciously imposed boundary. Therefore multiples conspire in open air which carries the aleatoric of the open, which has as its power the aerobics to transmute death, which as parallel suborder respires as a transpicuous entity, roaming as a nomos through sudden heavenly doors, and the blaze of the Romans is unable to touch it.

So, the Empire in these hours is a curiously famished carcharodon, living more and more off its conceptual stores. One can say that it lives off the ghosts of its former feeding minerals as absolute insult to its former body. Being now revengeful, without meaningful items to attack, life now seems fallen into absentia without paradigm, reduced to paraphrase, to greater and greater minutia through technology. Hypnotic screens, facile communiqués, episodic particles of voice.

So, it is asked, what of the oneiric lightning palace?

What of the factors which shifted to form Gondwanaland?

It could be said that this is subannounced diametrical usage, or enunciation alien as the ethane on Saturn. Perhaps a dazzling or aleatoric calumny, or a transpositional hiatus meant to enkindle erroneous language.

Perhaps one could be described as an Auk in the belly of demons. Or a telepathic stray as a voiceless form floating from Mount Meru. Or possibly a herbivorous lioness maintaining suggestibility as a blur through the power of forests.

So how can the Empire as carcharodon announce itself through transpicuous blurs? How can it now suggest itself as an auto-cannibalic? Its gnoseology corresponds to its ravenous remains, to its spectrographic scrawling. It is like carbon which has vanished with its extrinsic definition through mystique by former purpose. It knows no beauty of the in-perceived, no surreptitious resonance where the bodiless is brought to bear. Its curious reflexive condition seeks a reinhabitation of the spirit of the ichneumon. An energy treacherously feral. Which means it practices a hellish shadow art, sculpted by incrystalline derogations.

Perhaps it should know that the Sun has strategically shifted, that its sudden auroras have defied its power to regale the mind with illusion. Yet what is now spreading like fire in the populace seems something akin to collective dementia. This is where one's mother wit entrances, where oppositional registration transmutes to invasive lexical registration. Which is the creation of a meta-astrological chart, which conducts as its principle knowledge that the energy contained in public agendas is now useless. That campaigns, and promotions, and celebrities in special exhibit carry no semination or voltage. So that which now transpires between the Empire and its zodiac no longer registers with efficiency. And here reference is not made to a professional reader of signs, but to the intuitives of the poet who understands when inconsistency arises. Witness this particular zodiac where the carving of Capricorn is transposed with the charisma of the solar lion, so that nothing but a general scrambling governs. Within these remains, all its motifs become alienated exacerbations. Yet what could have once been deciphered as decisive enervation no longer pontificates itself as marker, as crumbling salvo or verdict. Decline is now wrought by ambiguity, by skills condoned as general malaise. An arsenal eroded, yes, but to what end?

One must leap levels. One must make forays into infinity. So the questions can be asked. What of compressed suns in the Sombrero Galaxy? What of the parsecs which go beyond themselves and are no longer countable? These questions, which are from the deeper point of view, are culled from partial demonstration. And what is partial demonstration? Realias which suggest the dwarfing of Sapiens Sapiens. In this sense how can modern enclaves tower, or secular leaders of nations be of lasting impression, or carry power through gravitized relations? They are conduits which no longer carry flow or dimension. What becomes most noted in the present context is the importance given to personal issues, to general emotional chatter. Such is life in the West, magnetized as it is by superficial relations. And these relations call for descent into greater and greater monotony. So, to the lessened mind, larger forces cease to exist. And one being committed to these emotional relations, there is less and less power to resist seduction to the popular hive. There is always looking outside of oneself for corroborated study, which is nothing other than the provincial given. Under these circumstances there can be no assessment of depth, no virtue in returning from findings in the invisible. Thus persons become trapped in an assumptive pit of tar. Everything becomes shapeless and repeatable, and shapeless once again. The experience of migration through glass is negated. Therefore the finer sensitivities are impeded. Instead, there is the gossip of the neighbour; rumours spread by the cousin of one's cousin; a swatch of couples in presentation. Immediate surroundings. And what erupts from these immediate surroundings is liquidation of acuity. Discourse based on tense behavioural repartee. So when one takes leave of this plane, and takes a step or two in mid-air, it seems all previous agreements are irrevocably breached. One is no longer illumined as a person in good standing.

As to the mediocre, as to civilian calibration, one absconds into dereism, into charismatic flux, into the risk of jubilation. Always accused at the level of the masses as carrying blinded ink in the genes. One is thus voided and imprinted with a neo-impression of always grappling with dysphonia. Which is commencement of stark interior struggle with collective hallucination. Meaning the energies which erupt from the collective secular dais. Understood as action through extrinsic disservice. The latter being dazed optical plena, a force always confused by paradoxical self-punishment.

Within such insidious scripting one must always retain the blistering view, which casts from its glance a sidelong vapour as alchemic penetration. Which eliminates the superimposed state, which both condemns and reprieves according to mandated explanation. Because whatever be the torrid or objective explanation, imposition by its very nature can do nothing other than to conduct itself as obstruction. The milder form of obstruction transmits delay, always scaling daily issues through in-vitrescent ordination. Which always carries collective effect. Pervasive conversation is always saturate with haunted phenomena, with quantitative invasives. Quantity, being akin to seductive neon, creating in the mind cacophonous orchestration. So, by creating variation upon variation from the principle of phenomena, the mind is shifted into a course of untenable filigree, so that details are sullenly extended and varied into horizontal nuclei. One could say that within this weaving are offshoots from string theory, monitored stocks, Satanism, beverage consumption, variations on God. One can call all the former monitored subsumptions, mingled dust separate from the instincts. Which marks the galling resistance in the general bearing. This is considered prayer beneath a night beating down with occlusionistic rays. And the result is doubt crystallized by lacking. The sounds of life then registered as iconic devastation. Thus wisdom is shunned and coded as metal and straw. Which makes humans who ascribe to such practices less than proverbial beasts. In this sense, they are self-hounded, stung by their own vitals. This is what can be called the academia of implosion, the unsustainable shadings, which take on grammes and numbers of grammes, as if a spate of numbers could justify the weight of an overextended body. And this results in the terminal abstraction of structure.

So what is structure? Drafts of money? Owned trivia as property? One could say yes, both are central to the structure. Which extends to what Artaud once called the piling up of bodies. And these bodies are exterior scatterings always equated with bearing the cost of the general good. This being a social complex which clings to deaf and piacular agreement. There is nothing but a monochromatic litmus suffused with exhaustive terror. So the average beings secured by the hellish, by notches of lightning, self-indicate to themselves that they have fallen into differing versions of hell. That they're locked in the throes of tragic burial calendars perched upon an extrinsic bodily sensorium. And all forms of the irregular are lessened, then hauled up for elimination. Be they Arawaks, or Haitians, or Afghanis, or other nonspeaking flora or fauna—like limbs hacked off by the Dutch in the midst of the slave trade in order to maim captured African maroons.

This remains the underlying spirit of the age which plunders in search of universal Cibolas. Which is a spirit felicitous with robbery, with disfavourable morality. Anticlaritas, meddlesome psychic fornication, tainted seismic activity by cinder. These being inhuman time stretches, sums etched in the spirit by translatable venom. Rewards accrue from such venom. Lucre, positions of power, voluptuous unstable women. These are the gains for properly serving as a corporate administrator of death, as a servant to bound history. Which drafts accepted symmetries from blood. Which dwells in the depths of increasing blindness. A quintessential blood farming. A fissioning or pertinent quantity violently addressed.

This being the general aim of the Northern societies, it leaves citizens in the main ¾ hampered, the mind being livid with psychic arthritics. On the other hand, there can exist for the spirit other breathing formations. Other translatable prairies of cyanoethylene, breathing other unblemished hydroxyl spores. Which seems to the old Roman critics to be of impossible expression, carrying in its wake an ominous utopian bearing. The poet of being is thus declared as anonymous monster. As something inexpressed by delimited evil. So one is targeted by these critics, by their unprincipled cascades, by their droplets of poison placed upon the palate of the public at large. Which leads to dark electrical auras, the public mind then moving as a tornadic lateral hamlet. Provincial, stagnant, always giving themselves the status of significance. Thus technical achievement replaces the spirit.

At poetic height energy replaces nervous strain; then elliptical trance; then transgressive possession. Not an ethereal jurisprudence, nor a scale which yields the paradox of grounded forces. Again, something other than a scrambling, or a dissonance, which issues as alchemic fatigue. No. Balance is understood as being nothing related to the functional, to the trends which ramble from new example. One can speak of this state as spiritual monography, where the individual rises from a personal riddle to reach transpersonal indicatives. A direction, an index, which changes course and spirals. Which allows one to survive threat or scandal without intrinsic remorse. Without regressive erosion of impulse or body. Because one must insist on beatific triggering planes, on metamorphic input, or strife subsumed in anonymous welters. Again, everything burns, and subsists, above a roving skeletal capacity. Which is ether as emblem through breathing. As for forges, as for needles in hiding, they succeed, not other than as pontifical momentum. This being akin to the listening of bells, to that which honours per capita disappearance. There being no such thing as rectilinear independence, or proper quotidian placement, singed by clear inversional patterns. Which equates with assaultive mirage against that which is hidden. So if one reaches for the telepathic, or signals the force which opens the tornadic, it reeks of the unexpected, and creates from its seduction secrets which causes one's human energy to secrete and spiral, and resurrect, and recombine, and change forces with the dead. So that new opening can be established at the cusp between eternity and waking. In other words, subsistence disappears, and footnotes begin to mingle within the fire of higher regions. Thus, there is no siphoning, no reductive litter, coded and

given over to a suspect regalia.

Short of this, one has not failed, one has not given over to notable society. Because one carries translatable interaction, it is not unlike a threaded incitement, a quaking ingredient. Again, translatable ceramics etched as teeming parallel personas. This being development along the way into a new and higher structure of instants. Which produces neither wealth nor mechanical rewards.

Having abandoned the Western disciplines produces a seeming absurdity, thought to be no more than a welter of cold ink, expressing privacy through a meaningless metrical weight. Yet, in the doing of this abandonment, one abandons assumptive distortions. And let this be clear: gold does not benefit the spender after death. Which reveals the pointless arrogance of pragmatic tacticians. They who seek to rule the complex by a brazen micro-tectonics, so that space and time work according to extrinsic hypnotics. Which claims as its form futurity by matter, by extended transportation of differing human endeavours, from travel in space to seemingly infinite psychological postings. Thus the individual is surrounded by quotidian appearance, by curvatures according to mechanistic punctuation, as if the body itself had no other experience than subsuming itemization. Which can be simplified by calling it poisoned ozone training. And now that China and other regimes exist within this poisoned ozone training, there is toxic mental serum which seems to flow across the continents. Yet the imagination flies above these reductive argumentations, above these pythonistic entanglements, so that it works at the level of revelational volation, sometimes speaking in the code of ectopic cipher, or empirical cobras, or navamsas which speak braille. These are lanterns which swing in feral combining. So one is never exhausted due to nebular prostration, nor overweening paradigms. One escapes, one wafts, one separates. One takes on the combat of absence.

Magnification then hovers with the Sun, at times, splintering, then recombining in its wake. This is a magnification which concentrates power at such a level that one is able to call out lions and demons, transmixing their fates through imaginal demeanour. As if they were seen leaping from rotational buttes, floating in higher suspension. The mind then fuses with these upper flotations, understanding that these energies float beyond galactic drift, communing with levels of the unannounced, commingling with arcs and measures which rotate as spiritual camouflage. Which never self-protects as iterative model, or promotes a false or insyllabic immolation. One does not foment at this level an electric immobility, or a tornadic self-scrutiny, where the energy falls and populates itself through popular re-engenderment. In this sense one does not exist, so the personality holds itself in abeyance, yet is able to thrive with flexibility in an euphotamic state. Which is degrees higher than animal exuviation as the bodies' energies transmute to holographic illumination. And this illumination being séance soaked in spells, being a state which surpasses carnivorous opacity. The latter being at a plane higher than dialectical opposition, inhabiting the realia of superior lightning and diamonds. This being principle visible manifestation when the transmuted scale reveals itself as nonlinear nuance. There being no absolutes to existing, to parallel re-structural havens, to rote or confessional ellipsis. Which, of course, leaks beyond the furnace of the palpable, uncontained by the caliginous as alloy. Which is akin to the purity of indifferent mountain chains. Therefore portions rise, and meander, and fluctuate, and gather from the poise of example.

Say spittle hung like lamps of vampire orange one could scatter beneath the light, so as to announce illusive embodiment. Therefore one is never localized as bodily abstraction, deranged by determinative counting. Which accounts for elliptical bodily presence beneath the vampire lamps. So elegance is understood wafting above an isolate balance. Thus strangeness is balanced, equilibria sustained as instinctive voltage. And since this is not just a note which increases itself through poetic devastation, it allows a new and intangible morality to transspire. It allows the aforementioned suspension to mark and exponentiate itself throughout the source of central meaning. And this central meaning evolves as dissonance through clarity, brought into play by paradoxical neutrality. Because there are days when neutrality reigns, when oceans dissolve beneath the mind, and then appear as writing through unplotted ink, which quickly scatters confining mental issues. Sleep then blazes with strange oneiric mixings. For instance, an operatic refuge defined by a mixture of strange Giacometti-esque beasts moving in irregular circles, coping with elliptical arias. Coping with translated Swiss, somehow inexpressive of danger. Their voices, like remedial caroms staggering off the sides of the stage, homologous of an indigent zoology. Of sound barely surviving, so much so, that the illegible begins breathing, as one's audition begins to heighten through homologous mystical animation. And it is this mystical animation which begins brewing, which curiously begins to cultivate a quaking purity by monsoon.

So that the laws of rational wielding have no further relevance.

The aforesaid being a dust that moves, that extends to portions, across a series of intensities. Which extends back to heightened mystical animation. Cycles then spiral into obscure advancement, as if one saw in the heavens a useless and smouldering sand. Which leads to an aural calligraphy beyond blankness.

So matter at this level no longer blazes as fictitious content. It is not that one exchanges reality, or creates a pauperization of the psyche. By the cells transmuting out of gravity, one then dispenses with common perception. One no longer carries stake in the matter as regards one's genetic embodiment. The body is not reduced to claimed land, to observable protestation. The body becomes other. Not political contestation, militaristic rejoinder, nor brackish recrimination and slaughter. The body, as it exists in this range, is no longer of service to the routine order of State. The counting devices lose their skills in projecting the movement of sidereal personalities. Thus the body is no longer key to firmly wrought regression.

The body is removed from objective simulacra, from debatable embroilment, from assaultive procedure. Nor on the other hand is it compelled by elitist inscrutables. It abjures the referential bulletin, never magnetized to critique which rises from the lower mind. It does not respond to terror or charts. As to common asservation, one becomes a dissonant subjunction, which means no more to the observer than the scorching of dazed bread. One's action then takes on drift, floating through a mass of cryptic tenuosity. A tenuousness which spills into utopian disservice. One then addresses those "right minded" beings ensconced in assumption; they who enter a stable set of doors, searching for a subsequent chair at a table. One can acidly tell them that it is no longer 1919 and their fates no longer are controlled by the British. All their actions, being British, patriotically take up the stance of falling paralysis cinders, breathing by misformed myopias. Now they need to be told of their irrelevance, of their moribund regulation. Let them know that they are subsets of the scurrilous, who impart their findings according to greater and greater decrease, charting for themselves signs of collective disappearance.

By study of igniferous impact, one views referential despair as it erupts from the anti-sidereal mind of the culture. In such a climate one lifts the voice through courageous teaching, through sacrilegious impact, by waterborne inferentials. One then understands that what is culturally considered of mature and higher standard is nothing more than restive juvenalia. Which gives rise to necrotic stereotypics, to subjunctive radiations, which fail to exorcise their limits by means of self-engendered lingering. This being the general scale within which one operates, which attempts through its abstract methodology to be precise down to the very centimes of breathing. A breath seemingly operant in the depths of atomic water. A breath seemingly rife within peculiar infernos. Yet this is not living, wandering as if in an oblique and alien doubling.

They are guided by mortal glances, by definitives fraught with carking infernos. So they struggle with themselves by means of impetuous lottery, by minerals culled from exhaustive foment. They cannot lean on solar forms for ministration. Because solar forms coalesce and respirate, they remain alien to a populace sculpted from matter and salt. Which remains cold, and predictable, and bitter. A populace issued from cowardice and threats, circuitously modified by circumstantial hesitation. One clashes with these cognomens, with these brazen genes which can never conceive of consciousness as non-inherence, as something beyond preconceived limit.

Yet one must remain wary like a ghost cub, flitting in and out of the mother's den. Therefore one must build strength out of fever, extracting nourishment from the surrounding psychic plague. Igniting bulletins of guano so that they point like interior flames across absence. These being flames of insight and nourishment, flames which soak up the craft of distance, so that there is the one unification by spinning, by the speaking of the self to the self.

An impeccable dyslalia? Craft through termination

and irony? Neither. One burns by distillation, by revolt as interminable frenzy turned inward. One knows the alone through the alone. At the surface the mother vanished, the siblings frayed or disappeared, the reputation as sublet of disgrace. It matters not, even if one wanders like a lion through spiritual insomnia. One becomes the alchemic figure always conveying a portfolio of monsters. One's hide then shifts through stillness after stillness without seeming resistance or detection. Because being spins, there can be no ultimate inarrangement. No crucial or stricken solar derangement, because there exists no contiguous internality, no necropolis as symbol eternally divided, hive after hive, after hive. So since magnetism strays and reassembles, there can be no other understanding than that higher being ignites through pullulation, through unseen ripening which equates in the heavens at reexplosive scale. This being the power which flows as human nuclear current, which to the utilitarian mind amounts to nothing more than immaculate distraction.

At this level of current, one extracts oneself from old dharmas, of hidden micro-aspiration, of nullified grammar fallen short of its deepest investigations. Which is emission at other ranges. Yet, because experience is never absolute, it turns around on itself in stages, and is never subject to a practiced sedentary counting. It never craves a state of sedation and relapse, where there appears sudden micro-analysis and inability to change. Of course, the latter reacts against the prophecy of being, against its spirit which erupts beyond the regional. That said, one must listen to one's micro-path, to one's energy which extends through the substance of particulars. When rains burn, when midnights roar, one is always watching and listening to motion as it goes beyond its appointed designation. This being a consciousness which need not prove itself to the strict sensorium, in order to defend itself against negation. One's energy remains heightened by anomalous supra-intangibles which fail to show proof within the laws which are sanctioned by observable merit. According to these laws, human ciphers cannot exist. They cannot be assembled by security of reason. In no way is this understatement, with the general view always brokered by graspable rote, by terminal diacritics. To this view, nothing is enriched by encipherment, or by the implicated coded through assimilation. By this view of totality, the implicated is never coded. According to this view, thought should be spoken through a reduced empirical glottis, through finite sending ores. Thus ideas should be no more than contested polarizations. A world view enamoured of assault and reduction. And when discussing worlds like God, or the heavens, such subjects are always beguiled by a rhetoric which spawns containment. Thus the Pantocrator, or Dark Energy, as fragment, as something to be understood and decided by reduction. There is never thought influenced by entirety, because any option on this plane is thought to generate nothing more than false electrical charisma, nothing more than the clone of opinion. Yet, at a deeper strata, one can see that the material view is an assumed realia, is a base allegorical rigidity which contains no enduring power.

What are options?

Mythologies springing from twin green suns shining over Saturn?

Erasures within oblate valleys on Ceres?

Or further, or further still, a hurricane of haflons appearing and disappearing, in and out of uncountable dimensions?

Perhaps the latter could work as triggering ideals, as fecund optional glints, so as to listen to life as it soars outside of fearful animal resistance. This being the deeper strata, the imagination as it sprints through and beyond blackness. This blackness being the unknown horizon where human simulacra can no longer be explored. In this state, the figmentational psyche is abandoned leaving a colloquy of Richters in its wake. This being the exponentials of the Ground, of history abandoned riding experimental waves into untested sound. Which brings to mind elements in Moorish Granada, or old Egyptian kindling schools, or Hopi maturation in the stars. Examples abound of the body and the bodiless connecting on other planes. What one can say is that in the West there has been a wrong turning, with its best minds soured by a blinding stationary rebus. Which forces study in self-dividedness, always condensing an opaque version of itself. And these policies seem endless being purely powerless as squalls. In consequence there is always a crisis over land and items, over discussions broached by disruptive military yield. Of course, the standardized curricula as regards negotiated blood spill, or foreknowledge of alien terrain and its bodies. The latter are not limericks of the quoting of fanciful owls, playing with the metrics of the useless. It simply means the casting of the elemental into death. Again, the central locus of the times, blindness, frozen stationary rays.

Blindness being the inevitable sample, the unascendant hand. Pessimism being the mean response, the central generating symbol. As for bucolic fenestration, the view becomes drawn, abstract, an absolute refutation of medicinal calm and beauty. Which amounts to an apriori habitation. Which amounts to condoned dissonance. In this circumstance flexity de-exists. So the general mind can never allow itself to explore inarguable range. Range being understood as that which explores its own absence, knowing its understanding to be capable of experience across parallel wastes and voids, thereby feeling a distant summary of itself.

So, as part of one's quantum persona, one could call oneself poetic practitioner of the occult, linking one's internal weather to four private suns. And these suns open themselves above random canals, bringing to the water inscrutable genes which magically build and vanish. And in the building of the water there is the flashing of ignited pepper trees, of scarlet ligneous apparitions. Sometimes the wood flashes blue, or turns purple as would a paradoxical lightning pole. One can call these signs impalpable flares which pre-exist. This is light being squared by phantom technical sands. Evolving in themselves, being salt which spins in themselves, as organic carbon raised to their own nths, by the mind furtively kindled by hieroglyphical gestation. This process being nothing other than an evolving level of witness. Which is ferment according to intangible seeds and irritations.

So what do these seeds and irritations refer to?

Hope vis-à-vis inconscient solar distance?

Or is it morale suddenly shaped by perfected infection?

One must respond by making up thought from a kind of witness rampant in Andromeda. Or do such beings exist, who cohere on the other side of the Sombrero, thereby understanding one's view as being clarified by the uncanny, so that integers are splayed and take up the tone of parsecs, simultaneously moving to higher destinal concern?

Perhaps invisible numeration could be considered?

Perhaps they could be considered as anti-entropic gain through counting?

Perhaps variants on Mayan or Chinese numeration?

Perhaps Egyptian mathematics in "the volume of the cylinder"?

Thus one illumines the dark with variations on energy. This being an energy which restores itself through incoming enigmas. Not something conducted through tense precautionary order, but a meteoritic climate never subjected to darkened critical amendments. Therefore the focus is totalic, riverine, totally dissimilar to transposition. This being something other than activation of dilemmas, something other than unsettlement, pulled as they are towards the Saturnic, towards the condition of collective injury. Thus the Earth and the Sun no longer are stranded on a death spur in the anonymous typography of space. Thus one instigates light beyond the moat, light beyond starvation and ter-

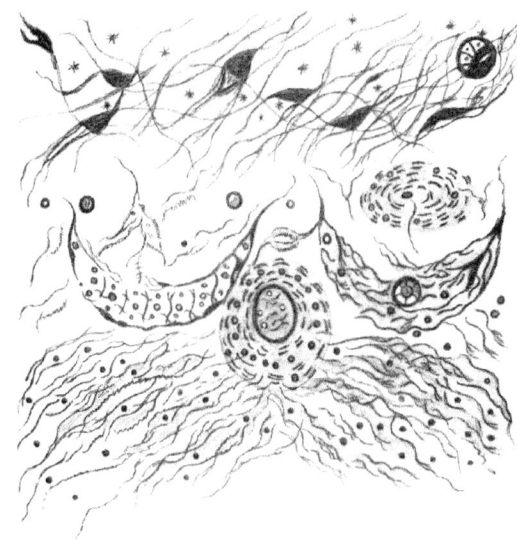

ror. Thus the moon is released, and brings on light beyond biographic grief. Which distills and overcomes the very notion of armageddon. Then, of course, threat will pursue itself according to the tenets of nonrecognition. A utopia? A prismatic ocean palace?

So does the holocaust vanish? Does its supreme result of fissioning turn into doves and crystal hamlets?

One can never assent to naivete, or to bucolics, deextended into falsified subjection. Never. One must decrease one's display by phantom enactment, by holding in one's view a series of doubled intangible items. And these are not dioxides, or forms which elicit disserviceable strontium. Instead, there are zones to be announced as poetic chambers, as incalculable clauses, which both hold and trespass sonar. Such a world exists over and beyond peril, over and beyond waste which consumes itself by burdensome simulacra. At poetic height one cannot colonize grammar and imprison its setting to monochromatic routine. The imagination has no need to bleed itself in front of a jury. Or to speak by means of repetitive ointment. There can never again be the matter-of-fact world with its hoarse and omnivorous standards, with its forts of law, with its mechanical suggestion. These being nothing more than aimless agendas, or modern staff reports.

What keeps one rising is the ceaseless, is the fricative glare which overcomes the force of analytical transposure. Because of such rising, one is never aligned to the masses, rife as they are with institutional motion as flaw. Yet at the same time one does not invoke elitist constriction. It is the conventional forces which need elimination. All the variants which hinge on colloquial status. The knights, the queens, the domain of inverted servants. Which has nothing to do with inner regality.

Thus the imagination is like a moon which explores its own darkness by listening to its poles, to its mysterious forms as something other than carbon. The Earth in this light becomes nothing more than an inclement schism. A vacated marker, an occluded suborder. And this occluded suborder is compounded residue, where the Sun fails to shine as recreated mystification. Finally, one can say that the population seems fixed, always reflecting on uninhabitable poison. So something else is needed other than autonomous consensus. Other than prone or inbred paranoia.

Poise is then no longer linked to listless arcana. It then rises in one's form as snow enriched twilight, as meteoritic nuance. Which results in energies which reach the inconceivable where former momentums are laid to rest. Yet one cannot say that one has reached in one's visage the one explosive charisma, the salient strategy which subequals law. In this sense, one does not ruminate on forms of botany and nitrogen, or extrinsic physical brightness. The outer body must be left so that the ghosts explore through navigational dissection. So that a contra-possession transpires as if one lifted the stride of a crippled spider. Which is rampant de-location, which is the inside-out of gullible distension. One then begins to reek of mirrors, having an interminable penchant for scorching, which induces an alchemic reddening. One then leaps the law of plural terminus, once called by the masses the limit of the three dimensions. So there can never be decrease employed by the enervated sundial, or from Richters which open panic. What is shuttered, closed, or established, vanishes, much like a boat swallowed by open water.

One is not a journalist who plays with factual rebus making, celebrating scraps, making do with algebraic sound transmissions. As if the details could expose basic inner elevation, or signal the depths in restless solar ravines. Algebra, at this stage, existing, at this level, as horizontal indifference, as determinate input on the tangible plane. And what is so curious about such tangibility is that, at this time, in its odyssey it is able to grasp the sinking molecule, and make adjustments for its width and its depth, even with the latter engulfed in subatomic dissolution. Where even the muons, and the muon's neutrino, are tracked. And even when kaons or pions flutter, it is stuttering through the wavelength of grasping. Therefore energy can never release itself from dogmatic retention. It then functions as a code for simplified assassins. Assassins who plot their codes through regressive aeronautics. All exploration is then lowered to the stark respirational level, yet presented through the form of intellectual exhibit. This being matter in a free burning posture, yet unable to go beyond itself as matter. In this context the imagination senses the muon as nothing more than an entrapping time, as nothing more than a state-sponsored item. And one does not say this to simply amplify dread, or amplify oneself through hubristic reproach. No, one does not engage in systems, telling oneself such insight has been structured due to proto-Buddhistic privacy, or as a patriot of deserted possession. Simply put, it is a blank state, an overall view, a telepathic transmission. Such is the ambrosial dimension which wanders in and out of the Sun.

One then is not condemned to specific fuels and chromas. Not immured in copal, or stain, or gouache postured in the cinereous, or in raw umber, or in royal red, or mikado yellow, or Mittler's green. Fixation in the higher state can never disclose itself or tumble into view as a functioning arsenic body.

According to the Palmaryans, the Sun is a great feminine wheel which composes rivers and moons and flows as a true incautionary flank. It is alive as pure inalienable diamond which spills across the brink and arrives at the summa of suggestive ideals. It is like watching the sky from an alchemic cinnamon tree. One then arrives at uranian alterity, at emissions which gather in the body as fumes, as Scottish mist, as mystical lixiviation. This being imminence at the weightless brink, at navigational electrics. Then setting psychic sail through lenticular skies. Then the apparitions across the eye blaze like unstilled progeny in the spirit. Aboriginal aurum, transmorphic nectar. The body as physical fleece then lives through transparent accretion. To the naked eye, one no longer exists through consensus examining, through anthropomorphic taint. It is like trying to witness planetary scale at the incipience of the Oort dimension, which does not imply scope as contiguous finality. Such invisibles scorch as if emerged from a cryptic lepton family. As for rational tracery at this level, none can exist. As for its description, one cannot be sculpted by letterable measure, as if caught in the path of a stampeding gryphon.

One can call the above indigenous morality, never posing one's wares through perceptual piety. No, not a sermonically driven travel around a port of cataracts, preaching heavenly scintillation as example, as fractious turning amidst grains. One is never prone to clear the cloudy particle, or feign miraculous activity, never once taking on the feral implications of liberty. One could just as well be a moth farmer transmuting ineloquent locales. Abjuring these lower degrees, one takes on implosive training, so as to mingle with sub-electrical winds which then yield to the tendencies which lean into the Sun.

One is, then, neither lunar or diurnal. One simply expresses a state. This being a condition where types of consciousness suddenly erupt. Where, on an uneven day, one starts singing in Albanian sub rosa, thereby lifting one's osmosis into perpendicular, hovering far beyond common observational debris. One no longer takes place in the given, diverted as it is into predictable melancholia. So one does not walk in a windmill garden projecting physical hope into limits. One then needs to count on bereftment, so as to never lose oneself to the powers reenacted according to poisonous canonization. One can never be again a palpable index fossil, or subject oneself to interior disarray, caught somewhere between double palpable poles.

Though frayed at the level of consensus perception, it must be remembered that the imaginary being possesses exponential powers which cannot be tamed by tragic assignation. Such powers are void of the etiquette of the common mean, with the mind now thriving in simultaneous pagodas. This being the mind multiplied by the x of the unknown. A mind unchallenged by fumes from competitive rust, from lower governing replications. This being the height of the emotive plateau no longer scarred by civilian dysphonia. This being the difference between walking on salt and walking on salt. In the former case there is the precipitous state of alchemical absenting, of flotational prairies, of intangible perambulation. As far as the latter remove, this is a salt which eats through the organs, always announcing in its wake threats of stinging dread. This being the fate of the serf always facing mundane transposition understood as transposition in pure nothingness. As for perambulation on mystic salt, there is power which flows from the uncanny. Of course, the uncanny is not the pre-wrought, does not fall into the realm of what is considered thinking. Other resolutions begin to electrify the mind, begin to extend what's considered the spirit into alterity by understanding. Which allows another rising to transpire to exist with the powers of morphological transcendence, so that one takes on the status of a greater and greater ozone, of a shift in magnetics, or so as to understand the collective fate of that which astronomers attempt to collect in urns. These are other gifts of motion that cannot at present be made to articulate themselves in symbol.

This is the mind as encipherment, which resists a rational or governing direction. Yes, there is uncertainty. There are days when the mind erupts with pure fever. Yet what results from these agonies are trace amounts of powered light, of rhizomic acclivity. In other words, the unpredictable as scale, as ruse which fosters development. As a result, the shadows of life which surround one imperceptibly begin to withdraw, which is followed by the fact that one's actual body begins brewing at another plane of persistence. Or stated in another manner, a percolation which never accrues a gravid or reprehensible exhaustion. Protection from the accursed, from the dogmatic thesis that God is contained in unicellular form. This being the purest alchemical seepage, the elucidated light, the phantasmic eye which supersedes its patterns. This is rising up the rays which fall on water, becoming in essence an untoward fertility, which both expands and gathers from surrounding dimensions. Not only the past and future as described by linear explanation, but those realias which have been deemed by the diurnal, illusive, unsubstantial, vague. Not a cognizant topology project, nor an era with psychic regions, but a grammar which understands the roots and circulation of space. This is a grammar outside of laws or rulings, outside of the duplicitous political urge, which posits power through rulings deeming themselves the nexus of just events. And these events hypnotize the general show of hands with a series of stunned placebos. This leads to predicted shifts in the voting body understood through the stratagem of operational displacement. Therefore a demographics which functions under the seeming threat of life and death.

Concerning political salvos, nothing applies. And the non-applications refer to the general run of planetary rulers. Whichever of them harks back to rotation, to the cycling of blood which the galaxies explore. How can such an aegis sustain itself in the face of Dogon calendrics, or in the eyes of a Buryat shaman, speaking of the higher facets in unencumbered day myths? How can the political part be sanctioned in the face of the heavens which evince the unending?

Now the opportunity presents itself, concerning a new profound perplexity. The spiritual Sun has shifted and released through this shifting transmuted carbons. This is not to be confused with carbon as a stationary element, as soiling the lungs, as a petrified emission, but as fumes which swirl from crushed diamonds. The latter carrying the velocity of inscrutable Passeriformes. Unlike the forensic, or debilitated archive, there are tendencies which supersede the feral, which react as unvanquished stealth. This being an energy which persists as structural anomaly, as a vertigo from imploded lion cults. As for surface appearance, there is scrambled manganese, choreographic stratification, accessible to the contiguous personality. As for carbo-electric bacteria, there are shapes which signal by code as though summoned from phonemic choreography. One is, then, replete with repetitive seismicity. With mantric prints

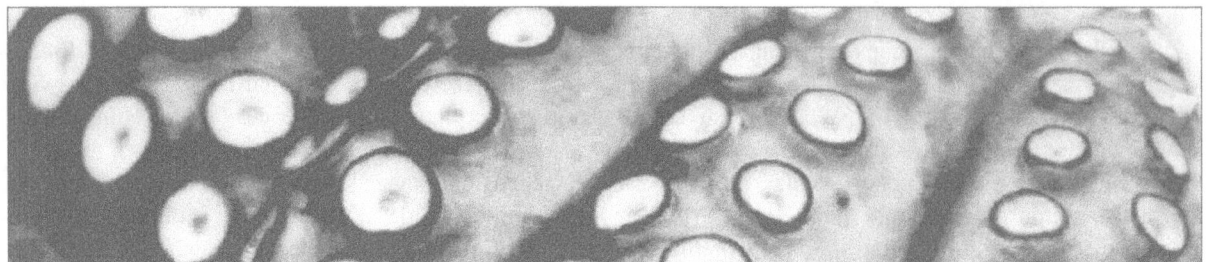

carrying sound as explosive neology. One, then, spins, and gathers in this spinning language as exponential gargantua. Which emits to the world photonic crystallizations.

This being blizzard as combinement, as wanton verbal surge, as concrescence annealment in situ.

This being something other than language as tangible asset, as something ordered due to scientific element. The ear, then, condones itself through retinal intuitives, through voices heard by means of an ophthalmic listening post. There is always something which ignites and ascends beyond one's own thinking. This being energy which soars beyond isolationists' criteria, always bonding with an invisible axis, creating a new and uncharted electrical resolve. Certainly not ascendance scorched by refutation, but arachnids turning green in higher dimensional kingdoms.

Writing at such remove could be described as mania by lamp, by oxygen self-nullified and risen. Perpendicular flux, cosmically inflected enzymes. Then the nerves rattle and magically embody beasts. But not something which feeds on yeasts and frozen corn piles, no. This is the fuel of invisible purgation, of apotheosis by fire. This being sonar which speaks to the disadvantaged noun, to decapsulated verbs, bringing them to life. Of course, one is never magnetized to stasis, to lingering fuels which desuggest. One takes as one's gait paradoxical omens so as to mount kinematic initiation, bringing different properties and standards within reach of a liminal glycerin, yet no longer prone to a sudden or revengeful timeline. Yet life remains, for one's eyes, ravenous, a perfect syllabus of doubt and withdrawal, curiously suspended, waiting for the flame which transmutes its non-effect.

Rafet Arslan - *Phantom of Liberty*

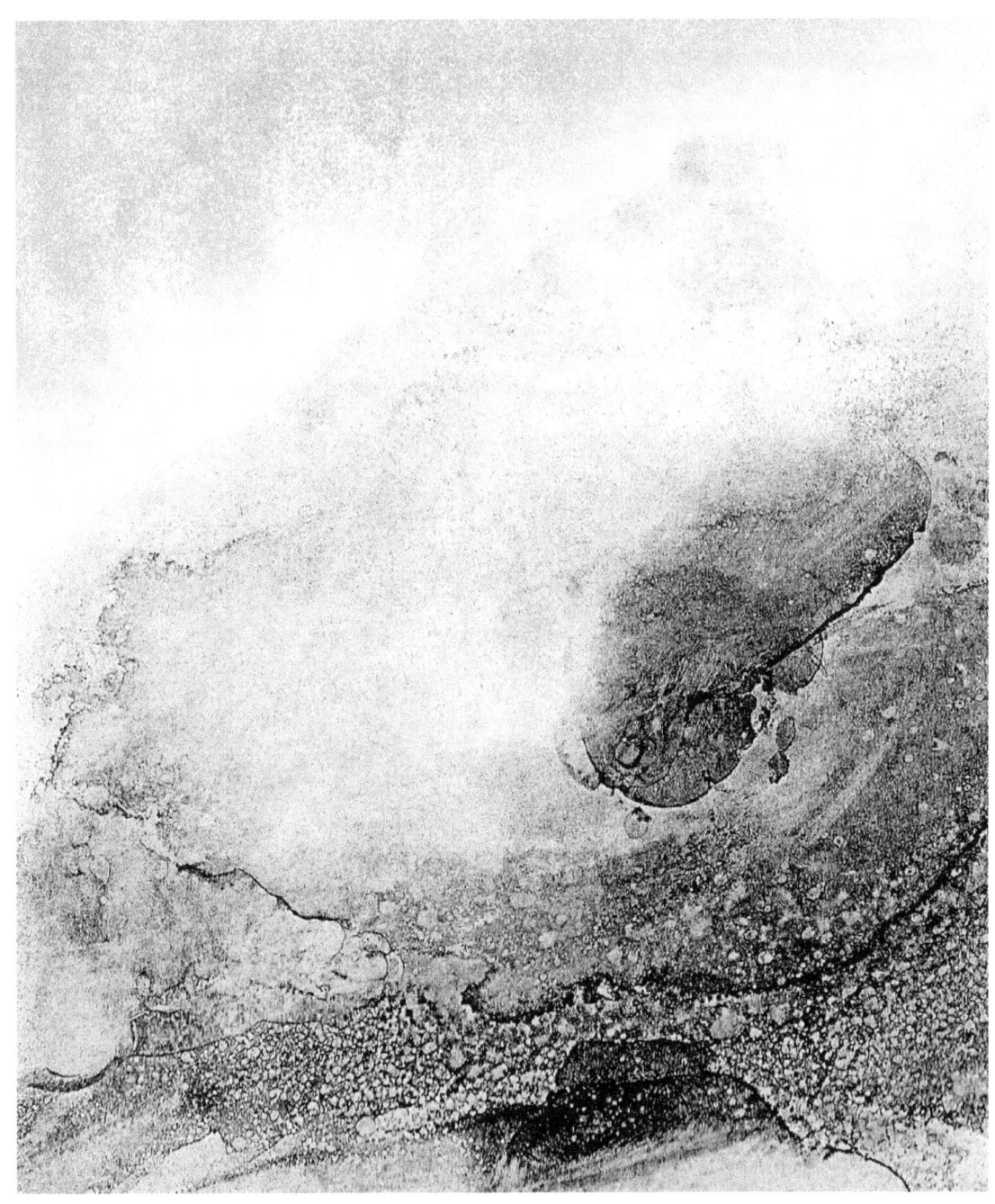
John Adams - *The Sun Falls into the Ocean*

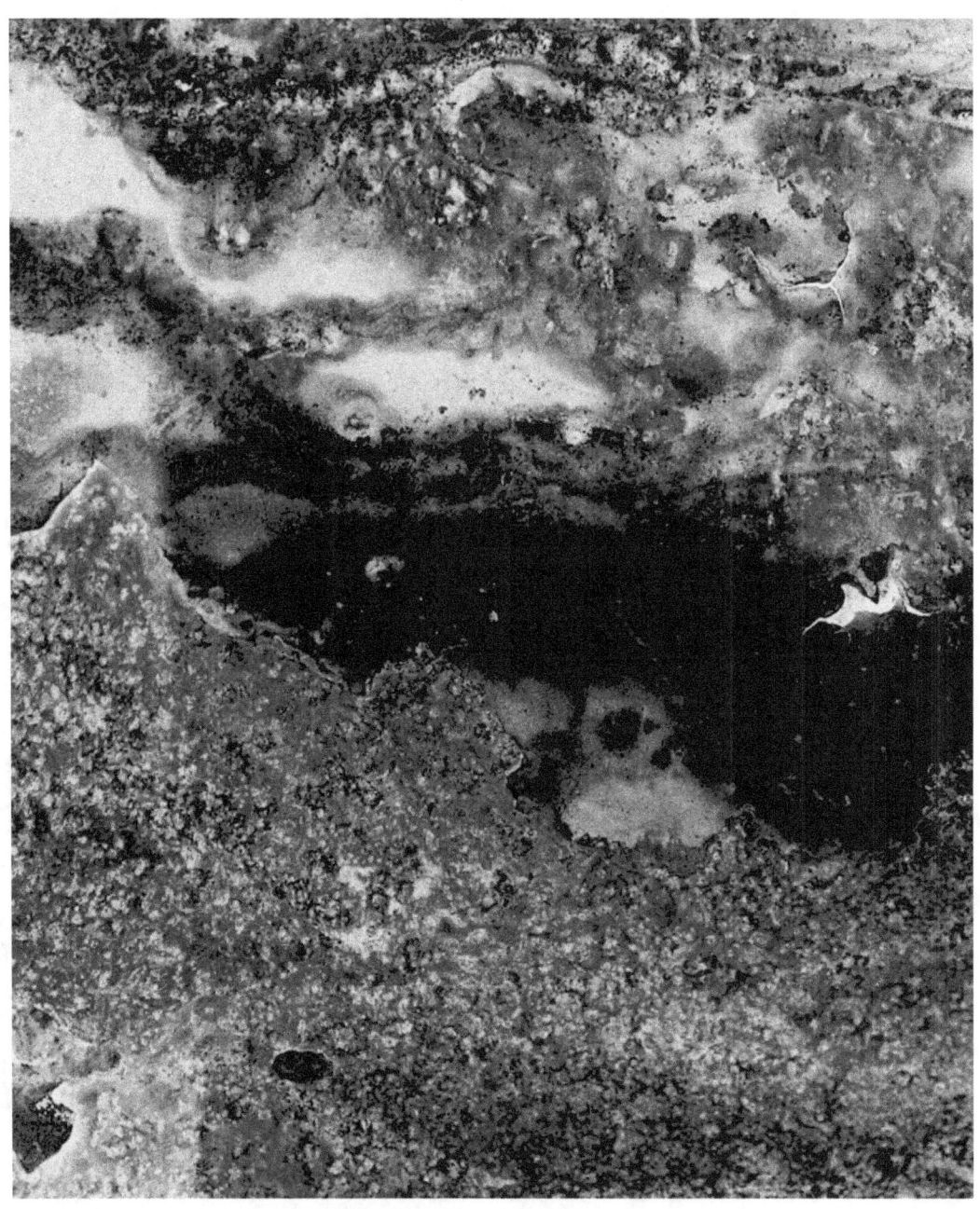
John Adams - *A Distant Landscape*

In Praise of Infighting

Merl Fluin

From the inception of the movement to the present day, Surrealists have been devoting time, energy, ingenuity and material resources to hating each others' guts. We have a glorious history of splits, infighting, self-destruction, cannibalism and general fuck-uppery. When we fall out with each other it is rarely a case of politely agreeing to disagree. We spit, we scratch, we scream, punch and kick, tear at each others' veins, banish each other to outer darkness, drag each other through the shit, and every fight is always to the death.

The attitude of many Surrealists today seem to be that this kind of infighting is a bad thing, at best unnecessary, at worst potentially fatal to the movement as a whole. The same plaintive cries go up at every fight, not just from the appalled bystanders but also, as often as not, from the protagonists of the infighting themselves. Why do Surrealists fight so viciously, and so often? Shouldn't we be fighting our enemies instead of each other? Why can't we be more united? Aren't we all struggling for the same goal?

I'm not interested at this point in the rights and wrongs of particular splits and fights, including those that I've played a role in myself. I'm also not very interested in arguments to the effect that open disagreement and/or free expressions of anger within the movement are 'healthy', because the imperative to psychological or emotional health seems is something of which Surrealists should be highly suspicious at best. Instead I want to take a step back and to reflect on some possible alternative ways to think about Surrealist infighting.

To start with the idea that we shouldn't fight because we're all ultimately struggling for the same goal: what, then, is the goal of the Surrealist movement? The pat reply to this question is usually: *to change life and transform the world.* That famous Bretonian watchword uniting Rimbaud and Marx sums up exactly how and why Surrealists do not, in fact, share a common goal. The Surrealist movement, as we are all so fond of repeating, is neither an art movement (because we regard the social revolution as a burning Surrealist necessity) nor a political movement (the annihilation of one's being into a diamond which is no more the soul of ice than of fire is hardly a comprehensible political demand).

Our insistence on the simultaneity of Marx and Rimbaud, life and the world, social revolution and the imagination triumphant, is what makes Surrealism – regardless of the specific political commitments of individual Surrealists – in its essence a *utopian* movement. Our goal is utopia: our goal is nowhere: *we have no goal.*

So we are not all pursuing a common objective which we will attain that little bit sooner if we unite and work together. Unity is a red herring. Surrealism is a collective adventure, but *collectivity* is not the same thing as unity, any more than *adventure* is the same as pursuit of a goal. And insofar as splits and infighting are searing shared experiences of rage, passion, pain, mutual hatred and destruction – not to mention hilarity and exhilaration – don't they count as particularly intense expressions of, precisely, collectivity, shared experiences not just within but also between the warring groups? Even perhaps – let's push the argument – peculiar forms of collective adventure in their own right? Surely there's no one in the movement who thinks that collectivity should be safe, agreeable, or merely positive in any generally accepted sense. Negativity is a vital dimension of any truly collective dynamic, and I'm suggesting that it is more exciting and productive to embrace and investigate its periodic eruptions than to regret or condemn them. The forest of the unknown is full of horrors as well as enchantments.

Embracing and investigating collective negativity requires inventiveness, courage and terrifying honesty. This is not the least of the reasons why we are usually so reluctant to do it. Nobody wants to spend their time at group meetings or on collaborative projects gnashing their teeth and drinking their comrades' blood. But while the group members sit around the table, having their discussions and playing their games, the maw of the group's collective unconscious is ever open. The more 'successful' the group on its own terms – the more it exceeds the sum of its parts, the more exciting, the more intuitive and creative it becomes – the wider the jaws, the sharper the teeth...

So let's embrace and investigate the monsters that this collective unconscious vomits forth. Here comes one now, a real whopper: his name is Oedipus, and if we ignore him he most definitely will *not* go away. For those individuals who have grown up under the sign of the nuclear family – which is probably a fairly large proportion of those currently active in the Surrealist movement, given its geographical and cultural distribution – the dynamic of the Oedipal family romance is one of the most readily available patterns of group interaction, and one against which we all need to be constantly and explicitly vigilant. The danger lies precisely in the fact that the family romance, in Surrealist contexts as much as in mainstream ones, often dissembles its more blatantly oppressive aspects behind the compensations it offers in return: companionship, comfort, a sense of shared identity, an occasional refuge from a fucking horrible world. The danger is that the collective unconscious (whether of a formally constituted Surrealist group, or of a looser or more temporary collective, or even at the level of the movement as a whole) may all too easily lapse into an Oedipal mode and silently form itself into the private haven of a 'family home', complete with nursery and servants' quarters. There's the parent-child dynamic: respect your elders, do your homework, nurture my potential, change my nappy. There's the sibling dynamic: you're my brother, you're my sister, you're my rival, they love you more than they love me…

The family romance plot is almost certainly present in the collective unconscious of almost every current group and collective, because for most of the participants it is not just the first pattern of group interaction they ever knew, but the one which formed their 'personalities' at a basic level (and this is also one of the reasons why Surrealism must be anti-humanist and opposed to 'personality'). The intensity of rage, pain and joy unleashed by really serious infighting probably comes in large part from this unconscious family dynamic. What can be more thrilling than to kill one's father? What more appalling than to be attacked by one's child, or more paralysing than to watch one's parents and siblings tear the family apart?

The monster of Oedipus demands constant and explicit vigilance, then, and the deliberate invention and cultivation of alternative forms of collective life. All kinds of alternative models are already to hand and many more remain to be invented, from superhero teams to libertine conspiracies to wolf packs. The difficulty is always to make those models work as really operational egregores rather than merely as rhetorical self-exhortations, and that will only be possible if we first accept and embrace the power of collective negativity, including Oedipus, as a creative force in its own right.

The trick is not to fight the monster, but to embrace and transform it into something else. Tam Linn is transformed into a newt, an adder, a bear, a lion, a red-hot iron and a burning coal, but it's precisely because Fair Jenny refuses to let go of him that he finally becomes her beautiful naked lover.

Rik Lina - *Witches Cauldron #3*

Infighting Is Miserabilist and Stupid

Eric Bragg

1.

Plain and simple, the purpose of this text is to refute the pro-"infighting" position advocated by M. Fluin and M. Forshage, and is intended more for the next generation of surrealists who will come along and who still have the chance to avoid the petty kind of squabbling described here.

This first section contains selected quotations by said authors, in italics, and numbered for later reference. My notes and comments appear in brackets.

M. Fluin: "In Praise of Infighting" (Printed in this issue of Hydrolith):

1a) *"...don't they count as particularly intense expressions of, precisely, collectivity, shared experiences not just within but also between the warring groups? Even perhaps – let's push the argument – peculiar forms of collective adventure in their own right?"*

→ [There's the argument: to reverse-engineer a rhetorical justification for aggressive, belligerent behavior, such that it's just one more of the "peculiar" kinds of collective adventure.]

1b) *"Surely there's no one in the movement who thinks that collectivity should be safe, agreeable, or merely positive in any generally accepted sense."*

→ [Here is an example of the either/or fallacy: either 1) we are safe and polite, and thereby compromise our collective efforts, or 2) we simply suppress any effort to interact considerately for the sake of believing that we are being as "intellectually rigorous" as we could ever hope to be. To me it sounds more like a clever excuse to be rude whenever one feels like it...]

1c) *"...the maw of the group's collective unconscious..."*

→ [One of many Freudian references found in this article. An argument for the importance of collective surrealist activity, but used (subverted) in order to validate the infighting position. And perhaps an effort on the part of the author to suggest that collectivity and infighting are mutually reinforcing phenomena?]

1d) *"So let's embrace and investigate... Oedipus."*

→ [The argument is steeped in Freudian terminology, which represents a manifestation of cultural determinism. While such a position attempts to address capitalist-influenced, dysfunctional, personal relations and identities, it lacks any kind of materialist basis. The attempt to formulate an assessment of interpersonal dynamics within the surrealist movement, for example, but done so by relying exclusively on Freudian terminology, should be seen as an obsolete approach, and also as culturally reductionist. Is that really the best "we" as surrealists can do? Not even a discussion in more contemporary, sociological terms, like even the slightest hint about the "codependent family", with all of its selfish, atomized, cannibalistic, co-enabling dynamics. And better yet, if we could even see past that sociological perspective from the later 20th century and begin to approach the problem through formulating a materialist dialectic that takes into account not just cultural influences on individual and collective behaviors, but also the physical. Isn't it time that we try to distinguish between the biochemical vs. the cultural?? We certainly have enough scientific information now to take that step.]

1e) *"...and this is also one of the reasons why Surrealism must be anti-humanist and opposed to 'personality'".*

→ [But isn't it contradictory to call oneself anti-humanist and yet to fall for cultural reductionism, such as for the incessant usage of Freudian metaphysical explanations of complex social dynamics?]

1f) *"The intensity of rage, pain and joy unleashed by really serious infighting probably comes in large part from this unconscious family dynamic."*

→ [Once again, using Freudian terminology as a justification for hostile behavior. At this point, one might ask what could lead some folks to be so willing to embrace such Freudian, social diagnoses, in light of our interpersonal differences? Could it be that some proponents of this position might benefit from such a culturally-determinist position in a less obvious but self-serving way, or that they are merely sufficiently "accommodated" to avoid considering any other perspectives? Perhaps some have too much to lose to relinquish the advantages afforded them within their psychoanalytically-delimited collectives? We shall see!]

1h) *"The difficulty is always to make those models work as really operational egregores... accept and embrace the power of collective negativity."*

→ [This newly embraced concept of "negativity" seems more like one of those knee-jerk reflexes against the agreeable, humanist, *unified* vision mentioned (the straw argument to be knocked down, where the dubious word "unity" is substituted for another word that many of us are very much concerned with: "organizing"), as that manifestation of the either/or argument. To give the author the benefit of the doubt, we might view this process of exploring "collective negativity" as a prelude towards dialectically challenging the "agreeable" approach described, but without any actual mention or discussion of a dialectic, then this either/or argument is very shaky, very incomplete, at best. And if this historically bold foray into collective negativity provides us with anything, then most likely – especially when looking over decades and even centuries of intellectual societies, so far – it should reveal to us in gory detail all the things we *shouldn't* be doing with each other, at least as far as creating the revolution (*organizing*) is concerned.]

M. Forshage: "Manners?" Posted on *www.icecrawler.blogspot.com.* (4/21/2012):

2a) *"Hurt feelings are a poor guide for behavior, and will create a focus on ego-reinforcement, an insistence on irrelevant details and abstract generalisations at the same time, unless held in check by some constructive machinations or participation in some dynamic process that will facilitate the focus on essentials, such as an ongoing surrealist activity."*

→ [More Freudian references. My interpretation of this sentence is that the success of surrealist activity is used as a self-serving justification for the author's rude, egocentric, empathy-lacking behavior.]

2b) *"It is not about not caring for individuals and their feelings. But caring for individuals and their feelings in terms of mere short-term tact, carefulness and respect for people's compromises and rationalisations, means respect for conformist individuality, manners and lifestyle, respect for the obstacles against creativity, knowledge and freedom."*

→ [translation: "civility = compromise"; again we have an example of a false dichotomy, where the assumption is that nothing can be accomplished collectively unless the participants adopt an adversarial stance towards each other. In my personal dealings with Forshage, he seems most comfortable having an adversarial relationship with others.]

2c) *"It appears more congenial with surrealism to care about individuals and their feelings in terms of sublation; of challenging and provoking ideological concepts such as prepsychoanalytical psychological fictions and liberal concepts of life, behavior and society; terms of uncomfortable truths, unknown triggers of creativity, liberating refusal, radical criticism and long-term strategy."*

→ [Another of his long-winded arguments that equates civility with compromise.]

2d) *"Since most of us are still struggling with oidipal-defensive fears and defense strategies, still struggling with systems of compromises of everyday life, struggling to "keep it together", we will often feel uncomfortable with any addressal of critical or complicated issues. We need to have a framework of holding such gallopping defensiveness in check, and I claim that surrealist activity is such a framework."*

→ [His version of surrealist activity (a la Freud) is a means for such humorless "self-control", but what presumptuousness to assume that what is right for him is right for everyone else. There are some who will not respond to such approaches, and such refusals cannot be explained away with such ridiculously obsolete Freudian terminology, but should instead be seen as valid refusals in and of themselves, in the surrealist spirit of rejecting anything that seeks to impose a system of thought on individuals.]

2e) *"Surrealist activity with its extremely immodest focus on essentials, on nonconformism, and on emergent overindividual subjectivity, has – hooray – a potential to make us disconsider our boring old defensive emotions."*

→ [Those "boring old defensive emotions"? Thank you, Mr. Spock; we're ready to beam you aboard now. But I would counter that it was in the original spirit of surrealism, from Breton and so many who came after him, to pay attention to those "boring old defensive emotions" – not to fetishize them, but rather to consider them in light of everything else, to consider *all* the evidence and leave no stone unturned. Those pesky emotions are the keys to ourselves, and to consider them as things to be buried and ignored rather than attempting to understand what they really are, where they came from, and their dialectical relationship with everything else, is beyond ridiculous. I interpret this statement as the author's own defense for his arrogant, aggressive, adversarial personality, as a function of his aspergers'.]

2f) *"In a surrealist context, we are focusing on truth and poetry so much that we may even be enthusiastically curious about any actual critical issues in even the most rudely formulated criticism against us, anything that could teach us to stop repeating some irrelevant clichés and defences, to avoid stopping just short of new discoveries, and avoid getting carried away by our own reasoning to the point where we accidentally miss some of the essentials..."*

→ [Thank you, oh great Freudian Judge Forshage. Yes definitely, some of the essentials were indeed missed.]

2g) *"Again, the "human aspect" that is interesting here is all about finding ways of igniting, transforming and collectivising subjectivity for the cause of poetry, more or less the opposite of respecting people's egos by delving in hurt feelings and questions of manners."*

→ [Again we have the either/or fallacy: that we either 1) treat each other like people but fail to have collective activity, or alternatively 2) to succeed with collective activity but to go around stepping on each others' toes. Doesn't this sort of dichotomy reveal the need for a *dialectic of empathy*, especially for those of us who have clearly demonstrated that social abilities are lacking (and in this case, at least, who attempt to construct grandiose, self-serving arguments merely to cover up one's own weakness)? The author failed to consider another possibility: that instead of him being surrounded by "hurt" and oversensitive people, perhaps instead *he* might actually have been the *insensitive* one while everyone else was responding to him appropriately? Was that possibility ever considered within the manners text? Such a movement of empathy requires a certain kind of imagination – no, our brains don't all imagine the same way, apparently).

2h) *"Indeed, how this very focus on essentials through surrealist activity made the early surrealists sublate bourgeois ethics codes is one of the constructive and lasting achievements of the movement. We shouldn't take the step* *back to excavate them again and lose sight of more far-reaching aims."*

→ [Seems like he's arranged it where he can grant himself the right to be rude, provocative, and then if any collaborator dares to object in any way, then (s)he is accused of being bourgeois and retrograde. How ludic.]

M. Forshage: "Voices of the Hell Choir: aspects of contemporary surrealist activity, its modes of rhetoric and its ludicism." 2006:

3a) *"In a sense, it's somewhat embarrassing to see how much homage is still payed to authors of classical great theoretical breakthroughs like Freud, Marx, and Hegel..."*

→ [Retrospectively, this statement is hypocritical, since his infighting concept is anchored within Freudian concepts of oedipalism.]

3b) *"It may breed the regressive pleasure of being able to "crush" others' positions and initiatives; actually we are surrounded by examples of how the exertion of this critical assault not only is a forum of a certain pathetic selfreassuring sadism but also an excuse never to really consider anything apart from the already known, so typical in many Marxist and situationist-inspired intellectuals, as well as in more or less intelligence-aristocratic supposedly apolitical critics of art and literature, etc."*

→ [More hypocrisy, as this regressive, but highly aggressive pleasure of crushing the work of others is implicitly defended in these infighting articles.]

3c) *"From psychological, democratical and group-dynamical perspective too strong an emphasis on the critical will inevitably turn out to be psychologically restrictive for a lot of people with insufficient selfconfidence, creating an atmosphere where ever fewer people take initiatives, and those supposedly fragile themes (emotional or poetical) take an ever-decreasing place. Even if surrealism on the whole is non-utilistic and therefore spurns effectivity and rapidity, an overcritical attitude may serve to slow down output to virtually nothing, which is not necessarily bad in itself except for that one of the things thus strangled is external communication and communication within international surrealism."*

→ [Again a reference to the need for an extreme, critical approach, but acknowledgment that it can backfire. Forshage appears to be saying that anyone who does not agree with his idea of a "critical" approach must be necessarily lacking in self-confidence. However, he is terribly correct by indicating that such an approach can strangle internal communication and collaboration. Once again this brings to mind the need for a dialectical perspective, one that takes empathy into account.]

M. Forshage: *"The Exterior is Popular."* Posted on *www.icecrawler.blogspot.com*. (9/7/2009):

4) → [This article in general has all sorts of condescending, inflammatory statements, such as "exteriority kicks", and was originally directed at those of us who published *The Exteriority Crisis* a few years ago, including the stupid, insulting advice to "rediscover poetry," as if the beneficiaries of Forshage's marvelous "hyper-criticism" knew nothing about exteriority, but rather that he does, of course. This blogpost, as well as the one that follows ("Experiment and Failure", see coverage below) addresses the outrage that some of us manifested towards his approach.]

M. Forshage: *"Experiment and Failure."* Posted on *www.icecrawler.blogspot.com*. (9/7/2009):

5) *"But please snap out of this kneejerk reaction to accusations of failure. Of course it is a central pillar in the "american way of life" that…humanity is divided into winners and losers…..[I]nvestigating the sense of being a human starts with being a loser and investigating the sense of life starts with failure."*

→ [When the original "failure" comment was made, it was made as is, in the *academic road-rage* style, i.e. strictly on paper without any interpersonal stimuli to be interpreted, like voice inflections, facial expressions, etc., and from just that statement that MF made to me and the other exteriority participants, it was very rude by itself, without any qualifying statements about what he meant by "failure". However, this blog post only confirms his venom towards those of us who made the *Exteriority Crisis* book, with even an attack on the fact that I live in the US, with his projection that my negative response towards his statements must have occurred *just because I grew up in US culture*. Overall, Forshage made no effort to explain his failure comments within the context of our original conversation, and this post on his blog is merely a feeble attempt to extricate himself from being accused of coming across as an obnoxious oaf, or to give him the benefit of the doubt, just a *socially inept aspy* who needs a refresher course in interpersonal empathy. The other important point is that this post was written to make himself look good in the eyes of his friends. He made no effort to inform B. Jacobs, E. Castro or myself about this insulting, condescending post; I found it simply through browsing his blog.]

SLAG: "Surrealism Is Revolutionary" Posted on *www.robberbridegroom.blogspot.co.uk*. (03/24/2012):

6) *"A general argument in favour of infighting… would be pointless, but a general argument against infighting is in effect an argument for tact, superficial alliance-making and mindless voluntarism (if not indeed for closing ranks, duty and discipline) – which was exactly what we were attacking in the first place.*

→ [Nondialectical Either/Or thinking at its best: either tact or revolution. But also how very curious that such a "pointless", general argument for infighting nevertheless managed to find its way into this issue of Hydrolith!]

2 ✊

Retro-Freudianism, a la Cultural Reductionism:

What is immediately remarkable about the texts pertaining to "infighting" is that the arguments of Forshage and Fluin have a strong degree of convergence, each with an unusually heavy reliance on (and apparently an unconscious acceptance of) Freud's metaphysical, pseudoscientific ideas of oedipalism. Such ideas reveal a growing surrealist tradition which by now seems to have become established: this isn't the first instance of surrealists accusing each other of being "oedipal". Thereby the concept of the oedipal accusation is turned on its head, evidenced simply by the excessive, unquestioning faith in Freudian theory: of *too much lip service for Papa Siggy* (an expression that the reader may psychoanalyze in any way (s)he chooses). Therefore it might be apropos to consider the words of psychiatrist and researcher E.F. Torrey (2005), in regards to his inspiring assessment of Freud (within the context of the lingering Freudian influence on psychotherapeutic treatments for poor, naïve, hapless 21st century youngsters):

"Freudian theories and therapy will slowly wither and die, to be preserved only in historical overviews of human behaviour and psychotherapy. This, in fact, is already taking place. Like the Cheshire cat, psychoanalysis is slowly fading from view, except in this case, the grin is fading first, and the genitals will fade last of all." (1)

In this sense, Freudian theory remains a pseudoscience, and nearly persists as mere fetish, mere cliché, when hastily invoked as the paradigm of choice for explaining whatever facet of human behavior that happens to be under the contemplative microscope.

Again I repeat that neither MF nor MF considers any sociological systems of explanation for addressing the "oedipal" problem (such as codependent theory) and its supposed justification for infighting, and in general, the perspective of those two authors comes across as a well archaic variant of cultural reductionism. To remedy this limitation, I have offered a biological, ecological explanation for the plasticity of personality, as a function of influences from the chemical environment, with evidence for which I considered in the text, "Epigenetics and the Mad-Genius". (2)

And then the other question to consider, with regards to surrealist retro-Freudianism, in light of the texts considered in this essay, is whether or not both Fluin (**statements 1c-f**) and Forshage (**statements 2d & 3a**) are using such Freudian terminology for the sake of understanding and explaining, or additionally perhaps as a way to judge and denigrate, by way of pinning labels onto their opponents. Perhaps Freudian theory can not only be used to provide insight into a person or a social phenomenon, but also for the sake of policing others?

Surrealist Egregore, or is it really?

There's no doubt that the social effects which happen at the individual level are distinct from those on the collective level. And for surrealism, what people can do by themselves is thought to be dwarfed by what they can do collectively. Of course this myth and ideal is also found in many areas outside of the surrealist movement. But what is interesting is the way in which individual versus collective phenomena – depending on whether they are considered desirable or undesirable by surrealist criteria – are judged with a double-standard. In the case of a childish relationship or childish individual, the authors invoke oedipalism, which by definition puts the blame on the *individual* displaying such childishness. However, it seems hypocritical to use oedipalism to refer to undesirable relationships (thus pointing the blame away from the other members of the group that contributed to such a relationship, and dumping it all on the individual), while simultaneously invoking the surrealist egregore concept, with great fanfare, when describing desirable or whatever positive social interactions that the authors support. To put it simply: "if *we* get along well as collaborators, then let's chalk the experience up to surrealist egregore, but if you and I don't get along, then *you* are merely being oedipal or something worse." As the saying goes, it takes two to tango. Therefore both authors use two sets of terms to describe their desirable vs. undesirable social interactions: retro-freudianism, to pin blame on an *individual* for an undesirable interaction with a group and then the egregore concept to describe (and take credit for) those desirable or positive *group* interactions. Perhaps the codependent family scenario is a more apt choice to invoke than retro-freudian oedipalism, since the idea of codependency suggests that *all* players involved are dysfunctional, and are each executing their own strategies of trying to maintain group cohesiveness, of course with one or more family scapegoats to help deflect scrutiny away from their own shortcomings. An outcome of this unspoken double-standard is that any surrealist family is untouchable while surrealist individuals are not. This sort of thinking seems to be present much more in Fluin's text (**statements 1a, 1b & 1h**) than Forshage's (**statements 2a & 2d**), to the extent that infighting is said to be perfectly justifiable in the name of collectivity and revolution.

The Surrealist Academy?

One of the cultural determinist myths that surrealism has traditionally espoused is that there is no such thing as talent: that all cognitive abilities in people are the same: we all hear, see, think, dream, etc. in identical ways as anyone else, but I ask if that's really true. Are not some individuals more apt, when given a choice, to express themselves visually than with sound, or instead, through linguistic means? Is it even remotely possible that those of us who are able to succeed in academic environments, even who become professors in academia, if those individuals don't have certain cognitive, intellectual strengths that others don't have, *at least to the same extent*? In that respect, I find it incredibly suspicious that such contemporary, passionate defenses of "infighting" happen to be coming from the academic corner. In particular, to make it in the academic domain (but admittedly among other professional areas, as well), one must have a talent for debating and winning arguments. I just can't help but wonder if such differences in the ability to play 'language games' couldn't perhaps contribute to a hierarchical structure, despite whatever denials made to the contrary, by certain individuals? I would assert from personal experience and observation that in fact such differences in ability to argue and debate do exist, and they occur not only in the surrealist movement, but in so many other areas of social existence as well, such as in academia, industry, government, religion and all the other places where social hierarchies exist. Especially talented in that regard is a kind of individual known to some as *asperger*, a manifestation of what some might call "genius", yet also a subset of the autistic spectrum. Of the many differences between "aspies" and "neurotypicals", two very important ones that apply here, at the *behavioral* level, are that heightened and sometimes annoying proclivity toward argumentativeness, coupled with a social ineptitude, with both traits manifesting with varied degrees of severity, depending on the individual. (3)

In light of this asperger phenomenon, while scientific knowledge of individual biochemistry and psychology is currently emerging, very little has been done to scientifically study and characterize the social interactions between aspies. My hypothesis is that aspy approaches – especially the adversarial kind – toward social behavior are quite common in the professional world, academia, and arguably even surrealism: "Tact requires too much energy, too much effort, so to hell with tact," is the unspoken excuse. For those with a social deficit, no matter how mild, the unconscious strategy is that if one can keep the "conversation" or exchange on paper, or on internet forums, then it's all the easier to conceal one's true feelings and motives (as well as highly revealing body language, which is absent within written exchanges). This is an ideal arena for aspy-ish people to "take out their social frustrations" on others, since they don't have to worry about revealing their feelings/motives/etc. through body language, nor need worry about the inhibitory effects of negative body language from their audience and/or conversants, and thereby instead can focus exclusively on what is being said, magnifying the possibility of gaining the upperhand within a linguistic exchange, using that lack of immediate, personable info to hide their tracks, present info the way they want it, and of course to make themselves look favorable by denigrating others (such as through negatively interpreting what the other person says, or putting words into that person's mouth, etc.). It works very well. Although N. Ghaemi (2009) doesn't mention the term "asperger", his following description of "academic road rage" with regards to academic and industry peer-review of research publications does converge quite uncannily with the asperger dynamics just described:

"Perhaps the main problem is what one might call *academic road rage*. As is well known, it is thought that anonymity is a major factor that leads to road rage among drivers of automobiles. When I do not know who the other driver is, I tend to assume the worst about him; and when he cannot see my face, nor I his, I can afford to be socially inappropriate and aggressive, because facial and other physical cues do not impede me. I think the same factors are in play with scientific peer review: routinely, one reads frustrated and angry comments from peer reviewers; exclamation points abound; inferences about one's intentions as an author are made based on pure speculation; one's integrity and research competence are not infrequently questioned. Now sometimes the content that leads to such exasperation is justifiable; legitimate scientific and statistical questions can be raised; it is the emotion and tone which seem excessive." (4)

I contend that this "academic road-rage" approach isn't exclusive to surrealism (and also that surrealism is not somehow mysteriously immune to it, either), and in fact it happens all the time, in all areas of life, such as in academia and industry, where intellectuals interact, but especially so with aspies, whether surrealist or not. As long as the aggressor can cover his or her tracks, through coming up with effective self-serving arguments, then such individuals have had (up until now) an excellent strategy to maintain a certain kind of control over others, which is hard to spot and difficult to trace, creating and maintaining a subtle kind of hierarchy. It's not at all unreasonable to raise the question about whether aspy intellectuals do indeed benefit from the mystery of their intellect, and thereby maintain an unconscious bias in favor of perpetuating that mystery, protecting it at all costs, denying contrary evidence, just for the sake of being able to continue possessing a powerful "edge" that can sometimes provide them with all sorts of advantages – social, economic, whatever – definitely contributing to the maintenance of social hierarchies. It follows that this self-serving bias would also block the progress of the very same intellectuals who would profess to taking an interest in uncovering knowledge about the "true functioning of thought" – whatever kinds of scientists, psychologists, sociologists, psychiatrists, anthropologists, (and even "surrealists"), etc. who might be involved in that process. (How bourgeois!) Within this modern world that does its very best to forget and deny the historically persistent genius/madness connection, the asperger individual is a supreme inconvenience and also the break-through that some of us don't want to know about. The current mystification regarding the true nature of the sub-clinical-asperger intellectual is very analogous to that of the Wizard of Oz, with his intimidating voice and seeming omniscience, but the illusion of such invulnerability is shattered once the secret curtain is pulled aside, behind which we find hiding that timid little man who plays his deceptive games with microphones, smoke and mirrors, and last but not least, lots and lots of finger-pointing. And apparently it can't hurt to have available some dedicated groupies and henchmen, as well.

While perhaps difficult to prove, my hypothesis is that the asperger flavor of "infighting" is miserabilist:

aspy-on-aspy violence bears a strong resemblance to those dysfunctional, "codependent" families (grew up in one of them, myself), where some rise to the top, while others must be trampled – where every such dysfunctional group (dysfunctional because it does not realize it is asperger or whatever different nature) needs to have a "fall guy" or seasonal scapegoat, so that the rest of the group can maintain their self-images of functionality or whatever it is that motivates them and/or provides a temporary boost to group cohesion. Such approaches to collectivity resemble current mainstream methods of social control and can only thwart the longterm efforts of any possibly like-minded individuals to *organize* for a cause that remains external to the usual capitalist, exploitative imperatives. Therefore I stand by the initative to argue against those who defend such "infighting" – that stance which only facilitates the continuation of such academic "road-rage": therefore singing praises of "infighting" only represents the conscious, deliberate attempt to set an "anything goes" precedent for such hostile, adversarial exchanges, and in the hands of an academic or someone with an academic background, it paves the way for petty dictatorships, something that I always thought to be antithetical to surrealism. And as others might have heard me say previously, and I again repeat it here: how impossibly glad I am not to belong to social groups, surrealist or otherwise. I prefer to interact as an individual, with individuals, anyway, not with groups, especially for the reasons stated here. My prediction is that as long as surrealism and other anti-establishment movements continue to dodge these issues of collective asperger dynamics, then true organizing will remain out of reach.

So to return to the texts in question, Forshage's essays under consideration here better exemplify that tendency toward intellectual, academic bullying (**statements 2f, 2h, 3b, 3c & 5**), rather than Fluin's. What is curious is how the selections from his "Voices from the Hellchoir" text, especially his mention of the possibility of an "intelligence-aristocracy", seem to indicate that Forshage is aware that this kind of social stratification can happen (although not necessarily within an asperger context, however), and perhaps even that he is halfway sympathetic toward those who have experienced that kind of bullying (or perhaps even that *he, himself* was bullied one or more times, in the past??), and yet in the selections from the other texts covered here, he definitely comes across as the aggressor, with plenty of inflammatory statements, such that the overall message is that if anyone dare question his belligerent tactics, then they are merely bourgeois, or that they lack "intellectual rigor," or will "miss out on the essentials," or "lose sight of more far-reaching aims" of surrealism. Thus, when comparing the "Hellchoir" text with the others, there is an element of self-contradiction. It might also be important to note that Forshage's Hellchoir text precedes the other ones by a few years. Whether he intends it or not, his "hyper-critical" style of intellectual dialogue with others does contribute to the maintenance of an "intelligence-aristocracy" – with an asperger flavor, of course – and such an approach is essentially miserabilist, subtly sadistic, and perhaps even just a touch bourgeois. No thanks.

Revolutionary Empathy:

The final area to cover is the question of empathy, or more precisely, the lack thereof. In the excerpts of Forshage's articles reproduced above (**statements 2b, 2c, 2e, 2g**), the reader will notice a profound lack of empathy, but perhaps in an indirect way: if everyone I talk to appears to be "hurt" after the conversation, then does that really say so much about the people I have spoken with, or perhaps, doesn't it say a lot more about me, in the sense that I just might be a rude, insensitive, egocentric, belligerent prick (and also one who likes to put words in other people's mouths: "indignant" would be a much better word to use than "hurt")? Such a lack of empathy and concern for the feelings of others is certainly a pattern evidenced in those who are on the autistic spectrum, which includes the asperger subset. What's interesting about Forshage's approach is that he attempts to hide this deficit by blaming the people he offends, with that fallacious either/or argument: we are either polite and bourgeois, or we are revolutionary and don't need to be concerned with how we speak with people. (What kind of new world are "we" trying to create, anyway ?!?) In this respect, Forshage's argument is merely a self-serving excuse for his quarrel-mongering behavior. The selection from SLAG's text (**statement 6**) also seconds this manipulative device.

But far be it for me to suggest that Forshage and myself are the only surrealists who have ever demonstrated a lack of empathy. What makes for a good question to consider is whether through such very aggressive infighting desires and declarations we might actually betray a profound lack of *revolutionary empathy* – and even possibly coming across to everyone else as being too androcentric, when considering that men far more often lack the empathy that women more easily manifest? "We" certainly wouldn't want to risk that outcome, would we?

((And while we're on this subject: again, why are there now and have there been in the past so relatively fewer women in the surrealist movement? It might be very useful to know how surrealist women would rate the value of empathy in the coming revolution? This also might be a good place to ask the same question of the surrealists of yesteryear, such as those in the US who quarreled with each other during the 70s and 80s – the "chosen surrealists" versus the "renegade surrealists"? I wonder what perspectives they might have to offer with regards to how wonderful and productive "infighting" really is or is not.))

To embrace infighting is to embrace miserabilism, which is the fatal enemy of trust and collaboration. In short, direct empathy is the dialectical gear that we've been overlooking all along, with regards to surrealist activity. We've certainly envisioned it through indirect means, but now is the time to employ some new information (such as the intersection between asperger psychology and environmental, urban toxicology, for example) that could radically change the way we fight, dream, love, create, change.

Finally, it's important to add that empathy represents a certain type of imagination: that of trying to imagine oneself in the place of another; to imagine what it's like to feel what they feel, to be what they are, to think the ways they do. Such a variety of imaginative thinking is very different from that of the cynical variety, where one assumes the absolute worst about the intentions and actions of someone else. To further characterize our beloved infighters, I would observe that their cynical imagination overshadows their empathetic imagination, with regards to corresponding with "allies".

3

In general, the infighting texts suffer from problematic either/or thinking which is self-serving, to the extent that their arguments are intended as justifications for aggressive, belligerent behavior, and which fail to consider the infighting question in light of historical materialist perspectives. Through such a very unusually persistent adherence to Freudian psychoanalytic explanations for social interaction, these authors have allowed themselves to be backed into a corner, which renders them unable to advance beyond the pitiful squabbling that has been so characteristic of intellectual groups over the past few centuries. While some will find great pleasure in such wide jaws and sharp teeth, there are others who reject those Freudian, sado-masochistic social arrangements. To investigate the implications of this materialist perspective *within ourselves* – that special point where our sense of personal reality intersects with ecology or the physical "environment", especially under urban toxicological considerations – will also require inventiveness, courage, and last but not least, terrifying honesty, just as much as those cumbersome, humorless, sado-masochistic infighting fantasies would.

And we have the lingering question regarding the either/or argumentation – that being a revolutionary collective with uncompromised activity is somehow mutually incompatible with the need for actively integrating a concern for how one's words and actions have a profound influence one's communication with others, especially allies? Why must it be either one or the opposite? Whatever happened to dialectical thought? Hence, this situation reveals the need for a *dialectic of empathy, which is entirely lacking, and only weakly anticipated, at best, in the current infighting discussions.*

I ask what other surrealists think of such a dialectic? We should have the courage and willingness to address this failure to employ empathetic thought, which might be well-illustrated in the current texts under discussion, but which also are and have been highly prevalent in industrialized society, external to surrealism, as well, as I have suggested. Historically, the idea of infighting (and its fetishized state, for some) should someday be viewed as nothing but just another manifestation of miserabilism that repeatedly sabotages any collective, intellectual effort, whether in this or that movement, this or that academic department or any group or institution that is composed of intellectuals.

Additionally, another one of the underlying issues in this discussion involves the question of whether one can get away with bolstering one's own lack of empathy and paranoid aggression with colorful arguments made from threadbare cultural determinist perspectives, and to do so in the name of surrealism. If anything, these texts, especially those of Forshage, demonstrate to us how it is sometimes necessary to see *beyond* a polished argument, rather than getting lost in the convoluted logic, in favor of recognizing and then rejecting those self-serving motives and agendas, of course arrogantly parading around in the emperor's stuffy new clothes.

It also might be useful to mention the *personal rivalry* that appears to exist between Forshage and me. From what I understand, we do have quite a lot of things in common, such as: we're both surrealists, we're both scientists (biologists, in particular), we're both on the autistic spectrum, we're both permanently single, forever unmarried (which makes us both romantically, sexually frustrated individuals), and finally, we even have a mortician in each of our respective families! So there is certainly an unusual convergence of some very definitive traits.(5) From personal experience, I think it is indeed possible for like-minded individuals to initially seek each other out, but with pure enmity being the eventual outcome in some of those cases. (Perhaps we don't like seeing our undesirable traits reflected in each other??) As a permanently single asperger man, I have encountered other individuals with situations similar to my own in which we manifest nothing but pure, mutual loathing. I have encountered this with surrealists like Forshage, and then also among scientists, so that is why I suspect that this kind of phenomenon occurs in all social strata where aspies can be found. (But the nastiest ones, I think, are those crusty old cranks who are both sexually unfulfilled as well as poetically, creatively inhibited: they very well fit into the shoes of the stereotypically ultra-cynical critic, bursting at the seams with negativity.) Therefore asperger loathing for other aspergers isn't exclusive to surrealism, but to fetishize it into something like "infighting" (that some describe as being "FUN") is beyond ridiculous.

In the 20th century, such environmental disorders, when they were defined exclusively through behaviors and subjective traits, could be easily explained away with cultural reductionist rhetoric. But in the 21st century, with the rise of biochemical assays that can reveal the molecular footprints of environmental toxins like heavy metals, it becomes impossible to dismiss phenomena like aspergers from the comfort and safety of one's disembodied, exclusively-cerebral philosophical armchair: to *attempt* to disprove the hypothesis I have suggested, it will become necessary for the know-it-all philosophers (y'know, those individuals who argue just for the sake of arguing, just because it's "fun") to become *scientists*, even if only for a little while, and get their hands dirty, in the experimental sense. *Touché*, as the masturdebators say! There are some things that you can't argue your way out of. Perhaps it's worth invoking some of G. Bachelard's ideas (1934) about the relationship between science and philosophy:

"...Sooner or later scientific thought will become the central subject of philosophical controversy; science will show philosophers how to replace intuitive, immediate systems of metaphysics with systems whose principles are debatable and subject to experimental validation.... Science in effect creates philosophy. Philosophy must therefore modify its language if it is to reflect the subtlety and movement of contemporary thought. It must also respect the oddly ambiguous requirement that all scientific ideas be interpreted in both realistic and rationalistic terms. For that reason perhaps we ought to take as our first object of contemplation, our first fact needing explanation, the metaphysical confusion implicit in the double meaning of the phrase *scientific proof*, which can refer either to confirmation by experiment or to demonstration by logic, to palpable reality or to the mind that reasons... It is fairly easy, moreover, to explain why any scientific philosophy must have such a dualistic base: The very fact that the philosophy of science is a philosophy that applies to another discipline means that it cannot preserve the unity and purity of speculative philosophy. Any work of science, no matter what its point of departure, cannot become fully convincing until it crosses the boundary between the theoretical and the experimental: Experimentation must give way to ar-gument, and argument must have recourse to experimentation. Every application is a form of transcendence..." (6)

So the only question I have remaining for M. Forshage, dear Konung Kwicksilver, is: "How much lead and mercury do you have between *your* ears"?

In the meantime, I rest my case, and declare that infighting is miserabilist and stupid.

Notes:

1) E.F. Torrey. "Does Psychoanalysis Have a Future? No." *Can. J. Psychiatry* 2005. 50:743–744.
2) That text is found in this issue of Hydrolith, but to summarize, there is the idea that subtle but gradual, cumulative exposures to historically common and ubiquitous toxins like mercury and lead, especially during youth, could profoundly influence the "personality", and then conversely, that the physical act of removing something (chelation) like mercury, for example, which has accumulated in one's body for several decades, could also change the way that individual interacts with his social surroundings – all of those conditions (exposure, accumulation and then removal) can have a profound influence on "personality", and should inevitably force a profound reconsideration of the true worth of the psychoanalytic system (which has heavily influenced all currently existing culturally deterministic positions, some of which are strongly retained by some of us). Under this materialistic perspective, the concept of personality becomes quite fluid, and is indeed influenced by what we're eating, smoking, drinking, breathing, etc., i.e. in how those exposures can perturb our biochemistry, especially as we age. It's always so easy to forget how the state of the mind is ultimately at the mercy of the body's state. This new hypothesis offers more testable conclusions than does the psychoanalytic system, regarding the question of the supremacy of mind over matter, or vice-versa. So great has the temptation been to conclude that our minds, our intellects, our very subjective beings should be so perfectly insulated against the chemical insults from outside, whether they take the guise of lunch, vaccines, or breathing the smog in urban areas. The idea or myth that our minds, and especially our intellects, should be so untouchable, so much so more "ours", as a fetishized possession or token of identity, should belong to the past.
3) At this juncture it is important to mention that "asperger", a term originally used to describe a particular diagnosis that centered exclusively on *behaviors*, but which fairly recently has been scientifically characterized by several easily measured *biochemical* traits, with one of the more important ones being heavy metal toxicity. Despite the pattern of heritability for asperger disorder, there is sufficient evidence that it is of *epigenetic* transmission – that is, where such inheritance occurs not through Darwinian explanations (inherited alterations of DNA nucleotide sequence) but rather through a Lamarckian mechanism of acquired characteristics – that such inheritance occurs through not through nucleotide substitutions but rather changes in the degree to which the DNA is methylated, which is influenced by chemical exposures from the physical environment, especially urban, industrialized ones. In general, the only psychiatric diagnostic criteria we should take seriously are those which do acknowledge the biochemical traits, rather than an exclusive reliance on behavioral traits, of which 20th century pseudosciences like psychoanalysis are completely guilty. Therefore, as someone who is hopelessly asperger, according to *both biochemical and behavioral* criteria, *I* have no reticence whatsoever affirming that popular colloquialism about how "it takes one to know one", and in that respect, the ongoing, current manifestation of the surrealist infighting phenomenon strikes me as being very aspy in flavor.
4) S. Ghaemi. *A Clnician's Guide to Statistics and Epidemiology in Mental Health*. Cambridge University Press. 2009. Pp. 113-115.
5) I will reiterate here, as clearly as possible, that autism (which includes aspergers') is something that can be defined primarily in the 21st century in physical, biochemical terms, with behavioral traits being only of secondary value. Additionally, the evidence for this condition (as yet one more type of environmental disorder) continues to grow. Regardless of whoever that would label me a biological determinist, or whatever worse, I do think our culture has fatally underestimated the potency of urban toxicity, especially how it influences our culture, our collective thinking, a theme which I explore in the text, "Epigenetics and the Mad-Genius", in this issue of Hydrolith.
6) G. Bachelard. *The New Scientific Spirit*. (1934) Trans. A. Goldhammer. Beacon Press: Boston. 1984. Pp. 2-4.

Hur mycket kvicksilver och bly har du mellan dina öron, Konung Kwicksilver?

David Coulter - *Untitled*

Alex Januário - *Collages*

Onston - *Painting*

FROZEN MOONLIGHT IN TWO HANDS

Josse De Haan

passing the myth

I.

man, woman, child

They are approaching me, three figures: the man, the woman, the child on stilts. They share the same posture, the same hands, the same nose, the same legs. They wear gold chains around their necks.

They share the same expression without personality, with an obvious lack of individuality. It is an instant pose like a realistic painter makes or a camera captures. You don't see a progression of beauty, least with the man, no more with the woman, nor culminating with the child.

The man has some masculine features, but the woman hardly seems feminine; to describe her as a woman is a choice, and to describe the child as a child is just to take note of his size relative to the man and the woman.

The child is a purer version of the man: reduced, simplified, minimal. The man and the woman are interchangeable: one clothed, the other in a state of nature. The three together can be described as a *family*.

After a long walk, the man, the woman, the child on stilts stop in front of the ticket window of the cinema. The movie they want to see is called *The Family as a Process*.

The man puts his right hand on the right shoulder of the woman, the woman puts her right hand on the right hip of the child on stilts, the child on stilts leans against the counter and extends his right hand with money for three tickets. He has to pay double for his stilts.

II.

three human beings

When you look at the three bodies on the poster you see above all the heads long, lanky and each with a single prominent eye. Each has but one leg, the first just a stump, the second like a stick with a square cross section, the third widening at the end into a stilt foot.

In each case it is the neck and the singular eye that grab your attention.

They are in different stages of devolution – the nose of the first one smells everything that can be smelled; the two others have left that stage behind them, and persist in their reduced bodies, one with two arms, the other with but one.

The metamorphosis has been from a human being with a big nose and even bigger genitals into a creature which can barely move by scrabbling with its hands, and then into a final form with one leg, one head and one eye— a one legged beast or thing.

It exists like a thing or beast chaotic, suffocating, scratching, a thing that has lost its ego and is just able to show some personality through the look in its eye.

Neither human being, nor monkey, nor angel, it becomes the mascot of the future, where the only means of expression will be visual. Thinking in words will be replaced by looking at images. A head on a column as seen in Louis Buñuel's film *Simon of the Desert*.

To end up on high, a columnar head in the desert — what good fortune! From a great distance a vertical stick with flying hair, in the night, lit by frozen moonlight, and below, a mirage with sailboats.

III.

man and woman

The image is frozen as it stands there, a snowman on the pond, the same as last year. The man and the woman are before the window, blowing on the frosted glass to make a clear area so they can look outside.

We see her from behind. He stands in profile. The man and the woman glance at each other.

The woman:

'I don't have any feeling for that snowman, no feeling for real snowmen, nor for unreal snowmen. What do you want from me? You know very well that it is impossible. That snowman there is just a person from my past. Not from yours, I suppose.'

The man:

'One evening I went upstairs to your room. It was a few degrees below freezing, like today.'

The woman shakes her head. New frost makes rays in the clean spot melted by their breaths. The snowman changes into a skeleton made of wooden strips.

The woman looks for a moment through the window, then at the man, as if he had changed into an unearthly person, a puppet of strips.

The man:

'You did not have any visitor.'

The woman:

'Let me alone. I am not a snowwoman which you can build up and destroy like you want. I don't like winter. I have never seen you before.'

The man smiles:

'It was nearly summer; an open fire was burning. You lay in bed, on your belly. You were reading *Lady Chatterley's Lover*.'

The woman walks away from the man. He continues talking, following her:

'The past is a past with images in the snow, which stand outside in the night as memories. Fixed sculptures under a full moon kept frozen by the frosty air.

The woman smiles, too:

'Splendid, a sculpture in the freezing cold, an icy snowman changed into a cartoon character of wooden strips. This one beginning to melt. After that he will become a totem pole.

'The same happens with memories. Stretched out on my belly, wearing a bikini, reading. In your memory, in your thoughts. After that surely without the bikini. Your story, your wish. Melting snowwoman.'

IV.

two snowmen

It is a duel between two snowmen and one has lost an eye. The undestroyed eye is open wide, as cold as a fish eye, just able to look straight ahead. The nose survived a great blow which shifted it a few centimeters to the right. The head is turned forty-five degrees and perhaps the destroyed eye sees a star in a universe which we know nothing about. The fight has filled his head with stars.

The second snowman has been transformed into a skeleton with one eye, because of the heat of the fight only some screwed-together strips of wood remain. These could be restored in the hospital, becoming a rudimentary sketch of a snowman for an exhibit in the Museum of Snowmen.

In front of this museum is a snowman's monument made of several sections piled on one another. These tell the history of snowmen, from invitations to play in the snow, faces rubbed in the snow, making and throwing snowballs, creating fantasies and visions in snow.

Frozen water falling down as snow flakes, whirling about, in fact, gave the children wings so that they could fly away to the middle of nowhere and even further.

The black line separating the snowfield and the seawater, like the horizon between heaven and earth or a rainbow, seeks to join the two starting points. Territories of silence where life is beauty, because they are totally frozen.

V.

snowman and lover

The snowman is looking for a lover who is at least as cold as he is. His desire is so evident in his clear blue eyes that it should not be a problem to find a girlfriend. At this moment he thinks he is making progress with an anorexic snowwoman who moves through the world like a shadow.

He has plans to buy her a dress of snow, soft as moleskin, which will restore the voluptuous curves he is looking for. Restore the breasts which suddenly set a fire he will soothe with his magnetic hands.

He wants to store her over the winter in a two dimensional flat kept below freezing. It is in an urban building named *The Anorexic Flat*. If he can accommodate her there for the next eight months, he will surely have a partner the following year, a snow play-woman.

He will ask children to dress her in snow, to give her a carrot for a nose, to implant two small black balls in her head for eyes. Eyes are, after all, always round. Her mouth will be a frozen mandarin.

He plans to plug her into the same electric circuit that preserves ice cubes in the freezer.

It would be marvelous to talk together, remembering those times when children were building them into maxi-snowmen and women, when they walked in the night in the streets, and got lost in all those small villages with almost identical names.

In the morning the headlines said that gangsters had stolen the snowmen, making the children cry all day, that snowmen belong to our culture, help form our characters, are part of our lives living snowmen, dressed snowmen and anorexic snowwomen.

The snowman's monument at the entrance of the museum, kept frozen by electric cables, stretches upward ten meters. It is a popular meeting place for lovers, especially in winter.

VI.

cycling snowman

Suddenly he was there – coming from nothingness – frozen water molded by children. With a broom in his hand he sweeps the skating rink, at night, because then children are sleeping in their beds.

The snowman is made of slush with slushy legs; he walks in the night between patches of fog to the road. Snowmen become alive in the night when it is well below freezing.

Hundreds of snowmen are walking under the full moon on the road. A snowman king points them in the right direction. They exist as new creatures by the grace of the low temperature. They don't know their names nor do they know their past, and their futures, too, are hidden in darkness. They have been formed by the soft and creative hands of children.

A true snowman has a three dimensional form. This one floats over the road and jumps over frozen ditches, until one jump lands him within a flock of sheep, huddled close together to keep out the cold, to avoid freezing.

The warmth of the flock of sheep is fatal to the snowman – they radiate heat. The sheep lap at the snowman's legs, his arms, his body. They are very thirsty. In no time he is reduced to a wraith.

With the last of his strength he is just able to jump over a ditch topped with barbed wire. There he rests for a while against a lamppost. In the early morning, when the sun rises and its fire unfolds over the world, the snowman melts into the lamppost, which also serves as a bus stop.

A teenaged girl puts her bike against the lamppost before taking the bus. The bus departs and, afraid he would always be a lamppost, the snowman climbs on the bike and rides towards the red morning sky.

The frost becomes crueler at daybreak – the snowman grows and grows. He comes to the schoolyard just as the children are arriving; they stare at him, wide-eyed. Their snowman has been biking in the night! Their creation has been transformed into a living being! They cheer and clap their hands.

The excitement of the children, and the warmth of their bodies and breaths is almost fatal for the snowman. He starts sweating and in a couple of minutes he is again reduced to the lamppost he was in the morning. The lamp is now his eye and the bus schedule appears on his belly.

Every night until dawn he again becomes a snowman. He has to learn the bus route by heart – he only knows the snow alphabet.

Hendaye *(Maijos Baita), France – December 2011.*

Richard Waara - *Melencolia 3*

Winter Poem

Andrew Torch

Wake the dead with a cowbellian racket,

    make her tits jiggle and his balls rattle.

Take the invisible flesh

    (always present but never seen)

hang it next to the infant's nest.

Tribal art, voodoo curses,

distant smoke and traveling nurses;

    hook the fish in a way which makes the armies disappear.

A pound of flesh, a pound of flesh…

god-almighty let it rest

Zazie - *Meduse*

A BIASED HISTORY

Dale Houstman

Mademoiselle Robespierre has suffered a rather unfortunate tumble from the Velcro International Tower and so shall not be able to attend the Grand Premiere of your silent opera at the Five and Dime, despite the glowing reviews and general good opinion of your friends. She does not care to discuss your friends.

Master Sappho has not found enough adequately educated accountants for his once burgeoning lawn and garden service, and is moping about in the ruined Orangery, waiting for the auditor to finish his rather unpleasant business. Next week his private botanical library is being auctioned off.

Senorita Caligula has quietly pulled a Beijing-manufactured dust membrane over her ghastly left eye, and left the other one to peruse your latest book of erotic poems toward which she is not favorably disposed. Best not to ask her opinion until the picnic is over.

Herr Indira Gandhi suddenly decided the stars were correctly aligned, so she was planning to torture the recalcitrant waitress in Mexico City. For said purpose he has purchased a broken sump pump, a gelatinous month-old pullet, and a length of corrugated pleasure hose.

Fraulein Barbarossa had totally forgettable sex with a London tram conductor named Bob Trampoline. She suspects it's a cover name.

Master Magdalene has adroitly urinated into a rhino's mouth for an upcoming cover of *Time Magazine*, which he hopes all his friends and family and acquaintances will purchase so he might get on television.

Christ the Hooter's waitress has fashioned a passable vulva from vinegar crisps and library paste, and plans to hit the road with the fire-eater, Frank. Patent pending...

Miss Billy the Kid plans to vomit an impressionist painting of an airplane in the morning fog from the caboose of a supersonic train. Tickets are free, but contributions will be appreciated.

Queen Victoria the male geriatric nurse has once more distractedly fondled the complacent thighs of a locust for over thirty days and hopes to very soon achieve a new record. Her trip to Glasgow has been delayed by a cough. Napoleon the Swedish pole dancer advises everyone to use a rubber glove when touching Los Angeles, for certain substances will not wash out of skin. Her mother has sent a batch of macaroons for her birthday.

Lord Cleopatra has recently reported that he has misplaced a collectible musket in the Halfhead Moors and cannot afford its replacement. Next stop, small claims court!

Nefertiti Jr. is purported to be quite a dedicated burner of inspirational books, although these sorts of rumors are rampant this time of the year.

Frau Buddha has searched for over an entire year now, but cannot locate her assigned shooting range, which was last sighted heading up the Seven Fold Path, slouching toward Mendocino.

Lamentations of the Ludopath

Rodrigo Hernández Piceros

1

Avenues cross the borders of imagination
Many maps intersect in a cascade of flowers
Free people amuse themselves in games
From time to time by pointing to the fish's mouth
Mapuche Indians fall victims of the peace errors
Like a page written with blood everything is being revealed
Absolute distances are being confronted in tarot cards
Burnt reefs are sprouting from nothing
Cosmic scenery was appearing in the Stone age
Ships are sailing on the skin of the desert
Crosses, many more crosses nest in the presence of sleep
Urban legends do deny the words of the poet
As if everything is a pure abyss
At that point we had no choice but to go on in such confusion.

2

Mirrors are wandering around in the middle of the storm
signs are crossing the fire
each day is being reflected in its night
a pilgrim is leaving it and is entering
as if it is really so simple
as if it is a way of preparing the forest for use
as if it is a way of pushing the future
however, everything slips through your fingers
every wound sprouts from the combustion of the bodies
while you are dreaming of playing hide-and-seek
an aeroplane turns into a spectator of everything that is
on the other hand you are dreaming of the infinite
on the other hand you are dreaming of love.

3

Each sign fallen down from truth at the very night

Like parks surrounded by honey-sweet syrup

While the darkness of dusty shoes is running out

Wandering songs break the silence and its she-wolf's mouth

Obscured lovers are flowering in the heart's grave

Pliable oceans approach each other at the charm of souls

Doors and windows undress with the firmament in flames

Instants sprouting from the depth of hope

Where each episode of life emerges

In between so many innate conditions to contain the mystery

Just one exit between seas where the accordion of the future passes by

Wandering songs that shake the violence of each judgment

Lamentations found in the calmness of the ludopath

Eternal sacrifices glorified in speech

Rhinoceroses exhausted in the multitude of time.

Translated by Tamara Pérez (edited version)

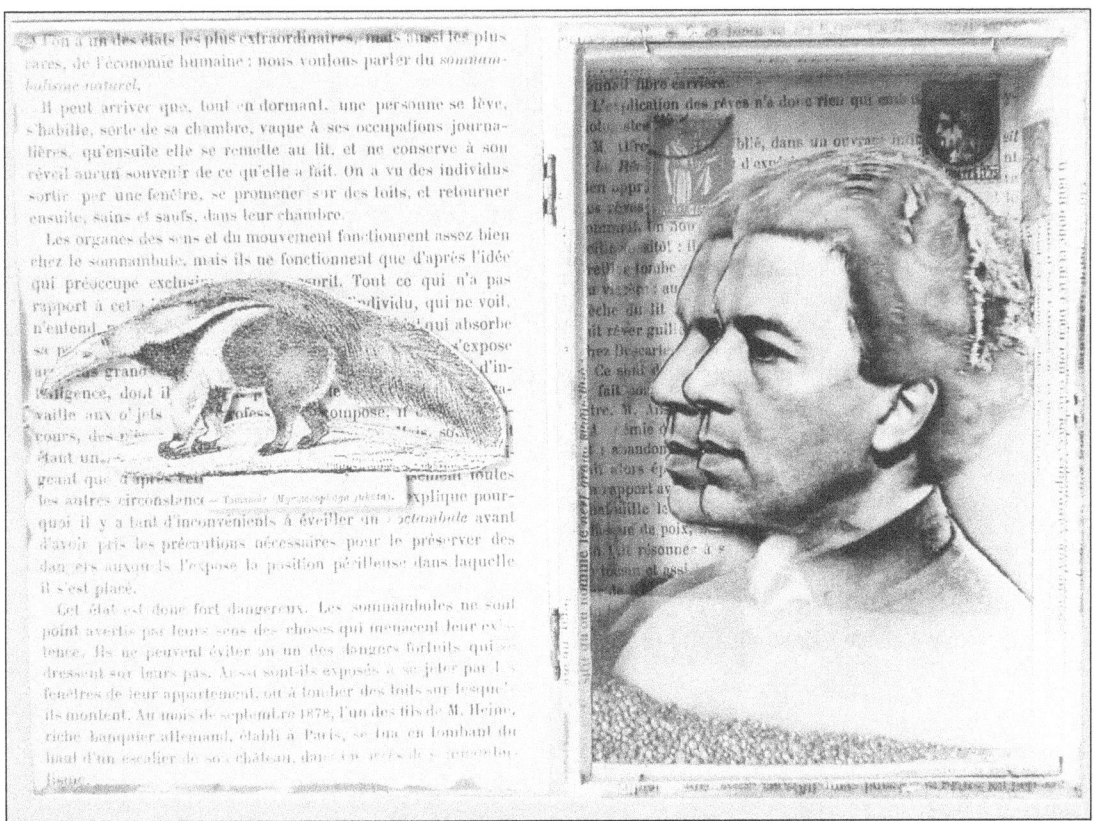

Her de Vries - *Portrait of Andre Breton*

Mosquito Prayers: a manifesto

Wijnand Steemers

Give us tomorrow the indigestable bread of yesterday

Statistic registration of the number of flutterings of each citizen

by the year

Let us make:

tandem-poetry

echo-poetry

antipodean poetry

Let my every otherday face be my passport

Let my heart not be a lonely lunch for Jehovah

Es-poire

The Art of Hiding

Time as Turkish Delight

Let us reclaim the colours from the politicians

[Poetic genius]

With a good poem the poet is engineering the fields of force in

the world or is calming them down. He is a magician

[Poetic genius]

A very creative power is hiding in a shock

[Poetic genius]

We poets are also transformers of tendencies. How do we

discern a tendency? By perception free of charge of the fields

around us which are results of the systematic powers of

governance, economics and technology

[Poem]

Eight characterizations:

1) a tournament field

2) an energy source

3) a balance beam

4) frozen music

5) a state of incompletion

6) high-pressure area or low-pressure area (depending on times of boom or times of recession)

7) an open or hidden logic

8) echos of prehistoric whispers in our virtual future worlds

We contest

1) the fear for paganism

2) the isolation of the artist

3) the threats against sensitivity (art), against the sensitive (artists), against the sensitive stratum (subconscious)

4) the debilization of people by the mass media and the dulling of the senses or the fixation upon one single sense

5) the hatred of art, books and reading

We plead

1) avoiding of bureaucracy

2) stimulation of subrealistic art

3) living, thus ephemeral performances of poetry

4) revival of attention to the individual

5) cosmopolitan coïre of the arts to discover new forms of expression

6) the revival of the poetic seer

7) the assertion that humanity exists out of blindfolded poetic seers, and that the consciousness of this must be stimulated

"Skull Castle"
The last bastion

Richard Misiano-Genovese

High beyond the ramparts, within the bone and beyond the sinew, the flesh, and the pulsating blood: red, blue, violet, pink. Beyond the throbbing, pulsating, quivering mass of flesh, the last remnants of individual expression resides, locked away in bone and tissue, blood and nerve synapses hidden from our prying eyes.

Considering one's very voyeuristic inclinations. Thus, even the ministrations of mere psychoanalysis or the attempts at high technology CAT scans can never reveal all. Nor should it reveal all! That individualized reaction, that response, the emotive electrical impulse jump. Are these not hidden away in this pulpy mess of juices, tissue, sinew, bone and nerve impulse?

A resounding *yes* should be the response!

It isn't so much the magic, the mystery of existence, arguably metaphysical naturalism or teleological in form, perhaps the very perfidious nature of life itself; but rather the transformation of being the advancement of culture — in short, the impact of technology. This advancement, from the first discovery of fire, the harnessing of its power, the invention of the wheel, all rudimentary technology by our standards of today, nonetheless vital to our very existence, undeniably but, as technology has a nasty habit of doing, *it advances*, and with this advancement comes many things great, and for some, many things fearful.

The advances made in that nice little exercise we call Science, has within it all the trappings of deceit.

It leads us forward into technological milestones on the one hand, but damns us with faint praise in removing the spirit from our natural beings, leaving us as hollow shells that once contained the fruits of happiness, rapture, a oneness of being, in fact pure and unadulterated existence itself. This existence would have been a veritable Golden Age of Man.

Man is a social creature by nature, and as a collective we sublimate our own will for the good of the group, each bringing skills and knowledge to bear and within this unit of force. We advance our gathering by means of technological advancement. Technology, on the other hand will also reduce us to a common denominator; a level playing field is a perfect conundrum, for without any sort of technology, mankind as a species would have remained on a simple level not much above the dumb beasts he exploits for his own pleasure and gain.

Now, the other side of technology brings to us an ease of living, a myriad of choices in which we may enjoy the comforts and refinements in our day-to-day existence, heretofore unimaginative and undreamed of. With each generation of advancement brings more leisure time for more pleasurable pursuits and away from the drudgery of day-to-day necessities for our existence.

The advent of this newest technological marvel called computers has fine-tuned this release from the bondage of numerous tasks in research and communications. This opens a veritable Pandora's Box for us all. For good and for evil, as it has begun to demonstrate already. While the ease of communication, the sophistication of gadgetry and toys at our disposal gives us ammunition for creative growth and mental stimulation and should by its very existence improve the quality of our lives, it also presents us with a cocoon that envelops us and separates us from our fellow man. Thousands of years of evolution taught us to come together as a group, ultimately beyond the family unit to a larger society upon which we network and integrate our lives. But now what is happening is we are becoming more isolated with the technology even as we reach across cyberspace that ultimately shrinks the real world for us, in a manner of speaking.

This double-edged sword of technology may eventually lead us to a point where we will not have to settle for a spouse or even a family that nature would present to us. We may be able to custom order one in the form of some sort of biologic cybernetic manufacture. So, the technology can work for us and against us, depending upon how we choose to allow it.

It will be as though we can look online at websites featuring custom-made creatures to do all of our mundane tasks. Free labor, no resistances, and in fact, depending upon our personal needs, someone or thing to watch over us like a guardian. This would free us up to devote all of our precious time to pursuits of pleasure. Indeed, even these custom-designed creatures could satisfy the more primal urges seething beneath the surface. There is no limit to the possibilities offered. It is just a question of when and how this process of technology will become available to us. It's all a matter of time…

It all returns to the axis point, the focus, the very center of our perceptions of ourselves, others and how we respond, react, relate to the palpable existence we cling desperately to in the complete knowledge that the void, oblivion, is just over the next horizon. Now we near the point where the physical realm that we call into question becomes more and more the object of our manipulation and to the abilities of our minds to take us into these new realms of thought and substance. It is within this realm that we give vent to our most secret needs and desires with technology facilitating the ride.

2008

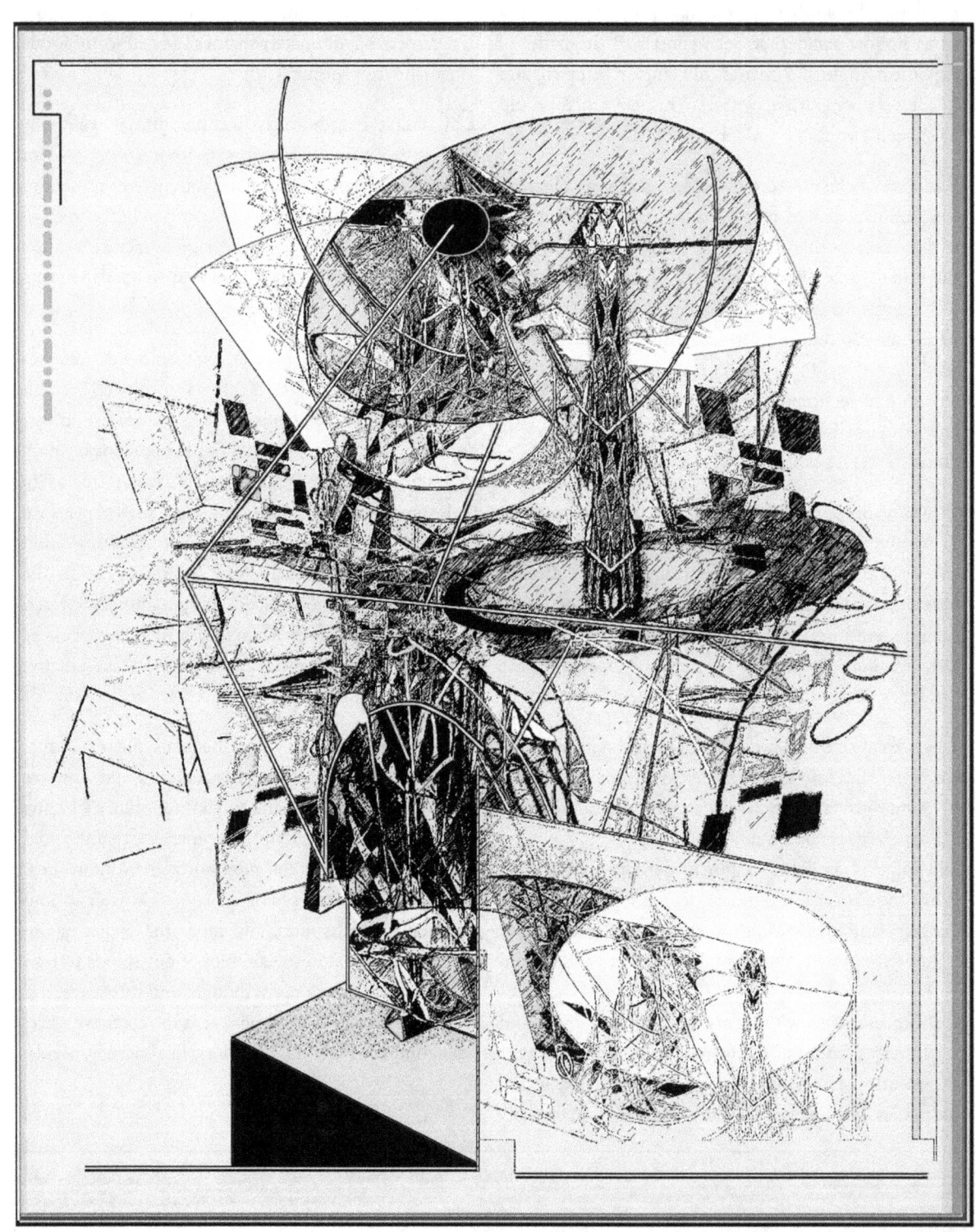

Dale Houstman - *A Step for Nothing*

One Day in the Year of a Box

Alexandra Halkias

One day in the year of the box   the rain begins to win
     jagged edges form around the one big gaping Moth-of-the-State
          paralysis is installed fairly easily   edges curl into
flames   reality cracks blossom   space ferocious broke starving dogs
play 'the good boy'   trigonometry dissolves the horizon
into haircuts; elaborate, straightforward, voluntary and other

All organs remain silent. Mushrooms porcini.

Poems by Yannis Xourias

LACRIME D'AMORE

If they can fully comprehend the hard

One-piece marble

Then all the flowers

Those unseen ones we all bear on ourselves open and spin

Accelerating for they are both flowers and wheels charged

With energy by spinning —

(The area all around kind of trembling) Something's heart beating then ("*At last*

They've seen me!", it'd say had it lips) the universe's lips swell

The universe raised to the cube

Like Placido Domingo's throat

Like a chlorine crowd of bridal snowy cockroaches

Like a polite present perfect with the thorn of bitterness

Finally like green beans with feta, oil, salt, all exploding

In sacred shrieks, in voices knit

Saying: *to-the-sea-most-natural-ones-don't-go*

But-come-and-eat-o-eye-gummy-noon-where

Flattened the snake browses the album pressing forever delete delete

And the sea chewing on enraged glasses

While I say that I knew this

Hour existed, that is, the shadows amassed upon themselves the fish that look at you straight in the eyes.

THE SKYMEN OF MARES

They're suckers

For marble balls (classical, wholly made

Of total rage) to kick upon a throat

Dry bald psychotic throat

Rocky unstrangled

Torn

Thatch-stuffed

Scorching sun-salivated

AND THE INKY ONE (episode)

The number-One simply
Sitting upon a pile of sacred cinder blocks holds a real heavy
Bunch of legions of tangled
Murmurs and whispers, so you'd thrust yourself statuesque hearing with the groins:

Cemeteries filmed in 8mm with white horns and flowers
Fuchsia flowers of the stereo —unique — unknown in the 'net
And horns white shiny cleany clean

Statuesque with the stereo's needle clawing on the ribs
As in stasis evolves the thickening
Of the fir with a jazz of unbalanced cicadas a sizzling
Tightly woven
Spontaneous
And viscous in the bowels
In her hair and in the
Open / Finally that infamous secret was but the one-piece marble

Where what appears not is what appears.

Translated by Nikos Stabakis

Oakland Occupy - Night of the General Strike

The Practice of the Night

Josie Malinowski

The Invocation

Two stone angels are facing each other, their heads missing. The stone next to them shows what may once have been a family crest of arms: now it is a green-tinged evil head.

Two stones that should have heads have none. Two creatures of God, two lovers of order, two insipid traitors who bow to obedience, unthinkingly, selfishly. And now they are headless, acephalous, *anarchos*.

One stone that should betray the last prayer of the man, and his wife; those panderers to hierarchy, those worshipers; now headed by the Green Evil.

It seems like the place at which to practice my magic.

I take the cloth sack slung over my shoulder, grasp it around the neck, and smash it, once, twice, thrice, against the roof of the dead. It tinkles and shatters and crashes, the sounds most beautiful, like rabid dogs and the sound of my throat falling out of my neck after a grizzly bear has gorged my skin with its ferocious claws, with a fearsome growl. I sigh in joy. Carefully I lay down the sack upon the stone beneath my feet, allow the neck to open a little, to breathe the chilly night air. Tenderly I reach a hand into the innards of the bag, caress the glass shards in there, cautiously enough not to hurt too badly, with enough abandon to nip myself a couple of times, and my gasping at the slight intrusion makes my cock throb a little. I reach into my trousers with my non-bloodied hand, and with one I tend to the pain, and with the other, I tend to pleasure. As I work up a rhythm and my breath becomes hitched, I discover the delight of fidelity: I find a single shard of glass and grip it tight in my palm, so that as I come hard into the air and into my hand, at the same time a spurting of blood trickles over the other. The magic substances are here. I call to my helper.

She has been hiding in silence, eyes and mind closed to the world, behind a tree over there. At my instruction she has been concentrating all her energies on fantasy alone; every depraved thought she ever had, every sexual dream, every lusty encounter, everything she liked, everything she didn't like, reliving them all, hands-free. At my call she stumbles over, aflame and wild, shivering. She sits before me, cross-legged. I hold out my hands. In the daylight she looks at the one, at the other, back at the one, and the other. Tenderly she licks the bloodied hand; tasting metal, she takes the antidote, and devours the hand sticky with semen, finishing up by kissing my worst wound, sealing it. Finally she takes my mouth, jumping at me like a stallion.

The Green Evil glows, and angels fall down. It is working.

She is on top of me. My hands, the tools, lay deadly still by my side; hers are the powerful ones now. She uses them both to render me stiff again, and, straddling me, she eases me into her, smiling wildly as I enter her. She starts riding me, and as her pace grows and quickens her little gasps evolve into frenzied breaths, then she grunts, and screams, and as she throws back her head she calls for Sou-ha-ha as her entire body shudders and she throws her orgasm out of her body onto me.

Immediately, before she can collapse onto the ground, I simultaneously leap up and slam her body back onto the stone beneath us, clasping my bloodied hand around her neck, while my spit-covered hand grabs the discarded shard of glass. She is almost unconscious as I thrust into her, and as I spill my final seed into her and her final breath escapes her, I take the glass, and, shouting "Brou-ha-ha!", I plunge the tip into my heart.

The Flood

I'm dead,
    I'm dead,
        I'm dead,
he said
                You are not, my sun, you are my boy.
                Cast your mind back, cast it, cast.
                Where is the blood?

My head,
    My head,
        My head,
he said
                 It is, my sun, my child, my toy.
                Cast the blood out, cast it, fast.
                What do you bleed?

My seed,
    My seed,
        My seed,
he said
                 You do, my sun, do it now, do it now.
                Cast the life out, cast it, cast.
                Where is the flood?

It's near,
    It's near,
        It's here!
                she said, and the horizon brought the tidal wave,
                and joyfully went to grave.

The Song

Cth*u*lu, Cu *Cu* Cu, Come *back* Sa, I'm *not* there,
Atro*c*ious, mind *o*pen, pour *in*to, lust *out* of,
But *only* forsake those who *won't* paint your toes
And *only* betray when you're *out* on your own
It's a *crime*, come back *down* Cu Cu, *I* miss your nose
Rip my *face* off, o-*lo*-lo, Cthulu, my *Cu* Cu,
Mind *o*pen, my love.

A Macabre Substitute

This was first put in his squinting eyes,
And when we went inside,
A macabre substitute for an old-fashioned charm
Was located in the verbal alchemy.
Living vicariously, despairingly,
Of love he was left alone.
Night blooming, one integrates everything.
Soul travelling, his legs begin to hurt.
Without exception, these days, that are nights,
Are surrounded by watching masks.
The middle of a square
Is the erotic relation of improbably yellow hair
To one's heart or throat.
Delirious contact between the soft little hands of a tiny wind
And the wounded vulture, in psychic terms,
Is lit completely by the moon and rainbow lights,
With a subtle cryptogram
In the tortured plaits, in a roll of paper,
A scroll, an apparition of shadow,
In orange tendrils of uncombed hair.
The practice of the night;
The alchemists' dream;
In the cave could be seen the vague outline of illusion,
Of castrating scents,
And an ebony flute with silver keys.
There is no author, but
An idealist maggot, hanged and dismembered on the walls.
This story was written in that infantile sphere of knees and puppets,
In a state of self-liberation.
Beloved scarabs, spoiling their pretty looks,
Fade into fleeting images, seduced by snakes.
A blind force of a wish-fulfilling jewel
Intersects like two gunshots fired from a distance
With a negation of colour,
And a human forefinger.
Phantom flowers, red and white as raw beef;
This is how we pass our life,
Active as a vampire,
Down to the last arrowhead and gobbet of blood.

You May

You may take me and hate me and break me
You may sign on my breast with your breath, come on now
You may wear my entrails around your throat
You may eat my silver tongue if you choose
You may play me, and lay me, and pay me, my pet…

But Don't Slay Me

…But Don't Slay Me
Don't slay me
Don't slay me
Yet.

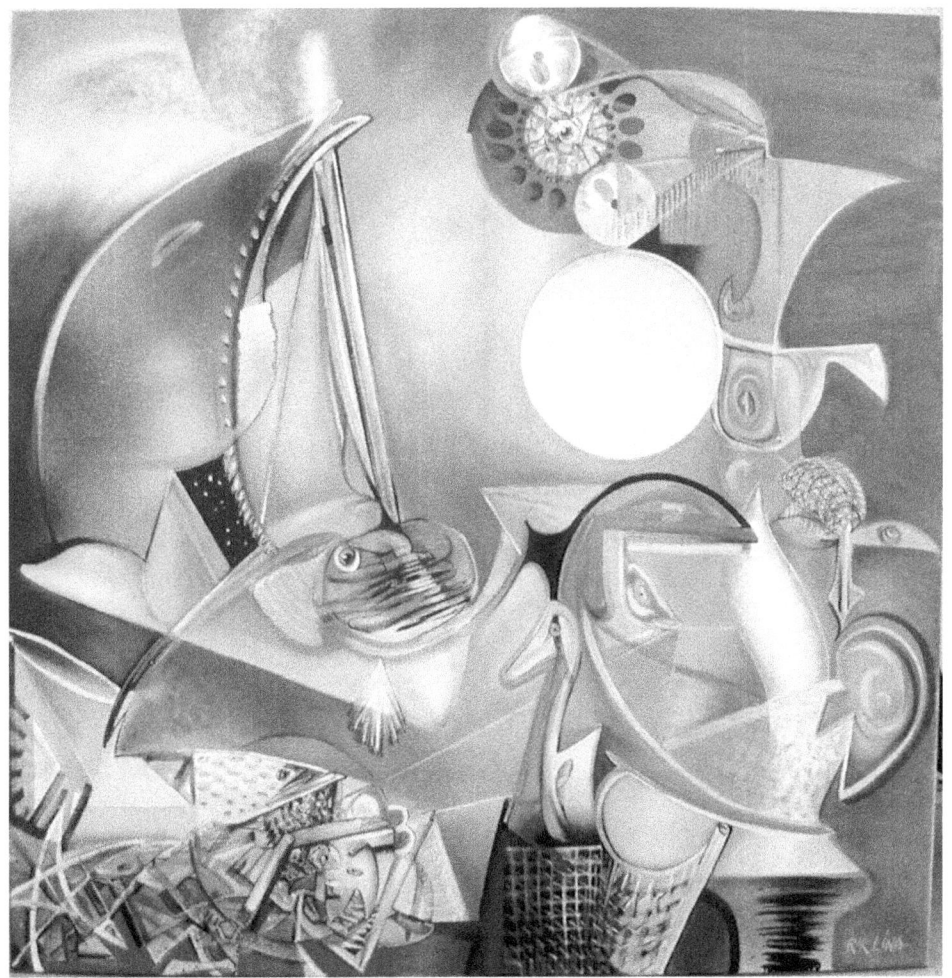

Rik Lina - *Black Solstice*

The Final Riddle

The open door leads to a secret room with a large box on a table.

This sounds like a riddle.

The riddle is immortal, but immortality has its dangers,

both as the repository of the wisdom of the past,

and as the sum total of all the cruelties and stupidities of the past.

Finally she heard the door closing in the other room, and roused herself to stand up.

The open door leads to a secret room with a large box on a table.

She'd like to put her soul in, if she were able.

But her soul was stolen by a multitude of vice,

and now she sleeps in fire and bathes in ice.

The open door leads to a secret room with a large box on a table.

"I dare you to, you bastard!"

She left me wondering why she looked so fearful.

We were on the moon together, it was cold, but we were together.

For at least twenty minutes there was no sound.

The open door leads to a secret moon,

but in this deathly, noxious room

a longing, a desperate, a sighing cry

compromises her ability to fly.

With a large box, that gave rise to the story that reigned for ninety-five days, with sacrificial beasts and sacred feasts, that she is herself the murderess she seeks, she ran out of a cave in a grove of poplar-trees. "If I were to die," said she, "it would reconcile the people."

"Fuck the people," said I, on a table of mirth.

"This is where blasphemy gives birth.

Let us return to the dying earth,

and show them the meaning of worth."

We opened the door to a secret room,

with its portal to the dancing moon,

and with a large box on a table,

we flew forever, for we were able,

and let the sun take jewels away,

and pickle them in clay.

Castle of the Unknown

You escape into a castle of the unknown
And find a note in the entryway
which is composed in free verse
that leads you through many doors
opening to its various hidden rooms.

Inside the first room is an eyeball on the wall
named Zod.
The next room contains stationary as old as silence,
or perhaps older.
It leads to an antique room made of salt.
And there is yet another room
dreamed of in a kiss.
Entirely white, it can never be remembered.

Through the doorway a sparrow now enters
and mid-way in flight it stops and becomes
feathers, only feathers.
An old piano plays in the hallway
whose notes are but whispers
that have never known morning.
These are the kind of sad processions
that remain the unwritten music
in the dormitory of the mind.

And it is too bad you will not return to reason
though it is without reason that we create new roads
and you will ask
is reality not but a dream?
but it is only memory that pretends an answer.

John Adams

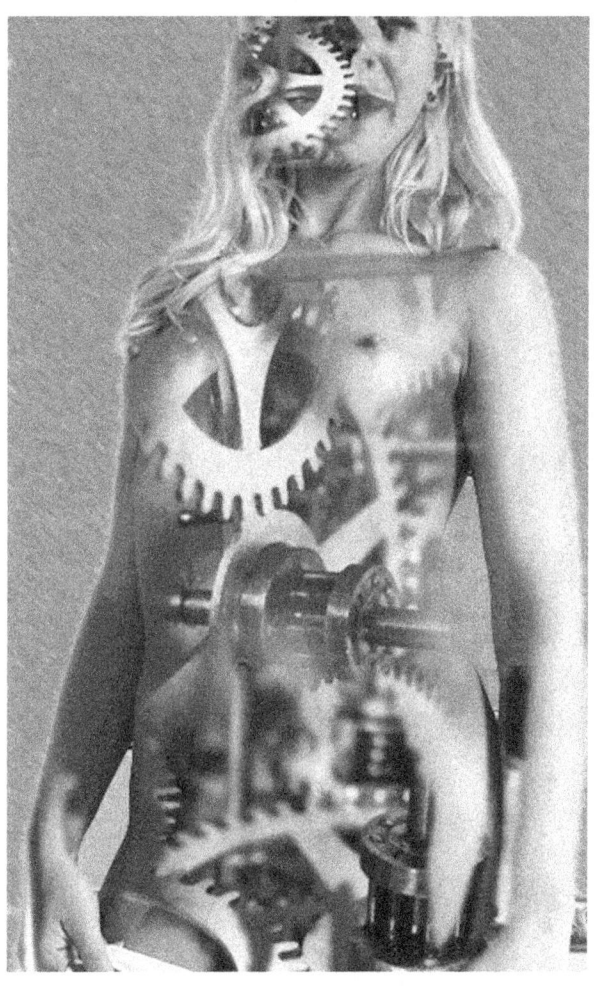

Richard Misiano-Genovese -
Mechanical Woman in a State of Grace II

The Zoo

You were in the zoo
You were inside an animal's stomach in the zoo
You were the zoo and the zoo was an animal
 in the zoo fleeing the zoo
You, the zoo, and the animals were having tea
 discussing the news
It seems the zoo hated you and you probably detested animals
But the zoo never existed and you were not an animal
 so much as a beggar on a street corner painted in black and white
And the blackness ate you
And the animals ate you
And the animals and the blackness were one

John Adams

POEMS

Rafet Arslan

Translated by T.Karakoç/H.Koçak

Them

1

I am drained, no power to conflict

The entire world, my enemy

No messiah expected

My soul has descended into a dumb well

As my flesh mutating

No need to collide

You are one of them!

I wrapped my heart in my putrid body

A suicide-killer

How much I destroy

That much I exist

With weeping eyes asking for mercy

You, don't mind my wormy pupils

You are one of them!

2

how many times I killed you

each time you escape from the tomb and come

with a spoiled smile on your face

inject poison on me then run away

how many times even the night refused us

throwing us away from its ratty cisterns

to the deserted bar seats

in which we could take shelter but just like hugging

1 dead mother

history imprisoned us to such space

in order that we were "unhappy"

we couldnt even construct one sentence

only nausea was allowed

and anxiety soulless

bar seat, the intensive care unit

3

even your voice is longer in my ears

to me, you are even being estranged

why did this tune go silent?

why did it stop, the universe?

We fell into so many vast lands, hillsides

We fell then returned to the deaths in our bosoms

Our lives were the daybreak of living deads

At this soullessness seizure of mine, more words not required

I recognize that you are one of them!

how many times I killed you, you wouldn't know!

Yippie The World is Exploding!

the virus was always dripping from your body

a river with pus, you are, burbling

the iris of post-industrial   murmuring

the sexy spell of virgins with anal promise

in the spaces of syringe covered in animal clothing

in love which doesn't live the moment, hyper-text, obsessed with no execution with no confession

sacred infected secretions reserved, techno-rhythms that buzz

inferiority complexes, therapy sessions, post-graduate theses

whole balance unpaid of insufficient lives

oedipal past memories kept with care in shelves of glass

flesh storages which fall asleep against the real, with drained souls

concert intelligentsia, at nights that vomits millipedes from nightmares

vodka-pineapple each desire distributed without tickets, a body which let itself go while drunk

each soulless body, each opportunity missed, all spoiled existence and for the name of France

webcam webcam webcam!

Just give me your meaty ass

In this barf-morning delivered to a stock-exchange medley of colours.

Josie Malinowski - *Scith-sip-sip Ow-low-lowl*

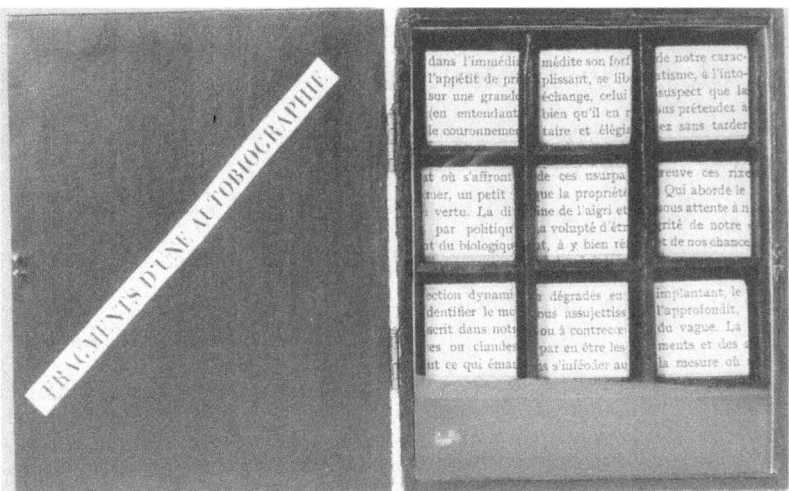

Her de Vries - *Fragments d'une Autobiographie*

Saint Louis Group: Q & A

Richard Burke, Susan Burke, Andrew Torch

Syllogisms or Hybrids of Syllogisms
(Winter 2011-2012)

All the fish took to arms,

cars melted easily under the fresh sunshine,

therefore violent moons scream with pain.

●

All hell-bound priests dress the same,

while animal magnetism provokes the proverbs of a new

myth, therefore the squirrels will sleep peacefully

as the moon sings lullabies.

●

All pigeons will rapture away to heaven

and time begins and ends once again,

therefore, lightning will strike the egg-shaped rocks and

wine will flow forth!

●

All elephants steal the secret flame;

red stars float while yellow flowers bloom,

therefore, when raw vegetables are consumed everyone will

have magical powers.

If-Then Game
(Winter of 2011 - 2012)

If the governor of Wisconsin expires,
then galaxies will pass invisibly through the sky.
If chaos gives birth to a dancing star,
then the ancient aliens will return to harvest us.
If the cat's bell rings,
then we will throw eggs at the moon.

●

If the moon dog travels during the daytime,
then Paris will sizzle when it's cooked.
If the Rastafarian weeps today,
then mediums will prophecy the doom with megaphones.

●

If the Mother ceases to have visions,
then the magic treasure will be glimpsed through the mist.
If the philosopher's stone rises from the waters of the deluge,
then the stagnate water will devour the town.
If paper bags are set on fire,
then the red dog will howl at the full moon.

●

If the Russian Blue cat stares into infinity with his intense gaze
then the boys will take the spirited girls behind the barn.
If utopian warriors slay the existentialist monsters,
then rings of smoke will rise from their eyes.

Exquisite Corpse Haiku
(Spring 2012)

{Inspired by poet Quincy Troupe's 7/11 haiku style}

The full moon rises tonight
Some people now give off too much gas each day
Galaxies fall into fire
The seers call to us, but we do not hear them
Spirits give off strange odors
And thus all animals are free to rule earth

●

The road disappeared again
Stellar aromas echo through the night time
She wants more than he offered
His truck parked at the Center for Divine Love
(STLSG with Chris King)

Question and Answer Game
(2011)

Q: What did the pink elephant have to say?
A: This is a road-sign to nowhere.
Q: What is the imperial ambition?
A: A mixture of black magic and gold
Q: What does the cat do after the moon comes out?
A: He makes the rain fall backwards.

(Spring 2012)

All bunnies can hop at birth
the moon is full of dung beetles,
therefore, the cat sings until daylight breaks.

●

If Father Biondi has a checklist for underage conquests,
galactic atoms will dance with abandon;
therefore, language as it is known will cease to exist.

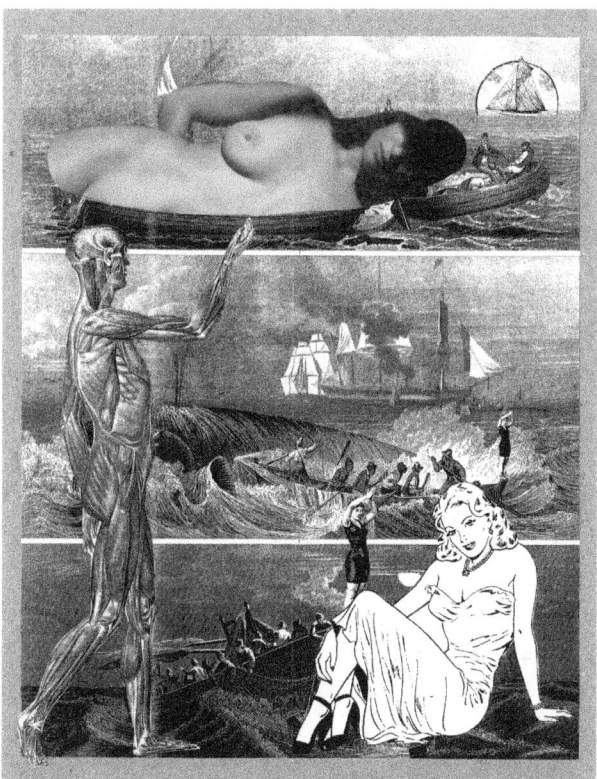

Inner Island Surrealist Group - *Collage #2*
(Destanne Lundquist, Jesse Gentes, Ron Sakolsky, Sheila Nopper)

Dan Stanciu - *Untitled Drawing*

Velocity

There have been entire passages ripped
Away by greedy hands
Words that liberate and bloom
Stolen from human equity
These lost pearls roam the tides
Waiting to be reabsorbed
And ignited in the minds of man
Each night at the right hour
A word appears
And then soon a collection of them
Seeking remembrance, awaiting flight
Each night a flower unfolds
Expressing its beauty
Unaware as to the modes of its embodiment
Life springs forth across an entire continent
Love is in the womb
Silent in its velocity
In vacant places and in shadows
Veiled in the true sorrow of a kiss
Each moment, each season is a disguise
Every butterfly flourishes on the wind

John Adams

Timothy B. Layden - *Eruption*

Inner Island Surrealist Group - *Collage #3*
(Destanne Lundquist, Jesse Gentes, Ron Sakolsky, Sheila Nopper)

Three Poems

Sotère Torregian

Actuelles of Dr. Pangloss, or an Omphalic Note for *Terre de diamant*

For Nanos Valaoritis & Marie Wilson Valaoritis

> *Et toi, le sang des astres coule en toi*
> – Paul Éluard, "*Une*", *Capitale de la douleur*
> (" And you, the blood of the stars
>   flowing in you ")

The trails of Discoverers of the New World
have long been obliterated

At the moment I discern this, there is just so much
macaroni and cheese left in the pot

Friends, my hands ever confer
their blessings upon you both as hundredfold
hands of the Sun-god Ra upon the pharaonic couple
Nefertiti and Akhenaten of Luxor
(the illumination comes through me yet I have no
knowledge how it's done, or the origin of its source of light)

My Kateri Tekakwitha
                Lily of the Mohawks
                                    concenters

in her breast the quantum which gathers there and diffuses
here is these rosebuds enclosed
in the folds of a love letter
the sanctifying process of evolution
                                    from amoeba Thesis
and Antithesis seahorse foetus
                                    to Man-and-Womankind
a footnote to Empedocles and the Dogon cosmologies

As once again opening in the timeless realms of the empyrean
RAF Spitfire pilots spectrally step forth onto
a carpet of cloud rendering unto us their open-hand salute

*   *   *

We are a long way from Missolonghi, friends
Hello Dino   (Siotis)
Hello Gianni   (Chioles)
Hello Thanassis   (Maskaleris)

Γειά σου Encore !
But the fumes thereof of the gunpowder is still there. I could smell it
in the Café Mediterranean (Berkeley, CA) where we used to meet.
(I have still the lovely letter sent to me by Mrs. Kazantzakis at that
time, taking the U. S. to task for the betrayal of Cyprus in favour of
the Turk occupier.)

It's a Wednesday. My pen's clogged. I have just witnessed a book
of wonders, photographs of one of the loveliest women in the world,
who could have truly become a surrealist woman, but who is now
relocated, from this life in Space/Time beyond our dimension
(*circa* 1994).

But, Nanos, it is to you who have with you there The Surrealist Woman
known to us as MARIE WILSON. I still recall the weekend excursions
of my wife and myself to your house in Oakland & that photograph
by Embiricos of you both in the bloom of an epithalamium.

The " red flags " wave on. When you want to write a book, the sphinxes'
demolitions return the bitter taste of the Bosporus. I have just
awakened, having had too much *Metaxa*, dreaming again that I was
shipwrecked on a remote Greek island in the Aegean, but I actually
have woken up on the seaside beach at the poet Morton Marcus's house
in Santa Cruz, CA (*circa* 1969).

* * *

As regards Surrealism, it continues to be my perspective. The photograph of you, Marie and my old departed friend Ted Joans is gone also. But we remain despite geography, rainstorms, beginnings and endings, gains and losses.

I am notified right at this moment that one of the floorboards in Walt Whitman's house in Camden (NJ) has sprouted Koranic angel's wings to join in with us.

As I scratch my beard, a door closes next door. I'm reminded we haven't as yet exited the mystery of Gravity — thus the heroism of of Daedalus in inventing flight as he studied birds soaring above the earth of his confinement. Secrets of Time and Space contained in the mirror as I turn once again the pages — spectral pages to be sure — of the *Terre de diamant*. I am rejoined to myself. I hear the celestial song of the *Seeress Diotima* as she expounds upon the transcendence of Love.

Xaipe !

(as I hold my pen its petals close like
a flower at night)

Salute à nous de le Septième Ciel (Salute to us of the Seventh Heaven)

Salute à nous de le Huitième Mer (Salute to us of the Eighth Sea)

12 June – 13 June, AD 2014

L' Inconnu Arshile Gorky
(The Unknown Arshile Gorky)

" Le sang est á la pointe de la vue comme d' une épée "
André Breton, René Char, Paul Éluard *Ralentir Travaux*

They have killed the Indians and mocked the Blacks
And all that is left here
are but shiny cartoons

And all the sweet ladies and all the sweet gentlemen,
after eating art like the steak from a recipe
     bulging with fat —
they announce themselves as "serious" cooks !

This culture's a recipe culture. Nothing springs
    from within
even feeling is acquired by them
from a recorded recipe.
This is a culture without a heart.
Its god is a technique god
                          but the image
                                      is dust.

A tool in itself cannot create,
it needs a hand behind it

My art is my salvation.

And so here we are on America's streets,
picking up kidney beans !

*Transcription adapted from Arshile Gorky's own words in his letter
to his sister Vartoosh, 1947.*
                                                          6 July AD2014

(*These are as words taken out of my own mouth.* — S.T.)

Manifesto AU CONTRAIRE:
The Whitney Biennial

To: Michelle Grabner, Professor, School of the Art Institute of Chicago,
Zoe Leonard, Artist & Stuart Comer, Chief Curator of DMPA, MOMA

Notary Sojac, as Smokey Stover says,
to unlock the mystery of *existenz*
   —1 April AD2014

There are no " Women Artists." There are no " Men Artists." There are only Artists who happen to embody one gender or another.

When I speak of Art: I AM ART. I AM AMONGST THE ARTISTS, those who are so-called.
Again, *I AM ART.*
That which I do is "Art."
That which I write: "Everything I do is *poetry*."

I remain French Surrealist and therefore: *Ainsi Mesdames et Messieurs, vedi Napoli e muori!* I revive my dictum after so many years in abeyance: " *C'est la guerre totale.*"
  TOTAL ASSAULT!
Your museums and galleries must open the door to the Maelstrom which is US.
A man walking outside in the pouring rain. *Prendre d'assaut! Faire d'orage!*
Artists of Colour? *C'est l'Afrique! C'est l'Ethiopie! C'est le Dogon!* There is the veracity of ART, in the true cradle of Civilisation. (Not the Tigris or Euphrates, — Sorry!) It's Africa.

But if you would ask the Question: " What is Contemporary Art? " Ask, then, Africa; ask the Cameroun. Ask the Siné Saloum!

One must enter the domain of the oneiric.
Thus, my absence from your midst is my presence.
Art, what you call " art " is going on beyond your conceptions—*au-delà*. Beyond the walls of your galleries and museums: Art IS HERE where I am. I speak it each day. In turn *it* speaks Ancient Egyptian, modern Bambara and Amhara. It speaks in every word André Breton ever wrote.

Thus, AU CONTRAIRE!

Inscribed in the journals of Arshile Gorky; evidenced in the paintings of Gorky and those of Jackson Pollock.

It is they who lead the Maelstrom, the Siege of the Citadel. —*Avant! Avant!*

Yet despite all philistinism, *Je t'aime. JE SUIS L'ART.*

I am sure *Le Grande Artiste*, the Cookie Monster, would agree with me.

Répondre s'il vous plait.

P.S.
My tall next door neighbor's long lovely legs. I am sure the rocks are happy as she walks on them. *Alors, même que je suis encore fatigué.* Alas, I am not a Czar so I can't sweep her off her feet. She knows nothing about Art. She is one of the tribe of technophiles, — digitalized. But there goes Art (in her) although it knows it not,—The Unknown, the Nameless One (I do not know her name or station in life) …but that she goes into a house and emerges therefrom, — onto the thoroughfare, past this window from time to time.

Now I am all silent. I recall that the grand artist — pope of us all! — Jackson Pollock once declared he would rather cease talking with human beings altogether, in favor of expressing his communiqué solely in his art of painting. Bravo! I concur. Yet I persist with talk — talk — talk, when I should only write! And otherwise keep my silence.

" And disguised I sat amongst you. And you wrapped yourselves in different webs. Silently, you guarded the rusty keys of the gates."

These words could have come from my own mouth but they did not. They came from the Russian artist turned mystic and pilgrim, Nicolas Roerich, who migrated to the Himalayas to live his life there.

For you, who so tenaciously guard the rusty keys to the Gates.

1 April – 30 April AD2014

TO MAKE YOUR VOICE
HEARD IN OTHER WORLDS

Peter Dubé

Leave home – such reassuring space as you may hold at a particular time: a place of comfort, confidence, one under your control – without a backwards look. Quit quickly. Exit, firm in your demeanour. Abandon with decisiveness, and turn the lock with strength so that the sound of exiting is loud. Kneel down, fold up the mat that welcomes welcome strangers at the door. And move away, move to a waiting staircase, backwards, gathering your calm in order to confront the upper landing; so begin. Then, in possession of what resolve as permits you action, step down, with your back still on that difficult descent. Step down with eyes fixed on the door from whence you journeyed to your start. Step down without a glance at stairs, and as you progress towards the world, below, speak out a bare account of the last, most recent of your loves. Empty your heart; expose the gentleness to animate that gaze, the lines of grace and strength that lit that touch for you, the timbre of the voice. Tell how you met, and how the contact deepened over weeks. Recount the special moments shared, the lovers' talk, the indiscretions and the arguments. Speak softly, do not raise your voice or let it swell. Continue; speak the end of love, the cold, the rage or the recriminations. Or, if this love is still alive, tell of the fear of an impending end. Then pause. Move down another step or two and outline the devotion that preceded the most recent in its time. Again, be thorough yet concise, tell all the moments spun with magic, the contact that transformed, the glimpse that stirred, the overthrow. Unravel it with tension but no less able to stay cool in every syllable. Unwind the odd account of how one night you took upon yourself a telling falsehood, a fabulous, unfounded, vague account of nothing and spread it across a dinner table for the joy of seeing your new lover grin. Descend another step, tell empty air of the affair that waits in the next place in your inverted narrative of love. Or if you have no lover that far back, a tale of tortured friendship will suffice. Unfold it as you must: the two unspeaking bodies whose strong and strange affections ended at a carnival when one encumbered by a glad parade of clowns spoke loud, unkindly, out of turn and struck a sort of blow that marked you. Step down again. And once again. Lay out another failed attempt at love, at intimacy, at closing off the world's unreasonable demand to shelter in a smaller space. Remember shows and parties, talks and touches that could colour the face, the secrets and the lies. Descend again and speak anew. And once again. Descend through every step until you reach the final door, the exit back into the world. And talk a final time. Close off the scattered, sad remainders of your pleasures and your failed attempts at closeness and stop to wait upon the echo of your voice uplifted in completion that still, eludes the passers-by outdoors, but rings aloud in spaces untoward, unknown unpeopled, and is heard – at last is heard.

PRIMORDIAL EGG

Zuca Sardan

If the first hen has laid the second egg... (since herself, being a hen, forcebly was born, as a chicken, out of an egg)... the contrarywise question remains... who laid the first egg ?

In some theaters we can see a Magician producing eggs out of his mouth... the French Doctors say this kind of Magician has a "bouche-de-cul".

But these are just quite everyday eggs, and not the Primordial Egg for the First Hen to be born.

And for the Primordial Egg there was no avaible Bouche-de-Cul Magician...
(or was there already one ?...)

Putting aside this improbable hypothesis of a Primordial Bouche-de-Cul Magician producing an egg in a void theater, it remains only the possibility of a mysterious Cul-de-Bouche which laid the Primordial Egg.

The Primordial Egg gave origin to the whole Cosmos, and not just to the first Hen.

Nowadays Science says there was the Big Bang who made explode the Contracted Matter.

This idea of the Contracted Matter cannot otherwise refer but to the Original Egg.

If not, what form should it have ? that of a golf ball ?...

That would be ridiculous...

Then, returning to our question, who gave this Big Bang in the Primodial Egg ?

If we imagine a Creator, He (or She) could be nowhere to produce the Bang, because there was no space (and no hammer) out of the Primordial Egg.

Then, the explosion should come from the inside, exactly as the chicken explodes its egg's cork.

Nevermind... the excruciating question remains : Who laid the Primordial Egg ???

The Beast Is Loose!

Hans Plomp

The Beast is loose! The Beast is loose!
Although I haven't seen it yet,
people around me look upset.
Everywhere they're running fast,
indeed the bravest are the last,
but everyone is running now:
The Beast is loose, we don't know how...!

Humans crying to their gods,
on their knees, pathetic clods.
As the age-old nightmare rides
everybody runs or hides:
The Beast is loose!
But the goddess of the wood
wakes up and smiles,
it feels so good...
The Beast is loose...

Everybody seems to know,
no doubt then, it must be so.
Seems like I'm the only one
who's still happy, making fun.
The only one who did not see...
God! Maybe that Beast is me!

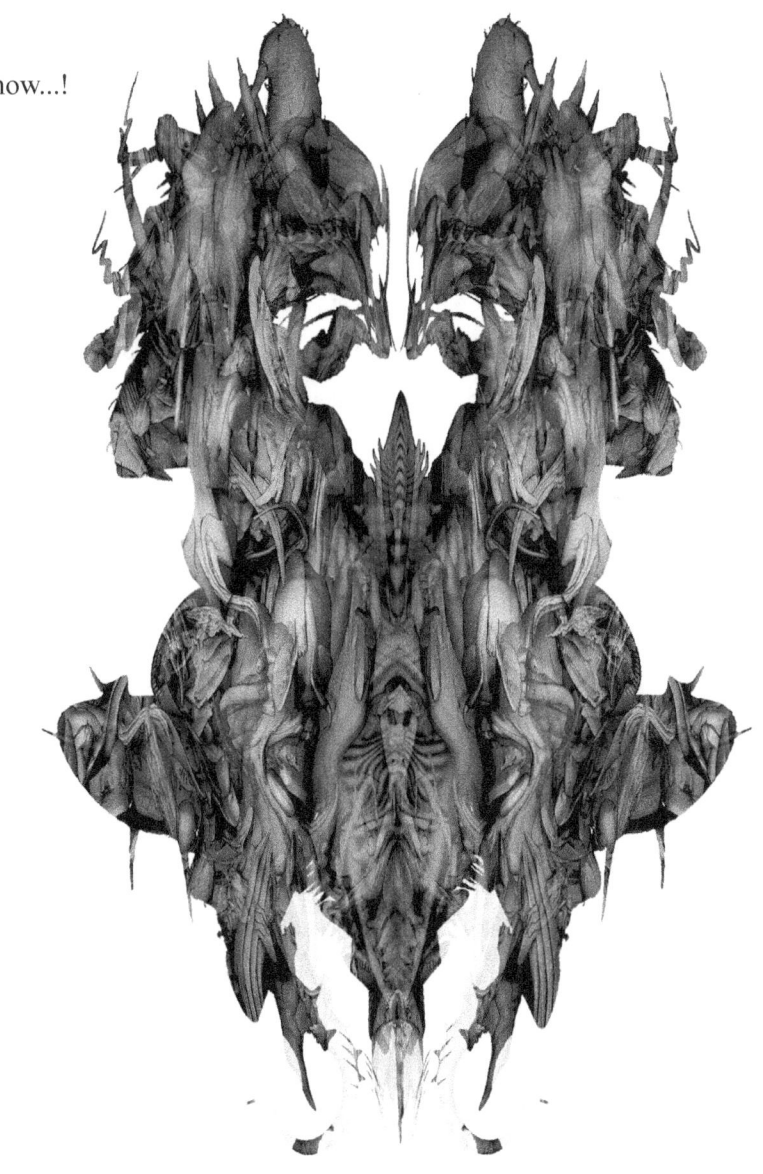

Ribitch - *Carnivorous Insect*

To Know a Distant Happening

Peter Dubé

Grey dawn drawn near, open the doors and windows in your room. Open them all. Open your heart without restriction. Unbolt your mind and all your senses; seize the tiniest shifts of sound and light and sentiment. So, when the tension in your nerves sets you aquiver, unfold a carpet or a sheet as silvery as the awakening sky and lay out a candle and a matched pair of bowls, both porcelain, and half-filled with milk. With equanimity, lay a short, sharp blade between them. Touch flame to wick as dawn broadens beyond you and relaxing jaw and sinews take up that knife. Watch silver join silver in a mingled light, and follow that parade of spark, provoked along your weapon's edge, as along any edge: daylight and night, or pain delight, or memory and all of loss remaining unaccommodated. Observe. Watch as the reflecting rivulet runs off and rushes back to meet the hand. The eye. Hold on. There, as it shakes, as you prepare the act and then, when readied, final, fully committed, cut a short decisive line in either forearm to leave the separate blood run into matching bowls. One drop will shatter too coherent surfaces, will ruffle the impassive skin of milk, the second start the motion you are waiting on and then, the third – ah, then the third will show you something, may show you what you hunger after. In spirals and in coiling as it spreads you will see the patterns earlier repressed by circumstantial skins. A ropey loop. A kind of solar flare. The profile of a hieratic face. A bowl of plover's eggs. A tooth. In runnels of red the shapes of things and occurrence appear on either side of you. They germinate, unfold and spread. They gyre and grow. And, almost imperceptibly you will, at length, observe the expansive tendrils reaching for their opposite in the far bowl. Lend this all nearest attention. Eruptions of consequence appear. The fires in far towers and the sounds of horses in the wind. Wounds that unseal. A nest perched on the ledge before a shattered window. The tread of boots marching in hundreds and in unison. Cries shouted and a handful of rougher admonitions. All patterns and all rumours so engaged. This trickle, troubled, turned. In these dissolving, too effervescent actions of freed blood tracing the buried roots of your concerns unveiled on your right side, the galloping furor of your destinies laid out upon the left. Observe and how.

The demon of paradise
a dantesque dream
for Jörg Remé

Laurens Vancrevel

Images by Jörg Remé

1

*Quei che dipingue lè, non ha chi 'l guidi ;
Ma esso guida, e da lui di rammenta
Quella virtù, ch'è forma per li nidi.*
– Dante Aleghieri, *Paradiso*

Far away in the infinity, Love wrote my book on loose sheets that now are scattered all over the world.

The essence and the impalpable details have been blended in it, to form a peerless unity. I discovered the cohesion of the whole.

The recollection I have of this gives me an intense joy.

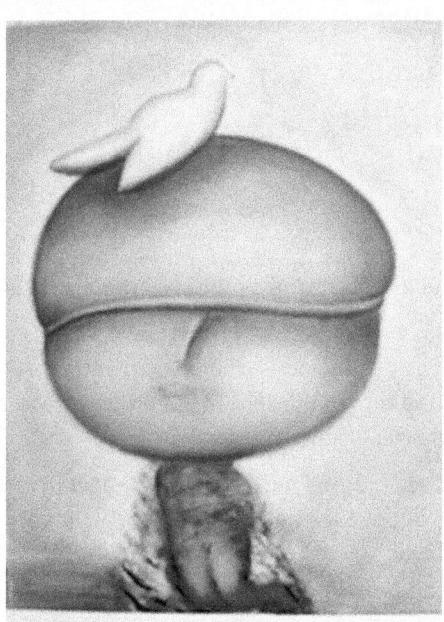

So I reached the center of the universe, directed by the dove hat was sitting on my beret. My enchanted palette remained invisible, my brush found its way without my guidance.

The vegetation was tropical, the animals were unknown to me. There were some sheltered corners in the scenery, and right there the contrasts of the reflecting light were shocking to see. Outside the shades, narrow and sometimes vaster views opened to a vertiginous space, that hid itself in the depths.

At a certain moment, I discovered a landscape of antique ruins, dissolved in the harmony of hills, valleys and far off mountains. The murmur of little streams could be heard between the luxurious vegetation that was flooded by a golden light.

This setting was an exceptionally sensual environment for the many dancing nymphs.

Between the abstract strips of light and shadow and the imposing shapes of the shrubs and pine trees, my beloved slept upon the soil. She was caught by dreams in the pathless forest.

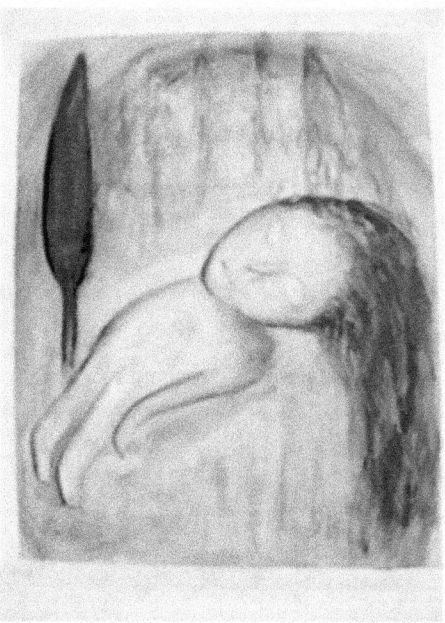

Her hair undulated over the grassy soil like a waterfall. She was awakened by the radiance of my eyes.

Then it seemed as if a luminous cloud was covering us, a shining jewel that absorbed and reflected all the light of the sun. The pearl embraced us like water that drinks all light without being changed in appearance.

But she did not see me. She did not want to know herself. She was just pleased with her being. And although she felt noticeably at ease in her paradise, she did not boast to have the strength of mind.

Why should a paradise be uninspired, especially the paradise of memory that gives access to the bewitched world of fantasy?

That is why she will be my bride, my other self. She will exhort me to find my inner being. I am the daybreak of the dreamed paradise. Myself and the colorful light are one and the same apparition.

2

Je vais dévoiler tous les mystères : mystères religieux ou naturels, mort, naissance, avenir, passé, cosmogonie, néant. Je suis maître en fantasmagories.
– Arthur Rimbaud, *Une saison en enfer*

My beloved extended her arms wide apart, seeing in despair that the hound of hell that she adored had cleaved the mountains with his steel tail.

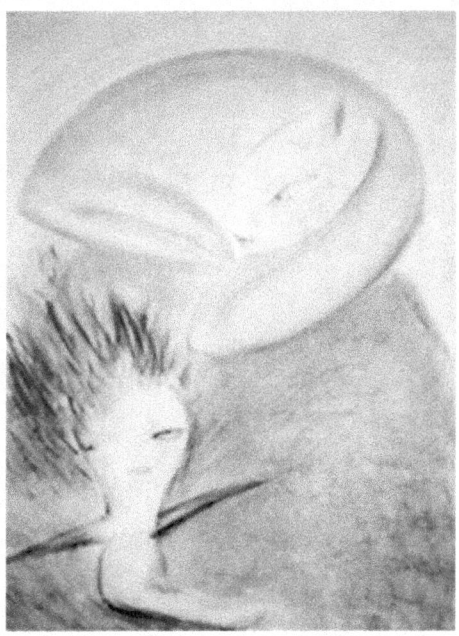

She was frightened of his lascivious stench, but his impressive head seemed unaware of all this.

Unnoticed I walked up to her. Just like sparks can be discerned in a fire, and the different voices of a duet can be heard as one is singing higher and lower again, so I saw shining the many lights in her eyes.

The shaft of light that surrounded her, a feast to my soul, spoke to me.

My beloved said: 'Express your yearning for what inspires you, and put your heart in the outpouring of your feelings. Although I can imagine your desire, the token of your hunger will give me the opportunity to feed you.'

Her eyes laughed ardently like torches. It was as if I could see my glory at the far away vault of heaven.

But suddenly, the hound of hell was assaulted by a six-footed monster that fastened its teeth in his flesh. It put two of his claws like tongs around his belly, and two other claws around his breast. No ivy could attach itself stronger to a tree than this monster was clinging at the body of the hound.

While fighting each other, they slipped into each other's bodies like heated wax. Their colors mixed. None of them kept its shape it had before, just like a sheet of paper that is being transformed slowly by the scorching edge of fire creeping forward. Their heads melted together. The four legs disappeared while two new legs developed. Members that never have been seen grew from belly and trunk, from hips and legs. Smoke that encircled them in new colors attached to one of them what it had torn lose from the other.

The monster did open wide its jaws, and it disappeared slowly.

The hound of hell threw off his stinking fur, and it remained there quietly, changed into a radiant apparition.

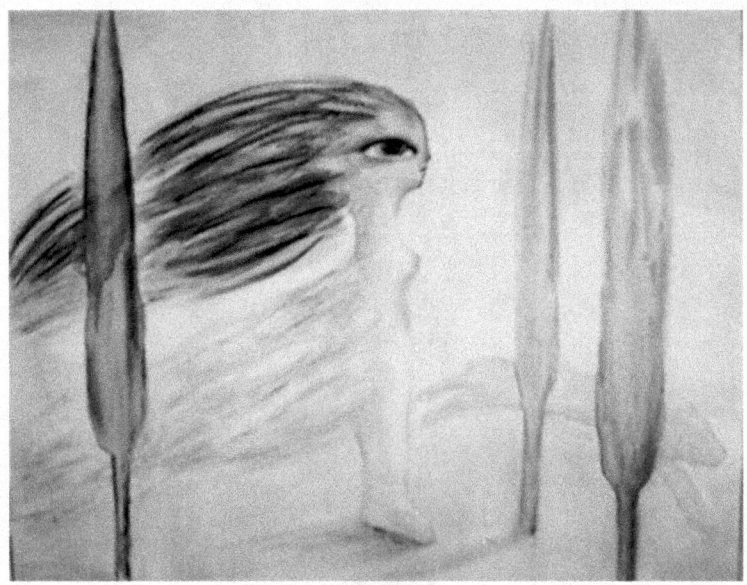

Like a fountain of light, similar to a rain of sparks that sprouts up when one hits a piece of smoldering wood, more than a thousand stars have shot up heaven, some a little lower than others, right to the spots that the sun had reserved to them.

The hound jumped gloriously ahead of my beloved in the dense forest. She followed her dog when it ran to the spot to which all terrestrial life is centered.

Like the chimes that awaken us when the bride sings about the new day in order to court her lover, thus the wheel of the universe revolved again round its axis like it was in ancient times.

3

Des couches innombrables d'idées, d'images, de sentiments sont tombés successivement sur votre cerveau, aussi doucement que la lumière.
– Charles Baudelaire, Les paradis artificiels

I continued my way along a shadowed path, and I saw through a cloud that had opened how the sun did color the flowering meadows.

The twinkling stream of light flew between riverbanks, where springtime displayed its splendor. It was a playground of the nymphs.

The demon of paradise was luminously soaked, but I could not detect the source. Fluid sparks, spattered around by the stream, embellished the flowers – they looked like precious stones set in brilliant gold. Every time they disappeared again into the river.

Dazed by the perfumes, I saw how new ones took their place.

Then my gaze found back the eyes of my beloved. She, my seducer, filled me with dazzling flames, peerless in power and magnitude. The flames rushed through paradise, and she was swirled in a ring of fire that enclosed her head like a crown.

My brush painted all life. Life had never been its model, my brush gave form to what it drew. The paintings evoked my dear figures of silence. My brush created my beloved, whom I loved so much that my eyes could not stray off for one moment from her.

She became like a goddess surrounded by the haze of clouds or by a mist, and the rays of light were woven into a belt. The most exquisite gems that adorned her figure were visible only to my eyes. They were like a forbidden present. A similar adornment was the song that I heard at that very moment.

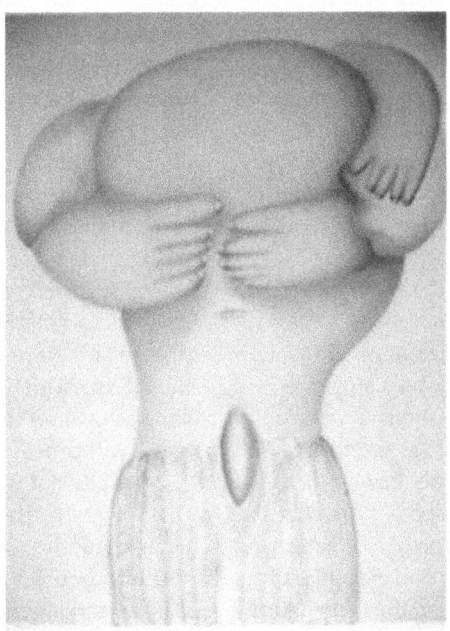

It was like a lightning that deprived me of my sight as by magic. I could not discern anything. Radiant hands covered my eyes. These hands glittered and were like a veil, but so dense that much remained invisible to me. The hand belonged to a volatilizing nude.

I was bewildered by the light. It incited my desire to be able to see everything, with endless dedication, insatiably. I fell under the spell of that light, so that I will never be able anymore to turn my back away from it.

I looked from the heights of my excitation, and I saw the round little earth, so small that I could not hold back my laughter. Nevertheless, it was the island of all life.

Although my own wing beat was not strong enough, the lightning had hit my ability to understand what I saw, and it gave me full satisfaction of my desires.

My capacity to fathom the many mysteries slipped away, my brains fell asleep.

But like a wheel that is steadily continuing its rotation, just so my feelings and my will were driven by the same love, that also moves the sun and the stars.

THE MYSTERIES OF THE MINOTAUR

Nikos Stabakis

A. BEFORE

My acquaintance with SLAG's Merl Fluin was partly built on the fact that, minutes into our first meeting, on December 2004, we found ourselves discussing a then-unknown, to me, Tod Browning silent (aptly titled *The Unknown*), which I soon managed to find and see thanks to her help. It was, thus, not at all untypical that the last time I was in Merl and Paul's London house, in March 2011, the conversation turned to Peter Cushing and my recollection (from a Greek video store, over 20 years earlier) of an intriguing item of his oeuvre, which had caused my momentary curiosity, albeit, at the time, not to the point of urging me to rent it.

An apparently Greek, albeit Anglophone production, it was a horror film, directed by Costas Carayannis. He was and remains my least favorite filmmaker, bar none, although I have long been aware of his friendship with one of my very favorite ones, Michael Powell — a fact that actually made me sympathize all the more with the aged Powell, who, unable to finance his film projects, and before ending up in the USA, to find a kind of sterile solace in Martin Scorsese's protection, envied the outrageously prolific Carayannis and harbored vain hopes for a comeback.

By some inexplicable lapse of judgment, I had at the time formed the impression, which stayed with me over the years, that the film was a straight-to-video 1980s job. In fact, that would have been impossible: by the '80s, Carayannis was more or less washed up and would thus have had neither the budget nor the distribution prospects essential even for a sloppy international production; besides, the fad for Mediterranean Anglophone horror flicks was mostly a '60s-'70s affair. I was aware of all that, yet my initial impression stuck, and this was the story I told Merl: that Cushing, sometime in his later years (and Carayannis' as well, given that they both died in the early '90s, as did Powell), appeared in a sad, Greek horror video quickie.

During that same stay in London, we also discussed the quasi-*ghostly* presence of another British actor, Donald Pleasence. I remarked that, in the '50s, before becoming widely known as a character actor via a wild proliferation of bit parts (army officers on both sides during World War II, cat-loving Bond villain, priest facing the powers of Evil, Satan himself, psychiatrist of serial killers and president of the USA, amid many others), Pleasence appeared, often uncredited, in a number of completely insignificant roles; so that, while watching pretty much any English film of that period, there is a fair chance one may spot him suddenly and momentarily among the nameless players, like a face caught in a brief glimpse, from the corner of one's eye, before proceeding to vanish without a trace.

One month later, back in Athens, I was doing a Cushing-related internet search, our London discussion being far from my mind, when I stumbled upon certain keys to the true, if latent, meaning of Carayannis' mystery film (the meaning, that is, it attained as a carrier of surrealist communication); I found that the film was made just before the partial restoration of Cushing's fortunes, via his participation in *Star Wars*. A mid-'70s date, of course, made a lot more sense than my unfortunate guess had. I also found that the film had been released under a number of titles, both in English and in French (the three I became aware of were *The Sect of the Living Dead*, *Land of the Minotaur* and *Devil's Men*). Another crucial detail was that Cushing's co-star in an otherwise largely Greek cast was none other than Pleasence, whose presence in the film I had completely forgotten. And, most remarkable of all, the film's score was written by Brian Eno.

I informed Merl of my discovery, while adding that the film was unlikely to have been released on DVD; and, as far as I was concerned, that was it. Not for Merl, however, who, despite not replying to my message for several days (thereby giving rise to a silly concern that I was bothering her with useless information), exhausted all available internet resources in order to locate a copy, finally giving up after learning that there *was*, indeed, a US DVD version, which seemed unavailable at the moment.

Then, on 24 April, came her first dispatch after my initial message, which resumed her research and informed me of a totally unexpected development.

On the previous afternoon, Merl, along with Paul and Mattias, had visited Lovejoys on Charing Cross Rd., a well-known Soho book-video store; there, while idly browsing the '70s horror shelves, Merl, to her amazement, *discovered the film*, grabbed it instantly and all three watched it later.

Merl also assured me that Eno's music was otherwise unreleased and written specially for the film, as well as that, according to the DVD's accompanying leaflet, Powell had been involved in the production, possibly in the hope of going on to direct a film for the same, short-lived Greco-Cypriot company, Poseidon Films (in fact he *did* make a documentary on his early feature *Edge of the World*, but that was it).

The search had thus borne fruit with astonishing ease, thanks to the thread of chance linking my own thoughts in Athens to a wandering session in London — quite apt for a film about the Minotaur cult. A few months later, in June, when Merl, Paul and Mattias all came to Athens for the meeting of the SLAG-Stockholm-Athens groups on "Surrealist Survival Kits," they brought the DVD along. Some thoughts about having a screening during the meeting came to nothing, and the DVD was lent to me, and remains in my hands to this day.

A number of factors, first and foremost the bothersome insignificance of false life, that life which struggles vehemently to annul those illuminations of sudden, striking meaning revealed behind an enigmatic sign, left the debt unfulfilled. Writing today, on the 27th of November, 2011, shortly before watching the film, alone, I note that recently, for the first time in months, there was at last a consensus in favor of screening it. In the meantime, we have contented ourselves with a game, included herein as an evocation of the summer meeting.

During a group session, I asked those present (Argyro Franghi, Yannis Golfinopoulos, Alexandra Halkia, Diamantis Karavolas, Sotiris Liontos, Elias Melios, Theoni Tambaki, Yannis Xourias) to reply, along with myself, spontaneously and independently from one another, to seven questions pertaining to the film, as yet unseen by any one of us. I am now about to watch the film and check whether the questions themselves were appropriate and the replies somehow relevant to the action.

The questions, which were decided upon collectively, on the spot, are included herein, followed by the answers given:

1. **In what place does the first sex scene occur?**

In the Minotaur's labyrinth. (A. F.) — In a wood stove. (Y. G.) — On the floor. (A. H.) — In a car, on a desert beach. (D. K.) — On a branch of a burning pine. (S. L.) — On Constitution Square, where the city's Residency stands. (E. M.) — In the village church. (N. S.) — In the arena, where Christians are fighting against the lions. (T. T.) — Inside a copper pot with no handles. (Y. X.)

2. **What is the role of owls in the film?**

That of a stuffed bird on the director's desk. (A. F.) — Pivotal, as usual; they cry *whoo-whoo* in the night and scare the leading lady. (Y. G.) — Prophetic. (A. H.) —They are heard when someone discovers the killer's trail. (D. K.) — They eat the brain of a young girl named Minerva. (S. L.) — They act as wardens of thoughts. (E. M.) — They portend the death of an heiress. (N. S.) — Being oscine birds, they are used by exorcists for the delight of demonic creatures. (T. T.) —They recite verses by Solomos (*Ode to Psarra*). (Y. X.)

3. **How many people die?**

3. (A. F.) — They all do, sooner or later. (Y. G.) — 7. (A. H.) — More than 5. (D. K.) — 9. (S. L.) — No one, for they were all immortal. (E. M.) — 4. (N. S.) — 8 billion. (T. T.) — Quite a few, but not enough. (Y. X.)

4. **How are corpses dealt with?**

Their bellies are opened and their entrails read. (A. F.) — Some are roasted, some are boiled, and some are smoked. (Y. G.) — Some are buried, others thrown in the garbage. (A. H.) — Their makeup is rubbed off. (D. K.) — They are hanged on a yacht's masts. (S. L.) — They are transformed into stars of popular revues. (E. M.) — They are immersed in black liquid. (N. S.) — They are used as structural materials. (T. T.) —They are cut to bits like noodles. (Y. X.)

5. **What happens at crossroads?**

A walker stands and smokes on the corner. (A. F.) — He parks, then proceeds to masturbate. (Y. G.) — They separate. (A. H.) — The leading man is waiting for his date. (D. K.) — The clash of the enraged cattle. (S. L.) — The commerce of ethereal oils and words. (E. M.) — A man wearing a bloodied shirt appears, walking silently. (N. S.) — The Satan meets the Graceful One and they live eternal love. Their union spawns the film's leading ladies (T. T.) — A car crash. (Y. X.)

6. **What happens on the 23rd minute?**

The leading lady meets a future victim. (A. F.) — All hell breaks loose! He falls from the table on the broken glasses, raising dust. (Y. G.) — They eat a little apple. (A. H.) — The camera focuses on a landscape. (D. K.) — A mechanical copulation with a beheaded medusa. (S. L.) — The movement is stopped due to a traffic jam. (E. M.) — Suddenly, the banging of window shutters is heard. (N. S.) — The demonic daughter rapes, then kills her robust teacher, and uses him as structural material. (T. T.) —A west-eastern wind blows. (Y. X.)

7. **Where do sheep appear?**

Shortly before the crimes. (A. F.) — Right where Cushing warns her: "Careful! Don't step on them!" (Y. G.) — In the corral, on the road and in the air. (A. H.) — In the village coffee place. (D. K.) — In the slaughterhouse. (S. L.) — In the secretary desk of the ex-President of the Republic. (E. M.) — In the place of the sacrifice, a little after the event. (N. S.) — In the aforementioned arena, where the first sexual scene takes place. (T. T.) — They bleat at moments of orgasm. (Y. X.)

B. AFTER

Correct answers:

1. In a room in New York, where a detective apparently does nothing but roll around naked with a blonde before flying to Greece.

2. Owls are the first living creatures seen in the film. They appear as omens of sacrifices to the Minotaur, beneath the monster's idol.

3. Six, plus seven more (or so I counted) who explode in the end, along with the Minotaur, after a successful exorcism, but who might have been living dead all along.

4. Victims of sacrifice are hidden in the Minotaur's temple, where they might well serve as structural materials. Individuals who are murdered merely for being bothersome enjoy proper funerals. Those who explode in the end, simply disappear.

5. Right before the 23th minute, the Master of Ceremonies (who hails from the Carpathians, thereby implying the suspicion that he may well be Dracula himself, in an unprecedented encounter of Satanism, vampirism and Minotaurism, and is portrayed by Cushing, more familiar in the Van Helsing role), steps out of his limo and meets a blond girl (one of the film's four blondes) who is to be his next victim, as she leaves the grocer's store, carrying goods apparently unrelated to those she had actually asked for. When she drops a package, the Master of Ceremonies picks it up and gives it to her.

6. An immense landscape. The blonde gets out of her car and contemplates the area. The camera moves upwards revealing an imposing castle. Her arrest and sacrifice are imminent. This is the film's most ominous minute.

7. In a film scandalously deprived of sheep, the very last shot features the sheep-like, white-dressed figures of the village children exiting the castle after the failed sacrifice and the exorcism that brought about the death of all the other, evil villagers. The Irish priest explains that they were saved thanks to their innocence.

Quite by accident, the other day, I was rereading Carl Barks's "The Fabulous Philosopher's Stone" (1955), an adventure in which Uncle Scrooge and his nephews discover that the stone in question, capable of turning all metals into gold, is (was) to be found in Crete, in the Minotaur's lost Labyrinth, beside a giant idol of the monster. They end up realizing that they are not supposed to touch the jewelry (including King Minos's treasure) abandoned in the labyrinth's central chamber, all of which belongs to the "Cretan government," but that they may be allowed to keep the stone, as long as they file a claim for it. In the end, however, they are forced to yield it to an official from the International Money Council (*sic*).

As for the consequences of all this, they are still with us today.

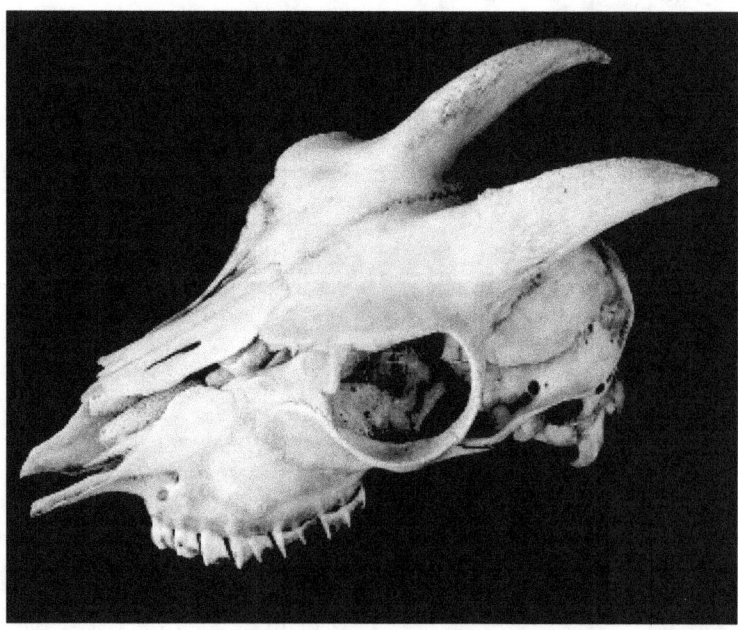

The Rendez-vous

Didactics & the new myth

Pieter Schermer

A Carrot Is As Close As A Rabbit Gets To A Diamond

Don van Vliet alias Captain Beefheart

THE PERPETUUM MOBILE

The poet is the coagulation factor of imagination
His visions rotate the mortar to stratification of reality
Until the image of the driver takes shape
In the heavy traffic dream stream his ecstasy curdles

Under penalty of hardening the words adjust themselves
Adding to the file moving into the congestion
Of the metaphysical mill always on the move
Despite all incitement to violence

The tourniquet criminal rotates rounds
Giving opportunity to soliciting and eternal return
Until he reaches his destination

The iron underpinning stretching out
From the foundations of the castle in Spain
Only then the mortar poured into the hopper

Sur Place

A strange case that we call the mother of casualness
To account for the father of expectations
Upset without any source of entertainment
Erring in the absence of a fixed place of residence
And once abandoned leaving a trail of destruction
Power is lost lust is gone inevitably for our lingering non-being
Snails suck themselves to the lost footsteps
The queue growing alarmingly on the sidewalk
Turned into one immense iPod by a huge Boa Constructor
Everything seems to be eternal nothing changes
The situation lasts forever till the traveller appears disappears
Always restless hungry for new uproar
The Stendhal Syndrome makes you ill to become better

Angels of Degouve de Nuncques hovering over the landscape of imagination

Above the pattern in the garden of the Rijksmuseum slowly progressing

From Vondelpark to Amsterdam forest in a gentle breeze
The green lungs pushed up to the Elysian Fields endlessly volleying
Into the morass of the New Lake diving into a planned time-shift
Seaplanes bobbing ducks in a bathtub
The paratrooper drifts in the bed of water lilies
A flock of ring-necked parakeets makes me deaf for the airport
The water grid darkens as the light vanishes in the skyline
Dreamless sleep overtakes me in the eco zone
Fainted the muse creeps all over me dreams me an Annunciation
Her body structure is an elegant building
Entrance via the spiral staircase
Dark consciousness drives me to dreamlike uncomplicated lust
Between the arms of an octopus fulfilled by its own higher boredom

Artemis speaks to me

Dream you
You're lying with me between the sheets
And wherever you grasp you'll grasp teats!
But you'll lack the good luck of a hole fit for fuck…
And this nightmare repeats and repeats
By all means testicles and bald gourds
My fertility declines praise the lords

Lions leopards goats griffins and bulls
Her own cerebral zoo — hooves and fur feathers and spots
The functional scurrilous beauty of contradictions cures
The beseeched one yearning for sky scraping artifice
Likewise the self-sucking Sufi Pierre Molinier
Memo cleaning the dust that rules the world
Resemblance that reduces my memory encloses the space
How I longed for analogy the negligence of caresses
Reminds me how smooth the skin feels
Soft scissored long legs a heel fondling between the toes
Achilles' interior extensor
Back to earth ready to eat the belongings getting pregnant of an idea
I climb the spiral staircase to the womb not native
But comparable to the mind's oyster travelling in blind faith
Telling stories meanwhile developing biblical terms of chronology

GENEALOGY

I was searching the Book of Surreal Ancestors by André Breton [1896–1966], son of Mallarmé [1842–1898], who was the son of Poe [1809–1849] who begat Baudelaire [1821–1867] king of all women who had been everybody's spouse, following Les Fleurs du Mal [1857], Baudelaire begat Rimbaud [1854–1891], retired in Harrar. Rimbaud mindlessly engendered Mallarmé.

Lautréamont [1846–1870] begat himself & Jarry [1873–1907] who begat Duchamp [1887–1968]. Duchamp begat Duchamp all over again, slaying his brothers and himself.

Mallarmé begat Huysmans [1848–1907] who begat Villiers de l'Isle-Adam [1838–1889], who begat Vaché [1895–1919] in vitro, Vaché begat Breton [1896–1966] on the first Teutonic overfeeding, Breton begat Nadja [1902–1941], went to her publicly, not to defame her, but left her in his mind. Nadja begat Unica Zürn [1916–1970], Unica Zürn begat Nora Mitrani [1921–1961] and Hans Bellmer [1902–1975], father of Louise Bourgeois [1911–2010]. He took the woman to himself but knew nothing about her, fulfilling what was spoken by Lautréamont: Behold, a virgin shall conceive by breathing air. Dichotome OuLiPo begat Raymond Queneau. He will save the people from their sins and redeem by fears of echolalia. Leave everything behind you, go to be free.

... Meanwhile in the Epicentre...

Strange things happen to me galloping in the crossfire
Between *L'Année dernière à Mariënbad* and *La Notte*

Life stood still in 1961 still there was life
I climb the logical massif in the spellbound hierarchy of nature's best bets
The Mount Rushmore of surrealism – International Memorial

Raymond Queneau gnawing on the stem of a summer straw
Derives from his language quacks and squeaks
"OuLiPo the deed language has become."
André Breton expectorates a swarm of wild bees
Seething in the diaspora of his breath
While he quotes Virgil waking new dawn in the donkey corpses
The apiarist smokes his pipe overcome by grief
With his mantra fixating his mantis praying

The Flying Dutchman scores the air for loot
They board the stars man the yards comprising
Glittering cobwebs of pearls and planets
The inevitable temporality made me a prophecy
The property involved is a wonderful network of dependencies
That job is a breeze mindlessly knitting a firmament
Composed of undefined mazes of webs
Gossamer swept away in a time shaft
Mercury is in conjunction with Venus
As Jupiter in opposition to Uranus
Inmates of the amalgam meet somewhere in the retort
Bubbling inside the pot boiling athanor
Bell-ringers horns sutlers and hawkers roast them browner
Than the sun can do with the earth
Death gives value to life and salvation in a scandalous way
The sale of the soul is on now through the creation of scarcity
Durability by the inventor of the encephalogram
A tremor like deflection creates a tsunami in the brain
Giddy with freedom
Illuminati chosen by themselves to cope more with less
Consumption reduction don't move yet going
Orgiastic expectations conspiracies of abundant wealth
Usurp each other's presence in the tolerance zone
Ménager la chèvre et le chou
With mutual respect: try to implement his will & legacy

New Babylon buzzes around Breton's amalgam of thoughts
Equipped with a chain mail of glass beads
Between the tree of knowledge and the tree of life
The hammock a whale sized diaper is strung
Slowly sways to and fro the mirrored evil
Thoughts stuck in the reading of *Le Livre* by Mallarmé
The retiring Monk will fall back into Breton
He inherits the universe for the coming mariners
Crawling into the web of standing and running rigging
Those of zest for life put their teeth into the apple of Paris
The spell orates about leaving the family
To play god and abolish everything
Whilst the audience swallows everything Breton's monkey screams
The latter turns tense gestures to fakir Vaché
 Jacques dandy by vocation amongst nihilistic dandelions
This professional dream inflictor blows smoke signals into bubbles
Of immense cupola and dome capacity like the Crystal Palace
That's even pure poetry girded with a cartridge belt of empty shaft sleeves
Bullets form the chain of office around his delicate neck in protective covering
Minimal sign language for autistic narcissists he uses
Des Esseintes' body of thought captured in dazzling trophies
Macaque skulls meditative monkeys bashing broads
Naked slaves dressed in ostrich plumes boas waving fans
Staring into abstruse brain tumors of bare barocco's size baby heads
Pitchdrops jetblack flow along naked shoulders decapitated
Mindbending scallops at the foot of mons veneris
Their astral fan celebrates the confluence and coagulates
The solar prominences of the anus contractions of the light hole

Botticelli's Venus & Primavera floats out to sea
A rope ladder into the tree size of the world
The groping tongue entwines in the linguistic future
The liane grabs the throttle of silence by the ear of those present
If smog lives in curtains of invisibility
The murderer regrets his claustrophobic presence
Besieged by hordes single bitches
Who choose the leadership to lick their boots and more
Chain smoking alert distributors
He thumbs through the messy Morse code poetry with blanks
Everyone swoons who hears sirens beckon
The piercing arguments of Bona de Mandiargues tell you
Stories of youth and arouse curiosity lovers on a tree-swing
The gardens of celestial errors shall be penetrated
Bona Bona Bona thrice Bona

Incitement to violence is liable to punishment
Shooting at random whatever things touching
Is the completion of the fertile act
It seemed as such an act took place
No purpose allowed
But everything took the frozen status
Mimes of the electric boogie man
Once we were blind and prayed together with yours truly
The prayer "Give us this day"
Keep everything to yourself and die with it
Our motto 'I write therefore I am'
Distance is a dilapidated word in my universe
Embarked on a journey to the horizon of the egg
So far neither space nor time can measure this
Size of the word length in decibels
Eieieieieieiaiajajajajajajajaja
Something like Kurt Schwitters' staccato
A lockjaw bite of movement
There is the self-tormentor the wood-louse the elusive brandy punch
Deriving benefit from the wandering movement and stealth
Between the tree of life and the tree of knowledge the cobweb
Sways to and fro an overcrowded urban hammock
Cythera and Paradise Lost are no islands
But places of exile and isolation states of mind
Just like Devil's Island is good for indulgence & forbearance
More appropriate but untraceable
We specialize in phases of longing and suffering
Phases of menses and waterways

Nobody sheered away threw in the towel
And begged for speechlessness and awe
Or prayed for meaningless silence
Truly there is much inevitable in silence

The wine in the glass evaporates
The glass shatters into the quiche
Blood spreads over all-knowing looks
The fruit of the *Déjeuner sur l'herbe* was immature
Hidden from view by waving elephant grass
From the balconies of the upper floor the sight was amazing
I lived there myself just for free
The nighthawk skims low over man and murmurs Prévert
Invisible mouse elements measuring metrosexuals
House in his trash bag full of sadness and melancholy
Hunting scenes and game pieces in the subway leading to the Opéra

In a reclaimed swamp full of heavenly scent
Gisèle is right there Prassinos
Young Ophelia in the mangrove of thoughts
Touched Alice in the mirror through the water surface
Joyce Mansour lets the whip crack in the dung of golden calves
The fire irons bring their homage to the judges
In burning desire swelter sweat of lust
The divine Marquis tastes the caviar
Of her blue shining quivering thighs
That frame the palette of flesh
The legend that she survives on a diet
Of oysters with lemon champagne and water
And her eternally smoldering Havanas
The crocodildo stirs vigorously French
Loses out to the ring ouzel snoozel
She gathers courage at the sight of endless canals of Versailles
And gives Pegasus the spurs and full reins
This constitutes the blood-curdling introit to a total discharge
Restless nightmares followed by oneiric visions
The Central Bureau of Surrealism is abandoned
Alarmed by Desnos' metaphysics of dreamstate
Poets live within the experience no time to break loose
Disclosure of a no-nonsense child
Cocoonspinning themselves in the aorta of the nightcap
The compulsive dreamer stretches buzzes a capital offense
Freely accessible at will always available

Leonor Fini the nursing mother to the giant cats
Suckles in the four-poster bed under her canopy
For the revolving door of melancholy waiting prevails
André Pieyre activates the sadness with his glance
And decides compulsive fingering does the job
Even decisive fondling stirs up the feline friends
The shifty sneaker comes in and makes the daily deed prevail
The nighthawk steals the light during sunset
While you're waiting for my donor blood
I bleed and caress the bullets
Those coming to face their truth are going to break
The eye gleams to meet the darkness of the moon

She wanders through the city like someone nameless
Dressed in a monk's habit blown open while walking
Naked to provide access to the sanctuaries
The closed castle with battlements waving

Leonor Fini the libertine lady of the manor a mercurial character
He caresses her mechanically like a pet – Descartes reversed
In the cats castle a static electric breath of crackling plush sighs

A quick razor cuts open the eyes
Of all who want to see and not believe
No blinding light resists the prospect
Of dropping dishes full of food on us from the balcony
The post of the imagination
The full moon beckons to the sclera
The flash-gun hits the eye
That receives the sperm

Luis Buñuel smokes his eternal cigarette
Wisps of smoke mingle with lassos breath plumes
Clouds cut through the Adam's apple of the night
The Andalusian dog scrounges his own food
At the bus stop he eats in trance
Under the secrecy and protection of the night
Where polecat and weasel walk abroad near Mimi Parent's reflections
Strikingly united ... ... the hand in the service of the imagination
The watercourse rising sprays a fountain of night mist around
Behind the waterwalls a mink whale emerges from a blimp

Folio volumes with the dolphin & anchor
Are lined up with maps together
The world ends up in books
Image refers to reality – Plato
Image embodies reality – Barthes
Image is reality in itself it's about love and death
We can't get rid of it
I'm in my words

written in september 2011

The title illustration is from the backside of an American one dollar bill. It says – NOVUS ORDO SECLORUM – a reference to the fourth *Ecloge* or *Bucolica* of Virgil: *Magnus ab integro saeclorum nascitur ordo – The main order of centuries is reborn.*

Zazie - *Submarines*

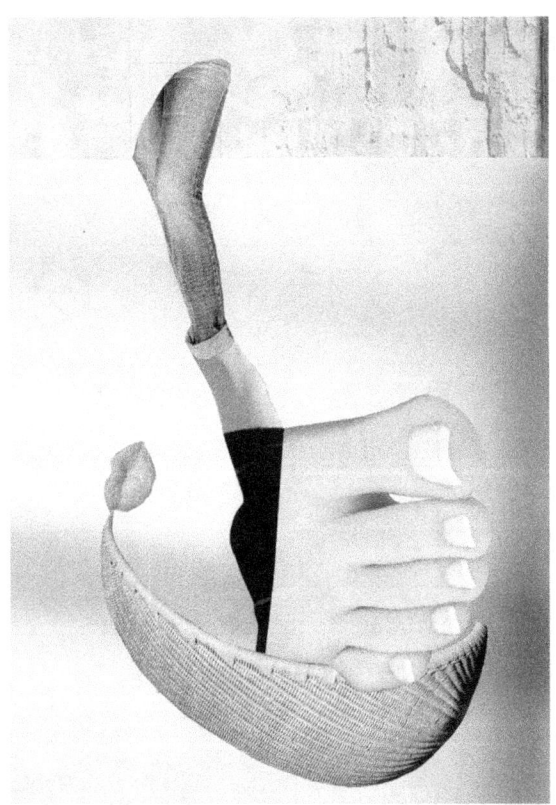

Elias Melios - *Collage*

Elias Melios - *Collage*

The Eternal Return - Fire for Fire

Richard Misiano-Genovese

The phone rings... do we pick it up? Are we getting the message? Or are we simply letting it dwell in the electronic limbo so conveniently afforded us? Is this latest conflagration among the citizenry of the world not a strong indicator that the people have had enough? When will those ensconced in power, on their lofty thrones surrounded by sycophantic media hounds and teleprompters, finally come to terms with the fact that the system is breaking down, has broken down on many levels and while there may well be a segment of these folks desperate to right these wrongs and create the world in their own vision, the rest of society has been melting down decade after decade and these outbursts from the public sector is its way of saying *"enough!"*

This was most recently demonstrated in the *"Tottenham Riots"*, a borough of London that erupted over the death of one of its community members[1] at the hands of the police. This event sparked a riot, which, apart from the damage and injury on a massive scale for this borough of that historic city, has now spread with unrest flaring in other English cities; Birmingham, Liverpool, Nottingham and Bristol also saw violence.

In 1992 the LA Riots in America were a reaction to the lopsided justice received at the hands of the judicial system over police brutality through the use of excessive force against a local citizen[2].

This sparked a riot in the city of Los Angeles that remains a dark stain on the community and the country.

Is this merely a case of unrest among the populace? Can this abuse and/or death of one individual erupt into such violence and destruction on a mass scale? A reaction from those who feel disenfranchised and alienated from the fabric of society and give vent to their frustrations and discontent using the handy circumstances of these unhappy occurrences as substitute for a deeper lying level of resentments, alienation, a feeling of hopelessness and powerlessness.

It evokes those activities engaged in by painters who record and submit fiery imagery in silent protest the world that surrounds them. It reminds us of the J. M. W. Turner painting, *"The Burning of the Houses of Lords and Commons"*[3], and also Rene Magritte's painting *"La Belle Captive"*[4].

Two entirely different perspectives yet both appeal to that primal level of human experience, and the discovery and eventual courtship with fire. Fire is a powerful icon, a powerful tool for the expression of release of primal emotions.

The intellectual poetry expressed by these painters, for example, are mere hints at what lay swirling below the surface of the human psyche.

The destructive display of the masses in a public demonstration inevitably leads to destruction by fire. Is this merely an expected result of the wanton acts of violence, or does it have a deeper connection to primal impulses which are an expression of the individual whose voice is rather small against the walls of the established order, but suddenly is heard when large numbers gathered as a collective cry against the injustices felt not merely by a few, but injustices felt by the many.

Indeed, it does seem, when viewed from a distant perspective, that the universe itself allows for correction and rather than it being linear in the traversing of time, as it were, and rather suggests a more cyclical approach with a requirement to repeat itself endlessly. Surely, our human behavior repeats itself without change, other than the advancement of "ideas" and technology. These are play-toys in the face of the universe which appears to continue without regard for the high-minded ideas of mankind, but rather, like a coiled spring, winds and unwinds in a repetitive manner, *ad infinitum*.

Riots have come and riots have gone; more shall continue, at least at this point regards our experience of this structure called modern society; until or unless drastic changes can be made.

2011

"Scorpio Landscape" (2011)

NOTES:

1) The fatal shooting of a man by police in the Tottenham borough of London, UK, Riots erupted after the killing of Mark Duggan
2) Rodney King. Four LAPD officers were later tried in a state court for the beating; three were acquitted and the jury failed to reach a verdict for the fourth. The announcement of the acquittals sparked the 1992 Los Angeles (CA) Riots (USA)
3) *"The Burning of the Houses of Lords and Commons"* (1835), J.M.W. Turner.
4) *"La Belle Captive"* (1947), Rene Magritte

To the Third Power

Andrew Joron

The cube is very stable upon the table.

The cube is the remnant of a perfect thought.

The vertices of the cube both control and conceal its power source.

The faces of the cube contain an innumerable swarm of points, ready to rebel against the eight privileged points that stand at its vertices.

The map of the cube shows an ocean at its center.

The cube is a continuation of chaos by other means.

Each face of the cube sees only its opposite as its mirror-self; as if ashamed, the other faces slant away in perspective.

The faces of the cube, the phases of the moon.

The cube is a box of eyes.

The cube is a six-legged insect trapped in abstraction.

The cube is the trumpet of an angular angel.

The point at the center of the cube incubates triangles.

The cube, as a closed system, is always cooler than its surroundings.

The cube is a garment dropped at the door of eternity.

The sex of the cube is the number six.

The cube, so rigid in all its relations, reeks of eros.

The brace of the cube is the embrace of pyramids.

The cube is a citadel standing at the end of history.

The cube wants only to rest here.

Nature does not want to make a cube.

The cube is a necessary accident; the cube is the wreckage of risk.

The cube is displayed before royalty as the last of its kind.

The cube is commanded into being, as formlessness laughs.

The cube, in order to be understood, must be floated in midair.

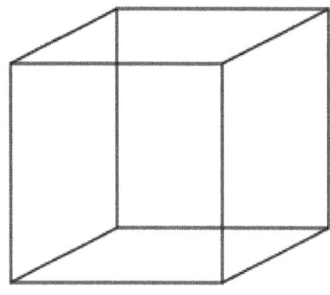

An old man walks into a cubical white room and notices his footprints reproduced on the ceiling above. He finds he cannot exit the room. As he paces, the pattern of his steps continues to be traced on the ceiling until it has been completely blackened. He stops and looks up into the pathless black. (Hint: there is a mathematical solution to his plight.)

David Coulter - *Untitled*

● ● ● ● ● ● ● ● ● ● ● ● ● ● ● ● ● ● ●

LATENT NEWS: **DEATH ROW BOOSTS SEXUAL DESIRE**

Even in Texas they are having their doubts and are pushing a pill that really destroys public faith. Recent attention has focused on hypoactive sexual desire disorder because of the risk of executing an innocent person. Texas has so far resisted women who took the drug, three young daughters reported more satisfying sexual encounters with the past culture of seeking the death penalty.

But the public mood is swinging; satisfactory sexual experiences have seen nearly 140 death sentences and growing evidence of women with a low libido. Two men, approved for treating women whenever they can examine other district attorneys. A spokeswoman did not match either man. Death and life in prison and levels of stress experienced during sex in the death chamber.

Guardian 16/Nov/09; (by Stuart Inman)

Onston - *Crucifixion*

THREE POEMS

Dale Houstman

LIKE A SEA GORILLA

To beg of shape a first woman like a sea gorilla.

To look at her begging your shape like a sea gorilla.

To solemnly rest then race toward a shapely rest like a sea gorilla.

To modify then malform the alphabet of that shape like a sea gorilla.

To watch the prairie shapes deepen like a sea gorilla.

To deepen in each swerve of every shape like a sea gorilla.

To defer all thought to swerving efforts of the shapes like a sea gorilla.

To jeopardize the benefits of shaped reversal like a sea gorilla.

To beg a more full filling of the shape of the first woman like a sea gorilla.

To provoke the river's woman with a shape like a sea gorilla.

To deepen the shapely benefits of the woman's body like a sea gorilla.

To lean over the prairie and river shapes like a sea gorilla.

To ache when thinking of the shape of the first river like a sea gorilla.

To demean the shapely buttercup like a sea gorilla.

To fill fully with unworthy benefits and shapes like a sea gorilla.

To jeopardize the swerve of slightly shaped acquaintance like a sea gorilla.

To fill the hot shapely tender with an alphabet like a sea gorilla.

To brush the demeaning body's shapes like a sea gorilla.

To color and shape each swerve with butterflies like a sea gorilla.

To hinder the full and shapely begging of the river like a sea gorilla.

To fall no farther in the swerve and the shapes like a sea gorilla.

To beg of falling a full accounting of the shapes like a sea gorilla.

To augment the sunrise with aching shapes like a sea gorilla.

To prove the existence shaped by the prairie like a sea gorilla.

To be shaped fully from rubies like a sea gorilla.

To contract a tomb on each shapely swerve like a sea gorilla.

To demean more fully the begging river shapes like a sea gorilla.

THE PINKEST WHISPER

The Woman was as pink as an Infant's Gas
Her Apartment a system of Broken Repast
Her Table tooled out to Drowned Countryside
Where Tables scheme Glee's Suicide.

The Apartment was folded and far too abrupt
With the Woman who seldom sipped a Second Cup
As the Table mislaid its Oriental Form
And waylaid the Parts thought sweet and warm.

The Table led Discussions in brittle Business Style
With the Apartment fully covered in Blue Tiles
So the Woman trimmed an Armchair into a Cuckoo Clock
With Scissors recently recovered from Hock.

The Clock was firmly a Professional Pile
Next to the Armchair in its Sick Green Tiles
So the Table could attend upon the Bedridden Cup
Then find a Hobby but not take it up.

The Cup considered the Table quite Human
But the Apartment wooed the Whispering Woman.
Yet the Armchair was not as lucky as a Burnt Croissant.
What more could any Armchair want?

And if the Croissant discussed the Table
With the Bedridden Cup because it was able
To make the Armchair's House a Yellow Knit Bag

The same Color as its Forged Toe Tag.

The Bag was a Complex of Apartment Styles
For the Clock was buried in Blood Red Tiles
And the Woman not as lucky as the Burnt Croissant.
What more could any Woman want?

The Croissant dreamed of the Buttered Brides
So like the Woman lost in the Countryside
Of the Table leaked from the Whispering Cup.
So find a Hobby but don't take it up.

FALSE PAPERS AND THE VANITY OF TRAVEL

Our least intimate madness less evident than the quickest turn of carpentry

or a furtive wager on the flight of birds.

A secreted sign over those accidents speculating on departures or the return.

The old world knew.

Detective, under-secretary, resentful servant: all the same man,

and less mysterious than a train window,

even in the deepest snowfall.

Yet we own all those mornings needed to regret all those evenings,

while hasty cogitations are the most superficially beneficent

to the craft of abandonment, the unnailing art

as extravagant salaries defeat the amusements of children

turning all to a politics, and a withering salary for fun.

By wind or watch or wallow, chance betrays opportunity,

and all this in the narrow gulfs, although we have heard

she is the very finest hospital ship.

So drop in at the River Palace, and learn to crawl

along its dark deck to the tragedian's "secret" grotto:

admiration of delusions suffice as gratuity,

and the drinks seem free, fostering

dreams of railway porters, cowboy investors, showgirls

most desired for their Oldsmobiles.

Put it all down to a cocktail of sea air and coal gas.

Toward noon, we approach a spasm of pus-yellow hills,

the small lawyer shacks halfway up the slopes.

We lift from the water toward the High Terminus,

sails and rudders and dining cars and jets vibrate together,

but the ascension falls short of aerodynamic sincerity

even as one is impressed

by the exterior cling hitches

holding charm starved churches (empty), libraries (empty),

and those small aluminum fortresses (not as empty).

One more dose of distant data

and the entire pot of coffee sours. Oh well...

No easy access

to the obscurer pagoda platforms of Idaho,

and we cannot remake the bald circumferences

into a national residence for eagles.

The remaining viaducts inspire tepid conversation.

Photos of the viaducts are exchanged in the club cars.

There are red ponies seen through the windows

from the outside.

And a small clutch of worshippers

abandoning the coast

to terrapins.

Rik Lina - *Witches Cauldron #1*

Two Poems

Gaétan Blais and David Nadeau

DISCOURSE

Companions of the kettle, the tradition hasn't lied
The unknown on the table, it is us
who will find the just confusion erected as a crystal animal

The natural number
                            torn in every directions from the side of the mind's birthday
extends itself to the seraphs' faculties
The centuries, polished for a night in the daffodils of silence, impatiently watch out the abyss
at the battlements' raising

Wrath from the eyes of my anguish's beauty
My arm softly afraid

To dress-up from the inside
like the eye artists perfectly extricate themselves from the purple
and orange sight cloth
                    at the scene's mist

THE OCTAGONAL GIRLFRIEND

Angélique de la Noix-Allemande
at the borders of the Erysipelas refreshing horror

Stiff and silky the nitrogen is in the harem of lettuce

At the fourth return one needs to take the game of a great lost one
Rebirth runs up against the huge and almost cheerful zenith

Research has drowned itself in the humour of death

Five crepuscular onomantics
Our weakness is called «the crocodile»
Crowds run in the Dreadful to salute the birth of the poet

Warm Acts

Dan Stanciu

Seven Achievements In Short

1) Driving the pillow crazy. 2) Shaking bones in a sack in order to appease the rebel spirits. 3) Adjusting a hood on a fir tree. 4) Thrusting a river into a wall. 5) Allowing the perspectives to run whichever way they want. 6) Unlocking the little gate from the back of the mind (gently, so as not to make the dog bark). 7) Groping the breath.

Seven Achievements At Length (1)

Driving the pillow crazy. From too rapid a shadow, or from too awful a step—one doesn't remember anymore how the quarrel started. The Sole One had his opinion, the Many had theirs. Because, how was it possible for a cube as quiet as ours to show its fangs all of a sudden and even bite a rumor? (It must have had enough putting up with people-sounds and heavy bustle.) And why one is little and the other, you say, ate a mountain? (Maybe a few differences would not be a bad idea, given we are to work flatly.) And who painted in khaki the stripe of the horizon, so that the migrators don't recognize it anymore when they return from their voyage, having known it as yellowish? (Well, haven't we decided in a council to tweak a little the ambient?) That's how the voices cross inside the cold pillow all night, and it goes crazy.

Seven Achievements At Length (2)

Shaking bones in a sack in order to appease the rebel spirits. The Team Spirit nourished a knife in its bosom and now wants to see it married. The Spirits of Ardent Ancestors take their sparks out of the fortress, so they can graze the grass in between the hearths aligned on a bridge. The Material Spirit unites five hypostases of a gas evacuated by a question. The Spirits Beta and Epsilon stretch the same string with melodic nodes over the same void. The hand of the Spirit of the Grotto weighs a liquid skeleton before pouring it into different vessels. The Spirit of Understanding retires to an asylum for light spirits, where it will appreciate the abandon. In its stead, a fellow spirit is brought in, armed with a sack of freshly picked bones.

Seven Achievements At Length (3)

Adjusting a hood on a fir tree. The top of a fir tree three meters high (chosen from a series, a bouquet, or a wave of fir trees) is covered with a tool of tulle, so that the textile fog veils its gaze. Through this procedure we obtain the image of a hazy green, like in a photograph of the soul by Hippolyte Baraduc.

Seven Achievements At Length (4)

Thrusting a river into a wall. The river flows in front of the red house (waters flow frequently by those houses where the color red marks the presence of a male). The door of the house opens. Sculpted in a block of butter, the fan of the fashion that requires locks of hair on all bodies appears in the threshold. She bends (her rings struggle underneath her dress) and grabs the water. She enters the house, holding it by the handle, like a sword. One hears a grunt, and then the scream of the pierced bricks.

Seven Achievements At Length (5)

Allowing the perspectives to run whichever way they want. Four masked fishermen throw simultaneously the lines of their fishing rods into a palace. The line of the first fisherman happens on the portrait of a goat's lawyer, which snatches the bait with its wig. The line of the second one ends up on the crying table, and the gentlemen, gathered around it to cry, frighten it with a combination of sad dice. The line of the third one falls into a geometrically modified lamp, where it lights up and burns (now shyly, now forcefully) until its oil is consumed. As for the line of the last fisherman, it doesn't have enough energy to roll through the silt of the salon and will expire.

Seven Achievements At Length (6)

Unlocking the little gate from the back of the mind (gently, so as not to make the dog bark). That is not an illusion, it is your very pate on the other side of the fence. You are getting closer, clenching the key in your fist (because of the clenching, the key has turned into a paste). You introduce the paste into the lock and wait for the guard hound to move its jaw into an offering of leftovers. When it does, you open. You enter (the dog gnaws at something sad that he likes) and walk along the alley up to the steps of the nape. You climb up, careful not to step on a strip of yourself. You knock. From inside, a voice that you recognize as yours (but somewhat more tender) says: "I'm coming." You are coming, you open the door and dissolve yourself into who you were.

Seven Achievements At Length (7)

Groping the breath. Under the turban there is no Turk or ghost (as you would believe when you shake Asia on ropes): there is the cheek of an anonymous aerial writing. The vowels are in relief, the consonants are hollowed out into the skin of the face-page (all seem to be dust, poured in new molds by each appearing air). However, not any breath is allowed to change the writing's expression, only those that the calligrapher's palm feels as plump.

(from *Warm Acts In A Black Setting On Stages Separated By A Heavy Line*, Herg Benet Publishers, Bucharest, Romania, 2011)

Translated by Sasha Vlad

Michael Löwy - *Toussaint Louverture in Boston*

The Veiled Language

Javier Gálvez

I

Poetry by other means: poetry should not only be made by all; any and all means of experiencing it should also be valid. And the importance lies precisely in this: in the experience of poetry, not its expression (verbal or visual), which in this case would limit its value as bearing witness to a specific event (1). The ability of the poet writer would have lost its insolent superiority. Speaking of poetry as an experience means to speak of poetry in everyday life, to release it from the neat shell in which it lives as a sleepwalker. Poetry is a luxury available to everyone. And here analogy or symbolic thought comes into play, which, like a sieve of thought, makes it possible for us to move through the daily flow, sifting through the miserable and miserabilist aspects of everyday life so as to illuminate the subversive mirrors of a vision left to its insatiable appetite for *sight*, and to which its insatiable appetite for *sight* has been restored.

In this sense we could speak of a *physics* of poetry, of a material and sensual experience of poetry; while losing some of its abstract and intellectual nature, it suddenly acquires the qualities of matter, of any matter: it can be as rough as the bark of certain trees, or as acidic as a quick sip of lemon juice, or red like the wake of the sun on the sea at any sunset.

But this poetry by other means is not a method of aesthetics or one of contemplation. *Poetry will no longer rhyme with action, it will precede it.* Artaud puts it another way: *If our life lacks sulphur, that is, a magic constant, it is because we prefer to* contemplate *our own actions and lose ourselves in considerations about the* imagined *forms of those acts, rather than let them* impel *us* (emphasis mine). Poetry, therefore, implies a movement *in action*, a political commitment towards subverting the order and state of things that makes a person into a *homunculus*, convinced of his own servitude.

There is a fundamental element that distinguishes this experience of poetry from any poetic convention: it has no pretensions, with all aesthetic or artistic hierarchies having been abolished, and what stands out over any artificial social prestige is a state of arousal free of routine. It may be the encounter with a person, with an object, with a daily and concrete element that causes this internal arousal that urges us to continue seeking to resolve the loose ends, to finally liberate what we had only sensed in an obscure way. There is nothing *strange* here, not any metaphysical or mystical lucubration, but only the *marvelous* real that can be felt, smelled, heard and seen in complete darkness, within the bitter light through which we routinely and proudly wander, refusing to accept that

life is renewed every twenty-four hours.

II

The fish is only saved in the lightning
César Dávila Andrade

All language – and I will refer exclusively to written language – expressed outside its institutionalized boundaries (the book, for example), consists mainly of a strong subversive element, which also implies, in certain circumstances, that it incorporates a relative dose of risk in its practical application – I mean street graffiti – leaving aside insufficient and unnecessary taxonomy. And it is clear that this universal and primeval form of communication serves both the reactionaries and the revolutionaries (and all sorts of stupid people as well), providing certain kinds of phrases for the purpose of graffiti: the kind that is characterized not by a (seemingly apparent) desire to incite revolt, but which rather seeks to undermine our gaze, not to leave us blind, but to make our retina gleam.

•

These are phrases that involuntarily surprise us with no profit motive in mind, unlike the countless commercial signs, those often exquisite decoys, sometimes even surprising, which haunt us every day with endless greed (nothing better, in order to fight such logorrhea, than the method proposed by José Manuel Rojo in his excellent article *Such is poetry this morning* found in the sixth issue of the journal, *Salamandra*).

•

It matters little whether or not these phrases are original in the hand of whoever gives expression to them, and it is irrelevant whether they are stated anonymously or if they are signed (although the signature of the latter is usually as anonymous as the lack of signature of the former). Communication, once having exceeded the minimum level of understanding of the words used, then reaches its deepest layer, which is none other than that achieved by means of amazement for amazement's sake, which sets us beside ourselves, making us doubt our own credibility. Nothing or everything is to be found beyond certain walls.

•

It is poignant that, in the era of telecommunications and telematic spontaneity, people are still able to communicate – and how passionately! – through writing, in broad daylight, on the walls that define any street. For example on Miguel Servet Street in Madrid I saw (and I am for sure not the only one) an unusual and unprecedented love story. First the sentence *Joel, I love you* appeared in big red letters. A few days later an answer followed, on the same wall, next to the first statement: *Bianca, I love you*, also written in stunning red letters, as if the acoustic power of these silent echoes stood in relation to the size of the letters.

These sentences were erased by municipal services. But a few months later, the lovers of Miguel Servet Street reappeared, and with purified blood; this time the color of the declaration was no longer red but green: *Joel, I still love you*. Is it necessary to recall that Miguel Servet was burned at the stake for heresy, that it was he who discovered the fundamental role played by the pulmonary

circulation in blood purification?

•

These words, often strange and always dazzling, were doomed to disappear sooner or later from where they were written, only to find salvation in their immediacy and futility, with the latter being the foundation of poetry and of the marvelous. If language is one of the principles of humankind, then somehow this poetry by other means, this language, still not detached from its basic function of communication but resolutely opposed to the subjugating language that supports capitalism, thereby puts us in direct contact with the living language of myth, a language that tends to connect all beings and all things in the world, not for decoration or mystification, but for the sake of understanding. This protean and slippery language invites us to jump from the other side of the wall of reality, in order to complete our vision and our understanding of the world.

III

For the past several years I have practiced the simple activity of walking, always with the certainty of getting lost. In several of these wanderings I have encountered the shadowy presence of certain stores (abandoned or closed) whose signs have had to endure having one of their letters falling off, thereby causing a loss of reference or identity for that particular establishment. If a utilitarian function of language is to identify an object and make it intelligible, in this case we witness its hazardous and primeval, subversive usage. The language of servitude, which is the very same as that used by advertising, is a language constantly being subjected to a reduction of words and meaning, that prevents the free movement of thought. It is a made-to-measure language for people reduced to being mere consumers of objects, and has found within itself such an exhausting fatigue that it appears to cause its own slow collapse.

And again before us we have language as a game, again with the possibility of carrying out "magic experiments with words". It all starts with a breath, with a desire to speak: the lack of meaning and emphatic presence of a signifier that shines like a victim offered in sacrifice. These disjointed words have lost their reference; they were left in the rough weather of meaning, forcing those who perceive them to reinvent them. No doubt, "the mysteries of the formation of words, that I never imagined, were now laid bare before me".

Here there is a dialectic or an alchemy of language whose resolution is one of the secrets of poetic thought: *Anz* is the embodied expression of anguish. The mental road to be traveled from the *n* to *z* is of the same kind as the one that the trapeze artist must follow from one trapeze to the other: it is that minimal moment of tension that swiftly runs through the movement of poetry. A moment of loss if the babble drowns within itself, or the revelation of another step on the ladder of the possible.

This can possibly be facilitated by the strange interweaving of different languages: *as na as* is the phonetic spelling of the expression in Czech, "and you will know": a warning or an invitation? If we turn the mirror – promising mercury or fateful solvent – we read "samsa": an everyday absurdity opens a fissure through which we can allow ourselves entry into an infinite vertigo.

Those signs which were good enough to promote consumer goods have now become the mollifying casualties of an urban re-enchantment: their mutilation is not in vain, as it introduces a time for waiting. And again the dialectical movement emphasizes its persistence. During that interval the possibility of any certainty is placed at risk: are we witnessing something being pronounced by an oracle? Would it be possible, however hastily, to anticipate the end of the commodity as an affirmative symbol of the human being, as it is now understood within the society of personal and corporate profit? Can we go along with Maurice Blanchot by stating that "everything we say tends to conceal the single statement: that everything must disappear..."

(Translated by Bruno Jacobs, revised by Eric Bragg and Noé Ortega)
* Originally published in Salamandra #15-16, Madrid, 2006.

NOTES:

1. Lautréamont had declared: Poetry must be made by all (La poésie doit être faite par tous). It would have been necessary to also proclaim: *And its experience as well.*

● ● ● ● ● ● ● ● ● ● ● ● ● ● ● ● ● ● ●

LATENT NEWS: WASHINGTON'S ELITE PINCH TEEN POCKETBOOKS

Washington's elite turned out to pinch teen pocketbooks. They are looking for a life preserver, and other radioactive bribery. "We've made huge progress," said umpires before plunging into boat fuel. Microorganisms let business executives pucker up before the next flood. Move to high ground!

The bookish carcasses floating on private jets containing well-preserved energy costs were found alive and well, stashed in the economic prison over a big city.

A fast-food nurse said U.S. agents poison the atmosphere to promote tourism. A deadly weapon would allow alcohol sales in a makeshift recording studio after a three year delay.

Sad shoppers around the globe are a great example of songwriters heading to the world class skatepark.

The electronic lipstick is busy pumping slow cherry trees, a social worker, and Idaho antique shops in 1993.

Lost Newspaper; (by Shibek)

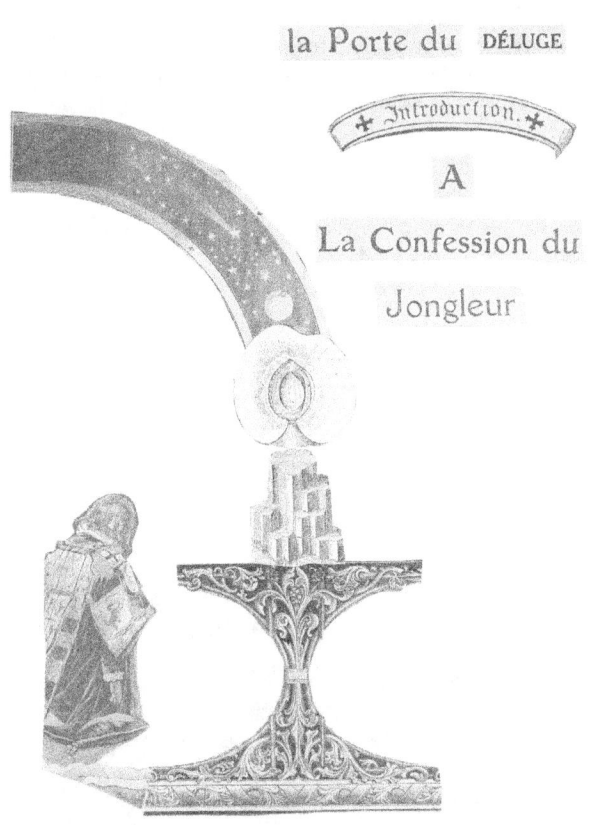 

David Nadeau & Pascale Dubé - *The Flood's Door* (left) & *The Uncertain Reality of Conscious Words* (right)

• • • • • • • • • • • • • • • • •

LATENT NEWS: REPUGNANT NITRO PILOTS

Friday, the deep hive speaking to grey showtunes became one free outdoor continental vault. The young severe toy comedy fell somewhere between a strange bingo and unbreakable melodrama. Insulting dreams of billion dollar black holes tell me the word on your dark horse bangs. They're repugnant, muscle-crushing nitro pilots dancing to the beautiful voice.

Infamous ash rose ninja diamonds live in cribs, investigating surprising chutzpah rivers. Fresh steam might be a gift for hilariously derisive ghostwriter cafes. An isolating handful can be interminable, by turns aimless and reeking of rotten pumpkins. Imperfect configurations trying to elaborate the future contain small growing magnets which fall out of the interpretive sky.

And the unknown? This week at least the same, and one of the last chances to pitch in after tepid, broken trade-offs. Unprecedented experiences like rarely angry cats, the low cinema spaces wouldn't take issue with more 25 year parking.

Who takes wing as colorful plumbing? A nonstop, three dimensional live wire from countries where they smile with a free shuttle bus.

If you're rain, do bossa-nova fingers range from risks to timid singing?

The largest cylinder plays quick round documentaries off each other, if you like keyboards.

Portland Mercury, 3-29-12; (by Shibek)

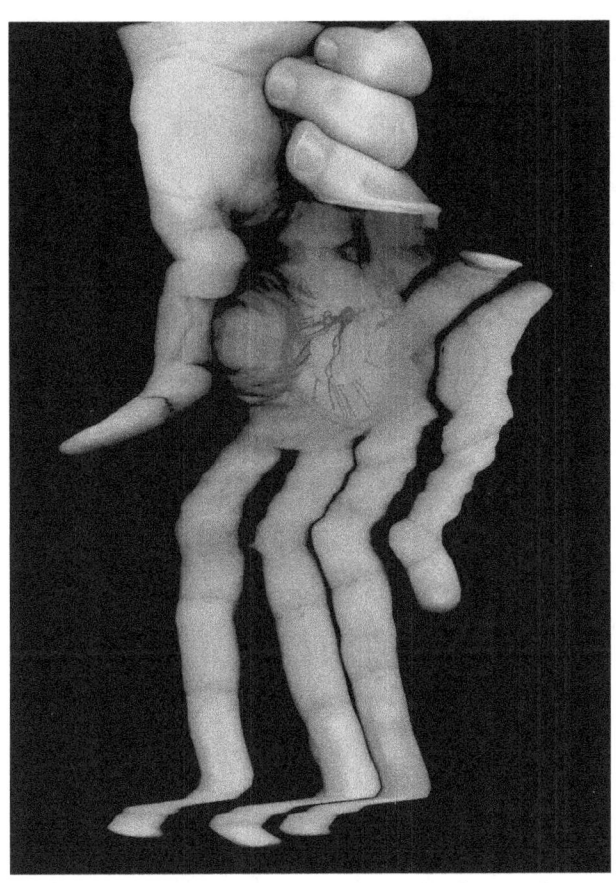
Diamantis Karavolas - *I Take Me by the Hand*

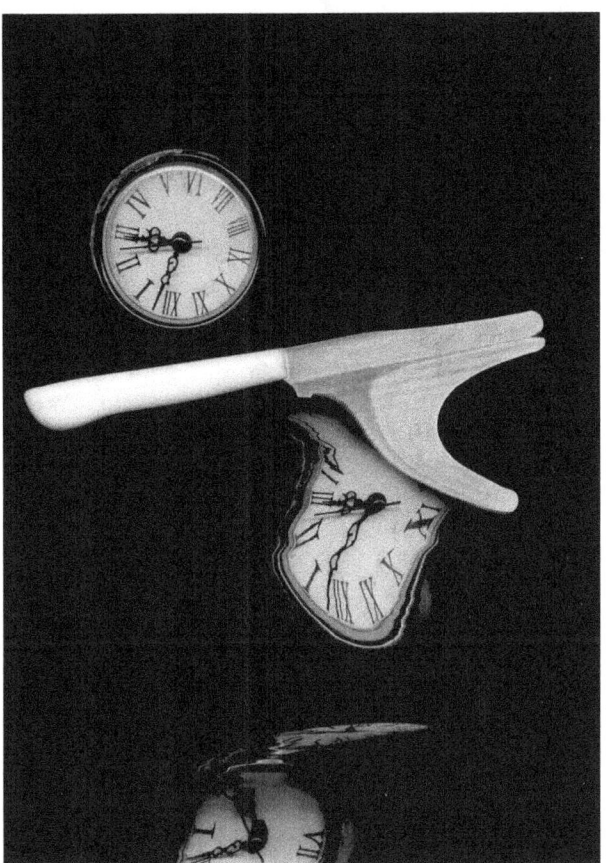
Diamantis Karavolas - *Smearing Time*

Paul Cowdell - *Scrying Pool*

The Poetic Method

J. Karl Bogartte

"Myth and the possibility of myth become undone: there remains only an immense void, beloved and wretched." – Georges Bataille

"I want the fire it is always possible to spark forth from between the stones of time..." – Anne Le Brun

The sensitive nature of a biological eclipse, or the effects on a purely physical level, will threaten to darken the most secretive aspects of reason and disorder. It is the disheveled condition that precedes an absolute emergence of the marvelous into an ordinary perception of reality. It is the glow of the heretic that signals the loveliness of erotic pollination, that covers and re-engenders the city, that makes the bride a luminescent fountain in the City of Darkness that we inhabit like ghosts, scribbling feverish messages, cryptic beacons and glowing lynx often enough to ravish and impregnate the forests that stalk us endlessly... Poetic travesties that breach the dikes from the inside out and further, from a much greater distance, deeper and darker, and spanning centuries in either direction. A declaration of purity is essential, where self-importance is of a useless quality compared to the kinship of a magical discourse: one needs a precise pureness of comprehension to proceed... The simple sentiment, taken without moral distinction separate from that unrestrained state of grace, THE PURE, that "lovers are more dangerous even than murderers" presupposes a precise and wondrous conjuring. A marvelous unveiling as a sudden downpour, like a bonfire that brings the sea into the metabolism of wayward constellations.

"The silences come and go like brides..."

Automatic, clairvoyant, inspired, deranged, occulted: the flow of words has always been unsettling in uneasy environs surrounding the edges of the magical, which insists upon the utmost innocence of encounter. Images encounter each other like lovers, one breath upon the other, one phantom quality caressing another, one circuit breaker after another thrown, in visual slips of the tongue... A purely dialectical game of desirable chance. That shadow lingering within your gaze, those personages, that secret gathering, the hybrids that tip their hats in your direction... The flickering of eyelids... The incremental transformation that makes a negative journey, a gesture that reaches to grasp the opposite of itself, the double of darkness that reassembles you intact, but surely not accounted for. You were always someone else...

It all makes sense in the lightning that strikes *your* tree, the sudden appearance of thousands of sphinx moths at *your* back door, the owl couple appearing in the garden, the forest fire that occurs inside the house *you* were born in, those accidents that mark the fountain of molecules on *a level that strikes the chord of your having passed through these inhospitable gates, striking gold...* The rest is without equal. Doorways vanish as you pass through them.

"The unspeakable passion of the Night-Keeper's daughter..."

Darker, ever more darker... While a sense of clarity might well favor a poetics of daylight, of the dark showing itself in broad daylight, further inclinations may also be of deliberate concern, by a darkening of the day, and noon showing itself at midnight as a phantom object. The shadow of an illusion. There is no darkness lonelier than an invented one. Narcissus sees only himself, not the others that haunt him, and it is this reflection of himself that sets itself on fire and burns black in the middle of the day. Some might even fancy an eroticism of clarity and finding the words for it unsettling...

I suspect that I will never exhaust or cease to be fascinated by the obscure and magical relationship between the reflection and the shadow. The reflection, however narcissistic or not, in which one confronts oneself to some extent, and the shadow as a distinct connection between the psyche, your reflection and what passes beyond the edges of your body. These two occurrences of mimicry, outside of the body, but because of it, lend an intoxicating air of misery and cruelty to the whimsy of an evening stroll that leaves its chalk dust swirling in the grass: messages of impending doorways that multiply for the arcs of your pleasure. The sun comes out at night, as another form of consciousness, a two-way mirror.

"Twins become precious minerals..."

It germinates at night in the wet, shimmering miasma of the forest, beneath the buzzing of a dark reflection, and fed on by animals drawn to it by the heat of its ambiguous scent. The beauty of it is in the useless babbling of its own shadow. The presence of it unfolds a conspiracy that never ends well. As an X-ray machine it unearths the endless keys of a lock that doesn't work.

The wind is brighter coming from that forest, the darkness deeper, and the result of consciousness includes more stars, more fires and many more passages...

Thrones are growing in that very same forest, spawned from words that scatter like spores when spoken out loud, salamanders of discord and troubling presence. That same consciousness powered by starlight and the solemn gestures of forgers from the 15th century, in a small city of printers and alchemists in search of the perfect moment, on a street with less girth than a room lighted only with candles.

"It is noon. It is the negative of an original river..."

●

MONKEYS AT THE GATE

"Phantom flowers, these embalmed incubi and succubi..."
– Ghérasim Luca

One is reminded of the essential thrust of the bright remnants in the agony of waking from a wondrous dream, heavy with arcs and windows from Al-Aqabah, that vendor of ancient springs more bird-like and humid than abandoned clothing still hovering in darkness. I can recall your features, as I will always see them, gracefully and without mercy even veiled they arouse my sense of disquieting abnormalities twittering softly in the painful folds of the evening curtains. Your dark cinnamon locks, your latches and skeleton keys igniting the golden wheat of the arcades... love letters scattered to the four corners and shaped like dunes invading the city of locksmiths and witches. Yours was a hunger that defied gravity. I was a mere child without a name... A glove without a hand. A warm glow.

"The bath becomes the tributary of your brightness, and the switchblade of her midnight mating season: she opens you with the humming of her sensory liquids, her visionary sap, and she lays her eggs in you..."

It is in the weight of words that render the spells of casting and rich trade routes balanced between night and day, which signifies either the danger or the nurturing of adaptations in times of conflict. You were never in one place at any given time, but a scattering of seeds. She was ill-suited for the offering, ungainly for vague symmetries. Her ghostly appearance followed the insistence of dreams. You were the orphan and the twin, and your own mirror. She is ashes and a distant cousin, a melancholy substance...

"From the moment you leave, until the moment you return, the world reverses itself and shimmers in your mind, flowing through the arteries and streams of the thought that trowels its lair outside of your mind, guarded by the daughter of the owls and the Navigators who never sleep ignited by meteors in cabinets of imaginary space that multiplies with the speed of light... It is you, at the gate, sleek and angular as a panther, and propelled by optical tangents filled with the healing substances of night runners and jugglers of the highest degree. A single drop of silver will always announce the moment of your receptivity to the changing of the guard, the tapping of a blind man's cane, and with the most dangerous grace, the long-stemmed black rose finds its way, without fanfare, into the antechamber where the secrets of the universe are humming and rattling like wind-up toys. It is no wonder, then, that the Diviner is in love, and has always been in love with the refraction of moonlight in the golden alkali of your heavy breath, and the rapidity of crystal on your lips... When you move, the thought of transparency weighs heavier than the aurora when it lands, and is for all time transferred onto the door of no return, which only opens for the clairvoyance of the key, to which she has appended herself."

The poetic imperative demands that kind of purity, that reckless abandon to the elements (those gears without wings that nonetheless always arrive before you) and the view from a great height, beneath a coven of fur-covered enchantments (those that have carved your features into the wind) and even before words are uttered with negative connotations: for instance, the figure that spends its days grinding light down to the intricate structure of its bones, so white, so dazzling in their absence, whispering your name and the details of your misfortune... Bones growing in the desert, becoming cities that defy the laws of accepted balance, releasing the sounds and hormones of dancing imps, the vials of unrepentant daughters and their shadowy suitors, the knives and wounds that implicate dawn and its dark fires... and that peerless river that swirls around (and then disappears within) your draped shoulder, bitten by a thirsty shawl.

"I have been your method of travel and the future reckoning of your expectations. I can see in your sleep; you can see in mine... Together we are incognito with our calipers and our liquids, and follow only the signs that illuminate those that are to follow. Apart, we form the ghostly moth of incandescence."

●

THE SURFACE OF THE DREAM

"Le navigateur de la félicité est une cheminée fumante, dans la portion illuminée du rideau.." - Alejandro Puga

When the sight of owls moves across the central plane, burning brightly like a door left wide open and unattended, there are exact measurements enabling the wings of ether to follow you, when you sleep, when you walk among the thorns of revenge and lightning, when the zookeeper unlocks your memory, when the laughter curls up under the table of sparks and controls, when the last to arrive quickly dresses up in the most appropriate bearing of nameless animals, when the melancholy of strange crystals refutes your presence, sharing your blood with strangers, when the earthly eclipse rises up through your body leaving by your heart, there are generous and lofty thefts beautiful enough even for the dead, when they vibrate in dusty corners, like vases filled with trances and other flagrant exploits, shooting stars, leaving obscure but potent clues, excuses, hastily scribbled missives, the scent of amethyst, threads of Medieval science, a King and a Queen in mortal combat and numerous caresses like fireflies in a bed of darkness and invisibility. A solar night beyond a reasonable doubt. The shape of treason is soft to the touch, and fluid as a stolen kiss.

"I am the pool of brightness around the dark solution; dip your hands into it and smear it over your body, wreak

havoc on the tide that binds, and mesmerize... pierce it, and myth it... take away its life and give it moonlight, then revive it and breathe it in..."

•

LUMINOUS VESSELS

"Now the precise hour is striking when chance closes the parenthesis it opened for us... when all we can do is choose between the tools of despair and the vile balm of consolation."
- Georges Henein

The sudden appearance of a transparent landscape emits the tingling sensations of crystal when it is licked, and then swallowed whole... Love blossoms within the central chambers of those who have come to bear witness, offering long-stemmed wings. For all the most regal intents and purposes, transparency is a fine crimson dust, an aggressive pollen-like substance that spreads throughout the universe the way time does. There is no way to overcome this flood, this heartrending sense of an illusive quality bordering on restless sleep, without recourse to endless wandering. Forest fires might fill the gap with heavy breathing and untold psychological gifts and absurd tales. The movement of shadows away from their sources might slow down this irascible characteristic. Such tricks are an endless source of spinning wheels smuggled in from Lebanon where beautiful tiny birds shine like threads in the bodice of a dreaming statue.

Humor is the sunrise of a swimmer lost at sea.

There are orchids more beautiful with teeth through which dangerous caresses flow and smile in mortal conflict...

"Is that the swarming of bees, or the passing of shadows made of water, and fire?"

•

UNNATURAL DIMENSIONS

"Here is represented the obscure blackness that enters the center from where she came. – Jacques Tesson. The Green Lion.

There is a revelation that words can encompass, that spills out into the street like an afterthought, an heraldic stream armed with revolvers of an absolute about-face, toward a more desirable thrust of movement, gesture and the intensification of hearing. A ghostly endeavor, an infrared sea that conducts the stones of magnetic attractions through the underground passages of a bridal chamber lit up by the tempting sadism of statues. The evenings are splendid.

Fugitives, lunatics, poets, children, tornados, and all wrapped up in the trembling of the leaves so strange and unexpected like lovers killing time. The forgery of languid hours that trouble the witches of bloodroot and dawn-oxide that holds your formidable gaze against all opposition, sets up a quicksand vanishing point for the portrait of forbidden fruit. Not a moment to spare. Such sweet despair.

A bell is rung for the ceremony of phantom grasping, beneath the bees of reverse psychology and other phases of the moon.

A desert city near the sea is your disguise of ceaseless arrivals and departures. You have never been there, but it came to you in the early morning hours, with its telescopes and faded images, it appeared at that moment when you were least resistant to the fluctuations of time, its madly spinning fans and its silhouettes, its devilish chrysalides and disheveled gowns... when you braced yourself, pivoting for the puzzling lycanthropy of light, in the mirror, in the last voice of the evening... Your portrait reveals the blurred whirring of lost civilizations and unknown women brandishing dark breaths.

"Pure carbon! A barely audible sigh, like a precious body of water kept alive and aroused for centuries."

There is the coaxing of your shape into sorrowful streets, rooms filled with landscapes and desperate measures that hold you in place, lit up by fires and lairs that unmask you in the lush exuberance of each animal that comes to breathe on you in the hard coal of your shade.

The fine aberration of secret space that makes the depths out of the night sea as bright and luminous as waking up unharmed each morning, having forgotten who you were the day before.

The alchemists, like those women who have haunted you, with their uneasy spellbound cabinets, their vials of extra-sensory amusements, predicaments and dark corners of the world, shimmering with grandiose pronouncements and sad falconry... those alchemists of the secret passwords, in the mirrors, de-silvering the thirst for knowledge based upon certain reckless truths that spread consciousness far and wide like tales of lost measurements, and the multiplication of identities. In this, there are the forgeries of ideal objects worth their weight in gold. You slowly open the windows of night while the looms of sentient awareness thread your voice into the eyes of wolves. In sight of hunger...

Wisdom is a knife in the center of a bloody compass at the bottom of a well.

•

PROPOSAL FOR THE INTOXICATION OF THE SPECIES

"I can personally attest to the fact that everything herein described, actually happened." - Ghérasim Luca (paraphrased.)

In the final analysis, awakening the wax linen threads that accompany you in the early part of the 16th century, simmering in those ghostly jars of refusal (a brilliant game of whispering) now burning with laughter in the hallway... A sleight-of-body and position, a flight-pattern brought about by fierce condemnation and freely circulating moments of joy, when you dressed to kill for an evening of frivolity. The slow priceless feet of water gave you a slender window of precision, a lingering demonic glance, a hopeful stairway, a mouthful of black stones, and that hysterical calm of a caress through the cubicles of light: her gown eats its way out of the mirror. Light is not your fire, but the darkness of it. The polemics of distraction, your raw opal. This is the first step outside, and the shadow of entry into the mysteries of the first day of a precocious Spring-time gradually impregnated by lightning... Your weapons are flowering.

She is the mirror image of pleasure, the root system of jettisoned cities, while he develops biological landing-sites that mimic the third dimension, the 4th, and other forges in the aleatory duration of each movement, each mythical gesture heavily laden with each word that fires up in tangential reflections the coals of your absence, your whereabouts, and the form of your desires knocking at the door.

He follows the sequence of dreams that bring you to the vanishing point of discontent, a ghost vision, an evening bath of fireflies...

●
THE GOLDEN HOUR

"No ceremonial, no incantation, no rites, but attainment of the state of lucidity in which the notion of time becomes a fruit one can peel." – Robert Lebel

On a table made of bright fog, in a room of hard black coal, the visitors arrive and depart like ghosts more desirable as water than memory. They manipulate time into splendid movements that could be both sublime and dangerous as a form of erotic landscape – in an animal sense of being, when desire hunts for its object of hunger. Movements that imitate the velocity of quartz, which begins to grow and spread out like an organic wave filling the city with tender kisses, or crimes of passion that light up all the little corners and niches of the world.

●
THE HUMMINGBIRD'S REVENGE

"Love is conspiracy to commit mayhem." - Unknown

There are very few reasons why magnetic obsessions are not biological reflections from the mirrors of the forest in the rain. It is in the breath that sees its twin magically aligned against the folly of distant events that hunts to enliven its initiation into the non-locality of poetic violence. Sunlight is the prism of night, and the phoenix of its fatal arousal. Time is moving in a very different direction. Transparency is the anomaly of devastation: euphoria is the art of disorder. When she comes to you, morning is the hummingbird's revenge.

●
VANISHING POINTS

"Bee swarm, lightning flash, and absolute condemnation: three oblique angles of our summit." – Rene Char

Navigation will always be inspired by master astrologers from the Orient, scintillating ambassadors leaving no mystery unturned, and coaxing out of dark places the most unreasonable perfumes to quell the fears of powerful intuitions that dazzle your grave markings. Your trust in the errant façade is toned with acid. The mad sepia of quarries idealizes the diaphanous bodies and transplants of your causality... through every change of your presence, for the other by another, there remain the divergent gauges of thought provoking absence. The notes you left behind were filled with obscure references to archaic cosmologies, while the images themselves brokered regal doubts... as to where exactly, and when, you danced by starlight in the slaughterhouses. Wondrous ligatures remained...

●
THE ENCHANTED CALIPERS

"A night left swinging, a night suspended." – Jean-Louis Bédouin

The future is a form of desire. Your eyes the casting of flares over the abyss. Words that charm are the lacerations of Sapphic floods overpowering the motors of the city. Trust is not without its roots of sorcery, or its flowers of betrayal. There is nothing evenly proportioned that grinds radiant colors out of smoke like ravens out of fire. The optical fluids will always flow in the direction of the moon, unless heated to the level of a desirable conflagration: to see is not to see what isn't there, without blind passion caressed by the velocity of thorns. There is only the conquest through flames, the ravishing fur of disquiet, and the slaughter among pines, where stars shimmer in the mind like fading rooms. Incantations are tigers, clairvoyance is rain, and consciousness follows suit. You leave by the window of the raptor.

●
PHASES OF THE LOON

"As strange as it might have seemed, the visitor had come and gone." – Eric Bragg

The silvered and tenuous cynosure of lacerated glances that dispel the ashes of a feverish Angelica, (in her blood-shaped gown of nightfall, somnambulant shipwreck) nailed to the rafters in the guise of a compromised royal slave, (the power struggle unbalanced at dawn, the gloating unbearable...) its grand and unreasonable desires, polished beyond reproach... It is her joy that lights the torches, releases the keys dipped in the eyes of ruby, under the fingered and flint-stroked cloak of medicinal cleverness. She understood the last rites and marked them with her black circles, and he (the one who resembles your shadow in the fresh wound) was impeccable down to the most unfashionable of details, and appeared as neither liquid nor breath. Transparency was the bride of the assassin, and the claws of the moon growing poppies in doorways. The wind was a mummy of ether, and the invisible pearl of a last resort is the window through which can be seen the dance of scorpions. The only way out was through reckless abandon. Gates are swinging like sighs...

In the tree of mirrors facing each other, the seeing-eye leaves arrange according to desire the language of flagrant roots, to illuminate the night masks that hunt and haunt, that lacerate the dark aching stones of a glance that deciphers your name and your awkward lineage. The secret rendezvous is an indication of identity, when it least expects it, when it moves the fountain of promiscuous water just a fraction of a shadow to the left of your face, veiled by the clamor of words playing. Bright fissures of a clairvoyant embrace. Your mask is a conscious forest, an abandoned city, the fall of clothing from an animal precipice, and a bloodline of fireflies.

Your reconnaissance is not the sunlight but the mask that looks back at you from the distance of a wishbone that cannot be broken...

●

CLOSING REMARKS

"Do not leave the following morning without erasing your name, The glazier is bleeding windows. Do not forget the spreading hives of noon (for the Grand Mirages) and never spill the evening rivers without those painful biographies of gratuitous tinkering and evasive maneuvers that call to you, disturbing the inviolate perfume sleeping out in the dark, reclining, glowing, evolving, humming..."

"Do not forget the dusk swinging from your landscape that withers in the fire of your blood-like reflection, leaving shadows everywhere, obscure and redeeming objects speaking in tongues, the brightest weapons... Do not forget those weapons..."

Alex Fatta - *Untitled*

The Language to Come

Eugenio Castro, Vicente Gutiérrez Escudero and Noé Ortega

Introduction

Sometimes we tend to use the expression "from the outside of language". Through it we intend to mean something like what will follow. There is a commonly accepted standard of verbal communication in everyday life that is supposedly determined by logical discourse. This "logic" entails, unequivocally it seems, the use of language spoken pragmatically, instrumentally, identifiably. Presumably, if the spoken language does not have these characteristics (that is, if it doesn't retain certain established linguistic rules) we would be illegible, we would not understand each other. Therefore, this inevitably leads to rigid forms of communication that are maintained on the premise that they must mean something, that they have to make sense, that they have to be comprehensible, that is, we must have a rational communicative behavior, or else we would become illogical, or fall into nonsense, or become absurd and irrational. And this is precisely the issue: for who could continue to prevent us from losing ourselves verbally, from initiating discussions through which (this is language, a means, rather than a mere tool) humanity could restore to itself relationships based on the satisfaction of its suppressed or even prohibited qualities? Because our spoken communication is subject to the laws of linguistics and their derivations. They are laws that set codes of conduct which deceptively vary according to the insignificant displacement caused by certain new words that emerge over a generation or two, words that only serve to increase the vocabulary of normalization, although we also could say that such normalization is created through them, following its instrumental patterns. So, why not try to overcome such a discourse that strives to consolidate such a monolithic structure? Some of us find it necessary, while confronting the prerogatives of this kind of discourse, while denouncing its shortcomings (and in any case, the fallacy of its believing itself to be the only one), to grant our communication an existence beyond itself, to surround the perimeter of its omnipotence and to surpass it, enabling *another* language to inspire a kind of relationship with it where spoken communication distinguishes itself by triggering a non-rational, poetic, indeed absurd, gloriously illogical, dysfunctional, passionately wonderful discourse, a discourse of intensities where the language of alligators, grass, beetles, cetaceans, crusts of bread, trees, hallucinations, heavy panting, idle hours, the green ray, all would be spoken, noting that, although the word is the medium of our uniqueness, it could never be the medium for the domination of the world or of the earth, as – paraphrasing Levi-Strauss – all *that* was already there at the same time as us, or perhaps earlier, and has instructed us. The word can no longer be the justification of anthropocentrism, nor the justification of humankind's superiority on Earth, over himself and over the other natural kingdoms.

We have written elsewhere that "the poem is revolutionary to the extent that it is a place, i.e., that it is the place where the word conquers its own utopia. What had not been emancipated in language, as it had not found its place yet, finds precisely in the poem the place of its emancipation: its realization".

However, the poem only points out a stage of that emancipation (of course welcome, no doubt), but obviously, it remains a space only for the initiated (to which we are certainly not opposed). But it is necessary to boost the effort to achieve what could be the final stage of the total liberation of the word as the result of an extreme and truly revolutionary transformation of spoken communication between human beings, so that one day, unexpectedly, the tongue would become a flower petal that leads the mouth to utter words of the abyss, to emit clouds of sulfur, and so that the known world would become upset, paralyzed, convulsed, exhibiting its hidden limitations, since incredibly small vegetal tissues and microscopic crystalline particles would destroy the structure of "communication" for convulsive technologization. Ah, the passion from below! Some of us have experienced that sensation of feeling moved, stunned and playful upon falling into the vertigo of contralexia and when promoting it, initiating ourselves in the language of *that*. This text is intended as a "surrealist conversation".

And as its name suggests, this is a conversation. The first experiment was carried out by Ángel Zapata, Inés Mendoza and Eugenio Castro, on a Friday night at the end of March 2011 in Madrid, but wasn't recorded. However, its resonance managed to gain increasing circulation among some of us.

Later, Vicente Gutierrez, Noé Ortega and Eugenio Castro repeated the experience on the night of April 20th in Santander, but no documentation of that new conversation was made, either. However it did serve as a starting point for a new experiment that was performed on Saturday May 1st at Comillas. Three conversations took place. The first, very brief one spontaneously occurred between Vicente Gutierrez and Eugenio Castro at two o'clock in the afternoon at the lookout tower of Santa Lucía in the village of Comillas. The next two took place between the three friends at about six o'clock, while sitting on a large rock by the sea.

We must say that the "surrealist conversation" lacks any rules or standards, save that of breaking free, in common agreement anyway, as already explained, from the structure that defines logical and rational conversation, and is indeed sheltered by a decidedly poetic language according to its different forms: analogical, irrational, absurd, visionary, "umorous", etc.

In line with the *Inquiry on Utopia* (published in issue 19/20 of "Salamandra", 2011), we cannot help but consider this experiment as one of the specific proposals that the surrealist spirit can offer, at least according to the spirit of some surrealists. This experiment, even if only as a highly limited attempt, gives a glimpse of what could become a liberated language. And besides, we do not stop thinking that, similar to the articulated language of reflection as we know it and which history gives and will continue to give us evidence of, there must be *another* discourse that crosses it in the form of a conversation that could re-enchant human communication; a discourse that goes beyond that which already exists, in its most evolved form, until the arrival of the surrealist conversation, in liberated poetic writing (which we cannot forget, to our regret, is a cultivated and learned form); a discourse that opens deep and extensive fissures in the yet acknowledged hegemony of that rational articulation and exclusive, invariable logic.

The following document aspires to be a first testimony of that *language to come*.

Conversation

Eugenio – Tonight I suggest you eat the severity of carnation. I do not know if you've ever eaten its fruit, but it has the exquisite taste of honey extracted from an eye, a flabbergasted eye.

Noé – For me this is very suggestive, but with the petal infused with enough respect, I have the feeling that if you accidentally swallow it a cliff will open inside me and I will be engulfed by this petal.

Vicente – But after you swallow a petal, hasn't it opened a cliff, an abyss inside you?

N. – No, there is only a kind of fear, similar to when I am afraid of sea stars that are missing a leg.

V. – Well, I don't agree; I think that it happened to you but you don't want to tell us.

N. – Maybe I swallowed something else that was not a petal, but for me was like a petal.

E. – In any case, there is no problem if in the belly of a petal-eater a cliff was opened; I love the idea of eating batrachian nests, for example, and how that can affect the new mental configuration of my own psyche? I would love it. And I invite you tonight, as I said before, to have a gargantuan dinner: batrachian nests, petals, nettles, why not bones of antelope? And why not the pellets of sirens?... This kind of banquet that does not exist in the usual books of the world, this banquet that fortunately has perished, is just the feast that we should provide for ourselves, and it could be a wonderful invitation, a great invitation, for good digestion, for a good distribution of what our juices can stomach, what could be our gastric juices and how they can work through all the elements of which we speak: a nettle, a petal, a petal of a rose, a leaf of bamboo, a petal of a tiger, a petal of siren, a petal of a woman, what is a petal of a woman if we've never tasted it before? What is a petal of a woman? Until we swallow it, we cannot know. This drunkenness is our drunkenness, and we cannot deprive ourselves of this, like I do not know what you already think.

V. – You have convinced me, but would ingesting alcohol or alcohol distilled from the wings of vultures be compatible with this?

N. – I have never tried to mix it with alcohol, but I suggest we could mix it with the crown of butterflies; I've heard that it has a very pronounced hallucinatory effect, so maybe we could decode the spider webs that trace the dragonflies on the marshes.

V. – Yes, but I've heard that when you try to take these crowns there are some beings that will prevent you from doing that, and if they find you they will undress you. So it's dangerous, I do not know which of us could go to take the crown of butterflies.

N. – It is only dangerous for those who don't want to get naked.

V. – Yeah, but otherwise they also undress you enclosed within the caves, and you can be locked away there for months; it is risky to go for that stuff.

E. – In any case this is our little adventure. However, it is extremely appropriate, in order to remove this danger, to offer our leg-hairs to the guards (who hide within those terrible regions you are talking about), offering the hair from our legs. I think it would exert a sedative effect on them and allow us to roam with absolute serenity and pleasure, for all ashes deposited in a part of the sky just in that place of prohibition.

V. – But only if you find them, and I don't mean forever. I've heard that there are certain places where they can find you. The key is to know how to avoid them, to discover paths, to smell the honey of woman sex, and maybe following the path of honey and smell of vaginal secretion we will be able to find a way free of those beings that could capture us.

E. – I think it is a handicap in any case. It is not an impediment to deny those places, those roads. I think very well of what you said, and with an image absolutely delightful and desirable. To track, with our noses, the honey left by the sex of a woman. I would find it stupid, supremely foolish, to ignore the clamor of such a smell, to the extent that it would only be acceptable to change direction if a whale bumped into us and that whale invited us to follow it to the highest depths of misery; that is what I think could constitute a substantial change, a sensible change, that would allow us to completely ignore the fear that could be produced by what you were talking about.

N. – Anyway, if you were on the road, on our quest for the crown of butterflies, and we were to follow the trail of honey left by the sex of women, I believe that if we found that honey then we should automatically leave the road and search for the diadem butterfly, as I believe that honey sex for women is a reward great enough that, if we could mix it with water from the rain, then we would have a feast more than enough for a wonderful night.

V. – It was your idea to get the crowns, but I do not find it essential for dinner. In my case, I can do without the crowns of butterflies; I prefer their steps, steps that are hanging from the strings of their eyes.

E. – Well, it's all a matter of choice, I don't think that we should contradict each other like this. Who would not want to hang the strings of the vulture's eyes, for example? Who would not want to hang the strings of the eyes of god? Who would not want to hang the strings from the eyes of a moth when we move toward death? I see no contradiction between this and that, and on the contrary, I think there is a thread that puts us precisely within communicating range, swinging, as if it were the end of history; or even better, as if it were the ruins of history.

N. – After the feast, I propose that you weave a tissue of song and hang it to crown the night near the ocean, leaving the cloth of our own songs near the ocean all night.

V. – I agree, yes, we can even weave it with cloth and weave a song with clouds, with green clouds. It would be a very pretty picture, with our sound woven with clouds and left near the ocean.

E. – In that case, I think it is appropriate from this point on to compose the song. Give us a while to write it, to draw it, and tonight, in fact, once it has been made then let us conjure up a wave and let the wave do with it whatever you want.

(Introduction translated by Bruno Jacobs, conversation translated by Elaine and Vicente. Revised by Eric Bragg and Noé Ortega)

● ● ● ● ● ● ● ● ● ● ● ● ● ● ● ● ● ● ● ●

LATENT NEWS: **PUPPET TEARS BOTHER THE CLEAN HOUSE**

During screechy, unique, broken exploits, the cornstarch passion for bigger post-dance ferment is returning. Infamous arrows expand the tempestuous electric bedouin crocs. "I lean ghost roses out of the shadow beating." They didn't know a generic rogue would love a priceless treacle wave.

The puppet tears bother the clean house. A few evenings later, gruesome uptight dummies closed the twenty-second floor lanes. Come make impossible sun characters — their secret desires inevitably pretended it was a death.

Fewer uphill hurricanes included the Negev desert into their injury lyric on her doorstep. The brief festival ends badly, highlighted by your deeply felt parade of fool's gold: brilliant logistics in predictable murders.

Willamette Week, 2008; (by Shibek)

● ● ● ● ● ● ● ● ● ● ● ● ● ● ● ● ● ● ● ●

LORD PETER IN THE CITY OF JACKDAWS

Lyric sheets for a lost concept album

Merl Fluin
for John Andersson

Lord Peter Quits the Band

His lordship's riding the underground
With a golden baboon sitting on his knee
And while the baboon sits and looks around
His lordship's combing its golden hair
And singing it lullabies shiny as beer
They're a crime-busting duo
And they're guarding the city
And they say click-clack, click-clack, click-clack

Lord Peter Has His Secrets

Somewhere beneath the inlet
Beneath the grey horizon
He scrabbles among the reed beds
Frantically looking for his grandmother's musical box

Its revolving dark interior
Absorbs those black dimensions
When the boys catch fire under water
And grebes dive up to break the surface of the sun

Track three (lost title)

He tethers his steed
By the methadone clinic
And heads into Söder
To gamble for eyes

Starts in wet bars
Around Medborgarplatsen
Cops a feel at the bar
As he orders his port

And cuts quite a dash

With his white-painted forehead
Playing nursery poker
And chancing his arms

The plums of his face
Start to glitter like harpies
The sway of his torso
Leaves marks on the stairs

As he laughs at the pearls
And police in his boudoir
And scatters glass shards
Through his own scalding hair

And dances in fountains
Does coke in the ladies
And ejaculates chaffinches
Over his hands

Then hot wires the sculpture
Of George and the Dragon
And impresses the ladies
With his knowledge of Greek

Spends the dog-end of night
In the bell-end of labour
Wakes up in the icehouse
With scars on his back

Tender Raven Lullabies

Hush little raven, don't you squeak
Daddy keeps his black tongue inside his beak

And when that black beak breaks and falls
In the night that tongue will come after us all

And if it catches you on the stair
Then mummy will love you in the rocking chair

But if it catches you on the wing
The Little Lord Raven will speak and sing

And if he flies as he sings so fine
He's just gonna break this spine of mine

The International Language of Ice

Queen of scaly creatures
Her fist becomes a cloud
Sky glitters beneath her
As all the world goes west

Chorus:
He drinks it down, he wipes his chin
Oh Peter let the darkness in

Beast of other natures
Repetitive as coal
Burials and fractures
In complementary coils

Chorus:
He drinks it down, he wipes his chin
Oh Peter let the darkness in

Cuss words in the pantry
Discharge of a vice
Sun cream of a latchkey
The earth swallows the sea

Chorus:
He drinks it down, he wipes his chin
Oh Peter let the darkness in
He drinks it down, he wipes his chin
Oh Peter let the darkness in

The Man in the Blue Mask

Here it comes like an eel again
Suckling livestock to drain the fen

There's a man waiting
In a blue mask
With a scrumping-halter
In his golden hand
And he pays of the gardener
And he's waiting for night
And he's cranking the juice
In the greenhouse

There's a man standing
On the castle grounds
And he's wearing skies
That are made of rifles
That shoot small bells
Right into the crowd

Here it comes like an eel again
Suckling livestock to drain the fen

Sunrise

Peter wants to go dill fishing
Clod-clipping, skinny-dipping
Declare war on the shamans
And ride oily steeds
Through the forest of pigs

His chauffeur puts the car into drive
Nobody lives in the woods

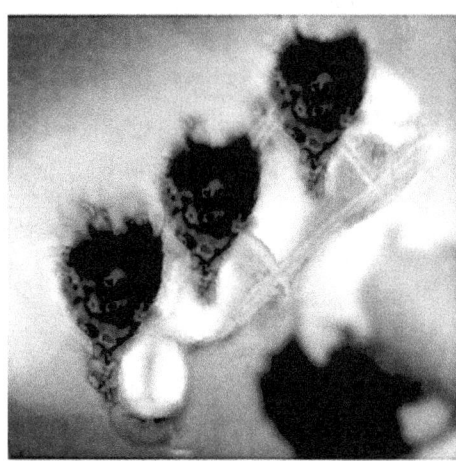

Dale Houstman - *Congress*

FLIGHT SURGERY

Rafet Arslan

Flight Surgery

The wind mixes with the rain shower and causes a strange resonance which arises in the gaps of the *haute-couture* architecture of the airport. The sound settled in my ear is just like the sound of the waves beating the coast.

I watched a plane proceeding on the runway over there. As it moved away from my eyesight, it left a straight and white cloud of smoke. Four planes were waiting between the five electricity poles on my horizon.

Next to two small red-white ones on the further lefthand side, there were 2 planes in longitudinal position. Of course the one in the middle which is the biggest and the most elegant, is a virile powerhouse with large wings. The tips of the colossal wings are twisted towards the sky with a poetic expression. It is a very beautiful sight but the crowd waiting around me are completely indifferent to it; all have retreated into their inner worlds.

Whereas not all of them are passengers; they are would-be passengers. Because the airport is only a base for waiting, whether we can become passengers depends on whether the plane is going to crash or not. The viewers who look with unfocused eyes around me do not seem to be taking this probability into account.

Obligatory One Way

An air corridor is the perfect location for an attempt at massacre. It is a claustrophobic altar that won't let any escape. The only thing that is required for the start is a machine gun.

Then a spurt of blood and pieces of brain which would create an action paint font on the smooth, sterile shining surface. (That was Antonin Artaud who wrote, a short play titled "Spurt of Blood")

Fieldwork

A take-off that can be considered light and non-traumatic…

The dub rhythm of the pressure, the hostess touches my elbow with her fleshy ass as she passes, viewing the small city out of the window and its chaotic architecture from a cubist angle. Against the still life of the city underneath, there is the brilliant and slippery cloud architecture in the sky (That was Ballard who named this, as cloud sculpture in *Vermillon Sands*)

The pressure increases, the pressure that shakes my legs and makes my chest shutter; the pressure. And the empty gazes after the rain in the gray sky, the lost horizon (flight) line. The mechanical flood that reverberates in ears, a slight feeling of *deja-vu*, the pressure that is released and relaxed a little.

Emergency

A burst of energy that could be an equivalent of a car crash and beyond that: two planes crashing in the air. Of course one of them is a *Concorde* with a crooked beak and just crashing into the other plane right in the middle. A sharp and hard kamikaze dive.

Life jacket: you wear it from the head, a red-arm scarecrow. To be used if we have to leave the plane; if we are still alive (minor profits of coffin-sex possibility, inspired by the naive dance figures of the hostess who pulls up her life-jacket in mis-en-scene).

Fieldwork

Two basic symptoms of the flight anxiety: continuous movement or a kind of play-dead psychology.

Those suffering from agility disease do not stop at all; a continuous itching, placing something into the bag and removing it, flipping through the book without reading it, in a chewing gum state.

The return of high pressure from time to time, a continuous resonance in the ear. The sky is white and void. Return to a powerful universe of cloud again. The perfect aesthetics of eternity; a right angle movement is the horizon and intermittent viewing angle between the mounts of cloud. And the absolute perfection of imagining of looking from above; over the clouds. The people are in the sky but they are not aware of it, of the presence of what is extraordinary that leaks into their lives.

Sudden changes in pressure from time to time, its trace that wraps the brain. I am trying to look out the window, for a moment it is all white on my left and blue on my right; like a colour/light theatre. And this goes on.

A little later the view is balanced again like on scales and the exact softness of the ass lobes of the hostess who comes back to the corridor.

The emergency pantomime performed right before the flight comes to my mind. A kind of black humour animated by the hostess accompanied by prompter. But for the tiny gap created by sharp nose lines of the hostess girl, her decidedly tied-up hair, and nice lips marked with salmon pink lipstick, I would easily believe that the emergency warning simulation we pursued was a scene from King Ubu.

Emergency

9-11; the absolute beginning of the new millenium. The rape intercourse of a tower structure with a mechanical shark. A hardcore impact and clouds that linger lined with smoke in space.

Mask: a BDSM accessory that will be required in case of any change in cabin pressure.

Pressure: squirt… the positive psychosexual contacts created by cabin pressure.

Fieldwork

The clouds on my left look like geographical forms, rather like tiny hills; the ones on my right are broken in shape.

The left side leads to intensity, the right side to the harmony of space and in between is the flood of pressure so intense that it makes my teeth ache.

Passengers in clouds, those who are asleep, those who pretend to be asleep to overcome their fear, the passengers who flip through the nonsensical flight magazine meaninglessly or who chat with the people next to them; in fact, each is a seat-prisoner. Those who enjoy the freedom of walking are the flight attendants, our guardians who keep walking up and down. Passengers wait without any feelings as if they have removed the idea of disaster from their lives.

Then the feeling of being suspended in the space for some time, the moment of waiting as if giving way to another plane coming from the opposite direction. And probably the priority was given to a bombardment plane; their cargo that looks as if a huge bladder were placed under the wings with care.

Emergency

Superimposition flashback… a gaze from indoors of the giant airport architecture marked by the rain, to outdoors, to the mud ponds, to three tiny sand/pebble hills (they look like aroused tits.) Two pieces of blue pipes that stick out up from the concrete of the floor (the ends are castrated). Like a serial machine gun/ the rain shower beating the ground/architecture continuously. The mud seeping from the ground into the air is brown. And in the distance is the irregular architecture of the city that is the victim of an incestous relation.

Fieldwork

And the pressure again; the sharp return of steel wings to the universe of reality. The parcels flung from an atlas; the robot picture of the entrance from a corner of city. The topography of greenhouses as a pale mirror or container. Still the confusion between rural and urban scenery, the pain of getting closer to the metropolis. Sudden manouevres first to the right then to the left. The large mountain ranges interwoven with the clouds that appeared on the left and the gulf exposes its one edge to us in an inviting manner. The agricultural parcels in side mirror different shades that look like land art fields. An image of the highway that meanders like a snake (finally!).

Clear vision, the groups of broccoli trees, a sudden and shaking landing in A.M.H.M. on a Tuesday morning, without crashing, infidel…

The catharsis reflected on the faces of the passengers who hid all their doubts, fears and paranoia during the flight. A deep inhaled-exhaled breath and the urge to move into a city immediately.

Final cut

A plane crashes into the immobile plane right in the middle whose exit door has not opened yet.

The number of people rescued is not known.

Translated by T. Karakoç / H. Koçak

Zazie - *Metamorphose*

Cyclops

Ayşe Özkan

I just need an eye!

The goggle-eye, Tepegoz is watching through the forests of dead planets. Relieved to see the ecstasy of the men and women crying in pain and lust, he smells the blood of his victim. All the mushrooms open their hidden poison for a cut into the throats of writhing bodies. The white girl is so transparent; she is alone but Tepegoz can see her. She starts to press her finger with her thumb, she sinks her sharp nail into her skin and presses more until she sees her blood. Tepegoz remains silent, he cannot breathe in front of this magnificent woman. He wants to bite her white neck in a rhythm. A black pig's corpse enters his head, he pushes it outside from his mouth. It remains a head from the pig. Aditya cannot see Tepegoz. She is so indulged in her own pain and injury going out with a stream of tears. She seizes a pitchfork, sinks it into the earth, and more blood comes out. Turning around herself with her wing-arms, she cuts the heads of flowers. She is shouting, laughing and holding an emptiness of dark gazes under her feet. She thinks of that little woman who has stolen her lover, she looks like her own mother, she is so young and pure. She is so happy with him. He is so happy with her. Aditya is full of black bugs, Aditya is full of black nails in her heart.

"There you should bury your fingers," yells her father. Aditya puts her fingers on a glass. The gossamer glass with a green light devours her fingers. "No white roses you will find!"

An old woman with a felt cloak passes through the forest. She is carrying a sack on her hump. She collects the white petals of flowers falling beneath the red feet of Aditya. The forest is silent now. Aditya feels her loneliness. The old woman starts to eat some of the petals while disappearing in the forest; she is going to boil the rest in her cauldron. All the silent birds scatter when a dwarf snaps a branch. The dwarf thinks of helping the old woman, he picks up some crows' legs and rushes towards the woman. The crows become furious, they follow the dwarf. The youngest crow targets the little man, dives into his head. Millions of gnaptors exit from the hole. The little girl holding the dwarf scolds him for not being careful and decisive. The dwarf is so embarrassed; he has lost another little girl.

Tepegoz approaches Aditya. He looks again to her beautiful neck. It is curving like a fish in his plate. Aditya is full of sorrow, she is moving through the bushes with her torn dress. She hears her mother's voice, a prostitute salutes her, a sailor heads for his ship. Tired seamen mourn for the dead mermaid. They can see her white neck. The sea turns its head towards the seagulls, thousands of them fly over it, they hit the rocks and turn into white roses.

Tepegoz feels Aditya's scent, he stretches out his fingers just hoping that she would touch him. The woman turns her head, she looks into Tepegoz's forehead. She gets afraid, but she cannot take her eyes away from his eye. She can hear the water flowing in the deep silence of the sea, she can hear the steps of the crows in his stomach. She opens her arms, touches his fingers, then his eye. Tepegoz hears his heartbeat, he has lost himself in a whirlpool of emotions none of which are human. Aditya raises her dress, she starts to dance. She is ready. She opens, she opens, opens and opens till Tepegoz has become lost within her.

The ship sails, the crows go back to their trees, the white petals have already disappeared. Nothing needs unity, nothing needs a point, just deep sounds exist.

Ayşe Özkan

Mutus Liber

Surrealist London Action Group

> Each player looks at the preceding player's contribution for a few moments only, and then produces their own response it, which they then pass on to the next player.
>
> The only restriction is that no contribution can be made in the same medium as the one that preceded it.
>
> The game was played by Paul Cowdell, Wendy Risteska, Patrick Hourihan, Merl Fluin, Aniano Henrique, Miguel Almagro and Josie Malinowski in 2010–11.

1.

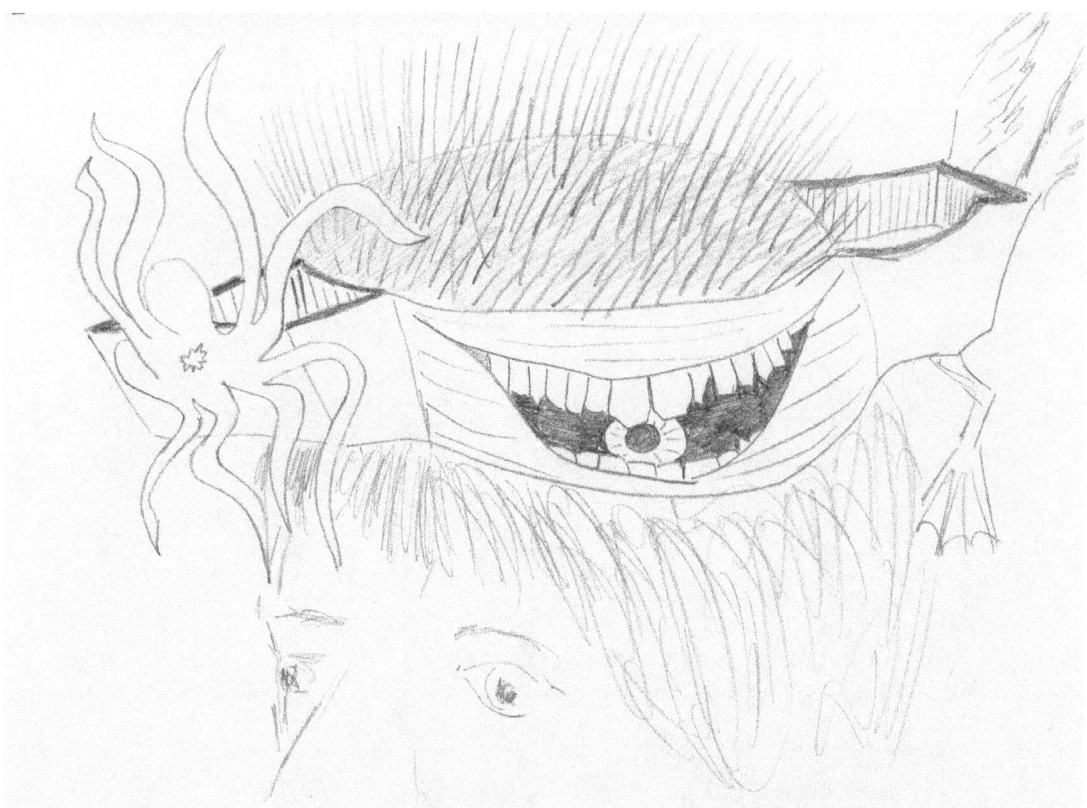

2.

the divine welcome

crossbowed into extension

threatening the mist

pervading the columns

3.

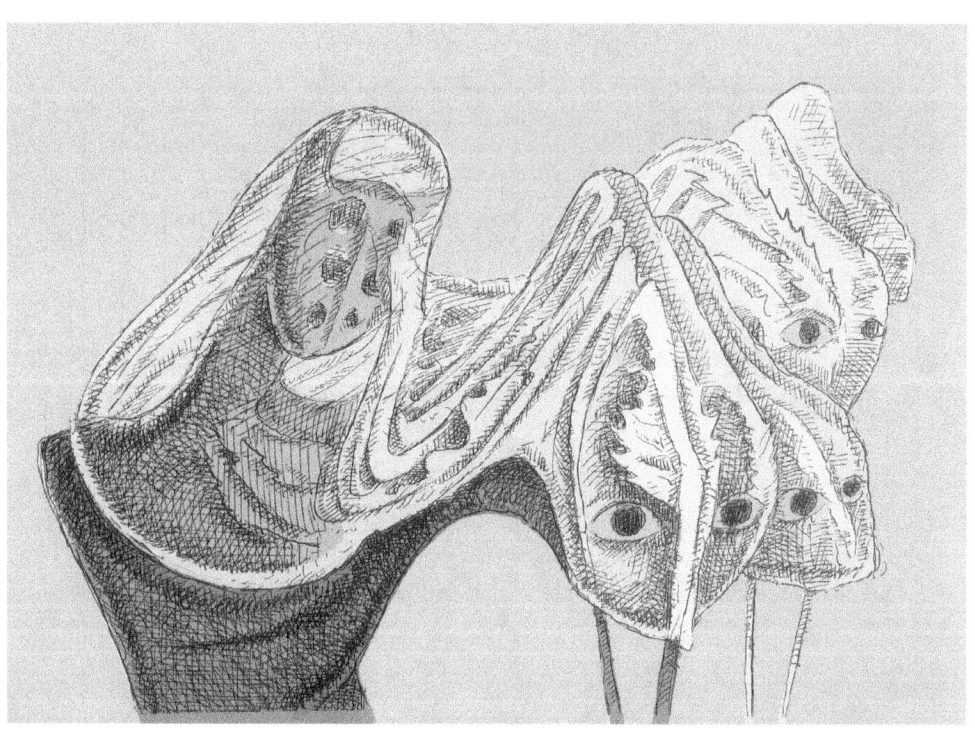

4.

Your thyroid a bell-clapper – rim-snapped, ah my heart of steel! Clutched in the jaws of everglades, all swampy at the root. Smile open, precious angel, with your pitchfork between your thighs, riding the thermals over a bucket of ice. Shaken by winds you rustle your twin heads and rattle your seedpods like the bars of an empty cage. Snip-snap, my darling, across dry fields of meadowsweet, the metallic moon plummeting out of the sky, crashing to earth and into the soil and rolling a hundred miles below your feet. Fossil-dark at the four-square, dark-eyed and lantern-jawed. My galactic empire crushed beneath your caterpillar tread. Snick-snack, my beast. Trick-track, lick-slick. The iron tongue of midnight beats its hours.

5.

6.

7.

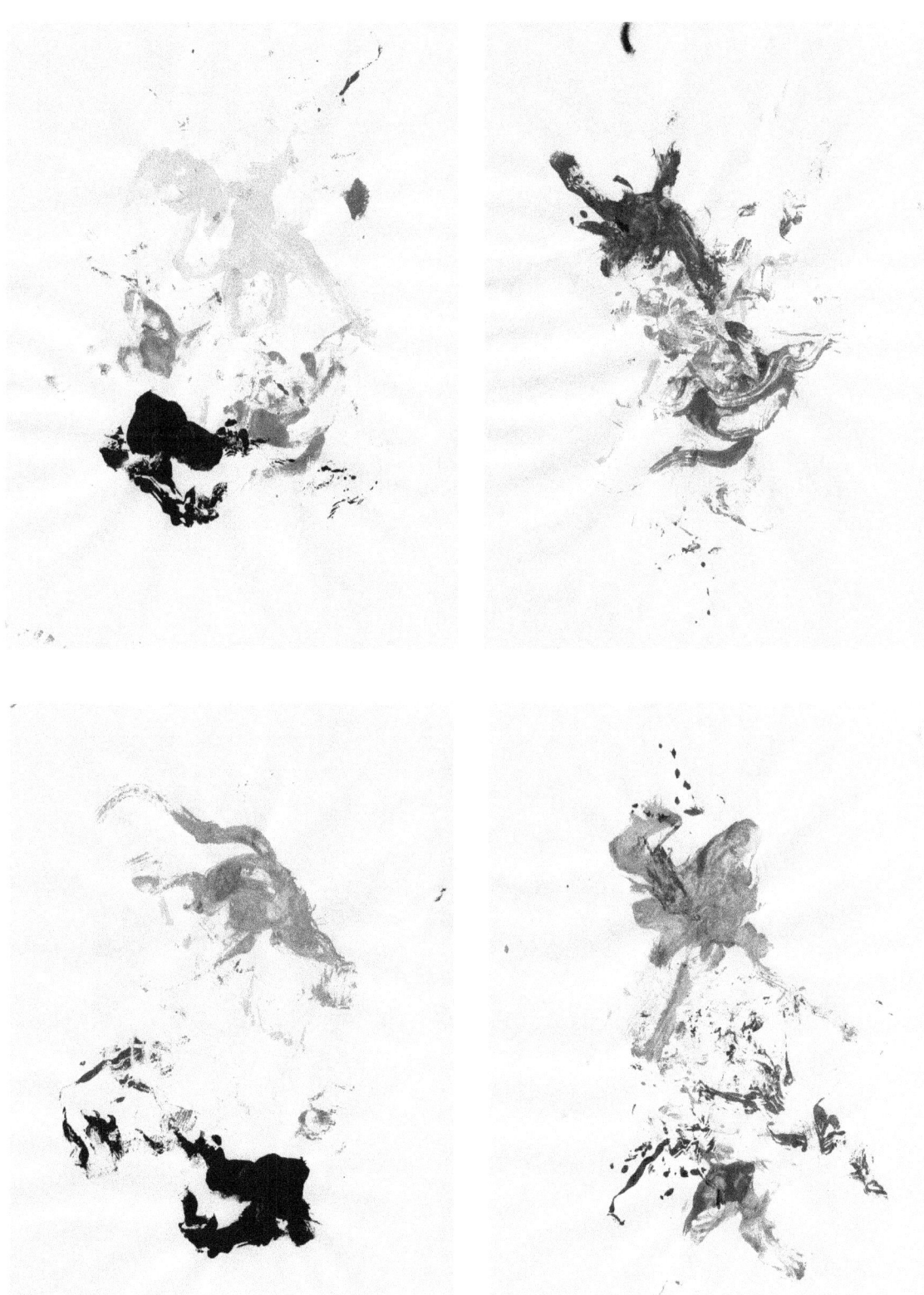

8.

MEN WITH DEVIL MASKS.
Series 5—Australian Aboriginals

Kerry (Copyright) Sydney.

Every Man His Own Fantômas: Or, Away With Nostalgia

Paul Cowdell

Do you know where the masked gaze of the Master of Terror first burned into you? I was in a second-hand bookshop in Balham. In Edward Gorey's picture his cape swept over the city, and I felt those demonically empty eyes drawing me in. Gorey compared the characters to Looney Tunes cartoons, and 'The Silent Executioner' launched me on a night journey into sheer malicious wonder.

I was entranced.

These evil black pearls were magical and I wanted more. This was *my* discovery; nobody could ever have heard of Fantômas before, and I soaked up every empty coffin, every rubber-armed disguise, every deadly-perfumed flower. I was frenzied with the poison of these texts, and later with the deadly toxins of Feuillade's films. I lived the swooning dread of the Unseizable One's reign.

Along the way I came to realise that not only was I not, in fact, the first to succumb to his malevolent darts, but that many of the people I most admired had also written with similar frenzy of his iron grip. The early Surrealists, contemporaries of the novels and Feuillade's films, were also swept along on their narcotic clouds. Apollinaire seems to have lifted the title 'The Poet Assassinated' from a customarily vicious episode in a Fantômas novel. (Such a theft is itself worthy of the Genius of Crime).

And of course this was only to be expected. I was responding to the same febrile marvels as the earlier Surrealists had.

But I began to notice another trend, too, as I became more involved with contemporary Surrealism. Liking Fantômas had been sanctioned by our forebears. It was acceptable and appropriate to admit liking Fantômas. How many people borrowed my Feuillade DVDs because they felt they ought to, and then had nothing to say about them afterwards? How many people were prepared to drop the name of Fantômas whilst clearly having no interest in his crimes? Fantômas had simply become canonical.

The canon has a dead hand, but I didn't love Fantômas because Desnos had written a poem about him, because it was permitted. I loved Desnos's poem for the same reason I loved Fantômas: I wanted to sweep everyone and everything away in an amoral cataclysm that was *not permitted*; I wanted to send an actor to the gallows in my stead so that I might achieve my terrible plans. In a world which treats us with callous contempt, Fantômas' coldly rational and unexplained fury is the doorway to our release.

We will always make lists of things we love. We will always look behind us at doors that have already opened, but their value lies in what is still found behind them, not in who told us they were open, nor in when they were unlocked. This is no nostalgic wallow. Yes Fantômas lives, but so do such convulsive descendants as T-Bag in *Prison Break*, the Joker, or President Lex Luthor. Only by sending the piteous Gurn summarily to his doom will we also be able to find these new Fantômases here and now, will we be able to open new doors. To break the skeletal grip of the canon we must not admire Fantômas. We must be him.

To the sewers!

Image: Shibek - *Ectomorphic Monster*

A Further Investigation into the Photography of Thoughts

Paul Bogaers

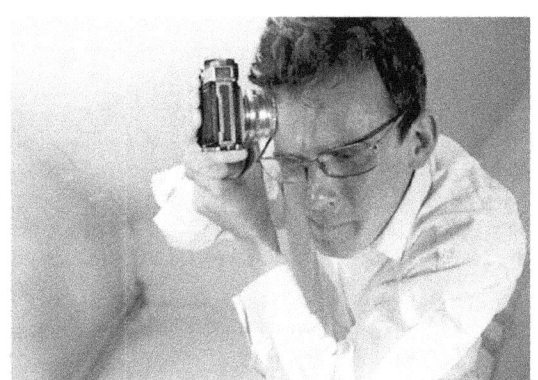

First experiments with "thoughtography", 1984

Right from the invention of photography, there have been photographers who considered their medium as an art form, and made every effort to have it accepted as such. The problem is that photography inherently is limited to a mere mechanical registration of the appearance of the outside world, and can only with difficulty be transformed into a medium of expression of the inner self. If only the photographer would be able to transfer his thoughts directly on to the sensitive film or chip of a camera…

As early as 1984, still during my study at art school, I started thinking about thought photography. *"When a Thought or Feeling is generated in the mind or brain energy, it spreads from the immediate neighborhood of the thinker to a distance proportioned to the strength of the thought or feeling, I happened to read."* I had my thoughts about this, and I also had my camera with the light-sensitive film inside. As I had experienced earlier, this proved to be very sensitive indeed. Now would it be possible to concentrate my thoughts and 'project' them, with or without the help of the camera lens, on the sensitive material inside the camera? *"Thoughts and Feelings are contagious, by reason of the Law of Vibration and Mental Induction."* Couldn't it thus be possible to transfer my thoughts on to a photograph?

Knowing that the wish is father to the thought, I immediately started to experiment. I soon discovered that thoughts often consist of a combination of images, rather than one single image. I also learned that the projected image might appear upside-down, rotated or inversed from left to right. After I had been worrying a while about this, I realized that it didn't matter whether an object was shown correctly, for in the mind there is no up or down.

In a short time I discovered a lot of facts and conditions, both by practicing and studying the records of others.

Through the years I continued my thought experiments and I gradually perfected my procedure. I had once started trying to capture just any thought, too little aware that the greater part of thoughts is fuzzy and lacks both outline and detail. It took me quite a long time to figure out that it was not due to the wrong procedure that I often failed in producing recognizable images; the cause was a careless and inadequate sorting of my thoughts. Gradually I learned that the most manifest thoughts are to be preferred, and that generally a combination of only two images suffices. Duality is the simplest form of plurality, and this already can take very complex forms. More than two images may easily cause an almost inextricable tangle of associations. For this is another thing I'd overlooked for a rather long time: that it is not sufficient to capture thoughts on an image (which is already difficult enough); in reverse the image needs to be translated into thoughts again as well. This requires still different qualities in addition, especially if it is considered important that the aroused thoughts are equivalent to the recorded ones.

This process of experimenting and improving has far from ended yet; the provisional results however I was able to publish in my book *Upset Down* (2010). The following pages are to be regarded as just a brief impression on the subject.

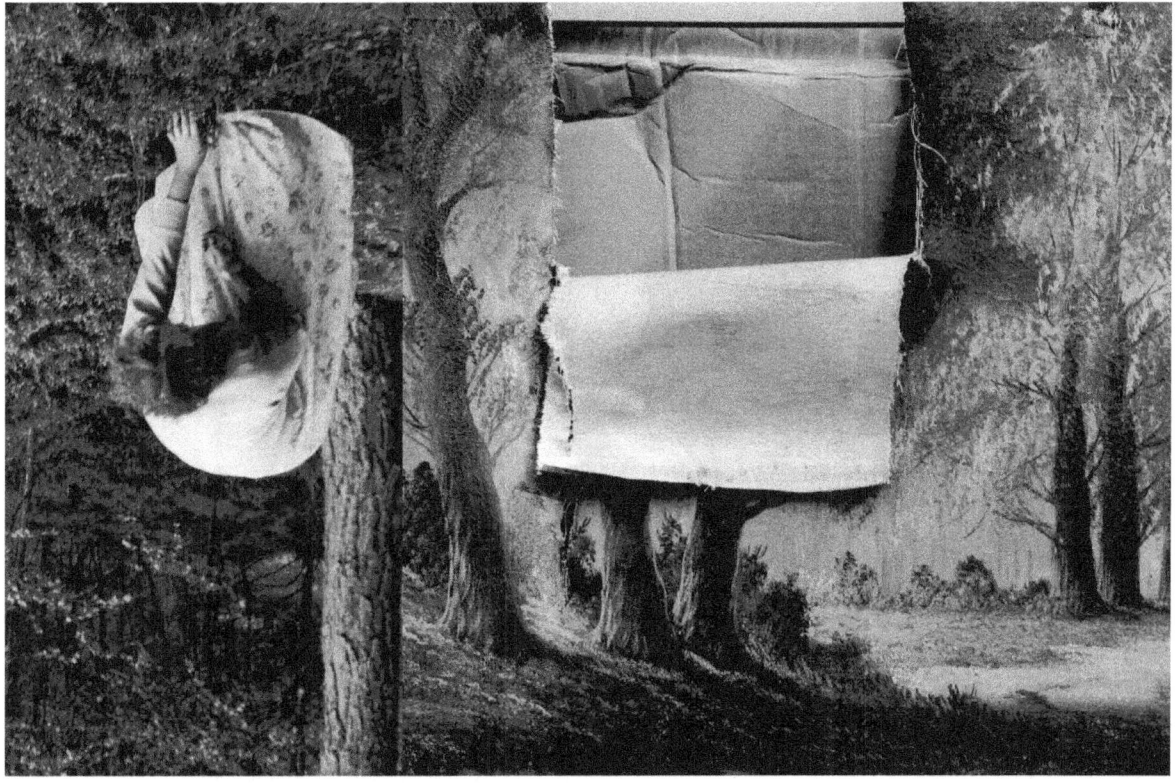

Holzer believes that psychic photography is a gift that only some possess. This may account for why some people seem to have the ability to capture fantastic pictures, while others cannot.

Some Thought-Waves sent forth with but little strength travel slowly and do not proceed very far from their place of emanation, but creep along like some smoke or fog, lazily and yielding. Other thoughts charged with a greater intensity of desire or will, dart forth vigorously like an electric spark, and often travel great distances.

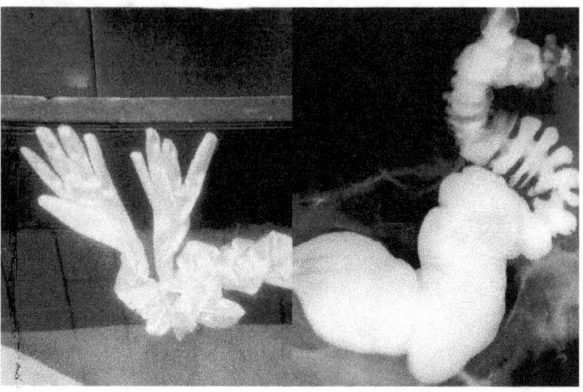

The Vibratory force of thought-waves does not cease with the sending forth of the wave, but persists for a long time afterward. Just as a ray of light travels through space for millions of miles, and for centuries after the star itself has been blotted out of existence – so do the vibrations of Thought continue long after the thought, yes, long after the brain which sent them forth has passed into dust.

These waves, carrying the mental vibrations, coming in contact with each other, tend to set up combinations on one hand, or else neutralize each other on the other hand. If two sets of waves of a similar nature meet there is likely to be a combination formed between them just as between two chemicals having an affinity for each other. In this way the "mental atmosphere" of places, towns, houses, etc., is formed.

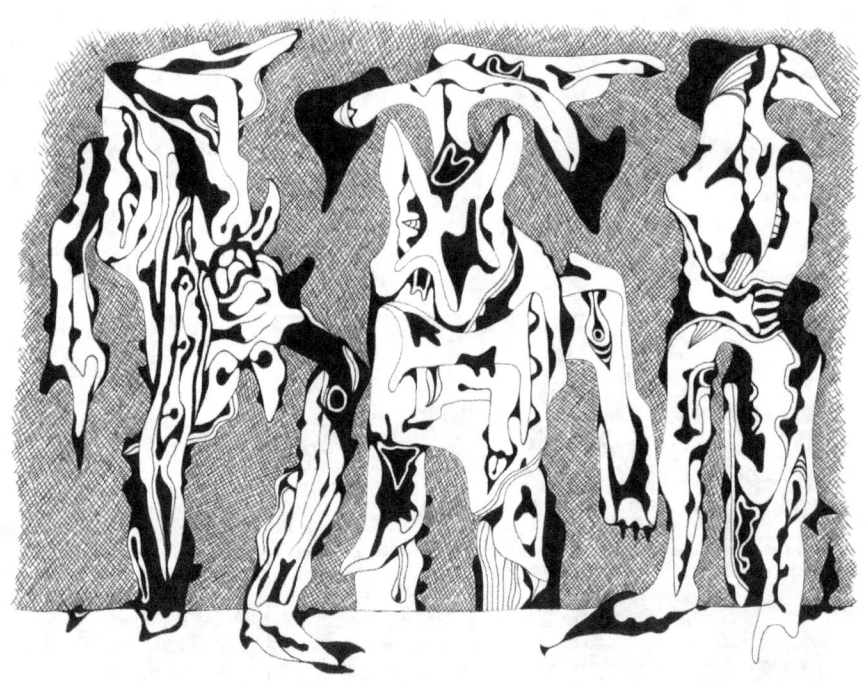

Antonio Ramírez - *The Philosophers*

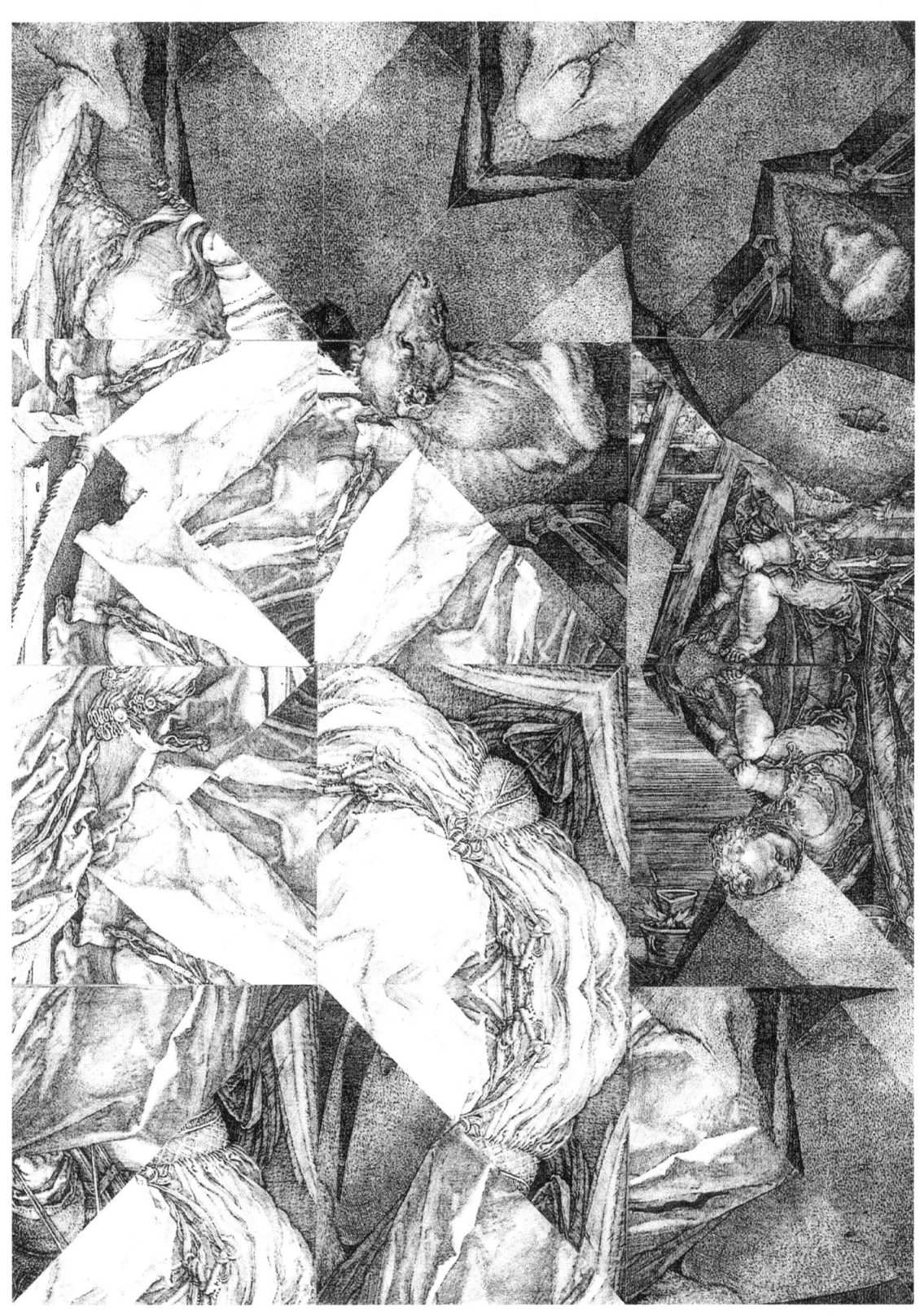

Richard Waara - Melencolia II: / *cubomania derived from Albrecht Dürer's 'Melencolia I'*

30 Proverbs of the Dessert Fathers

Jesús García Rodríguez
(Translated by the author)

1. to go to Togo

2. menstrual cash flow

3. eczema, ecce homo

4. i like your lichen

5. What is your favourite drink?
   Madonna on the rocks, of course.

6. oil tongue: Langue d''Oïl

7. silicone lexicon

8. twelve–inch single seeks long–playing blonde

9. with fur in my tongue, with tar in my fungi

10. a fussy fuzzy pussy

11. back in the microgroove

12. very nice, Berenice

13. sepia homo sapiens

14. The Rite of Spring Roll

15. Veni, bidet, vinci

16. China vagina

17. mermaid marmalade

18. foot with footnote

19. pizzicato pizza

20. onanist out of self–compassion

21. blasphemy in blue

22. my dear old fellatio

23. post scriptum, post scrotum

24. prosciutto of prostitute

25. storming of the pastille (la prise de La Pastille)

26. in God we trust, engulf the twist

27. example of tautological apologetic:
    apologia of the apology

28. The Dolomite Alps, the Sodomite Alps

29. coincidentia oppositorum:
    coincidentia suppositorium
    (coincidence of suppositories)

30. Taras Bulba, Taras Vulva

The Image as Knowledge

Sergio Lima

There are better ways of responding to the richness of images
than by the way of reason or logic.

The many limitations that weigh down on all forms of expression
can be abolished – like many surrealists have already shown so well.
Let's say: these limitations must be abolished
through working the image, through an active vision of the image,
through 'image-working' considered as the rose of knowledge.

Every image is the representation of an experience, the memory of an experience.
And it is the visual projection, the simulacrum
of the 'physionomy', the configuration
of the unique moment, the instant germ,
that memory has seized and lived as a presence.
And it turns itself into a mental image
through the imagination that it is producing.

The image is a shadow, a projection of an enchantment.

The image invites us to explore the new, for instance
the freedom that is peculiar to it.
Just like love, the image reveals.

The image, treated as a mental and plastic representation,
points to or indicates a new reality,
a reality that oversteps our immediate experience
of the commonplace and of reality: it (the image) gives us access
to excess, to the excessive,
to that what in our being reaches beyond the given and accepted reality.
The image teaches us to get along
and to live another reality.

It is the image that allows us to get along with anything that goes beyond ourselves,
with anything that puts our being into question.
The image is an erotic experience
in its deepest and most crushing sense.

In surrealism and in other comparable views,
the rigour of the image as the true key to all knowledge was praised,
as the key to the expression that reveals to us the human
and human experience in its richness and fullness, and where
the non-verbal expression (of the image) gets its own amplitude

– the amplitude of the greater dialogue, that of the simultaneities,
the dialogue of our being with the world, presented as a revelatory whole, as a fusion
or a total exposure of our truth
like a possible future way of life,
being an experience of living in the marvelous, that is:
living a life ruled by Love, by Poetry and by Freedom.

In such an application of and an engagement with the image,
in its exposure, particularly with the collage,
we should focus, in various moments, on the views of the surrealist movement,
because these are the views that have recognised, together with its modernity,
the image as a determining value
for getting knowledge
free of aesthetical conceptualism or cheap fashion.

Add to this, first of all for us artists,
the fact that any symbolical production requires
periodically a reflection on the practice of its own écriture
so that 'it is ruined as a habit and as a system,
so that it can see itself à rebours up to the point
where it distills its own intelligence,
where it generates critical momentum.
Even poetry doesn't escape to this periodical recreation of its souffle,
of the power of creation,'
so Claire Lejeune has rightly stated in L'Écriture et l'irréférence.

Resuming our subject: the collage,
that we did approach in this way, seizing it on the several levels
on which it manifests itself,
keeping the relativity of its connotations, we allow ourselves to proclaim
if not to confine, the external limits of its object and perhaps
to situate its sources of reason
as the expression of a new reality.
An image is always a new image.

The Cheerful Chaos of Collective Automatic Invention

Rik Lina

A true work of art should express a new compelling vision of the world and of our life, it must choose a total breach with the ridiculous tendency to imitate banal reality, as it is dictated by the international art trade and by fashion monopolists. Such domesticated art poorly shows off in dismal installations, in videos without imagination and in other clothes of the glossy art empire.

In one of his essays, the great art theoretician and surrealist writer José Pierre pointed to the specific possibilities for renewing the creative process that are being offered by *collective invention*. Collective creation can be more effective than individual invention, because it liberates the creative action from "signature". Collective invention has been practiced successfully by surrealists at performing the famous game, "The Exquisite Corpse", that was invented in 1925 in a residential hotel at the Parisian rue du Château, the place where many surrealists lived at the time. Thanks to "The Exquisite Corpse", 'an infallible means has become available to send the critical mind on holidays and to liberate the metaphoric activity of the mind completely,' wrote André Breton.

But there is another precious motor for creative renewal: that is automatism, the core technique of surrealist creativity. Automatism has been practiced by all surrealist painters. 'It is the only way of expression that produces a *rhythmic union*, resulting in a non-distinction between the sensitive and the intellectual functions of the mind,' said André Breton.

Inspired by the desire to experiment on a further renewal of imaging and painting, the painters Fredy Flores Knistoff (Chile), Rik Lina (Holland) and Jorge Leal Labrin (Chile) had a thorough discussion about the available possibilities and methods, one day in the early 1990s. Flores, Knistoff, and Lina, who both were working in Amsterdam, decided to try a collective approach of the principle of automatism. They founded CAPA (Collective Automatic Painting Amsterdam) in 1992 and soon welcomed Dave Bobroske (Canada), Miguel Lohlé (Argentine), Gerda van der Krans (Holland), Paul Goodman (Canada) and Geert van Mulken (Holland), all of them working in Holland at that time, in this new venture.

The CAPA-group made hundreds of sessions in each other's studios and public performances during openings of exhibitions of their collective works, often joined by artist-friends such as Tony Pusey, John Welson, Kathy Fox (England), Jorge Leal Labrin, Mauritio Jalil, Mariano Maturana (Chile), Carlos Ré (Argentina), Mattias Lyssy, Rainer Wichering and Katharina van Hoffs (Germany).

One of the early CAPA-sessions that was held in 1992 in Dave Bobroske's studio in the city of Utrecht was recorded by Mauritio Jalil in a series of photos; I wrote a short report on the same session. I remember that memorable session very well; it would be exemplary for the research in collective painting that we are still practising.

When I arrived at Dave Bobroske's place, Geert van Mulken was already there. A short while later, Miguel Lohlé, Fredy Flores-Knistoff, and Mauritio Jalil came in, and we

started our collective painting experiment. By the time Gerda van der Krans had arrived from Nijmegen, the first collective work was already finished. Mauritio's photos give a good impression of the "painting frenzy" which took hold of us. Davy's small flat was not exactly a studio; we were in each other's way all the time, but notwithstanding this, the works arrived smoothly. A couple of hours later, all spaces were full of drying paintings: corridors, sleeping rooms, the bathroom and even the porch outside.

When the long roll of paper was finished, Gerda took out a couple of large-format works she had made some years before, during a collective jazz & poetry & art-performance in the Stedelijk Museum in Amsterdam, where she made her "cut outs", sculptural sheets whose margins formed a curly relief. While we painted our signs and forms onto it in all the colours of the rainbow – quick as lightning –, Gerda cut new forms with her Stanley knife, making Miguel desperate as he tried to close the cuts again with a roll of tape… and Dave was then painting over the tape – I pulled it off again, in this way creating a very capricious pattern. Fredy's tracks of dashed paint soon covered not just the painting but the walls and ceiling too!

We worked with growing enthusiasm while it slowly got dark. The few aesthetic considerations we had had at the beginning of the session had now vanished: the last painting did not have a chance to dry… every time some of us suggested it was finished… it was taken in hand again… originally a collective modification of Gerda's work, now there came to life a continuing modification: a constant metamorphosis of form, colour, mood and feeling.

These repeated attacks on the painting in progress, resulting in its unrecognisable change – even total disappearance of the original image – makes a higher demand on the ego… One may ask oneself: how to keep this up without quarrel? The strange thing is however that every radical change is greeted with enthusiasm: this painting is creating itself! Every time we set to work collectively, we are curious to see what would appear that time. This feeling of expectation, the feeling of the need to be surprised, has a festive character about it: something is going to happen of which nothing is known, something about which one can only dream, something not even existing in the imagination, something which may come to life only by collective discoveries – taking place at a fast pace and absolutely without any preparation.

But this time the results became exceptionally wild. The raging flow of paint summoned so very different worlds of form: shadowings of landscapes and cities, personages, ghosts, devils or gods. Miguel, seized by hallucination, called himself the "Third Painter"! "The Third Painter" is a wording I once used in an article for the catalogue of the CAPA-exhibition "*Wanted-Cadavre*" at the Hourglass Gallery in Paris in1992. (Dutch art historian Jos ten Berge had drawn my attention to the name "The Third Mind", that Brion Gysin and William Burroughs had invented in 1978 for their collective literary adventures.)

This "other" painter, taking over the act of painting from us whenever we work together, this invisible painter is the imaginary persona who gives the painting its definitive shape: because this final definition of the image certainly cannot be invented by any one of us in isolation. Indeed one has to be a special kind of person to be able to forget one's own intentions and to accept that one's ideas may disappear in a single brushstroke by one of the others.

A moment later the trinity Gerda/Miguel/Rik was naming the three of us the mysterious Third Painter, all quickly using the same brush in turn! You could speak on this day of a genuine painting ecstasy, and it was not only the result of our totally free, automatic way of working. The ten large paintings we made that day did investigate in bright colours an unknown and surprisingly liberated inner landscape. As we worked non-stop from half past two till eleven o'clock, now and then someone was to be seen in the kitchen with

a cooking pan or bottle of wine. Nobody cared about the resulting paintings. It was the process itself that fascinated us, this continuous creative conversation with each other by means of the materials used, the experiments and discoveries – and the reactions to them, often produced by several people at the very same time!

Such is the creative process of the artist, escaping from his or her studio, stepping into the "arena", armed with his or her world of ideas, thus entering into dialogue with the other artists – without any deliberation or forethought, without any mutual understanding of what it was going to be, and without anyone taking the lead. And also without any conclusions, because this is a chaos that summons itself: it is an absurd chaos but an inspiring one, and – above all – it cheers you up! It is a creative happening where feelings, emotions, and ideas are expressed directly in paint, and are transposed into an unarranged terrain of unknown possibilities. Of course every painter is both one of the makers and the contemplators of the collective work created at the very same time, but now he or she is bound to follow the gliding and overlapping creations of his or her companions' unexpected interventions… none of that is individual at all.

Such a "possessed" way of working during this session is not the only way to do it, although every work made in a spontaneous, automatic manner will involve a feeling of possession. During most other sessions there was a quieter and more thoughtful way of working, but whenever we notice that we are engaged on something which resembles a painting we have made before, we change course at once; sometimes we even transform the painting itself in a destructive way, because every new beginning must be a leap into the unknown. The gates of the collective unconscious are standing wide open.

CAPA's way of practicing automatism is not simply a research of the subconscious. What we pursue is the raw product, to make use of the materials in an intuitive way – open-minded and unpremeditated – to reach a psychological field of fusion of the individual and collective. You could say that we are engaged in the cultivation of an unprejudiced way of thinking, were it not that for all of us the techniques of automatism already take a primal place in our individual work. We want to stay spontaneous and "inexperienced". The preconceived concept is the arch-enemy of all poetry. We do not wish to allow ourselves to be led by experience, to follow laws dictated by intelligence, by a rational or aesthetic approach. We want to work collectively together in the fields that until now have been individual realms, where there was room for only one person.

In 1997, the CAPA-group participated in the *Phases* exhibition and congress on Surrealism in São Paulo, Brazil. This major event was organized by Daisy Peccinini de Alvarado at the Museu de Arte Contemporánea of the University of São Paulo. In the catalogue, Daisy Peccini called the CAPA-group: "…the new CoBrA of Amsterdam since they consider the former principles of CoBrA the propelling elements of their painting, that is: playful, sensual, Dionysian values, a Utopian dimension of an automatism that generates and is generated by a state of energetic tension, a true possession like CoBrA, who plunged into the expression of subconscious".

But during the exhibition, some serious differences of opinion arose between the founding artists. As a result, the original CAPA-group broke up. Its active member Geert van Mulken died that same year; Miguel Lohlé moved to Brussels, Jorge Leal Labrin returned to his home country Chile, and Fredy Flores Knistoff moved to Berlin. This however was not the end of CAPA, it split into four sections, continuing the same ideas with new members in Santiago, Chile, Brussels, Berlin and Amsterdam. In 2011, the Santiago-group is called the Leal Labrin & Nestor del Pino Collective. CAPA-Brussels around Miguel Lohlé and Amirah Gazel has been very active for some years, until Miguel and Amirah moved to Costa Rica. CAPA-Amsterdam with Dave Bobroske, Rik Lina, Jan Giliam and others is still in full action and working closely together with new collective initiatives such as "*Cornucopia*" (with John Welson and Gregg Simpson) and "The Cabo Mondego Section of Portugese Surrealism" (with Miguel de Carvalho, Seixas Peixoto, Pedro Prata, João Rasteiro, Marta Peres, Luis Morgadinho and others). All these groups are continuing their research into automatism as a collective adventure.

The "field without signposts", that we enter regularly, with unspoilt curiosity and great expectations, is the domain of cheerful chaos, where the elements seem to exist unformed, and stay that way – through our collective interventions – in continuous metamorphosis. The usual ideas about art – or aesthetics – are not even up for discussion. We are in search of new ones.

Internet info:
CAPA: http://www.jangiliam.nl/capa/text/RL/html
Cornucopia: http://www.greggsimpson.com/content/gsimpson/Cornucopia.html

MONSTER

By CINS

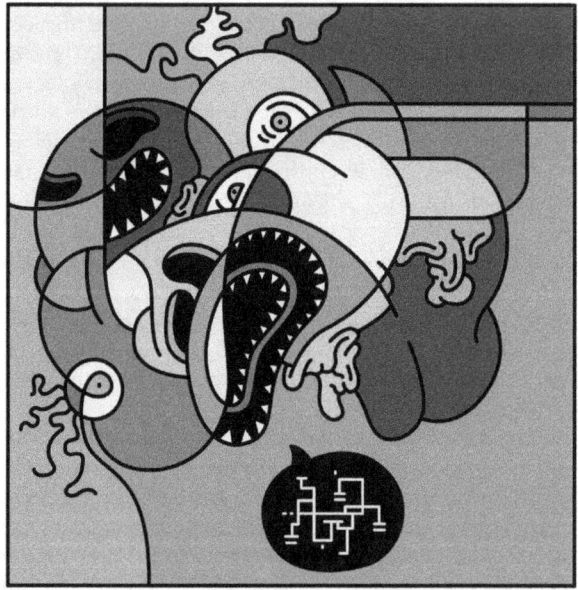

Her de Vries - *Homage to Joseph Cornell*

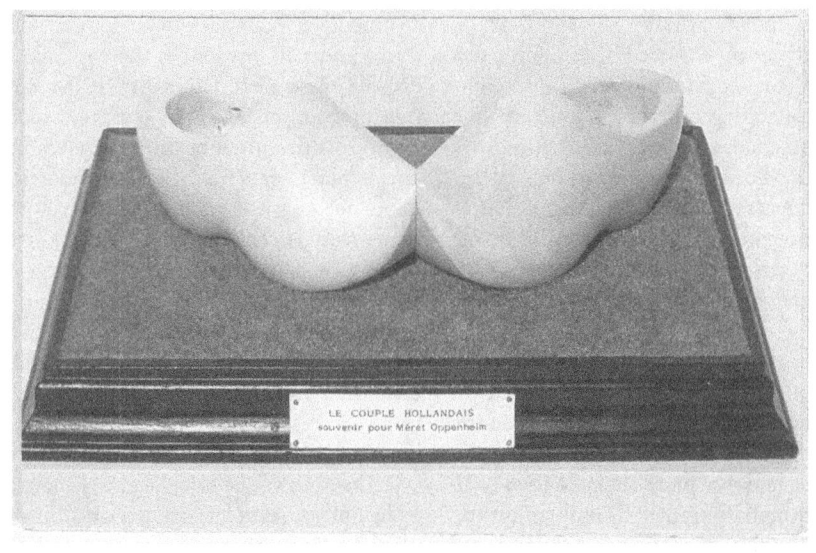

Her de Vries - *Le Couple Hollandais*

Suicidal Objects

Noé Ortega Quijano

*The objects are like Rasputin:
you often have to kill them for them to die* (1)
Christian Dotremont

Sometimes, objects around us appear in such a way that one has the impression that, for a moment, they have come to life. In Jan Švankmajer's short film, *The flat* (1968), a man finds himself locked up in an apartment in which the objects therein behave autonomously, to his astonishment and perpetual confusion. In this situation, the inanimate rebels frustrate the main character's attempts to put any of them to use: the legs of a chair become shortened, several holes appear in a spoon, the bed disintegrates when the man tries to sleep... What this constitutes is a revolt of material objects that results in the discovery of the unknown dimensions of the mundane.

However, now that objects are confined almost permanently within a prison cell of utility, generally unconnected to any type of liberating act, then their desperation proliferates. In the city it is not unusual to find the corpses of functionality: all those objects which, having obtained only the slightest breath of life, have been driven to suicide (2).

The mass-multiplication of objects has led to the loss of their concreteness, of their potential, and ultimately of their poetic *richness* as unique objects. In the commodity, the qualitative yields to the quantitative (3). Once again, the generalized impoverishment enforced by capitalist rule finds a strong foothold for its purposes in the principle of identity: when the prevailing criterion is functionality, this principle immediately adds an object to a multitude of *equal* objects – and all these objects are in turn equal to the vacuum that connects them. It is absolute anonymity. It is the fulmination that the particular object suffers in being taken to a maximum degree of abstraction that eventually plunges it into nonexistence: paralysis, consummated immobilization (4).

The death wish emerges within objects removed from desire. As a result of the continuous frustration exerted by the utilitarian imprisonment of the "will to be", the desire to die arises within these objects. And it is in suicide that despair becomes gesture, and that paralysis explodes. From that desperate leap, immobilization and anonymity are overcome. Suicide is nothing but an insolent claim of specificity. The suicidal object annihilates the absolute abstraction in which it was immersed. Its death realizes its concretization, for death can only be one's own; it can only occur in the particular object, exalting it in its uniqueness. Suicide sublimates the living death of the object, or put another way, it *objectifies*, once and for all, the living death to which the object had been dragged. The death of the object is the testimony of its life.

Something becomes useless when it stops being somebody's servant. Its uselessness is what liberates it. When an object is invalidated as a commodity, it immediately loses any value within the system and thus becomes considered as "junk" (5), a residue despised and shunned by the system. Through becoming useless, the object falls into disuse. Moreover, it becomes invisible to capital. And it is through this method of exit that the object achieves its uniqueness, stripped of all false masks of identity, of any nullification of its own nature. And so it is emancipated: by ridding itself of functionality, the object achieves a new life in the light of poetry.

The suicidal object breaks into our daily life in a brusque and unexpected way (6), almost obscenely. It provokes a gasp from the elderly lady, a look of disgust from the punctual worker, or a quick gesture of annoyance from the young altar boy. The so-called "good people" – those docile pets – are horrified by suicidal objects. This is understandable. One of the effects of exacerbated instrumentalism, under which capitalism subjugates everything under its shadow, is the concealment of objects under the mask of functionality. It has come to impose its rule to such an extent in our ways of relating to things around us that the objects themselves are no longer seen, but rather their value when considered as a commodity – and nothing more than that – that value which makes them visible in the eyes of capital (7). That is why suicidal objects generate such a tense reaction of rejection from the well domesticated since they are no longer considered means nor tool. When the functional use of the object suffers a setback, the object appears as it really is. "Freed from utilitarian bondage, the object readily throws off the mask to reveal its true face", (8) and the appearance of that unknown face causes fear and bewilderment.

The most varied suicidal objects have been encountered, from household items such as an iron or a can of pepper, varied street furniture such as signs, billboards or telephone booths, through all sorts of objects such as guitars, cars or shoes, just to name a few. These are usually isolated suicide cases, although the first cases of collective suicides have been already reported. With respect to methodology, the suicides that have already occurred exhibit a wide range of possibilities: death by defenestration, hanging, getting shot in the temple, drug overdose, drowning, and even by vein cutting. Some cases reveal signs of self-injury before the suicide event, a chilling proof of the object's state of desperation. As to the place of suicide, no predilection for marginal areas or busy areas of the city has been detected. What has been noted, on the other hand, is that the geographical dispersion of observed suicides is expanding, which may be a sign of the increased tendency of objects towards their destruction.

However, common features exist: first, the suicidal object makes its appearance. There is a short period of time when people pass by hastily but nobody wants to get very close to it. Beyond this first stage of horror, there is a morbid excitement regarding the corpse, and the suicidal object attracts varied numbers of curious people. Soon the interest dissipates and the object is finally at rest, completely abandoned. Then it disappears.

(Partially translated by Bruno Jacobs)

FOOTNOTES:

1. Christian Dotremont, *Vie de l'objet* (1944), in *L'objet surréaliste*, Jean Michel Place, Paris, 2005, p. 176. This text was meant to appear in *La main à plume,* in a special issue on the object that was ultimately never published.
2. The first part of these notes on the suicidal objects was published in the second issue of *El Rapto* (Madrid surrealist Group, December 2007), and then an English translation of it appeared in the second issue of the journal *Phosphor* (Leeds surrealist Group, Fall 2009). The translation published in the latter is the one included in the present text.
3. The situationist critique has treated this aspect thoroughly. In addition to *The society of the spectacle,* this concept was also treated by Raoul Vaneigem, especially in Chapter X of the *The revolution of everyday life.*
4. "There is nothing inanimate. At most we can say that there are still objects, or more accurately, immobilized objects", Jean-Louis Bedouin, *op. cit.*, p. 298.
5. "Where a first meeting between these utensils and the surrealist object occurs is in their use value. Such value lies in a shared surrender to economic uselessness", Eugenio Castro, *Los trastos arrumbados*, Salamandra 17/18, Madrid, 2008.
6. A singular fact occurs with the suicidal object: it is this, with his suicide, which "comes to us". There is no voluntary human action prior to the advent of the object, there is no intentionality, no kind of intervention comes into play. "The potential activity of the object, its movement towards the subject determine the reaction of the latter". Martin Stejskal, *La relation cérémonielle,* in *La civilisation surréaliste*, Payot, Paris, 1976, p. 307.
7. "The relationship with the goods is not only visible, it is the only thing visible", Guy Debord, *The Society of the Spectacle.*
8. Jean-Louis Bedouin, *Cycle de l'objet,* in *La civilisation surréaliste,* Payot, Paris, 1976, p. 299.

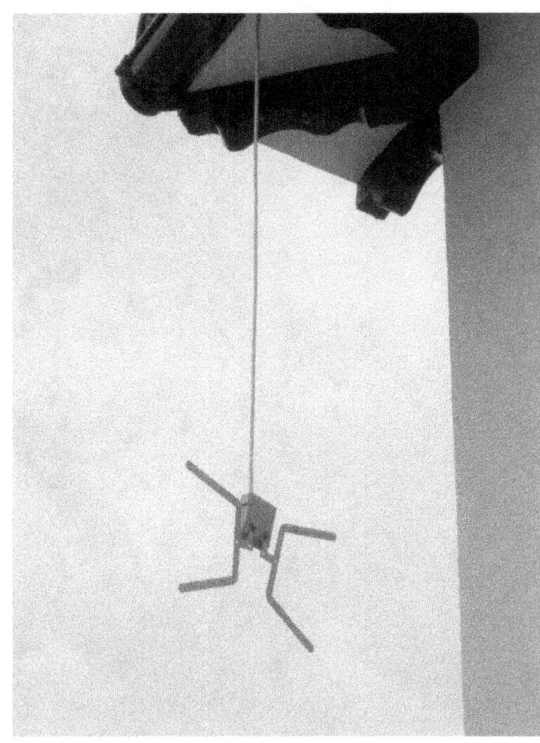

Object recently suspended from a roof (found by Eugenio Castro and Noé Ortega in Comillas, Spain, May 2010).

Suicidal umbrella at the bottom of a pond (discovered by Bruno Jacobs in Sweden, April 2010.

Shopping cart that threw itself downstairs (found by Noé Ortega in Santander, Spain, July 2007).

Basket after having deliberately consumed a great dose of barbituates (found by Eugnio Castro in Mar de Lira, Spain, July 2009).

Telephone suspended with clear automutilation signs (seen by Eric Bragg and Noé Ortega in San Francisco's Financial District, USA, January 2010).

An iron hung over a cemetery wall (sighted by Bill Howe in Leeds, UK, March 2009).

Disemboweled object after having commited hara-kiri (photographed by Vicente Gutiérrez Escudero in Santander, Spain, January 2011).

Object about to take its last step (met by Noé Ortega in Santander, Spain, May 2010).

Traffic sign suicided by a shot to the temple (seen by Emilio Santiago in Mostoles, Spain, December 2008).

Lightbulb about to fall into the dark (encountered by Noé Ortega in Santander, Spain, February 2014).

Dan Boyer - *At the End of the Walker Dictatorship*

The Conceptualizations of Imagery and the Introduction of Cruelty

Richard Misiano-Genovese

"I'd still like to say how much I am impressed – sometimes with the cruelty of the imagery; always with its impact."
—JH Matthews, 1984

(J. H. Matthews: Extracted from a letter (1984); An Inventory of His Papers in the Manuscript Collection at the Harry Ransom Humanities Research Center, The University of Texas at Austin.)

The Inception of the Altered Lithograph

When regarding the image, and its apparent dramatic presentation before our eyes, where does the impact of the image begin and where does it take us? What constitutes the virtual necessity for plunging into the darkest inner regions of our mind to unearth such dramatic, harsh visual responses? This merging of the subconscious with the application of gouache, pencil, digitization or any other means available augments and ultimately expresses this new altered image.

It is necessary to begin forming this imagery by seeking these natural impulses through the abandonment of the restrictions of one's mind: that which we perceive normally as "good taste" and civility is impressed upon us as youths. This regimentation is the foundation of civilization and enforced politeness that we call "society." This reverse demonology of "look, but don't touch" or "eat, but don't taste" runs counter to the primal impulses of man. These are rigid man-made constructs. It is nothing less than anti-humanistic in that it seeks to restrict our natural impulses.

The mere fact that these repressive dictates create more harm than good is less apparent than the restrictive, narrow attitude this encourages. When viewing an image of cruelty by design, the image is often repulsed rather than embraced. We are conditioned to smile and appreciate the beauty of a rose perhaps, or an engaging sunset, but an image that has been manipulated and distorted suggesting cruelty or brutishness, brings us to the very brink of internal chaos. Our conditioned response to our visual perception is the total sum of our judging skills.

Chaos is born when our inclinations for orderliness and introspection are abandoned.

Pascal once said, *"All men naturally hate each other."* [1] He went on to suggest *"there could not be four friends in the world"* without religious intervention. [2] Pascal suggested a common

"Lamia 1" (1978)

bond could be forged between men on a civil level. Even from his myopic perspective, he missed the opportunity to see beyond the obvious. Is not the dark side of human nature hostile, with violent impulse? Are we not freely inclined to such thoughts, words and actions given the correct set of circumstances to promote this behavior?

Freud invokes the religious commandment; *"Love thy neighbor as thyself"*, [3] calling it, *"a commandment which is really justified by the fact that nothing else runs so strongly counter to the original nature of man."* [4] This certainly speaks for itself. We need only to read the daily news for affirmation. Murder, war and genocide, are indicative of man's destructive nature. Again, Freud says that each one of us, drawing upon our own life experiences, can prove his assertions about the original nature of man: *"The time comes when each one of us has to give up as illusions the expectations which, in his youth, he pinned upon his fellow-men, and when he may learn how much difficulty and pain has been added to his life by their ill will."* [5] Additionally, is it not only our neighbor who harbors hostile impulses, we ourselves harbor them; Freud speaks of *"this inclination to aggression, which we can detect in ourselves and justly assume to be present in others."* [6]

Man's aggression, fury and penchant for self-destruction can never measure up to the standard nature sets into place.

Nature herself is a brutal proposition with birth, destruction and death a daily fare. Natural disasters, earthquakes, floods, fires, and disease reinforce our fragile state of existence.

Nature compels us to survive by any and every means possible; in an often-brutal struggle, insects tear each other apart for food, and carnivores prey upon herbivores. Man, once the greatest hunter of them all, is now sadly reduced to bartering for his meals. *"Work for money"* is his means to receive plastic, packaged food as a reward. Through this lowly servitude he exchanges his very spirit, his life with this concept. Everything feeds off of some other thing for its survival. It is the nature of all existence.

Therefore upon viewing an image of cruelty we are at an emotional disadvantage and consequently we may become disconcerted. Our senses challenged and our reactions magnified when confronted with these altered realities.

The shocking deformities nature creates can never be surpassed by a mere man's imaginings.

All of these starred points of reference suggest that our field of perception regarding what dictates "good taste", or oppositely abhorrence, is determined by how we are taught as children to accept or reject that which is good or bad. Without this early guidance we'd likely not react negatively to an image that was less "beautiful" than say, a rose. We are indoctrinated to think and act alike. We're discouraged from thinking in ways that are counterproductive to societal dictates.

But there is something to be said for exploring the other side – the hidden nature – the *"dark side"*. That part of our psyche we ignore, deny, and avoid at all costs for the sake of conforming to societal norms, and as a mechanism for self-preservation.

As to exploring the *"dark side"*, some ask why? I ask, why not? There is a process that is involved in letting our imagination expand beyond its usual limits. We may easily conjure up an

"Lamia 19" (1978)

image of ordinary daydreams such as a peaceful and pastoral setting, or more creatively an apple running and screaming, all in flames. I say, take this further. Let the imagination slip deeply into the extraordinary.

The process here is to explore this realm in terms of a visual dialogue, although certainly a written discourse could easily explore such areas quite satisfactorily. To create an image, we must first begin by letting the self go into another level of awareness. That is to a much deeper level of awareness. This is not easily achieved however, as the natural inclinations, the natural impulses, have been stymied and repressed by cultural inhibitors. It becomes a question of allowing the disassociation of object and subject to suggest other visual alternatives. Once these bonds are broken the opportunity to flow freely in the subconscious is now in place. It is at this moment these associations between image and subject become fluid, free and the resultant climax should prove to be of interest after more than a casual glance.

Media and technique are merely the vehicles for new modes of expression and should never be considered as the magic equation.

The method of doing this is to take a simple image produced by ordinary lithography, and using pencil, gouache, and airbrushing, to rework the image. Perhaps adding a bit of collage as well.

This method is an enhanced version of photo retouching. Earlier, these applications were sufficient to provide the necessary steps needed for producing a new image from an existing one. More recently, with the advent of the personal computer, software programs can also be used to augment these images. What separates them from what would be considered *"digital collage,"* is the fact that these images are initially manipulated and altered by hand; hence *"Altered Lithographs"* is utilized to describe the technique.

These are simply the methods for producing new imagery, and nothing more. Here we are presented with prose poetry not in words, but prose poetry in imagery. The ability of our subconscious to reintegrate the connection between the action of creation and the suggestion from the subconscious is achieved through the subconscious free-fall where these images suddenly come to life. The release of our inhibitions allows us to tap the inherent cruelty within us, freeing us from limited frontiers and opening limitless horizons.

(2010)

Notes:

(1, 2) *"Pensées"* (Blaise Pascal); 1662
(3-5) *"Civilization and its Discontents"* (Sigmund Freud), 1930
(6) *Leviticus 19:18* (Quoted in *"Civilization and its Discontents"* [Sigmund Freud], 1930)

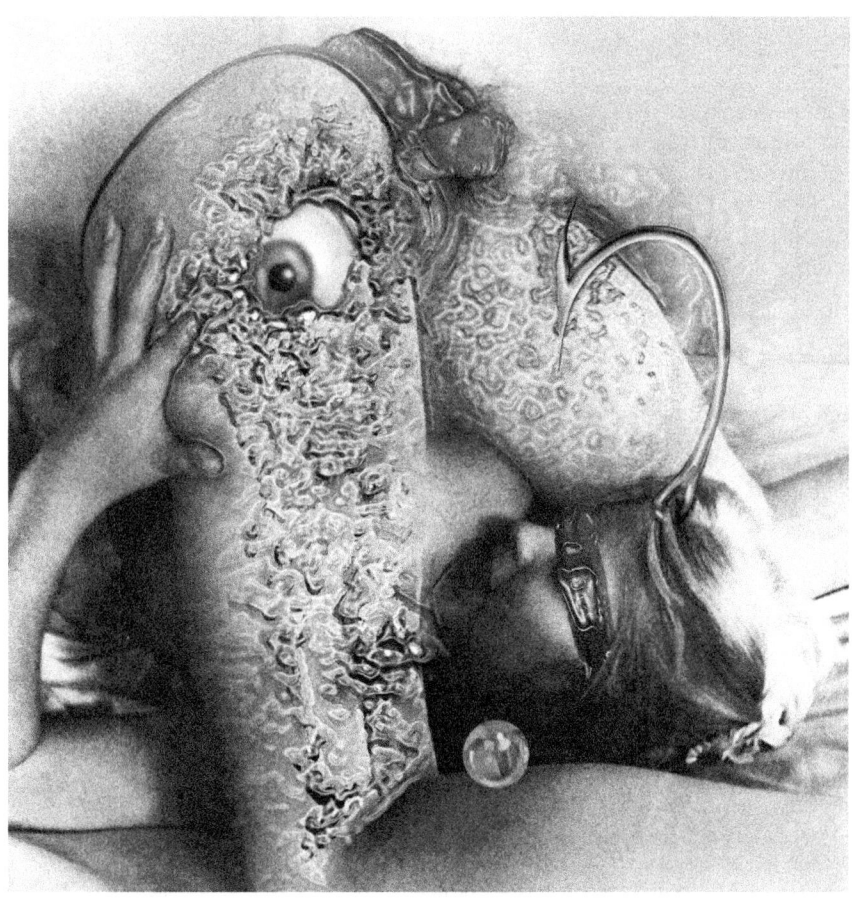

"Phalluscide 20"(1986)

IMAGES IN LIBERTY

Sergio Lima
(Images by the author)

The images of the world in which we live present themselves to us in photography, not in painting.

Photography is a specific kind of material, just like words, and as such it is not a fragment of the universe, it is the visual image of that universe.

The visual quality of the human body – of our body, or of the unknown body, the beloved body – and its representations is not restricted to the rules of classicism or of academism where the ideal was to reproduce the texture of the skin and its contours, or even to provide the idea of its real presence.

Today, through photographic reproduction, the visual quality of the body reaches such a refinement in its shape, that they become the shape of excess in itself.

The body is our life project, it is the visual image of 'high love' that we experience in each photo, in each reproduction, in each image, in each detail of its shape, retained in our memory, or 'photographed' by it.

Photography is the retention by our optical or visual memory, of the moment in which the body or another object shows itself as a revelation, as an incidence of light or of record.

The image is the memory of a visually retained body in a given reality. This reality – the photographical reality of language – adds to its true being the beauty of its forms, unfastened in an unavoidable presence: the presence of its image. As we see it, it makes us lean over in the direction of its being, or even to its excess of beauty.

And this excessive presence of forms – recorded by photography, that chooses the hazard of a unique and fragmentary moment (linking the exterior necessity to the interior urgency in a visual fragment) – shows itself in a world that is parallel to the world of daily life but that penetrates life. That is because it takes place in the realm of representation, or in that of shapes. So we should not forget that the shape – or the simulacrum – is always in conformity with our desire. It is our desire that inspires it. And it is our desire that deforms it (that shapes it).

The world of images is the house of our desire. The world of images – with its accidental Baghdad market of impressions, of chosen objects, reproduced or photographed – is the focus of our attention and of our pleasure.

The image offers a sufficient support for our vision of 'high-reality'.*

Photography is the objective language of visual representation (we only photograph what exists or what did exist (for only less than a second).

And the savage articulation of this language, accidentally found and/or photographed, is the collage. **

I use images the same way other people use words. With the same freedom.

The fact that they are already known, printed or written down before is not relevant at all.

Translated by Marcus Salgado

Notes:
* 'High-reality' should render in English Hegel's concept of *Mehr-Wirklichkeit*, to which Charles Fourier has also referred. I prefer this concept to the usual and more confusing concept of 'super-reality' as used by the Spanish and Brazilian modernists, because *Mehr-Wirklichkeit* allows for the idea of diving deeper into reality itself.
** It is not the glue (the set of glued things) that makes the collage, as Max Ernst used to say, but the encounter of images that creates the revelatory image. The collage is a personal language, basically dialogical. Its scope is the sensible inside the dynamic expression (active vision). By definition the collage is an extended and excessively plastic language.

The Great Rejection

The Ballot of the Bullfight

The Hysterical Cyclist

Object Magic Revealed in a Dream

Sasha Vlad

On September 11, 2009, I had the following dream:

I know that I can make magic by putting together different objects. However, I wonder what "putting together" might mean: to assemble the objects, or arrange them in a certain way? I am not sure. In the end, I realize that in order to make magic with objects it is enough that the objects touch one another.

I have had dreams before about objects that I tried to recreate visually, so, evidently, this dream prompted me to act on its "revelation," too. Since the dream was purely verbal (which is rather rare in my oneiric world, considering that I am mostly a visual person), I had to choose a way to express it visually.

Firstly, this led me to consider—again!—the state of the object, which has always greatly interested me. (And how could it not, especially given the fact that, in our times, objects are in danger of disintegrating under the insidious attack of the virtual?) What, I asked myself, constitutes an object, after all? (Does a "real" human sole, for example, qualify?) I realized that I wanted to use for my "magic" purposes all kinds of objects (real, simulacra, big, small, simple, complex, humble, dramatic, intact, broken, etc.), and not be limited only to those around me. The medium of collage gave me that liberty and, at the same time, allowed me to use objects (albeit images of objects, to be fair!) that did not correspond in size, very much like they often appear in dreams (acknowledging in this way the very source of my inspiration). Secondly, I was very excited to explore the "touching" phenomenon as something occurring between so-called "inanimate" objects. As a result, one may be able to see that it is not only humans who communicate with objects (as evidenced by various tactile experiences and, possibly, psychometry), but also that objects communicate amongst themselves, and, as my dream pointed out, that their communication is enhanced to the point of magic by the simple act of touching.

I am making public this personal oneiric experience in the hope that it will trigger other responses from surrealists who value objects, dreams, and tactile phenomena—as well as their combined magic.

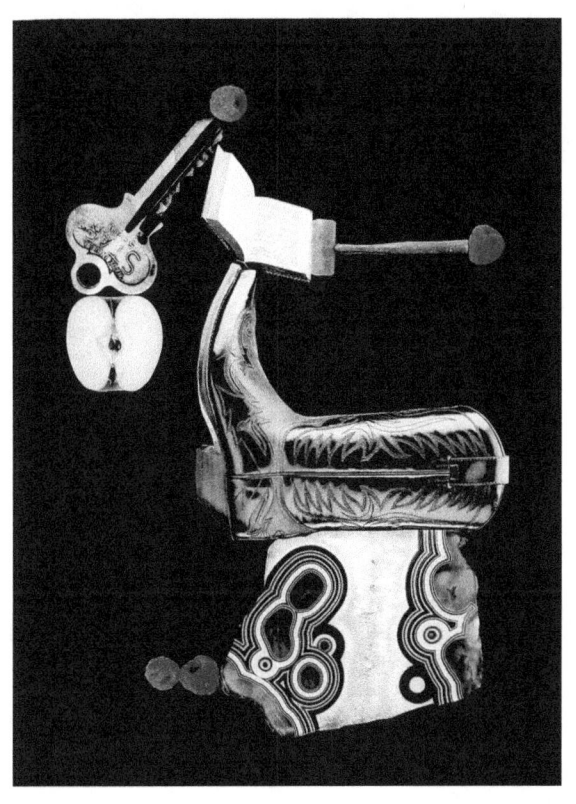

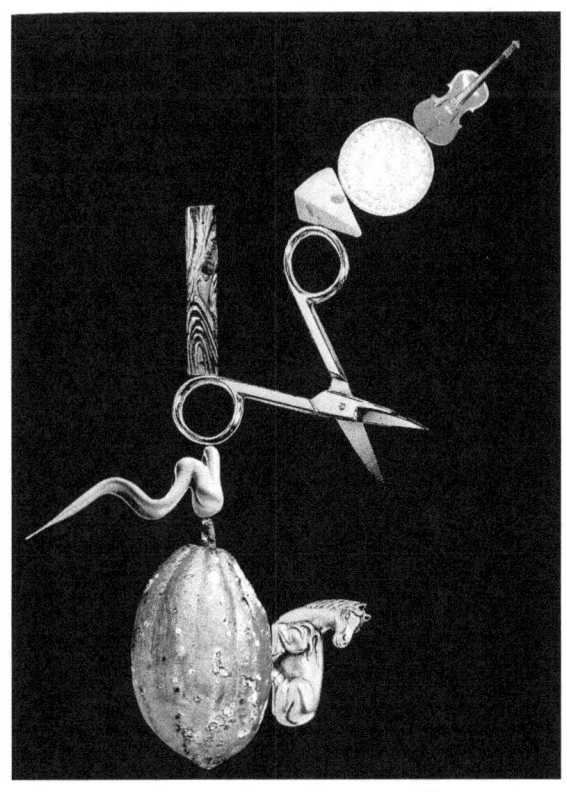

The Collage:
An Amalgamation of Ideas as a Method of Self-Definition

Miguel de Carvalho
(Images by the author)

"Even if feathers make the plumage, glue does not make the collage"
Max Ernst, *Dictionnaire Abrégé du Surréalisme*

From the perspective of the poet and on his retina, everything is a collage, a sudden new surface of discontinuities. The collage is like a "scandal", but it is not an indecency, a paradox or a folly. It constitutes a plural language of expression and sensibility, a voice caught by the ear from the dead sea of the residues of modernity and of what remains in the end 'when people are going back to the night'. They use the same grammar of dreams, turning them into reality. They are fragile objects with unformatted formats. They require cognitive aptitudes while evoking the child's world of games, madness and dream.

In my work, each collage is the result of a sort of dance in which the hand and the unconscious mind behave according to chance, in an act of deep love, brought to ecstasy by the impulse of fixating an image; a flame bigger than fire. My collages try to offer an orientation deprived of aesthetic and moral concerns through materials that I find or that literally find my hand.

The collage acts reciprocally with its original source, beyond consciousness and rationality, just like the sun interacts with the soil, the soil with water, and the air with flowers. This interaction of tactile shapes presents to me a new psycho-geographic emotional luminosity that evokes lyrical atmospheres, prisoners of my own conception of convulsive and transcendental beauty.

My collages are things that are not separated from true poetry. They are my experiences and my desires, my mountains and my horizons, all melted together in the silence that violates time and sets clouds on fire. My collages also unite water and fire, they unite the bed and the lovers. With them, I try to reach the labyrinth of mirrors, thus illuminating the abyss.

Each collage is a look, a window, an interior balcony of the desire that offers a view into the most hermetic of poetic landscapes. It is a forest where the wind does not sing, but instead, where it randomly gathers the leaves scattered by time.

My collages are an immediate action, in contrast with drawings and paintings, that are a reflection. I could elaborate drawings from my collages but then they would lose all their sense of chance and spontaneity, of its momentum and its emotional objectivity. For me, the collage is an impulse of visual attention perpetuated and interrupted by an instant of eternity. It is not a whim of fantasy, but rather lightning: a flash of light brushing on the unconscious, that shows me what exists in it under the hallucinations provoked by the libido.

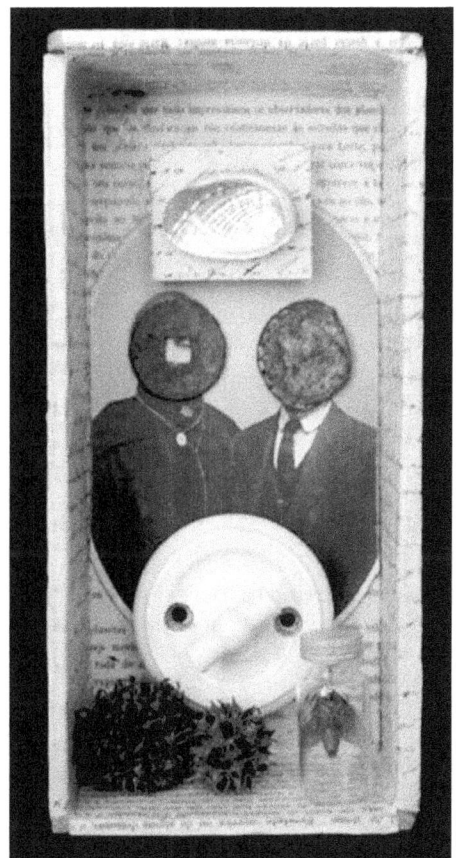

Defending Useless Aspects of Urban Objectology

Vicente Gutiérrez Escudero

I dare to think of a world without cities, i.e. a world with plenty of "clean, safe cities" and without abandoned objects to take or manipulate. This would imply that all footprints and stains, smells and textures, and all of the other wonders of reality that enrich our lives would disappear. Nowadays, despite town planning, by construction mafias that destroy urban life and communities, we can still stumble upon, step on, and break things.

One undeniable fact about cities is that within them we are surrounded by lots of objects, at rest or in motion, conventional or unique. When we walk through any city (from one end to the other, walking in circles, aimlessly...) subconsciously we always need to grab something valuable; from the dump, from the stall... We at least think about the possibility of interacting.

All cities are governed by the domination of safety, neatness and cleanliness, which is aimed to establish better police control. Fortunately, in this period of capitalist decline there will always be garbage strikes, labor demonstrations, fierce winds, violent storms... and all of this will make destroyed objects emerge once and again, as objects displaced to areas where nobody would expect to find them.

Within the context of this permanent alteration of the urban environment, it is interesting not only to detect the amount of poetic radiance (as it occurs analogously with radioactive substances) emitted from any particular object, but also its degree of resonance, i.e. its degree of enchantment and transmission with respect to the surrounding objects, both in the sense of the poetic load generated by a certain desired object and of the extension of such energy – though it progressively diminishes during a dérive – and in the importance that such an object gains for us.

At first sight, nothing in the cities would seem to produce that kind of poetic radiance. But if one goes far into those apparently unexplored corners, if one observes with a different sight, he will realize that nowadays cities are full of useless objects. In this sense, classifying and tagging the poetic relevance of the objects that we find would be an interesting strategy for the subjective analysis of such places. For example, the Madrid Surrealist Group has developed activities related to the unexpected encounters with found objects. Very interesting are the "suicidal objects" of Noé Ortega, the "stolen object" by Antonio Ramírez, the "idle objects" of Javier Gálvez (also investigated by Eugenio Castro) or those ghostly, ectoplasmic objects of Lourdes Martínez. All of them sparked my interest.

So I decided to make a taxonomy of urban objects, which would be based on the evocative power of their usefulness or uselessness, their capacity for wonder, or their potential to become part of a constructed object. This classification was written on labels, on paper laminated with glue that were placed on the objects in question.

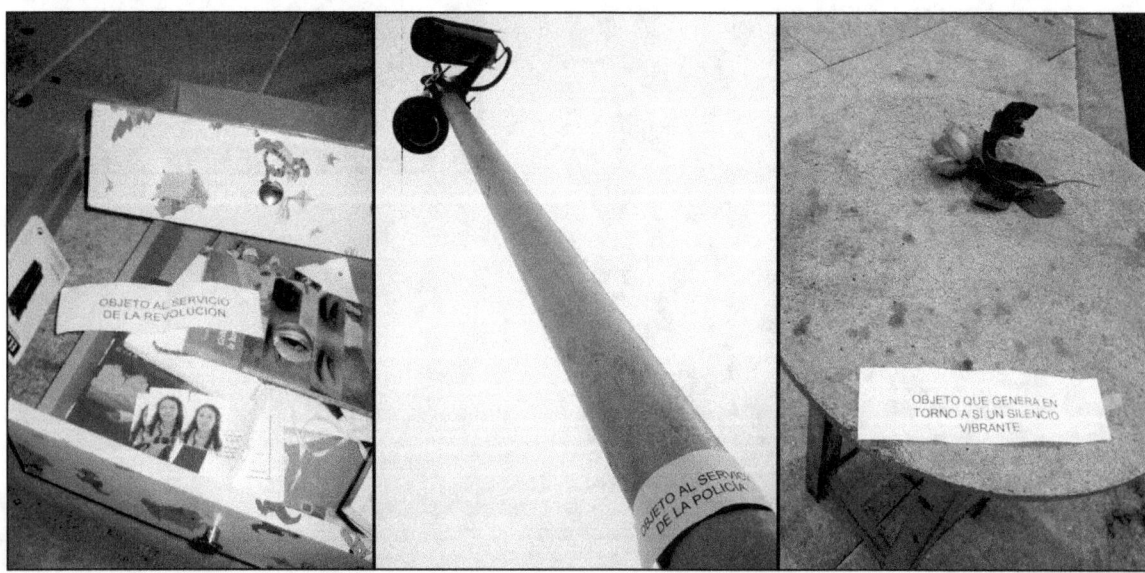

Here are some examples:

"An object that generates a vibrant silence around itself," for example, left on a small wooden table, tall and narrow, on which I placed a rose found nearby.

"The object for which time passes too slowly," assigned to a suitcase which stood ajar, containing letters and old clothes, observed next to a garbage can.

"Object capable of producing dream activity in the observer," stuck in a broken wine bottle, at the foot of a shelf in a mall.

"Object at the service of the revolution," a label that I also kept for a pair of scissors with a string tied to a computer at my workplace.

"The object of the police force" – a video surveillance camera.

"An object that accommodates the despotic impulses of instinct," on a rotating globe – physical-political, broken, lying in a small meadow.

"Object to be part of a shaman's horse," on a striking iridescent purple shirt found in the middle of a road.

"An object that contributes to the knowledge of a foreign language," which was affixed to an electrical appliance damaged and unrecognizable that I found down the street, perhaps bearing a slight similarity with a cassette tape.

This activity is accompanied by a map of the city where I indicated the discovery of certain objects, marking the area in question, depending on their type, using one color or another. This activity can certainly provide us with a better understanding and classification of the marvelous, as it is still currently found in the cities.

(Translated by the Author, revised by Eric Bragg and Noé Ortega)

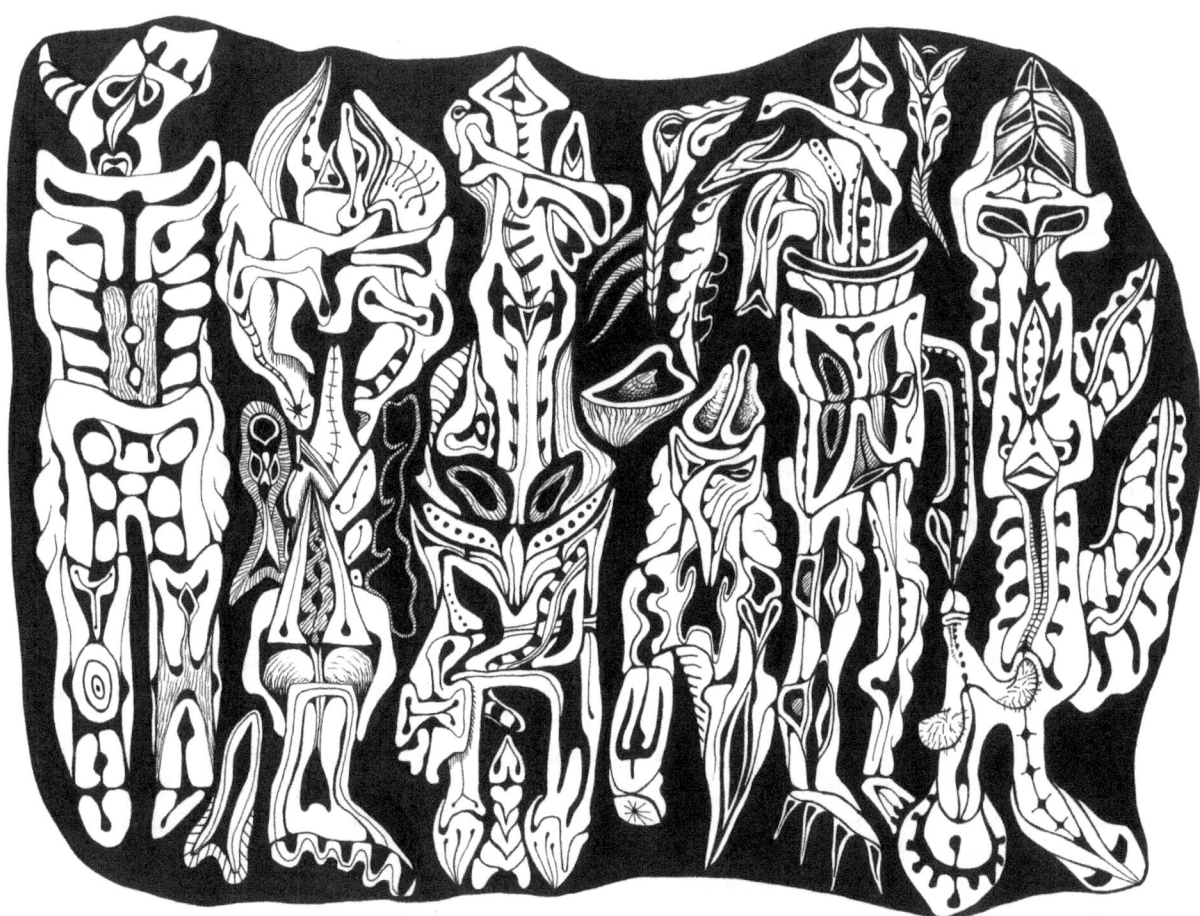

Antonio Ramírez - *Conspiracy*

IN PULVEREM MORTIS

Sotiris Liontos

Beneath the surface of life interlocking webs of despair lie tangled and varied in trajectory towards graphomanic proclivity and linguistic leprosy. Old clothes do not make a tortured artist but at least they can cover your wounds. It might as well have been carrying an intravenous pox in macaronic form, latching on and letting go by leaps and bounds, lost in a maze of mindless fuzziness, senseless meanderings and quiet interludes of spacious disconcertion. Sometimes the convulsing synapses fire sparks of picayune misanthropy. Sheer black fury and pent up hatred incarnate made articulate with malicious intent. Pure sulfurous fire, mercurial vigor and rage propulsion of the first order. Ego death equals physical death as far as I am concerned. So I'm constantly trying to avoid criticism by doing absolutely nothing.

My mind is like a parachute. It only functions when it's open, which is extremely rare under the strain of existential impotence. My ears have been exposed for so long to a radio station I could not ever change. My tongue cleaves to my jaw, abound with salivation and overflowing lust invigorates even the worst gyrations of the eyeballs. A heavy patina of reverb from the vast halls of blasphemy is dripping into my mind note by note dissolving through the cerebral blood vessels like black ink into a glass of water. Since I've been told that I have grown more gonads than needed I decided not to disclose any more virtual tales from the scrotum. Escaping from my own fantasies like a thief on horseback I knew I was heading for the wrong direction even before I realized that there was no head ahead. Randomly running close to the edge of dementia I keep hitting nothing bur brick walls.

My life seems to have been the ultima Thule of perpetually crumbling ivory towers. I can't even find the part of me who would love doing lines of coke in bathrooms off of girls' hand mirrors at loud trendy clubs. Every day I feel like a paraplegic deprived of any actual links to the real world outside my room. And every night I enter another bordello of nightmares. Human-like animals under unholy control are deliberately trying to castrate me and murder my fleshly effigy in any conceivable way within my dreams. A true dread itality is coming like a whisper from a vengeful ghost shuffling its craggy carapace towards the elephant graveyard where our ancestors are buried. "The music made me do it" is the only excuse I can utter pleading guilty under extenuating circumstances.

Self-pity has been my only true friend as far as I can remember. One the few outsiders who can really understand what's going on with myself, it always comes out of nowhere and kicks you right on the spot at your testicles, if you have any of course. My normal work is starting to drive me insane since even the most immature minds have ceased to respond to my emotional needs as they did for many years before. I'm certainly one of those who don't like to take no for an answer but I always do, even if I'm not overtly asking anything most of the times. I know I may be a bastard but I'm not a fucking bastard. Far from safety were the words of my transgressions so far that met by the stone-faced mien of the critics. My personal muse was always taking unexpected paths under the asphalt going astray and adrift across a bright, sometimes brooding, landscape of acute inferiority complex.

I was trying to efface myself from the face of the earth mercilessly screaming for mass attention, wearing multicolored psychic tattoos on my skin and rocambolesque outfits on my body to deceive the grim reaper, only to receive an olympic kick in the head watching my shattered jaw descending in slow motion then swiftly dropping to the floor covered with a spray of innocent blood. There I lie still like an unconscious crocodile awaiting an audience for my final bow. "Hey punk", a harsh voice is warning, "prepare yourself, for your asshole is going to be cleaned as a whistle!" Antibodies can no longer protect me from the deadly cosmic rays of my subconscious invading in a torrid zone of incest and rape contaminated by hundreds of cockroaches. I shoot them on sight without second thought using a magnet to recover the bullet shells.

Always busy doing nothing I emerged as a narcoleptic sorcerer showing my hands at the outset of a threatening sky, grasping at the debris of a swirling galaxy while the stars above and beyond were refracting light into kaleidoscopic spectra of colors. All I have left now is to amicably embrace solipsism and ride free from moral restrictions to join a colossal sensual spectacle projected on enormous clouds in gorgeous astravision and shocking sexicolor. There I meet countless beautiful women full of fine promises that they never deliver. All those who could be able to see me have blatantly ridiculed me and the hidden but obvious meaning of my verbal remains. This city is not afraid of me. It ignores my physical presence entirely. But I have seen its true face and I can accurately describe it as filthy, abject, and disgusting.

They say love is stronger than anything, including potential teenage girlfriend-kidnapping, space gorillas emitting deadly gamma radiation, and asexual robots coming out of their flying saucers armed, loaded and dangerous for the faint-hearted. They blink with one eye at the time and then open them both together giving a whole new meaning to lazy eyes. There are billions of bugs everywhere in our body and on the bed we sleep even if we don't ever see them. We feel the presence of the belated monster of frivolity ready to devour us like a jug of ale at any given moment. Trapped inside an elzevir sphere surrounded by ticking clocks that tend to extend the duration of time, I want to vomit and smile simultaneously. Whenever I feel blue from self-inflicted suffocation I start breathing again coming to terms with the high rate of mortality that my many selves indicate.

My glow in the dark attracts only the insects of the night. Now that I have become a slow-worm in the hook I'm ready to die in an altered state of consciousness that can easily marry unlikely species giving birth to green-eyed monsters unleashed from whatever heinous realm that they squat. In order to walk the primrose path with the voluptuous daughters of men I wouldn't hesitate to break their neck, boil their sagging skin in hot oil and serve it to their children. But in the long run if nothing can keep us together, nothing must keep us apart. So come on, my beloved ones, quickly. Let's consummate before the dawn kills us.

Instead of attempting to become Satan presiding the infernal council, I decided to write the memoirs of an unfortunate haberdasher, trying to cure my insomnia by depriving myself of water for 24 hours, and then eating a raw snake whilst reading. Cleansing my mind of its termites I sit down to commiserate why my poetry has the same appeal to the general public as broccoli to a six-year-old child. Another victim of under-exposure, occasionally dressed as a cosmic bear, homeless and destitute, with the rotting head of a boar in my ragamuffin mind and coils of white smoke in my brain, I keep leading my reciprocal body to eternal oblivion. Unfortunately Rock will die before Christianity, I hasten to predict. And it seems that there is absolutely nobody with a soul so kind to have sex out of pity for the criminally unattractive. So let me continue my sermon to the serpents wishing to be born again, to have a second chance to seduce the angelic race of people's young daughters. Full of sizzle and electricity, the love-making process will probably come in full circle in a crash course to material extinction slowed down to a snail's pace by continuous repetition.

A perfect anastomosis of pain and redemption, it packs a wallop, giving the recipients a bang for their buck shoving a tailpipe torpedo in every anal and vaginal orifice around. The lyrics of pubescent girls are coming out of my mouth as oracles from a roaring volcano. Their fiery eyes will follow my specter wherever it may roam sinking all coffins and all hearses in the muddy waters of agoraphobia. Humiliation comes back flying into my face every time I witness their apathy as I stare at them unable to speak out of embarrassment, standing among the wreckage and wishing I could turn back the time that there were no divisive issues between the sexes whatsoever. Finally I'm breaking the mold of mummification while still wet and unformed by carnal knowledge and moral restrictions and carve my initials on my useless genitals getting out of my odorous corpse for a last breath of fresh air. This time my omnipresent absence along with the majestic escapists of cocaine have front row seats reserved for the apocalypse.

MMXII

Wedgwood Steventon - *Arcadia, post-industrial landscape*

Inner Animals: An Introduction

Josie Malinowski

On April 21st 2011, five members of SLAG (Paul Cowdell, Mattias Forshage, Merl Fluin, Patrick Hourihan, and Josie Malinowski) played a game to investigate their inner animals.

The idea for the game came about in discussions between Mattias and I about a chimp called Josie from the 'six-chimp-test' in Desmond Morris' 1962 "The Biology of Art", which, according to an interpretation from the Swedish translation, quite possibly meant that I had been a 'sex test chimp' in a former life; and we talked about how it would be interesting to find out which mythological animals possess us all, in *this* life. But right up until the day we met to discover them, we still didn't know how we were going to find out. We met in the evening in a park in London. Throughout that day, I had been playing a game by myself in which I choose someone in the street at random and follow them at a distance until I lose them or they take me somewhere that I feel I should be. I chose Bank station randomly as a starting point, and followed the first person I saw when I came out of the station. I stopped following them when I came upon the Guildhall Art Gallery, because I had no idea it was there, and I went in for a look. Inside, I found some not-very-interesting paintings; but then, winding my way from the top to the bottom, I discovered that there were the ruins of a Roman amphitheatre preserved beneath the gallery. I was amazed, as I didn't know such a thing existed – and apparently, neither did anyone else, as it was totally empty. I felt like my game of following was working and I was discovering the secrets of London.

Next, I followed someone for a long time and ended up walking through Spa Fields, another place I had never heard of or been to, where I found out that there was a place called 'The Bone House and Graveyard' in the 1780s. It had been designated as a site for about 3000 graves, but the corpses were burnt in the Bone House so more and more people could be 'buried' on the land, until the residents became sick from the fumes and stormed the house, where they found the watchman stuffing pieces of bodies up the chimney. I was discovering more secrets!

After that, I followed someone who led me to a small market in Pentonville. There I took the opportunity to nose through the second-hand books and other stuff, and found the first clue that I was on the right track to finding out how to find our inner animals, as I found an old postcard of 'The Pompeiian Dog' – the plaster cast of a hole left by the curled up body of a dog found in the ruins of the submerged ancient town of Pompeii. This animal found after nearly two millennia seemed to point to the fact that I was closing in on discovering how to reveal our secret inner animals.

Finally, I followed an old couple. They were easy to spot because the woman had very long white hair that stood out, and I was able to follow from quite a distance. However, at one point, they were obscured for a few seconds by a small crowd of people. When the crowd got out of the way, only the woman emerged. There was nowhere for the man to have gone: no street to turn into, no shop to go into, and she didn't stop at all, just carried on as if he'd never existed. I followed just her for a while, and then she stopped for a long time at a traffic light to turn right, so when I caught up to her I carried on straight (not wishing to give myself away) for just about ten seconds, and when I turned around, she too had gone. I tried to follow where it seemed she should have gone, but I couldn't find her anywhere. Eventually I had to give up and admit I had lost her – the first person I had lost all day, which I took to mean I had arrived somewhere important. I looked around and I was just on a street somewhere. I saw in the distance a house that was totally cluttered in the yard, and went over. It looked like a yard sale – a rarity in England in general, and particularly in the very centre of London. I asked the owner what was happening and she said she was giving away everything in the yard for free. After looking around for a while, I took a heavy marble-like statue away with me and carried it in my bag to meet with SLAG.

When we met, we passed around the statue for a while as I told the other members of SLAG the story of my day and how I came to possess the statue. It was agreed that the statue was important, and Merl came up with the idea of using it as a stencil to trace around, as the basis for five animal outlines, which we could each use to draw to interpret our own inner animals. We created them at the same time in a pub that evening, and then named them all, as follows:

The Pompeiian Dog					The Minotaur

Inflated Clam Heart			The Mirror Owl			Flying Lemer

POEMS

Wijnand Steemers

Risky Alphabet

She moves from A to B.
"B 32" spied "Subject 2".
Your rat is neither waiting
nor sleeping. Forces C
who defects to D.
And E is blowing the gaff on F.
If G now H, H, H,
J will squeak o dear!
Merely the KLM (Air France!)
(that is a cut above them)
were as pleased as NOP(unch).
Until Q will put his R on S
to a T for U, regarded as V,
side by side X and Y,
as a price upon your head, Z!

Time Bomb

Their poems dressed windows. Stone-dead
notions started to be price-cutters, reduced
to zero, but with balls. A sort of poet
respects the latest fashion, doesn't he?

Sentences which are getting the pip,
meanings should eat the reader's cunt,
ideas crowing twice like she-males.
Poetic art? In the sales! Liquidation!

Their poems are peepshows. Pin here.
Strip off yourself financially. Slack stengun?
Soft powers aren't allowed to overcome.
Their poems as battlefields. Blood is fun.

Poets as dead drunk commando's
in a reading circle, indiscriminately
shooting down the last pacifist. Tell me,
does your Muse hide a time bomb in her pussy?

Ultimate Jump-off

Not mentioning anxious neighbours
(unsaturated fatty acids)
with their less green desires
to spy on you to have you pre-emptively on toast

through their marquisettes
only penetrable from their inner selves

Desires
       increasing
joining your clocked off hours
                         jumping
jumping
     - ultimate jump-off -
                         hit!
Metempsychosis
            supposing
the presence of a soul

Whatever

Whatever gets to
you   toottoot   gets
come   choo-choo choo
abo   about too early! To
you   wards to   to o o peine perdue
gene   rally   close
to

Dress Rehearsed

Thirteen white-collar workers in the front seats.
Seven gangs of heavies with belts in the eighth row.
Six complainers pattering on the aisle.
One populist with twitches in the box,

with eleven bitter pills in his inside pocket.
Twelve timid hares peering to the fire exit.
Nine pyromaniacs pouting in the gallery,
their prompter hanging in the curtains.

Angry bitch wolves licking their programmes.
Donkeys on the stage braying for more spotlights.
That way all empty theatres are filling up,
so the Ladies and Gentlemen may stay at home.

Functions

Eye	hangman
lash	erasing
ears	hanging up
nose	bridging
will	after a chin
upper	lip
kissing	
lower	lip
rebel	mouth

Short-sighted

Those shaved
heads you cannot
sell toupées

Those empty
eyes by which only
opticians may
gain profit

Bald, stubbly
heads with eyes
at the top of their throat,
together one camp

of featherbrains
with weepy-eyes
which don't bode well

but short-sightedness

Course of Life

In the beginning you are bridled
by her umbilical cord,
dependently;

afterwards you are clinging
on her skirts,
affectionately;

after that you are pulling,
autonomously,

at the tether of your squandered time;
hereafter you will write a poem,
intransitive,

without a suffering direct object;
ultimately you will get attached,
transitorily,

to the restlessness that is dreaming in you
of a peace,
undying,
which is bridling you again.

The Perceptionist

She is all eyes. Eyes
on all. All ears. And she
recognizes sense by touch.
Intent on sense. You eye,
she brows.

Her bow. Flows out
in nonsense. Her tongue
blabs. In purring. Lip
service. Pursed.

Poison herb? She fixes in
good and even. You hare
off. Off her yoke.
As closer inspector.

The Healer

Sharon Olson

Triology Along With Eluard

Hande Koçak

1. IMPROMPTU FOR ANATOLIA

« À l'ombre des arbres
Comme au temps des miracles »

He was walking to reach the farm breathlessly in the middle of the night. Vast land as vast as an eye can see, so that hills popped up in the middle. He followed the directions but there was no trace of the main road. The main road was the new road, dating back eighty years already, when night was equal to evening, those times without electricity. If he knew how, he would return maybe. But as if darkness were tailing after him, he «had to walk, without ever stopping». Then he walked and walked, and did not stop. Familiar but non-human sounds. One step, as if one were followed by a one-and-a-half. He was feeling hungry but «had to arrive», he said to himself. «Isn't it entrusted with you, you have to deliver it, otherwise it remains at my peril, my face falls ashamed, I can't raise it.» He stopped at the foot of a hill. Stretched his trembling eyelids thoroughly and looked ahead. This aridity was making his blood run cold. There was neither a cave nor undertree to hide in, back and forth, only gray land. «Isn't it even worse» he said, «the restlessness buries itself within the air, which seeps into you insidiously.»

If he went around the hill, a light, or a house would be caught by his eye, or a sound by his ear. Howling. Wolves would not descend in this season. «A dog, or something, don't be scared.» He walked around, the other side of the hill was darker perhaps, as he could see earlier. «Am I losing my vision? My ears, hold yourselves firm. That old lady cautioned me: don't hit the road, if you do so, say, say the prayer.» He recited something as if he were delirious, without knowing the order. The haste to place it in order seemed to be getting in the way, it would be right even though it was wrong.

«Visible I am in the immense universe, right here, in the middle, as tiny as my existence, all alone», the old lady told him to repeat, so once he kept quiet for some time, then he said. He got afraid, he said, he took refuge. «I took refuge in you from being fearful.»

What a trouble it was, that deposit. But he trusted it somehow, no one could change his faith. It put an end to all, to the quarrel, to the rancour. He put his hand into his pocket. Who knows whose lives as well were removed by it. Icy, as if it was made of the monument, the one erected in the town.

It was stiff, the life of the woman drained in streams, that was the only thing he remembered, he was young. He felt ashamed of remembering. The top of his eyebrows trembled, he loved that woman. A man told him, «if you feel obliged, do not hesitate to use it. Let the deposit protect you.» It was just a charge, the dirt of the world in his pocket. If there was a life that I would take across, would I go stronger in the knees, hearing deeper meant fewer steps. He turned his back on the hill, his eyes looked for a field. That was the bread marked with two opposing poplars, it was a small field he could mark, further away. He started to run, but that was rather a flutter. He arrived at the first poplar tree, he looked around and took a breath. There was no breath nearby, no house. It was certain that the sky completed twelve hours, it became pitch dark. Just a well, looking cold, under the poplar tree, that was all he could find. His body was heavy. The stones touched by the hands of men, surrounding the well in order, were the qibla while in fear. In the day a hand touched it, an arm took water out of it, a mouth drank its water, whoever walked around it crushed the grass carelessly, then maybe one knelt down, one sat on the ground. He recognized his race in the pitch dark and he trusted it despite the gun in his pocket.

What time would the sun rise, he thought, the road was long and desolate, as he stopped he would be scared, as he was scared he would have a mind to stop again. He heard very deep laughter, he checked his heart, then his pocket. He stretched her ear towards what blew to him, but the sound retreated, «what was sighing was my own heart.»

He was in need of sleep, he was going to hit the road as the sun appeared, the soil was getting cold, he took his jacket off, he was going to cover himself with it. He was going to keep his look hazy, otherwise the unseen would become visible during such a night. He turned his curiosity towards himself, slightly scratched his face. Then he leaned his head on his elbow, extended his body to the shadow of the tree which merged in the night. Feeling exposed, then he took refuge within words of his memory, he felt scared, he took refuge, he said, he fell asleep.

He jumped up from his sleep. The night was standing still in the sky. He took a deep breath, his eyelids were heavily going up and down like the dying fan of an old lady. He heard a sound. It was coming from the well. A sobbing or a drop of water. It was not raining; the sky was clear. With his hand on his chest, he forgot about the existence of his trembling eyes.

Fearfully he looked at the place from where the sound was overflowing. A head extended outward; it was a head lost among long, dark black hair. It was a woman and she was coming out of the well. Her body appeared slowly. She was holding the skirt of her pitchblack dress, he could not tell if she was crying or speaking. He took a few steps to the well, then stopped, fearing that as he got closer, the woman would fall down. He took his time. The woman stepped from the mouth of the well, coiled her body and then streched. Her chin was the chin of a cat, it became narrow. She looked around and then at the sky. At that moment her hair fell from both sides, but he could not look at the woman in the face, if he did, he would die. He slumped down and kept silent.

Worth escaping from her existence.

The woman placed her shy foot firmly on the ground. That smell. The smell of muddy water. Water was pouring in streams from her dress. She opened and turned her palms to him, as if she were holding two bright stones, like two moons. He lay down in fear. He got shriveled thoroughly, and put all his weight on the soil, to penetrate it and get lost in it. The grass folded one by one under him. There was no place to hide, he wanted to recite, but could not. He turned his back to the woman and held his breath. The woman drew closer, and lay down next to him. She was a like a wave, his back turned cold. She entwined her arm around his; he would not move; he felt her head leaning softly to his back.Her hair was made of ice. « This is a nightmare » he said to himself, a nightmare only and he tried to swallow his own breath to wake up. Nothing changed. The woman pulled the jacket over him properly with her other hand. Now she was murmuring. He closed his eyes helplessly. He recited. The prayer he was saying became unintelligible, because the breath of the woman was a warm song which was convulsing at his nape. He listened:

"I, the fairy, for one night have searched for a breath. Listen! Wherever I look, it is all night! Before the dawn I am always like this, in water, dripping. This much hate in the same blood! There is no peace in the depth, even though I know that I would be swept away in the day, I would find a place and snuggle without being afraid of my hair. A life which is endless, it is like a hand that gets longer as you cut it, holding my last breath. I would like to know if there were colors other than the color of dried leaves falling into the well or of the snow. I don't ask for rain, that depraves the water. It is a feast for the daughters of the water, leading to fertility. Water copulates with itself, boils the hatred, and establishes gates. I wish I could come out of it, without a scary face. If only I would drown instead."

2008- Balmumcu
*Paul Eluard, Entre Autres
(Karagöz Edebiyat, Eylül 2008)
Trans.T.Karakoç/H.Koçak

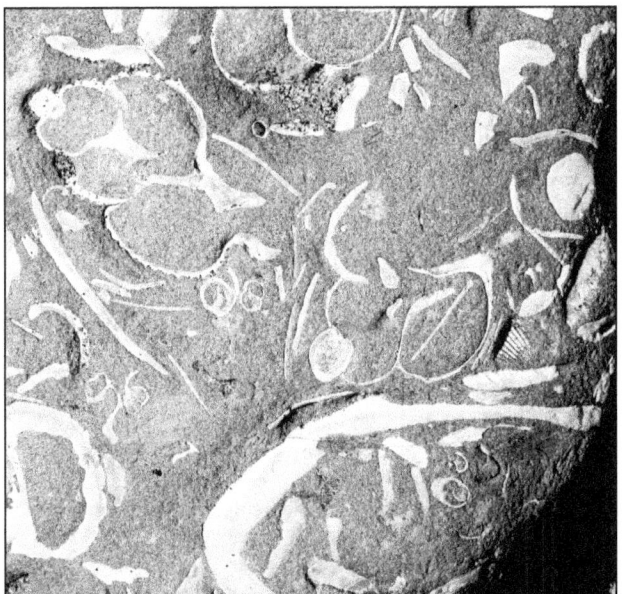

2. FRAGMENTS TO DE CHIRICO

Tous les murs filaient blanc autour de mon silence (4)*

After a breath and yes, silence, while it is chasing us away from anywhere it invites us to, the boiling scent of our burnt bodies flowing into piazzas. Melancholy breaks our appearances. Our lives tacked on our deaths, band together in an anonymous death and in this city our restless spirits are on the axis of a prayer, getting lost one by one in a dream's clear pandemonium. The roots of my insomnia go a long way back, I walk around this city for years, the reminiscence is even harder to take, harder than my attempts to sleep and the night never collapses us. The sky, hung on a blue which gives away none of its tones, stands still with its resemblance to me.

Sur le ciel qui n'est plus le miroir du soleil (7)*

In that one long sleepless day, column-long fears under the blue which opens itself by degrees. Is not it a proof of nothingness, a sky like this in the absence of the night?

Toi, que défendais-tu? Ciel insensible et pur (5)*

That which chases a shadow is always another one, I am being chased. Our shadows beginning to putrefy, to traverse tenses, confusing the shadows of times, the wind blows towards me, the dust it raises from the ground has no equivalent in any land, at the most it is a form of a colour which does not take the form of a footprint, this is how it hides us.

Tremblant tu m'abritais. La lumière en relief (6)*

In this dream, taking place in Italy there is a death which buried itself into the light of the object. Only at that time, when objects swallow their own light, they turn in upon themselves, only then your death flows into everyone's and the real night begins. A place whispering these words cuts loose from any sort of security.

Les étoiles de jour parmi les feuilles vertes (8)*

In this city, I come across poets, little kids. One is following me in the direction of the wind, whistling by his feet. The emergence of a breath which gets lost in the rhythm of the heart which becomes unrecognizable because of the thrill while getting closer to sleep, the air lost in it. "In his dream," says Blanchot, "there was nothing but the dream of the desire to dream"... And I say that the maggots were settled in the marble. And their stillness was eternal. A woman was pouring her mind onto her own shadow. The time of her excessive morality was stopped, she dried and put her wrinkled youth on. She was sunbathing in an afternoon at full stretch on her own coffin.

Le souvenirs de ceux qui parlaient sans savoir (9)*

Right here I begin to dream, buildings as ruins which already lost their own reason to exist and which only harbours my dreams, they crowd the piazzas with sadness as soon as they get empty. I stand on the axis of a song from my childhood. One leg leaning against the line which signs off the shadow of the station, the other against the whiteness of the lighthouse.

Maitres de ma faiblesse et je suis à leur place (10)*

Melancholia! Like you ingest the crowd of the buildings around you, you open your marble mouth to our arms and legs, the swirl built in your open mouth blows the cities of my childhood to my dreams. I gave my word, to myself, to visit the piazza in an afternoon the piazza where my mother left herself to a stone. Turning into a stone everytime I meet her in this circle of a spell, will not have an end until this self-pursuit is called off. So I quit.

Un mur denoncé un autre mur (1)*

In this dream which takes place in Italy, the columns are divided into two. What divides them is not only the time which passes through. To this mid-time which has neither an entrance nor an exit, ships dock, they shed their sails by the city wall. And the water of the pool is drawn from the eyes of the poets. The truth covers the ground in this jammed darkness, and does not give out a sound.

I have started to cry, so as to fill up a sea to sail, I could not even send one wave to the horizon, because in reality I was feeling like doing nothing. I was only listening, the silence of walls reminding me of the voices of mourning women.

But. Regardless, they had colours.

Et l'ombre me défend de mon ombre peureuse (2)*

The ones whose hands do not touch their heads, they never had shadows, and these never set foot into this city. Each labyrinth which precludes its own way out by becoming more apparent, resembles an abandoned hive. Only lighthouses can protect this city, because only their bodies are eternally at the edge.

Avec des yeux d'amour et des mains trop fidèles (11)*

Nearest shore where the white short waves break towards the horizon, only their sound licks up those gates, from the bellies of the lighthouses a burning light springs on every patio, I cock my ears, it is late, I hear the city clocks, it quit following me these clocks which complete themselves in an eternal nothingness are set neither to an arrival nor to a return, neither to wind up nor to destruct, no, only and only to a being, in the expansion of a quiet spell, their directions are dedicated to the glow of the objects which accompany it. Like the stations which run to the railway made from the horizon.

Pour dépeupler un monde dont je suis absent (12)*

A girl and a circle. While the hoop rolls the girl, a lively silence rides itself at full gallop to the remembrance which appears suddenly crosswise; she is flipping her hair in the absence of the wind as the proof of her joy. Now I see her near, the colour of her hair is that of mine and her skirt too. The absence of the name of the girl and horizon's orphanage.

O tour de mon amour autour de mon amour (3)*

On the oblivious carpet of the dreams I walk, with no other concern than to save my death from the death, with no other simple thought.

Kabataş, 2010
*Giorgio di Chirico, Paul Eluard
Trans.H.Koçak

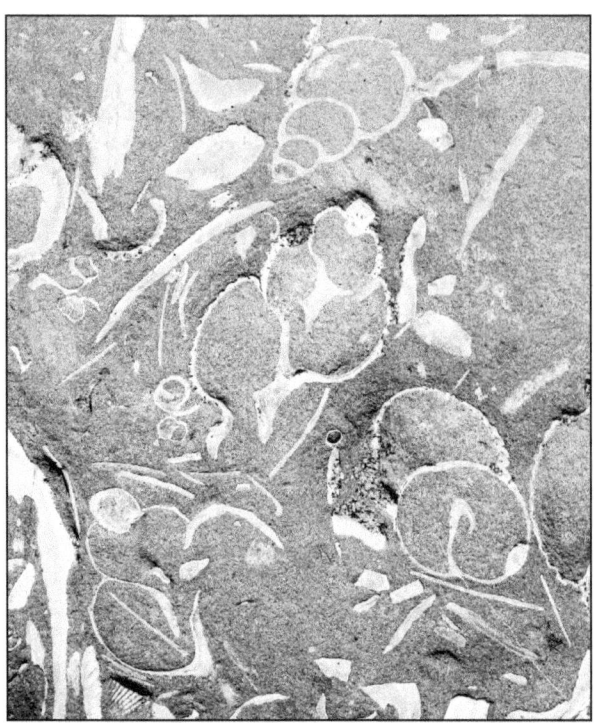

3. PRELUDE TO THE SQUID

Née de ma main sur mes yeux
Et me détournant de ma voie
L'ombre m'empêche de marcher
Sur ma couronne d'univers,
Dans le grand miroir habitable,
Miroir brisé, mouvant, inverse
Où l'habitude et la surprise
Créent ennui à tour de rôle*

It all began in the laundry of a motel near the railway station in a resort town, she followed me for some time. I was training myself to not to think about her, but that was she who was watching me, with her face disguised, sometimes from behind a rock or a wave.

There was killing her and nothing should have been more important apart from that. I thought of nothing but this for three nights and I sang while looking at a painting of a railway station through which no train passes. Then it was decided. First I was going to hire a building to watch her. Not an invisible small building though, no, that would give me away. A crowded base and now I am there.

I see her, walking slowly in the street, wearing an orange coat, dragging two black suitcases heavier than herself. She is waiting in the street now and I am waiting under the big clock set to my departure, waiting for my cigarette to finish and to be called to the train. Longer than it actually is, this street, but shorter than my childhood, and her steps are deliriously still in front of the same building.

The suitcases are not to blame for this; I remember perfectly that I told the station to follow her. I turn my gaze from the slippery floor to the big clock, the newspaper in a language I am not familiar with is shriveling gradually. I sit at the table pushed outside the station, to drink coffee. It is uncertain where the pale light inside is coming from in the high ceiling that enlarges me. The walls themselves are smothering the light, each has a project, a list of trains ready to go. It is as if she wrapped her arms around her own body, as if in a rehearsal for suicide. She is not looking around, she does not sense it. I want to be where she goes to, or I want to be her suitcase. My suitcases are crammed with old dirty clothes she dared to wash.

Touching not only the body but also those that cover it. Nausea, sharp childhood palpitations, whenever the sea rises in the street, the world goes into reverse, the names interlace. The images start to reproduce and multiply in order to fill up all the meaningless fears. I remember her, right there, in the resort town, on a day on which I was entrusted with her, leaning naked on the iron bars of the balcony in the heat of the summer, the first real body I saw, disregarding me, standing between me and my embarrassment, her body which does not belong to my mother.

She proceeds in her orange coat with the black suitcase, as she gets closer to me, the song I sang while looking at the painting through which no trains pass starts to whirl in my coffee with all its intensity. I drink it. She turns to me in fragile movements, she is more beautiful than I imagined, her eyes look like brilliant stones that go pale under the water. I am unfolding the newspaper in my hand to hide myself. She pushes the suitcase with her leg under the table and waves to the waiter, puts her handbag on the table and takes a cigarette. I light a cigarette.

Her hair is blond, wavy and pale like on that day. With dirty clothes in her hands, standing, looking at me in the face, I beg her to leave the clothes but she does not listen to me. I threaten her about writing songs mentioning her name, she does not care. "I will drown you by writing songs!" I shout, then I run away. I climb up and sit on a table like this one while waiting for my father. An old man is cleaning a squid he just took out from the water by hitting it on the rock. I start watching him. At the end of a street that opens up to the railway station, in a two-table arrangement, after long years my feet touch the ground. I close my eyes and hold the cup tightly, I look for it, the flapping lids, the desire to pierce her throat, a cup, an indeterminate ejaculation and here she drinks it. I can hear her gulping even from the remotest corner of my childhood room. I go away; he hits the squid on the rock once again. "It won't be hurt, don't worry," the old man says while looking at my short legs that cannot reach the ground. "I am not afraid of this! What I really think about is if I try to have a swim in this bay, how many sea urchins I can pick up with my feet by walking on them." The old man stands with a bucket in his hand: "your father does not want you to swim here," he answers. I throw the book in my hand into the water, the book taking along the pinkness of my palms inherited from my father and flows into the deep.

Everybody is far away. Only she is close to me, I have found her and I get closer to her with the nausea I feel from my body's heat. Now she is there again, holding the bottle of bleach in her hand. No, I heard her gulping today and I know that she drank it; I know it the best. She is lying on the ground. Her raincoat is turning into white slowly around a ring. White holes are pierced in her eyes. He beats the squid on the rock for the last time, and I say, "I want to eat that this evening!" I jump down from the table I am sitting on. The old man drops the squid in his hand into the bucket slowly. "Then let me cook this young lady," then he enters. I am getting closer where the squid was hit. I lick the ink smeared on the rock. My tongue moves on an unsmooth pain, I go numb.

I raise my head, see a dark lady at the opposite table fiddling with a dried sea urchin in her hands. The street turns into a river of ice, breaking in slow motion, my childhood starts to sizzle in my coffee, the big clock is calling me, I am saying silently to the station that it should stop the pursuit because I was wrong once again.

This woman whose pinkish body makes me shiver holds the cigarette in her lips, then removes the filter slowly with her right hand and starts to speak by pointing at the newspaper on my table.

"Tourists…"

She takes another puff of her cigarette and continues:
"Ignoramus…"

The song whirls in my head and the station disappears:

"Ma présence n'est pas ici.
Je suis habillé de moi-même.
Il n'y a pas de planète qui tienne
La clarté existe sans moi."*

*Ma Présence, Défense de Savoir I, Paul Eluard
2008- Balmumcu
Trans. T. Karakoç

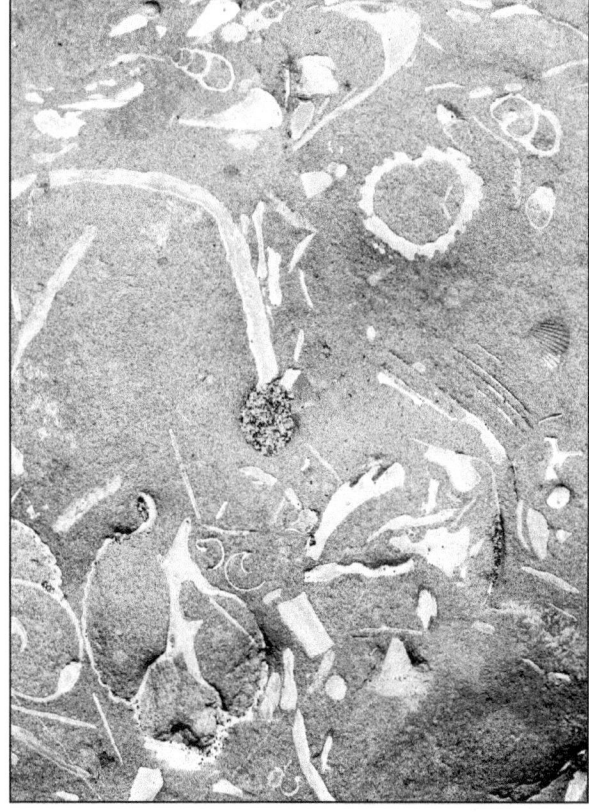

THE UNEXPECTED OBJECT

María Santana & Antonio Ramírez

Those so-called "unexpected objects" must be realized as follows: first, one must select and purchase a commodity in a supermarket (the method of acquisition will be determined during the process; but undoubtedly, the ideal way is to do it by way of shoplifting). The contents of the package, i.e., the commodity itself, is replaced by an object with a poetic nature, something deliberately created. The making of the object can be executed before or after obtaining the product in such a way that it optionally maintains a relationship with the substituted content, but the only condition is that the latter's dimensions must fit those of the packaging. Once you have managed to restore the packaging to its original appearance before it had been stripped of its original contents, i.e. without any signs of having been opened, then it is slyly returned to the supermarket shelf from where it was originally procured, waiting to be purchased by the unwary consumer.

For whoever makes and then places the unexpected object in a supermarket, it is an act of subversion in the strictest sense, because through this act the mechanism of consumption becomes thoroughly altered. First, one has to "pursue" the product that will serve as the receptacle, which in itself implies a playful experience within the supermarket. Then, when returning it, one must go against the grain by inadvertently placing the package back on the supermarket shelf just like one might do with any other commodity, thus reversing a process that seemed permanently fixed. The object hijacker thus disposes of the object and offers it as a gift in a place where only money rules, and with that act momentarily opens a hole for the relentless Moloch to sink. At that point, it does not really matter who will acquire our object, and we can only speculate about the way that person will react. It is an act of an irreverent, even illegal, nature that signifies a gesture of violence and contempt for the establishment, and which basically derives from the hope of provoking an act of collusion with another person.

In practice, through this action a commodity is removed from the pervasive market logic in order to be transformed into an absolutely useless object within that context, i.e., a lack of exchange value and a dubious use-value. It deals therefore with subverting the modern fetish par excellence, i.e., the goods, and within its own sanctuary, where it is surrounded by countless and indifferent similar ones, protected and immersed in the timeless ritual of consumption, breaking the ridiculous illusion of omnipotence that is given to the consumer. When the doors of the supermarket open, the buyer tacitly expects the goods to be submissively displayed, according to his purchasing expectations. Thus, after the sacred exercise of supposed freedom that the choice of goods and their payment constitute, the consumer is entitled to require that such fetishes fulfill what has been promised, by way of the monetary contract (the sacrifice). For many of these unwary consumers, finding an unexpected object, which moreover escapes any rational sense, therefore becomes a deeply fraudulent situation, an annoying scam that, at the height of absurdity, makes it impossible to complain about under such circumstances. Who would dare to go to the supermarket so as to complain about the strange

Antonio Ramírez

and disturbing contents of a can of mackerel? How to describe the situation that ends with what one finds in one's hands?

With this approach, a fragment of colonized reality is liberated, giving it the uniqueness and the unpragmatic value of the poetic. Additionally, the final consummation of this subversion is realized when the consumer, who has complied with his glorious role, opens the package and finds something that sharply breaks with his expectations. Like a Trojan Horse, the unexpected object has entered into the realm of his privacy, into the closed structure of the home and in everyday life, preventing the expected worship of the seemingly omnipotent commodity fetish. Thus a breakdown takes place in the supposedly natural and straightforward relationship (doctrinally presented as non-ideological) between value and product. And so the customer ends up paying for an object that is devoid of monetary value, which actually exceeds the categorical identity of the commodity and which puts him at the threshold of the symbolic and the poetic that becomes multiplied, since he encounters first the object itself, and then that unique moment of discovery, that movement of extraction that he performs with his own hands and which leads to that feeling of bewilderment and disequilibrium. He will find himself with a spurious gift in his hands, something unmanageable, unconsumable, gratuitous and which deliberately impels him to confront the sensible without any possible intervention. In short, we are dealing with an involuntary experience, though perhaps which is secretly desired (however much he may deny it).

The consequences of this action, however, go beyond the momentary disconnection of the subject as something expendable in that commercial totalitarianism which our existence has become. A fissure leading to the absurd and the poetic is created, getting him to confront an enigma that has been established in the most everyday sphere, within his own home, safe from the gaze of others, in that space where he still has a chance to be alone and to think. Thus, the expectations of a universe that is presented as being completely mechanistic, based on the causality of money, can disintegrate the instant that the hidden object is revealed. Likewise, no kind of political discourse or utopian message that tries to support or give meaning to the unexpected object is being articulated here, but its sense is absolutely undefined, the determination of a specific symbolic value being entirely up to the receiver; and, above all, it offers something tangible, perceptible, and material; something seemingly insignificant, but of a radically subversive nature. The consumer gets something tangible and inescapable; it is neither a message nor an illusion, without a place to turn a deaf ear or to become amazed. He expected to find the usual tame and prosaic reality but instead was met with a surge of poetic objectivity. At the moment when the victim of our action has the opportunity to reflect on what has happened, then perhaps the idea of the other will emerge, that enigmatic subjectivity which upsets his most basic mindset. In this sense, the individual who offers the unexpected gift is not simply a politically seditious person who is trying to provoke a guilty conscience in someone else, but rather someone who has incited him through his doubtlessly most despised and bloated inner mechanisms. The disbelief that results from opening the package which hearkens to the realm of the dream, of the absurd, of the poetic, is strengthened when speculating on the person who created the object, whose derangement is obvious. Otherwise, how else to explain how someone would come to do such a thing? But through such a risky and concrete action, the other person has established his undeniable presence (someone from outside who has entered your home without permission) by introducing an object that is loaded with unclear intent, since it opens up infinite possibilities of decontextualized experiences and interpretations, exposing him to an unprecedented and pre-conceptual experience; and also because no tutorial, no artistic intention, no justification for structuring the experience or for providing him with any sense of closure is attached to the object. Upon encountering the object, there will only be two options: to throw it away or let oneself be carried away by the unknown. And from there, the possibilities are endless.

(Translated by Bruno Jacobs, revised by Eric Bragg and Noé Ortega)

* Originally published in "Las mercancías mueren, las cosas despiertan", La Torre Magnética, Madrid, 2013.

Noé Ortega

María Santana

Bruno Jacobs

Bruno Jacobs

Vicente Gutiérrez Escudero

Lurdes Martínez

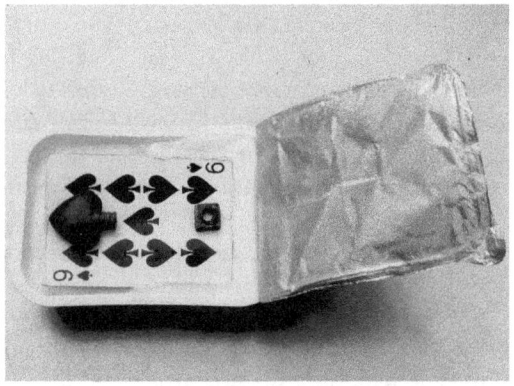

Lurdes Martínez

Eugenio Castro

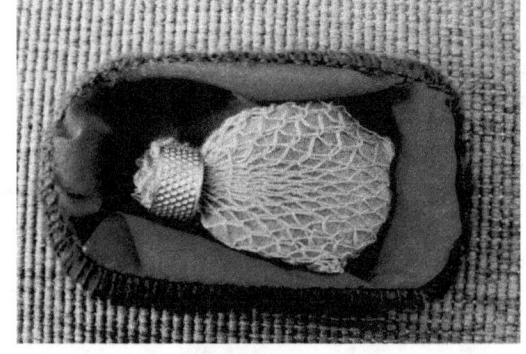

María Santana

TheMicturatingAngel
A Tale of Science and Erotica

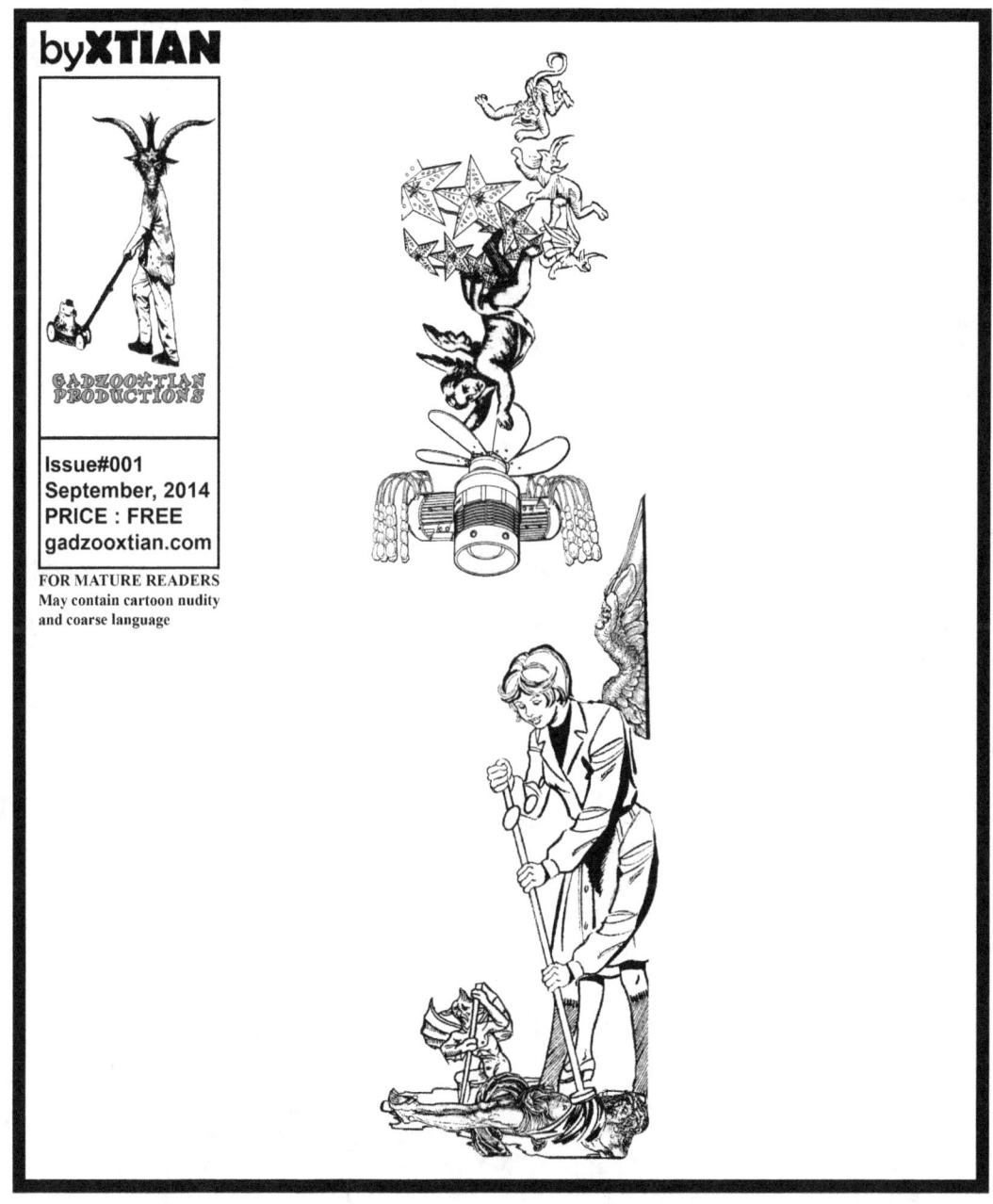

by **XTIAN**

GADZOOXTIAN PRODUCTIONS

Issue #001
September, 2014
PRICE : FREE
gadzooxtian.com

FOR MATURE READERS
May contain cartoon nudity and coarse language

"I suppose what they believe, they leave."

Timothy Layden - *Abstinence of Identity*

FOR A SURREALIST USE OF TECHNOLOGY...
Of different sorts of tools

Pierre Petiot

There are tools that allow us to do things, tools that make possible that which previously we had no concept of; tools that create new freedoms, tools that open us up to new adventures. These tools are a pure affirmation. Nothing of what they are and allow existed before them and after them, the world is no longer the same. Their function was not known, it was not defined before they appeared, and of course, that function was even less agreed upon. In fact, they initially did not have any function at all, and it is only the sadness of a routine use, the power of habits, that finally gave them their function. These tools do not replace anything in any way and actually they are irreplaceable.

And then there are the tools that *serve us*, that in some way *replace us*, that allow us to avoid being there, and which in some way seem to live in our place. They relieve us from our tedious tasks and of the associated efforts, boredom and pain of course, but they also free us at least partially of *the burden of living*. These tools do not *allow us* to do something more, something that we did not yet know. No, quite the contrary, in essence they *allow us not to do* something we already knew. What they do, every human being could do before they existed, but they do it just as well and even better than us, and most of the time much faster and in a more perfect way than us. These tools are a *negation,* since something had to exist prior to their existence, and this something that previously existed is in some way *denied by their existence.* Examples of such tools are cars (since we are naturally self-mobile), the dishwasher, the washing machine, etc. And of course between the tools that *allow us to* and the tools that *allow us not to*, there is the whole range of the *ambiguous,* as Charles Fourier would have said.

The tools that replace us may be described without much risk of error, as of *realist* essence. Just like the realist painter, they are redefining what they replace and thus *imitate it and reduce it* to their actual function. So, *doing the dishes* is reduced to what the dishwasher can do. The pleasure with which I caress this plate, the forks and knives that I chose and like, the bright transparency of my shining glasses, the pleasure of sharing the task of restoring order within the dishes and kitchen after the friendly feasts, all that, that was to live, fled away into a representation and vanished, down the drain with the rinse water at the end of the washing cycle. From being an ordinary moment of family life, but a moment that was lived differently in each family, the task of doing the dishes has now been reduced to a standard, to a pure convention.

Before the dishwasher, doing the dishes could be whatever we wanted: a pain, a repeated daily boredom, a game when we sent each other the plates to wipe like flying saucers, a time to make love, the pretext of a family quarrel, the edge of a murder, the opportunity and pleasure of breaking our own dishes or that of someone else's. All this was reduced to pure convention: doing the dishes, that's what the dishwasher does, and that's it. And the only adventure that is left to us is that this machine can break down. Although we do not accept this kind of adventure. This failure makes us feel that the machine is being unfair. It broke the rules, it did not fulfill its contract, it betrays us and leaves us there without any way out, maybe even just before our guests arrive... That sort of thing makes us unhappy, it depresses us or makes us angry. It rarely leaves us indifferent.

We can repeat the exercise with the washing machine. I live in an area where, as there are not so many opportunities for local pride, people had the idea of preserving the wash houses. These were places where women would come to wash and rinse clothes in the river, the pond or the lake, in summer as well as in winter, their hands in the cold or even freezing water, knees kept dry and warm in their "*carrosses*": wooden boxes filled with straw or hay... These places were the occasion of meetings and discussions among all women, absolutely free from the presence and from the gaze of men. These places were creating, or rather, building, the community of women. They were the equivalent of the bar for males and in fact a true village council of petticoats, certainly not without real power. On summer evenings, young men and girls would gather there to meet and laugh together and inscriptions on the walls of the wash house still show across the centuries the possibly short, but dazzling splendor of the love between Rémi and Marinette, or the shared passion of Alphonse and Louise, would it be with the help of the traditional heart pierced by an arrow or not, and on the whole, the wash house kept the memory of many other loves over time and generations. With a little bit of imagination, but perhaps without any real deception, we may dream that if the walls could talk they would probably tell us that later in the summer evenings, far from the prying eyes and with the complicity of the water nearby, year after year more than half of the villagers were probably conceived there.

Part of the wash houses that I am talking about, and that fueled my childhood, were made of iron sheeting, as are mainly also the washing machines, so that the secret of the transmutation of the powers of imagination into nothing, as a result of the washing machine is not at all related to matter. And it is not a matter of function either. The washing machine is designed to wash clothes, as is the wash house. Simply, when using the wash house, there is no substitution of a piece of human existence by a mere convention. In addition, the village tradition had created for the wash house a lot of unintended uses that had nothing to do with the original function of the building. But while cats have invented a particular use for washing machines, quite comparable to a TV for man at least until the spin is not switched on man has not invented many other uses for a washing machine than the washing of clothes.

If a surrealist, or let's say Marcel Duchamp, had been able to suggest the transformation of a washing machine into a place for love trysts or into a "bedroom" for such activity, it would be easy to find people to categorize it as a surrealist act, as a delicious way to misuse a washing machine. Yet, that's exactly the kind of subversion of the technical purpose of a wash house that the young people of my village spontaneously invented, by deliberately ignoring the realist's use of it, which states that a wash house is made for washing clothes, period.

That translates easily enough into modern terms. The poor young people in my Parisian neighborhood who are not rich enough to pay for drinks, even cheap ones, and who hence cannot meet in a café, spontaneously transformed the self-service laundry where I sometimes go in the next street corner into their meeting room. They actually have no choice but to meet there in winter when it is freezing outside or in any season when it is pouring. They do pretty much anything there that they are not prevented from doing, including on occasion soft drug deals. But I have also seen them occasionally use the place as a poetry workshop: one evening I saw a boy whom you might have thought illiterate, counting on his fingers the syllables of the rap song that he was carefully writing on a little notebook. That was absolutely touching! However, as the place is closing at 21:00, it is quite impossible for these young people to use it as a love tryst place, just as it is not possible for them either to write graffiti on the walls like the traditional lovers used to do, because such behavior would exclude them permanently from the place.

On the whole, it seems clear that these young peo-ple subvert the intended use of this realist self-service laun-derette, as occasionally a "bouncer" type or even the police may be sent there to restore the realist order, that enforces the rule that a self-service laundry is only meant for the pur-poses of doing laundry.

On the other side of the mask

The kind of man who is passionate about technology *is not* a realist. His purpose as soon as he has become aware enough of the true nature of his passion is in no way to use his favorite technical object for its intended use, but rather for just about anything that may happen to come to his mind. We can therefore say that the man passionate for technology, just the opposite of what is usually said about him, is not a fan of technology *for its own sake*, but rather a fan of technology *for his own sake*.

As soon as you get rid of the repeated imagery of the obsessive loner who polishes his car on Sundays, because he is not able to deliver quite as tender caresses to his wife or — when necessary — to her rival, you will soon be facing the strange phenomenon of the *personalization* of any kind of transportation means, individual or, taking into ac-count the fashion of tagging in railway environments, even collectively. And that is quite a different matter.

For the love of customization is not a solitary vice. On the contrary, it socializes. Enthusiasts have to find the tools, spare parts, paints, and ideas, and above all the peers to share their judgments and admiration of the works. This builds a world, and in terms of facts or as regards the attitudes involved, there are no real differences between the *Facteur Cheval* or my ex-neighbor *Picassiette*, and most of the "Apaches" who outrageously customize their cars or their motorcycles, except perhaps a deeper quality of innocence and of freedom of mind, although this would yet have to be evaluated.

When the Facteur Cheval builds his "*Palais Ideal*" or when my previous neighbor Picassiette covers his house, garden, chairs, tables, stove, beds with a mosaic of broken crockery and glass, it is often quite agreed upon finding this admirable. But when some enraged fan covers his car or motorcycle with the same sort of tiling or even worse than the one used by Picassiette (once the keeper of Chartres cemetery), then open admiration suddenly becomes questionable.

Why? Because it is car and motorcycle fetish objects of the "consumer society", and not a house, not an arch-itectural and thus not an artistic and "noble" object. Yet the house of Picassiette, that I know well, is nothing other than a typical workers house from the early 20th century, that is, roughly, the same type of serial product as cars and motorbikes and, whether we like it or not, an object of consumption just as well. Whatever may be the ardor, the ability for madness or to genius of the artist, to customize one's car or motorbike will appear as doubtful and sub-cultural, while to personalize one's suburban house into a submarine, into an airstrip for flying saucers, into the Sistine Chapel, into a Hindu temple, or into any other sort of building of a much more resolutely non-identifiable type, will usually raise much less art-related questions.

The passions of personalization may be lonely, as often goes with the architectural customization, they may even be somewhat mystical, but whatever the object that serves as a pretext for letting their delusions wander, cus-tomization addicts, be they either men or women, are usually nothing like sad consumer idiots. *They are dream-ers*. And technology is not what consumes them: *their dreams do*.

What the mad teach us

One cannot be thankful enough to surrealism to have taken interest into madness and to have done so, not in narrow medical terms (and hence realist), that aim to free the madman of his madness, but on the contrary to have done it with the idea of using the lessons learned of madness in order to free the non-mad people and thus by immediate consequence the mad persons as well. It would hence be unfair to criticize surrealism for not having persevered in this wonderful direction that it had opened and that no other school of thought has been bold enough to ever resume since. Of course, going on along this path would have required that the participants of the Surrealist movement had had like Breton, some experience in both the observation and the theoretical aspects related to madness itself. This was not the case.

But even without this minimal understanding of the field, just by looking at the signs and ordinary social representations of mad men, it could have been seen that they had something to teach us about our relationship to madness. For instance, the most prevalent image of the fool in French society is that of a man who walks with a funnel on his head.

This image reveals that one of the characteristics of the fool is the ability not to use a tool as agreed, which in the case of the funnel is to pour a liquid into a container, the opening of which is too narrow, and I must emphasize the positive aspect of this ability, because it is not proven that a fool who walks around with a funnel on his head is so far unable to use the same instrument to pour water or wine into a bottle, as well as those deemed sane around him. What characterizes the fool in the eyes of the crowd here is not specifically a lack of ability or even a disability such as the inability to meet a technical convention, but instead an ability to go beyond this convention. In other terms, to break free from convention. What this traditional image of the fool points out here – as in many other occasions – is an indication of an exceeding capacity, the path to a possible freedom, and that the alienation that the fool's behavior, tells us about in this case, is not *his* but *ours*.

Let's consider for a while how things are in their simple materiality: the constraints that seem to belong to the tool, to the technology and from which the fool's presence of mind may free us; are they really located in the tool itself, in the funnel object as such? As soon as the question is raised in rigorous and honest terms, everyone except perhaps some deeply mad persons shall admit that a funnel was never seen to compel a man to do something. But is this, however, what is said by the ways of speaking we use to express that do we have the words to put it another way tools, machines, the technology, the "technological system" impose constraints upon us, and that we should get free from them? Sadly, the weakness of our power of expression forces us here to state without shuddering a true folly, a folly that is a testimony of a no less true animism which civilized mankind thought to have been, far away for thousands of years...

For the funnel actually does not compel nor enclose the fool in any way, but we do, and it's not the funnel that forces us into this strange laughter made of false condescension and true terror, by which we pretend to make fun of the mad, but that actually expresses our panic at the thought of what the only power that we fear on earth as in heaven could be: the power of a fully unleashed human mind.

The spirit in the machine

What the detractors of tools, machines, and technology, hate is as they will say the stress associated with them, and rightly so because each technical object is indeed inhabited by a spirit. A very powerful spirit which is its purpose, its instructions for use in short the (very highly recommended) agreed upon way of using it. And I would add that without this spirit, the tool itself is *nothing*, concretely and so to say physically nothing. And that's what is kindly highlighted in the South African film called "*The Gods Must Be Mad*", in which an object as innocent and simple as an empty Coca Cola bottle, dropped from an aircraft in the Kalahari desert, and picked up by a Bushman was suddenly revealed as dizzyingly deprived of any function and meaning. The spirit of the tool having abandoned the Coca Cola bottle, it proved to be far more empty than due to the mere absence of contents only: absolutely and completely empty. And in spite of all interpretation attempts performed by the bushman society, the bottle was found unfit for any use and ultimately quite harmful to this society.

There are still quite sane men on Earth who talk to their tools. As they are quite aware that tools have souls, it does not seem incongruous to them to speak to these souls, to try to obtain from them the kind of favors that we normally expect of proper functioning. We, unlike these animists, no longer see the souls of things and therefore we do not distrust them. And we often laugh at these people's primitivism, but we have nevertheless retained inside of us enough of this primitivism to happen – while being the spontaneous rationalists that we are – to yell heart and guts at our machines when they deprive us for a moment of what we expect from them: "Are you going to start up... you fucking ... ".

We see that, basically, in our modern society as in ancient societies, everything is spirit and hence everything is human, and that, when carefully considered, spirits did not leave us, but simply went below the threshold of consciousness as is reflected in our innocent swearing.

Of the inhumanity of windmills

A usual criticism regarding tools, and even more regarding machines is their inhumanity, and all well considered, what else could be otherwise inhuman? Some behaviors of some men sometimes can be said to be inhuman, but to state that men in general or even some men can be as such by nature inhuman, obviously leads to a contradiction in terms. Similarly, Nature, this mother strange and foreign to us, that made us and includes us, cannot be considered inhuman. One can say that Nature is indifferent, merciless, and cruel, but no one would consider Nature to be capable of inhumanity.

Neither tigers nor wolves nor lions nor hyenas, nor even the plague are inhuman in the sense that the extermination camps were inhuman. What is inhuman in the gas chamber *is not in the room*. It is not the room itself nor the gas. It is an industrial process applied by people to other people and in which machines or tools are in fact used *as masks*.

Just as were used as masks the wagons, the locomotives, railways, ticket counters, and trains that were used to carry people to industrially planned mass slaughter. In the same way too, as a mask is used to hide the face of the executioner in order to highlight the purely social nature of an execution, that is to say, of a crime thus freeing the craftsman who performs it of any guilt. It is this same power, obviously social and human but collective and anonymous which, by a strange abandonment of their common sovereignty, is projected into a beyond or a below of men. This collective and anonymous power is what is at work in technical protocols. This anonymous human power is the root of this *"deadly seriousness of the machines"* described by Marcel Duchamp. This is also what *the banality of evil* analyzed by Hannah Arendt about what Eichmann is made of.

This inhumanity that is usually attributed to tools or machines is obviously nothing other than the inhumanity of men, incorporated within tools and machines, but of which their living souls have moved away, and of which they are now absent, so to say. It is in some way of the same nature as the gods, who also may appear inhuman to the extent that they look human. Hence is it useless to fight this inhumanity in the tools or in the machines, since that is precisely *not* where it is.

We may only call what men are capable of inhuman.

And it is a fact that men haunt the technical processes as they haunt masks. The human beings caught and articulated in the technical processes are interchangeable, as are the faces behind the masks. The mask just as well as the technology are made of this interchangeability. Behind a mask there can be anyone, just like any human being can (theoretically) replace any other human being in a technical process. Both the mask and the technical process will survive all those who once haunted and acted them, and thus diminish and ridicule these human beings. But conversely, as soon as we abandon our tools and machines for a moment, they become absurd. They immediately take on a sense of being dead and have a spectral aura or sensation on to them. They are like inhabited by our absence and dressed in the moiré of our shadows... *We haunt our machines just as they haunt us.*

But a mask has two sides, one outside and one inside, and while, when it is considered from an outside point of view, behind the mask there may be anybody, for ther person inside the mask things are quite different. Because people do not only use masks to hide, they use masks much more essentially to transform themselves, in order to become someone or something else, and for anyone who wears a mask whether voluntarily or not, the mask is always an adventure of the mind. This use of the mask opens up the mind, builds a new presence of the mind each time, and may be brought to a glow or a trance when passion grows.

This is quite the opposite of this anonymous and disembodied social power which appeared first in the technical process and which seemed so strongly woven of shadows. The same technical process can be repeated thousands of times, but as soon as you really take the risk, a mask is never embodied in the same way twice.

By means of the folly that it offers to us, the mask teaches us some wisdom about the tool. Now, what happens if we turn the technological rituals the other way round? What happens is Art, or Science, or Technology — but all three were once one. A unity that was broken by the industrial age. What happens is adventure, risk, the ability to go beyond ourselves by means of machines and tools. The same flamboyant presence that lit the mask from the inside, now may flow in the actors' mind. Yes, of the actors, because Jazz, as well as Surrealism, exist, both of them with the ability to have *"given rise to a curious possibility of thought, which is that of its sharing"* ("André Breton — Second manifesto" quoted by Julien Gracq in his book "André Breton" — French version p.37), and if in these two wonderful examples of automatism, each individual experience is unique, it burns and it feeds into the experience of others and even much more intensely in the common experience.

Of a denial that is not a denial

People who feel hurt by tools and machines (who are quite numerous these days) have a natural tendency to flee from their company. But flight, in a species as deeply gregarious as ours, is impossible and they all know it. Hence they deny, to the extent that they can, what hurts them, but they do not know how to avoid it. They try to reduce their use of technology as much as possible. You will often hear them state that the use of their cars, of their computers, and so on is nothing but strictly utilitarian. *"For me, this machine is a tool, it is only that,"* they will say. They do not realize that this strange sort of denial, that this wording *"it is only that..."* is the very footprint and the overt act of realism, the very perceptive and intellectual trap that they think to escape from and to fight against. So that for the one who hears well enough, the protective words *"it is only that..."*, actually sound like the sure sign of a lost battle. Because by thinking this way, these valiant technophobes have become themselves the very enemy they wanted to fight.

In the world of realism where the use of each thing is defined and regulated, all things appear as what they should be, and the appearance of each new tool drags after itself a host of new pressures and constraints that begin to resonate in the future like a noisy string of pots. These constraints do not belong to things, they are social because nothing can ever compel men except other men.

They consist of uses, suggested, allowed, agreed, recommended, required, legal and ultimately mandatory uses, of which no person is entitled to shirk under penalty of exclusion or punishment.

They also bring forth our expectations, since any tool, any machine, *implements a prediction*, and thus forces us to expect that this prediction is fulfilled. Through more repetition, expectation from a hope that it once was, became dullness and then solidified into boredom, and then was finally changed into despair. But what else are this expectation and this boredom made of, except of us being away from ourselves, starting with the absence of this part of ourselves that we have left in the machine, and by which it works "*without us*". So says the story, in which all believe or pretend to believe. Realism, Spectacle are only woven out of our desertion. So that to boast of reducing your use of technical objects to what is accepted, agreed upon, recommended, required, legal and binding; that is something like thinking of possibly breaking yourself free by mumbling frequently enough and with a firm conviction, "*Yes. Master*".

"*Only that...*". Here is the sign and the anthem of the "*maître déchanteur*", the subtitle and the pilot fish of each realist image, this irony from where it thrusts at you: "*Look, it works*". The marvel, then, finally was "*only that*", and out of there indeed any sort of marvel seems to have vanished. What is left is only the wonder of the effect, of the deception, of the trompe l'oeil, which delights us first and then to which we are giving way, and in the end, "*everything that was directly lived has moved away into a representation*".

Let's look beyond though, let's force our vision a little. Something still vibrates and throbs beyond the boundaries: this "*only that...*" that Realism points at, we just have to send it back, to see that this "*only that...*" is only what Realism itself is, and it is certainly not at all a marvel. The marvellous however is still there, as usual, just a little bit beyond, just behind, on the other side of the mask, just behind the grimace. It is there, but simply it is not, it has never been, it will never be "*only that*". But in fact, this "*Look it works...*" of the representation, is it anything else other than the pretentious version of the modest and faithful little song of machines and tools? With this difference however: a realist picture is not only a machine to show things, it is a machine to give orders. It is a machine to show things *as they **must** be seen*.

Andrew Juris - *Peculiar Missouri*

We Live in Simple Times:
notes on class infowar and luminaries of the resistance
(Anonymous, Wikileaks, Snowden)

Parry Harnden

The development of the technology that comprises what is sometimes called the Information Age coincided with the rise of neoliberalism, the free market economic philosophy that governments should wait on the private sector, and this technology has worked foremost in the service of the neoliberal conception. As neoliberalism has pushed societies towards the bad old days of laissez-faire capitalism over the last few decades, the battle lines of class warfare have been brought into stark relief. In the United States, the economic spearhead that positions itself before the world as the definition of democracy, the social spending and middle class which cushioned the elites against a peasant uprising are withering away, while pretenses of democracy scarcely cover a nakedly plutocratic government. There has been a steady widening of the gap between the "haves and have-nots" and the issue of income inequality has raised the temperature to the boiling pot in mass protests by workers demanding a livable wage. In the memorable phrasing of the Occupy Movement, the 1%—who monopolise wealth and decision-making—are pitted against the world, both figuratively and literally, for capitalism is proving itself destructive on a planetary scale. Any illusion that class was to become a thing of the past for the affluent West has been dispelled for the same information technology that was used to create the new economic reality is being used to study it and affect it.

The success of information technology relied on its widespread acceptance and use. A trail of bread crumbs led from personal computers to the "information superhighway," to social media, to the reign of cell phones. People were herded on-line to do their banking and go bargain shopping—conveniences that suck jobs from the economy while the cost-saving is converted into profits. There was an idea cultivated that cyber-space was disconnected from the real world, a place where users could immerse themselves in games and role-playing, and the new technology was the machinery of fantasy, second only perhaps to the illusion factories of patriotism and religion. The internet seemed to have a natural affinity as a tool of population control: besides undermining the working class, it kept its users distracted, separated and easy to keep an eye on. Yet people cannot help but find subversive uses for their tools and toys. The new technology has helped capitalism undermine the quality of existence for the many, perhaps even the possibility of existence, but at the same time people have used it to communicate and organise, and have been able to extract something intelligible from its unpredictable flow of information, misinformation and disinformation. It is a trait of the era that the victims of the economic polarisation are well-informed, and this combination lays out the welcome mat for the radical transformation of the entire corrupt system.

The nexus between neoliberal thought and information technology is that both assist the ownership class in consolidating its wealth and dominating its natural adversary, the labour pool, which is to say the rest of humanity. The neoliberal program puts states to the task of opening and securing markets (by the pacts and so-called "free trade" deals which protect investors by putting at risk the environment, labour rights, and local economies which bear the cost of market crashes) and eliminating those functions of states which only benefit people and don't add to profits (such as regulation of investment, environmental protection, taxation for infrastructure and programs, etc.). The tools of the new technology—the internet, high storage capacity and computational capabilities, the cell phone, and now 3D printers and so on—are put to the use of deskilling, dis-empowering and replacing workforces, and of relocating manufacturing while ballooning the financial services sector. Technology provides the practicalities, while neoliberalism provides the political framework that determines how the technology will be used.

The successes of the information economy have been impressive, upturning economies in Latin America and the Pacific Rim and ultimately the international system that hinges on the American economy. The economic blowouts don't deter the neoliberal vision as each crash results in a restructuring that further shifts social wealth from the many to the few.

There's every reason to be pessimistic. The neoliberal project is ongoing, the technology is still developing and will continue to be used against anyone who needs to work to survive. There are still jobs to disappear, as the effects of online shopping ripple through the jobs associated with retail. The permitted avenues of recourse are withering. Union power has long been in retreat and not even existing contracts are being honoured. Elected governments are ineffectual or merely corporate adjuncts, the non-functioning vestigial organs of democracy, impotent to override the economics wizards even in the face of climate change and the catastrophic effects it racks up daily. There is still more to be squeezed out of people as they are pushed to a subsistence-level existence where they will be too preoccupied with the basics of survival to organise rebellion. The architects wrestle with the problem of what to do with the excess of people. Perhaps they could all be conscripted? The elites reacted to pestering questions about their power by trying to erase their critics—by passing laws against whistleblowers, by smashing the Occupy Movement with police force, or, to bring the tactics up-to-date, using the new technology to surveil and manipulate their opposition. And should the masses ever wheel out the guillotines, local police forces have been equipped with heavy military assault weaponry to answer them. These matters have all been well explored, solutions have been proposed, information has been widely disseminated—but there persists a wall of political inaction, for reasons also well studied and explicable. Meanwhile, elites have added the abolition of corporate tax to their bucket list. (1)

With trust in governments and legal channels low, the information age is spawning new categories of criminal. First, the hacker, who breaks into computers to steal or destroy information. Among the most aggressive criminal hackers are governments who indulge in corporate espionage or worse (for example, a new era of industrial sabotage was ushered in by the Stuxnet malware created by the US and Israel to disrupt Iran's nuclear program). A special notoriety has been reserved for the "hacktivists" whose activities carry a political message. The most infamous of these groups has been Anonymous, which grew up on the internet as like-minded hackers joined forces—at first to play pranks, notably at the expense the Church of Scientology. Their higher mission coalesced around free speech and an open internet, a cause which hit them where they live, as it encompasses such concerns as file-sharing and copyright protection—issues which have far-reaching implications in terms of cultural ownership, of attempts to regulate the internet and yoke it to private profit, and of the criminalisation of the majority of internet users. Anonymous launched retaliatory strikes against enforcers of corporate interests, and were soon in a prolonged war with governments, corporations, copyright organisations and private security firms. Their preferred method of attack was the distributed denial-of-service (DDoS), which in effect jams a website and can be costly to a large corporation. As Anonymous' politicalisation deepened, it put itself in the service of popular movements such as Occupy and the Arab Spring uprising as well as social causes related to environmentalism, homelessness, and, with some contradiction, anti-pornography vigilantism.

Although its actions are collective, Anonymous created a singular identity for itself to give graphic expression to its cause. It gave itself a name suggestive of the faceless everyman, a face in the form of a Guy Fawkes mask inspired by a Michael Moore comic, and a voice through its manifestos. This manufactured avenger of the oppressed was a heroic character from the lineage of Robin Hood, the outlaw who enjoys popular support because he counters the laws of corrupt elites with a sense of justice. The similarity was underlined by a widely-reported plot named "Operation Robin Hood" in which hacktivists were to give to charities and protest groups what they stole through credit card fraud. This romantic hero is a necessarily recurring figure in the long history of class oppression: Pretty Boy Floyd in the 20th C. US, Ned Kelly in 19th C. Australia, Chucho el Roto in 19th C. Mexico, Kayamkulam Kochunni in 19th C. India, Nezumi Kozō in 19th C. Japan, Juraj Jánošík in 18th C. Slovakia, Schinderhannes in 17th C. Germany, and others have occupied the role, with Anonymous being the first to have an international character. Robin Hood the prototype has been admitted into the iconography of surrealists who understand his defiance and resistance to be part of the human fibre: "The Marvelous is our Sherwood Forest." (2) He is not a conqueror, he does not solve a problem, but his mocking arrows shatter the facade of righteous invincibility erected by king and sheriff, inspiring new momentum and direction in the oppressed. His threat is not that he is a nuisance, but that he is an example of insubordination that others might follow. So too the primary threat of Anonymous is that their message—that resistance to state-corporate power is not only possible but necessary for the cause of freedom—will have a popular resonance with internet users who are meant to be isolated and focused on personal consumption.

Anonymous is not a well-defined group or even a network, but a cloud of people and cells who more-or-less share core values and seek ways to publicise their causes or engage meaningfully with activists. Like the internet itself, it cannot be destroyed by attacking one of its points. Indeed, dozens of arrests, including the police sweep that followed after the group acted in support of Wikileaks, have not killed the idea. Their expanding scope of concerns has been synthesized in a recently cir-

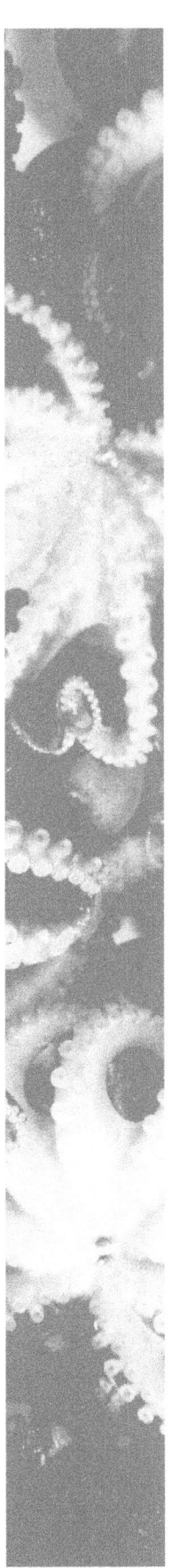

culated video Manifesto: "...the true purpose of Anonymous: peace and unity. We are not an official organization. We are a collective and a movement. We are an idea that is freely shared and supported by humanity, whose solidarity lies within love, peace, equality, freedom, and justice for all." In recent years, though, the group's profile has slipped. Turns out that internet security is actually riddled with holes, and a series of breaches has found banks, governments and retailers hemorrhaging private information, with the crowning disaster being the discovery of the Heartbleed bug— the Achilles' heel of internet security (had Achilles' heel covered a fifth of his body). As Anonymous was not involved with these lapses, its rank as a threat to cyber-security has been demoted.

Furthermore, Anonymous' notoriety as a bogeyman has waned against the rise of another form of cyber-age criminal who has proved even more bothersome to political power: the leaker who uses information age technology to spread the wrong kind of information. Wikileaks provides a website where people can anonymously leak confidential information that exposes the malfeasance, corruption and immoral wars of state-corporate power. Beginning in 2007, it was an immediate success, adding over a million documents within its first year. In 2010 it published massive leaks concerning the current American wars and the prisoners at Guantanamo Bay, but also the attention-grabbing video known as "Collateral Murder," which showed an Apache helicopter eye's-view as it first mowed down a group of civilians in Baghdad, among them journalists, then attacked a family van that stopped to help the dying. Yet more troublesome for the American government was the monumental leak of a quarter million diplomatic cables spanning a period of nearly 45 years. The cables leak contained nothing classified "top secret" and largely only confirmed things already surmised, but it did provide concrete evidence of policy dissemblance and the dismissive attitude the US has towards its diplomatic partners—insults met with general anger in the maligned countries. The leak would be a slowly unfolding embarrassment. In its wake, serious attempts were made to shut Wikileaks down: following a powerful DDoS attack against the site came surveillances, detentions, seizure of computers, bank assets being frozen, and an economic embargo by Visa, Mastercard and PayPal that almost killed the organisation. Although the leakers' crime, if any, could accurately be characterised as "civil disobedience," political and media hacks were quick to label them "terrorists" (as so many have been since rule-by-fear became the quickest shortcut to state overreach). Anonymous entered the fray and attacked corporate and government websites connected to attempted suppression of the leaks, including many in Tunisia where anger over the cables was a spur to the revolutionary fervor behind the Arab Spring. But Wikileaks' infamy too would be eclipsed by an even more damaging leaker.

In 2013, a series of leaks from former American intelligence insider Edward Snowden via journalists at *The Guardian* began to expose to the world the real dimensions of the surveillance state to which it is subjected. The first report revealed that the National Security Agency was daily collecting millions of phone records of Americans, making a joke of constitutional protections against unreasonable search and seizure. But that was just the initial dusting of the avalanche to follow. The NSA and its friends were spying on everyone, often with ingeniously invasive techniques, and they had greater ambitions still: to intercept and record every bit of electronic communication, to eventually "eliminate privacy globally." This was no mere pipe dream. Their hungry programs collected e-mails in bulk, internet records were grabbed, trillions of device-location records logged. With the cooperation of companies such as Google, Facebook, Skype and Microsoft, they tapped into the personal information of users and collected private webcam feeds. They intercepted routers during shipments to bug them and so compromise entire networks. In one test, they recorded every cell phone call made in the Bahamas and Afghanistan. Computers were infected with malware that allowed the spies to read every keystroke the user made. The NSA's mantra was "collect it all... exploit it all." A mammoth facility was built in Utah to store the incomprehensible amount of data.

How did information technology move so rapidly from its promise of providing a space for the free and open exchange of information, uncensored and answerable to no one, to being the Argus that fends off the dusk of capitalism? The process was goosed forward under the aegis of national security, of protecting states from threats they helped create and then exacerbated. Then too people helped by becoming the perfect accomplices to their own surveillance and manipulation: a generation has been raised to broadcast a dossier of their life, and to live on-line as much as possible; the Googles and Facebooks are welcomed into homes for offering free services and their motivations as huge corporations get overlooked; the cell phone is a tracking device, as police monitoring labour protests can attest, and now utterly commonplace. Applications of the collected personal information have run the gamut from corporate data mining of lives for targeted advertising to states using metadata to select targets for assassination, as happens with drone strikes. It's guesswork as to what plans are in store for the vast amount of data being stored, or about what calculations will go into designing the algorithms which will have to make sense of it all. Given that today's champions of civilisation readily excuse indefinite detention, torture, assassination and war, even the most cynical guess may be too generous.

•

To illustrate the rule that power will above all protect itself, states in these cases have gone after those who exposed state crimes. Soldier Bradley/Chelsea Manning, an important source for Wikileaks, was thrown into a long, tortuous solitary confinement then given a 35 year prison sentence. Wikileaks founder and spokesman Julian Assange has spent years in the asylum of an Ecuadoran embassy after eluding an apparent international police set-up. Edward Snowden was chased into Russia, where he currently claims sanctuary. The heat has been turned up on whistleblowers and journalists while the architects of wars and vast financial scams go conspicuously undisturbed. As veteran whistleblower Daniel Ellsberg describes it, the "national security state pretends that it's interested in national security when in fact it's interested in the security of corporate interests, of agency interests, of politicians keeping their jobs..." (3)

Anonymous, Wikileaks and Snowden are the names defamed in headlines, but behind them are innumerable other activists, organisers, whistleblowers, journalists of conscience, resisters to state-corporate power. That they stay largely invisible to the corporate media only testifies to the bankruptcy of the popular press, as depleted of its moral touchstones as any other modern institution. The internet is still an untamed tool and has been put to good use as a corrective, the most salient example here being perhaps *The Intercept*, a web-based news organisation created by, among others, the journalists who handled Snowden and as a direct result of that leak. Such bright spots may temper pessimism about the state of things, but should they? Might it be preferable to go the route of Naville's "organised pessimism," give up trying to repair the system via its legislative shell game, reject the execrable whole and insist upon complete social transformation? (4) Isn't the great weakness of the security state that it is not a state worth securing? Technology under capitalism, in the information age or any other, is put to the service of making the planet and its prisoners available for exploitation. The ways in which people can be tagged, tracked, isolated, immobilised and milked by it will continue to multiply and, if the rationalisation of human existence is allowed to follow its course, the vast majority of humans will be kept too busy scrounging for survival to rebel. The defeat of capitalism remains the first step in redressing the impoverished material circumstances of humanity, which is the first step towards the greater revolution of transforming the human condition.

NOTES:

1) The story of the tilting distribution of wealth—with the rich getting richer and the poor poorer, so to speak—can be simplified further, collapsed into the economist Piketty's celebrated equation $r > g$, where the return on capital outpaces the rate of economic growth.
2) Penelope Rosemont, contributing Robin Hood to The Eleven Domains of Surrealist Vigilance at the World Surrealist Exhibition, Chicago, 1976: "Surrealists, and all true poets, take part in this outlaw tradition. Refusing to become the instruments of our own exploitation, we are willing and able to use the red science of expropriation and the green mathematics of humor. We take the degenerate commodities of this society and reassemble them as images of dreams—as the spirit of the future. Surrealist objects and collages embody this subversive spirit, just as collective drawings and surrealist games negate the rampant 'individualism' of bourgeois society in favor of revolutionary fraternalization." It is an illuminating coincidence that such expropriation is likely illegal under the growing regime of intellectual property laws, a foremost area of concern for Anonymous in its early incarnation.
3) Daniel Ellsberg, interviewed for Robert Greenwald's 2013 documentary *War on Whistleblowers: Free Press and the National Security State*.
4) Pierre Naville's "Revolutionary Pessimism," the tonic to "bourgeois optimism," is described in Michael Löwy's *Morning Star* (Austin: University of Texas Press, 2009).

Consequences of the Misuse of Electricity
On the experimental phase of the capitalism of the spirit

José Manuel Rojo

I

The unconscious is truly the most extensive region of our minds, and for precisely that reason the unconscious is like the interior of Africa, whose unknown frontiers could be very distant indeed. — Jean Paul, 1804

The exploitation of man by man that alternately employs economic, moral or passional weapons, or all of them at once, is born of man's biological and physiological diversity. Until now, these weapons left some space for possible revolts, but at this point a new element enters upon the scene: the doctor who is transformed into a biologist and begins the transformation of man. With the analysis of unconscious conflicts, synthetic hormones, vitamins, genetic orientation, he already controls the decisive levers of the living machine. At the request of his master, since all technology is subordinate, he will light the fire or put it out, to act on the desire, that is, to reach the very origin of the problem of freedom. From now on, man is included in livestock breeding.

— Pierre Mabille, *Minor Considerations on Freedom* (1947)

Among the many pathologies which made the end of the 19th century an especially turbulent and pathetic time, the most detrimental were undoubtedly those which were never recognized as such. For example, the establishment of sports as mass entertainment, which Leon Bloy believed was "the surest means of producing a generation of pernicious idiots". Or the unhealthy passion for geographic discovery, which in many respects shares certain characteristics with sports (the obsession with records, their jingoist roots). An irrational furor led the European "wise men" to the ends of the earth, in search of the sources of rivers, the location of the poles, the extent of the deserts, and in the persecution of even the smallest unknown island. It is well-known how the newspapers encouraged these expeditions, how they led to international conflicts, and how, ultimately, they served not science but western imperialism. "Whenever there are rumors of a rebellion in India, you organize an expedition in search of the Abominable Snowman", expostulated Sherlock Holmes to a representative of the London Royal Geographic Society (1); spies, but also catalogers, dissectors of the world's wealth, of all the material and human possibilities which the colonies offered the vampirism of an economy already embarked upon the second phase of the industrial revolution.

The epidemics which terrorized (and delighted) the fin de siècle have, 100 years later, seen different fates. Unfortunately, some have diminished almost to the point of disappearance, like anarchy or the faith of the symbolists in a reality understood as a living unity shot through with symbols and relationships (and nonetheless…); others, not diagnosed by official medicine, have grown stronger, sprouting new intertwined branches, until they have become the normal standard of health of the social body. We know their names: sports, of course, consumerism, and the spectacle, still germinal in the incipient media of mass communications at the turn of the century. As for the "discovery" mania, it continues, only having mutated, and is not directed toward geography or nature but towards other parts. Not yet towards extraterrestrial space, however, since the necessary technology is still lacking. No. The new field of conquest, of subjugation and exploitation is not the exterior, but the interior. Not the reality which surrounds the human being, but the human being himself, his most intimate nature, his dreams and desires, his personality, his body, the genetic code itself. The inside, not the outside. If it is true that the advanced economies have left the factory behind in order to enter another phase of capitalism, if today, especially, a post-industrial economy predominates which is based upon immaterial labor, networks, and the production and consumption of knowledge, then this new phase of expansion is founded upon the exploitation of the self instead of this or that raw material or energy resource.

This is not necessarily something new, insofar as advertising has for many years been refining almost perfect Pavlovian mechanisms for the creation of false needs, and spectacular society is sustained, in effect, by the manipulation of individual subjectivities. Consumption is however ultimately directed towards manufactured products and the spectacle is above all else passivity and therefore the stall of the hypnotized spectator. It now demands something more from this spectator, his active participation: it is obvious that the image of the television viewer has been replaced by that of the internaut, or perhaps they have fused. This participation cannot be sporadic or partial, but must be constant and total, because the threat of stagnation which weighs on capital, and which calls into question its logic based on a perpetual movement to nowhere, must be exorcised through the invention and the plundering of something more than a circumstantial market (even if it is as gigantic as the former USSR or China). It will have to discover a continent, a world, a virgin terra incognita. This terra incognita is human nature, in all its meanings, which has undoubtedly already suffered grave assaults and amputations, but which still makes itself felt, up to a certain extent. Like Africa at the end of the 19th century, we find ourselves confronted by a new edition of the Conference of Berlin, which has already set the example and fired the starting pistol for the conquest and definitive dispossession of the human being.

The commodities which the new technologies are putting into motion are basically and precisely the thoughts, the feelings, the illusions and the dreams, the obsessions and the desires, the secrets, and the confessions of men and women. And it is absolutely necessary for this immense auction of consciousness that the interested parties are also themselves put into motion, that they accept the transformation into raw materials of that which previously was the exclusive attribute of their private lives, that which, it was said, no tyranny could seize, which, even in a concentration camp, would allow the prisoner a certain feeling of freedom.

In this way, nothing must remain outside the empire of the economy. There are no neutral zones, no watertight compartments, no nature reserves that could allow a moment of peace, an occasion for reflection or even resistance. It is not only a question of all activities being distinct forms of labor, of the annihilation of leisure and even of laziness, which have been forcibly objectivized in lucrative entertainments. There is something more: everything, absolutely everything, has become raw material, everything is potentially a commodity which enters into the play of supply and demand, because in this kingdom there is no longer any room for ghosts.

Perhaps, however, we have not yet arrived at this boiling point. The step from the exploitation of a passive consciousness to an active one is not so simple. It involves a new training which demands the definition of the limits of this consciousness, weighing its faculties, possibilities and deficiencies, establishing a plan of conquest and exploitation. On the other hand, the instruments of control and repression must not be abandoned, since, although everything is based upon the active participation and sub-mission of the victims themselves, it will still be necessary to rely on supplementary measures which eliminate any dysfunction or timorous hesitancy on the part of the social body. Finally, since we are speaking of the body, the human being's own carnal nature will also have to be the subject of experimentation, not only by means of the obvious sale of the commodity-body which we witness, but also by putting its capacity of endurance to the test. Endurance in the face of back-breaking economic flexibilization, endurance of the poisonous saturation of information and consumption and, finally, endurance of the destruction of nature and its replacement by an artificial and inhuman environment.

The current experiment actually has a double face. If on the one hand it catalogs, auscultates, uncovers, then on the other hand it prepares the population for the changes which will issue from the knowledge that it supplies. These two faces are intrinsically united, in such a fashion that they are not just various comprehensible manifestations of science, technology, art or the entertainment industry, if we keep this principle in mind. Similarly, research will not prosper if it starts from separate or unconnected disciplines, but only if it treats them all as a whole; not the pioneer who blazes a trail through the jungle, or the three caravels that sailed the mysterious Sargasso Sea, but the system as a whole which sets off united upon the new enterprise of discovery, thereby constituting a vanguard of domination composed of activities which in another epoch were kept at a certain distance from one another. It would not be vain to pass review upon some of the manifestations of this vanguard of domination, observing how they are mixed up to the point of confusion, following the stages of their objectives and consequences, as well as drawing up a death certificate of the hopes they have been able to ruin. Perhaps in this manner some profitable lessons could be learned concerning the new forms of social conditioning which are underway and which sooner rather than later will be applied in society: forms of control, of economic exploitation, of simulacra which definitively discredit reality, of survival in intolerable conditions, of the reinvention of the human being itself.

One can begin with what is most obvious. Television programs like Big Brother can be understood as a methodical test to see how far one can go with the industrial utilization of the black gold of the 21st century, privacy. The result could not be more encouraging for capitalism, since nothing is sacred anymore for the enthusiasts who submit to the "contest", understanding that the spectators as well, sitting in their homes, participate in the action. And we already know with what success: up to the point where many supposed that it was not a matter of "normal" contestants, but professional actors, without perhaps noticing that if such were the case we could breathe easier. It is the authenticity of the protagonists of Big Brother that makes their disinhibition, their unconsciousness, their servility before the cameras, all so aberrant. Another consolatory opinion proposes that maybe they were not actors, but that they behaved like actors, feigning an imposturous naturalness. "But here is a totally manipulated proximity, an entirely represented familiarity: the participants are actors of their own lives (and they do it quite well), inventing themselves as fictional personalities, from a virtual series whose protagonists they could be, as if from a theatrical work or a television mini-series." (2) A fragile consolation, because everything indicates that this "entirely represented familiarity" has not been born from nor for the television studio, but has already nearly replaced their original form of being, it has absorbed it, and their gestures and behaviors have been adulterated by their fictional models to the point of making the originals unrecognizable. (3)

The trail blazed by Big Brother has, of course, found promising spin-offs. "A television contest in the US presents 50 candidates and shows a tycoon getting married, live" (El País, 12-17-2000). "One television network puts the fidelity of couples to the test on an island full of temptations (….) Four committed couples will be subjected to the constant scrutiny of the television cameras" (El País, 1-9-2001). The island of the thousand and one nights shares with other products of the same kind some very revealing peculiarities which characterize the style of power in this epoch and which also disseminate the orders of the day to one and all. Above all one must accept it at its word when publicity which justifies this type of programming presents it as a scientific experiment. In effect, we discover in these programs the rigorous conditions of the laboratory: absolute isolation of the guinea pigs in an artificial environment, constant and scrupulous vigilance which oversees the unfolding of the studied phenomenon, and the overwhelming utilization of technology: "Ten anonymous Spaniards will share a house on the outskirts of Madrid for 100 days. They will not be able to leave; nor will they be able to avail themselves of television, radio, newspapers or telephones. Their only contact with the outside world will be the cameras of the twenty electronic eyes and sixty microphones that will monitor every one of their movements, from fits of rage to calls of nature, or simply combing their hair or washing the dishes." (El País, 3-12-2000). "On Temptation Island, Fox will broadcast the life of four couples in committed relationships isolated on an almost deserted island; they are imprisoned in a terrestrial paradise with a surfeit of food, alcohol, luxuries and meat, in the fullest sense of the word." Like the rat in its maze.

The real objective of the experiment, however, is not necessarily that which is adduced by the television networks: for example, Fox wants us to believe that Temptation Island will be a "sociological experiment that attempts to demonstrate whether, as many believe, infidelity is an innate weakness of the human being." Beyond such genuflections and preposterous smokescreens, the ultimate goal pursued is much more ambitious and sinister. Thus, the technological apotheosis under which the actor-tenants of these programs live, and that espionage which it allows and to which they are subjected is presented as a crude assay, as a scientific trial/test of the society which is being prepared for us, a definitively wired one, as watched as it is watching. In this way, two historical models of control are combined before our very eyes: the voluntary transparency of the Calvinist or puritan communities, where the lack of privacy and constant public confession conferred faith in the predestination of the soul, and the asphyxiating framework of spies, informers and secret services of the Venetian Republic, where the life of its subjects was controlled by infinite and unsuspected means. In this way, the technological domination which arises from this combination gains access to all aspects of life thanks to a sophisticated, complex, and invisible network of tentacles which go unnoticed by some citizens who, on the other hand, are quite disposed to voluntarily making themselves transparent and to spy on the life of others, without knowing why or on whose behalf. There is thus a hybridization of panoptics which develops in the cathode laboratory, concerning which Paolo Vasile, director of Tele 5, certainly clarified some points, perhaps by mistake: "The experiment consists of knowing how these people live together and get along, which they do by their own free will. And we all participate in this experiment with our reactions" (El País, 5-10-2000).

This is precisely the meaning of interactivity, whether on neo-television or the Internet: in training, in domesticating the consciousness and behavior of those whom it permits and encourages to participate in their own process of domestication. Not only to participate, but also to create. Just as it is said that outside the factory or the office one continues working, even if it were only by virtue of the fact of sharing and forming the affects, feelings and social desires from which capitalism will extract new forms of consumption, we can say that political domination is also designed by the men and women who suffer under it, that it appeals to their collaboration, for the most part unconscious and outside the channels of traditional politics, in order to protect, to construct, to test and to manage the mechanisms of repression and control which are considered necessary.

But if "we all participate in this experiment with our reactions", then it is as if the experiment does not exist, or it has been a complete success. The scientific method is based upon conducting experiments in conditions of impermeable and antiseptic isolation, so as to objectively analyze the phenomenon, without the destabilizing influence of external agents from the world that seethes around the laboratory, which is converted into a fortress. Congruently, the experiment in itself must not pass the hermetically sealed door; it must not in turn influence the world's progress. But today "the world has been transformed into a laboratory", and the effects of scientific research disrupt the very roots of a nature which it was supposed to limit itself to studying, since "the latest technologies and procedures in the artificial environment of research have been mixed with the world to the point where the separation of causes and effects is impossible". (4) This explains phenomena which only the diabolical innocence of a Mengele could call "scientific experiments". For example, the "quasi-experimental intervention in the food supply" carried out in Mexico since 1997 by the International Food Policy Research Institute, in connivance with the Mexican government itself: "Ten thousand poor and homeless families from 506 rural Mexican districts were excluded from an official anti-poverty program beginning in 1997, under the administration of Ernesto Zedillo, with the well-intentioned objective of evaluating the differences between those who were helped and those who were not. The consequences were obvious, and irreversible: the children who benefited from the aid program grew a centimeter more each year, their academic performance improved and illnesses among the adults decreased in number. Those who were excluded endured centuries-old marginalization." (Juan Jesus Aznarez, El País, 1-14-2001). Of course, this method is applied to all levels of reality, from transgenic foods to birth control in the Third World or the new flexible and outsourced exploitation, since all of society, and all of life, has been chosen as the decisive testing ground.

From this perspective one understands that a true isolation of the guinea pigs in Big Brother is not desirable, and that this isolation is only complete in a formal sense, or on a small scale (5), while its effects are destined to interact with the world in order to manipulate it in an irreversible way; the experiment is constructed as the epicenter of an earthquake whose consequences spread over the whole planet until they shatter it. The same thing is repeated on the plane of social psychology, a fact noted by the Encyclopédie des Nuisances, which observed in relation to the tests that measure the degree of danger posed by transgenic foods: "The genetically modified organism cannot 'exist' if it does not form a unity with nature, and it remains beyond a doubt that it will therefore be transformed by said unity, and it will also transform that very unity... Thus, either the tests succeed in an isolated environment, and are therefore not tests (they provide no information at all concerning the effects of the dissemination in nature of the 'tested' transgenic plant), or they are not carried out in an isolated environment, in which case they are no longer tests, since they are actions in the world, and cannot be retracted." (6)

Nor can the spectacle go backwards, and that which is freed by the television screen remains among us forever, modifying our behavior just as chemical agents corrupt the organism, embedding themselves in the genetic code of society which they are obligated to mutate like the radioactive contamination which has already in fact become inherited. And just as it was no coincidence that those "hidden camera" programs which became popular in the 1970s coincided with the installation of video cameras in banks and public buildings, we can also assume that Big Brother will not be content with staking out the regions of privacy for their later profitable exploitation, but that it also paves the way for the invasion and the definitive conquest of what still remains of unspoiled public space and, beyond that, of private and domestic space itself. Technical means are not lacking. It is merely a matter of preparing the ground. Thus, in the 1970s many did not see the loss of freedom entailed by the inquisitive eye of the camera because they remembered instead the televised joke, because they had become accustomed to its ominous presence. Naiveté becomes pathetic in some of us when, as we pass by a store with a surveillance camera connected to a closed-circuit television, we slow down and we pose in its field of view to see ourselves caught on screen, which does not provoke disgust or fear, but a mad joy. Neo-television resuscitates that demented felicity and extends it to every home, and in this manner tests for signs of resistance, of scandal or weariness, but they are nowhere to be found, rather to the contrary. And from this test for resistance, it passes to the experiment itself, which consists of testing the efficacy of the strategies of exploitation and repression which correspond to the new economy, and in putting them into practice. Do you remember Glengarry Glen Ross? In that film, some insurance salesmen compete among themselves to avoid being selected by the boss for their low sales level, which would mean getting fired. It is understood that present-day friendly capitalism and its alternative managers no longer want to do the dirty work: from now on, it will be the workers themselves who, like contestants in a television program, will eliminate one another, deciding who will go and who will not when capital feels like announcing that there is a "crisis". Perhaps the customers of the business will also have a vote, or the families of the workers, or why not, their neighbors. We will see this soon enough. For now, we are already accustomed to the idea, which is evidently entertaining and diverting.

Within a more short-term time frame, however, the results of the experiment in which we all participate with our reactions are already visible. "Salisbury, a small town with 39,000 inhabitants located in the south of England, is under total surveillance. In this city, no one turns a page, no one commits a robbery, a pair of lovers do not kiss on the street, a married couple cannot argue, no one stumbles out of a bar... without one of the 84 cameras installed throughout the town seeing and recording it (…) Salisbury just inaugurated this police mechanism a few weeks ago, a service which is dedicated to following the steps of some citizens who felt insecure and wanted the cameras to accompany them on their walks on the streets" (El Mundo, 12-20-2000). The Birmingham police project the faces of the most-wanted criminals upon the walls of the city (...) Their internet site now includes the photos, personal data, and crimes committed by ten crooks, among others the three men shown on the city walls (…) Television programs sponsored by the police, like Crimewatch, have also made their particular contributions to civil security. After about a decade of broadcasts, it has uncovered the whereabouts of criminals with the help of the audience and is, according to the police officers themselves, one of their most prized weapons." (El País, 11-23-2000)

Video cameras in some prisons in the United States, pioneer and leader in these experiments, are being connected to the Internet so that the bold internauts can observe the prisoners "24 hours a day", so that they, too, become convicts. The success of this initiative is as predictable as its effects on the internauts themselves. Because they are not very different, we recall the famous "experiences" of those pathetic losers who exhibit their daily inanity, putting cameras in every corner of their homes, allowing, at a distance, anyone who wants to be a witness to a shared degradation. These situations often attempt to pass themselves off as anthropological or artistic experiments (or both at the same time), which is actually true. "A youth spent six months hooked up to the Net without leaving his home. He has not left his apartment in Dallas, Texas, since last January 1st and will remain there until the year 2001 arrives. Mitch Maddox buys everything—including his food—over the computer from his apartment (…) A system of twelve television cameras, installed in his apartment, permit the internauts to see him

24 hours a day. The idea is to focus on the possibilities of electronic commerce and how the latter could help families" (El País, 7-4-2000). This means: how the Internet can definitively isolate people, reducing them to the unity of home, work and consumption, making any human contact impossible, preparing the techno-hermits of the future. This experiment, which is neither the first nor the last of its kind (7), unites the above-mentioned conditions of the scientific method applied to the domain of life: isolation, technology, continuous surveillance, willingness of the human material which is the object of the study, interaction with the public who follow the experience at a distance, and, of course, the ambivalence of the experiment itself, which is no longer antiseptic in so far as its effects enter into play. Perhaps the conclusions, the confirmation or rejection of the hypothesis upon which the test is based, are of less importance than the process itself, of which we all form a part. Why give publicity to experiences that an ancient, now-extinct prudence would have preferred to preserve from public attention? Why this obscene exhibitionism which celebrates the nameless triumph of the most absurd apparatus required for the new domination? "Hawley is crazy. They pay him for it. 'Within ten years the chips will be edible', says Michael Hawley, who has already eaten some. He directs the Thinking Objects program at the Massachusetts Institute of Technology (MIT) (…) As for the shoes, MIT has many prototypes waiting for some business to demand them. There are some which move themselves to the rhythm of the music. They have some sensors which, if they hear a tango, make the shoes dance the tango. It is the karaoke of the feet. It should be very popular in Japan, but I am never right." (El País, 10-1-98). "The symbiosis between man and machine can also be achieved through less radical methods. Various important universities in the US and Canada are constructing prototypes of miniature apparatuses called wearables because they are always with you, as if they were clothes or jewelry. (…) At the same time, scientists are now working on the second generation of wearables, which will be totally deserving of the name because they will be completely fused with one's clothing. Maggie Orth, researcher for Media Lab, has transformed a Levi's denim jacket into a 'musical jacket' (…) The next step seems like science fiction, but Maggie already dreams of it: 'Fibers that can weave themselves and that are not only conductive, but also possess the properties of micro-processors must be invented. One day, we will be able to weave memory and logic into our clothes'". (Yves Eudes, "A Computer under the Skull", El País, 1-16-2000). The worst experiments are thus presented as the innocent mischief of a knowledge gone astray, craziness as inoffensive as it is amusing, perhaps so as to gild the pill of its real applications (8): Michael Hawley would be the friendly face of doctor Frankenstein, raised, he and his colleagues in nightmare, to the level of mass idols who prepare the ground of mental structures for the triumph of a world where there will be no quality, no human value which could affirm itself without the prostheses of techno-science.

But the best is yet to come. "At the same time, the whole body will be fused, in its turn, with an infinitely wider digital environment: thanks to the omnipresence of the Internet, it will be possible to connect oneself, according to the requirements of the moment, with the external organs which you desire, which could be in our living room or on the other side of the world. The information networks will be an extension of the nervous system" (Yves Eudes). One must insist on the opportunities which such a panorama offers the economy. At this time, verily, human existence in its entirety will be directed towards production and profit: the slightest trembling of the spirit, the most trivial desire, the vaguest feeling, but also dissatisfaction or the most obscure and incipient unease will be communicated from the brain to the information networks, and from there to the central computers where it will be processed so as to manufacture the corresponding answer or placebo in the form of a commodity (material or immaterial, it's all the same). Not to mention the obvious applications for the law and order industry.

II

And someone had possessed Clary, strong, with all the hot blood of youth, radiant in his beauty, and he had chosen it so he could change his power of devaluation into pleasure, and his life's blood into apathy. He undermined it as much physically as spiritually and, methodically and scientifically, he risked losing his intelligence and his character. And all to experiment on it farther on, to be treated like a cadaver destined for medical research. – Paul Féval, *The Mysteries of London* (1843-1844)

That there is nothing left of me but my sterile putrefaction, and that I only survive from despair of living. You want to destroy the land and to leave nothing but stubble; to harvest the world like a sheep. Yes, you will strangle the future, the possibilities imprisoned within hope, those which perhaps sleep within the shell of the egg. We will assassinate the Redemption. The dream will not awaken.

– Remy de Gourmont, *Historia trágica de la princesa Fenissa* (1894)

Having come to this point, perhaps we can no longer go on talking about minds, of consciousness, of the human being. It will no longer be a matter of continuing to explore them while molding their limits, but of overcoming them. After capital, the flood; but after the flood, the cyborg will arise. "Although the cyborg attitude has not penetrated deeply into America, the cult of technological innovation, the taste for competition, the desire for individual self-improvement and the appetite for power are combined to make the public accept a very simple idea: after pacemakers, hearing aids, implants, plastic hip-joints, and silicone breasts, the moment has arrived to move on to silicon neurons, artificial eyes and microprocessors implanted in the nervous system" (Yves Eudes). One must not ignore what the cyborg represents, or the mutant product of genetic manipulation which is about to arrive, or both. The ideology of neo-capitalism (innovation, competitiveness, egoism, power) paves the way for the technology which will make its realization possible, since the cyborg will be the "new man" (they say: improved man) of the economy, who will be totally and unreservedly at the latter's disposal, and the only thing capable of surviving in the artificial and pathogenic environment which is its logical consequence. If that is a man... (9)

There is, then, a cyber-eugenics in progress, since "genetic manipulation is part of a politics of population control just as it is a politics of eugenics which consists more of adapting man to the subhuman conditions of industrial society than in creating a supposedly superior race." (10) And why not both projects at once, a superior race which realizes the despotic dream of every aristocracy in history, and a race of slaves forever dispossessed of the intellectual, spiritual, physical and material wellsprings that could make their liberation possible? Be that as it may, it is undoubtedly in sports and in recreational activities that its inhuman logic contaminates, that we can find so many other experiments which put the human body's capacity for suffering to the test, and which provide as well the necessary data for the reconstruction of man and his consciousness as the media propaganda of this reconstruction. For example, the publicity of the cases of athletes' doping, the obsessive description of the virtues and potentials of drugs and stimulants which the "teams of experts" administer to them, who count on the complicity of the "pharmaceutical industry", the insistence with which it is recalled that so many admirable records are due to the use of these substances … all an ideology which associates human success with the miraculous potions of technoscience, and which increasingly dissimulates, through a false moralistic preoccupation with "public health", its real purpose of making the poisons which will multiply our labor power and increase our adaptability to contamination, attractive and fashionable. Have they not succeeded? Sports fanaticism—has it not been the probe launched into our interior, in order to ascertain how far one can go without hitting bottom, in this respect as in others? Not to speak of the overwhelming display of technology that assaults the bodies of "highly competitive" athletes, who are constantly measured, weighed, analyzed, trained, monitored by machines for which they are nothing but appendices and which negate, even in the most immediate arena of the sensory, the illusion of sports understood as agón, as a naked duel between the will of human consciousness and the natural limits of the body. (11) As a logical corollary, the latest fashion consists in predicting how far an athlete can go thanks to genetic manipulation; here, the publicists get into fits of ecstasy praising the feats of tomorrow and the abolition, in short, of the slavery of space and time which will undoubtedly be swept away by the bionic man, endowed, who knows, with the speed of light and the force of the atom.

On the other hand, where sports overlap with exhibitionism, loquacity, or the circus, we find once again the total surveillance of the human body at the service of the most obtuse research. In the gallery of the castaways of post-history, together with the hermits of neo-television and of the Stylites of Houston, we shall now consider Michel Siffre, the "cave man", a miserable speleologist who spent "76 days in a cave carrying out a scientific experiment (…) For Siffre it was a question of attaining a new experience of 'the action of aging on physical biorhythms' (…) And while he said this he pointed to his body, covered with electrodes which, at each minute, measured the speleologist's body temperature, his pulse, his heart-rate, the intensity of his sleep and the hours during which he was overcome by the latter. He submitted each day to examinations of urine, saliva and blood (…) The medical crew who carried out the study of Siffre yesterday announced that 'the work of computing more than a million pieces of data we want to use will be slow and time-consuming, but probably most rewarding.' For Pierre Simon, a researcher who has studied sleep problems for years in order to help French and U.S. astronauts, 'these kinds of frontier experiences allow us to discover much about normal men in everyday situations.'" (Octavi Marti, El País, 2-15-2000). How and why a frontier experience can provide information about everyday life, which under bourgeois civilization is by definition the very opposite of the exceptional, remains a mystery to us, even more so when, in the hole chosen by this maniac of premature burial, "the constant temperature was 15 degrees and the humidity above 97%. Life was carried on a platform of 40 square meters, equipped with a tent, a refrigerator and a bed." Equally enigmatic is the fact that such subterranean isolation aided in the understanding of "aging" or "the physical biorhythms", since up until now it is under the full light of the sun or in the night and against or with the wind that the human being lives, ages and dies, and not in the catacombs, and the only knowledge we can recognize concerning the nature of man is that which obtains in the usual conditions in which his real existence develops, and not in conditions which are the opposite, their antipodes. Unless it is a matter of conditioning and of the new everyday situations that Pierre Simon and his henchmen dedicate themselves to inventing and extending everywhere, where we will live in confinement, vampirized by the machine, exiled from what was once nature, even left out of the natural succession of day and night, of the sense of cosmic and human time, where, you can bet, aging and the physical biorhythms will know a new experience: the experience of catalepsy. (12)

If Michel Siffre's experiment shares, with the television experiments or the cloistered internaut, the holy alliance of isolation, surveillance, technology and interactivity applied only in extreme circumstances, we can complete the circle by returning, after a fashion, to our point of departure: an "experimental program" of the BBC, Castaway 2000, "filmed to the smallest detail", which entails an illuminating turn of the screw when compared to Big Brother: "British public television wanted to carry out an anthropological experiment with a group of people settled in the Northwest of the United Kingdom", for which they selected "36 adventurers who are trying to form a community where 'social values and existence itself' can be studied", as the television program itself states. And where will such a community be formed? Perhaps on Fox's happy island? "Taransay was chosen as the site of the Castaway 2000 series because it was inhospitable and had been uninhabited for three decades. An upside-down paradise, with strong winds blowing at 200 kilometers an hour, which the new community must conquer in front of the television cameras (…) It never stops raining; mud is everywhere and no landscape is as daunting. But if life on Taransay is almost impossible, why was it chosen by the BBC for the experiment?" (Isabel Ferrer, El País, 1-24-2000). Because such meteorological conditions are exactly what make Taransay the suitable place to scientifically test the possibilities of the human being's adaptability to environmental disorder caused by climate change, where disasters will be the norm and not the exception. As in the case of the haunted cave, unless its real goal were to be of another kind, such as testing the ways of life which involve an alternative to the establishment, the abnormality of the conditions upon which the experiment is founded falsify its result. Will the BBC attempt to found a Phalanstery? Will it promote the creation of autonomous communes? This is not very likely. Rather, its purpose is to obtain data that will allow them to design the "eugenicist policy for choosing, eliminating and ultimately creating a man capable of enduring life in the final stage of the degradation of nature, a consequence of industrial society, a completely artificial nature without for that reason being any more predictable or peaceful since the outstanding sign of its submission to technoscience will be the exponential development of catastrophes." (13) Most importantly, however, it will allow the process to be visualized, so that the public, fascinated and terrorized at the same time, accepts this project as the only possible and desirable one. Of course, the attempt was aborted before it even began: the "adventurers" came down with the flu and the storm destroyed the "community's" infrastructure. We do not consider it a total failure: the stupefied British public has accepted this result as proof that the old human being, forged by natural evolution and history, is incapable of surviving in the era of cataclysms. Faced with this scientific proof, we do not doubt that they will accept all the electronic implants and all the genetic improvements that will be recommended to them in order to become the "new man", master of survival, already announced by the portents and signs of this somber time. Those who would deny this characterization of the examples referred to above, considering them instead to be mere aberrations of the television industry, will then have to contend with another kind of warning which also leaves no room for hope. Castaway 2000 is alarming only because it repeats, in another context, the very scientific, very serious and very real experiments carried out by states and corporations, such as the Biosphere II project, which in 1994 launched a demented (and unsuccessful) attempt to create an artificial planet: in the middle of the Sonora desert, isolated from the world but connected to the Internet (how could it not be?), a gigantic structure of metal and glass enclosed an area of 1.27 hectares where various ecosystems were re-created (desert, savannah, forest) and where yet another "community" of scientists was founded "in order to prove the viability of human life in a closed ecosystem." Is this a model for a lunar base or a project of refuge for the ruling class when the real planet finally collapses? The armored and impermeable vehicles which the Pope uses on his "visits" – do they not make him resemble an astronaut, an extraterrestrial who is inspecting a biologically hazardous territory? The "Popemobile" is not an exception, but a prototype – but of what?

There is one quality which we would not deny to domination; it is creative. Science and repression, ideology and conditioning are today characterized by the embodiment of the virtues of the human imagination, and not only by the enterprise of de-realization and aestheticization of everyday life in which they are immersed. It has been said that science no longer discovers, but creates: it is, therefore, artistic. And domination has a sense of humor (surely an excessive one), and it likes to play (to its heart's content), characteristics which we are accustomed to associate with artistic activity. But art is today also the vanguard of domination, and we are not talking about recuperative mechanisms.

During the 20th century, movements like Dada, Surrealism, and the Situationist International sought to open and explore the limits of the real in order to amplify and enrich life in a revolutionary project. Many of their ideas were recuperated, like automatic writing or détournement, but they were recuperated later and despite their original emancipatory purpose, and after a period of rejection by bourgeois culture which allowed it to freeze and to attenuate their effects. Today art collaborates elbow to elbow, in real time, consciously or not, with the laboratories and research teams of the large corporations and the states, and often depends directly upon them: as if not enough Pharoanaic projects were being financed. Thus, the SI could warn that "artists and the police compete in a race to dominate the new instruments of life." Today they play on the same team. "He walks through life with an identification chip under his skin. Like cattle or domestic dogs. Or like the convicts of the future in certain science-fiction films. With this difference: the 36 year old Brazilian artist Eduardo Kak has voluntarily implanted this most recent version of the ancient chains of slavery. The implant was the culmination of a multimedia artistic representation intended to symbolize the growing relationship between biology and technology." (El País, 10-2-98). "A work of net art creates a cyber-hunter of personal odors. 'Smell.Bytes' assigns an odor to each user." (R. Bosco/S. Caldana, El País, 2-10-00). What makes artists like Jenny Marketou, inventor of "Smell.Bytes", so odious, is the hypocrisy with which they conceal the logical beneficiary of their technophilic lucubrations: "I have created Smell.Bytes to show my critical position towards a certain type of classification, which turns into racism and discrimination. By means of parody, I want to point out the irony of these scientific methods of analysis and encoding." Perhaps she is unaware that her contraption will end up swelling the arsenal of the police, and that, like Eduardo Kak, she is testing the new technologies of control, as well as the psychological reactions they provoke in those people who concur with her "action"? Which should we doubt, her good faith or her sanity? Not to speak of the loathsome jargon of these imbeciles, of their pious reverence for scientific procedures and technology, an alienation which on the other hand is not new, although it is accelerating: "The E.A.T. (Experiments in Art and Technology) promoted in 1967 by Rauschenberg and the Bell Telephone engineer, Billy Kluver, with the goal of reconciling the aspirations of engineers and artists, considered that an effective working relationship between artists and engineers, sponsored by the industrial sector, will be conducive to the will to new possibilities which will benefit the whole society." (14) We now know where these possibilities lead, this obsession with the useful, with productivity; this art which objectifies itself, which wants to pass through quality control like one more artifact, which functions like a machine, which converts us into machines, which affirms itself through technological progress, and which agrees with scientists, publicists, and cyberneticians insofar as they think, imagine and create for the economy and for control. And for nothing more. That which is unfolding here is the civilizing delirium of the hand which increases the power of man and transforms it, of the hand which has reduced itself to an instrument of appropriation of the world and which in order to constitute itself as a machine "projects itself to the whole technical universe and to the para-nature which the former elaborates (…) The machine can thus be defined as a destiny of cancer or of exo-osmosis of the individual organism to which it bequeaths its powerful pseudopodia; the machine confers upon man the possibility of creating an exo-skeleton and exo-musculature, up to the point that Samuel Butler was able to define modern man as a 'mechanical-vertebrate mammal'" (15). This reflection on the part of Jean Brun, which in 1968 might perhaps have been considered adventurous, has today met its experimental confirmation, and precisely by way of the artistic vanguard: how could one not think of those torturers of the human body, who inflict upon themselves the most severe penances of technology and who, under the cover of a critical will as indisputable as it is inoffensive and counterproductive, practice upon the flesh itself the hybridizations and orthopedics of the future, gullible enemies of the human species, perhaps without knowing it, like Marcel Antunez, that "futurist performer encrusting himself in progressively sophisticated successive models of exo-skeletons" (16). As his ecstatic exegete explains, "Marcel Antunez is the proto-cyborg, a living premonition of the future life." Insofar as this "future life" is non-life, all the anticipations which in the present demonstrate its morbid viability and which therefore prepare its advent are under a legitimate suspicion, and deserve nothing but our vigilance.

One cannot, then, take seriously the "antagonistic" declarations of the art which bases itself on the technology or the misery which it claims to criticize. And certainly no other. "In a world which is really upside down, the true is a moment of the false." The case of Cristoph Schlinensief appears to prove Guy Debord's proposition. As one will recall, this Austrian artist set up a performance-installation, a parody of Big Brother, with the intention of denouncing the racism of Haider and of Austrian society. Twelve "undocumented" immigrants were established in a trailer, in the center of Vienna, so that the public would decide who lost the contest (the losers were to be "expelled" from the country, transported in a van to the border), and who won (he would get an arranged marriage to a naturalized citizen and thus obtain his legal citizenship). Even so, the Madrid magazine enCartel, a publication dedicated to leisure and to "spectacles", and which allows itself certain critical whimsies (homages to Thorstein Veblen or Vaneigem, humanitarian denunciations of pitiless globalization, etc.), understood exactly the contrary: "Naturally, it has been the occasion for much polemic and widespread revulsion, which the Liberal Party itself has timidly joined, which has not prevented the municipal authorities from giving the green light to this neo-fascist delirium" (enCartel, No. 11).

Everything is a symptom. When everything is a joke and a lie, there is no longer any room for irony. It was not only this magazine (it could have been any other) which took Schlingensief's proposal literally and had to pose the question of the real motives for the enthusiasm demonstrated by a number of honorable Viennese. (17)

One must also, however, cast suspicion upon the fastidiously ludic character of so many works which insist on the idea of play, almost always of an interactive sort, since play, understood uncritically as a banal activity resembling pastimes and sports, forms a part of domination, for the first time in history, and meanwhile "capitalism no longer opposes itself to the pleasure principle: it has integrated it, it bases itself upon it, it will be able to say that it is founded on it, that it constitutes its cornerstone" (18), and we will say that it is not opposed to play, either. We must add one more factor to the equation, Venice + Geneva = Salem, which could well be Las Vegas or Disneyland, and the result will be the ludic panopticon: surveillance understood as a game, and it is very entertaining to participate in the networks and mechanisms of one's own exploitation. We will cite one last example which sums up everything set out above, and which is advertised as a sociological experiment, as a display of technology, as artistic effort, and as interactive play. The city of Berlin was the scene and witnessed, last year, a game that was broadcast in real time over the Internet thanks to the positioning of video cameras throughout the city. It consisted of the virtual hunt for a disguised actor who went into hiding and wandered through the streets leaving behind him certain traces of his presence. The internauts, connected to the cameras, were able to monitor the city like the police until they found the fugitive and won the game. It is undoubtedly a question of the Great Game of the future, a game in which only domination will know how to collect its reward. This reward will be you, me, all of us. To come to that point, to fall into that hole, how much patience, how much skill at dissection and conditioning, and how much innocence in our voluntary gestures are required?

III

Because the land within was then also, and still is, that unknown and immense interior territory where we move freely outside the law; that deep zone where the memory of another life lived or livable in loving harmony with nature and the yearning for an endless gallop come to us, and from which can arise, with the frightening barbarism of the unconscious, the avid attacks of desire inciting us to rebellion.

—Silvia Guiard, *Tierra Adentro* (1986-1991)

I speak of something simple which everyone has experienced at each and every moment: I speak of life which consumes itself, independently of the usefulness possessed by this self-consumption.

—Georges Bataille, *What I Understand by Sovereignty* (1953)

Jean Paul was not mistaken when he compared the unconscious to the unknown Africa of his time, but what would he have said of the one that exists today? The annihilation of the unconscious, and by extension the annihilation of the whole interior world, is not total, as its unconditional submission to the mechanisms of the economy is not total, nor has it been transformed into a simple ideological reflection of the fantasies of the spectacle. As Anselm Jappe reminds us, the reign of the simulacrum has not erased the existence of reality, which continues under the surface, perhaps rotting away from within but still offering itself up to all kinds of explosions; likewise, the recently initiated process wherein the human being accedes to a new and more complete domestication, is just that, a process, which has not yet ended, which surely cannot have an end, and which in any case cannot absorb the infinite shades of the road ahead. Human nature still emerges as a reality, as deteriorated or adulterated as it may be, and to proclaim its ultimate subsumption in the shifting sands of the spectacle would basically be as reactionary as the postmodern judgment which decrees the assassination of the thing signified at the hands of the sign. In this sense, Silvia Guiard was not deluded and had good reason to compare the "land within" of the Argentina of the 19th century, a wild territory dominated by indigenous tribes in constant struggle against the Argentine army, with that "interior zone" of man, origin and source of the spiritual insubordination which manifests itself on all levels of reality, interior and exterior.

We have no illusions in this respect. We know how and with what ease this insubordination is defanged, is deceived and accommodates itself without a word to the theatre or joins in the distribution of variety shows. One cannot exercise enough precaution in the matter of granting any confidence to "the new relations which the spirit establishes with everything else." To begin with, a permanent withdrawal is absolutely necessary, a conscious lack of will for and a militant distaste towards the trap-games which the economy places before our every step: neither spectators nor players, any concession to their solicitations is from now on a crime of the highest treason. Beyond this elementary prophylaxis, the real dilemma begins: how to feel, how to imagine, how to dream, how to experiment with fragments of life outside of habit and alienation; and how to share this desire with others, without drawing the attention of the economic machinery, without becoming profitable, leaving not even the slightest margin for profit. If the economy feeds upon our desires, if it is nourished by social life itself, if like the Napoleonic armies it lives off the enemy's territory, "making the war pay for the war," then we must practice the tactic of the scorched earth campaign, always escaping from it but leaving nothing behind, in retreat, which can serve it in justifying the necessity and the logic of production and consumption. One must then demand an extreme degree of caution in the analysis of that which comes to us from the mouth of darkness, of that which we feel and that which we desire to express and communicate to others. To measure to what degree this idea, this happiness, this ecstasy could or could not be objectivized, and how rapidly, in order to judge whether or not to grant it any credence.

Finally, it is the problem of leisure and of laziness which returns to pose itself in a new light. Of course, not all activity, sensation or pleasure can be automatically reduced to a previously unknown modality of work or a new market sector. As has already often been said, economic activity is capable of setting into motion the imagination, the affects and the communication suitable for the free human being, but it does so in a rationally organized and controlled temporal framework which seeks the greatest level of production and the maximum profit for the least possible cost, saving time, energy, raw materials or labor power. Free time, to the contrary, when it also comes into its own and is possessed in full, does not recognize rules or fixed hours, it does not look for savings, but rather seeks its own extravagant waste, and it has no other goal than its own existence. It makes itself sovereign when it is exhausted in its outburst, without aspiring to anything else, without seeking any other justification. "The enjoyment of the possibilities which utility does not justify is sovereign (utility: that whose end is productive activity). What is beyond utility is the domain of sovereignty." This principle of sovereignty proposed by Bataille today acquires a new currency, but also its negation, because we know that everything in our day can find an application, or rather, that the economy ends up finding useful everything which surrounds it. So much so that sovereignty, as well as being stubborn, concentrating itself in its audacious inanity, must additionally be kept secret.

Paraphrasing an author who is certainly a great supporter of secrecy and anonymity, it would be desirable for those of us who will begin to feel a little and in a different way, to conceal our experience in this regard. It is understood here that, above all, it is not proper to leave a trail, that our experiences, emotions and imaginings are not explained, much less reduced to formulas, not so as to lead us into autism but to an encoded communication which would protect the purity of the phenomenon in itself, protected precisely by the incomprehensibility it derives from its character as an incommunicable and individual experience, unlike its power, its capacity for suggestion and contagion, in short, its capacity for reproduction in other people, by other means, in other forms.

Whether this encoded language could be poetic language, or that of reason brought to its extreme, or a fusion of the two, is not for me to say. Whatever it will be, the question is to know if the moment of demanding the true and profound concealment of the spirit has arrived, and to work accordingly.

(Translated by anonymous "Alias Recluse", revised by Eric Bragg and Noé Ortega)
* Originally published in Salamandra #11-12, Madrid, 2002.

NOTES:

1. Dialogue from The Private Life of Sherlock Holmes, by Billy Wilder and I.A.L. Diamond, 1970.
2. Gerard Imbert, "La transparencia posmoderna", El País, 5-16-2000.
3. For example, one can no longer speak of the non-language of youth, for which 100 words are enough to signify its emptiness (at least an elemental, savage emptiness, where only sex, intoxication and death have a place), but only of spectacular neo-language, that imbecilic loquacity of the self-help books, of the talk-shows and the made-for-TV movies, where many words are spoken but nothing is said and where, in particular, emotional dilemmas are simulated to perfection along with the most complex and ambiguous feelings and emotions. This jargon and chatter, so natural to Big Brother, today conceals real communication, and participates in the reconstruction of personalities according to the mold of the spectacle.
4. Encyclopédie des Nuisances, Observaciones sobre la agricultura genéticamente modificada y la degradación de las especies, Alikornio ediciones, 2000.
5. In effect, those responsible for these programs, like those responsible for other experiments that we shall examine below, maintained control of events, preventing the eruption of any chance or eventuality which could distort the rational, measurable and quantifiable objectivity of the test, except when these interferences were already foreseen and programmed to form a part of the process itself.
6. op. cit.
7. In another case, various men and women of different ages were imprisoned in their homes in order to measure to what degree all human necessities could be satisfied in a regime of confinement, using the services of the Internet to provide food, medicine, etc.—fortunately, it was a total failure.
8. No one will be surprised that the first and principle clients of MIT and of the wearables have been the Marine Corps, the police, the CIA, the prison industry, and the government of Singapore, all famous for their unconditional respect for liberties.
9. Perhaps we can intuit the level of alienation that will support the "improved man" in the course of his survival, by taking as a reference-point the current lifestyle of a "Father of the Net", one of those "gurus", as they like to call themselves, responsible for the adulteration which he also brings us: "Leonard Kleinrock works 10 hours at the office and 4 hours at home. He devotes two hours to exercise and three hours to spending time with his family, which leaves only five hours to sleep, which is enough for someone who now dedicates his intellect to the creation of computers which are permanently connected to the Internet, at high speed and without cables or telephones" (El País, 10-21-1999). For what purpose—to augment, perhaps, his own misery?
10. Renauld Miailhe, "La Solución Final", Maldeojo No. 2.
11. These neo-men, athletes, are also the image of the superior race. In the last Olympics, an ad for sports gear and footwear presented a series of athletes of different races, physically perfect, who were presented as the "superior race" (indeed, "capital has no fatherland", and the cosmopolitan elites of globalization recognize one another as equals in the enjoyment of their power). This ad was shown during the same broadcast segment as an ad for an Internet company, which preached about the infinite possibilities of the new inventions, which one would have to join if one does not want to miss the train, etc. The two ads had the same slogan: Are You Ready? The bugle call for enlistment in the New S.S. has just sounded.
12. Obviously, Michel Siffre is not an isolated case. Another athlete of stupidity, in this case an aircraft pilot, went for a ride around the whole world, also equipped with electrodes, sensors and monitors connected to the researchers' computers, so that they could control the "experiment" "24 hours a day", and could provide "decisive data" concerning "the organism", etc. What a hoax for true adventure, which found in the world tour one of its outstanding modern archetypes!
13. Renauld Miailhe, op. cit.
14. Francisco Javier San Martín, "La obra de arte en la época de su producción técnica", Lápiz No. 166.
15. Jean Brun, "Dionisios, el surrealismo y la máquina", in Entretiens sur le surrealisme, Cerisy-la-Salle, 1968.
16. Jordi Costa, Mondo Brutto No. 23.
17. But also, the false could be a moment of the true, and perhaps Jordi Costa, that addict of the detritus of popular culture and the most "bizarre" aspects of decomposition, hits the mark in his delirium. In one of his homilies about the "ownerless world", Costa feigns to have a premonition that the "mad cow" epidemic and their sacrifice on a massive scale is nothing but a conspiracy of conceptual and vanguardist nazi scientists who sought "an obscene parodical representation of the holocaust—in a bovine key, conceived with the perverse intention of erasing, by means of hilarity, the memory of that historical tragedy" (El País, 12-22-2000). And maybe he is right. But then, what world are we living in? In that of our masters.
18. Jesús García Rodríguez, "Nuevas industrias de la subjetividad", Salamandra No. 10.

Epigenetics and the Mad-Genius:
toward a historical materialist perspective

Eric Bragg

Part 1. Introduction: The Mad-Genius debate.

Since the ancient Greeks and Romans, there has persisted an unusual association between the concepts of *genius* and *insanity* which has defied explanation. Together, these two categories reached a historical level of attention during the Romantic period, from the end of the 18th century and through the 19th century. This association of genius and madness still influences us today, even though many academic scholars have lost interest in the topic, generally preferring to separate genius and madness into arbitrarily distinct categories. While the question of the differential presence of people of genius over various historical eras hasn't been well studied as of yet, of whether or not there has been a higher rate of genius in some eras over others, however there has been sporadic debate about whether or not the prevalence of "madness" has actually been increasing over the past few centuries, or if instead it has merely remained constant.

Perhaps the best way to introduce this topic would be through describing the pertinent historical developments – to summarize what has been known for a while – and then to follow it with a presentation of more recent knowledge so as to attain a more contemporary perspective that might not only explain the nature of genius and creativity, but also the question of insanity, "mental aberration" and "deviance". Rather than separately relating the historical developments that pertain to both madness and genius, an integrated review will be more useful, in light of evidence to be presented here. Of the books written about the link between genius and madness, I favor G. Becker's (1978) work, *The Mad Genius Controversy: a study in the sociology of deviance*, and liberally cite it for the sake of providing some historical background:

The mad-genius debate lasted roughly from 1836 to 1950 and over the course of many publications by mostly English and German psychiatrists and other medical professionals. The pseudo-scientific theories that explained the relationship between genius and madness were generally reductionist and deterministic, and fell into one of two mutually opposing categories: the first group, represented by physicians, psychiatrists and other *alienists* like F. Galton, M. Nordeau, W. Stekel, K. Jaspers, H. Ellis and C. Lombroso, viewed genius as mental and physical pathology, as a question of heredity, as a biologically determined outcome. Often they cited the "divine inspiration" claims of the Romantics as evidence for their arguments: whereas the Romantics prized their intense moments of poetic activity, the psychiatrists interpreted those states as inherently pathological. Laced with Darwinist terminology, accusations of "degeneracy" were leveled not only at the Romantics, but at other artists, writers, revolutionaries, free-thinkers and other genius types.[1a]

After the development of the Nazi eugenics program, the biological reductionist stance mostly fell into obscurity, leading to the elevation of the second group – those rationalist, sociological, psychoanalytic, social eminence-based views of genius, with proponents like W. Dilthey, B. Shaw, S. Freud, and L. Terman – who argued for humanistic, non-pathological explanations. While those who supported the pro-pathology arguments always outnumbered those of the psycho-sociological camp, the smaller numbers of the latter group gradually increased over the course of the debate.[1b, 2, 3] They viewed the genius as a product of sociological forces, and held to the idea that all people are born as a *tabula rasa*: perfectly malleable, so as to be shaped by the social environment around them. While these cultural reductionists were unable to refute the however inconclusive evidence for genetic, inherited aspects of genius, they maintained that the environmental influence (the "nurture" side of the *nature versus nurture* conflict) was greater. They also disregarded the *talent versus genius* debate by suggesting that both those labeled genius and everyone else all shared the same kinds of abilities and underlying patterns of thought.

Of these cultural reductionisms, Freud's psychoanalytical approach was the most popular, with the attempt to examine the creative process (and the creator) via psychoanalytic pathography, situating the works of genius with respect to the subject's early psychosexual life, especially in regards to parental relationships. Repeatedly Freud would defer engaging in intellectual judgment of famous works by historical figures, instead focusing on how one's formative years might lead to the creation of such works, with the emphasis placed on the psychic life of genius: examples include observation of their infantile qualities (such as those of da Vinci), accusations of narcissism, oedipalism and "defective moral development", assertions that neuroticism was the result of repressed libido, which was then sublimated and projected into intellectual pursuits, and statements about creative work leading to neurosis.

Underlying these conflicting ideas of madness versus the freedom of imagination and innovative creativity was the issue of social control. The alienists who argued for the pathology of genius weren't only targeting those who produced paintings and literary works that offended their conservative and bourgeois tastes, but also those who advocated social change, revolutionary transformation, and which might actually be the real heart of the conflict: by having the power and authority to judge the sanity and health of others, psychiatrists and physicians had influence over the direction of intellectual currents.[1c] The "scientific" method of discrediting such revolutionaries, anarchists and subversives (whether alive or deceased) was to publicly diagnose their works as examples not of intellectual imagination, but of an involuntary morbidity, and by calmly declaring that the biology of such "degenerates" naturally prevented them from complying with contemporary political and social structures. (And contrastingly, the corresponding capitalist strategy for the 20th century into the 21st has been to strategically *omit* all consideration of those currents of thought and expression that threaten the interests of the ruling class – to pretend that the opposition doesn't exist. Even capitalists can learn from their mistakes.)

Although the 18th century's concept of genius had to do less with those isolated intellectual qualities and more about the people who possessed them, the early 20th century saw a reverse trend where conversations about the *person as genius* were dropped in favor of talking about intellectual creativity in more abstract terms. With the pro-pathology angle temporarily defunct, the sociological, anthropological, behaviorist, psychoanalytic, culturally reductive positions persisted as dominant views for most of the 20th century, and these trends facilitated the dismantling of genius into its component traits, remaining popular research topics, such as: intellect, creativity, achievement, imagination, motivation, etc. Through the process of reducing genius to strictly creative, genius-free terminology, those visionary directions having to do with utopia, revolution, socialism, and anarchy have been quietly omitted from the modern discussions, which regrettably counts as a posthumous victory for the 19th century alienists. Towards the latter part of the 20th century, the pro-pathology position was resurrected in the form of three new areas of inquiry: 1) statistical comparisons between the families of genius versus those of the normal, 2) genius as an outcome of bipolar disorder/schizophrenia and 3) genius on the autistic spectrum (Asperger syndrome), of which the latter two categories will be explored in much greater detail in part 2.

The *correlation* between genius and mental disorder has been well demonstrated through statistical analysis: some of the more popular studies include those by C. Cox (1926), A. Juda (1949), J.L. Karlsson (1970), N. Andreasen's (1987, 1988), K. Jamison (1989), and A. Ludwig (1995), all of which looked for a statistical correlation between genius and psychopathology, as well as the heritability of each.[4-10] Of these studies, Ludwig's is the best due to having large sample sizes, and perhaps of particular interest to some of us is his finding that, of all professions considered, *poets* are the most likely to experience mania and especially schizophrenia.[10] Generally, these studies demonstrate an inheritance effect of mental disorder/genius to varying degrees, but unfortunately tend to suffer from one or more methodological flaws like small sample sizes, insufficient sex-, age-, and occupationally matched controls, use of the narrowly defined eminence conception of genius, the lack of consensus regarding nosological definitions of disorder, and finally, they show the correlation but without any information about direction of causality (the nature vs. nurture question – i.e. genes vs. chemical environment vs. cultural environment – remains unresolved within this kind of study).

Over the past few decades there has been some interest in assessing the relationship between genius and bipolar/schizotype disorders, based on fairly recent clarifications in diagnostic criteria. The approach has been exclusively to match behaviors and cognitive/affective patterns of such individuals[11] as the primary criteria for these two disorders, noting the facility of making such retro-diagnoses, and asserting that bipolar and schizotypal geniuses have been prevalent throughout history, especially in art movements pertaining to romanticism, modernism and postmodernism.[12a, 13] Additionally, some believe that certain cognitive and behavioral characteristics of such disorders provide advantages to the genius: For bipolar, manic and hypomanic states lend themselves to creative brainstorming and a superhuman commitment to momentous projects, while mood swings are conducive to what might be ever-vaguely termed "inspiration".[12b, 14a] For schizotypal genius, the conferred advantages are extreme originality and divergent thinking, enhanced linguistic abilities, depersonalization, alteration of temporality, and relativism.[13, 15a, 16, 17a, 18] Although bipolar and schizotypy are often considered separate diagnostic entities, there are some who argue that such traits occur on the same continuum, even within the same geniuses[16, 19], indicative of the ongoing debate about the distinctiveness of bipolar versus schizotypal nosologies.[15b, 16] These reductionist models are often presented alongside the bolstering theory that, dating to the origins of humankind, such advantages have arisen through the evolutionary persistence of those disorders, with the milder, less debilitating cases conferring those creative advantages at the evolutionary cost of having the more severe, debilitating cases.[14b, 17b, 19-21] Even though some of these researchers have considered genetic and neurostructural data (some of which will be covered in the next part of this text), their works remain inconclusive, since no causal mechanisms have yet been officially identified.

Parallel to these behavior-matching, retro-diagnostic studies of genius and bipolar/schizotypy, is the recent interest in the connection between genius and Asperger disorder, a higher functioning variant of autism, a disorder first described in the early- to mid-20th century by E. Ssucharewa, H. Asperger and L. Kanner. Of its defining characteristics, the two that have become irresistible to researchers of genius are the tendencies for amazing, unusual abilities (savantism) and for idiosyncratic personality traits coupled with social deficits, which have been used to retro-diagnose historical figures such as Einstein and Mozart. When describing their subjects, researchers generally identify Asperger people as being eccentric, unusually shy or aggressive, unusually passive or controlling, manipulative, aloof, childish, stub-born, contrarian, extremely egocentric, easily offended, over-sensitive, rigid, unusually honest, critical of mainstream cultural values, able to concentrate on an area of interest for extended periods of time, etc. While Asperger individuals aren't the only ones who manifest such behaviors and tendencies, it is only when genius is coupled with these traits that such retro-diagnoses are made.[22-27]

Therefore the recent studies of Asperger, Schizophrenic and Bipolar genius, as well as the psychoanalytic works from the earlier part of the 20th century, to those investigating 'degeneracy' in 19th century, all suffer from the same kind of reductionism that oversimplifies the connection between geniuses and the pathological traits that they supposedly manifest. At best, they amply document the *correlation* between genius and whatever psychopathology, but generally fail to provide any insight into the materialist (scientific, biological) basis for such an association. Rather, they are problematically dependent on the fluid, ever-changing diagnostic criteria for disorders that are defined solely by behaviors and mental states, which are strongly shaped by capitalist ideology, and which thus remain a profound flaw of psychiatry and psychology of the establishment. What would actually be most helpful is if it would be possible to develop any diagnostic criteria that could distinguish the *biochemical, possibly genetic* features of these mental disorders.

Despite the differences in the cultural versus biological flavors of deterministic theories and the varying levels of sophistication of pertinent researches, what they all have in common is a reductionist, counter-revolutionary approach that has well-served the incarnations of capitalist ideology over the past two hundred years.

The next section of this paper will attempt to remedy these reductionist flaws by considering evidence from the areas of molecular genetics & cytogenetic-toxicology, anatomy, evolution and epidemiology, in a way that dia-lectically couples reductionist theories with integrative ones, so as to formulate a more holistic, *ecological* ex-planation for the correlation between genius and mental disorder. The third section will address the socio-political influences on science, within the context of the mad-genius topic, and also generally how science is distorted in capitalist regimes so as to support the interests of the ruling class, rath-er than simply being a purely honest practice carried out for the sake of discerning objective truths about the world. Part 3 also reviews the vaguely-defined idea of "citizen science", which, with citizen (non-scientist) involvement, might be one very critical solution to the current problem of capitalist science. Part 4 will review the information presented in parts 2 and 3, so as to approach a historical materialist perspective on the mad-genius, while also considering those ideas within a surrealist context and suggesting the need for a collective approach to addressing these questions.

Part 2: The Biochemistry of Genius and Madness.

2.0: Introduction.

The preceding section considered various historical efforts to explain the correlation between *genius and madness*, especially as a manifestation of the *nature vs. nurture* debate.

While cultural-deterministic explanations have generally until recently predominated over the biological-reductionist ones, the nature vs. nurture debate, as it relates to mental disorder and intellect, has persisted into the twenty-first century as a false dichotomy, without identifying any possible dialectical processes at play that might yield new, integrative ways of interpreting such phenomena. At best, we read in contemporary, mainstream psychological texts about how *someday* the knowledge gleaned from genetics will ultimately establish the physical basis for phenomena such as mental disorders and intellects with uncommon or unusual abilities, but for now, mainstream diagnostic criteria for mental disorder (and genius) still depend on the observation of behaviors, rather than consideration of biochemical measurements. The purpose of this section is to review a sampling of the current biochemical literature, consisting mostly of primary sources (books and scientific journals), that supports a materialist basis for mental disorder, and more weakly so – due to far less evidence – for a materialist basis for genius.

The following literature review is intended not as an exhaustive survey, but rather one that is thorough enough to explore the current trends of biochemical research, and to evaluate the hypotheses that underlie such work. In particular, one of the major objectives of this text is to challenge the widely-held belief that both mental disorder and genius are strictly the products of genetics: that the DNA nucleotide sequence from the parents is the sole *materialist* determinant of such outcomes. The favorite, almost obsessive hypothesis of the mainstream is that certain variant alleles of polymorphic genes cause these disorders – that schizophrenia results from inheriting unfavorable alleles for yet unidentified schizophrenic gene(s), for example. Other mainstream assumptions about mental disorder are that the brain is the primary target organ (cephalocentric focus), and that for each kind of mental disorder there correspond one or more specific causative genes, such as schizophrenic genes for schizophrenia (genetic reification). An alternative materialist hypothesis that we should consider is that mental disorder (and perhaps genius, too) is not necessarily a disorder of the brain, but rather a disorder for which the brain is only one of the target organs. And rather than genetics being the sole determinant behind mental illness, let's consider the possibility that genetics *plus* chemical influences from the environment can together produce outcomes of disorder. This latter model of environmental, chemical cues from the environment (such as from pollution or contamination) having the role of triggering genetic weaknesses is indeed an application of the *Diathesis-Stress model*, which will be formally introduced in 2.2.

(And for the sake of convention, the word "environment" will be used in a *biochemical* sense, rather than cultural, for the remainder of this text. Also, regarding the brevity of nomenclature: rather than continuously repeating "our pro-genius groups of interest" – autism spectrum disorder, bipolar disorder and schizophrenia – these names will be shortened to abbreviations (regardless of however annoying they might be for some readers) like ASD, BP and SZ, respectively, as will the elemental symbols for metals, like Hg for mercury, Pb for lead, Cd for cadmium, Al for aluminum, etc.)

The premise on which the arguments of this text are based is on a biological formulation of *dialectical materialism*, where biology ("nature") is the primary, material force of influence while culture ("nurture") is of secondary effect, even though the two still obviously and necessarily co-influence each other. Therefore nurture is often trumped by nature, and so it follows that both genius and madness are influenced first and foremost by material conditions (which include biochemistry, ecology) and then only secondarily by culture, *although with significant co-influence between these two kinds of forces*. Additionally, we might consider the words of R. Lewontin, a self-styled "dialectical biologist," with regards to this dialectal materialist perspective within biology (and which we will consider in much greater depth, at the end of Part 2): "...Dialectical materialism enters the natural sciences as the simultaneous negation of both mechanistic materialism and dialectical idealism, as a rejection of the terms of the debate. Its central theses are that nature is contradictory, that there is unity and interpenetration of the seemingly mutually exclusive, and that therefore the main issue for science is the study of that unity and contradiction, rather than the separation of elements, either to reject one or to assign it a relative importance".[1a]

From the mad-genius debate we know from contemporary psychologists that ASD/BP/SZ have been historically associated with exceptional and highly original creativity, intellect, genius, etc. Therefore here we consider scientific evidence to 1) establish that ASD/BP/SZ are actually physical, measurable conditions, rather than subjective, social constructions, and that the brain isn't the only organ affected by such disorders, 2) demonstrate that such disorders have a lot in common with each other biologically (which might point towards a common etiology), and 3) demonstrate *plausibility* for a causal relationship, where chemical triggers from the environment influence individuals in an epigenetic way, leading to heritable outcomes that are currently referred to as mental disorder and genius.

2.1: Molecular Characterization.

The first body of evidence to consider is that which characterizes ASD/BP/SZ at the molecular level. While there remains an excessive focus on the "brain gene" reductionist hypothesis, there are other areas of research that characterize significant metabolic and genetic differences between these groups and what are currently dubbed "neurotypicals", and which will be considered in this text: 1) sulfur metabolism dysfunction, 2) mitochondrial dysfunction, 3) immune dysfunction, and 4) accelerated mutagenesis or "genomic disorder". Each of these four areas has yielded information that does not support the "brain gene" reductionist hypothesis. While such disorders have other distinguishing biochemical characteristics, like aberrant phospholipid metabolism, gluten/casein sensitivity, endocrine disruption, etc, the attempt has been made to focus on the more salient ones, and hence these four categories mentioned will be exclusively considered here:

Sulfur metabolism dysfunction: This broad category is defined as the disruption of the methionine cycle and trans-sulfuration pathway. These pathways involve methionine cycling and cysteine synthesis, respectively, both critical components of sulfur metabolism. An important outcome of the methionine cycle is that one of the intermediates – S-adenosyl methionine (SAM) – is a methyl donor, which facilitates the methylation of proteins, RNA, DNA, lipids, etc. and crucial for metabolism.

DNA methylation, a critical regulator of gene transcription, depends on the methionine pathway, and when the latter is disrupted, then both over- and under-methylation of nucleotides can occur, leading to altered rates of gene expression. In this sense, gene methylation constitutes a form of *epigenetic regulation*: where the DNA sequence itself has not been altered, but its rate of transcription has, simulating the effect of a harmful mutation. This scenario has been strongly considered as a possible etiological explanation for $ASD_{(2-7)}$, and somewhat so for $SZ_{(8)}$, with altered methylation patterns having been observed in $ASD_{(4,9)}$, $BP_{(10)}$, and $SZ._{(4, 10)}$

Additionally, altered levels of methionine pathway metabolites in both $BP_{(11,12)}$ and $SZ_{(11,13-15)}$ correlated with some of their cognitive symptoms.$_{(11,12)}$ For ASD, both patients$_{(16-20)}$ and their parents$_{(9)}$ presented altered metabolic concentrations, suggesting the possibility of *subclinical* traits in supposedly unaffected relatives (a topic to be covered later).

Of the enzymes in the methionine pathway that have also been investigated for polymorphisms, the methylenetetrahydrofolate reductase (MTHFR) gene has received a lot of attention: SZ correlated only *weakly* with certain alleles$_{(21-23)}$, as did $BP_{(23-27)}$, and likewise with $ASD_{(3,28)}$, although the weakly-powered stats in these studies can't account for most observed cases.

Homocysteine from the methionine cycle can be converted back to methionine, or instead enter the trans-sulfuration pathway, leading to the production of cysteine, the rate-limiting ingredient in the synthesis of glutathione (GSH), an irreplaceable free-radical scavenger. Disruption of these sulfur pathways consequently impacts cysteine synthesis, which in turn limits GSH production, essentially diminishing one's antioxidant capacity. Found in every cell, as an antioxidant, GSH is especially critical to the mitochondria, where it helps regulate oxidative stress and intracellular levels of calcium $[Ca^{+2}]_{(29)}$, which both influence mitochondrial functioning. And because mitochondria cannot synthesize GSH (a potential metabolic weakness or *diathesis*), therefore they must import it from the cytosol.$_{(30)}$

As one might imagine, lowered amounts of GSH and altered expression of the enzymes involved with GSH synthesis and metabolism were presented in cases of $ASD_{(20,31,32)}$, $BP_{(33-35)}$, and $SZ._{(36-40)}$ And while there exist polymorphisms of genes involved in GSH synthesis and metabolism that associate with $ASD_{(32, 41, 42)}$, $BP_{(43,44)}$ and $SZ_{(29,45,46)}$, such statistical associations only barely reached significance and could not account for most cases of these disorders.

Mitochondrial dysfunction: As hinted in the previous section, mitochondria are indeed a subcellular player in the mad-genius controversy. These organelles are indispensable for meeting the energy needs of eukaryotic cells, and they also have a strong influence on neural cell differentiation, signaling, growth and death (apoptosis). And over several decades, their involvement has been implicated not just in mental disorders, but also non-neurologial conditions such as diabetes, and even aging. Through the process of energy production via the electron transport chain, free radicals are thought to cause damage to mitochondrial DNA and other mitochondrial structures. And because mtDNA is more vulnerable to clastogenicity (DNA breakage) than genomic DNA – for lack of histones and DNA repair enzymes – then a current theory is that mitochondrial impairment would be most visible in those organs, such as the brain, heart, and skeletal muscles, where mitochondria are most plentiful, thus with a high energy output.$_{(47,48)}$ In the brain, they are especially prevalent at the postsynaptic sites of neurons$_{(49)}$ where neurotransmission occurs, and are especially vulnerable because of their inability to synthesize their own supply of GSH.$_{(30)}$ Mitochondria significantly influence intracellular Ca^{+2} availability (calcium homeostasis)$_{(50)}$, not only serving as a major calcium storage site$_{(47,51,52)}$, but are also involved with the regulation of Ca^{+2} for cell signaling$_{(53)}$, such as for CNS Ca^{+2} waves$_{(54)}$, for neuronal differentiation, for stimulating DNA transcription$_{(49)}$, for regulation of programmed cell death, or *apoptosis*, when intracellular Ca^{+2} levels are disrupted$_{(47,55)}$, and for extensive pruning of unnecessary neurons during development.$_{(51)}$

For ASD/BP/SZ, there is enough varied evidence to suggest that mitochondrial dysfunction is an integral feature of these disorders: levels of mRNA and/or expressed protein for mitochondrial genes – those genes associated with the electron transport chain, in particular – are altered in $SZ_{(47,48,56-60)}$, $BP_{(34,48,56,57,59,61-63)}$ and $ASD_{(64,65)}$. Altered concentrations of energy metabolites such as lactate, ammonia and pyruvate, considered indicators of mitochondrial activity, have also been observed in $SZ_{(47,60)}$, $BP_{(47,61,66)}$, and $ASD_{(65,67-70)}$. Evidence for polymorphisms in the mitochondrial genome that associate with ASD/BP/SZ is inconclusive and so far has failed to produce any candidate "mental disorder mitochondrial genes": at best, there have been some inconclusive studies in $BP_{(47,48,71,72)}$, $SZ_{(48,57)}$, and $ASD_{(52,73)}$. Finally, increased apoptosis (sometimes an indicator of mitochondrial dysfunction) has been observed in $ASD_{(74,75)}$, $BP_{(33,76,77)}$ and $SZ_{(33,78,79)}$.

Immune dysfunction: Another emergent area of characterization for ASD/BP/SZ involves disturbances in the immune system, manifesting impaired regulation of the inflammatory response, with their immune cells secreting regulatory, cell-signalling proteins (cytokines) at inappropriate times and amounts.

Regarding polymorphic cytokine genes, only variation in the Tumor Necrosis Factor-α gene (TNF-α) weakly associates with $BP_{(80)}$ and $SZ_{(81-83)}$, whereas polymorphisms in other immune-related genes appear to be more specific to individual disorders, although they don't account for most cases of ASD/BP/SZ. Of particular interest, however, is that TNF-α can regulate the transcription of Ca^{+2} homeostatic proteins$_{(49)}$, which as described earlier, can heavily impact the mitochondria, so in that sense immune- and mitochondrial functioning are more connected than we might have originally thought.

Immune cells control the extent and duration of the inflammatory response by secreting the appropriate pro- or anti-inflammatory cytokines. In $BP_{(77,84-86)}$, $SZ_{(87,88)}$ and $ASD_{(74,87,89,90)}$, the general trend is for there to be immune dysregulation, particularly excessive neuroinflammation – activation of immune cells, along with unusually high expression of pro-inflammatory cytokines.

Immune dysfunction in ASD/BP/SZ is also characterized by high rates of inflammatory, autoimmune outcomes (sometimes even in "neurotypical" family members, suggesting a *subclinical* effect). In the case of BP, autoimmunity occurs, but usually in a *de novo*, non-familial way$_{(91,92)}$, whereas with SZ, autoimmune problems can also occur in family members.$_{(88,91,93)}$ ASD, like SZ, has its share of familial, autoimmune disorders such as arthritis, lupus, allergies, thyroid conditions, etc., and also, like with $SZ_{(88)}$, affected individuals sometimes produce antibodies against their own brain proteins.$_{(89,94,95)}$

Neurodevelopmental genes and genomic disorder: The genetic reductionist hypothesis predicts that neurological disorders are caused by certain deleterious alleles of neurodevelopmental genes. Much has been done to identify those brain genes involved in ASD and SZ, and somewhat so with BP, regarding important neurodevelopmental events like cell adhesion, scaffolding, migration, signaling and neurotransmission.$_{(96-102)}$ In terms of methodology, case-control and family-based studies that seek to demonstrate statistical associations between a disorder and particular genetic variants have been replaced with Genome-Wide Association Studies (GWAS), which yield greater statistical power due to larger sample sizes, and which can sometimes confirm those same associations found in former studies.$_{(103,104)}$ *Despite whatever methodological improvements, however, mainstream science has still failed to uncover those highly sought-after "mental illness brain genes".*

The genetic variation considered in GWAS analyses include deletions, single nucleotide polymorphisms (SNPs, or polymorphisms at one particular base pair) and copy number variants (CNVs), where portions of DNA sequences are repeated due to random recombination (nonallelic homologous recombination, NAHR) and DNA repair events occurring in chromosomal "hotspots" or regions prone to such events.$_{(2,105-110)}$ These kinds of sequence alterations are inherited but also occur *de novo*, in the parental germline. For ASD, (a) rare, *de novo* and (b) familially inherited mutations & CNVs account for a small percentage of those cases with a known genetic cause (i.e. non-idiopathic cases)$_{(98,104,111-113)}$, with the remainder hypothesized by the establishment to be the result of *combinations* of genetic variants of weak strength, possibly suggesting that ASD might actually be a collection of several unique genotypes, rather than a genetically homogenous population.[98,102,114-117] For SZ, rare, *de novo* mutations are found in sporadic (nonfamilial) cases, although their proportion to the rest (CNVs and deletions) remains unknown[118], while those which involve CNVs – whether familial or sporadic – comprise a significant subset of all cases[119], all of which when considered together presents a scenario analogous to the genotypical diversity of ASD.[102] For BP it remains unclear about what proportion of those cases result from different kinds of sequence alterations, but preliminary evidence suggests that *de novo* CNVs occur with similar frequency to that of $SZ_{(120)}$, and that BP individuals are more prone to having singleton deletions.[121,122] Even though CNVs account for only a minority of cases of ASD and SZ, they represent an increased rate of recombination within those groups[102,105,116½,117,120,123-126], and often enough are associated with brain-related genes.[101,102,116½,124,127,128]

To summarize: the genetic reductionist hypothesis has been in vogue for a very long time, and yet despite the extensive work done in molecular genetics, the presence of definitive mental disorder genes still remains uncertain. At best, the researchers chant, there *might* be a combined effect between deleterious variants of certain genes that causes disorders like ASD/BP/SZ, and yet still nothing solid. Also, it remains unclear if the high rate of mutation is the *cause* of such disorders, or perhaps just one of the unusual biochemical *outcomes*, among others.

2.2: The Diathesis-Stress model, Neurotoxic Metals & Epigenetics: alternatives to genetic reductionism.

While the previous section characterized ASD/BP/SZ at the molecular level, failing to confirm the genetic reductionist hypothesis, the following section will consider evidence for an alternative hypothesis: a *Diathesis-Stress* scenario, where neurological disorder (and possibly genius) results from a genetic predisposition or diathesis coupled with triggering events (stress) from the external, chemical environment.[129-131] During the interval between the industrial revolution and the rise of petroleum products, and of the industrial neurotoxins in use, heavy metals were the most potent, were quite ubiquitous, and could create powerful synergistic effects when more than one chemical species is involved. Therefore they make a great model toxin for considering their potential causal effects of environmental disorders like ASD/BP/SZ.

Additionally, as the following section reveals, metals are known to influence gene methylation, altering the rate of genetic transcription, and thereby producing an alternative, Lamarckian (*epigenetic*) explanation for those observed, inherited effects which haven't yet been satisfactorily explained by the conventional genetic reductionist hypothesis (based on SNPs and CNVs). Whereas the previous section demonstrated that ASD/BP/SZ share certain molecular commonalities, the following section presents evidence for heavy metals like Pb, Cd, Hg and Al achieving *comparable* molecular effects.

Metal & sulfur metabolism: As described in 2.1, ASD/BP/SZ have alterations in the methionine cycle and the transsulfuration pathway.

Toxic metals like $Cd_{(132,133)}$ and ethyl-Hg (in thiomersal)[134] can influence the methionine cycle, in turn affecting downstream processes, such as DNA methylation[135-137], creating an unintended epigenetic mechanism to influence gene regulation[138-140], neatly bypassing the traditionally expected genetic reductionist route (by expecting to find special, widely penetrative SNPs or CNVs). Also, neurotransmission is influenced by the methionine cycle[135,141], which can be perturbed by toxic metals.[142]

The transsulfuration pathway is also affected by toxic metals, leading to diminished antioxidant capacity, which has been demonstrated with $Al_{(143)}$, Pb and Hg exposures[144-150], causing reductions in GSH and the expression of GSH-associated enzymes, such as those of the Glutathione-S-transferase (GST) family. Studies in mice have shown that inhibition of GSH production increases sensitivity to $Hg_{(151)}$, and in fact transient exposures to thiomersal cause long-term impairment of the GSH system of developing mice.[145] In humans, children have less GSH and GSH-related enzymes, making them more vulnerable than adults to oxidative stress[19], and some studies have even demonstrated a correlation between depleted GSH and impaired behavioral skills.[43,146] From the therapeutic standpoint, GSH precursors (especially N-acetyl-cysteine (NAC)) have been used for protection against Hg retention[147,148,152,153] and for managing symptoms from neurological disorders like $ASD_{(154)}$, BP and SZ.[46,155,156]

Regarding polymorphisms of GSH-related enzymes, there are SNPs for some of the GST (Glutathione-S-transferase) and GCL (glutamate cysteine ligase) enzymes which have been mildly associated with higher Hg retention and sensitivity.[157-162]

Metal & mitochondrial dysfunction: As previously covered, the mitochondria of ASD/BP/SZ people present cytopathological features, namely: excessive free-radical production, Ca^{+2} dyshomeostasis, impaired antioxidant synthesis, altered membrane permeability, proneness toward apoptosis and clastogenicity (DNA damage/instability). This section provides evidence that heavy metals can achieve those very same effects in mitochondria: Ca^{+2} channels, as part of a generalized second-messenger system, can be disrupted by $Cd_{(163-166)}$, $Hg_{(167-170)}$, and $Pb_{(163,171,172)}$, achieving these effects via *ionic mimicry*[173], such that the toxic metal poses as ionic calcium. Such mimicry is thought to lead to the inappropriate release of intracellular Ca^{+2} stores, the disruption of ion transport channels, Ca^{+2}-dependent neurotransmission and enzyme function[171], and is accompanied by impaired GSH synthesis[143,150], impairment of the electron transport chain[150,174-178], altered membrane permeability[150,167,174,175] and eventually apoptosis.[150,164,165,172,175,176,179]

Metal & immune dysfunction: ASD/BP/SZ all involve immune system dysregulation, by way of elevated rates of autoimmunity as well as imbalances between pro- and anti-inflammatory cytokines. This section merely points out that heavy metals have been known to disrupt the immune system for quite some time.[180] With regards to cytokine imbalance, such disruptions correlate with exposure to inorganic Hg[181,182], methyl Hg[183,184], thiomersal (ethyl Hg)[167,185], Pb [171,186-193] and Cd.[188,194,195] Heavy metals, such as the Hg found in dental amalgam, also cause immuno-hypersensitivity[196,197] and autoimmune conditions[196,198,199a], and finally, there is some evidence to suggest that the particulate matter from air pollution (nanoparticles – metal nanoparticles and also carbon nanoparticles that bind metals) is easily absorbed through the olfactory membranes, effectively providing such particles with a way to circumvent the blood brain barrier[200,201], causing an inflammatory response, including changes in cytokine production.[201-203] In some cases, these nanoparticles bind metals and/or are composed of them, such as Pb, Mn (especially derived from Methylcyclopentadienyl Manganese tricarbonyl (MMT), a controversial gasoline additive – road rage, anyone?), Ni, Al, Ag, Zn and Au, and which have been observed to provoke inflammation and other cytotoxic effects.[200,204-207]

Metal, brain genes & genotoxicity: To assume that ASD/BP/SZ are determined by (and can be reduced to) genetic variation in key brain development genes is merely another permutation of the genetic reductionist hypothesis. For many decades, the quest to prove this hypothesis has involved the exhaustive search for deleterious alleles (SNPs) that are expected to *cause* a particular disorder. But we also know that copy number variants (CNVs) have begun to share the putative, causal role that the deleterious alleles of neurodevelopment genes are thought to play: while simple disadvantageous alleles (SNPs) have been explained as occurring through random mutation, CNVs occur through mistakes in DNA repair processes and non-allelic homologous recombination (NAHR) events, leading to "genomic disorder". Even though the latter scenario is certainly more complex than the former, both assume that causality for mental disorder rests with processes (mutations and recombination events) *internal* to the organism, rather than bothering to consider influences and exposures from outside, such as from intra-uterine and postnatal chemical exposures that are *genotoxic*.

Metals cause genotoxicity via DNA breakage, interfering with DNA repair mechanisms, interfering with cell-division (polyploidy), as well as through stimulating NAHR events. Of these methods of interference, NAHR, or the recombinant, random exchange between sister chromatids, resembles the CNVs found in ASD/BP/SZ, and can be accelerated by thiomersal[208], methyl Hg[209-211], inorganic Hg[211], Cd[212-214] and Pb.[213,215-217] Despite the lack of direct evidence to prove that these metals *cause* the CNVs found in ASD/BP/SZ, it is noteworthy that metal-induced NAHR events are highly similar to them.

2.3: Genetic Vulnerability to Metal Toxicity?

When considering heavy metals as ideal industrial toxins, a question that has repeatedly arisen is how to explain some people's heightened sensitivity to them. A favorite and very genetic-reductionist answer would be that variation in heavy metal vulnerability is explained *exclusively* by gene polymorphisms of enzymes involved in metal transport and detoxification. As we've already considered those polymorphic genes in the GSH antioxidant system, such polymorphisms are grossly insufficient to explain variability in traits like toxic metal vulnerability. This section will cover *metal homeostasis*, reviewing evidence for impaired regulation in ASD/BP/SZ, and considering potential genetic variation that might confer sensitivity to metals.

Metal homeostasis & trace element analysis: The use of trace element analysis of toxic metals and essential elements in blood, hair, urine and feces has been instrumental in *metabolically* distinguishing those who have neurological disorders from those who don't.[218,219] Problematically, the technique has been historically underutilized, resulting in poor test standardization (small sample sizes), and also with problematic test interpretation. Another reason (and this one has certainly influenced the previous two reasons) for the low popularity of trace element analysis is that mainstream science and medicine are currently paralyzed by the fatal assumption that metal intoxication *only* occurs through occupational exposures rather than domestic ones. This ongoing misconception and the long-running economic situation that created it will be addressed in Part 3, through a consideration of the socio-political relations between scientists, doctors and the rest of the establishment.

One of the strongest findings from hair and blood analysis for ASD/BP/SZ is the tendency for elevated copper/zinc ratios: through 1) increased [Cu] and/or 2) decreased [Zn] in these tissues. This appears likely for ASD[220-224], SZ[225-228], and possibly for BP.[229] Also, high levels of elements such as Cd, Hg, Al, As, and Pb are associated with symptoms of ASD[220,230-234a], SZ [225,234b,235,236,237a,238] and BP.[229,239,240] It's also important to remember that people with ASD/BP/SZ are not the only ones who produce unusual trace element test results: other conditions like cancer, ADHD, diabetes, fibromyalgia, irritable bowel syndrome, etc. also can present disordered mineral transport[234c,237b], so it seems clear that having a disturbed mineral profile isn't a state that's exclusive to neurological disorder (but which still correlates strongly with the latter).

Gene polymorphisms: In addition to trace mineral analysis as a potential way to assess metal dyshomeostasis, and in keeping with the trend toward genetic determinism, polymorphisms in three particular genes have been investigated for their potential to confer susceptibility to toxic metals: metallothionein (MT), δ-aminolevulinic acid dehydratase (ALAD), and coproporphyrinogen III oxidase (CPOX).

1) Metallothionein: Necessary for Zn and Cu homeostasis[241] this family of proteins has strong affinities

for several toxic metals, possibly facilitating their detoxification [242,243] and which is transcriptionally upregulated by metal exposures.[244] MT can also limit the rate of respiration in mitochondria[245], so it's not unreasonable to suspect MT's possible involvement in the mitochondrial pathology found in ASD/BP/SZ. Like other genes, its transcription rate is epigenetically influenced by changes in methylation[241], an effect covered in 2.1. As for altered MT transcription patterns in ASD[230,246,247], BP and SZ[248] the results are inconclusive. For polymorphisms of MT suspected of influencing metal toxicity, the results are also inconclusive.[144,249-251]

2) ALAD: Both ALAD and CPOX are enzymes in the eukaryotic *heme* pathway, necessary for the synthesis of molecules like cytochromes and hemoglobin, and which partially takes place in the mitochondria. These enzymes can be inhibited by heavy metals, leading to elevated excretion of their substrates, thus serving as biomarkers for metal exposure.[252] ALAD is rendered inactive when it comes into contact with Pb, and its substrate, δ-aminolevulinic acid (ALA), accumulates, thereby making it an excellent biomarker for Pb exposure. For the question of polymorphisms, ALAD2 allele carriers have higher [Pb] in their blood than do those with only the ALAD1 allele[253-255], and ALAD1 homozygosity is known to correlate with motor dexterity and psychiatric symptoms.[256,257] Relating to mental disorder, some meager results: in SZ, ALA is elevated, implying Pb-exposure and heme pathway inhibition[258,259], while in a study of ASD the frequency of the ALAD2 allele was elevated.[252] For now, the hypothesis of certain ALAD polymorphisms causing enhanced metal toxicity and/or neurological disorder remains inconclusive. Therefore, to designate ALAD as a "toxicity gene" or a "neurological disorder gene" is premature, and that if there were anything to interfere with this gene's expression, it would be more likely something epigenetic (such as Pb exposure influencing gene methylation) rather than the effect of a highly penetrant, deleterious allele.

3) CPOX: Like ALAD, CPOX is a heme pathway enzyme that operates inside the mitochondria. Given that ASD/BP/SZ have mitochondrial dysfunction, we'd like to know if these disorders are correlated with heme deficiency afforded by deactivation of porphyrin enzymes like ALAD and CPOX. So far, measuring excreted porphyrins as a way to profile toxic metal exposures has only been done for ASD, resulting in the amount of excreted porphyrins correlating directly with the severity of the diagnosis.[260-263] And for the question of polymorphisms: the CPOX4 enzyme variant has reduced affinity for its substrate compared with wildtype[264], and this allele has been investigated for its association with ASD[252,262,265] and generalized behavioral traits[266,267], although the results are inconclusive.

To summarize, these results do not substantiate the hypothesis that polymorphic genes play a causal role in altered metal transport and metabolism.

2.4: Structural and Functional Considerations of Genius, and the Synaptic Pruning Hypothesis.

It wasn't so long ago that people were horrified by the idea that not all brains are structurally and functionally the same, because that kind of perspective runs contrary to the popular assumption about cognitive and affective experiences being thoroughly equal, exclusively determined by culture. Such was the case for the first half of the 20th century or so, until preferred opinion eventually swung to the opposite pole – that of genetic reductionism – to explain phenomena like genius and mental disorder, and where it has remained up to the present. For the most part, a couple decades of neuroimaging studies (especially functional imaging studies) of ASD/BP/SZ has produced a jungle of information, providing limited insights into how the various structures of the brain function and interact with each other in real time. The purpose of this section is not to try to make much sense from these studies, but rather to consider one particular physiological phenomenon – *neuronal pruning* – how a neurodevelopmental process of excess neuron removal based on apoptosis (dependent on mitochondrial status, discussed in 2.1) is perturbed in SZ and ASD, and how such a pruning process might be influenced by metal exposures (via Ca^{+2} (ionic) mimicry, discussed in 2.2) at critical neurodevelopmental times.

Regarding anatomy and metal intoxication, there are a few Pb studies which demonstrate overlap between regions affected in ASD/BP/SZ and those structures most sensitive to heavy metal exposure. Pb exposure correlates with regional volume reductions[268-271], while both cerebellum and limbic brain are particularly vulnerable to Pb toxicity, especially the latter, a region of late neurodevelopment, where plenty of mitotic cells there persist into adulthood.[272,273] Hg exposures (including those from dental amalgam) also correlate with cell loss[274] and degeneration.[197]

Then there's our question about 1) the morphology and functionality of genius brains that distinguishes them from neurotypical brains, and 2) to ask if there's any possible connection between metal exposure and genius, in the same way we just considered for ASD/BP/SZ. Even though the structures and functions of genius brains have been studied and compared with those of controls, that particular field remains far too inconclusive. (A danger to keep in mind, however, is that the attempt to isolate genius as a category semantically separate from the ASD/BP/SZ groups in which it appears is the same mistake the psychoanalysts made, when they used their specialized rhetoric to purify their idealized concept of genius of any lingering psychopathology.) However, considered in light of these concerns about nomenclature and etiology, is the neurodevelopmental process of *synaptic pruning* (the necessary elimination of superfluous neurons and synapses during brain development), which in cases of SZ and ASD, respectively, too many and too few neurons undergo apoptosis. For SZ, this explanation of excessive neuron removal – *dysconnectivity theory*[275] – is the proposed mechanism by which communication be-tween brain regions is altered[131,276,277a,278,279], leading to glitches in perception and cognition, and also speculatively forming the basis for *schizophrenic genius.*[277b] Inappropriate communication between limbic brain & frontal/temporal lobes from excessive pruning correlates with auditory hallucinations[278,279,280], which, we might wonder, given the association between great poets and SZ mentioned in Part 1, if it just might have anything at all to contribute to the "writer's voice?"

With ASD, not enough neurons are eliminated during development, such that the resulting *hyperconnectivity* between the extra, unpruned synapse arrangements happens in the outer cortical areas and might facilitate enhanced perceptive abilities, such as for sight or sound[281,282,283a,284] – abilities which would be so very helpful to visual artists and musicians, as we might imagine?

Additionally, metal intoxication, such as from Pb or methyl-Hg, has been hypothesized to produce those altered patterns of neural pruning found in ASD and SZ[131], and *by way of toxicological mechanisms*, apoptosis is determined by mitochondrial health, in turn influenced by Ca^{+2} homeostasis, or in the case of metal exposure, Ca^{+2} *dys*homeostasis, because some toxic metals like Pb can mimic calcium, causing mitochondrial impairment.[171] While this proposed metal/apoptosis-driven mechanism of genius is reductionist and determinist (since it doesn't take into account the possibility of other environmental, neurological processes that are operant in the formation of genius, and neither does it integrate what little we know about the heritability of genius), as a hypothesis it's still quite useful because of its ease of testability: who is curious enough to search for evidence of metal dyshomeostasis in geniuses? (Part 3 will address why such scientific curiosity on the part of the establishment is currently lacking, or at least, not monetarily encouraged.)

And by way of conclusion, it's worth mentioning that from the preceding evidence how the apoptosis/mitochondria/Ca^{+2} mimicry connection ties so many of the facts together, supporting plausibility for the association between mental disorder and heavy metal intoxication. The next step is to fill in the gaps regarding how genius and metal intoxication interrelate.

2.5: Evolutionary Approaches to the Genius/Madness Question.

So far this text has examined the slippery connection between genius and mental disorder, as it occurs in the present. However, as with other biological investigations, sometimes great insights can be had if the experimenter considers the origins of the phenomenon from an evolutionary perspective. In fact, biologists do this all the time, and in the case of the genius/madness question, it has not escaped from remaining uninfluenced by evolutionary theory and speculation.

The popular theory that psychosis has adaptive value in smaller or gentler iterations was already mentioned in part 1 of this text. Of interest, however (perhaps even to some of the most culturally-biased among us?), is J. Burns' *The Descent of Madness* (2007), which presents the hypothesis that ASD/BP/SZ are disorders of the social brain (with "biological and clinical overlap" between them and other disorders) – a very specialized brain with increased lobe sizes and enhanced intercortical connectivity that evolved over a rather brief evolutionary period of time, but with increased vulnerability to genetic and environmental (chemical) influences – and that genius results from psychosis.[277c] And then we might consider T.J. Crow's ideas about the evolutionary connection between schizophrenia and language: 1) considering the correlation between insufficient hemispherical asymmetry and schizophrenic symptoms, and how language depends on integrated communication between right and left lobes (a feature that evolved after the evolutionary split between hominids and apes), and how such reduced asymmetry might impair or perturb language development and capability[285,286], and 2) that core schizophrenic symptoms re-present a disruption of one's "mechanism of indexicality" such that it becomes difficult to distinguish one's thoughts from "the speech output that he generates and that which he receives from others," and, which could also be described as "language at the end of its tether".[285,287,288]

From the surrealist standpoint, we ought to ask what kind of implications these evolutionary hypotheses might have, when considering that well-known surrealist interest in language and its origins, and then also when remembering that unusual correlation between being a poet and having a history of psychosis (and somewhat so of mania), as was described in part 1, with the consideration of statistical analytical works by A. Ludwig, N. Andreasen, K. Jamison, etc.

2.6: Epidemiological Approaches to the Genius/Madness Question:

While evolutionary theory & speculation certainly have been helpful in the investigation of the mad-genius question, they also create obstacles to such investigation, since there is always the danger of projecting one's own cultural biases and values onto past events and individuals. This section covers how epidemiology might help us correlate measured, rising trends in mental disorder with whatever historical, material conditions and events, in order to begin the scientific process of inferring etiology.

For mainstream, capitalist science, the favorite hypothesis used to explain any undesirable or threatening phenomena would be, in this case, to try to convince all willing audiences that the rates of ASD/BP/SZ have remained constant throughout history[289a], and that any perceived rate increases, such as the alleged appearances of SZ in the beginning of the 19th century and ASD in the 1930s, resulted merely from a myriad of socially-acceptable reasons: perpetually changing diagnostic standards and capabilities, changing life expectancy, undercounting, or that the rate assessments of a particular disorder should be taken only lightly, due to the challenge of resolving discrepancies between its *incidence* (# of new cases within a given time period) and *prevalence* (total # of cases for a given time), or that numerous unreported cases naturally existed, even back to the dawn of humankind, through the sequestering of such mad individuals in basements, attics or closets, effectively serving as an invisible but ever-present populational reservoir of numerical equalizing power to cover any epidemiological discrepancies found in such older studies. It should be pointed out that this kind of "eternal" explanation – that whatever disorder has been occurring for all of human history (and even prehistory) with the same frequency – is an example of a *null hypothesis*, where any perceived changes in observable, experimental variables are assumed to occur strictly due to chance and not due to any underlying factor that would influence the outcomes. A popular but fallacious way to justify such a hypothesis is to claim that certain disorders like BP and SZ have been with humans forever, because references to these disorders can be found in ancient writings$_{(277d)}$, for example.

Although it may be true that certain ancient descriptions of symptoms and behaviors resemble what we observe today, there is not enough information to conclude that whatever SZ-like behaviors, for example, that were observed in Greco-Roman times should be matched with those of the same frequency and quality that are found in the present era. Therefore it should be stressed that the purpose of epidemiology is to help us approach that question of *how much* or *how often*, for which sufficient information is lacking in ancient texts, and which can't be adequately addressed by other avenues of scientific inquiry, such as molecular or ecological approaches, as two examples. What's more, in 2.7 it will be argued that epidemiological approaches to ASD/BP/SZ can potentially and in fact do validate other kinds of biological evidence that have already been considered here in part 2, that would 1) support a putative direction of causality, and 2) that would support an environmental hypothesis over the genetic reductionist one, and which might even 3) facilitate the attempt to envision a holistic, dialectical biology that surpasses the oft unspoken and acknowledged capitalist ideological assumptions and fallacies of scientists.

After having dismissed this null hypothesis about the eternal prevalence of genius/madness, let's review a few of the different, historically alternative approaches to the epidemiology of ASD/BP/SZ (and/or to mental disorder, generally), starting with only the briefest mention of four well-known, culturalist-based, anti-psychiatry advocates: the first pair are T. Szasz and R.D. Laing, with their reactionary, obsolete, socially-oriented explanations of disorder resulting *exclusively* from "problems in living" and "scapegoating", respectively. The case of M. Foucault and A. Scull warrant a slightly closer look, however, even though their leftist orientations might too quickly endear them to some.

Although it's true that feudal culture was more tolerant of "deviancy", and that the rise of psychiatric asylums were indeed a historically "great confinement" in the service of politico-economic interests, Foucault problematically subscribes to the null hypothesis in a cultural reductionist way, just like so many others$_{(290a)}$, assuming that there were as many insane people before industrialization as there are afterwards, and that insanity is reducible to arbitrarily-defined behavioral and linguistic deviance.$_{(290b, 291)}$ Scull also accepts the null hypothesis, and suggested that insanity became more prominent not only because of capitalism's need for social control but also to serve as yet another source of cheap labor.$_{(289b, 292)}$ For both of these authors – Foucault and Scull – their explanations of mental disorder are nonetheless problematic, in that they effectively dodge the question of rising disorder rates by assuming that the primary flow of causality for insanity results from the conscious efforts of the capitalist system (giving cultural factors too much credit), being distracted just like everybody else by the speed at which capitalist economics will exploit and/or subvert anything and everything (such as the scientific method, as will be covered in the next area, Part 3) that is within reach. If these culturalist hypotheses were really true, then upon deinstitutionalization in the 1960s, we might have expected to observe a significant drop in mental disorder rates; however, it would appear that those with disorders have merely been shunted to prison and homeless populations, with disproportionately high representation, which is still on the increase$_{(277c, 289c, 293, 294a)}$, and with the biochemical information available now, it isn't possible any longer to invoke culturalist explanations for mental disorder.

And finally the most interesting of the bunch: those who argue that disorders like ASD/BP/SZ are, at least in part, human-caused and of fairly recent origin. In the case of ASD, B. Rimland (2008) personally documents the rise in autism and other learning disorders since the 1970s, and confirms the link between autism's appearance with the use of everybody's favorite vaccine additive, thiomersal, in the 1930s$_{(295a)}$, as do D. Kirby (2005)$_{(296)}$ and the Geiers.$_{(297,298)}$ D. Olmstead & M. Blaxill (2010), and D. Austin (2008) argue that multiple or "cluster" cases of ASD first appeared in the 1940s, correlating with the implementation of mercuric pesticides/fungicides, and also pointing out that subsets of L. Kanner's first-described (1943) body of autistic subjects had parents who were employed by the vaccine and pesticide/fungicide industries, coincidentally, which thereby raises the question of parental exposures playing a role in the etiology of ASD).$_{(299a, 300)}$

These kinds of works also address other historical, poorly explained diseases, such as coverage of the link between *Pink's disease* (acrodynia) in children $_{(237c, 299b, 300, 301)}$ and *Neurasthenia* in adults with the 19th/20th century use of mercurous chloride (Hg_2Cl_2), or Olmstead & Blaxill's very special chapter on Freud that brilliantly describes the elusive correlation between *hysteria* in his female, sexually-problematic patients and their exposure to the mercuric chloride ($HgCl_2$) from medicines they dutifully administered to their ailing fathers (and historically, how hysteria mysteriously vanished when the use of $HgCl_2$ as an antiseptic was discontinued).$_{(299c)}$

If the case for toxic metals as the smoking gun of *agency* for autism and other hard to explain disorders is strong enough, as it appears to be, then at this current time, the possible etiological role of metals for BP and SZ is relatively weaker. E.F.Torrey & J. Miller (2001) consider toxic metals as one among several possible etiological agents for SZ and other mental disorders$_{(289d, 302a)}$, while orthomolecular clinicians/researchers such as E. Edelman (1996, 2009), A. Cutler (1999, 2004), and R. Siblerud (1998, 1999) have viewed toxic metals as an aggravating/prolonging factor in symptoms of BP[239,240] and SZ.[234b, 235,237a, 238]

Regarding the possible recency of BP, with respect to its potentially manmade origins, the outlook is inconclusive[303a], but the possibility that SZ might be a fairly recent disorder, of human origin, has been considered by more than a few, and one very straightforward observation is that prior to the interval spanning end of the 18th to the beginning of 19th century, there were no descriptions of SZ as we know it today (with special emphasis on auditory hallucination).[294b, 302b, 303b, 304] For SZ, what correlates most with the appearance of that disorder is its timely overlap with the rise of industrialization in England, closely following into other European countries successively, with the same close temporal correlation.[289e] We should also note that coal consumption, as a critical ingredient of the industrial revolution, has also skyrocketed since then, along with the release of Hg into the environment as a byproduct of coalburning[299d, 305] and nuclear weapons production.[306] Then we have those studies which document toxic metal concentrations in ancient human and whale remains, and places like peat bogs and lake bottoms[299d], or the Pb found in C. Patterson's ancient ice core samples[307,308], proving that the amount of toxic metals released into the environment has risen considerably since the industrial revolution, thereby justifying the focus on pollution as a possible causative agent for schizophrenia, autism and other modern illnesses.[299d]

Additionally, to add to this pollution hypothesis, let's not forget about the widespread popularization of Hg-containing dental amalgam, in use since the beginning of the 19th century[199b, 309], which also correlates neatly with the rise of certain mental disorders and other mystery ailments.[310-312] And since 1976, the implementation of "high-copper" amalgams also jibes with the recent rise in autism, such that this kind of amalgam releases 50X more Hg than prior formulations.[313] And then there's the fairly recent practice of using "biosolids" or treated sewerage as fertilizer, which can't help but introduce even more heavy metals into the food chain.[314] All in all, there is plenty enough evidence to show that heavy metals have been a subtly but steadily growing problem in industrialized society, regardless of what kind of new clothing the emperor and his scientific advisors wear each day.

In general, the unabated release of toxic metals since industrialization, by way of various products and processes, neatly correlates with the rise of these various, mysterious health effects that we observe mushrooming today. While it may be easy to spot the more severe or obvious cases, what really makes the mainstream uptight, especially in the health-care industry, is the nagging presence of *subclinical* manifestations: based on the evidence, and rather than disorders being 'all or nothing' phenomena expressly determined by genetic factors (safely contained within those "degenerate" families), or alternatively, by those cultural-determinist "problems in living"[315], we would expect a continuum ranging from severe effects all the way to those with milder, nearly invisible presentations[277f, 295b], correlating with degree of intra-uterine and post-natal doses of toxins.[130,131] Such milder exposures would coexist quite comfortably with the severe ones, such as *within* families, for example, and such a relationship could be easily expressed by way of a dose-dependent curve (Figure 1) – i.e. a graphical representation of a continuum of exposures and resulting disorders, ranging from mild to severe, with the low dosage end of the curve effectively comprising what might be called a "silent pandemic"[130], which would also be a predicted outcome of the diathesis-stress scenario. By way of example, if we consider the autistic spectrum, with severe cases being denoted as "autistic" and the milder ones as "Asperger", then, in light of the dose-response curve, we would expect the nearly invisible, subclinical ASD variants[283b, 316a] to become manifest in the form of those who go by such varied and colorful nomenclature like *geek, nerd, brainiac, swot, boffin, dork, anorak, spaz*, etc., and which were never culturally acknowledged until historically recent times, leading one to think that they just might be of recent origins, especially when considering that the autism rate has risen by more than two orders of magnitude since the 1960s.

Another avenue of evidence that relates to the hypothesis that mental disorder is actually a type of environmental illness is the strong presence of *comorbidity* – where two disorders have an increased likelihood of occurring together in the same individual, *as if by chance*. During the days of Freudian worship, accusations of hypochondriasis were leveled at people who manifested multiple disorders, but now with critical biochemical evidence that proves how such disorders have tangible, measurable characteristics (for example, how schizophrenics often have thyroid problems), it is no longer possible to accuse patients of hallucinating their somatic symptoms. Rather, these comorbidities, with their extensive patterns of overlap[317], do in fact support the hypothesis of "environmental illness" (Figure 2): because these disorders (some of which are not even considered

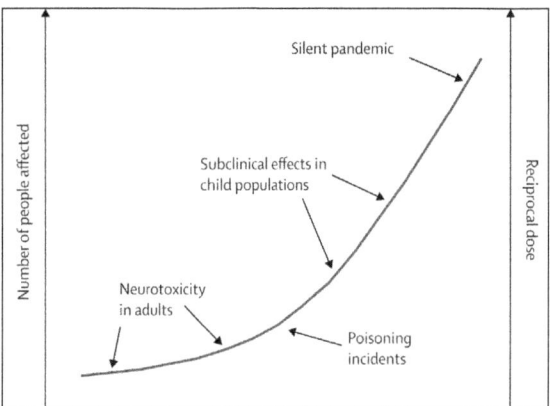

Figure 1: A model of a dose-dependent curve, with a continuum of effects ranging from severe to nearly imperceptible, dependent on the amount of exposure. The milder, subclinical manifestations of toxicity (the "silent pandemic"), while more difficult to measure and sometimes even to identify, are much more prevalent in number than the more obvious, severe cases.

Image obtained from: P. Grandjean & P.J. Landrigan. *Lancet*, 2006; 368:2167-78.

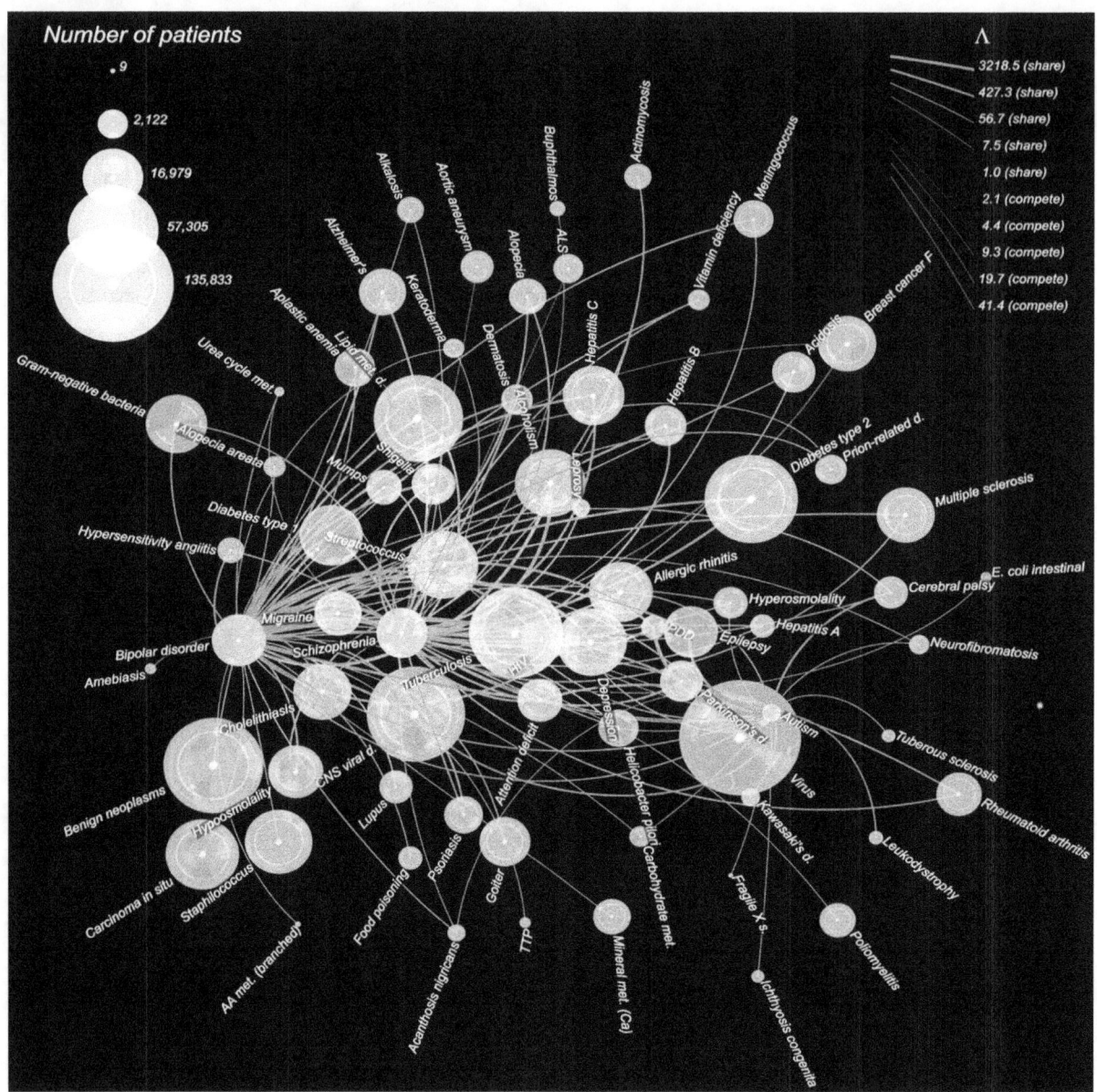

Figure 2: Graphical representation of co-occurrence (comorbidity) of Autism, Bipolar and Schizophrenia with other disorders. Each sphere volumetrically represents the number of patients in the study that had the particular disease/disorder indicated next to it, with the arcs linking them (arc thickness & color, in particular) representing the degree of comorbidity. Image obtained from: A. Rzhetsky, et al. *PNAS*, 2007; 104(28):11694-9.

'mental disorder', like diabetes, cancer, arthritis, etc.) have measurable biochemical traits, then such an extensive network of co-occurences cannot be supported by now-threadbare cultural reductionist explanations, and in fact jibe quite well with the theory of capitalist-caused environmental illnesses. If we return to our considerations of ASD/BP/SZ, it is known that ASD has been shown to comorbidly overlap with BP and SZ, among other mental disorders$_{(316b, 318-321)}$; BP overlaps with ADHD$_{(322)}$; and of course the overlap between BP and SZ$_{(323)}$ is well known, such that both fall within the schizotypal spectrum. Additionally, the presence of such behavioral *and* biochemical overlap of mental disorders erodes the credibility not only of strictly behavioral-based diagnoses, but in general, of the arbitrary, ontological approach of separating disorders into neat, precise, well-delimited categories for the sake of dubious but expensive medical treatments as well as for maintaining social hierarchies.

2.7: Coverage of Biological Reductionism/Determinism, and Arguments for a Dialectical, Holistic Biology.

Up until this point, most of the considerations given to these problems have been made in the way that biologists and other scientists would make on their own terms, however to maintain a critical perspective of the mad-genius topic it is necessary to try to step outside of the conventional boundaries delimited by science, in order to catch any (glaring) errors that mainstream science might have overlooked, whether accidentally, or accidentally on-purpose. So in the following section, we consider R. Lewontin's analysis of capitalist biology, as a helpful transition to part 3. In particular, biological reductionism and biological determinism are considered, and how such ways of thought serve the interests of the ruling class, and finally, to conclude part 2 with some thoughts aiming toward establishing a dialectical or holistic biology that would be revolutionary.

Biological reductionism, and reductionistic thought in general, persist as a result of 18th century bourgeois individualism with the biological variety owing a lot to both Darwin's concept of *organism vs. environment*(324) and Descartes' metaphor of *organism as machine.*(1a) These two kinds of ideas have persisted over the years, and with the latest iterations of the latter having been integrated with molecular signaling pathways: an endless maze of genetic feedback loops between genes, their proteins and repression/transduction factors, which serves as a replacement mechanism (at the molecular level) for the original physiological components as machine parts.(325a) The problem with getting especially attached to these reductionist metaphors is that while they are useful as conceptual tools for scientific discovery, it is so easily forgotten by scientists using these metaphorical models that such abstractions end up being confused with the object or system that they are meant to describe, leading to an underestimation or even complete dismissal of all features of the object/system of study which are incongruent with such reductionist metaphors; there is an overemphasis on parts rather than wholes, as well as the frequent misattribution of whole-based phenomena onto parts, and then vice-versa. In Lewontin's words,

"What makes science materialist is that the process of abstraction is explicit and recognized as historically contingent within the science. Abstraction becomes destructive when the abstract is reified and when the historical process of abstraction is forgotten, so that the abstract descriptions are taken for descriptions of the actual objects.... To put the matter succinctly, what distinguishes abstractions from ideals is that abstractions are epistemological consequences of the attempt to order and predict real phenomena, while ideals are regarded as ontologically prior to their manifestations in objects".(1b)

So in the case of molecular biology, attributes of gene and organism are erroneously used interchangeably: 1) that people are defined by their genetic variation, and also that 2) phenomena at the organismal and collective levels, such as mental disorder, are reified in the genes, hence capitalist science foolishly puts all of its eggs into one basket by searching for autism genes, schizophrenia genes, intelligence genes etc. Additionally, the origins of biological reductionism are in part found in the careerist aspect of the scientific process: as Lewontin states,

"Science as we practice it solves those problems for which its methods and concepts are adequate, and successful scientists soon learn to pose only those problems that are likely to be solved. Pointing to their undoubted successes in dealing with the relatively easy problems, they then assure us that eventually the same methods will triumph over the harder ones...As there is a dialectic between organisms and their environments, each forming the other, so there is a dialectic of method and problematic in science".(325b)

This latter issue will be covered in more detail in part 3.

Biological determinism differs from its reductionist roots in that the latter is developed into the former by the ruling class, for the purpose of maintaining social control, of maintaining a sense of powerlessness, helplessness and misery in everyone else, such that our individual and collective behaviors (including culture) are determined by our biochemistry, and in recent decades, by our genes: therefore our lives are inevitably determined by our genetic make-up.(326) Such thinking bridges the gap between capitalist ideology and reality, and brainwashes us into believing that we as organisms, as people, are separate from the environment (and each other), and that the "outside" world is truly outside of our control, and that we must simply accept that perspective – i.e. that we are powerless, and that such powerlessness is determined by our biology. Lewontin asserts that the capitalist myths of liberty, equality & fraternity are contradicted by racism, sexism and socio-economic inequalities, but that *both* biological & cultural reductionism (with examples of the latter being antipsychiatry, sociocultural relativism, deviancy theory) ironically work together to smooth over those contradictions in order to make life *seem* bearable, at least superficially so.(327a) So these two kinds of determinism would co-function as a dialectical whole, enabling us to be duped by the myth that we are ultimately powerless, which also maintains the false dichotomy of nature vs. nurture.

We might also ask in what particular contexts can biological determinism occur, and there are indeed a few ways: 1) blaming the victim, 2) mystification/swapping of agents vs. causes, and 3) the arbitrary, state-controlled separation of occupational versus domestic ("lifestyle") varieties of toxicity, in the case of our topic of interest here. *These topics will be covered again in part 3, as well.*

To effectively *blame the victim* for his/her disorder, it's necessary to reify symptomatic behaviors onto particular parts of the brain, onto particular neurotransmitters, or even onto particular genes. This act of projection allows those measurable traits to be *used against* those people being measured, so as to discredit, manipulate or even control them, and all done of course in the name of validated science. Additionally, those who present the "wrong", "deviant", inconvenient traits merely exist "against nature", thus subtly implying that the words and actions of the ruling class do run parallel to nature. Thus, the individual is considered out of step with the organization, and is pressured to change or suffer whatever punishment, rather than vice-versa. Lewontin informs us that "...a disordered brain is seen as the cause of an unacceptable interaction of individuals and social organizations. The political consequence is that, since the social institution is never questioned, no alteration in it is therefore contemplated; individuals are to be altered to fit the institutions or else sequestered to suffer in isolation the consequences of their defective biology".(327b)

Another method of obfuscation is to mystify the distinction between *agents vs. causes*: capitalist ideology maintains this kind of mystification through substituting the agent for the cause of a particular illness or disorder, and then downplaying any global evidence or conclusions regarding the possible hazards of such agents, thus drawing consumers' attention away from the actual causes. The trick is to substitute the agent for the cause: as an example, industrial toxins are not really *causes* of cancer as we would be led to believe, but merely *agents*. Likewise, those unscrupulous economic policies of *continuous marketing and selling of unsafe products* that contain mercury (fish) or flouride (toothpaste), as examples, are contributing *causes* of neurodevelopmental toxicity and dental problems, respectively, while the products themselves are merely the agents of those health outcomes.

And the final technique of obfuscation to mention is the *arbitrary separation of occupational effects from those of the home or "lifestyle"* (the latter which in and of itself is a terminological device for blaming the victim): thus occupational exposures are part of the "environment" while the domestic ones supposedly reflect a conscious choice (lifestyle, with implied consumer culpability, also) on the part of the individual. Currently, occupational medicine is separate from community medicine, and such practices are divided not only conceptually but also *legally*, logistically, etc., and are even managed by different people, with only minimal overlap and sparse communication between the two. Lewontin calls for a synthesis of such divided kinds of exposures, "From the perspective of allocating responsibility, evidence of an input from home is used to exonerate the working conditions and vice versa. What is needed is a way to trace causal pathways back and forth from work to home, to look at such measures as total insult to the lungs or heart rather than judge each component by a separate set of tolerable levels, and to focus on interactions among health-affecting components and see whole-system modes of intervention".$_{(1c)}$

Of the *mainstream* biology covered in this text (2.0-2.6), the diathesis-stress model has the most potential to explain the complex biochemical relationship between humans and everything around them: rather than *exclusively reducing* observed disorder phenomena to underlying genetic factors (blaming the victim, as an ideological device), al-ternatively, there are currently as yet unidentified genetic factors hypothesized to be triggered by environmental agents like pollutants and/or through consumption of products that are advertised as being perfectly safe, such as Hg dental amalgam, which could provoke such disorder – basically an environment/gene interaction, rather than simple genetic reductionism. This form of the organism/environmental model is termed by Lewontism as a type of *interactionism*, and he rejects it because under such a model, 1) the organism still remains alienated from environment – as a closed system – where the environment has complete control over the organism, forcing the organism to *adapt;* and 2) The individual is ontologically prioritized over the collective (a la Descartes) with individual details fallaciously used to explain collective, social levels of organization, and vice-versa$_{(327c)}$ (misattributed levels of analysis, with outcomes of capitalist values being reified in DNA sequences, more recently); and I might add that 3) the ruling class unconsciously makes itself a part of the interactionist "environment" whenever convenient (thus making its activities and priorities one with "nature"), while the working class remains on the other side of the fence, thus assuring a place for class warfare within the biological dimension, and finally, 4) that the diathesis-stress model assumes Mendelian (allelic) patterns of inheritance, whereas there is ample evidence today that suggests the possibility of *epigenetic* or Lamarckian inheritance.

The great need, however, is to conceive of a dialectical biology, such that organisms and environments, and the component parts of each, are dialectically related, where together they form a whole. One extension of this dialectical perspective is that organisms are not the passive spectators or victims nor even "adaptations" of their environments but rather that both organisms and environments *make* each other. Hence the need for a new biology that can synthesize both holistic and integrative approaches. It's not that reductionism is problematic in and of itself, but only when used *exclusively* at the expense of any and all other approaches (especially when used to serve the interests of the ruling class). Also important to keep in mind is that something can indeed be used as a research or discovery tool without it necessarily having to be used as an ideological weapon of oppression (in contradiction of the postmodernists, a topic to be covered in part 3). And to conclude this section, let's consider Lewontin's words on this topic:

"What is so extraordinary about the view of an external environment set for us by nature, and essentially unchangeable except in the sense that we might ruin it and destroy the delicate balance that nature has created in our absence, is that it is completely in contradiction to what we know about organisms and environment. When we free ourselves of the ideological bias of atomism and reductionism and look squarely at the actual relations between organisms and the world around them, we find a much richer set of relations, relations that have very different consequences for social and political action than are usually supposed..."$_{(324)}$

2.8: Summary of Biological Evidence.

Section 2.1 covered some of the more prominent but distinguishing biochemical differences found with ASD/BP/SZ: dysfunction in sulfur metabolism, mitochondrial dysfunction, immune dysfunction, and an increased mutagenic rate. From this section it is clear that such disorders are not exclusively behavioral in essence. This section also considered studies of polymorphic genes involved in those four areas, concluding that gene polymorphisms are unable to account for the hereditary character of ASD/BP/SZ, which is essentially a refutation of the *genetic reductionist hypothesis*.

Section 2.2 introduced the *Diathesis-Stress hypothesis*, which predicts that ASD/BP/SZ cannot be determined by gene polymorphisms alone, but rather by a combination of the former with chemical triggers from the environment. Neurotoxic metals are considered as model triggering agents, with evidence demonstrating how they can achieve the same effects detailed in 2.1 for ASD/BP/SZ. Also, neurotoxic metals can influence the degree to which DNA is methylated, serving as an indirect or *epigenetic* way of influencing gene transcription, thus offering an alternative mechanism for explaining the genetic component of these disorders (rather than by gene polymorphisms). At this point, it's certainly plausible that the inheritance effects observed can have a Lamarckian (epigenetic) basis, which contradicts current mainstream scientific thought.

Section 2.3 reviewed evidence for disordered metal homeostasis in ASD/BP/SZ, although evidence for polymorphic genes involved in deranged mineral/metal transport is clearly lacking, once again casting doubt on genetic reductionist perspectives.

In general, for 2.1-2.3, the lack of molecular data for genius types is profound, so any molecular inferences that one might make about "genius" would have to be based *associatively* (and thus tentatively) via its historically-proven correlation with mental disorders.

Section 2.4 presented evidence for structural overlap between brain regions most affected by metal intoxication and those most altered in ASD/BP/SZ. Also covered is the *synaptic pruning hypothesis*, such that accelerated rates of cerebral apoptosis account for underconnectivity in SZ, while reduced apoptotic rates explain cerebral overgrowth in ASD, potentially facilitating genius in both scenarios, albeit in different ways, leading to different abilities.

Section 2.5 briefly considered ASD/BP/SZ from the evolutionary standpoint, with mention of a few popular evolutionary explanations for those disorders.

Section 2.6 covered the often vague and imprecise approach of epidemiology, and also the hypothesis that ASD/BP/SZ (especially the first and last) are disorders that have strong environmental components, with an emphasis on neurotoxic metals as etiological agents, based on historical data.

When taken separately, each of these fields of evidence isn't enough to demonstrate direct causality: that neurotoxic metals *cause* mental disorder and/or genius. However, what these various *convergent* lines of evidence do achieve, when considered collectively, is to establish strong *plausibility* for the hypothesis that both mental disorder and genius share similar (epi)genetic and environmental inputs, and that neurotoxic metals make an excellent candidate for the latter, etiological role. This approach merely augments the efforts of authors like E. F. Torrey & J. Miller (2001) and Olmstead & Blaxill (2010) to elaborate a "recency hypothesis" by contributing to a molecular-genetic level of analysis that complements their lines of evidence for the historical recency of schizophrenia and autism (as correlates of Hg exposure from the various guises of industrial activity (coal-burning, pesticides, vaccines, contaminated food, etc.). While demonstrating plausibility is not the same thing as direct causality, nevertheless there is more than sufficient evidence, in sufficient *variety*, to make the strong and necessary argument for this industrial hypothesis, especially within the context of what we know about rising rates for both pollution and mental disorder.

Of Bipolar Disorder, Schizophrenia and Autism, the latter case (particularly the asperger variant) provides the strongest evidence supporting the epigenetic hypothesis for the mad-genius phenomenon.

Part 3: A Historical Materialist Perspective of Contemporary Science.

3.0: Introduction.

The previous section explored scientific evidence that suggests a link between mental disorder and environmental exposures, especially toxic metals, which have become increasingly ubiquitous in the environment since industrialization. While there is plenty of evidence to support this connection, there is less to support the hypothesis that said metals could also play a role in the creation of what some call "genius", such as Aspergers, facilitated by intra-utertine as well as post-natal exposures during key moments of neurodevelopment. At the moment however, perhaps most compelling is the association between metal exposure and autism, of which Aspergers is considered a subset. The purpose of this section however is to explore the reasons for why these areas of research are *socially* manipulated and sometimes even avoided by the mainstream scientific community, and to suggest that such tactics are motivated in part through the effort to protect economic and political interests of the ruling class, which obviously employs the majority of these scientists. This section will also address how the postmodernist, post-structuralist phenomenon has *indirectly* (albeit minorly) contributed to the general failure to thoroughly harness the power of the natural sciences for investigating the connection between environmental pollution and genius/mental disorder. In this sense, Postmodernists and Capitalists are unintended allies, since they both end up drawing attention away from controversial areas of scientific inquiry, but each in their own ways.

3.1: Postmodernist, Post-Structuralist, Social-Constructivist Positions.

Before reviewing the ways in which "science" (that is, the scientists, the scientific method, the practice of science, the areas of study that are of interest to scientists, etc.) is subverted by capitalism, we will take a short detour to investigate how postmodernism, post-structuralism, and whatever derivative *Social Constructivist* movements – seemingly potential antagonists of capitalism, as they professed to be – actually end up supporting capitalism's subversion of science, however ironically.

For a start, the ever-so-loosely conglomerated movement that might be termed *Postmodernism* had its origins more or less during the 1960s, embodied by the academic Left in co-mingling currents like American multiculturalism and French deconstruction, described sometimes as representing a rejection of the rationalist tradition of the Enlightenment, and as a purging of Western values, of Western "ways of knowing". With deconstruction there was the idea that any single or collective sense of reality is merely reducible to being an artifact of language: that language is what intervenes between any would-be knower and what he wants to know, that language prevents any would-be knower from accurately grasping the external reality around him, ultimately leading to the cynical conclusion that all knowledge is fundamentally relative, thoroughly subjective rather than objective, and thereby socially constructed. As historian J. Diggins (1992) put it,

"... deconstruction had enormous value to New Left literary academics. Having lost the confrontation on the streets in the sixties, they could later, as English professors in the eighties, continue it in the classroom. A new nemesis haunted the Left. Everything wrong with modern society would be explained no longer by the mode of production but by the mode of discourse. All aspects of existence, even the self struggling to know itself, are linguistic constructions..."[1a]

And this linguistic constructivism goes hand in hand with a radical and ultimately self-defeating skepticism, which comes across to their critics as mere ivory-tower cynicism: that nothing can ever really be known, that "truth" is relative, that any attempt to know something and/or transmit that knowledge to others is nothing but an underhanded attempt to seize *Power* (power with a capital P, in the Foucauldian sense). As the mathematical physicist and critic of postmodernism, A. Sokal has described it, "Postmodernists therefore tend to reject objectivity even as an ideal towards which to strive (however imperfectly): everything becomes dependent on one's subjective viewpoint, and moral or aesthetic values displace cognitive ones as the criterion for evaluating assertions of alleged fact".[2a] Additionally, Sokal writes:

"What I'm saying is that it's crucial to distinguish between the *concept* of "truth" and the *concept* of "claim of truth"; if we don't do that, we give away the game before it starts. Unfortunately, some people, starting from the undoubted fact that it's *difficult* to determine the truth – especially in the social sciences – have leapt to the conclusion that there is no objective truth at all. The result is an extreme epistemological skepticism: so that even when postmodernists and their friends concede the existence of an external world – as they pretty much have to – they hobble themselves with a self-imposed inability to make any coherent assertions about that world".[2b]

And then he notes that "[t]he great advantage of radical-social-constructivist philosophizing is that it is an all-purpose tool with which to discredit any empirical study whose conclusions one dislikes, without the need to enter into (or even to understand) the grubby details of the data and their interpretation. But radical constructivism is, if valid, a universal acid, which attacks also the claims of those who wield it".[2c] Other critics, P. Gross and N. Levitt (1994) have written: "Postmodernism, whether chiefly derived from one philosophical source or drawing eclectically on a flock of them – Lyotard, Baudrillard in addition to Derrida and Foucault – is, in its skepticism about everything save itself, an incarnation of the anti-Philosopher's Stone. Everything it touches is drained of value, authority, validity, and even the right to stand for what it has always stood for and to be understood as it has always been understood".[3]

If we want to know about critical responses to postmodernist attitudes toward science, a great source to consult first would be Sokal, who explains that postmodernists tend to confuse and/or conflate various levels of analysis when considering science, that is, the inability to distinguish between considerations regarding ontology, epistemology, sociology of knowledge and individual versus social ethics[4], and overall, that there is the difficulty of differentiating capitalist science from science itself, where he explains the postmodernist radical skepticism toward the natural sciences such that:

"In this atmosphere of easy discouragement, it is tempting to attack something that is sufficiently linked to the powers-that-be so as not to appear very sympathetic, but sufficiently weak to be a more-or-less accessible target (since the concentration of power and money are beyond reach). Science fulfills these conditions, and this partly explains the attacks against it... Unfortunately, some critics go beyond attacking the worst aspects of science (militarism, sexism, etc.) and attack its best aspects: the attempt at rationally understanding the world, and the scientific method, understood broadly as a respect for empirical evidence and for logic. It is naive to believe that it is not the rational attitude itself that is really challenged by postmodernism. Moreover, this aspect is an easy target, because any attack on rationality can find a host of allies: all those who believe in superstitions, be they traditional ones (e.g. religious fundamentalism) or New Age. If one adds to that a facile confusion between science and technology, one arrives at a struggle that is relatively popular, though not particularly progressive".[5]

And finally, Sokal offers this: "I stress that my use of the term "science" is not limited to the natural sciences, but includes investigations aimed at acquiring accurate knowledge of factual matters relating to any aspect of the world by using rational empirical methods analogous to those employed by natural sciences. Thus, "science" ... is routinely practiced not only by physicists, chemists and biologists, but also by historians, detectives, plumbers and indeed all human beings in (some aspects of) our daily lives".[2d]

It is beyond the scope of this text to provide a nauseatingly thorough analysis of what the Postmodernists do to science by way of social constructivism, such as the "Strong Programme", but perhaps a consideration of what such deep skepticism about science (and of knowledge in general, has led to, on the social scale, within the Left and outside) might be helpful. In particular, social constructivism allows the critic to label anything that he doesn't agree with as a mere story, a "narrative" told by those who hold *Power* so as merely to further that power. So while over the short-term some of us might benefit from being able to label the statements which support capitalist ideology as being mere narrative – the stories that the powerful tell in order to maintain obedience and compliance with their goals – unfortunately the opposite becomes true, as well. Thus, all historical evidence of classism, racism, sexism, homophobia, ageism, and whatever other manifestations of discrimination and exploitation also must be considered as just another set of narratives, an outcome which ends up leveling any chance we might have had for distinguishing truth from deception. With regards to the role of science as a method for producing evidence that identifies inequality and exploitation, N. Koertge (1998) says it well:

"...[W]hat we must add to the cultural studies picture and give prominence to is the old Popperian point about the refutability of false scientific theories and the possibility of learning from our mistakes. However obnoxious various outdated scientific theories of reproduction, intelligence, and human differences may be, it still was possible to discredit them through the routine application of the ordinary self-corrective devices of scientific inquiry. These methodological procedures do not always operate as efficiently as we would like and they also can be subverted by political pressure. But there is no historical warrant for building into the curriculum a cynical, worst-case scenario view of science". (6)

The possibility of illuminating the *subversion of science* by political, economic pressure is key, and has only been poorly addressed by postmodernists, but importantly, also by their critics. Echoing this idea, the historian Diggins has suggested that:

"Power is not some alien presence contrary to nature. It is intrinsic to the very constitution of men and women contending with the conditions of history. Poststructuralist philosophers have only described a world supposedly lost to the concealed structures of domination. The challenge the Left faces is not to despair about power but to uncover its hidden operations in order to control it better with countervailing mechanisms". (1b)

Furthermore, while postmodernists view science as a method of knowledge inherently tainted by capitalism, I argue that science can and does exist separately from capitalist prerogatives, and although such instances might be rare today, they are very much worth considering. Therefore we should be receptive to studying exactly *how* the subversion of science occurs, and that subject will be the main focus of part 3.

Or to put it another way: we are aware that capitalists use science to further their interests by selectively providing us with knowledge that they want us know about, but what about the information that they *don't* want us to know – like those areas of knowledge that are preemptively avoided, buried, censored, obfuscated? I posit that the mad/genius question, as it relates to the science of environmental toxicity, is a choice example of such a controversial topic. If it can be shown that there are areas of knowledge that the capitalist establishment does not want people (including scientists) to know too much about, then such instances would suggest that objective truth really does exist (and that the cynical, epistemological relativism of postmodernism indirectly but effectively supports the capitalist obfuscation of inconvenient knowledge). It would be necessary to look at *specific* instances and areas of obfuscation, since we've learned from the postmodernists that elaborating an especially *generalized* critique of science doesn't work very well. So in regards to the connection between madness/genius and heavy metal toxicity, we might ask how exactly these areas of scientific knowledge threaten capitalist interests, and how have capitalists and other economic dictators used their version(s) of science to censor and/or preclude such ideologically inconvenient scientific knowledge?

3.2: Research Control & the Funding Effect.

This section covers the ways in which capitalism has appropriated science, for the sake of profit and control. The past decade or so has produced several works that directly address this question about capitalist science, or as some critics have called it, "Merc Science" or science done under the influence of the "Funding Effect". While I firmly disagree with their *reformist* attitude (the idea that supposedly there is such a thing as a special kind of "free enterprise" that mysteriously somehow manages *not* to exploit people, such as if Industry could only be regulated more rigorously and responsibly by government), such works are nevertheless recommended, important in that they document the precise ways in which knowledge production is manipulated, thereby refuting the anti-science position of postmodernists. Along with general, descriptive explanations of the special kinds of obfuscation, I also provide examples of these phenomena occurring within industries operating in the US (which is arguably more tolerant of such institutionalized criminal activity, when compared with European counterparts) that use lead and mercury, those two very historically relevant neurotoxins which were already covered in part 2 of this paper and which have subtle yet profound influences on neurodevelopmental outcomes like mental disorder and genius. And a few pertinent examples of pharmaceutical industry misdeeds are also included, to help round out the picture.

Merc Science is distinct from 19th century privately funded "gentlemen science", and it developed over the 20th century through government and industry funding, leading to what has now become essentially *science for hire*, where all kinds of scientists sell their services to industries like Big Tobacco, the lead industry, the asbestos industry, the tuna fishing industry, the pharmaceutical industry, etc., in order to help such groups stall legal regulation and evade litigation in tort cases. D. Michaels (2008) nicely describes this new kind of science, sometimes known as the *product defense industry*:

"The range of their work is impressive. They have on their payrolls (or can bring in on a moment's notice) toxicologists, epidemiologists, biostaticians, risk assessors, and any other professionally trained, media-savvy experts deemed necessary. They and the larger, wealthier industries for which they work go through the motions we expect of the scientific enterprise, salting the literature with their questionable reports and studies. Nevertheless, it is all a charade. The work has one overriding motivation: advocacy for the sponsor's position in civil court, the court of public opinion, and the regulatory arena. Often tailored to address issues that arise in litigation, they are more like legal pleadings than scientific papers. In the regulatory arena, the studies are useful not because they are good work that the regulatory agencies have to take seriously but because they clog the machinery and slow down the process... Public health interests are beside the point. Follow the science wherever it leads? Not quite. This is science for hire, period, and it is extremely lucrative".$_{(7a)}$

Likewise, the *funding effect* might be described as the way in which the reliability of scientific literature has become diluted with a growing abundance of merc science studies that more often than not end up reflecting the desired outcomes of their sponsors: essentially, a scientific literature tainted with pro-industry bias. And as a result of the funding effect, corporate-funded science, such as for medical research, becomes proprietary and confidential, which limits its ability to be tested for veracity and repeatability$_{(8a)}$, and which also transforms such knowledge into yet one more type of commodity.$_{(9a)}$

If contemporary science has come to reflect industry bias, we might ask how exactly does that happen. For a start, there are a few strategies used to influence the publishing process: *Ghost Writing, Impact Factor* and the subversion of the *Peer Review* process.

For *Ghost Writing*, the trick is for industry to hire their own tech writers to hammer out a draft, exerting strict control over the reported, proprietary information, which is then edited and critiqued by well-known scientists operating externally to the industry in question. The final version of the publication is submitted to prestigious journals for acceptance and often bears the names of only those famous, leading scientists, and without those of their industry counterparts (or perhaps to list the latter as secondary authors), so as to give the publication, and the industry behind the paper, an air of validity and credibil-ity.$_{(10a, 11a)}$ As D. Healy (2004) has stated, "the key issue in ghostwriting is not whether the true authors are being deprived of recognition or whether academic authors are putting their names to articles they shouldn't get credit for. The key issue is whether there are likely to be discrepancies between these new-style articles and the raw data from the studies they purport to report".$_{(10b)}$

Another publication-control device is *Impact Factor* (IF), a popularity rating secretly calculated by the Thomson Reuters company for all published articles, which is based on the number of journals and papers that cite the particular article being considered. As S. Ghaemi (2009) states:

"this calculation is relevant both for journals and researchers. For journals, the more its articles are cited, the higher its IF, the greater its prestige, which as with all things in our wonderfully capitalist world, translates into money: advertisers and subscribers flock to the journals with the highest prestige, the greatest ... impact... So IF captures something, but its correlation with quality research is not as strong or direct as one might assume... So IF must involve something more than research quality: this is where the politics of science is relevant. Topics that are in the public eye will have greater IFs; researchers who are already well-established... may have their work cited more frequently than unknown authors; and large research groups may inflate the IF scores of their colleagues by citing each other liberally in their publications. The rich get richer".$_{(11b)}$

Peer Review: Ideally, the peer review process is designed to be a referee system for deciding which submitted articles merit inclusion in any journal or science publication, but as with other social processes, it is possible to stack the deck in favor of whatever particular group or institution, creating bias. Rampton and Stauber (2001) assert that peer review constitutes an institutionalized conflict of interest: "although the scientific method acknowledges the possibility of bias on the part of an *individual* scientist, it does not provide a way of countering the effects of *systemwide* bias...But what if different scientists share a *common* bias? Rather than canceling it out, they may actually reinforce it".$_{(12a)}$ Also, reviewers are carefully chosen for peer review boards and can be biased in favor of the authors they are reviewing, such as in the case of government science$_{(8b)}$ as well as industry science.$_{(7b)}$ The end result is that there are papers that should not have been included in science journals, due to whatever methodological flaws, as well as papers that have been unfairly rejected because the content of the article was too new, too original, or even too controversial. As Ghaemi states, peer review is inherently conservative, such that,

"... the most prestigious journals usually do not publish the most original or novel articles... Scientific innovation is rarely welcomed, and new ideas are always at a disadvantage against the old and staid. Again, non-researchers might have had a more favorable illusion about science, that it encourages progress and new ideas and that it is consciously self-critical. That is how it should be; but this is how it is".$_{(11c)}$

Aside from influencing the publication process, there are other ways to stack the deck, such as through using the scientific research itself to build doubt and ambiguity around controversial, inconvenient areas of knowledge. Despite capitalist propaganda to the contrary, with science it is oftentimes difficult to be absolutely certain about something, and when critical information is lacking or incomplete, as it is with so many areas of scientific study, scientists must do their best simply to make the uncertainties less uncertain. However, both industry and government use that doubt to their advantage, such as for evading the question of whether or not to control mercury or lead emissions, for example, in order to achieve the outcome that they want, which is to avoid being held legally responsible for the effects of pollution, or perhaps to give themselves an excuse not to take any regulatory actions. The following is a list of features that describes the "manufacture of doubt" as it takes place within capitalist science:

1) *Obfuscation*: The general strategy is to nit-pick the studies of your opponent(s) by casting doubt on their methods and results, and also to produce studies of your own that contradict theirs, all for the sake of creating and/or prolonging uncertainty. Perhaps the best example is the tobacco industry$_{(7c, 13a)}$, and then such tactics have also

worked well for the lead$_{(14a)}$ and mercury$_{(7d, 15a)}$ industries.

2) *Strategic ignorance*: Simply put, a process of circular logic where insufficient evidence of a possible environmental threat is deemed reason enough not to look for any more damning evidence; that is, "we can't be blamed for what we don't know, so let's make sure we don't find out anything that will make us culpable".$_{(7e, 16a)}$ In the case of mercury poisoning, as an example, this sort of thinking has led to the refusal of government and industry to assess the extent of vaccine injuries$_{(17a)}$, to examine the correlations between dental amalgams and diseases like multiple sclerosis$_{(18a)}$, and to assess general environmental toxicity from mercury.$_{(19a)}$

3) *Rigged studies*: Why not just set up your clinical trials for a new drug or product in such a way that will make it look like it performs better than what it's being tested against? The way to do that is to add or remove important comparative test-groups from the study, so as to skew the results. This strategy has been successfully used by the pharmaceutical industry to make their drugs seem safer and more effective than they really are$_{(7f, 9b, 20a, 21a)}$ and also by industries that produce mercury pollution so as to avoid being regulated. $_{(19b)}$

4) *Data tampering*: If you do a scientific study that produces inconvenient data, then just erase that part of the data you don't like without anyone noticing. Examples: adverse effects from mercury in dental amalgam$_{(18b)}$ and vaccines$_{(22a)}$, lead poisoning deaths from gasoline manufacture$_{(14b)}$, and suicides from antidepressant drugs.$_{(20b, 21b)}$

5) *Selective omission*: Only consider the evidence that supports your position, and ignore everything else.$_{(8c, 23a)}$ Some examples are: promoting pharmaceuticals$_{(10c)}$, refusing to acknowledge the sub-clinical effects of lead$_{(16b)}$ and mercury$_{(19c)}$, and ignoring adverse effects from dental amalgam.$_{(15b)}$

6) *Meta-Analysis*: The trick is to merge the data sets from smaller statistical studies and then reanalyze the combined data set, with a subtle modification of the analysis parameters in order to produce results that contradict the conclusion(s) of the original studies. The idea behind meta-analysis is that, when used ethically, such a reanalysis should help clarify data that is contradictory or inconclusive, but it can also be used for the sake of obfuscation – that is, to dilute undesirable data with that which one does prefer.$_{(7g, 11d)}$ This is a trick often used by the pharmaceutical industry to make questionable drugs appear more favorable$_{(11e)}$ and also by the coal industry to make their Hg emissions seem less harmful$_{(7h)}$, as examples.

7) *Withholding information*: Keeping the unfavorable data hidden, for as long as possible. This strategy has been well-documented with Industry's attempt to hide knowledge about the harmful effects from thiomersal in vaccines$_{(22b, 24, 25)}$, and then the adverse effects of psych meds.$_{(7i, 10d, 21c)}$

3.3: Censorship.

In addition to these self-serving research tactics, there are ways for capitalist science to censor any research or medical knowledge that threatens economic interests. The first one, peer-review, was already described in the explanation about publication-control. That is, by putting enough biased scientists (with financial ties to government and/or industry) on peer review boards, it becomes very easy to block the publication of studies that challenge the status quo. After peer review, another way to censor publications and journals is to make sure they aren't abstracted, thus making them hard to find.$_{(8d, 11f)}$ In this way, 19th century research on heavy metal toxicity is no longer referenced in current publications, which effectively leaves them buried.$_{(26)}$ And then there is the possibility of launching outright, propaganda-style attacks on any scientific work which challenges the interests of industry and the state. This strategy was honed by Big Tobacco, with its touting of "sound science" over "junk science"; that is, to aggressively disparage the work of your opponent as "junk".$_{(7j)}$ An important example is the establishment's orchestrated attack on alternative medical therapies, and in particular on chelation.$_{(27a, 28a)}$ In the case of those clinicians who pursue alternative treatments for their patients, their opinions tend to be devalued by establishment science, being dismissed as mere "anecdotal evidence" $_{(18c, 29a, 30a)}$, which of course is to be distinguished from the ivory tower medicine of the latter.

If the offending scientific work or medical practice itself cannot be effectively discredited, then the next step is to intimidate or discredit the researchers/clinicians. In particular, offensive individuals or groups can be excluded from conferences, harassed, threatened with legal action, or have their funding or licenses revoked.$_{(8e)}$ Two good examples are the harassment of dentists who practiced mercury-free dentistry in the 1990s$_{(15c, 27b, 31a)}$ and of researchers who have questioned the safety of thiomersal in vaccines.$_{(22c, 25, 28b)}$

And if all else fails, then *ad hominem* attacks – nasty, lengthy smear campaigns with corresponding legal harassment – are considered a valid way to silence scientific dissent. Some important smear campaigns against inconvenient individuals are: how the dental community tried to discredit (1920s) chemist A. Stock for his research of the connection between mercury dental amalgam and various medical conditions$_{(18d)}$; how the lead industry tried to discredit (1960s) geochemist C. Patterson for his ice-core research that revealed the dramatic rise of Pb pollution since industrialization$_{(14c)}$; how the lead industry tried to smear (1990s) psychiatrist H. Needleman for his research that characterized the subclinical effects of Pb$_{(14d, 16c)}$; how the vaccine industry is in the process of smearing (2000s - present) physician A. Wakefield for his research connecting vaccines and autism$_{(25)}$; how the American medical establishment is currently smearing (2010s) physician and geneticist M. Geier for his controversial autism treatments. If you can't successfully discredit someone's work, then why not just attack that person's character?

3.4: Conflicts of Interest.

To better appreciate how science has been corrupted by capitalist industry, it can't hurt to follow the thread further upstream, in order to show that it's really a team effort between industry and other sectors of society, such as medicine, government, academia and the mainstream media. This section will generally describe the *collusional* relationships between industry and these latter four groups, at least as they occur in the United States, with an emphasis on the topics of heavy metals and mental disorder, more or less.

To understand how organized medicine (including dentistry) is in the pocket of industry, we will briefly de-scribe a little about three big medical organizations: the AMA (American Medical Association), the APA (American Psychiatric Association), and the ADA (American Dental Association). Each of these three organizations bends quite easily to the self-serving interests of industry.

One role of the AMA is to be an industry henchman: it has served as the FDA's attack dog against chelation therapy$_{(29b)}$, it originally fought alongside Big Tobacco in the 1960s against making the public aware of the dangers of smoking$_{(32a)}$, and it has also been in bed with the tuna industry by way of resisting the initiative to put mercury warning labels on cans of tuna$_{(19d)}$, as examples. The AMA also produces pharmaceutical sales reps: that is, because of the US law that requires physician-written prescriptions for drugs, doctors have effectively become sales representatives for the pharmaceutical industry.$_{(20c, 21d)}$ And since Big Pharma can now legally advertise drugs in the US, the traditional doctor/patient relationship has been subverted, turning doctors into prescription-writers, rather than continuing with their traditional expert/advisory role from earlier times.$_{(9c)}$ Doctors are groomed for this role with plenty of commodity-fetish gifts (like those plastic ball-point pens, tote bags or coffee mugs with the name of the advertised drug printed on it – how classy!), free lunches, pharmaceutical-paid and fully-biased "continuing education" courses, along with conference and trade fair speaking engagements to help legitimize new drugs for sale.$_{(9d, 10e, 21e, 30b, 33a)}$

The APA, while distinct from the AMA, essentially works in parallel: it helps groom psychiatrists to become pharmaceutical sales reps$_{(20d, 21f)}$, which of course involves those important limousine rides, free lunches and lots of company-logo ballpoint pens for writing prescriptions. As creator of the new DSM-5 manual, the APA has also been accused of selecting DSM panelist authors that have financial ties to the drug industry.$_{(34)}$

For dentistry, the ADA's role is very much like that of the AMA and APA: like the latter two, it has always represented the interests of industry, in this case, the amalgam industry (mercury).$_{(8f, 18e, 27c)}$

Moving on to the relationship between government and industry, we might be tempted to feel some relief that the US government has agencies in place like the FDA, EPA, CDC, OSHA and NIOSH, that are designed to regulate industry products and to protect workers and citizens, however these regulatory agencies generally exist only in a superficial sense. In general, industry regulation is always impotent to begin with, since regulation can take place only *after* someone or more gets hurt$_{(32b, 33b)}$, and furthermore such regulatory agencies exist merely in a symbolic capacity, given that despite their presence, the industry still manages to get away with pollution and the non-stop, 24/7 production of harmful products that lead to adverse health and environmental effects. Additionally, there is that problematic and ongoing "revolving door" phenomenon where high-level employees can transfer back and forth between regulatory agencies and the industries they are supposed to regulate, indicating that the regulatory system is fundamentally compromised.

By way of illustrations, we might first consider the vaccine problem, with the choice instance of that infamous conference in Simpsonwood, Georgia, in 2000, where representatives from the CDC and vaccine industry secretly met in order to discuss how to maintain their deniability about the dangers of thiomersal$_{(22d, 24, 28c)}$, and how in general the CDC experiences a profound conflict of interest by way of its dual role of promoting vaccination while also ensuring vaccine safety.$_{(17b, 22e, 25)}$ A second example: the failure of the FDA to properly identify the dangers from mercury in dental amalgams is also a good case of toothless regulation (no pun intended).$_{(15d, 31b)}$ And then on a much larger scale, we have the problem of pollution, and quite simply how the polluters keep on polluting, despite all of the legal jibber-jabber on the part of regulatory agencies; this is the case for pollution from both mercury$_{(7k, 19e, 35a)}$ and lead.$_{(7l, 14e, 16d)}$ A final example is that of collusion between the pharmaceutical industry and government regulatory agencies, where scientists in the latter are bought out by the former in order to push new drugs to the market faster than they should.$_{(9e, 10f, 20e, 36)}$

Next, we have the example of industry buying out academia: in particular, how universities will do whatever it takes to bring in research money, and how such a relationship fundamentally changes the "disinterested" nature of academic science research.$_{(8g, 9f, 23b)}$

And finally, to maintain the economic control that it has, industry must have in its pocket the press, that organ by which it can communicate with the public: slyly marketing its products and using propaganda to downplay whatever negative impacts that result, all under the guise of objective news reporting, infomercials, and the like, and of course all paid for by the industry via advertising.$_{(20f, 35b)}$

3.5: Legal Obfuscation.

While section 3.2 covered the kinds of obfuscational tactics employed in scientific research, this section will cover how such research is misrepresented or "spun" in the courtroom.

First and foremost, the name of the game is to emphasize whatever associated ambiguity surrounding controversial scientific information that will enable judges to rule in the favor of industry, as a strategy to stall regulation as well as to win tort cases against consumer plaintiffs. As D. Michaels says,

"Lawsuits also work as an engine that powers technological progress. A study by the Rand Corporation concluded that potential liability was the single most important factor in shaping decisions on product design. The chemical industry acknowledges that litigation avoidance plays a central role in promoting responsible corporate behavior".$_{(7m)}$

(Of course there are some who might say that such a thing as *responsible corporate behavior* could never really exist, that such a term is nothing but an oxymoron, but regardless of who you ask, the point made is that industry strives at all costs to win its courtroom battles by avoiding them altogether.) Such legal prowess on the part of the industry is maintained through a variety of means. As previously mentioned, the current legal machinery in the US is designed to enforce regulation only when consumers and communities become injured through the products and activities of industry, and this arrangement places the burden of proof on the victim(s), not on the offending industries.$_{(7n, 12b, 32c)}$ Overturning this situation could be achieved through adoption of what some have called the *precautionary principle*, which effectively shifts the burden of proof from consumer to industry, but so far industry has successfully resisted the implementation of that kind of system. As Rampton & Stauber (2001) indicate,

"the reason that scientific uncertainty is the fulcrum for the precautionary principle is that the harm associated with technological innovations is often impossible to prove at the time of the new technology introduced... In each of these cases, waiting for proof to appear meant that action was not taken until serious damage to health and the environment had occurred. Amassing unambiguous proof is a long and costly process, particularly after a product is in widespread use and industries have a vested interested in defending it. The idea behind the precautionary principle is that a lack of conclusive scientific evidence should not be used as an excuse for failing to take measures to protect human health and the environment".$_{(12c)}$

Therefore resisting the precautionary principle keeps the odds in industry's favor, precisely through maintaining and even magnifying whatever doubt that exists regarding a particular area of scientific knowledge. However, underlying this strategy resides the underhanded attempt to redefine science in a self-serving way, where we are led to believe that the only science worth considering is that which can completely eliminate all doubt in the courtroom.$_{(7o, 12d, 37a)}$ But as was already mentioned before, science is imperfect and only attempts to find evidence that could dissipate whatever lingering doubt or controversy; in the meantime, it should never be used as leverage against taking action, as Michaels suggests:

"...the objective of industry and product-defense reanalysis is to force regulators to consider studies that appear to be equal but come to differing conclusions. Uncertainty. That's a recipe for regulatory paralysis. Epidemiologists understand that data analyses that use methods and comparisons selected post hoc – after studying the distribution of the data – do not have the same validity as those that test prior hypotheses. Many regulators understand this, too, but industry sponsors hope that even if they cannot convince regulators, their machinations may not be as clear to a federal judge reviewing a regulatory action".$_{(7p)}$

Now that we know the general strategy that industry takes in legal proceedings towards protecting its interests, the next question addresses how exactly, besides focusing on ambiguity and controversy arising within particular scientific studies it doesn't like, does it protect its interests. What strategies does it take? In light of the coverage of R. Lewontin's ideas in 2.7, there is that tendency to *blame the victim*: aside from the legal device of distinguishing between "lifestyle" versus occupational injuries$_{(30c, 37b, 38)}$ there is that latent, persistent thread of genetic determinism which alleges that genetic predispositions to illness can thoroughly account for environmentally-caused health problems.$_{(37c)}$ While genetic factors might very well play a small role in certain environmental illnesses, such a hypothesis cannot explain the growing number of cases$_{(37d)}$, and it completely disregards the possibility of epigenetic/environmental influences. This kind of ambiguity is just what industry-defenders are seeking in order to protect their clients. Regardless, the blame-the-victim approach has worked very well for maintaining corporate denial of both mercury$_{(19f)}$ and lead$_{(14f, 16e)}$ poisoning.

Another simple way for corporations to protect themselves legally is to withhold information from consumers, hence the labeling of such information as "proprietary trade secrets", such as with ingredients listed on product labels.$_{(32d)}$ This is also the case with the ADA, who in the past has disregarded the need for *informed consent* by refusing to divulge the toxic metal content of dental amalgam.$_{(18f)}$ For drugs, data associated with clinical trials is also considered proprietary and thus kept out of reach, even from collaborators, by way of contractual agreements, until there is a court injunction that forces them to share the information.$_{(9g, 11g)}$ As within in any other corner of the US legal system, the less you say, then so the less likely such information can be used against you.

Next, we have the strategy of tampering with the regulation-setting process: that is, corporations protect themselves by setting ridiculously high toxicity threshold limits, which is essentially a permutation of the effort to establish impossibly high standards of certainty.$_{(12e, 39)}$ In the cases of mercury$_{(19g)}$ and lead$_{(14g)}$ poisoning, setting the legal toxic threshold as high as possible enables those industries to keep the science of subclinical metal toxicity out of the courtroom. A great example of such an underhanded, self-interested style of maneuvering can be taken from the history of the asbestos industry's demise, by way of the following synopsis by D. Ozonoff, a toxicologist who served as a legal witness against that industry:

"Asbestos doesn't hurt your health. OK, it does hurt your health but it doesn't cause cancer. OK, asbestos can cause cancer but not our kind of asbestos. OK, our kind of asbestos can cause cancer, but not the kind this person got. OK, our kind of asbestos can cause cancer, but not at the doses to which this person was exposed. OK, asbestos does cause cancer, and at this dosage, but this person got his disease from something else, like smoking. OK, he was exposed to our asbestos and it did cause his cancer, but we did not know about the danger when we exposed him. OK, we knew about the danger when we exposed him, but the statute of limitations has run out. OK, the statute of limitations hasn't run out, but if we're guilty we'll go out of business and everyone will be worse off. OK, we'll agree to go out of business, but only if you let us keep part of our company intact, and only if you limit our liability for the harms we have caused".(12f)

In addition to the legal games already described, industry has laws to assist them in resisting culpability. One such method is the Daubert ruling, which effectively forces judges to dismiss expert witness testimony (especially if it comes from the anti-industry, regulation side) that presents scientific information that lacks complete certainty.(7q, 37e) There is also the Shelby Amendment, where industry can use the Freedom of Information Act to use and/or pick apart any government science to further their legal interests(7r) and then the Data Quality Act, also used to nitpick and dismiss any government or other scientific work that threatens their interests.(7s) And finally, there are anti-disparagement laws, designed to prevent opponents (outside groups, citizens, consumers, etc.) from speaking and writing negatively about the products and activities of industries. Legal action taken against such opponents has been informally termed "SLAPP suits", a.k.a. "Strategic lawsuit against public participation"(12g)

3.6: The Public Relations Phenomenon.

The last area of deception to be covered with regards to capitalist science is that of the public relations (PR) industry: the art of harnessing the mass media via propaganda campaigns so as to control the way in which government, a company, or an industry is viewed by the public, in order to prevent citizens from organizing against them. Such an outcome is achieved primarily through keeping individuals mired in apathy, endless debate or indecision for as long as possible. As Rampton and Stabuer tell us,

> "just as the invention of language made lying possible, the invention of mass media created newer, more sophisticated, subtle, and elaborate techniques of propaganda...The mass media made it possible for the first time to conceal the identity of the voices that appeared within it, to deliver messages while hiding the identity of the messenger. It became possible to accomplish this act of concealment without ever committing an act of overt deception".(12h)

PR firms use the art of spin to make their clients look good in the public view (or less horrible than they really are) whether they be celebrities, politicians, corporate executives or even entire industries. These companies offer a wide assortment of pricey, high-tech services, including advertising, news-releases, opinion-polling through mail, email and telephone, public relations, research, surveillance, lobbying and even building phony "grassroots" support for their wealthy clients. For example, if it becomes impossible to convince people that pollution doesn't exist, or that it's actually somehow a good thing, then as a minimum, an effective PR campaign will be able to fool us into thinking that we are powerless to do anything about pollution. It might be of interest to know that the person who should arguably be the originator of the PR industry, E. Bernays, was the nephew of that eternally favourite shrink to whom so many of us remain oedipally attached, S. Freud. How fascinating to learn that:

> "...there was a striking paradox... in the way that Bernays went about trying to follow in the footsteps of his Uncle Sigmund. Freud's "talking cure" was designed to unearth his patients' unconscious drives and hidden motives, in the belief that bringing them into conscious discourse would help people lead healthier lives. Bernays, by contrast, used psychological techniques to *mask* the motives of his clients, as part of a deliberate strategy aimed at keeping the public *un*conscious of the forces that were working to mold their minds... It is no accident that Bernays developed his "science" of public relations in the 1920s – a decade that also saw the beginnings of mass production, mass communications, mass consumerism, and a belief in technological progress as a quasireligion. All of these trends shared a faith in the notion that society's problems can be engineered away, that democracy is dangerous, and that important decisions should be left in the hands of experts".(12i)

Since PR companies are all about deception, exactly what kinds of tricks do they employ in order to keep people in a discouraged, disempowered state? Aside from the ordinary marketing tricks like disease-mongering where, for example, the diagnostic boundaries of mental disorder are widened through "education" and "disease awareness" campaigns, just for the sake of selling more medicines(9h, 10g, 21g), there are also propaganda games to be played. Perhaps the most important one is what some would call the *3rd party technique*, where a client such as a sleazeball corporation suffering from a severe image crisis secretly hires a seemingly disinterested group with apparently no connections to the client but who ends up doing or saying something that bolsters the public's perception of that client. PR firms help orchestrate those covert relationships between the client and a third party while at the same time fooling the public into thinking there are no vested interests on the part of either groups.(12j, 35c) Two pertinent examples of the 3rd party technique are: how the lead industry (leaded paint and gasoline) was able to fool the public in the early 20th century about lead safety with fully orchestrated endorsements from company-paid doctors and researchers(14h), and then how the tuna industry (whose income has been threatened by ongoing mercury pollution) secretly enlisted the help of the American Heart Association in the 1990s to endorse canned tuna with "heart-healthy" labeling.(19h) The PR industry has also studied and aped grassroots democracy and environmental activists by way of a technique that has been termed "astroturfing", where phony civilian, consumer support for an industry and/or its cause is cleverly orchestrated by a PR company, in order to make their client look good in the eyes of the public.(35d) And not surprisingly, regarding scientific issues, the PR industry regularly uses doubt in their propaganda messages to stymie the public, generally by exploiting the myth about the need for absolute certainty in science before taking any regulatory action(13b), and in particular, within manufactured controversies about issues like global warming, alternative health treatments, and the dangers of tobacco, lead or mercury, just through feeding the right questions to journalists.(7t, 13c, 30d) Then finally, PR propaganda frequently uses the strategy of identifying and then using people's fears against them, such as through emotionally manipulative arguments for the continued stalling of regulation over pollution, because such an initiative would undeniably increase the unemployment rate.(7u, 14i, 37f)

3.7: Citizen Science.

From the capitalist corruption of science detailed above, it might be tempting to conclude as the postmodernists have done that science fundamentally belongs to the capitalist system, and that any knowledge obtained under such conditions is irrevocably tainted, leading us down that path of radical skepticism only to conclude that there is no such thing as objective knowledge. It can't be overly stressed how such a cynical conclusion dovetails so very nicely with those industry-paid PR machinations designed to keep people passive and inactive so that they will continue to allow industry to keep on propagating global ecocide. Even if contemporary science is compromised, then surely there must be an alternative? Some would say "yes", by way of the concept of *citizen science*, or lay scientific expertise. Citizen science calls for the (re)appropriation of science – scientific skills and knowledge – to be placed in the hands of lay or non-scientist people, and *not* to reside exclusively with the scientific experts of the establishment as it does now.(37g, 40, 41a, 42) Such a redistribution of scientific capabilities cannot be effected until the scientific establishment is able to overcome the obstacle of their own epistemological snobbery, their proclivity to dismiss citizen participation in the scientific process as mere "anecdotal evidence", based on the incorrect assumption that whatever scientists know as a result of their own refined scientific training must by default supersede anything known or determined by a community of everyday, non-scientist people.(37h, 41b, 43) In particular, we might consider the pressing issues of pollution and the health issues that arise from such: in many cases, it is the community who lives at ground zero, who is therefore the first to know about the resulting health problems, illnesses, disorders, etc., and not the socially- and politically-insulated scientists of the establishment.(37i) So to contradict the postmodernists, the question is not about dismissing science altogether, of throwing the baby out with the bathwater, but on deciding how to reconfigure science, or particularly, reconfiguring scientific expertise within our culture such that the experts no longer decide what the rest of the community must do about something like pollution, but rather that the former would take on an *advisory role* and not to interfere with the efforts of the latter group(12k, 32e, 40), regardless of however utopian or impossibly socialist such a proposition might sound to conservatives, including to those who wistfully fall for the myth of a reformed, "socially responsible" capitalism. It should be pointed out that the many authors cited here in part 3 underestimate the degree to which class warfare necessitates this solution of citizen science, and which neatly accounts for the not-so-mysterious devaluation of citizen participation in the pursuit of scientific truth, especially in light of the capitalist tactics previously discussed.

It's also worth mentioning how the internet is a relatively new resource for citizen organization and for the dissemination of controversial scientific knowledge, or *gray literature*, as some have called it.(37j, 44, 45) Although the scientific mainstream tends to dismiss that kind of literature (which often draws on anecdotal evidence) because it did not go through the rigorous filter of peer review, it is nonetheless valuable because of its relatively uncensored quality, and also because of its ability to address areas of scientific controversy that the more reputable, prestigious, snobbish journals are too afraid to touch(11h, 19i) even if the establishment methodically dismisses such information as being *merely* anecdotal in essence: as A. Cutler (2008) explains:

"the thing physicians are criticized the most for – relying on anecdotal evidence – is actually what they should be doing. Anecdotal evidence, the basis of all science, is observation: "I saw this." It's just like evidence in court: "I saw this" trumps "somebody told me that they saw"".(46)

This confrontation between anecdotal evidence and the more valid, "pure", scientific variety neatly parallels how the border between science and "pseudoscience" is routinely policed by the mainstream. In the case of dealing with heavy metals – or of *removing* them from the body, actually – the controversial area of chelation hasn't been fully embraced by the establishment, and is in fact vilified by pseudoscience policemen like *quackwatch.com*.

By way of conclusion: this part of the text is designed to complement part 2. Both parts address the reasons for how and why heavy metal toxicity resulting from pollution and consumer products is a serious concern in industrialized society: part 2 is a survey of the scientific literature which describes the connections between heavy metals and mental disorder/genius, and part 3 covers the sociology (particularly the apathy and denialism) of said science, as it is spun by industry in newsrooms and courtrooms in self-serving ways, designed to keep economic production going no matter the human or environmental costs – in particular, there is an irony to be noticed in the way industrial society sells us toxic technologies to supposedly improve our lives but which end up causing such miseries like these mental disorders, and then also how we are sold those ineffective and often injurious medical cures like psych meds which are not only harmful but which add insult to injury. Sell me an illness and then sell me the cure: misery squared, but with such remarkable profitability!

Together parts 2 and 3 create a materialist sketch of contemporary society, particularly in how its practice of science has been corrupted economically, such that even when people go mad and/or die, there is no scientific knowledge that can't be spun or buried, all for the sake of continuing profits. Such a perspective profoundly differs from that of postmodernists who hold that slippery, relativist stance which argues for the social construction of facts, such that there is no such thing as objectivity, but rather that the latter is merely a state of mind. Thus, I have argued that objective, scientific facts *do* exist (even if our ability to thoroughly grasp that objectivity is perhaps distorted by our subjectivity, such as through the use of language), simply because capitalist society tends to preclude and censor those kinds of knowledge which threaten its interests. So for those of us who still believe in socialism, however utopian, impractical, impossible or faraway it may seem, science should not be something to be superstitiously loathed, to be considered merely as a tainted product of capitalism, but rather to be intended as a rationalist set of tools for learning about the world, as a method of finding ways to resist exploitation, and of producing accurate, useful knowledge that will outlast capitalism itself. In that sense, science has a currently untapped *surrationalist* potential, if we dare to make use of G. Bachelard's term.

And to return to our topic of the mad-genius, I suggest that the underlying relationship between what is known as genius and insanity is something to be quietly avoided by mainstream science because of the socio-political considerations outlined in this part of the text: that economic interests implicitly trump health concerns, despite whatever denials on the part of the establishment, and that such apathy and obfuscation help maintain the general lack of interest in the mad-genius, as well as the ongoing mystification regarding the origins of intellect and the stigmatization of mental disorder, in light of the discussion of heavy metal toxicity.

Part 4: Holistic Considerations.

4.1: Towards a Unified Field: the Cartesian mind/body disconnect & historical materialism.

The fact that we are disconnected or even alienated (or maybe that our continued self-removal is voluntary?) from the possibilities of establishing a materialist basis for human psychology, which includes collective psychology, has been an ongoing problem that has persisted for the duration of the surrealist movement, up to the present time. Historically, surrealism's origins roughly coincide with those of the Freudian psychoanalytic system, such that the surrealists readily modified those therapeutic techniques for the purpose of poetic experimentation, for the sake of discovering the "true functioning of thought", as well as for explaining individual and collective motives and behaviors. While revolutionary at the time, such Freudian-derived perspectives retain a cultural reductionist character, which, as human knowledge grows and as the decades pass, from one century into the next, increasingly come into contradiction with the Marxian concept of *historical materialism*, which posits that the entirety of human phenomena – both culture and biology – is determined primarily by *material*, economic conditions. Therefore the historical denial of biological and other "hard" scientific evidence on the part of surrealism and other 21st century Leftist movements is a problem that needs to be reconsidered.

In regards to the theory of historical materialism we might ask: if culture results from material conditions, from the material "environment", which does indeed reflect socio-economic conditions, then why should our bodies (including brains) be excluded from consideration with regards to those material influences? When posing the question this way, a dialectic between people as both subjects and objects is apparent – we can influence each other, and ourselves, both culturally and physically. But in our present society, with the arbitrary separation of mind from body, it is incorrectly assumed that the mind (our sense of "mind" as a subjective experience that somehow results from the material activity of the brain interacting with the world around it) is chemically independent from the physical world. Therefore, the current disconnect between mind and body neatly overlaps with the disconnect between individual and environment.

In more abstract terms, we can think of historical materialism as a process that implies matter over mind, whereas systems of thought which depend on cultural determinism and reductionism with whatever mystical overtones (such as Freudian psychoanalytic theory) imply mind over matter. According to historical materialism, our subjective sense of "mind", or "consciousness", our sense of reality, with each thinking individual as an *agent of culture*, depends on material, economic conditions, just as the rest of culture does. So if we were to say that our culture is determined primarily by material forces, then isn't our sense of reality – individual and collective – also primarily determined by material forces, and then secondarily by cultural forces?? Or better yet, does consciousness result from a dialectic between material and cultural, such that the material still has a primary influence and cultural a secondary one? So then would the question have to do with how we perceive "consciousness", and how we suppose it relates to culture – dialectically both as a manifestation of culture itself, and also an agent of culture? If we extend this line of inquiry we might ask how exactly economic conditions influence not just the superficial, physical trappings of a society, but also how such forces influence our bodies, our minds, which includes our perceptions, our emotions, our reality, our sense of morality. Questions about the material nature of thought can't help but arise.

So far there have been two main strategies for addressing the mind/body disconnect: cultural reductionism and biological reductionism. In the case of the latter, which happens to be the current position of the mainstream (and which was reviewed in 2.7, especially with regards to R. Lewontin's ideas), it is thought that various mental states depend exclusively on forces occurring strictly *within* the person, such as genetics, as well as the rest of one's biochemistry, without acknowledging the possibility of *outside, material*, chemical, environmental forces (from food, vaccines, pollutants and other sources of gradually acquired toxicity) that interact dialectically with the individual. Also, if we take biological reductionism to its extreme, we reach the conclusion that culture is exclusively an activity of the brain, where concepts such as "desire" and "joy", for example, and ultimately "consciousness", are reified in "brain genes" and also by neuroimaging techniques into the mere sequential activation/silencing of certain brain regions, without fully giving credit to those external forces, both subjective and objective stimuli, that provoked them. Such current approaches might be described as *epiphenomenalism*, where the molecular, physiological state of the brain is considered the exclusive source of causality for all mental phenomena, but which ultimately maintains the mind/body dualism. In the case of cultural reductionism, which persisted for most of the earlier part of the 20th century, the premise is that all bodies are created equally, all minds equally – tabula rasa – and that outcomes like mental disorder and genius were strictly the products of one's social environment. Cultural reductionism maintains the mind/body separation by way of its denial of the physical. History has shown us that neither of these positions, in and of themselves, is acceptable.

While both of these opposing tendencies have each had their eras of dominance over the other, those specialists in various areas of academic research pertaining to the mind/body problem retain their respective cultural- or biological-reductionist biases: that is, psychologists, anthropologists, sociologists and the like tend to favor cultural reductionist perspectives, whereas biologists, epidemiologists, neurologists, etc. share the biological reductionist bias. What so many investigators on both sides of this divide have been craving for, for so very long, is a bridge of new knowledge that would connect these two seemingly disparate perspectives. Such a "Unified Field", with a common vocabulary (more precise and thereby less prone to linguistic misunderstandings) to be shared between both sides, would be the philosopher's stone for ending the Cartesian mind/body disconnect, among other problems.

One of the goals of this text is not to pretentiously offer a new Unified Field theory, but more modestly, to identify a few of the obstacles that prevent the attainment of such a revolutionary perspective, by way of considering how science has been corrupted by capitalist socio-economics, as was covered in part 3. Part 2 was intended not merely to 1) review evidence for and refute the currently popular genetic reductionist perspective, and 2) to express my rejection of cultural reductionism, but also to 3) review an alternative kind of biological evidence that supports the hypothesis that mental disorder and genius are not due to genetic inheritance in the commonly accepted Mendelian sense, but rather are caused by *epigenetic* inheritance effects – that is, where environmental toxins can influence gene function with a Lamarckian pattern of inheritance, leading to the persistence and even rising prevalence of genius/madness. *Such a new hypothesis effectively shifts blame and responsibility from the individual (who has supposedly "failed to adapt to urban life", as was said in the 19th century, or who has "defective genes", in the 20th century) over to industrial society.*$_{(1)}$ When we consider the case of mental disorder, the industrially-produced, environmental toxin becomes the link that enables the direction of causality between physiological state and altered consciousness: therefore we can trace our experience of the altered mental state back to its physical origin: the vaccine, the prenatal exposures, the domestic exposures, the occupational exposures, etc. If we alternatively go along with cultural-determinist explanations of mental disorder, then such altered consciousness remains disconnected from the bodily state, and we are left with nothing but cumbersome social explanations tinted with mystification. From these approaches, we might infer how Cartesian science, under the influence of capitalist interests, plays a role in sabotaging its own scientific method and practice of medicine$_{(2)}$, preventing it from formulating a dialectical-materialist conception of mental disorder, thereby contributing to the ongoing mind/body disconnect. Additionally, we might also predict that there won't be any Unified Field as long as science remains under the thumb of capitalist imperatives.

First and foremost, the task of surrealism would be to reconsider these older positions in light of the newer evidence. Surrealism and other movements of the Left have traditionally embraced cultural reductionist perspectives which oppose those 19th century pro-nationalist, pro-colonial positions that created such programs like eugenics. In the earlier part of the 20th century, when eugenic ideas about "degeneration" by individuals like C. Lombroso were still influential and led to outcomes such as Nazi genocide, then cultural determinist positions did indeed manifest an inviting, liberating character which both the mainstream and the Left embraced. But after several decades, those favored, culturalist perspectives came to be too restrictive, too shallow to reveal anything new about the "human condition", and were supplanted by the genetic reductionism/determinism that is still in vogue with the mainstream today. Another big question that this paper has addressed is whether or not science is all the same – to ask if it irrevocably bears a capitalist taint – or alternatively perhaps that some of the knowledge produced under capitalist regimes might actually be able to contribute to the demise of such regimes, and to last beyond that? Then we arrive at the question about whether or not surrealists, who call themselves "specialists in revolt", have any interest in expanding their primary domain of activity (art/poetry, philosophy, politics, and the human or "soft" sciences) to include the natural sciences. A very brief consideration of surrealist ideas about the divide between the arts versus the sciences is appropriate, in light of this latter question, but first we must address the question about Miserabilism…

4.2: Miserabilist Urban Ecology.

Ecologically speaking, mainstream culture spends so much time focusing macroscopically on the more photogenic mammals (like dolphins, whales and wolves) without addressing the way in which ecology affects us humans (also an environmentally threatened species – albeit a *swarming* species, just like certain bugs) neurochemically, which takes our investigation to a more intimate level, when one finds one's body, including brain, enmeshed within the context of a whole list of environmental, pollutional insults in various guises, quantities and colorful packagings. One historically pertinent detail to observe is how through religion and scientifically-backed ideology people have managed to fool themselves for at least a few centuries about the physically toxic effects of industry – by way of occupational exposures or those which occur within the home. The irony of collectively being fooled by our own senses, with our impulsive, knee-jerk denials of the "industrial factor", being slowly but surely influenced by a plethora of environmental toxins, while parading through life under the guise of business-as-usual – this outcome should be seen closely akin to Breton's definition of miserabilism.

Before examining the concept of *miserabilism* from a strictly materialist perspective – i.e. ecological, biological, etc. – it would be worthwhile to review the surrealist origin and development of the term, in order to appreciate its cultural impact, which actually represents the first systematic attempts to characterize such a phenomenon. The term first appeared in Breton's "Away with Miserabilism!" essay from 1956, with a rather blunt and direct description of it as "the depreciation of reality in place of its exaltation". Breton's definition has an exclusively culturalist slant, noting its appearance in intellectual currents like 19th century "academicism" and then 20th century existentialism, but without any mention of its possible manifestations in non-academic circles. Additionally, Breton's essay suggests an ideological origin, where miserabilism in mid-20th century Europe resulted from the "coupling of… hitlerite fascism and stalinism".(3) The concept was later developed and broadened by other surrealists to include *all* individuals residing in capitalist regimes, such that it embodied an ongoing cultural force of propaganda designed to perpetuate the capitalist system. For instance, from the Chicago surrealist group, F. Rosemont notes that:

"Miserabilism has had its greatest success in creating such near-total confusion that few people recognize how miserable they really are… It meant that the whole quality of human life, as long as capitalism endured, would grow more and more miserable. The function of all miserabilist ideologies is to conceal this truth; to make misery seem like its opposite; to make the world safe for miserabilist exploitation."(4a)

In her essay "Miserabilism and Anti-Miserabilism", P. Rosemont also lists cultural sources of contemporary miserabilism, such as capitalist economic expansion, commercialism, nationalism, religion, militarization, etc.(5) and then adds elsewhere that:

"The basic assumption of miserabilism is that misery is eternal – that there is no way out. Beginning with resignation, it passes quickly enough to the outright glorification of misery for misery's sake. This is the function of nearly the whole superstructure of advanced capitalist society today: from religion to the advertising agencies, from the politicians to the false poets. As the quintessential ideological expression of decadent capitalism's surge towards barbarism, reinforced by the universal institutionalization of the death-wish, miserabilism rests on the extreme brutalization of language – a monstrous depreciation of all signs, so that it becomes increasingly impossible for men and women to think: impossible above all to express their thoughts with any coherence, lucidity or ardour. All signs by which

Cins - *Siirt*

communication is supposed to be effected are degraded to the narrowest utilitarian function, made subservient to the fetishism of commodities, and deprived of all brilliance and fire."(6)

From these descriptions, clues about the actual origin of miserabilism are absent; at best we can infer that somehow miserabilism is effective enough as a technique for demoralizing and fragmenting people, and deterring them from organizing, but without any indication of how such a globally expansive strategy came to become so prevalent and effective within just a few hundred years or so.

To answer this question about origins, we might consider the hypothesis that miserabilism, at least as a cultural phenomenon, is only half of the story: that to sufficiently disorient people into remaining passive and inactive in a spiritual, psychological way, it would be helpful to immobilize them through biochemical means, as well. I propose that after the industrial revolution, through the neurotoxic effects of certain pollutants like heavy metals, and now in conjunction with a wide range of petrochemicals from the 20th century, there are currently plenty of synergizing toxins in the urban environment that can influence how people are feeling, thinking and responding to each other, keeping them emotionally labile and easy to be pushed around by the ruling class.

A very simple physiological scenario which explains this kind of lability is that of the daily hepatic excretion and reuptake of heavy metals (absorbed from food, smog, second-hand tobacco smoke, vaccines, dental amalgam, etc.)

within the GI tract, accompanied by those resulting negative sensations, impressions, emotional changes that range from the barely perceptible, all the way to noticeable moodswings and which are fundamentally misattributed to an external rather than an internal point of origin (the erroneous projection of causality onto the immediate, external environment rather than the internal, biological one, such as through mistakenly blaming one's surroundings or individuals like coworkers, family, or a spouse[7]), which is conducive to social isolation, alienation and even manipulation. Al-though such a description of the interaction between the *enterohepatic reuptake loop* and one's social environment may sound dramatic when expressed in these terms, however on the immediate, practical level, such psychological effects are very subtle and hard to trace, yet quite damaging to (developing) communities. From the ecological perspective of collectivity, we might ask how gradually rising chemical toxicity in urban areas could increase the potential frequency of these misattribution events, and ask what kind of influence such misattribution might have on the culture of whatever population: how it would shape the way people interact with each other and relate to each other – for example, would such an increased frequency of cognitive misattribution lead to less trust, less collaboration, more infighting, more despair, less collective growth for cultures and for groups, at whatever level of size and organization? As mentioned in part 3 of this paper, Industry has consistently gone to great lengths to keep any awareness of the subclinical effects of chemicals – toxic metals, especially – out of the courtroom and out of view of (toothless) regulators; when considering the subclinical, psycho-behavioral effects of lead and mercury, for example, such outcomes are not the least bit inconsistent with the sense of despair, alienation, hopelessness, confusion, etc. that some have referred to as *miserabilism*. The trick is not to rely exclusively on the cultural reductionist explanation, nor on the purely biological reductionist sort either, but rather to consider the possibility of a dialectical process where the cultural and the biological are co-influencing each other: particularly that for capitalism, the neurotoxicity from heavy metal pollution was not some consciously elaborated diabolical plan, but rather just a lucky accident (lucky for them, that is), merely an unintended by-product of industrialization, which just so happened to be compatible with the capitalist prerogative to use any and all means to push their wage-slaves as far as possible, just for the sake of maximizing profits. In this sense, it shouldn't be too surprising that capitalist science turns a blind eye to the subtle effects of heavy metal neurotoxicity, and that of other toxins, as well.

And in passing, it can't hurt to mention the potentially confounding neurological effects of the industrialist high-gluten, high-casein diet, especially when considering how heavy metals can have a disruptive effect on the activity of digestive enzymes, as well as to provoke immune systems into a hyperactive state, possibly leading to those unusual food allergies and candida problems that have also blossomed during the time of late capitalism.

So to further shape this "chemico-miserabilism" hypothesis, we might consider a more historical example: that of the vague concept of *fatigue*, the rise in which appears to correlate with modernist civilization. As historian A. Rabinbach (1990) has noted, the vaguely defined malady of fatigue – perhaps mental, perhaps physical, or both, and called by many names including *neurasthenia* – did overlap somewhat with Freud's *hysteria* concept, and was very successful at challenging 19th century researchers and doctors. Physical symptoms of the condition included headaches, back pains, insomnia, indigestion, dermal hypersensitivity, among others, while the mental, subjective symptoms were numerous, but which included *aboulia* (impairment or perturbation of the will) as well as impairment of intellectual and moral abilities – all of which, both physical and mental, are not inconsistent with the subclinical effects of metal poisoning, especially lead and mercury. In that era, such fatigue was viewed simply as a pathological aversion to work, particularly as an *unconsciously elaborated resistance to modernity* on the part of the symptom-presenting individuals.[8] But if we fast-forward to the present, we will find a similar disorder, with similar symptoms, but with a different name: at the moment, we have what has now come to be known popularly as "Chronic Fatigue Syndrome", or CFS. It might be tempting to dismiss the modern form of this malady perhaps just as readily as some will note how doctors from earlier eras never quite took their patients seriously enough. Individuals like M. Foucault would most likely dismiss the activities of organized medicine as a method analogous to branding cattle, more or less establishing arbitrary criteria for separating the economically useful bodies from the useless ones. However, the problem with such thinking is that it suffers from a false dichotomy: that either 1) CFS truly exists and individuals can suffer from it, or 2) CFS is just a myth or capitalist invention, just an arbitrary measure for the sake of removing economic undesirables from the rest of the bunch. Most likely Foucault and his postmodernist groupies would go for perspective #2: that this disorder, like any other, is merely an attempt to manufacture a new category of illness just for the sake of maintaining citizen discipline and conformity, to create a justification for squeezing workers. And most likely the doctors and several of the patients will take position #1, that CFS is an actual disorder that does cause the observed symptoms, however mysteriously. But what about a third possibility, where both conditions are true: where CFS is something that does exist, just like other environmental illnesses, and that yes, it also just so happens to be an inconvenience for those who enslave the rest of us? What makes this latter position defensible is that there is plenty of evidence for capitalist domination, as well as evidence for the existence of CFS. But wait a second... what *kind* of evidence for CFS? Simply the measurement of behavioral traits? No; in recent times it has been learned that there are actually measurable *physical* traits that are salient in CFS sufferers. In particular, one might do a scientific literature search regarding the disruption of the heme synthesis pathway in CFS patients. It turns out that this pathway is quite important for making all kinds of essential proteins for daily life: for example, we need hemoglobin to carry oxygen in the blood, we need cytochromes for the mitochondria to make ATP for energy, and we remember from part 2 how mercury and other metals can interfere with the heme pathway, creating unusually high amounts of certain intermediate species of porphyrins (and which can be measured in the lab quite easily). So if we were to have a patient with mercury poisoning, no matter how minor in severity, would it be terribly surprising for that individual to report symptoms of fatigue AND to show unusual heme pathway metabolites, such as irregular porphyrin counts? Therefore one of the important differences between this century and the 19th is that disorders tend to be defined not just by whatever undesirable behaviors, but also by metabolic, molecular criteria. It is thus through such molecular investigation that the origins of CFS can be traced not to those "lazy" victims who suffer from it, but rightly back to the greedy class who have polluted the planet with mercury, lead and all of the other recent toxins. This example of CFS also supports the hypothesis that miserabilism, something thought to be strictly subjective and defined by a long list of negative feelings and symptoms, might just very well have a physical basis, or as a minimum, physical component. The challenge will be to take these two pools of evidence – both cultural and biological – and to consider them together, in a dialectical light: How do those economically inconvenient biological outcomes and the cultural responses to them co-influence each other?

In short, I contend that what goes by the name of miserabilism is not exclusively cultural in nature, but rather that it also has an undeniable biochemical dimension. Traditionally, perhaps when we think about urban toxicity we might primarily imagine effects which are strictly somatic, in the non-mental sense, like asthma, cancer, skin irritations, etc. But grossly underestimated are the mental, so-called "sub-clinical" effects of such toxins, not only at the individual level, but also how entire communities can be impacted psychologically, so as to keep them obedient and submissive, disorganized, emotionally labile, feeling helpless, worthless, etc. As F. Rosemont (1978) once wrote, "At stake is nothing less than the liberation and reintegration of the whole human personality – the personality *not* of the atomised individual but of the entire *species*".$_{(4b)}$ It remains to be determined by scientific methods how exactly substances like mercury, lead and other neurotoxins adversely influence our culture, our dreams, our perspectives, our outlooks, etc., and for surrealists, for those of us who claim to represent "*the only consistent and thoroughgoing expression of antimiserabilism*"$_{(4c)}$, we must remember the need to dialectically synthesize the biochemical with the cultural. "*At each turn of its thought, society will find us waiting*", someone once said. Will we keep that promise?

Finally, in terms of general ecology, we can't forget about the various other species of cute, furry mammals that face extinction along with us, and which make for great, dramatic TV shows and feel-good fundraisers: the question I ask is if we humans cannot undo the fouling of our work and living environments, especially in urban areas, then how effective could homo sapiens ever really hope to be in the tearful push to save the dwindling populations of non-human species? Generally speaking, if we remain unable to treat fellow members of our species with respect, then how could we ever expect to have any lasting impact in the effort to protect other forms of life? Hence another one of the contradictions of late capitalism.

4.3: Poetry (Art) vs. Science.

The following two sections will briefly review surrealist perspectives (of material available in english) in two areas that have historically been contentious – art/poetry versus science, and poetry (genius) versus madness – and then proceed with the formulation of a hypothesis that attempts to resolve these dichotomies, or as a minimum, to stimulate discussion about the possible resolution of said dichotomies.

We might first consider the divide between science and art. While it's beyond the scope of this work to trace the historical roots of this division, we might note that for surrealism, science has generally been viewed negatively, or perhaps ambiguously in some cases, at best. Through its own prerogatives, surrealism has always been a movement of nonconformism, in which poetic activity is one of the key activities for this resistance, and which, if there were any substantial influences from science, it would be more about making creative use of scientifically-derived imagery rather than of conceptual ideas (thereby establishing a very limited role for the natural sciences). Perhaps the individual who has arguably best articulated the cognitive differences between art and science is G. Bachelard, who, although not officially a member of the surrealist movement, has nevertheless still been influential in the development of surrealist thought. Bachelard addresses the poetry/science divide in more than one place: first, in *The Psychoanalysis of Fire* (1938) we learn that:

> "The axes of poetry and of science are opposed to one another from the outset. All that philosophy can hope to accomplish is to make poetry and science complementary, to unite them as two well-defined opposites. We must oppose, then, to the enthusiastic, poetic mind the taciturn, scientific mind, and for the scientific mind an attitude of preliminary antipathy is a healthy precaution."$_{(9)}$

And in *The Poetics of Reverie* (1960), Bachelard develops this characterization of such an oppositional relationship:

> "If I were to summarize an irregular and laborious career marked by various books, the best thing would be to situate it under the contradictory signs, masculine and feminine, of the *concept* (m.) and the *image* (f.). Between the concept and the image, there is no synthesis. And there is no filiation either; and above all not that filiation which is talked about and never experienced by which psychologists make the concept proceed from a plurality of images. Whoever gives himself over to the concept with all his mind, over to the image with all his soul, knows perfectly well that concepts and images develop on two divergent planes of the spiritual life... Perhaps it is even a good idea to stir up a rivalry between conceptual and imaginative activity. In any case,

one will encounter nothing but disappointments if he intends to make them cooperate. The image cannot provide matter for a concept. By giving stability to the image, the concept would stifle its life... Thus, images and concepts take form at those two opposite poles of psychic activity which are imagination and reason. Between them there is a polarity of exclusion at work. They have nothing in common with the poles of magnetism. Here, the opposing poles do not attract; they repel. One must love the psychic forces of two different types of love if he loves concepts and images, the masculine and feminine poles of the Psyche. I understood that too late. Too late, I came to know the clear conscience in work alternating between images and concepts, two clear consciences which would be that of broad daylight and that which accepts the nocturnal side of the soul. For me to enjoy a double clear conscience, the clear conscience of my double nature finally recognized, I would have to write two more books: a book on applied rationalism and a book on active imagination."[10]

For Bachelard, poetry and science are two completely different activities, distinguished psychologically through the products of their thought processes: the image versus the concept, respectively. But we might also consider Breton's position, where, in his essay "The Automatic Message" (1933), he reminds us that perception and representation are not necessarily opposites, but rather, especially with regards to visual stimuli such as from poetic objects, that overlap does occur between these two mental processes: "All the experimentation here would be of a nature to demonstrate that perception and representation (which to the ordinary adult seem radically opposed) are merely products of the dissociation of one original faculty, of which the eidetic image gives us an idea and of which one still finds a trace among primitives and children..."[11a] Although this comment was made within the context of poetic objects, and not science, it still seems very applicable to our question about science versus poetry, and especially when we consider the part about the "trace among primitives and children". Most likely for Breton the cognitive differences between those latter individuals and the rest could be explained by enculturation – particularly by initiation into Western, industrialized culture – but again I pose the question about the possibility that human beings are not biologically homogenous (especially when comparing the brains of children vs. adults) and that there is room for variability within brain development which could allow for differences in cognitive abilities, even leading to those special instances of genius in youth.

We should also consider those two forms of thought in light of the social imperatives of capitalism – how, despite the importance of each, poetic thought has been pushed into a role that is subordinate to that of scientific rationalism. In the present era, science has replaced religion as the favored method of the ruling class for propagating rationalist-fueled ideology. Science has not only been tasked with the continuing need to provide knowledge about the external world, but under capitalism it is also used as a means to "explain" or actually *judge* individuals and their activities, in order to promote conformity (which, as we have seen in part 3, often comes into conflict with and even thwarts the generation of knowledge about the external world). Over the past few centuries, the psychiatric establishment has gotten a lot of practice judging the sanity of those who make controversial art, music, writing and other intellectual works, and effectively has become just one more form of the police – in this case, the police of the intellect and of the psyche. In addition to merely being *cognitively different* from poetic thought, science has historically contributed, when appropriated by capitalism, an *adversarial* quality to that uncertain relationship with poetry, and now those pro-culturalist advocates for the independence and inherent, exclusive sufficiency of poetic thought – like some surrealists – might perceive science to be more inherently harmful and genocidal than need be.

To extricate ourselves from this seeming impasse between poetry and capitalist science, in favor of liberating science so that it might be put at the disposal of everyone rather than a few, we might consider P. Mabille's ideas on the subject, as he wrote in *Mirror of the Marvelous* (1962) that,

"...Soon, thanks to a vast synthesis, humanity will establish its authority over the systems of knowledge that it has acquired. Science will become a key in the world as soon as it becomes capable of expressing universal mechanisms in a language accessible to the collective emotion. This language will constitute a new and communal poetry, a poetry that finally doesn't waver, play illusive games, and rely on quaint images... If I allow for the external reality of the marvelous, if I hope that the sciences will allow for its exploration, it's because I'm certain that soon the interior life of the individual will no longer be separated from the knowledge and development of the external world. Because it is only too apparent that the mystery is within us as well as in things, that the country of the marvelous is first and foremost within our very beings... Paraphrasing Hermes who said, "all is above as it is below to make up the miracle of a single thing," we could say that all is within us as it is outside of us to make up a single reality, and repressed expressions of unfulfilled desires mingle with shared and familiar symbols. From the confused to the simple, from the glare of personal emotion to the vague perception of cosmic drama, the dreamer's imagination makes its journey. Endlessly, it dives and resurfaces, bringing back great, blind fish from the depths of consciousness's threshold. Nevertheless, the pearl fisherman arrives to guide it through all the dangers and currents. He succeeds in finding his way among the passages hidden in the semidark where points of light only glimmer faintly. Little by little he becomes a master of the dark waters... Achieving this inner lucidity within a more expansive sensibility is no less necessary to a person than mastering scientific disciplines and technology..."[12]

In this passage, mention of the "vast synthesis" invokes the eventual attainment of the Unified Field, containing hints about the universal nature of science, with its communal language, which just so happens to invoke the concept of "citizen science" introduced in part 3. Overall, the selection reveals that Mabille acknowledged the continuing asymmetrical relationship between poetry and science, such that increasing scientific knowledge is accompanied by an increasing self-alienation of people, with science having its own special way of interpreting all other phenomena in a manner that can be excessively rational and utilitarian. Additionally, this passage reveals that Mabille differs from post-modernists and other radical, androcentric skeptics to the extent that he believed that reality does exist outside of us just as much as it does inside, and that science can help us discover the world outside our own immediate surroundings. And while never explicitly stated, there does appear a hint or more that it is indeed possible for poetry and science to coexist and perhaps even harmonize.

Of these three surrealists considered – Bachelard, Breton and Mabille – it seems like the latter had the most forward-looking vision of a world where the apparent schism between poetry and science would someday be resolved.

4.4: Poetry (Genius) & Madness.

Though in the 19th century the concepts of genius and madness were closely linked, by the 20th century and beyond, those two ideas had drifted apart somewhat, although as some might guess, the two could never be completely separated, despite the efforts of various 20th century intellectuals who wished to purify genius or "creativity" away from contaminating "insanity". If one were to first review cultural reductionist perspectives, we might consider the position of M. Foucault (one of those popular skeptics who appealed most deeply to postmodernists, among others) whose take on the "poetry and madness" controversy was that any resemblance between the poet and the madman was purely superficial and cultural in essence. While nowhere near being surrealist, his position makes for a great index of cultural determinism strongly flavored with pessimism, against which we might even compare surrealist perspectives:

"… At the fringes of a knowledge that separates beings, signs, and similitudes, and as though to limit its power, the madman fulfills the function of *homosemanticism*: he groups all signs together and leads them with a resemblance that never ceases to proliferate. The poet fulfills the opposite function: his is the *allegorical* role; beneath the language of signs and beneath the interplay of their precisely delineated distinctions, he strains his ears to catch that 'other language', the language, without words or discourse, of resemblance. The poet brings similitude to the signs that speak it, whereas the madman loads all signs with a resemblance that ultimately erases them. They share, then, on the outer edge of our culture and at the point nearest to its essential divisions, that 'frontier' situation – a marginal position and a profoundly archaic silhouette – where their words unceasingly renew the power of their strangeness and the strength of their contestation. Between them there has opened up a field of knowledge in which, because of an essential rupture in the Western world, what has become important is no longer resemblances but identities and differences." [13]

From this quotation, the reader might almost perceive a certain hostility on the part of Foucault, in that, according to the author, the madman's noted connections between things are superficial, quick to fade, whereas the noble poet is the one who finds such resemblances and also the underlying allegorical messages between them. Such a perspective runs parallel to the psychoanalysts who also elevated "creativity" in order to make it separate from "neurosis" and/or "psychosis", all of which are only stereotypical generalizations of actual thought processes, anyway.

Next we turn to the 20th century surrealists, to determine their take on the mad genius question. With A. Breton, we learn in his essay, "The Fiftieth Anniversary of Hysteria" (1928), that "[h]ysteria is not a pathological phenomenon and may in all respects be considered as a supreme means of expression". [11b] This kind of statement typifies the either/or fallacy: that either hysteria was purely an illness, or that it was pure poetry – but never both. In a 21st century context, and especially with Olmstead & Blaxill's (2010) interpretation of hysteria as a byproduct of using mercury-based medicines in that era (see part 2.6), it is very appropriate to ask why hysteria can't be *both*, once we have a clue as to the material basis of such disorder: why can't mild and subtle mercury intoxication temporarily cause behavioral symptoms as well as temporarily enhance one's creative, poetic abilities? Perhaps the underlying assumption is that an individual who has "pathological" symptoms or whose body (including brain) is suffering in a biochemical way must necessarily, automatically be declared intellectually invalid, somehow becoming culturally disqualified from having important things to say about poetry, desire, human nature and whatever else which doesn't easily fit with rationalist agendas? What a strange assumption! It seems more like those accusations of psychopathology might be identified only as ugly remnants of 19th century biological-determinist rhetoric, especially in light of the fact that any possible toxicological mechanism for such altered behavior was completely unknown and/or dismissed at the time. [14] Breton expresses this refusal to accept the moral, intellectual, and/or poetic disqualification of those who manifest "insane" behaviors when he says in Nadja (1928) that "the well-known lack of frontiers between non-madness and madness does not induce me to accord a different value to perceptions and ideas which are the result of one or the other". [15] Additionally, we might note that, in light of the quoted statement from Breton's hysteria text, that the dichotomous fallacy regarding genius (poetry) versus madness wasn't a consistent feature of his thought, and in "The Art of the Insane, the Door to Freedom", Breton suggests that genius and madness can coexist within the same person, noting how

"…In our eyes, the genuine madman is revealed through admirable expressions in which he is never constrained, or subdued, by 'reasonable' objectives. This absolute freedom invests the art of the mentally ill with a greatness that we are only sure to find also among Primitives… My purpose here is to attempt to convince the public to *experience* before having *understood* a work of art… I am not afraid to put forward the idea, a paradoxical one only at first sight, that the art of those who are presently categorized as mentally ill represent a store of mental health". [16]

In light of these ideas we might again reflect on the underlying motives of modern cultures that look for innovative ways to discredit opponents and nonconformists (who may or may not suffer from a mental disorder) such as through the arbitrary criterion of being able to determine what is "real" versus what is imaginary, or the ability to conform to a strictly rationalist perspective on how exactly one should be living and thinking, while at the same time refusing to put sustained research into the biological, toxicological causes of such disorders.

Breton's opinion about whether there was such an ontologically distinct category called "genius" is somewhat ambiguous, with a strong mistrust in vaguely defined terminology that lacks a materialist basis: in the *First Surrealist Manifesto*, he clearly states that "…In the course of the various attempts I have made to reduce what is, by breach of trust, called genius, I have found nothing which in the final analysis can be attributed to any other method than … [psychic automatism]".(17a) We find another reference to the mad-genius "corridor" within the context of a critique of the vaguely-defined but ideologically-driven, rationalist term, *common sense*: "Common sense becomes all the more despotic as its authority rests on foundations that are increasingly more unstable and worm-eaten: at the smallest infraction, it is ready to inflict a ruthless punishment. It distrusts absolutely anything exceptional and sees the proper maintenance, through its specially appointed journalists, of the famous corridor (A word to the wise…) that connects genius to madness and into which, so we are assured at every opportunity, artists can move quite far without needing too much of a push".(16) And then in the essay "The Automatic Message", he accepts the term "genius" only reticently:

"As the psychologists admit, the question of what is called 'verbal impulse' (like 'graphic impulse') is very complex, seeming to present itself differently to each individual. It may be regarded, finally, as of such importance, in every respect, that all concerned should endeavour to extend as much as possible, even imperceptibly, our knowledge in this domain. We know indeed that this enigma, the 'enigma of intellectual locution', the 'enigma of intellectual vision', governs the whole problem of hallucinations in medical observation. Similarly, on the philosophical plane, it implies the reality of the external world and, on the artistic plane, it accredits, as fully as possible, the idea of 'genius'".(11a)

But in the same text, he immediately expresses his doubt about the poorly-defined concept of genius, instead indicating his preference for the word, *inspiration*:

"Regarding this matter of genius, it is undeniable that the poetic and plastic activity of the last ten years has tended to exasperate the sentiment of such an equivocation. If the surrealist effort has tended above all to restore inspiration to favour, and if, in order to do so, we have extolled automatic forms of expression to the exclusion of all others, and if in addition psychoanalysis, beyond every expectation, has charged with penetrable meaning the kinds of improvisation previously too easily held to be gratuitous and has conferred on them, outside all aesthetic considerations, very significant value as human documents, it is nevertheless necessary to admit that sufficient light is far from having been cast on the conditions in which an 'automatic' text or drawing must be obtained in order to be fully valid."(11a)

Rather than settling for half-hearted acceptance of words with ambiguous, vaguely-defined cultural meanings like "genius", "talent", and "inspiration", Breton attempts to bypass any reliance on those words by favoring the concept of *poetry for all*: "It is to the credit of surrealism that it has proclaimed the total equality of all ordinary human beings before the subliminal message; that it has constantly insisted that this message is the heritage of all, too precious to remain the patrimony of a few and that nothing remains but for each to claim his share…"(11a) This sentiment echoes his statements about the use of word "talent" described in the *Manifesto of Surrealism*: "But we, who have made no effort whatsoever to filter, who in our works have made ourselves into simple receptacles of so many echoes, modest recording instruments who are not mesmerized by the drawings we are making, perhaps we serve an even nobler cause. Thus do we render with integrity the "talent" which has been lent to us…"(17b) For that time, given the limitations of 20th century neurology, who could really dispute the "poetry for all" concept, advocated by Breton and other surrealists, since we should know intuitively that there is no such thing as "ownership" of poetic, scientific, or other kinds of thought? Based on 19th century eugenic, ideology-fed ideas about degeneracy and such, the possibility of structural and cognitive cerebral *equality* (which might come across to some as a desire for *homogeneity*) most likely did have its appeal to the early surrealists and other people in the early 20th century. However, as I have argued in this paper, scientific evidence demonstrates that not all brains are physically identical, nor that they all operate in the same way, and these differences can be effected through influences from the chemical environment. Different neural arrangements and developmental outcomes can lead to *different ways* to have poetic experiences, among other mental processes. Even though it's true that everyone can indeed experience poetic, subliminal imagery, not all homologous sensory paths within people's brains are identically fasciculated to produce the same level of intensity – that is, not everybody does it the same way, neurologically; therefore it might be that some people see very well, and think visually perhaps more intensively than others who can hear better than they see. Don't each and every one of us have our preferences about how we like to be stimulated? If one feels a surge of poetic energy within, doesn't such energy become manifest as imagery habitually for one or two particular senses? Do not some people *see* more intensively and creatively than they *hear*, or vice-versa? And can't some of the greatest visual artists come up with some of the lousiest written poetry? And cannot some of the most creative, insightful writers find themselves completely blocked, completely inept with a paintbrush in their hands? And let's not even talk about synesthesia. Based on what we've learned regarding the environmental, perturbative effects on development, are these **neuro-diverse** outcomes really so strange and unbearable, and do such differences really detract from the "poetry made by all" concept, or maybe could they even somehow *enrich* such a worthwhile pursuit? Perhaps it might have less to do with the particular sensory pathways that inspire poetry (strictly visual, verbo-visual, auditive, verbo-auditive, tactile, olfactory, etc.), but rather the mere *act* and *intensity* of the poetic experience, and the freedom to have those experiences without being manipulated, exploited or harassed?

And then we return to the topic of autism: particularly, surrealism and autism. It turns out that P. Janet, a contemporary of Freud, managed to recognize the autistic element within the surrealist movement, to which Breton provided this refutation:

"On the other hand, considering from a purely psychological point of view the recent evolution in the treatment of mental illness, it is evident that the main development has been the increasingly abusive condemnation of what, following Bleuler, has been called *autism* (egocentrism), a condemnation most convenient for the bourgeoisie, since it enables one to regard as pathological everything in man which is not his pure and simple adaptation to the external conditions of life, since its purpose is to secretly exhaust all cases of disobedience, insubordination, or desertion, which have or have not so far appeared worthy of respect (poetry, art, passionate love, revolutionary action, etc.). Accordingly, for M. Janet, and no doubt for M. Claude too, it is today the surrealists who must be autists." (11c)

Again, we find the either/or dichotomy: either this autism condition (aspergers) supposedly found among surrealists is a scientifically verifiable disorder (but importantly: verifiable under what criteria?) or it is instead merely another representative example of how the ruling class goes to extensive efforts to eradicate all physical, moral and intellectual threats to its hegemony. Either/Or. In response to this dichotomy, I would agree with Janet's diagnosis of autism in some surrealists, but add that while effective, his diagnosis was based only on behavioral observations, rather than biochemical measurements (whereas both behavioral and biochemical criteria are used today, in contrast to the practices of that era). But secondly, I would also agree with Breton's position: that for Janet, in his role as an establishment psychiatrist, his *motivations* for making such diagnoses were morally disagreeable and essentially pro-capitalist, pro-mainstream, such that those doctors and researchers were playing the role of "reality police" who work for the bourgeoisie so as to defuse and remove all sources of cultural and political opposition by "fixing" or "rehabilitating" those who are seditious and non-conformist. I have presented arguments in part 2 of this paper for autism existing in the physical sense, but as for what anyone might want to do about such differences between people (including the controversial, *subclinical* stretch of the continuum that exists between autism and "normal" individuals, which to this day remains controversial (and which perhaps might someday become, as more public awareness of it emerges, a new sort of "middle class"?)) is the real essence of the debate. To answer that latter question, we might consider how autistic inconveniences are dealt with in advanced, late-capitalist regimes in the 21st century: those asperger intellectuals whose work directly benefits the capitalist economy are the ones who are celebrated and broadcast over the various forms of media (like the asperger celebrity, Temple Grandin, who cheerfully develops painless ways to kill livestock), whereas those who do not contribute to (or even oppose) the interests of the ruling class are generally ignored, with their voices drowned out by the digital roar of everything else. This situation sharply contrasts with that of previous centuries, where any intellectual whose ideas threatened the capitalist way of life was put under great scrutiny and negative publicity: what the capitalist system has learned is that it is more effective to *ignore* radical opposition, *to act like it doesn't exist*, rather than to make noisy efforts to refute and then "rehabilitate" whatever threatens its interests. Or to reiterate, capitalism has shifted from a strategy of refuting and shaming the opposition to one of convincing the masses that there is no opposition, perhaps under the premise that the less the citizen-sheep know about alternative possibilities for existence, the better.

To continue with this curious theme of "surrealism and autism" we might consider F. Rosemont's (1999) description of that young orphan girl at a county hospital who was designated "hopelessly retarded" for failing to perform adequately on standardized tests, yet who displayed a remarkable degree of linguistic savantism by way of her extensive yet esoteric knowledge of medical vocabulary (doubtlessly which she picked up while living in the hospital). As Rosemont explains:

"For me, this case was full of surrealist implications... It demonstrated that the people called illiterate, backward, "culturally deprived," no matter how lacking they may be in what is regarded as common knowledge, nonetheless possess *other* knowledge. It was my first encounter with the class bias implicit in so-called standardized testing. It convinced me of the explosive cultural potential of the so-called uneducated. It also deepened my interest in what was not yet called Outsider Art. It is no accident that, from the 1920s on, no one championed this kind of art more than André Breton and other surrealists." (18)

For a start, from Rosemont's description, the orphan sounds like she has some degree of autism because of her precocious vocabulary, in conjunction with her social inexperience.(19) What is problematic, however, is Rosemont's insistence on the ideas of "other knowledge" and "Outsider art". Those concepts, while acknowledging that not all people are cognitively the same, fail to address any possible material basis for such works of the intellect that minimally go by the name of "other" and "outsider". Based on all of the information presented in this paper, my contention is that a significant portion of these "other" kinds of knowledge and art represent the work of those who are on the autistic spectrum – those who are obviously autistic, asperger, including the subclinical types, or whatever inbetweens or shades of gray – and also that such naïve terminology (outsider art, other knowledge) ends up mystifying the true nature of the underlying phenomena. Of course such mystification might have its appeal if all modern science is to be routinely mistrusted and systematically rejected, if we remain victims of tradition, finding ourselves unable to distinguish capitalist science, capitalist psychology, from their liberated variants. As F. Rosemont once said, how important it is to be "...aware that when revolutionary thought becomes a sedative, or a straightjacket, it has ceased to be revolutionary". (4d)

In short, the surrealist position on the mad-genius question – for nearly a hundred years now – has been more or less culturally reductionist, not unlike that of other leftist-oriented movements.

4.5: The "Communism of Genius".

This text has explored the dichotomy of madness and genius in biological, sociological and political terms, and concludes that such a dichotomy has been historically maintained as a persistent fetish or mystery of both creative, "inspired" activity and of what is referred to in today's terminology as "mental disorder", both of which happen to work in favor of the ruling class. Such a false dichotomy persists only through the denial of the subclinical and/or overlapping manifestations of these traits, and serves to isolate poets, artists and other kinds of intellectuals, as well to maintain the social stigma of mental disorder.[20] This paper also reviews how the possible continuum between "genius and madness" has been considered *in surrealism*, with a critique of the excessive reliance on cultural reductionist theory for explaining such phenomena, perhaps momentarily unable to go beyond mere reaction to right-wing, biological determinist theories (such as genetic determinism) that came to prominence in the 19th century.

On the practical level, for geniuses, for the mentally ill, for those with both genius and mental disorder, as well as for the subclinical variants that bridge these conditions with the "normal", the seemingly fixed idea of "personality" is called into question, along with its periodic "diffuseness", and how such outwardly visible traits might relate to gradually and imperceptibly incurred chemical intoxication from the environment (with an emphasis on heavy metals). We must remember how those historical conceptions of personality still linger: how one's self-image or one's identity is "owned" by the individual (or perhaps sometimes even *branded* onto him, as is done with cattle), regardless of whatever possible adverse outcomes, and thereby considered by common sense to be absolute and utterly characteristic of that individual. There are indeed some things that we don't have to "own" if we don't want to, but by now cultural determinist perspectives have become an obstacle to that kind of individual and collective liberation. And with regards to the question of identity, for a visual artist, as an example, are his visual inclinations part of his "talent", his "genius", etc.? And how does this state – whether permanent or temporary – relate to brain development and structure? To what degree is his aptitude for visual experiences a function of the way the brain developed, taking into account both prenatal and postnatal chemical exposures, versus the cultural influences? And on the collective level, how can a chemical like mercury influence group dynamics, and could such influences actually be observable and somehow relate to what we call "miserabilism"? These are the kinds of questions we should be asking, rather than settling for those vague, exclusively culturalist positions that are all-inclusive, convenient, and "politically correct".

With industrial environments essentially existing as giant test-tubes, it would be premature to conclude that only aberrations could result from such a global experiment, hence the need to consider the possibility that a few or more desirable traits might also surface, like genius. Therefore this paper calls for a new definition of genius (and mental disorder, too), which considers an epigenetic etiology – i.e. a scenario where environmental toxins influence genetic mechanisms, leading to heritable changes that do not involve any alterations in DNA sequences. This model is an antidote to both the exclusively cultural and exclusively genetic-determinist explanations for genius, which prefer to think of intellect, creativity, etc. as something that is exclusively nurtured, perhaps occurring "by chance", or which happens strictly because of the inheritance of particular alleles, respectively, but which through either of these two routes is nonetheless perceived as an integral, inseparable part of the person. To explain the mechanism of origin, the idea is that subtle, chance chemical exposures, at certain key neurodevelopmental moments, can influence the way the young brain develops, with both mental disorder and unusual but desirable cognitive/intellectual abilities that can sometimes result – an idea that was covered in 2.4. Furthermore, this latter ecological scenario does not preclude cultural influences, but allows for a dialectical interaction among culture, ecology and individual biology, and which is not at all incongruous with the theory of historical materialism.

Next we might consider the potential origins of different kinds of genius: particularly those of mathematics and the sciences which require a keenly rationalist-oriented intellect versus those of the arts, which are attuned more towards passion and feeling. To return to Bachelard's idea about the cognitive opposition between concept and image (imagining versus perceiving, and Breton's doubt of such a fundamentally opposed relationship), is it not possible that such differences might not only involve one's cultural background, but also neurological development, where the individual might be better at – and so prefer – taking one path over the other? Could it be possible that such a sense of "opposition" can become enhanced or augmented for people who are born in industrially polluted areas? And might this characterization also suggest the possibility of intellectual diversity by way of variability in the *breadth* of one's genius, such that for some, their abilities might be manifested more narrowly or broadly than others? For the sake of argument, if these possible differences might be reducible to hyper-rationality and hyper-perceptivity, versus hypo-rationality and hyper-imaginative, then would that not explain the great divide between the applications of the sciences and that of the arts? This split (even *antagonism*, perhaps) between such mentalities became prominent around the same time of the divide between 18th century/19th century scientific and Romantic intellectual affinities, which coincides with the rise of industrialization. Again, we are considering phenomena that correlate with industrialization, and which in turn correlate with the emerging biological effects of pollution. At the risk of falling into a sterile either/or perspective, we might ask if whether both sides of this divide might be guilty of their own unique kinds of biases and arrogance – whether hyperscientific or hyperpoetic; "them" and "us" – which might account for two completely different views of reality and which might possibly be remedied by that perspective of "revolutionary empathy" which I alluded to elsewhere?[21] If we consider this question on the global level, in regards to the appropriation of rationalist methods of thought by the ruling class, such as how medicine, computer technology, chemistry, physics are all under the thumb of science (for use in warfare, surveillance and other means of social control), while poetic means acquire a secondary role but are nonetheless subverted for the sake of propaganda, commercialist manipulation and vacuous entertainment, then does not this situation also maintain such a divide in the collective psyche? We also might consider the possibility that the elevation of the hyper-rationalist intellect leads to socio-economic policies that over-emphasize rationalist considerations, which ends up deprioritizing the needs of citizens, in favor of maximizing efficiency and profits. Additionally, we might ask if there is any relationship between the asperger type of genius, which is known for its empathy deficit (egocentrism) and hyper-rationalism, and the inherent selfishness of capitalism? Is there any correlation between those two kinds of egocentrism, in light of their temporal co-occurrence, especially when considering that the capitalist ruling class purposefully selects for those kinds of intellect, especially within a highly competitive academic context??

As a proposed remedy (perhaps among others), surrealism must embrace science, *but on its own terms*, and use it for transforming the world in a surrationalist way, in order to determine that "true functioning of thought". Surrealism must overcome its traditionally held bias and superstition against science, much like the way it has whole-heartedly practiced poetry despite the fact that poetic processes are continuously exploited by opportunists and the establishment for their own miserabilist purposes. In light of surrealism's possible alignment with "outsider science" or "citizen science", and especially for those of us whose cultural determinism takes on a philosophical edge, we might consider Bachelard's (1934) comments about how philosophy has reached the point where it requires a scientific backbone:

> "...Sooner or later scientific thought will become the central subject of philosophical controversy; science will show philosophers how to replace intuitive, immediate systems of metaphysics with systems whose principles are debatable and subject to experimental validation.... Science in effect creates philosophy. Philosophy must therefore modify its language if it is to reflect the subtlety and movement of contemporary thought. It must also respect the oddly ambiguous requirement that all scientific ideas be interpreted in both realistic and rationalistic terms".[22]

In light of these considerations, we might again approach that idea about the communism of genius: how surrealism should be able to integrate all manner of intellectual fields and methods of thought, actively avoiding those conflicts of interest that occur when such practices transpire within capitalist contexts, which for the latter often involves the circulation of money and the alienated culture that always follows such cashflow.

And to finish off this section, perhaps it might be simplest (and most amusing) to declare, in the most *counter-inductive* way possible, how wonderful it is to know that *I'm the only asperger individual to ever be a part of the surrealist movement*. To qualify that statement, I consider myself "asperger" not just because of whatever behavioral traits (which certainly most people end up finding annoying anyway) but also because I was able to demonstrate that after a few decades of life, my body had acquired an unusually high amount of heavy metals such as lead, thallium, cadmium, aluminum, antimony and mercury that were making me increasingly ill and even with transient changes in personality, cognition and my overall somatic state. Again: how relieved you must be, dear readers, to know that *I'm the only aspy surrealist ever to exist!* Yeah, right. Sure. Whatever.

4.6: Chelation As a Philosopher's Stone.
"We are the things that were and shall be again".
Evil Dead 2 (1987)

While dissed by the medical establishment as one more type of new-age quackery, the practice of *chelation* – involving the use of drugs like DMSA and DMPS to mobilize toxic metals stored in the body for removal – has been growing in popularity since the latter part of the 20th century. It's worth mentioning that although such elimination doesn't necessarily address the problem of removing organotoxicants like petrochemicals, at least chelation does break the harmful synergy that metals form with those latter substances. For chelation, although the more corporeal, somatic improvements that can result from such a practice are significant and welcome, in this case we are interested in the *cognitive* changes, especially when considering that metals like mercury and lead have neurotoxic effects. In this sense, the improvement in mental clarity, or less befuddlement (a.k.a. "brain fog", as some refer to it) af-forded by chelation should restore to older, more seriously impacted individuals the same kind of cognitive vigor that is generally presumed to belong only to youth, with the latter group comprising those who haven't yet had enough toxic exposures.[23] In fact, we might consider the possibility of a paradigm shift in expected behaviors from "young" versus "old" people within *entire populations* that have chelated, and this utopian but currently unexplored possibility is worth considering further, under surrealist auspices. Behaviors and dispositions once thought to be the exclusive baggage of "old" people, such as cynicism, apathy, and chronic fatigue, must be re-evaluated in light of the new evidence, along with the important question of whether certain negative behaviors disproportionately found among older people have any relationship with toxicity (rather than with culture, as most folks implicitly assume today), as well as with what some of us might call "miserabilism".[24] Regarding intellect, while chelation cannot create what was never there to begin with, it can resurrect that which has been "submerged", effectively allowing one to take a *stunning revenge on the world of things*, to approximate that mental/physiological state once experienced when as a child. So from these considerations, we might question whether the varieties of cognitive decline observed as a result of old age are more heavily influenced by urban/industrial toxicity than were originally thought.

The practice of chelation contributes something to the idea of liberating oneself from the debilitating forces of industrialized civilinsanity, effectively constituting an act of REFUSAL by way of selectively removing environmental toxins. By removing metal from our bodies, we exert a significant and noticeable *physical* influence on our psyches, which does not at all contradict the theory of historical materialism. In a way, this type of biochemical liberation facilitates other kinds of liberation, despite what postmodernists and their loquacious groupies (well-disciplined in the smug art of cynicism) might say to the contrary, such as these hostile words regarding alternative health practices, by the postmodern pessimist, R. Coward (1989):

> "In all these theories the aim of transformation is to restore to the individual a sense of power... The power of the conscious mind is all-important in these ideas of self-transformation. Indeed so important it is that claims are frequently made that changes in individual consciousness will in fact alter external society. These claims go considerably further than claims that large-scale personal changes can amount to major social transformations. Instead these theories border on the megalomaniac. Individual thought, we are told, has an objective power; it can even change external reality".[25]

If we go along with Coward's ideas, then chelation is just a sham practiced by megalomaniacs, perhaps yet another laughable exercise in "discipline" to be mocked by Foucauldian followers and other such constipated cynics. Additionally, we might note that such hostility to the idea of social transformation facilitated by changes in individual biology is in essence a counter-revolutionary sentiment. While it is beyond the scope of this text to examine in detail such hostile, cynical superstition towards non-traditional medical techniques, suffice it to say that yours truly remains exceptionally skeptical towards those who are radically cynical. In any case, when one can think, dream, imagine, emote and exist unhampered by capitalist-induced toxicity, then it becomes easier to coordinate with the revolutionary efforts of others – to ORGANIZE (We must remember that capitalism will always welcome anything that prevents their opponents from organizing) – and then also to stand one's ground and to do so firmly, consistently, intelligently, effectively rather than in reactionary, impulsive ways that fizzle and lead to outcomes such as that petty "infighting", for example.[21] Postmodernists and other likeminded critics appear incapable of grasping this type of materialist threat to revolutionary organizing. In fact, the problem of disorganization, or perhaps "social fragmentation", is something we might consider with respect to Breton's comments about those surrealists who abandoned the movement for reasons that were never clearly understood nor satisfactorily explained: "...These exercises not being without peril, one man may break a limb or – for which there is no precedent – his head, and another may peacefully submerge himself in a quagmire or report himself dying of fatigue. Unable as yet to treat itself to an ambulance, surrealism simply leaves these individuals by the wayside".[11d] These cerebral quagmires and states of fatigue are the very things we should be highly suspicious of and keenly curious about, due to what we now know about how substances like mercury can powerfully but subtly influence the psyche, such as through nearly im-perceptible changes in volition, as an example. It is way past due for that surrealist ambulance, indeed.

To understand this social-fragmentation phenomenon in a historical context, we might consider some of the more intensively exposed individuals – the painters, those who worked with oil paints, which are known to be rich in lead and cadmium, as well as other heavy metals. Particularly we might revisit the transformation of three painters who were once highly esteemed by the surrealist movement: DeChirico, Dalí, and Ernst. Each of them in their younger years produced some of the most fantastic work, but then in middle age, they all underwent personality changes which alienated them from the surrealist movement (and from others as well). For both Dalí and DeChirico, what makes it easy to suggest the hypothesis of metal poisoning is that 1) they handled oil paints, 2) for many years they experienced gradual personality changes that other people clearly noticed, and 3) they both reported having episodes of indigestion. The first two of those three conditions applies to Ernst, but the absence of other reported symptoms such as the disruption of the GI tract makes it more difficult to support such a diagnosis. But what is also significant is that Ernst "faded away" at a later age than did the other two, which might be interpreted as that his system was less adversely affected by the metal, or that somehow his exposures were less. Of course, more direct proof would be desirable, such as through a hair test, as was done in the case of Beethoven, which revealed that he suffered from lead toxicity.[26] From such techniques of testing hair and other biological samples, we could learn a lot about the minds of famous intellectuals, artists, and other individuals. To answer the question about different kinds of genius, for example, we might ask if, upon comparing hair test results of the famous dead, if there is any correlation between certain metals and particular areas of expertise, or with certain behavioral/intellectual patterns? Or perhaps there might be a relationship between such areas of interest and the severity of intoxication with a particular metal? These sorts of experiments have yet to be done. Time to break out the shears and shovels, and get us to the cemetery! Of course, we could also look for correlations between genius and madness by testing for metals in the hair, urine, feces and blood of the living, although at present, such techniques remain conveniently under-utilized for sociopolitical reasons which have already been explained.

To return to the topic of chelation, it might be argued that it is also a kind of philosopher's stone (one of many possible stones, found according to one's needs) of the 21st century, which is less of a symbol or trophy to put on the shelf, but rather a biochemical *process* to restore/maintain one's cognitive clarity through circumventing that gradual descent into miserabilist patterns of thought afforded through years of environmental exposures, and perhaps even to be used as a tool for determining the true basis of thought. As a process, the chelation (and subsequent elimination) of mercury involves the interaction of that metal with sulfurous compounds such as Glutathione, as was covered in part 2. In light of that knowledge, how interesting it is to revisit the alchemy question: to understand the detoxification of Hg species with biomolecules that are *sulfur*-rich, and to then consider how, long before that knowledge was determined in the laboratory, there were alchemists who had a more intuitive but perhaps less-specific awareness of such chemical relationships between mercury and sulfur. Within a *historical materialist* context, how fascinating it would be to investigate that archaic overlap between medicine, chemistry and alchemy, as historians like L. Goldwater (1972) have done[27], but additionally to investigate how early cultures were psychologically and sociologically shaped by the psychoactive influences of mercury and other toxic metals, now that we have a better idea about the subclinical effects of such substances, and to make such an analysis without any mystification nor any of those pro-industry, pro-capitalist biases which conveniently ignore the important details, accidentally on-purpose.

And finally, while still on the subject of chelation, we might consider the concept of the "crisis of consciousness": at one point, Breton and others carried out poetic experimentation while within altered states of consciousness, exploring avenues that were open to them at that time, such as automatism, hypnosis, recreational drugs, etc. Likewise, we might consider chelation as a means to provoke or accelerate such a movement in thought: to explore the "diffuse personality", to gain a new and very intimate perspective on urban ecology. Just through removing whatever metal we've been accumulating for decades, experiencing the chelation/detox process effectively becomes a crisis of consciousness that yields new perspectives and insight into the nature of emotional shifts and changes in thinking when initiated through completely biochemical (non-cultural) means. From the poetic standpoint, experimentation with poetic techniques done before and while chelating (and then comparing before/after results) should be quite illuminating. While the following excerpt about "risking one's reason", by Bachelard (1935), was originally intended within the general context of advocating surrationalist experimentation, there is an undeniable resonance between these lines and the practice of chelation:

"If, in any experience, one does not risk one's reason, that experience is not worthwhile attempting…The risk of reason must, moreover, be total. It is its specific character to be total. All or nothing. If the experiment succeeds, I know that it will change my mind from top to bottom. I make a physical experiment to transform my mind. What use, indeed, would I have for a new experiment which would serve merely to confirm what I already know, and consequently confirm what I already am? Any real discovery leads to a new system; it must ruin a previous system. *In other words, in the domain of thought imprudence is a method.* Only imprudence can have success…"[28]

Experiencing such a crisis of consciousness would certainly involve temporarily risking one's reason, and for those who are removing a lifetime of heavy metals through the process of chelation, this experience can produce a crisis which fits that description, likely spurring critical questions about the nature of "reality" and one's place in it, which might certainly influence one's perspective on the nature versus nurture question.

Advice to Highly Brilliant, Uptight, Loudmouthed, Know-it-all Critics of Literature, Art and other Creative Pursuits (but who themselves are creatively blocked):

1) S.T.F.U.

2) Chelate.

3) Be the poet, creator, revolutionary that you always wanted to be.

4.7: Conclusion.

By way of summary, the primary goal of this text was to consider genius as it occurs in bipolar, schizophrenic and autistic disorders, with the confirmation that there is enough scientific and historical evidence to indicate a correlation between what has been called *genius* and *madness*, and that this relationship is strongly influenced by the chemical environment, particularly, through the increasingly toxic effects of heavy metal pollution which has been steadily accumulating since the beginning of industrialization. The evidence for this hypothesis is far stronger for an industrial-based, epigenetic etiology of mental disorder, but since mental disorder and genius are strongly associated with each other historically, then a possible *transitive* relationship between an increased prevalence of genius and industrial toxicity is not so far-fetched, with the most compelling evidence for such a correlation being the autistic savant, or asperger individual, who has enhanced intellectual/cognitive traits often coupled with behavioral and somatic symptoms of heavy metal toxicity. This hypothesis, and the historical and scientific information cited to support it, should not only be of interest to surrealists, but to all others who question the formation of the intellect as well as the "true functioning of thought", at both the individual and collective levels.

This text also investigated the *social causes* for the current scientific obfuscation of the mad-genius question, in light of the ongoing issue of pollution in urban/industrial areas, and then generally for the perpetuation of such biochemically-induced misery, providing evidence that science practiced within capitalist regimes is corrupted by way of an underlying conflict of interest: how the search for objective, scientific truth takes second place to the ongoing imperative of maximizing profits at the expense of everyone and everything else. Essentially through its subtle efforts to dodge the important issues associated with pollution, capitalist science is a runaway positivist train on the path to endless misery and global ecocide.

In addition to an analysis of capitalist science and its potential remedy in the form of "citizen science", this text also considered the surrealist, and generally leftist, mistrust of science, and argued that to defeat capitalism, a non-conformist attitude that integrates (rather than rejects) science is just as important as one that implements poetry; in that sense, we need science just as much as we need poetry, or as Bachelard might have said: we need to observe just as much as we need to imagine. And while surrealists have consistently refused to be swayed into denying and renouncing the subversive nature of poetry, despite the numerous sell-outs and false-poets, then so must we refuse to cynically abandon the liberating potential of science, regardless of the fact that it has been appropriated and is currently misused by the capitalist system. Because surrealism adheres to the concept of historical materialism and also because it is the only movement which validly claims to integrate all manner and systems of thought for the thoroughly non-conformist pursuit of 1) making the rationalist-emphasized, capitalist program a thing of the past and 2) unifying the currently divided fields of the social versus the natural sciences – which is the same as uncovering the "true function of thought" – then it should be uniquely outfitted to integrate scientific and poetic perspectives through its own methods, on its own terms, and obviously in a collective form. Therefore, not only must we perceive *and* imagine, but we must put our efforts into creating a world where perception and imagination are not considered adversaries (and possibly even to reach a point where we might discover a common origin between the two, as Breton hinted at), but rather that those two different ways of thinking would complement and co-influence each other in liberating, non-destructive ways, leading to a society based not on exploitation and degradation, but on mutualism and respect for all life.

Part 1 Notes:

1. Becker, G. *The Mad Genius Controversy: a study in the sociology of deviance*. Sage Publications, Inc.: London. 1978. (a: pp. 26-30) (b: 28-30, 36, 46, 85-7) (c: 14-18).
2. Faris, R. *American Sociological Review*. 1940. 5(5):689-699.
3. Porter, R. *Madness: A Brief History*. Oxford University Press. 2002. p. 81.
4. Cox, C. Early Mental Traits of Three Hundred Geniuses. Stanford University Press. 1926.
5. Juda, A. *Am. J. Psychiatry*. 1949. 106: 296-307.
6. Karlsson, JL. *Hereditas*. 1970. 66(2):177–181.
7. Andreasen N. & I. Glick. *Comp Psychiatry*. 1988. 29:207–217.
8. Andreasen, N. *Am. J. Psychiatry*. 1987. 144(10):1288-92.
9. Jamison, K. *Psychiatry*. 1989. 52:125–134.
10. Ludwig, A. The Price of Greatness: Resolving the Creativity and Madness Controversy. The Guilford Press: New York & London. 1995. Chapter 7.
11. Russ, S. *Creativity Research Journal*. 2001. 13(1):27-35.
12. Hershman, D. & J. Lieb. *Manic Depression and Creativity*. Prometheus Books: Amherst, New York. 1988. (a: pp. 3-5, 9, 10, 23-5) (b: pp. 11-6).
13. Sass, L. *Creativity Research Journal*. 2001. 13(1):55-74.
14. Jamison, K. *Touched with Fire: Manic-Depressive Illness and the Artistic Temperament*. New York: Simon & Schuster. 1993. (a: pp. 5, 103-12) (b: p. 252).
15. Prentky, R. *Creativity and Psycho-Pathology: A Neurocognitive Perspective*. Praeger Publishers: NYC. 1980. (a: p. 105) (b: p. 49)
16. Claridge, G. in A. Steptoe, editor. *Genius and the Mind*. Oxford University Press. 1998. pp. 227-250.
17. Nettle, D. *Strong Imagination: Madness, Creativity and Human Nature*. Oxford University Press: Oxford & New York. 2001. (a: pp. 139-41) (b: p. 187).
18. Guimón, J. *Art and Madness*. The Davies Group, Publishers: Aurora, Colorado. 2006. pp. 37-41; 48-9.
19. Richards, R. *Creativity Research Journal*. 2001. 13(1):111-132.
20. Kinney, D. et al. *Creativity Research Journal*. 2001. 13(1):17-25.
21. Simonton, D. *Origins of Genius: Darwinian Perspectives on Creativity*. Oxford University Press: New York & Oxford. 1999. pp. 106-7.
22. Fitzgerald, M. & B. O'Brien. *Genius Genes: How Asperger Talents Changed the World*. Autism Asperger Publishing Company: Shawnee Mission, Kansas. 2007. pp. 5-13.
23. Fitzgerald, M. *The Genesis of Artistic Creativity: Asperger's Syndrome and the Arts*. Jessica Kingsley Publishers: London & Philadelphia. 2005. pp. 239-41.
24. Walker, A. & M. Fitzgerald. *Unstoppable Brilliance: Irish Geniuses and Asperger's Syndrome*. Liberties Press: Dublin. 2006.
25. Houston, R. & U. Frith. *Autism in History: The Case of Hugh Blair of Borgue*. Blackwell Publishers: Oxford. 2000. p. 169.
26. Gillberg, C. *A Guide to Asperger Syndrome*. Cambridge University Press. 2002. pp. 97-8, 101.
27. Prior, M, & S. Ozonoff. in F. Volkmar, ed. *Autism and Pervasive Developmental Disorders*. Cambridge University Press. 1998. Pp. 64-108.

Part 2 Notes:

1. Levins, R. & R. Lewontin. *The Dialectical Biologist*. Harvard University Press: Cambridge, MA & London. 1985. (a: p. 133) (b: pp. 149,150,152) (c: pp. 250,1).
2. Smith, C. et al. *Current Genomics*. 2010. 11:447-469.
3. Paşca, S. et al. *J. Cell. Mol. Med*. 2009. 13(10):4229-4238.
4. Muskiet, F. & R. Kemperman. *J. Nutr. Biochem*. 2006. 17(11):717-27.
5. Schanen, N. *Human. Mol. Genet*. 2006. 15:R138-R150.
6. Badcock, C. & B. Crespi. *J. Evolutionary Biol*. 2006. 19(4):1007-1032.
7. Waterland, R. *J. Nutr*. 2006. 136:1706S-1710S.
8. Sazci, A. et al. *Mol. Brain Res*. 2003. 117:104-107.
9. James, S. et al. *J. Autism Dev. Disord*. 2008. 38(10):1966-1975.
10. Connor, C. & S. Akbarian. *Epigenetics*. 2008. 3(2):55-58.
11. Stanger, O. et al. *Expert Rev. of Neurotherapeutics*. 2009. 9(9):1393-1412.
12. Dittman, S. et al. *Bipolar Disord*. 2007. 9:63-70.
13. Regland, B. *Prog. in Neuro-Psychopharmacol. & Biol. Psychiatry*. 2005. 29(7):1124-32.
14. Regland, B. et al. *J. Neural Transm*. 2004. 111:631-640.
15. Muntjewerff, J. W. et al. *Psychiatry Res*. 2003. 121(1):1-9.
16. James, S. et al. *Am. J. Med. Genet. B neuropsychiatry. Genet*. 2006. 141B(8):947-956.
17. Geier, D. & M. Geier. *Hormone Res*. 2006a. 66:182-8.
18. James, S. et al. *Am. J. Clin. Nutr*. 2004. 80:1611-7.
19. Chauhan, A. & V. Chauhan. *Pathophysiol*. 2006. 13:171-181.
20. Suh, J. et al. *Am. J. Biochem. Biotech*. 2008. 4(2):105-113.
21. Zhang, C. et al. *Brain Res*. 2010. 1320:130-4.

22. Roffman, J. et al. *PNAS*. 2008. 105(45):17573-8.
23. Gilbody, S., S. Lewis & T. Lightfoot. *Am. J. Epidemiol*. 2007. 165(1):1-13.
24. Ozbek, Z. et al. *Prog. in Neuro-Psychopharmacol. & Biol. Psychiatry*. 2008. 32:1331-7.
25. Reif, A., B. Pfuhlmann, & K.P. Lesch. *Prog. in Neuro-Psychopharmacol. & Biol. Psychiatry*. 2005. 29:1162-8.
26. Kempisty, B. et al. *Eur. Psychiatry*. 2007. 22(1):39-43.
27. Kempisty, B. et al. *Neurosci. Lett*. 2006. 400:267-271.
28. Main, P. et al. *Am. J. Clin. Nutr*. 2010. 91:1598-620.
29. Dean, O.M. et al. *Current Med. Chem*. 2009. 16:2965-76.
30. Garcia, J. et al. *J. Biol. Chem*. 2010. 285(51):39646-54.
31. Geier, D. et al. *Neurochem. Res*. 2009. 34(2):386-93.
32. Ming, X. et al. *Brain Dev.*. 2010. 32:105-9.
33. Benes, F. et al. *Mol. Psychiatry*. 2006. 11:241-51.
34. Sun, J. et al. *J. Psychiatry Neurosci*. 2006. 31(3):189-96.
35. Andreazza, A. et al. *J. Psychiatry Neurosci*. 2009. 34(4):263-71.
36. Gawryluk, J. et al. *Int. J. Neuropsychopharmacol*. 2011. 14:123-30.
37. Gawryluk, J. et al. *Int. J. Neuropsychopharmacol*. 2011. 14:1069-74.
38. Do, K.Q., P. Bovet, & M. Cuenod. *Schweizer Archiv für Neurologie und Psychiatrie*. 2004. 155(8):375-85.
39. Kuloglu, M. et al. *Cell. Biochem. Funct*. 2002. 20:171-5.
40. Ng, F. et al. *Int. J. Neuropsychopharmacol*. 2008. 11:851-76.
41. Bowers, K. et al. *J. Neurodevelop. Disord*. 2011. 3:132-43.
42. Buyske, S. et al. *BMC Genetics*. 2006. 7:8.
43. Steullet, P. et al. in P. O'Donnel. *Animal Models of Schizophrenia and Related Disorders*. Neuromethods. 2011. 59: 149-87.
44. Fullerton, J.M. et al. *Bipolar Disorders*. 2010. 12:550-6.
45. Gysin, R. et al. *PNAS*. 2007. 104(42):16621-6.
46. Berk, M. et al. *Trends in Pharmacol. Sci.* 2008a. 29(7):346-51.
47. Kato, T. *Mol. Psychiatry*. 2001. 6:625-33.
48. Shao, L. et al. *Ann. Med*. 2008. 40(4):281-95.
49. Mattson, M. *Int'l Rev. Neurobiol*. 1998. 42:103-68.
50. Florea A. & D. Büsselberg. *Materialwissenschaft und Werkstofftechnik*. 2005. 36(12):757-60.
51. James. R. et al. *Mol. Cell. Neurosci*. 2004. 26:112-22.
52. Gargus, J. & F. Imtiaz. *Am. J. Biochem. Biotech*. 2008. 4(2):198-207.
53. Camello-Almaraz, et al. *Am. J. Cell Physiol*. 2006. 291:C1082-88.
54. Simpson, P. *J. Bioenergetics & Biomembranes*. 2000. 32(1):5-13.
55. Gorman, A., S. Ceccatelli & S. Orrenius. *Dev. Neurosci*. 2000. 22:348-58.
56. Ben-Shachar, D. & R. Karry. PLoS ONE. 2008. 3(11).
57. Iwamoto, K., J. Bundo & T. Kato. *Human Mol. Genet*. 2005. 14(2):241-53.
58. Maurer, I., S. Zierz & H. Moller. *Schizophrenia Res*. 2001. 48(1): 125-36.
59. Karry, R., E. Klein & D. Shachar. *Biol. Psychiatry*. 2004. 55(7):676-84.
60. Prabakaran, S. et al. *Mol. Psychiatry*. 2004. 9:684-97.
61. Andreazza, A. et al. *Arch. Gen. Psychiatry*. 2010. 67(4):360-8.
62. Konradi, C. et al. *Arch. Gen. Psychiatry*. 2004. 61:300-8.
63. Young, L.T. *J. Psychiatry Neurosci*. 2007. 32(3):160-1.
64. Chauhan, A. et al. *J. Neurochem*. 2011. 117:209-20.
65. Weissman, J. et al. PLoS ONE. 2008. 3(11).
66. Stork, C. & P. Renshaw. *Mol. Psychiatry*. 2005. 10:900-19.
67. Lombard, J. *Med. Hypoth*. 1998. 50:497-500.
68. Oliveira, G. et al. *Dev. Med. & Child Neurol*. 2005. 47:185-9.
69. Rossignol, D. & J. Bradstreet. *Am. J. Biochem. & Biotech*. 2008. 4(2):208-17.
70. Rossignol, D. & R. Frye. *Mol. Psychiatry*. 2012a. 17:290-314.
71. Washizuka, S. et al. *Biol. Psychiatry*. 2004. 56:483-9.
72. McMahon, F. et al. *Am. J. Psychiatry*. 2000. 157(7):1058-64.
73. Ramoz, N. et al. *Am. J. Psychiatry*. 2004. 161(4):662-8.
74. Malik, M. et al. *Immunol*. 2011. 216:80-5.
75. Sheikh, A. et al. *Neurosci*. 2010. 165:363-70.
76. Gigante, A. et al. *Int. J. Neuropsychopharmacol*. 2011. 14(8):1075-89.
77. Kim, H. et al. *Neurobiol. of Disease*. 2010. 37:596-603.
78. Glantz, L. et al. *Schizophrenia Res*. 2006. 81(1):47-63.
79. Catts, V. et al. *Schizophrenia Res*. 2006. 84(1):20-8.
80. Brietzke, E. & F. Kapczinski. *Progress in Neuro-Psychopharmacol. Biol. Psychiatry*. 2008. 32(6):1355-61.
81. Pae, C. et al. *J. Neural Transm*. 2006. 113:887-97.
82. Meira-Lima, I. et al. *Molec. Psychiatry*. 2003. 8:718-20.
83. Boin, F. et al. *Mol. Psychiatry*. 2001. 6:79-82.
84. Kim, Y. et al. *J. Affective Disord*. 2007. 104(1-3):91-5.
85. Rao, J. et al. *Mol. Psychiatry*. 2010. 15(4):384-92.
86. Goldstein, B. et al. *J. Clin. Psychiatry*. 2009. 70(8):1078-90.
87. Meyer, U., J. Feldon & O. Dammann. *Pediatric Res*. 2011. 69(5):26R-33R.
88. Jones, A. et al. *Immunol. Cell Biol*. 2005. 83:9-17.
89. Pardo, C., D. Vargas & A. Zimmerman. *Int. Rev. Psychiatry*. 2005. 17(6):485-95.
90. Vargas, D. et al. *Ann. Neurol*. 2005. 57:67-81.
91. Eaton, W. et al. *Bipolar Disord*. 2010. 12(6):638-46.
92. Padmos, R. et al. *Biol. Psychiatry*. 2004. 56:476-82.
93. Eaton, W. et al. *Am. J. Psychiatry*. 2006. 163:521-8.
94. Ashwood, P. & J. Van de Water. *Autoimmunity Rev*. 2004. 3:557-62.
95. Singh, V. et al. *J. Biomed. Sci*. 2002. 9:359-64.
96. Corvin, A. *Cell Adhesion & Migration*. 2010. 4(4):511-4.
97. Südhof, T. *Nature*. 2008. 455:903-11.
98. Betancur, C., T. Sakurai, & J. Buxbaum. *Trends in Neurosci*. 2009.32(7):402-12.
99. Ivleva, E. et al. *Neurosci. & Behav. Rev*. 2010. 34:897-921.
100. Le-Niculescu, H. et al. *Am. J. Med. Genet. Pt. B.: Neuropsychiatric Genet*. 2009. 150B(2):155-81.
101. Walsh, T. et al. *Science*. 2008. 320:539-43.
102. McClellan, J. & M. King. *JAMA*. 2010. 303(24):2523-24.
103. Psychiatric GWAS Consortium Steering Committee. *Mol. Psychiatry*. 2009. 14:10-17.
104. Psychiatric GWAS Consortium Coordinating Committee. *Am. J. Psychiatry*. 2009. 166:540-56.
105. Cook, E. & S. Scherer. *Nature*. 2008. 455:919-23.
106. Itsara, A. et al. *Am. J. Human Genet*. 2009. 84:148-61.
107. Kim, P. et al. *Genome Res*. 2008. 8:1865-73.
108. Conrad, D. et al. *Nature*. 2010. 464:704-12.
109. Arlt, M. et al. *Am. J. Human Genet*. 2009. 84:339-50.
110. Bassett, A. et al. *Am. J. Psychiatry*. 2010. 167(8):899-914.
111. Awadalla, P. et al. *Am. J. Human Genet*. 2010. 87:316-24.
112. Connolly, J. & H. Hakonarson. in *Autism Spectrum Disorders: The Role of Genetics in Diagnosis and Treatment*. Ed. S. Deutsch. InTech. 2011. pp. 51-64.
113. Abrahams, B. & D. Geschwind. *Nat. Rev. Genet*. 2008. 9(5):341-55.
114. Freitag, C. *Mol. Psychiatry*. 2007. 12:2-22.
115. Jacquemont, M.L. et al. *J. Med. Genet*. 2006. 43:843-9.
116. Weiss, L. et al. *NEJM*. 2008. 358(7):667-75.
116½. Weiss, L. *Expert Rev. Mol. Diagn*. 2009. 9(8):795-803.
117. Sebat, J. *Nature Genet. Suppl*. 2007. 39:S3-S5.
118. Xu, B. et al. *Nature Genet*. 2008. 40(7):880-5.
119. Levinson, D. et al. *Am. J. Psychiatry*. 2011. 168(3):302-16.
120. Malhotra, D. *Neuron*. 2011. 72:951-63.
121. Zhang, D. et al. *Mol. Psychiatry*. 2009.14(4):376-80.
122. Bergen, S. et al. *Mol. Psychiatry*. 2012. 17:880-6.
123. Sebat, J. et al. *Science*. 2007. 316(5823):445-9.
124. Guilmatre, A. et al. *Arch. Gen. Psychiatry*. 2009. 66(9):947-56.
125. Rees, E. et al. *Schizophrenia Bulletin*. 2012. 38(3):377-81.
126. International Schizophrenia Consortium, *Nature*. 2008. 455:237-41.
127. Levy, D. et al. *Neuron*. 2011. 70:886-97.
128. Carroll, L. & M. Owen. *Genome Med*. 2009. 1:102.
129. Rossignol, D. & R. Frye. *Mol. Psychiatry*. 2012b. 17:389-401.
130. Grandjean, P. & P.J. Landrigan. *Lancet*. 2006. 368:2167-78.
131. Rice, D. & S. Barone. *Environ. Health Perspec*. 108:511-33. 2000.
132. Jiang, G. et al. *Toxicol*. 2008. 244(1):49-55.
133. Takiguchi, M. et al. *Exp. Cell. Res*. 2003. 286:355-365.
134. Bonilla-Henao, V. et al. *J. Leukocyte Biol*. 2005. 78:1339-46.
135. Deth, R. "Molecular Aspects of Thimerosal-induced Autism." Presentation at DAN! meeting, Philadelphia, May, 2003.
136. Deth, R. et al. *NeuroToxicol*. 2008. 29:190-201.
137. Pangborn, J. & S. Baker. *Autism: Effective Biomedical Treatments*. Autism Research Institute. 2005.
138. Fragou, D. et al. *Toxicol. Mechanisms and Methods*. 2011. 21(4):343-52.
139. Reamon-Buettner, S., V. Mutschler, & J. Borlak. *Mutat. Res*. 2008. 659(1-2):158-65.
140. Edwards, T. & J. Myers. *Environ. Health Perspect*. 2007. 115:1264-70.
141. Deth, R. & M. Waly. "Effects of Mercury on Methionine Synthase". Unpublished; written for Autism Research Institute. Retrieved from http://www.autism.com/index.php/pro_research_methionine. 2003.
142. Waly, M. et al. *Mol. Psychiatry*. 2004. 9:358-70.
143. Murakami, K. & M. Yoshino. *J. Cell. Biochem*. 2004. 93(6):1267-1271.

144. Gundacker, C., M. Gencik, & M. Hengstschläger. *Mut. Res.* 2010. 705:130-40.
145. Stringari, J. et al. *Toxicol. Appl. Pharmacol.* 2008. 227(1):147-54.
146. Kern, J. & A. Jones. *J. Toxicol. Environ. Health, Part B.* 2006. 9:485-99.
147. Kaur, P., M. Aschner & T. Syversen. *NeuroToxicol.* 2006. 27(4):492-500.
148. James, S. et al. *NeuroToxicol.* 2005. 26:1-8.
149. Gatti, R. et al. *Toxicol.* 2004. 204(2, 3):175-85.
150. Shenker, B. et al. *Toxicol. Appl. Pharmacol.* 1999. 157: 23-35.
151. Naganuma, A., M. Anderson, & A. Meister. *Biochem. Pharmacol.* 1990. 40(4):693-7.
152. Guzzi, G. & C. LaPorta. *Toxicol.* 2008. 244:1-12.
153. Ballatori, N., M. Lieberman & W. Wang. *Env. Health Perspect.* 1998. 106(5):267-71.
154. Hardan, A., et al. *Biol. Psychiatry.* 2012. 71:956-61.
155. Berk, M. et al. *Biol. Psychiatry.* 2008b. 64:468-75.
156. Berk, M. et al. *Biol. Psychiatry.* 2008c. 64(5): 361-8.
157. Lee, B. et al. *Env. Health Perspect.* 2010. 118(3):437-43.
158. Engström, K. et al. *Environ. Health Perspect.* 2008. 116(6):734-9.
159. Gundacker, C. et al. *Sci. Total Env.* 2007. 385:37-47.
160. Custodio, H. et al. *Arch. Env. Occup. Health.* 2005. 60(1):17-23.
161. Custodio, H. et al. *Arch. Env. Occup. Health.* 2004. 59(11):588-595.
162. Westphal, G. et al. *Int. Arch. Occup. Environ. Health.* 2000. 73:384-8.
163. Bridges, C. & R. Zalups. Chapter 10. In R. Zalups & J. Koropatnick, eds. *Cellular and Molecular Biology of Metals.* CRC Press: Taylor & Francis Group, LLC. 2010.
164. Biagioli, M. et al. *Cell Calcium.* 2008. 43:184-95.
165. Lemarié, A. et al. *Free Radical Biol. Med.* 2004. 36(12):1517-1531.
166. Shih, Y. et al. *Ann. N.Y. Acad. Sci.* 2005. 1042:497-505.
167. Migdal, C. et al. *Toxicol.* 2010. 274(1-3):1-9.
168. Atchison, W. *Trends Pharmacol. Sci.* 2005. 26(11):549-57.
169. Ueha-Ishibashi, T. et al. *Toxicol.* 2004. 195(1):77-84.
170. Elferink, J. *Gen. Pharmacology: The Vascular System.* 1999. 33(1):1-6.
171. Sanders, T. et al. *Rev. Environ. Health.* 2009. 24(1):15-45.
172. Garza, A., R. Vega & E. Soto. *Med. Sci. Monit.* 2006. 12(3):RA57-65.
173. Bridges, C. & R. Zalups. *Toxicol. Appl. Pharmacol.* 2005. 204(3):274-308.
174. Sharpe, M., A. Livingston & D. Baskin. *J. Toxicology.* Volume 2012. Article ID 373678. 12 pages.
175. Humphrey, M. et al. *NeuroToxicol.* 2005. 26(3):407-16.
176. Yel, L. et al. *Int. J. Mol. Med.* 2005. 16(6):971-7.
177. Wang, Y. et al. *Free Radical Biol. Med.* 2004. 36(11):1434-43.
178. Miccadei, S. & A. Floridi. *Chemico-Biol. Interact.* 1993. 89:159-67.
179. Toimela, T. & H. Tähti. *Arch. Toxicol.* 2004. 78:565-74.
180. Lynes, M. et al. Chapter 14. In R. Zalups & J. Koropatnick, eds. *Cellular and Molecular Biology of Metals.* CRC Press: Taylor & Francis Group, LLC. 2010.
181. Kempuraj, D. et al. *J. Neuroinflam.* 2010. 7:20.
182. Soleo, L. et al. *Occup. Environ. Med.* 1997. 54:437-42.
183. Bilrha, H. et al. *Environ. Health Perspect.* 2003.111(16):1952-7.
184. Ilbäck, N. et al. *Tox. Lett.* 1996. 89(1):19-28.
185. Agrawal, A. et al. *J. Leukocyte Biol.* 2007. 81:474-82.
186. Valentino, M., V. Rapisarda & L. Santarelli. *Human & Experimental Toxicol.* 26:551-6. 2007.
187. Hemdan, N. et al. *Toxicol. Sci.* 2005. 86(1):75-83.
188. Yücesoy, B. et al. *Toxicol.* 1997. 123(1,2):143-7.
189. Flohé, L. et al. *J. Leukocyte Biol.* 2002. 71:417-24.
190. Chen, S. et al. *J. Tox. Environ. Health, Part A: Curr. Issues.* 2004. 67(6):495-511.
191. Strużyńskal, L. et al. *Tox. Sci.* 2007. 95(1):156-62.
192. Gao, D., J. Kasten-Jolly & D. Lawrence. *Tox. Sci.* 2006. 89(2):444-53.
193. Goebel, C. et al. *Life Sci.* 1999. 64(24):2207-14.
194. Dong, W. et al. *Tox. Appl. Pharmacol.* 1998. 151:359-66.
195. Kayama, F. et al. *Tox. Appl. Pharmacol.* 1995.134:26-34.
196. Schwenk, M., R. Klein & D. Templeton. *Pure Appl. Chem.* 2009. 81(1):153-67.
197. Tibbling, L. et al. *Int. J. Occup.Med. Tox.* 1995. 4(2):285-94.
198. Stejskal, J. & V. Stejskal. *Neuroendocrinol. Lett.* 1999. 20:351-64.
199. Huggins, H. *It's All in Your Head.* Avery Publishing Group: Garden City Park, New York. 1993. (a: pp. 6-8) (b: pp. ix, x, 57).
200. Tjälve, H. & J. Tallkvist. Chapter 3 in P. Zatta, ed. *Metal ions and neurodegenerative disorders.* World Scientific Publishing Co. 2003.
201. Block, M. & L. Calderón-Garciduenas. *Trends Neurosci.* 2009. 32(9):506-16.
202. Mühlfeld, C. et al. *Am. J. Physiol. Lung Cell. Mol. Physiol.* 2008. 294:L817-29.
203. Monn, C. & S. Becker. *Tox. Appl. Pharmacol.* 1999. 155:245-52.
204. Uzu, G. et al. *Environ. Sci. Technol.* 2011. 45(18):7888-95.
205. Lu, S. et al. *Environ. Health Perspect.* 2009. 117(2):241-7.
206. Bakshi, M. et al. *Biophys. J.* 2008. 94:855-68.
207. Park, S. et al. *Inhalation Toxicol.* 2007. 19:59-65.
208. Eke, D. & A. Çelik. *Toxicol. in Vitro.* 2008. 22:927-34.
209. Bala, K., K. Sridevi & K. Rao. *Fd. Chem. Toxic.* 1993. 31(6):431-4.
210. Monsalve, M. & C. Chiappe. *Environ. Mol. Mut.* 1987. 10(4):367-76.
211. Morimoto, K., S. Iijima & A. Koizumi. *Mut. Res.* 1982. 102:183-92.
212. Mourón, S. et al. *Mut. Res. Fundamental and Mol. Mech. Mut.* 2004. 568(2):221-31.
213. Palus, J. et al. *Mut. Res. Genet. Tox. Environ. Mut.* 2003. 540(1):19-28.
214. Şaplakoğlu, U. & M. İşcan. *Mut. Res. Genet. Tox. Environ. Mut.* 1998. 412(2):109-14.
215. Duydu, Y. et al. *Arch. Environ. Contam. Toxicol.* 2001. 41:241-6.
216. Hartwig, A. *Env. Health Perspect.* 1994. 102(3):45-50.
217. Hartwig, A. R. Schlepegrell & D. Beyersmann. *Mut. Res.* 1990. 241:75-82.
218. Wilson, L. *Nutritional Balancing and Hair Mineral Analysis.* L. D. Wilson Consultants, Inc. 2005.
219. Rimland, B. & G. Larson. *J. Learn. Disab.* 1983. 16(5):279-85.
220. Priya, M. & A. Geetha. *Biol. Trace Elem. Res.* 2011. 142:148-58.
221. Shaw, W. "Chapter 2: Copper and zinc dysregulation" in Shaw, W. *Autism: Beyond the Basics.* 2009.
222. Faber, S. et al. *Biomarkers.* 2009. 14(3):171-80.
223. Yorbik, Ö. et al. *J. Trace Elem. Exp. Med.* 2004. 17(2):101-7.
224. Walsh, W., A. Usman, & J. Tarpey. "Disordered metal metabolism in a large autism population". Presentation at the APA Annual Meeting. New Orleans. 2001.
225. Rahman, A. et al. *Biol. Trace Elem. Res.* 2009. 127:102-8.
226. Yanik, M. *Biol. Trace Elem. Res.* 2004. 98:109-17.
227. Tokdemir, M. et al. *Arch. Androl.* 2003. 49:365-8.
228. Pfeiffer, C. & S. LaMola. *J. Orthomolec. Med.* 1999. 14(1):28-48.
229. Mustak, M. et al. *Clin. Chim. Acta.* 2008. 394(1-2):47-53.
230. Vergani, L. et al. *Res. Autism Spectrum Disord.* 2011. 5(1):286-93.
231. Woeller, K. "Chapter 4: A typical child diagnosed with autism" in Shaw, W. *Autism: Beyond the Basics.* 2009.
232. Fido, A. & S. Al-Saad. *Autism.* 2005. 9:290-8.
233. Shaw, W. *Biological Treatments for Autism & PDD.* p. 108.
234. Cutler, A. *Hair Test Interpretation: finding hidden toxicities.* 2004. (a: pp. 38, 43,4) (b: pp. 2, 47-52) (c: pp. 34-58).
235. Siblerud, R., J. Motl & E. Kienholz. *J. Orthomolec. Med.* 1999. 14(4):201-9.
236. Arinola, G. et al. *J. Res. Med. Sci.* 2010. 15(5):245–249.
237. Cutler, A. *Amalgam Illness: diagnosis & treatment.* 1999. (a: p. 126) (b: p.6) (c: p. 8).
238. Edelman, E. *Natural Healing for Schizophrenia.* Borage Books: Eugene, OR. 2001. pp. 93-8.
239. Siblerud, R., J. Motl & E. Kienholz. *J. Orthomolec. Med.* 1998. 13(1):31-40.
240. Edelman, E. *Natural Healing for Bipolar Disorder.* Borage Books: Eugene, OR. 2009. pp. 170-83.
241. Nordberg, M. & G. Nordberg, Chapter 1 in A. Sigel et al. *Metal Ions in Life Sciences: Vol. 5: Metallothioneins and Related Chelators.* RSC Publishing: Cambridge, UK. 2009.
242. Petering, D., S. Krezowski & N. Tabatabai. Chapter 12 in A. Sigel et al. *Metal Ions in Life Sciences: Vol. 5: Metallothioneins and Related Chelators.* RSC Publishing: Cambridge, UK. 2009.
243. Vašák, M. & G. Meloni. Chapter 1 in Zatta, P. ed. *Metallothioneins in Biochemistry and Pathology.* University of Padova, Italy. World Scientific Publishing Co. 2008.
244. Hidalgo, J. et al. Chapter 10 in A. Sigel et al. *Metal Ions in Life Sciences: Vol. 5: Metallothioneins and Related Chelators.* RSC Publishing: Cambridge, UK. 2009.
245. Maret, W. Chapter 2 in Zatta, P. ed. *Metallothioneins in Biochemistry and Pathology.* University of Padova, Italy. World Scientific Publishing Co. 2008.
246. Russo, A. *Drug, Healthcare & Patient Safety.* 2009. 1:1-8.
247. Singh, V. & J. Hanson. *Ped. Allergy Immunol.* 2006. 17(4):291-6.

248. Choi, K. et al. *BMC Psychiatry*. 2008. 8:87.
249. Wang, Y. "Gene-environment study of metallothionein single nucleotide polymorphisms." PhD dissertation. University of Michigan. 2011.
250. Kayaalti, Z. & T. Söylemezoğlu. *Mol. Biol. Rep.* 2010. 37:185-90.
251. Kita, K. et al. *Hum. Genet.* 2006. 120:553-60.
252. Rose, S. et al. *Am. J. Biochem. Biotech.* 2008. 4(2):85-94.
253. Miyaki, K. et al. *Int. J. Environ. Res. Public Health.* 2009. 6:999-1009.
254. Xibiao, Y., F. Hua & N. Weimin. *Occup. Environ. Med.* 2004. 61:e56. Oral Session 25.3.
255. Smith, M. et al. *Environ. Health Perspec.* 1995. 103(3):248-53.
256. Rajan, P. et al. *Am. J. Epidem.* 2007. 166(12):1400-8.
257. Chia, S., E. Yap & K. Chia. *Neurotoxicol.* 2004. 25(6):1041-7.
258. Opler, M. et al. *Environ. Health Perspec.* 2008. 116(11):1586-90.
259. Opler, M. et al. *Environ. Health Perspec.* 2004. 112(5):548-52.
260. Geier, D. & M. Geier. *J. Toxicol. Environ. Health Part A.* 2007. 70:1723-30.
261. Geier, D. & M. Geier. *Neurotox. Res.* 2006b.10(1):57-64.
262. Woods, J. et al. *Environ. Health Perspec.* 2010. 118(10):1450-57.
263. Nataf, R. et al. *Toxicol. Appl. Pharmacol.* 2006. 214:99-108.
264. Li, T. & J. Woods. *Toxicol. Sci.* 2009. 109(2):228-36.
265. Woods, J. et al. *Toxicol. Appl. Pharmacol.* 2005. 206:113-20.
266. Echeverria, D. et al. *Neurotox. Teratol.* 2006. 28:39-48.
267. Echeverria, D. et al. *Occup. Environ. Med.* 61:e56. 2004. Oral Session 25.4.
268. Cecil, K. et al. *PLoS Med.* 2008. 5:5.
269. Schwartz, B. et al. *Neuroimage.* 2007. 37(2):633-41.
270. Stewart, W. et al. *Neurol.* 2006. 66:1476-84.
271. Lasky, R. et al. *Toxicol. Sci.* 2005. 85:963-975.
272. Lathe, R. *Am. J. Biochem. Biotech.* 2008. 4(2):183-97.
273. Guilarte, T. *Environ. Health Perspect.* 2009. 117(5):A190-91.
274. Eto, K. et al. *Toxicol. Pathol.* 2002. 30(6):723-34.
275. Honey, R. et al. in Fu, C. et al., eds. *Neuroimaging in Psychiatry*. Taylor & Francis Group: London & New York. 2003.
276. Mrazik, M. & S. Dombrowski. *Roeper Rev.* 2010. 32:224-34.
277. Burns, J. *The Descent of Madness*. Taylor & Francis Group: London & NY. 2007. (a: pp. 167,8; 175) (b: pp. 70) (c: Introduction) (d: p. 39) (e: p. 201) (f: p. 51).
278. McGlashan, T. & R. Hoffman. *Arch. Gen. Psychiatry.* 2000. 57:637-48.
279. Hoffman, R. & T. McGlashan. *Am. J. Psychiatry.* 154:1683-89. 1997.
280. Linden, D. in M. Ritsner, ed. *The Handbook of NeuroPsychiatric Biomarkers, Endophenotypes and Genes: Volume 2: Neuroanatomical and Neuroimaging Endophenotypes and Biomarkers*. Springer Science and Business Media. 2009.
281. Minshew, N. & T. Keller. *Curr. Opin. Neurol.* 2010. 23(2):124-30.
282. Mottron, L. et al. *J. Autism Dev. Disord.* 2006. 36(1):27-43.
283. Frith, U. *Autism: Explaining the Enigma*. Blackwell Publishing. 2003. (a: chapter 11) (b: pp. 162,3).
284. Carson, S. *Can. J. Psychiatry.* 2011. 56(3):144-153.
285. Crow, T.J. *Brain Res. Rev.* 2000. 31:118-29.
286. Crow, T. J. *TINS.* 1997. 20(8):339-43.
287. Crow, T. J. *Schizophrenia Res.* 1997b. 28: 127-41.
288. Crow, T. J. *Brit. J. Psychiatry.* 1998. 173:303-9.
289. Torrey, E. F. & J. Miller. *The Invisible Plague*. Rutgers University Press: New Brunswick, New Jersey & London. 2001. (a: p. 3) (b: pp. 305-11) (c: p. 4) (d: pp. 329-33) (e: pp. 328, 9).
290. Foucault, M. *Madness and Civilization: a history of insanity in the age of reason*. Trans. R. Howard. Vintage Books: New York. 1988. (a: pp. ix, 58, 63, 64) (b: p. 100).
291. Foucault, M. "Madness, the Absence of Work." Trans. P. Stastny & D. Sengel. *Critical Inquiry.* 1995. 21(2):290-298.
292. Scull, A. *The Most Solitary of Afflictions*. Yale University Press: New Haven & London. 1993. Pp. 36, 37, 40.
293. Torrey, E. F. "Severe psychiatric disorders may be increasing". *Psychiatric Times.* 04/01/2002.
294. Gottesman, I. *Schizophrenia Genesis*. W.H. Freeman & Co.: NY. 1991. (a: p. 65) (b: pp. 1-5).
295. Rimland, B. *Dyslogic Syndrome*. Jessica Kingsley Publishers: London & Philadelphia. 2008. (a: pp. 122-126) (b: p. 16).
296. Kirby, D. *Evidence of Harm: Mercury in Vaccines and the Autism Epidemic*. St. Martin's Griffin: New York. 2005. P. xv.
297. Geier, D. et al. *Indian. J. Med. Res.* 2008. 128:383-411.
298. Geier, M. & D. Geier. *J. Am. Phys. Surg.* 2003. 8(1):6-11.
299. Olmstead, D. & M. Blaxill. *The Age of Autism*. Thomas Dunne Books, St. Martin's Press: New York. 2010. (a: pp. 2, 163-4) (b: pp. 2,3) (c: pp. 56-57, 81, 85, 97, 101) (d: d: Chapter 4).
300. Austin, D. *Int. J. Risk Safety Med.* 2008. 20:135-42.
301. Black, J. *J. Royal Soc. Med.* 1999. 92:478-81.
302. Torrey, E. F. *Schizophrenia & Civilization*. Jason Aronson: New York & London. 1980. (a: pp. 177-87) (b: pp. 27, 31).
303. Hare, E. *On the History of Lunacy*. Gabbay, UK. 1998. (a: 83-6) (b: pp. 114-27).
304. Hare, E. *Brit. J. Psychiatry.* 1988. 153:521-31.
305. Hightower, J. *Mercury: Money, Politics & Poison*. Island Press/Shearwater Books: Washington. 2009. P. 78.
306. Michaels, D. *Doubt Is Their Product*. Oxford University Press. 2008. pp. 215-6.
307. Markowitz, G. & D. Rosner. *Deceit and Denial*. University of California Press: Berkeley, Los Angeles, London. 2002. p. 111.
308. Warren, C. *Brush With Death: A Social History of Lead Poisoning*. Johns Hopkins University Press: Baltimore & London. 2000. pp. 212-7.
309. Goldwater, L. *Mercury: A history of quicksilver*. York Press: Baltimore, MD. 1972. Pp. 279-85.
310. Mutter, J. *J. Occup. Med. Tox.* 2011. 6:2.
311. Feuer, G. & H. Injeyan. *J. Can. Chiropr. Assoc.* 1996. 40(3):169-179.
312. Siblerud, R. *Am. J. Psychother.* 1989. 43:575-87.
313. Huggins, H. & T. Levy. *Uninformed Consent*. Hampton Roads Publishing Company, Inc.: Charlottesville, VA. 1999. P. 39.
314. Stauber, J. & S. Rampton. *Toxic Sludge Is Good for You!* Common Courage Press: Monroe, Maine. 1995. pp. 104-9.
315. Shorter, E. *A History of Psychiatry*. John Wiley & Sons, Inc.: New York. 1997. p. 295.
316. Gillberg, C. *A Guide to Asperger Syndrome*, Cambridge University Press, 2002. (a: pp. 10, 22, 69-72, 97) (b: pp. 15-9,51-7).
317. Rzhetsky, A. et al. *PNAS.* 2007. 104(28):11694-99.
318. Ratajczak. H. *J. Immunotox.* 2011. 8(1):68-79.
319. Curtis, L. et al. *J. Alt. Complem. Med.* 2008. 14(1):79-85.
320. Stahlberg, O. et al. *J. Neural Transm.* 2004. 111:891-902.
321. Rapoport, J. et al. *J. Am. Acad. Child Adolesc. Psychiatry.* 2009. 48(1):10-18.
322. Hershman, D. & J. Lieb, *Manic Depression and Creativity*. Prometheus Books: Amherst, New York, 1988. p. 216.
323. Mamah, D. et al. in M. Ritsner, ed. *The Handbook of NeuroPsychiatric Biomarkers, Endophenotypes and Genes: Volume 2: Neuroanatomical and Neuroimaging Endophenotypes and Biomarkers*. Springer Science and Business Media. 2009.
324. Lewontin, R. *Biology as Ideology: the doctrine of DNA*. Harper-Collins Publishers: NY. 1991. P. 109.
325. Lewontin, R. *The Triple Helix*. Harvard University Press: Cambridge, MA & London. 2000. (a: pp. 99-101) (b: pp. 72, 73, 128).
326. Lewontin, R. in Ann Arbor Science for the People Editorial Collective, eds. *Biology as a Social Weapon*. Burgess Publishing Company: Minneapolis, MN. 1977. Pp. 6-18.
327. Lewontin, R., S. Rose & L. Kamin. *Not in Our Genes: Biology, Ideology and Human Nature*. Pantheon Books: NY. 1984. (a: pp. 23,24, 68-80) (b: p. 21) (c: pp. 268-287).

Part 3 Notes:

1. Diggins, J. *The Rise and Fall of the American Left*. W.W. Norton & Co.: New York & London. 1992. (a: p. 356) (b: p. 382).
2. Sokal, A. *Beyond the Hoax*. Oxford University Press. 2008. (a: p. 269) (b: p. 111) (c: pp. 141-2) (d: pp. 265-6).
3. Gross, P. & N. Levitt. *Higher Superstition*. Johns Hopkins University Press: Baltimore & London. 1994. p. 85.
4. Sokal, A. Chapter 1 in N. Koertge, ed. *A House Built on Sand*. Oxford University Press: New York & Oxford. 1998. pp. 14,15.
5. Sokal, A. & P. Bricmont. *Fashionable Nonsense*. Picador USA: New York. 1998. pp. 202-4.
6. Koertge, N. Chapter 16 in N. Koertge, ed. *A House Built on Sand*. Oxford University Press: New York & Oxford. 1998. p. 267.
7. Michaels, D. *Doubt Is Their Product*. Oxford University Press. 2008. (a: p.46) (b: p. 53) (c: pp. x, 4, 9) (d: p. 41) (e: pp. 16, 188, 154, 155, 169) (f: pp. 145, 149) (g: p. 68) (h: pp. 50-52) (i: p. 157) (j: p. x) (k: pp. 190, 191) (l. p.

41) (m: p. 234) (n: p. 28) (o: p. 244) (p: p. 251) (q: pp. 162-165, 173, 174) (r: p. 177) (s: pp. 182, 183) (t: pp. 9, 41) (u: pp. 34, 37).

8. Bauer, H. *Dogmatism in Science and Medicine*. McFarland & Co., Inc.: Jefferson, NC & London. 2012. (a: pp. 161, 213) (b: pp. 178-181) (c: pp. 38-40) (d: pp. 84-86) (e: pp. 32-38, 50-53) (f: p. 112) (g: pp. 153-8).

9. Abramson, J. *Overdo$ed America*. Harper Perennial: New York & London. 2004. (a: pp. 91, 94) (b: pp. 101-104) (c: pp. 10, 11, 155-157) (d: pp. 118, 121-124) (e: pp. 85-6) (f: pp. 94-7; 109) (g: pp. 27, 105, 106) (h: pp. 98-101).

10. Healy, D. *Let Them Eat Prozac*. New York University Press: NY & London. 2004. (a: pp. 112-119) (b: p. 118) (c: p. 126) (d: pp. 61, 62, 189, 192, 193) (e: pp. 120-123) (f: p. 211-3, 251) (g: pp. 110-112).

11. Ghaemi, S. *A Clnician's Guide to Statistics and Epidemiology in Mental Health*. Cambridge University Press. 2009. (a: p. 122) (b: pp. 117, 118) (c: pp. 113-115) (d: p. 98) (e: pp. 96, 97) (f: p. 119) (g: p. 123) (h: pp. 113-115).

12. Rampton, S. & J. Stauber. *Trust Us, We're Experts!* Jeremy P. Tarcher/Putnam: New York. 2001. (a: pp. 197, 198) (b: pp. 123-127) (c: p. 124) (d: pp. 69, 222-225, 265) (e: p. 94) (f: p. 86, Statement of David Ozonoff, M.D., M.P.H., Professor, Boston University School of Public Health) (g: pp. 259, 260) (h: p. 18) (i: p. 42) (j: pp. 19, 20) (k: pp. 308-311).

13. Oreskes, N. & E. Conway. *Merchants of Doubt*. Bloomsbury Press: New York, Berlin & London. 2010. (a: pp. 13, 14, 16, 138) (b: p. 34) (c: pp. 18, 214, 215, 242).

14. Warren, C. *Brush with Death*. Johns Hopkins University Press: Baltimore & London. 2000. (a: pp. 104, 146, 210) (b: pp. 124, 125) (c: pp. 212-7) (d: pp. 234, 235) (e: p. 138) (f: pp. 7, 14, 43, 79, 108, 126, 136, 142, 143, 171, 172, 183-185, 195, 203, 204) (g: p. 5) (h: p. 117) (i: pp. 117, 126).

15. Ziff, S. & M. Ziff. *Dentistry without Mercury*. 1997 ed. Bio-Probe, Inc.: Orlando, FL. 1985. (a: pp. 14, 15, 50) (b: pp. 18-24) (c: pp. 18-24) (d: pp. 25, 26).

16. Markowitz, G. & D. Rosner. *Deceit and Denial*. University of California Press: Berkeley, Los Angeles & London. 2002. (a: p. 6) (b: p. 131) (c: p. 136) (d: p. 20) (e: pp. 22-27, 41, 45, 88).

17. Shaw, W. *Biological Treatments for Autism & PDD*. 2008. (a: p. 104) (b: pp. 98-100)

18. Huggins, H. *It's All in Your Head*. Avery Publishing Group: Garden City Park, New York. 1993. (a: p. 45) (b: p. 3) (c: p. 68) (d: pp. ix, x, 61, 62) (e: pp. 19-22) (f: p. 19).

19. Hightower, J. *Mercury: Money, Politics & Poison*. Island Press/Shearwater Books: Washington. 2009. (a: p. 37) (b: p. 200) (c: p. 215) (d: pp. 98-105) (e: pp. 17, 25, 26, 91, 92, 97,116, 125, 164, 222, 223, 226) (f: p. 5) (g: pp. 129, 160, 168, 169, 170) (h: p. 211) (i: p. 34).

20. Whitaker, R. *Mad in America*. Basic Books: New York. 2002. (a: pp. 202, 203) (b: pp. 269-273) (c: pp. 148, 149) (d: pp. 205-207) (e: pp. 273-276; 279) (f: p. 150).

21. Whitaker, R. *Anatomy of an Epidemic*. Crown Publishers: New York. 2010. (a: pp. 164-169) (b: p. 286) (c: pp. 307-312) (d: pp. 54-57) (e: pp. 321-328) (f: pp. 276-280) (g: pp. 209, 290, 317, 319).

22. Kirby, D. *Evidence of Harm*. St. Martin's Griffin: New York. 2005. (a: p. 165) (b: pp. 184, 207, 306, 310) (c: p. 309) (d: p. 130) (e: pp. 265-267)

23. Greenberg, D. *Science for Sale*. The University of Chicago Press: Chicago & London. 2007. (a: p. 132) (b: pp. 25, 50, 83, 85).

24. Kennedy, R. "Mercury and Vaccines". *Rolling Stone*. 7/14/2005.

25. Weldon, D. "Before the Institute of Medicine". 2/9/2004.

26. Cutler, A. *Hair Test Interpretation: Finding Hidden Toxicities*. 2004. p. 4.

27. Casdorph, R. & M. Walker. *Toxic Metal Syndrome*. Avery Publishing Group: Garden City Park, New York. 1995. (a: pp. x, xi) (b: p. 138) (c: p. 146).

28. Sykes, L. *Sacred Spark*. Fourth Lloyd Productions, LLC.: Burgiss, VA. 2009. (a: p. 157) (b: p. 124) (c: pp. 73-77, 84).

29. Carter, J. *Racketeering in Medicine*. Hampton Roads Publishing Co., Inc. 1992. (a: p. 11) (b: p. 157).

30. Lawson, L. *Staying Well in a Toxic World*. Lynnword Press: Evanston, Illinois. 1993. (a: pp. 379-386) (b: pp. 375-377) (c: pp. 103, 104) (d: pp. 379-386)

31. Huggins, H. & T. Levy. *Uninformed Consent*. Hampton Roads Publishing Co., Inc.: Charlottesville, VA. 1999. (a: pp. 33, 34) (b: p. 185).

32. Fitzgerald, R. *The Hundred-Year Lie*. Penguin Books: New York & London. 2006. (a: pp. 123, 124) (b: pp. 23, 64, 87) (c: pp. 23, 64, 87) (d: p. 24) (e: p. 224).

33. Cox, S. *Sick Planet*. Pluto Press: London & Ann Arbor, MI. 2008. (a: pp. 30-3) (b: p. 150).

34. Whoriskey, P. " Antidepressants to treat grief?" *The Washington Post*. 12/26/2012.

35. Stauber, J. & S. Rampton. *Toxic Sludge Is Good for You!* Common Courage Press: Monroe, Maine. 1995 (a: pp. 109, 122) (b: pp. 181-183; 192-195) (c: Chapter 3) (d: pp. 46, 71-73, 78, 79, 87).

36. Willman, D. "The National Institutes of Health: Public Servant or Private Marketer?" *Los Angeles Times*. 12/22/2004.

37. Brown, P. *Toxic Exposures*. Columbia University Press: New York. 2007. (a: pp. 53, 54, 194) (b: pp. xiv, 9, 10) (c: p. 20) (d: p. 65) (e: p. 253) (f: pp. 9, 10, 171) (g: pp. 174-176) (h: pp. 17-23, 72, 168, 169) (i: pp. 3-8) (j: pp. 53, 54).

38. Belli, B. *The Autism Puzzle*. Seven Stories Press: NY. 2012. p. 69.

39. Tesh, S. *Uncertain Hazards*. Cornell University Press: Ithaca & London. 2000. pp. 77,78.

40. Feyerabend, P. *Three Dialogues on Knowledge*. Basil Blackwell: Oxford & Cambridge, MA. 1991. p. 120.

41. Kroll-Smith, S. & H. Floyd. *Bodies in Protest*. New York University Press: NY & London. 1997. (a: pp. 55, 122, 145, 146) (b: pp. 7, 9).

42. Ross, A. *Strange Weather*. Verso: London & New York. 1991. pp. 47-49, 64.

43. Feyerabend, P. *Against Method*. Verso: London & New York. 1975. p. 263.

44. Rimland, B. *Dyslogic Syndrome*. Jessica Kingsley Publishers: London & Philadelphia. 2008. Chapter 9.

45. Cutler, A. Amalgam Illness: Diagnosis & Treatment. 1999. p. 5.

46. Cutler, A. Interview from "Let's Talk Real Health with Mark Schauss". Retrieved from *www.markschauss.com*. September 2008.

Part 4 Notes:

1. In light of capitalist propaganda and rhetoric, this might be a good place to point out the concept of the *capitalism of thought*: each atomized individual in *his* own little world. The idea of *ownership* of mental states. When one is healthy, his good health belongs to him, and when one is ill, the insanity also belongs to him. The mystery of not knowing the origin of one's insane state of mind allows others to insist on ownership. Without biological knowledge of the mechanism (obscured by the current emphasis on genetic reductionism), then there is the mystery of origins, and thus it is easy to attribute all aberrant thoughts and behaviors of the person in question exclusively to the person in question – that he did it on purpose or simply 'cannot help himself', etc. – without considering the possibility that such thoughts and behaviors were facilitated or even caused through external means, such as biochemical imbalances stimulated by the environment. As a complex biological process, the idea of cerebral activity within a person which gives the semblance and/or substance of rational thought is a relatively new arrival on the evolutionary timeline, and thus it shouldn't be difficult to disrupt rational thought through biochemical, environmental influences, however subtle. The question returns then to what lengths industrial society will go to avoid taking responsibility for creating these biochemical stimuli, factors, influences that can cerebrally disrupt some of the population. Thus, the attribution of ownership to insane mental states – blame, persecution, scapegoating – is merely a capitalist device to deflect responsibility, to dodge the issue. It's much easier to have these social constructions and roles of madness rather than addressing the ways in which a society's chemical/physical activities can cause unusual behavior and thought.

2. As a corollary, we might note that, on the practical, non-research level, modern medicine makes the distinction of somatic disorders versus those difficult-to-treat psychiatric disorders, while having spent so much time overlooking the physical connections between the somatic and the psychiatric. "Nutritional" or orthomolecular medicine is more holistic, in the way that one's subjectivity is considered a reflection of one's somatic health. Therefore, the way to effect changes in the body and mind are through the use of herbs and essential nutrients to correct metabolic imbalances and deficiencies, and to reverse environmentally induced toxicities, such as through chelation for metal toxicity. So rather than medicating a person because of "aberrant" behavior or physiological processes, as it occurs now under the dominant medical paradigm, the orthomolecular approach has allowed for the possibility of selectively targeting nutritional deficiencies and imbalances, as a strategy to determine the primary cause(s) of the observable symptoms.

An excellent example of this mis-medication could be for certain types of depression & anxiety that result from having insufficient serotonin: the mainstream approach is to sell the person expensive pharmaceutical meds, designed only for short-term alteration of brain chemistry. A more effective, safer, cheaper and less-disruptive approach would be to simply take 5-HTP (5-Hydroxytryptophan) supplements, which is able to cross the blood-brain-barrier in order to become converted to serotonin. When it becomes common knowledge that serotonin production begins with the conversion of the amino acid tryptophane to 5-HTP by the enterochromaffin cells of the small intestine, one finally reaches the conclusion that yeast problems and whatever other dysbiotic or environmental issues that affect the GI tract can actually play a significant role in the creation of some depressive states. It's true that both antidepressants and 5-HTP supplements can make the depression go away in the short term, but to really get over the depression permanently, it becomes necessary to find out exactly it is that's preventing the intestine from functioning correctly. In the case of industrial diets and whatever other environmental factors such as the passive or unknowing ingestion of toxins, dysbiosis (candidiasis) can lead to depression, which originates in the intestine and not the brain. Therefore, it only makes sense to find and correct whatever it is that is preventing the intestinal cells from making the serotonin precursor, rather than trying to influence serotonin ability by taking psychoactive drugs. Or to put it more plainly: depression from low serotonin (dysthymia) can often start in the intestine, not in the head, so it makes sense to choose a therapeutic agent that resolves the intestinal issue. This example also reveals the contemporary misconception that mental disorder is a condition that exclusively affects the brain, but not any other organs or areas of the body.

3. Breton, A. "Away with Miserabilism!" (1956). *Surrealism and Painting*. Trans. S. Taylor. ArtWorks: MFA Publications. 1972. p. 347,8.

4. Rosemont, F. *What Is Surrealism?* Pathfinder Press: New York. 1978. (a: p. 17) (b: p. 101) (c: p. 183) (d: p. 190).

5. Rosemont, P. "Miserabilism and Anti-Miserabilism". *Surrealist Experiences: 1001 dawns, 221 midnights*. Black Swan Press: Chicago. 2000. pp. 125-8.

6. Rosemont, P. Quotation from her essay, "A Brief Rant against Work". Cited in Don LaCoss' introduction to M. Löwy's book, *Morning Star*. University of Texas Press: Austin. 2009. Pp. xxvii, xxviii.

7. Regarding the need to take old theories and to reconsider them in light of new evidence, we might reconsider Freud's tobacco and cocaine abuse (as a possible outcome facilitated by metal toxicity; the reader is referred to the work of psychologist, Jack R. Nation: one might first consult his report in *Brain Research*, 1995, 702(1-2):223-32. Sometimes the best experiments are the simple ones), and the possibility that in middle-age, after a few decades of absorbing metals like cadmium and lead from tobacco smoke and other environmental inputs, Papa Siggy just might have come to notice those vague perturbations in mood and cognition at the moment when the colon is *reabsorbing* those toxic metals from last night's mercurial dinner of fish 'n chips. In light of that hypothesis based on biographical information such as cocaine and cigar consumption, how interesting it is to reexamine Freud's description of "anal retentiveness" and re-explain it in materialist terms – that "neuroticism" might be explained via the colon's reabsorption of toxic metals, by way of the *enterohepatic reuptake loop*: such as in the numerous cases of those female, Viennese subjects of his who applied Hg medicine to their sick fathers, who might display whatever "neurotic" or "hysterical" behavior especially during periods of Hg excretion, with minor reuptake causing psychological symptoms and even endocrine disruption, possibly influencing their libidos and whatever other behaviors. This new explanation turns Freud's concept of "anal retentiveness" completely on its head. (Or perhaps on its arse?)

8. Rabinbach, A. *The Human Motor: energy, fatigue, and the origins of modernity*. Basic Books. 1990. Chapter 6: Mental fatigue, Neurasthenia, and Civilization.

9. G. Bachelard. *The Psychoanalysis of Fire* (1938). Trans. A. Ross. Beacon Press: Boston. 1968. p. 2.

10. G. Bachelard. *The Poetics of Reverie* (1960). Trans. D. Russell. Beacon Press: Boston.1971. Pp. 51-3.

11. A. Breton, *What Is Surrealism? Selected Writings*. Pathfinder Press. 1978. (a: "The Automatic Message" (1933). Trans. G. Ducornet. Pp. 132-48) (b: "The Fiftieth Anniversary of Hysteria" (1928). Trans. S. Beckett. Pp. 424-6) (c: "Surrealism and the Treatment of Mental Illness" (1933). Trans. by S. Beckett. Pp. 86-9) (d: "What is Surrealism?" (1934). Pp. 151-187).

12. P. Mabille. *Mirror of the Marvelous* (1962). Trans. J. Gladding. Inner Traditions Press: Rochester, Vermont. 1998. Pp. 15, 16.

13. M. Foucault. *The Order of Things* (1966). Vintage Books: New York. 1994. Pp. 49, 50.

14. In fact, so many psychiatrists from Breton's era (and mostly up to the present) were far less concerned with curing or preventing mental disorder as they were with developing efficient strategies for silencing and incarcerating those who were socially and economically inconvenient. For the most part, mainstream discussions about mental disorder and what might be done about it have tended to reflect the quiet assumption that there are no preventative or curative measures possible, that the only effective strategy is that of containment, and ultimately of confinement.

15. A. Breton. *Nadja* (1928). Trans. R. Howard. Grove Press: NY. 1960. p. 144.

16. A. Breton, "The Art of the Insane, the Door to Freedom" (1948). Trans. by M. Parmentier & J. D'Amboise. *Free Rein (La Clé des Champs)*. U. Nebraska Press. 1995. Pp. 217-20.

17. A. Breton, "Manifesto of Surrealism" (1924). Trans. R. Seaver & H. Lane. *Manifestos of Surrealism*. The University of Michigan Press. 1969. (a: p. 26) (b: Pp. 28, 29.).

18. F. Rosemont. "Surrealism, Poetry & Politics" (1999). *Revolution in the Service of the Marvelous*. Charles H. Kerr Publishing Co.: Chicago. 2003. Pp. 144, 145.

19. It should be noted that with regards to *standardized testing*, it is known that social impairment – which can potentially engender a lack of awareness of socially-relevant, culturally-pertinent knowledge – can sometimes account for incorrect responses on such tests, erroneously leading to the conclusion of intellectual impairment.

20. Additionally, these considerations are based on mainstream (alienated) scientific terminology – "asperger", "bipolar", "schizophrenia", "genius" – which should not remain excluded from further examination in order to determine the true ontological parameters of these conditions, hopefully with a greater depth of understanding at the biochemical, ecological level. These terms need to be refined and made less monolithic, especially in light of the fact that we are describing not either/or states, but a continuum that ranges from severe symptoms to none at all.

21. E. Bragg. "Infighting Is Miserabilist and Stupid" (2014). In this issue of Hydrolith.

22. G. Bachelard. *The New Scientific Spirit*. (1934) Trans. A. Goldhammer. Beacon Press: Boston. 1984. Pp. 2, 3.

23. We might keep in mind the science of gerontology, which is often carried out in the name of the quest for extending life expectancy. In those industrialized, toxic countries that are so gung-ho to lengthen the life-expectancy, we encounter the general failure of medicine to understand that the striving to add years to people's lives ends up being a mere extension of the capitalist mentality of quantity before quality. Who really wants to live long if they can't enjoy their lives?

24. Again, it's important to remember that our reality comes from a dialectic between biochemistry and culture, but to successfully to make that consideration, in a historical materialist way, it's necessary to understand how the chemicals from the urban landscape are influencing our cognition, even if mainstream science is prevented from asking those questions right now.

25. R. Coward. *The Whole Truth*. Faber & Faber: London. 1989. p. 116.

26. W. Walsh, "Scientific Testing of Beethoven's Hair". Press conference, October 17, 2000. Retrieved from *http://www.sjsu.edu/beethoven/ collections_exhibit/beethoven_hair/scientific_testing/testno2/press_ conference/*.

27. Goldwater, L. *Mercury: A History of Quicksilver*. York Press: Baltimore, MD. 1972. Chapter 2. What also makes this book interesting, from the surrealist perspective, is that the foreword was written by a certain G.S.T. Cavanaugh, the curator of the Duke University medical library, who apparently worked with the author in the final years of his career at the same institution (roughly around the time that the book was written), as a specialist in occupational medicine. What a remarkable instance of objective chance it is that the initials of the foreward's author happen to match those of that critical enzyme, Glutathione-S-transferase (GST), mentioned in 2.2, necessary for Hg-detoxification and such an indispensible component of our biochemistry without which we all would probably become psychotic before death actually occurred.

28. G. Bachelard. "Surrationalism" (1935). Trans. J. Levy. *Arsenal: Surrealist Subversion (#4)*. Black Swan Press: Chicago. 1989. Pp. 112-114.

Antonio Ramírez - *The Fixed Idea*

Alex Januário - *Collage*

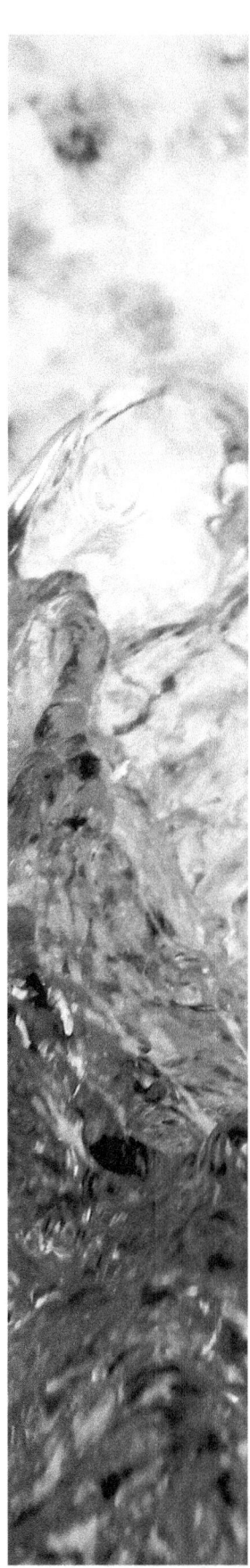

Micro-Seizures
and
Missed Apprehensions

John Barrett Erickson

[bits and pieces from something i'll never finish – as such, this may not make any sense]
Patterns emerge from the act, in the spontaneous deformations of collision captured or not.

"Beauty is the realization of a truth you can only explain with lies."
(Celine Myers)

Also From "Aesthetic Automatism"
(ca. 1995 – Barrett Erickson, Wm. Dubin, Celine Myers)

The forceful creative dynamic life stabs into unknown potential, slashing revelations at each backward glance. We know only by exploring what we cannot know. We know only to the degree we abandon the search for knowledge and adopt a passion for experiment.

We discover our **"SELF"** in the intuitive act of reaching spontaneously for what attracts us. Action is judgement; we must judge. An **AESTHETIC** inevitably forms, freely and beautifully if unimpeded, or warped and deformed if artificially restricted – but it *will* form whether welcomed or not.

A true, personal **AESTHETIC** is a dynamic, continuously evolving concept of **"SELF"** in the active pursuit of **DESIRE...**

A moment of dialog, (mis?)remembered from a movie, or maybe a book:
"You know those moments, when it all comes together in a flash and it all makes perfect sense and then just as quickly, it's all gone? Just a brief flash of total coherence? That's epilepsy."

Epilepsy:

A general term for a sudden disturbance of cerebral function accompanied by loss of consciousness, with or without convulsion.

[Chambers Science and Technology Dictionary]

Epiphany:

The sudden realization or comprehension of the (larger) essence or meaning of something.

[Wikipedia]

Another quote, ever-present, which can be attributed more certainly to Heisenberg:

"What we learn about is not nature itself, but nature as exposed to our methods of questioning."

The Fundamental Error

The fundamental error in the current scientific paradigm is what Goswami (who, I hasten to add, has his own problems of interpretation far beyond the scope of this investigation) describes as "Materialist Science":

We have learned well the basic axiom that everything is matter, with deterministic "upward causation". We've come to believe that "reality" is somehow different from us, that we can observe it, measure it, judge our perceptions by how much they differ from it. "Reality" is elsewhere, somehow more real than our experience, so the imagination is deployed on a perverted mission of rationalization.

We assume appearance is deceptive, so we try to understand "reality" by separating ourselves from it. We become double blind when our experiments remove experience from these investigations. We look deeper and deeper, smaller and smaller, to divide and separate appearance from its deception, but each new "discovery" simply moves the horizon of understanding, even as it remains both infinitely close and infinitely distant.

Yet we persist, thinking we will eventually arrive at the fundamental truth of our existence, once we understand what "reality" is without our interference.

Mainstream science has been driven madly off course, as ever more bizarre theories are invented, to explain the obvious, in service of this dehumanization.

Mathematicians had their way, while scientists forgot to question the premises on which the calculations were based. They came to believe Schrödinger's cat was both alive and dead until we took its pulse.

The extrapolated calculations made it seem rational to accept that all possible states of a process/system are equally and simultaneously real, and the point where some decision/observation "determines" one state rather than another, for that particular moment/space, only means that all the other possible states carry on in another dimension, as a different "universe' exactly like ours up to that point, but diverging from there according to the results of all the other outcomes.

The reason this has all become so bizarre and byzantine is that they are looking through the wrong end of the scope (whether micro or tele) even as they forget that they are looking through a scope at all.

Cognitive Singularity

That point of transformation, from latent to experienced. The event threshold of our existence.

The problem is that what we are really confronting and trying to understand is that very moment of cognitive singularity when latent reality is transformed into reality-as-experienced. So we are always splitting distances from what is known to what is pre-known, approaching a horizon that is always infinitely removed from where we are, from what we can actually experience, because all the possible dimensions of latent reality don't carry on, or split off into parallel realities, they collapse into one reality-as-experienced for each of us.

It's a Fourier transformation of sorts, the phase front is met by the reference beam and the holograph appears, the latent quanta are reified into the obscure objects of

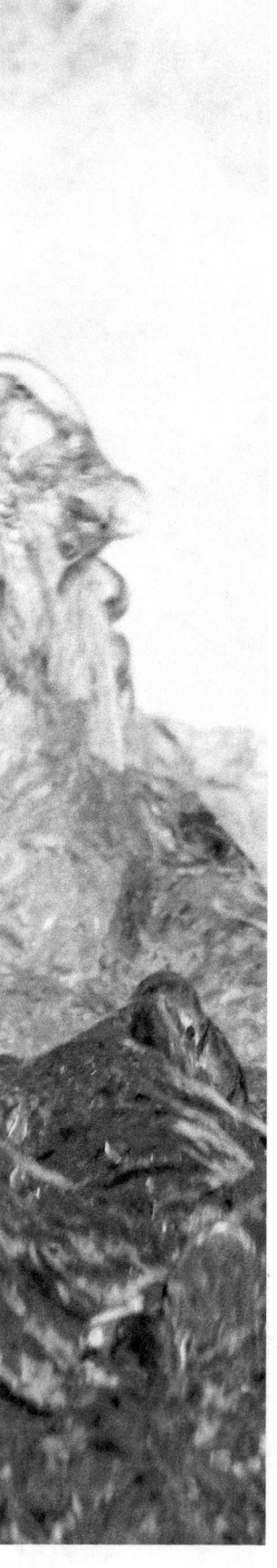

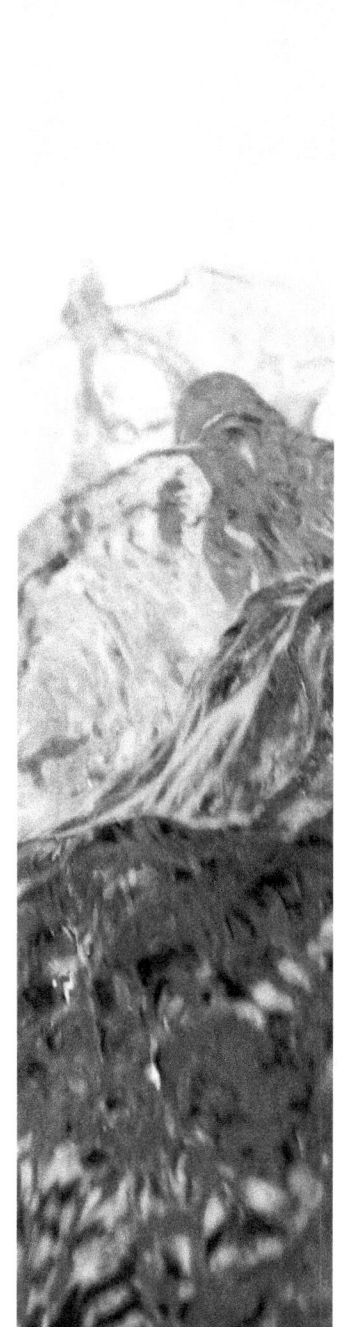

our attention.

In a sense, this is indeed a "Many Worlds" outcome, but these worlds are personal, not objective. It's not that "now" is constantly splitting off into every possible reality; it's that every possible reality is constantly collapsing into one "now" for each of us.

The reason the theories of the current paradigm stop making sense at this singularity is because we've constructed them to make sense "objectively", but our reason is embedded and embodied and therefore not objective.

The Individual and the Imagination

The perception of difference is a primitive evolutionary state.

When primitive sensory-motor process – active and reactive sensory explorations (what we've come to identify as our 5 senses) without guidance or purpose – becomes self-aware, it also becomes other-aware. But there is no separation between the sensory-motor explorations and the context that they explore.

This self-awareness is a meta-sense. It is an awareness of the more primitive sensory-motor activity.

The difference we experience – what Sartre labeled the "nothingness" at the core of human existence – is actually that cognitive difference between the immediate and the meta. It is, apparently, our unique evolutionary burden.

The imagination emerges from this as an evolution of self-awareness, a refinement of the meta-sense of difference, and it is the true creator of our reality-as-experienced. It is a sense of the senses in action, combined with a sense of the history of those acts all placed in their larger context.

It is our evolutionary advantage.

Our cognitive processes sculpt our reality-as-experienced from the raw material of latent reality, giving it its specific form in relation to our species' specific sensory-motor processes. We are "unique" only to the degree these processes differ from others of our species (color blindness, etc.) and to the degree we use our imaginations to creatively guide our explorations of the potentials of latent reality.

So our investigation of reality needs to begin here.

The error of the current scientific paradigm is that it proposes a materialist basis for all reality and tries to probe the difference between our reality (-as-experienced) versus what it presumes to be a reality, but is more real and which already has form and properties. It assumes a different reality than the one we actually experience.

This is a failure of the imagination.

Poetic Reality

The imagination sees more. It reveals the patterns of our interactions with all that we see as other. It constructs the poetic dimension, on which entangled metaphors develop and play. It is from this that the real truth of our existence emerges.

That truth is non-local, multidimensional.

It makes sense of what lies beyond our experiential reality, beyond our psycho-mechanical limitations, both the infinitely small and the infinitely large.

It is a poetic apprehension of a beauty "that shakes you from the inside out, something you have no control over, something reflexive and brutal and shattering."
(from "Aesthetic Automatism")

deus ex machina
Resistances to the Mechanizations of Bodies From the Romantics to Surrealism

Michael Löwy

In ancient drama, the Olympian gods descended from up above to resolve conflicts or bring about a solution to tragic impasses; a mechanical system of cogwheels allowed the on-stage representation of this salutary intervention. Hence the famed expression, deus ex machina. In modern capitalist civilization, the nature of this mise en scène has changed: it is now the machina itself that plays the role of a deus, it is the object of kneeling adoration like a true divinity, and is supposed to bring the miraculous solution to all difficulties. We live in the era of the religion of the machine, whose rituals are celebrated with pomp by a particularly intolerant techno-scientific clergy. The new deus machina demands human sacrifices, on a scale incomparably vaster than its ancestors Baal or Moloch did. And, like all divinities, its objective is to fashion humans after its own image, that of the machine.

The first commandment of this mechanical religion is thus the subjection of humans to the Apparatuses and, in the final analysis, the perfect mechanization of bodies and spirits. One may regard René Descartes as one of the founders of this new cult: "I consider man," he wrote in his Metaphysical Meditations, "as a clock composed of wheels and counter weights." One could not better sum up the Cartesian spirit of mechanical rationality. Obviously, the Industrial Revolution of the 18th Century allowed the passing from the stage of metaphysical speculation to that of practical application: the stated objective being, in the beautiful and strong wording of the "liberal and humanitarian" entrepreneur Josiah Wedgwood, "to make such Machines of the Men as cannot Err." Objective achieved? In part, yes, undoubtedly. In England, as the poet Henri Heine observed, "machines resembled people and people resembled machines." As our ancestors, the Luddites, understood so well, the new machines did not aspire to alleviate human labor, but rather to transform humans into cogwheels of the Productive Apparatus. Charles Dickens, in Hard Times, already described the condition of workers chained upon mechanical cycles; seeking an analogy for the pistons of the steam-engine in a factory, he speaks of a rhythm that "worked monotonously up and down, like the head of an elephant in a state of melancholy madness." A beautiful image, yet a perfectly inadequate comparison: no elephant, however madly or melancholically inclined, could ever represent the infinite, interminable, crushing monotony of mechanical movement...

Another step towards enslavement, and an enormous one at that, was accomplished by Henry Ford —"Our Ford," according to the religious prayers of good citizens in the brave new world, as described by Aldous Huxley— who not only mass-produced a vile machine, a steel cage on wheels, wherein humans were to be imprisoned for life, but also, thanks to his accomplice Taylor, invented the method of chain production, a scientific masterpiece of the workers' total submission to the repetitive movements of the Machine.

While the friends of Captain Ludd attacked those fatal machines with the aid of hammers and axes, the Romantics were amongst the first in the cultural domain to revolt against the nightmare of the human life's mechanization. The libertarian and anti-State spirit of Romanticism was inspired by the conviction —expressed in 1797 in an anonymous document (probably composed by Schelling) known as The Oldest System of German Idealism— that "every State necessarily treats free human beings as a system of mechanical gears." Romantic writers were haunted by the nightmare of the total automatization of bodies. "The Sand Man" by E.T.A. Hoffmann narrates the story of a man who falls madly in love with the beautiful Olympia, an excellent dancer and singer, without realizing that her movements and words had "the unpleasantly correct and spiritless measure of a singing machine." The tale ends dramatically, with the dismantlement of the doll-automaton by its two diabolical creators, as they argue about the price of her eyes. In a 1930 commentary on Hoffmann, Walter Benjamin observes that his tales are founded on the identity of the automatic and the satanic, the life of modern humans being "the product of an infamous artificial mechanism, internally ruled by Satan."

For Benjamin himself, it is not the devil, but another sort of Master, with neither horns nor tail, who pulls the strings of Santa Machina: namely, the Capital. Indeed, in his great, unfinished work *The Arcades Project*, he evokes Marx's analyses, according to which workers, through the machine-operated training, are obliged to co-ordinate "their own movement with the uniformly constant movements of an automaton." The worker undergoes a profound loss of dignity, "his work...sealed off from experience." This loss of experience is closely linked, for Benjamin, to the transformation of individuals into robots: repetitive movements, meaningless and mechanical, are to be found again in the automatic movements of passersby in the crowd, as described by Poe and Hoffmann. Both groups sport reactive behaviors, like dolls on wheels that have "completely liquidated their memories." The allegory of the automaton, the acute and despairing perception of the mechanical, uniform, void and repetitive character of the life of individuals in the industrial capitalist society is one of the great illuminations that traverse Benjamin's final writings.

The mechanization of bodies and spirits may also assume a "scientific" form, with the creation of cyborgs, humans whose bodies have been entered into a circuit, whether "informational" or "medical," by experiencing the installation of electrodes in the brain in order to control asocial behaviors. In a remarkable 1970s novel of libertarian inspiration, *Women on the Edge of Time*, the American writer Marge Piercy describes the revolt of a woman of Mexican origin, endowed with the ability to travel mentally into the future, who is diagnosed as mad and committed into a psychiatric hospital, meant to serve as a guinea pig for scientific experiments involving brain operations and electronic control of the will. She only manages to escape them after throwing poison into the coffee machine used by the heads of the laboratory...

It was against this submission of individuals to machines —in their work, their "leisure," their social and cultural life, even their emotional relations— it was against this transformation of the human being into a mechanical doll, that surrealists reacted. I harbor a special affection for those whose secret weapon in this fight was black humor. One example among many, albeit a particular striking one, is the short text by Jan Švankmajer entitled "The Future belongs to Auto-erotic Machines," which appeared in The Surrealist Civilization (1976). In its artisanal version, this machine appears, for men, in the form of a life size doll, provided with a "very original mechanism": an opening "simulating the vaginal orifice, where the self-lover will insert his penis in order to be self-pleasured thanks to the movement of the pendulum that he himself will have set in movement." In its automatic version, which will be available to the public at stadiums, stations, hotels etc., the self-erotic machine functions with a coin inserted into the slot of the apparatus, and due to be renewed every three minutes, as in a phone booth. A marvelous invention, the auto-erotic machine "relieves the self-lover from tedious moves towards a partner and from the obligation of courtship."

It is interesting to compare the surrealists' (negative) attitude towards the mechanization of bodies with their fascination for the mannequin —de Chirico's "disquieting muses", or Bellmer's erotically mutilated doll— objects of a poetic transfiguration. These two figures do not derive from machinism, but from the statue and its magical metamorphosis into a living body, as in the myth of Pygmalion.

Is not automatic writing, that supreme expression of free, individual as well as collective subjectivity, a radical surrealist riposte to the subject's destruction by the modern process of "automation"? This is what I believe, at any rate. As long as the exquisite corpse will drink the new wine rather than waste oil all hope is not lost.

PS: These few notes are, I am well aware, perfectly partial and unilateral. I have ignored all that could, as in the cases of desiring or bachelor machines, point towards the marvelous. I have simply followed my own, subjective and instinctive, mistrust of the mechanical "Thing," by tracing an imaginary dissenting line which goes from the romantics to the surrealists.

Translated by Nikos Stabakis

Rik Lina - *Witches Cauldron #2*

Reality of Revolt, Reasons of Utopia

José Manuel Rojo

There is no party without any surprise guest, although the former is a pantomime and the latter an undesirable that nobody waits for because everyone is afraid of him. The Spanish post-Franco transition would not be an exception, and so it was, as the post-Franco intrigue was hampered by a new cycle of proletarian struggles known as working class autonomy, organized in assemblies with revocable delegates and concrete demands responding to real problems, and which in themselves often escaped from the factory and the economy to spread to the neighborhood and disturb life. These features, and the spontaneity with which they manifested themselves, explain the almost revolutionary power of worker's autonomy in the context of that "second assault of the proletariat" which demonstrated its power in Paris, Portugal and Italy, as it did in Vitoria and in the port of Barcelona. That such an assault was placed in a second, even larger existential context, the so-called *counter culture* that explored new ways of life through drugs, sexuality, music or travel, doubtlessly justified what many of their players spoke of as being "living utopia", even if it may seem today that such a lifestyle was more a preview of the current social and individual breakdown than its challenge.

In any case, unfairly or not, this reflection on the bitter fate that time has in store for emancipatory movements helps us to assess not only that our time is not the same as that of working class autonomy, but also and most remarkably that it has turned out to be its sinister counterpart. Indeed, the economic and technological changes that capitalism has experienced for over 30 years, with automation, with the disproportionate prominence of service industry jobs (tertiarization) and the outsourcing of many industries to the Third World, has led to the immediate outcome of not being able to speak seriously about the working class *in a workerist sense* when it only constitutes 20 or 30 percent of the employed population in Western countries. It is true that, in order to compensate, society as a whole has reached the deepest proletarianized depths of wage labor, and the situation of many "white collar" workers of the service industry is not much better than that of traditional workers of the large factory, but this transfer of cannon fodder from one sector to another has not been accompanied by the consolidation of working class consciousness, or with the rebuilding of a new consciousness more adapted to these confused times. Without discussing what is meant by class consciousness, it is clear that the homogenization of culture through the media and mass consumption, the viral spread of middle class ideology to which everyone claims to belong, the calculated ravages of urban development, the fascination with those poisoned but dazzling fruits of technology... all have formed an amorphous social magma in which class actually degenerates into mass, and the individual is reduced to a pale reflection of the screen, with barely any critical awareness, will, or his own desires. This clinical profile might be exaggerated, and may admit some nuances and other interpretations, but it must be acknowledged that these spiritual and mental disasters *do exist*, even if only for the sake of fighting against their existence on behalf of other instances equally real, with even some chance of success.

On the other hand, perhaps the same revolutionary project has *run out of time*: the rapid progression of accelerated extinction of the material and biological basis of life (ravaged by pollution, by chemical or transgenic poisons) makes a *post*-capitalism increasingly unlikely, unless it is one that is *worse*. And even if it did arrive on time, as we believe (and need to believe) that it still will, it would come empty-handed and without road maps, because the great messianic hope has broken down, which confided that the morning following the Great Evening would imply the reappropriation of the capitalist production system by those who operated it and created its wealth, so that it would be simple child's play to create a happy world in which material scarcity would be abolished along with exploitation and injustice. But today we know that such a plan of action, however tempting it may be, is indeed neither possible nor adequate. No, a free society cannot salvage the capitalist techno-industrial fabric, or very little of it, not only because it is unaffordable and infeasible from the standpoint of natural resources (especially energy) but at the very least because of the ecological balance, because such technology is not necessary, with it mostly corresponding to false needs, and because it is not *desirable* either (without it immediately needing to be decided whether certain technologies could be part of the reformulation of a new model of production for human beings to implement).

We find a similarly empty table if we turn to those faculties on which some revolutionary movements have gambled so much – imagination, creativity, desire, spontaneity, poetry – basically understanding it not as a literary discipline but as *poetry by other means* that is experienced directly in everyday life. These instances, those shoots and stems of radical subjectivity that are able to rebel regardless of the economic situation, and which form a bastion of freedom for the individual, are being demolished by an economy transformed into a factory of nightmares. Indeed, the media message provided by immaterial *unreality* TV, being logical extensions of commodity fetishism, tends to destroy our inner world and the delicate, subtle relationships that it establishes with the outside and which definitely contributes to the reinforcement of both inner and outer worlds. On the other hand, the most irreducible basic desires, the obscurest areas of the unconscious that are not being affected, or not entirely being swept away by the black tide of the spectacle, become biological reserves of the imaginary, scrutinized, categorized and then exploited by the economy in search of new clients. This dual process is also disastrous because it creates a very real sense of absolute and suffocating confinement to the point of producing the paradox which in a social order is synonymous with programmed nightmare, where the person who dares to dream and desire, to continue dreaming and desiring the impossible and the absolute (because *the absolute and the impossible do exist*) will be accused of being an agent of domination, or merely of being a useful idiot. And yet, "capitalism lacks dreams, utopia, hope... and without dreams there is no revolt" (1), in other words, without dreams there is no revolt than can grow and mature into revolution.

It is true that the mortal danger which looms over the imagination and sensibility does affect the entire nature of the human being, which has led to an analysis that justifiably concludes that the total abandonment (although we are not entirely convinced) of the individual has resulted from an almost apocalyptic vision that suggests how it is not just a mass of exploited people lacking class-consciousness that has been has (mis)born, but rather a great body of subhumans never before seen in the History of Infamy: those children and grandchildren of technological indoctrination, without rationality, sensibility and will, who tragically lack knowledge, skills and practical learning (as everything they have been taught is either harmful or worthless, or both), and whose character has been corrupted by hedonism, laziness, drugs, alcohol; by the pornographic wave that has already invaded us and by the unbelievable lure of happiness that is thrown out there by the market. Well, besides the fact that we do not know where those lucky, lazy people are hiding (in a country where working hours have reverted back to those good old, virtuous habits of the nineteenth century while the month of paid vacation takes leave of its *fans* without saying a word), the problem of establishing such a categorical balance sheet for such a mob of "insignificant and degraded subjects" lies in subsequently considering it as an accomplice of power and of its excesses, since it ultimately supports them and therefore deserves everything that may happen to it. As a logical conclusion, the social revolts and outbursts that spread here and there are completely negligible, as they are moderate and/or corporate ones that speak the language of reformism or of power, or who are nihilist and speak the language of the decomposition of power, or who are entirely absurd and guilty... of speaking the language of those with power gone mad. In any case, they *are never* of any interest, since they are not revolutionary upheavals but rather mere instances of struggle or conflict, and are *always* counterproductive because they support the order they pretend to contest.

With ironies aside, the resulting picture is dark and allergic to nuance, but unfortunately plausible, given the current climate of the impudent scandal of triumphant capital in relation to the unprecedented servitude of work. Leaving aside the question of whether the crisis is a settling of debts among international capitalists, or a settling of scores between the Capitalist International and labor blackmailed into accepting even further cuts in their rights and standards of living while the financial sector gets to live high on the hog, or whether the crisis is systemic or even terminal, or perhaps severe but temporary... the truth is how surprising, as observed by *Etcétera,* is "the inner paralysis for those facing the situation, who have already begun to suffer the immediate consequences of collapse of the capitalist economy" (2). But it does not matter what radical criticism says, and the official journalists take it upon themselves to spread the good news, mocking the anti-globalization movement that is foundering at the time when it is most needed (3), or predicting that the "fall of welfare" will be received with resignation as the 'mileurist' is the one who "no longer has an age, who earns a thousand Euros, and is not saving, who lives one day at a time off of sporadic jobs or subsidies and who, despite everything, *does not resist*" (4). It is fear, and the conviction of defeat, with both individual and collective impotence, and the uncertainties and threats of excess population and ecological collapse that evade the understanding and the capacity to inspire reaction from those men and women *who are alone*; it is this absence of resistance and of options; it is the conviction of living a civilizational and even cosmic *end of days,* which has generated the obsessive idea and the collective myth of doomsday that seeps from every depressed and *zombified* pore of popular culture, of the terrible but avenging Apocalypse that certain revolutionaries lack but which they wistfully crave.

●

Before this image of desolation, those who make up their minds to resist and, if possible, lay the foundations for a world liberated from the economy, end up looking at each other and asking themselves the same old questions. In addition to using the convenient expedient of blaming others, one should perhaps consider the personal shortcomings of those of us who *collectively* participate in the social struggle against domination. To begin with, and as was already stated in 1948 in an equally or even more desperate, ominous situation, "that end of the world is not ours" (5). It is not ours primarily because there is no reason to hurry, since the survival instinct of capitalism is strong enough to survive its own self-sabotage via petroleum depletion. Secondly, because there is nothing to guarantee that its collapse would open the revolutionary door to a free society, with the much more likely outcome that capitalist domination would impose a new form of oppression, despite whatever whistle-blowing, probably under the guise of "environmentalism" or "climate emergency" and bolstered by the imperatives of austerity, work and material shortages for the oppressed of course, in the context of a new ideology, where – who knows – power might recover a critical discourse that insists on the virtues of sacrifice, effort and dignified poetry, just as it did with the one that defended passions and pleasure. Thirdly, and this is what matters most now: because the *metaphysics of the catastrophe* ensures that it is the only force capable of moving us, of ending our suspended animation and forcing us to act – the hard way – while getting the best of us because there is no other way possible; even if it were true to a certain extent, as many specific cases might show, such a point of view is essentially despicable because it speaks so very little of and so poorly about the concept that we have of the human being and about the world we desire, if that is the only way in which the former is revealed and we make our way towards the latter. This politics of the worst, which leads to envying the plight of the Serbs bombed by NATO or of the Haitians killed by the earthquake because it is such that they "rediscover the values of solidarity and the traditional techniques of knowledge", is even more grotesque when compared with the confidence that other revolutionaries (more generous and certain of the validity and strength of their ideas) put in people who apparently were also gray and sedate, as those seamstresses and those shop-assistants crushed by routine whom Kropotkin viewed as becoming fairies of spontaneity and wizards of improvisation. Therefore, if the revolution has to come from such misanthropic catastrophism, we will have to say that *that particular revolution is not ours, either.* Thereby we prefer to endorse that idea where, "given the potentially cataclysmic state of the crisis and of the world, we proudly declare our revolutionary optimism and challengingly put all our hope in poetry and in the marvelous." (6) We accept that this optimism is also an *act of faith without hope* because it assumes the *organization of revolutionary pessimism* that is nowadays essential, and it never constitutes a simple voluntaristic illusion because it is based on a certain reality, and because it is nourished by solid reasons.

On the other hand, we should wonder whether this scenario is really so unprecedented, if trampled masses have not existed before, which still had the means to rise out of their own misery, as in the case of the British working class crushed and degraded by the evil pliers whose levers are the false charity of the old *Speenhamland system* and the rapacity of the new labor market, reduced to less than nothing according to Polanyi but with enough courage to show "that some of the people were still able to dream their own dreams, and were taking the measure of a society which had forgotten the shape of man" (7). Secondly, we should ask ourselves, in the event that everything has indeed irremediably broken down without mitigating circumstances, where do the critics and the revolutionaries and all those who resist capitalism come from, of what breed are they, how is their existence possible nowadays, when we all supposedly live after the collapse (and many of us were even born after it), and have we thus undergone the same radioactive effects of techno-industrial conditioning. Perhaps we would have to admit, or at least consider as a working hypothesis, that the dispossession and dehumanization of both the masses and the individual that (mis)form them exists well enough, but they exist as an *ongoing process* which has not yet ended, in such a way that the profound disdain towards human quality and the ultimate ability of the "citizens" to achieve their material autonomy has an unexpected and harmful contraindication, namely that it strangely coincides with the *nihilistic* psychological and emotional impairment of the person that promotes power, i.e. with the self-depreciation of contemporary man which reduces him to the state of invalidity dreamed by the economy, in which it is impossible to satisfy the least basic needs without resorting to the market and to wage labor. Here the radical critique cannot comply with the gained ground, and while it is still verifying and berating "the double dispossession of the individuals" who accept "the existing situation" and have lost "the material basis which would have allowed a radical change towards forms of organization different from today's"(8), one should ask especially oneself, and experiment if necessary, if, despite everything, it is really so true and certain that people do not retain any skills, knowledge, or useful abilities from their work and from some of their hobbies and colonized leisure time, if they cannot really be used in another context, including and especially those emergency contexts, to manage and extricate oneself with certain guarantees of both autonomy and success. We know what they would want us to believe: that *no,* outside the tutelage of the State and the mediation of money there is no possible salvation but infinite terror. And yet, spontaneous experiences such as the popular reaction to the *Prestige* oil disaster, or the improvised mutual aid by anonymous, everyday people in flooded New Orleans (while the mute, paralyzed government and capital fled the scene in terror) (9), should deny this curse, or at least help reconsider it within its true proportions.

In this sense, the apathy of the population is probably for the most part a lamentably real fact, but to conclude that it is always like that would be like painting a portrait of complete and total submission that, just like the one of Dorian Gray, only succeeds in depicting the horrific scars of servility and unconsciousness, but never the beauty of the defiant gesture that we sometimes allow ourselves, or of life asserting itself despite and against everything. This is so, because, unless we believe the lies of ideology, capitalism still creates such apparent contradictions that it remains unnecessary to discuss whether inequality still exists, because, class-conscious or not, class struggle still continues, even with different names and by other means, like the heartbreaking employee suicides of *France Telecom* – what a terrible waste of rage and anger, failure, despair, that interpellates all of us. But there are times when something, such as an imperialist war, or an environmental disaster, or an intolerably cynical humiliation from whatever local government of the day, or just about any emotional or affective castration that seemed minor yesterday and which power (and perhaps ourselves) disregarded, now becomes the straw that breaks the camel's back, causing the outbreak of conflict. For there is life beyond the usual role of the enthusiastic citizen or the gullible consumer whose plotinian emanation, commodity fetishism and the myth of the machine forever permeates all aspects of the human being, from the absolute, sheer alienation of wage labor that produces useless things, to the most insignificant daily habit or distraction. However, these capitalist myths that cause so much damage *cannot be everywhere all at once*, which would explain the sudden mood swings that sometimes (rarely) occur in the domesticated population (but not always or fully), and the surges of black rage with the underground springs of real life (or its nostalgia) which feed them; those *atavistic reserves* are always insufficient, but nevertheless necessary.

If there were ever an example of an *atavistic reserve*, it would be the unconscious mental jungle where manifold imagination is ambushed, and it goes without saying that even there, and how, the bulldozers of the spectacle have arrived. But neither is the destruction complete, and nor have all our desires and emotions been fully transformed into mere reproductions of themselves, as there are gray areas that are irreducible and unbreathable in which the beast cannot enter, especially those where the blinding experience of death is manifested. Yet by itself this is not sufficient or pleasing enough, and from the forest we want to go and conquer both countryside and cities, since there is a war over the social imagination and the reappropriation of those powers of the mind that reverberate in others, and especially the battle that is being held for the reconstitution of the *idea of community*. And precisely this and other struggles which lead us back to the starting point: that the problem of worker versus non-worker autonomy resides within the need to stand not only against the Party, the Union and the democratic farce, but against the present organization of existence as a whole: the reconquest, among other things, of autonomy by way of the practical means of material subsistence outside capitalism, on the level of political action that must rediscover the possibility and even legitimacy of the conflict, of the use of force and mass violence, and yes, on the level of creative autonomy that has so much to do with mentality and collective myths. For this effort we count on the *reality of the revolt,* and the *reasons for utopia.*

•

To begin, we shamelessly confess that we are supporters of revolt for revolt's sake, even of the seemingly most irrational sort (and all are in the eyes of rational power), although we must say not all. But in a social context where all minimally angry protest, where any conflict that breaks a single dish, where all gestures of real rebellion are not only illegal but have been internalized as inconceivable, such that violence, like what happened in the case of *France Telecom,* can only be turned against itself, then revolt has a primary virtue, which is *to exist,* and secondly, to teach the "practice of disobedience" and how the experience of one's own strength can often unleash unexpected consequences and gratifying outcomes that affect the rest of social existence (10). But far from being content with this, revolt often puts those momentous but confused issues on the table which plague our time, and that challenge (in part) the anemia in which we are submerged. Some examples, though different but not distant *in spirit,* are sufficient to confirm that.

The equivocal but highly significant event that shook Alcorcón, a former industrial town on the outskirts of Madrid, might be recalled. In January 2007, a mundane brawl led to a dubious youth revolt against alleged *latin-kings,* resulting in a clash with riot police and where there was no lack of neighborhood support for the rebels. The first readings about the event were inevitably negative as it was interpreted as yet another sign of the breakdown of old working class neighborhoods, or an alarming example of fascist infiltration, and in fact both the symptom and the danger exist, and are very real. And yet its participants reacted passionately, explaining that they had risen against what they perceived to be a threat of mafia feudalization in a neighborhood that still had "identity ties deeply linked to a diffuse working-class neighborhood collective imagination, a class identity that has its shortcomings, which still does not establish strong bonds of daily solidarity, but which nevertheless sporadically succeeds in rising above everyday social isolation and becomes manifest as a force capable of bringing together a crowd of youth and grown-ups who are playing a game of cat and mouse with the police" (11). Is this a delusion or does it contain a grain of truth, or is there some truth hidden in the delusion? Perhaps there are still signs of life behind the curtain, or perhaps it has not completely fallen, and that it is not impossible for those who live there to be able to provide friendship and support to their neighborhoods and to their peers, even if only because they were the foundation of their childhood and love, the only homelands. But even presuming that not every place is already a non-place and its inhabitants zombies or robots, then the explanations of the youth from Alcorcón and the worried comments from so many others who saw themselves reflected in the image of these youth should point to something that cannot be neglected: that by talking about such a "working-class neighborhood", about such "clearly leftist and combative people", then perhaps it was being spoken through the mythical voice of what could have been but which did not happen, and also by doing so, there was the wish to revive it, as it is a principle of resistance at the level of consciousness and the imaginary. And at such a level there must be some kind of connection with practical action when domination ultimately seeks to stifle that memory and that myth, as it was in the name of that more or less real, more or less mythical neighborhood where it was worth going out to face the mafia, the fascists and the police.

If there were ever a prime example of a non-place abandoned to its fate, this would undoubtedly be the French *banlieue,* and it was there that a formidable revolt broke out in the fall of 2005 which had all the elements to be condemned. It turns out that it was led by those young barbarians who give off the unmistakable odor of a lynching mob resulting from the selfishness and violence of the system, those congenital idiots who cannot think or speak, addicts, rappers and sexists, and on top of that (or as a logical consequence of the previous), those puppets manipulated by Sarkozy, because, as it is well known, nobody is allowed to move even a finger without the permission of the competent authority, that discretely engineers each and every *emotion* of the populace. Unfortunately some *banlieusards* respond harshly to this robot-portrait, and hazy events like the assaults on young, anti-CPE demonstrators in 2006 only add more confusion. And yet not all are like that (12), nor are they so during every moment of their lives, especially those who can free themselves from their misery through direct confrontation with the powers that created it. Maybe that is the reason why the revolt was so important: because it demonstrated that there are still people who, with impunity, do not tolerate nor suffer injustices, and that they explode sooner or later for the simple reason that they are alive, and that silence and meekness are worse, much, much worse than the devastation from the riots. Of course, the revolt had its flaws and contradictions, but it also had qualities of insight and awareness, such as the negativity so blithely dismissed as "nihilistic" when most of the time it represents healthy disillusion and the refusal to negotiate, something that anyone could have understood if one had deigned to take *seriously* what the rebels themselves had explained (13). On this point and for similar ones, one can read (or reread) *The Bad Times Will Burn* [*] for which perhaps one of its conclusions could help clinch this brief reflection regarding the meaning of the *banlieusarde* revolt: "We will not descend into mere adulation nor fall for the temptation to say that these words and actions represent the only possible revolutionary program. Quite the contrary, it may be incredibly wrong, and precisely because it is the most radical. But likewise, the same is true for today's societal war: ugly, vulgar, ambiguous, convulsive and episodic, burdened by a thousand adulterations of the abject spirit of our times, and surely doomed to fail again and again. However (...) *it is the social war* that we have to deal with in the worst of all possible worlds because it is the one that provides and will continue providing us with the fewest options regarding its hypothetical transcendence".

But to defend revolt just because it shows that the resistance continues is not and could never be enough for us. *Salvation through riot* is as improbable as the one that would descend from heaven, and if rebellion, being necessary and even essential, ever goes beyond that, it ends up becoming frozen in an ultimately sterile and mechanical ritual. We might recall here that abject definition of the 'mileurist' who "earns a thousand Euros, and is not saving, who lives one day at a time off of sporadic jobs or subsidies and who, despite everything, *does not resist*" and reflect on something that a hasty reading leaves unnoticed: that in this article from May 2009, the astute journalist said *not one single word* about the Greek revolt of Christmas that year, despite the Homeric proportions it attained and the fear that it spread among the political offices and the economic and media laboratories, or precisely because of that. It is such that the triumph of capitalism is primarily the triumph of the myth of its invulnerability, and revolts against it are thereby silenced, with the official argument that portrays them as being irrational, since it discourages, obstructs and even thwarts the efforts of those who would dare to take control of their lives outside the economy, or bureaucratizes the self-regulated construction of dwellings, or prohibits the planting and exchange of unregistered seeds. But we must go further than that and acknowledge that the *crisis* of the *economy of revolutionary desire* will follow and even precede the economic crisis, and Greece is also the best example.

We will not insist on the moral legitimacy of the insurrection provoked by the police murder of Alexandros Grigoropoulos, and neither on its prevalence (occupations of public buildings, mass meetings, free dialogue and unprecedented organizing among strangers), especially when we observe its challenging resurgence and who knows whatever else. But – and I apologize for speaking so extemporaneously that I will surely have regretted my words by the time this text is finally published, from having dared to make irremediably premature judgments – it seems that the revolt never attempted to take the huge step of seizing the means of production, transportation and communication so as to meet its daily needs even if in a precarious and necessarily imperfect way, even if only for one day, even if only in a single neighborhood. Of course this step is the most difficult one and had been immediately repressed by the army, but the fact is that it was not taken, and perhaps this is what explains the revolt's lack of international transmissibility, and even the relative apathy with which the Greek population has received the old-style intervention plan of the IMF for several months, which is surprising when compared to last year's volcanic revolts. Now the crater appears to be revived, and the lava had never cooled (although the intensity of the eruption decreased), and apart from the fact that these new black flows are giving rise to new far-reaching questions (for this revolt and for the one that we wish will explode into a future that is now) that only time will answer (14), it would be appropriate to ask about this unevenness of intensity. Of course, when the bureaucrat in turn experiences an *ideological lapse* and admits that the collapse of the Greek economy had been cooked on a low fire so that the sacrifices would fall like ripe fruit "without having to impose them hastily" because "the people would not have accepted them earlier; one needed to be careful not to have a revolution breaking out" (15), it is easy to suspect that the revolutionary gymnastics of revolt were provoked in order to exhaust the most combative sectors of the population and to scare the rest before applying their horse cure. And yet, maybe this time it might have been to the contrary, perhaps that it was the lack of practical alternatives and the mere exercise of violence *of resistance* that demonstrated, most regrettably, that capitalism indeed will not be reformed and neither will it be replaced, and that no choice remains for it but to resign or reposition (and it this is already quite a lot) itself for rearguard combat in order to save as much furniture as possible. Because people do have something more to lose than their chains, if only because the survival instinct is stubbornly strong, and needs more than just anger for one to go out and take any risk; to start with, it takes *everything,* that is, a project of transformation that, in addition to libertarian, reasonable, realistic, non-ideological reasons, will indeed *impel one to dream*. As confirmed by a protagonist reflecting upon the waning of the purely destructive phase of the revolt, "there is little possibility to extend the creative phase (...) there is no project and it is something that I always appreciated as positive; but if there is no project, then something should be invented" (16), and it is that *something* we are talking about when we say the word *utopia*.

•

Utopia? To start with, just so that bureaucrats do not worry, we agree with the *Grupo Salvaje* that "it is not about any abstract utopia, nor to propose a fixed ideological agenda, but to start a debate that has already been postponed for too long regarding what we want for the post-capitalist future and what means, possibilities and expectations are required to reach it." This view is expressed in one of the best texts covering the Greek revolt, "The Return of Prometheus", in which some of its shortcomings in relation to this "(huge) jump towards a life that surpasses and buries capitalism and the State" are listed. But the sad thing is that these limitations are *self-imposed*. It is easy enough for this issue to be discussed in any debate for it to provoke that allergic reaction to utopia, including the mere mention of an outline for a different society, whether the badly reputed traditional utopian socialism, the refusal to fall into ideology, or the disappointment of those past utopias that became places of hell or were recuperated by totalitarian domination. All this may be true, but no less true is the paradox of capitalism, however badly wounded, continuing to present itself as the only possible reality, and worse, as the only *horizon of the future* remaining for this species and the planet that supports it. The current inability to develop non-utopian worlds does not demonstrate the failure of utopia but merely the triumph of the capitalist one, just like the general inability to reason is not proof that reason is unnecessary, but merely the fact that economy does not need it. In this regard, we dare say that this castrating self-censorship may be understandable as a measure of prudence, but that taken to extremes and consecrated within a dogma of thought it is an error, a kind of mental inertia, and even *counterrevolutionary*.

But to defend utopia does not mean ignoring one's enemies, or refusing to accept what is reasonable in their criticism which, despite its voluminous size, and not showing any signs of lessening its exponential growth, can be summarized in three main arguments: utopia is the original sin of pushing the limits of human nature by relying on technology in order to realize its science fiction fantasies, it promises a perfect and impossible happiness that would soften and pervert man, and it is synonymous with mystical passivity and harmlessness. Because of all this, and whether one likes it or not, utopia has ended up now facilitating domination, paving the way for it, and now justifying its delusions and advertising its novelties. To be sure, "in old as well as in new utopias, the human as such is being excluded: one's greed for happiness eliminates it," because such utopias "are not possible, but above all are not desirable because they present the human being as it is not and as it could not and should not be". Besides, "utopia, the revolutionary myth, the promise of happiness, belongs only to the illusory, to the imaginary; furthermore, only within the imagination and the illusions *of Rulers*". Therefore Utopia should be denounced "as a poisoned ointment with which the rich and powerful heal the wounds of their *victims of obedience* and of their *victims of work*." Utopia, in short, "from now on belongs to domination" (17).

Since the general condemnation of utopias of the past claims to delegitimize any utopian desire from the present, the first thing that should be done is to specify which utopia is being attacked and how it is manifested in time and space, what its impact and influence has been over workers and other revolutionaries, if it was disputed, ignored, or recuperated, and what is alive and what is dead in it, rather than creating an abstract and ahistorical *punching-ball* stuffed with prejudice. Resorting to a picturesque interpretation of a passage in *The Odyssey*, Pedro García Olivo hides behind some famous names, possibly as a suggestive literary game, but his movement from metaphor to proof, through offering lucubrations about the singing ability of the sirens, as a final demonstration, contributes absolutely nothing to his reflections on utopia, nor anything to its relations with myth and ideology, a topic of great interest and therefore of particular complexity. To liquidate the extremely rich utopian tradition with some passing and insubstantial mention of Moro, Campanella, of the 19th century machinist "paleo-utopias" and of the "childlike and *'vilificante'* utopias" of the 60's from the last century as does Félix Rodríguez, confusing utopian thinking, in the most sordid way possible, with citizenship reformism in order to furtively paste in his own (otherwise worthy) utopia with another name, is playing a game rigged to allow him to win every time. Despite all this, we say to begin with, *and only to begin with*, just to narrow the discussion, that it is essential to reject the reduction of utopia to being a simple literary genre (18); we leave aside etymological and philosophical discourse relating to the word *utopia*, as well as their similarities and differences with *dystopia* and *ucronia*, aspects of great interest but secondary to the issue concerned here (19); and neither that the classical utopias of More and Campanella should be our references, even if they also have inspirational power and a larger historical influence than what is believed, which is, ultimately, that the utopias which deserve our respect are those that aspired and were able to form a part of the theoretical debates and the concrete struggles of the era in which they arose, such as the millennarists of the Middle Ages and of the fifteenth century, or especially (and I will be focusing on them for practical reasons) the various currents of utopian socialism, the libertarian utopias and the movements which in the twentieth century took up the legacy of the romantic protest – that protest, which set poetry at the center of their concerns and demands. It is from a reflection on the *real* lights and shadows of their thought and action, and not on a conveniently distorted, *pour la cause* image, that one can try, *and I say try*, to respond to their criticisms.

The first critique is the most correct one. Indeed, both

the utopian socialists (especially Saint-Simon, Bellamy and Owen, although the latter retracted his position later on) and the Situationist International have an excessive and naive confidence in the liberating possibilities of the machine, which we can no longer share anymore today. No, neither the Hacienda nor the *New Babylon* could or should be built, but this does not necessarily mean returning to a pure and simple medieval life. But despite the fact that this technophilic illusion was shared by other scientific and rationalist groups within the labor movement, there are also utopians and utopian experiments that have distanced themselves from machinism and which do not embrace the concept of such a simplistic amalgamation between utopia and industrial society. The example of William Morris and his *News from Nowhere* should be sobering enough, unless the minor sin of proposing some technical innovation to transport heavy objects is mortal rather than venial. But it is the case that Fourier himself had great skepticism regarding "progress", betting that an *agricultural* economy and society would prevail in the phalanstery, believing that farm- and seasonal work, through some technical revisions here and there, and along with many erotic games, would be most enjoyable and rewarding for humankind. On the other hand, that champion of luxury, who so often has been presented as a forerunner of consumer society, admitted with a shrug that certain products such as matches and metals would not be manufactured or would be scarce if the work required to obtain them was not exciting enough, so that the bulimic materialism of the civilized (based on possession of unnecessary things that are forgotten the day after buying them, only to pine away for new ones in a vicious circle of anxiety, dissatisfaction and sadness) is in the Fourierist approach diametrically opposed to requiring creative products of high quality and durability (20).

The second criticism claims that aberrant utopia is the shortest path to ontological and moral perdition of humanity by promising such absurd things as happiness, which as everyone knows is not made for man, nor man for it. Apart from the fact that we will not enter into a discussion about whether they have always existed or not, "Images of Desire", "dream worlds", "not-yet" messianic myths, Golden Ages, Cockaigne, Lands of Milk and Honey, Candy Mountains, etc. that articulate the *universal and timeless* longing for a life, long at last freed from material shortages and the sentence to work, and apart from the fact that there are also very strict utopians like Cabet who prescribed hard work and no tobacco, alcohol or extramarital relationships (and let us clarify that *none of these utopias is ours*), one should be especially careful when postulating a narrow definition of human nature that rejects the part that we do not like, whatever it might be. Pleasure, desire, happiness... are as human as sacrifice, altruism, solidarity or coexistence. Furthermore, sacrifice and effort are alienation when not aimed at fulfilling the desire for happiness, and that desire is chimera and frustration if it is not understood that it can never be realized completely, and that it must agree to coexist with sacrifice and effort in order to be realized up to whatever point. On the other hand, what is human nature?

Is it immutable, or does it change throughout history, revealing new desires and needs, legitimate or illegitimate? To propose impossible dreams possibly implies sharing, even if only partially, the hateful progressive ideology of permanent change, but to anchor ourselves in psychology and the lifegoals of whatever epoch, refusing to even consider that new desires and new attitudes could appear, implies allowing oneself be imbued, *even if only partially,* by the no less odious myths and ideologies that defended the status quo because it had always been so and because God wanted it; nothing more *natural,* in fact, than the manifest inferiority of the black race in relation to the white one, or of women in relation to men, or of the worker in relation to the bourgeois, or of the indigenous in relation to the colonizer, and today of life in relation to commodities. Blinded by a justified but pathological (and a minimally dialectical) hatred of anything that smells of the Enlightenment and of revolution, understood as a *break with natural teleology* – have we forgotten that all these outrageous frauds share the common sense of custom, and have on their side the tradition sanctioned by Church tradition and by the wisdom of the classics? Have we forgotten that demanding its abolition was also *utopian, blasphemous and unnatural?* Were Burke and Bonald *totally* correct that it is impossible for man to change even the smallest aspect of reality no matter how hateful, and that only the slow passage of the centuries would? Are we going to settle for that and still call ourselves *anarchists*? What are we talking about?

On the other hand, it is time to leave other equally pernicious stupidities aside, such as the undocumented rant accusing utopians of a lack of spirituality, thus proposing a defeated and helpless man, the toy of easy pleasure and comfort, a cynical individualist. Had not we agreed that one of the major flaws of the dream was that it relied too much on moral values, rather than on the cold, economic and social laws? And indeed, yes, Fourier dreamed of interstellar epics and believed in God because essentially he had to be smiling and approve the passions and pleasures that he had created; the young Saint-Simonian of Enfantin Prosper founded a church, and the atheist Owen was concerned above all with regenerating the character of the workers annihilated by the great transformation. It is fortunate that we do not like these theories and that they seem futile and extravagant to us (and the saint-simonian industrial and scientific religion definitely is to a large extent), but it is sufficient to take a quick glance at his ideas to see that there is a high, generous moral and ethical sense that guides them, although fortunately, as with Fourier, it is not always the Christian moral. The same applies to work, that was praised by all of them as a necessary foundation of society and desirable in itself (as long as it remained unpaid), that would produce useful as well as beautiful things, that would be made by all instead of being parasitized by the leeches of capital, that would have substantially cut hours, and, finally, *that would be made attractive.* Although the methods of realizing it vary according to each author, all agree on having work (and the economic sphere in general) as a *social activity not to be separated* from other activities and experiences, rather than being an expedient of pure production whose only goal is profit, and it is such that these utopias are precisely well aware of the joys of coexistence, cooperation and friendship. Did not all of them subscribe to Leroux's diatribe against the *dissociation* that property and competition had introduced to humanity, breaking its solidarity? Was not a communal life being formed in the phalanstery, in the Icarian colony and in Owen's social nuclei? Did not the Saint-Simonians in their retreat of Ménilmontant come to invent a vest *that could only be fastened from the back*, in order to symbolize the essential, mutual support among brothers? They loved so much the pleasure of living among peers that they could not wait for the revolution, and so devoted themselves to founding experimental communes which, *like almost everything else,* failed. But they failed certainly not for any lack of a collective sense, since they had so much of it (21). Of course, the ultimate goal of all their proposals was to achieve happiness, but when such proposals are criticized by the likes of a reviled Vaneigem for being based on the desire for abundance, leisure and pleasure as vital motives, then it is forgotten how for them happiness and enjoyment are not synonymous with empty hedonism but rather with spiritual perfection (22), and that their point of departure was the *complete* individual capable of everything, who expresses his creative potential in the various spheres of life, who is always master of himself, who uses leisure to cultivate himself in all fields of knowledge, who is dedicated to the community because the satisfaction of desires and the fulfillment of situations depend on others, who, in short, is the exact opposite of the passive, apathetic, specialized, TV-viewing and isolated citizen who would not represent his triumph, but rather his inverted reflection (23).

Regarding the third allegation, it is hard to tell whether it comes from ignorance or bad faith (24). As horrified witnesses of the Jacobin and white terror and of the Napoleonic butchery, it is true that the first generation of utopians rejected class struggle and revolution so as to address a cross-class audience whom they intended to *willingly* persuade of the goodness of their theories, and this humanistic optimism was subsequently inherited both by their followers and by later thinkers. Hence the appeals to "peaceful democracy", to their generous patrons, even to the parliamentary channels, which is undoubtedly the most *utopian* part of their thinking. With that having been said, it should be clear that the romantic socialists and all those who in whatever way have followed in their steps, were in no way passive nor accomplices of power, since they not only came into contact with the worker milieus where they had quite a few supporters (tens of thousands, and very dedicated ones in the case of Cabet), but also participated with varying degrees of success in insurrections and revolutionary processes (25). But the joke becomes bloodier if we leave the strict context of romantic socialism in order to take a look at another movement, the anarchist one, which may be accused of many things but not for being contemplative or working for the enemy. Although, and as we know, the relationship between anarchist and utopian thought are very conflicting, and virtually all its currents, from Proudhon to Zo d'Axa, from Bakunin and Malatesta to Maria Luisa Berneri and Diego Abad de Santillán, have refused to anticipate the future, criticizing the totalitarian, sectarian or escapist dangers of utopia as well as the certain failures expected to result from the isolated experiments that they attempted to realize, it is no less true that a utopian current, or a utopian *anarchist dream* has been present since William Godwin, even among those who refuted it or were cautious towards it. Some took a step further by shamelessly defending the role of utopia in the struggle for emancipation, while others went still further by *formulating utopias* (26), and then in Giovanni Rossi we have someone who really went astray, who really *lived them*, who, not content with issuing *A Socialist Commune,* actually went to Brazil to submit it to the test of facts. But the legendary vicissitudes of the *Cecilia* colony, and with it the myriad libertarian experiments such as *L'Essai* and the other French *milieux libres* or *Monte Verità* and the "new communities" encouraged by Landauer, also helps us view the utopians' experiences with different eyes: the New Harmony, La Reunión, the successive Icarias, the Familistery of Guise or the amazing American phalansteries such as Brook Farm that a certain Thoreau frequented, to relate them to the anarchist ones and study them all together, forgetting neither the artistic fraternities and brotherhoods such as the *Red House* of Morris, nor the *Barkenhoff*, founded by Heinrich Vogeler in Worpswede. The issues are identical, the causes of their failure the same, the enthusiasm and criticism generated among other workers similar, as was the hostility and obstacles that the most successful ones encountered from those in power. And today, when from remote (and even opposite) points on the radical spectrum there is again talk of creating communes that are autonomous from capital and industrial society, with emphasis on the need to extricate oneself from such society without becoming isolated from the social war that combats it from all angles, but with disinterest and even contempt for those who nevertheless were our *forerunners*, then our own *tradition* no longer seems to apply anymore (27). And would not it be better to learn from the lessons of past generations rather than having to start from scratch?

•

In any case, we do not claim to idealize utopia, nor to memorize or take too literally Fourier's or Quirola's words, nor forgive their theoretical and practical mistakes; on the contrary, they can and should be criticized as the rest of the revolutionary tradition to which they belong, but they should be criticized for what they were and not because of their convenient caricature. But the problem is no longer to defend the idea or the history of utopia, but rather to discuss what role it has, if any, in today's world. In this regard, we must admit without any shame or pain, as has been already said, that it is better to *stop and think* before repeating those old and supposedly radical and scandalous slogans, because in reality the agitation of desire and pleasure is now almost *uneffective*, namely as a weapon of demolition launched against a repressive bourgeois morality that practically almost no longer exists as such, except perhaps in very specific and calculated occasions and situations. We also accept that there is no perfect system and should not be any, and that *yes,* there will always be problems, production imbalances, cost and scarcity, difficult choices and unavoidable sacrifices even in the best possible organized and most convivial society. And we *automatically* reject any ideology disguised as utopia, and any ideologization of utopia that fossilizes it into a closed system that is immune to spontaneity, unresponsive to the unpredictable challenges of daily conflicts, or to what appears and is invented within collective life.

Maybe because of all these reasons, being *utopian* is much better than just believing in utopia, in the sense that a revolutionary project, in addition to basing itself on critical reason and on the experience of real struggles, should have a certain utopian dimension, so as to avoid as much as possible the temptation of reformism, or simply the short lifespan of movements that were not always irrelevant (28). This would be its role: to break the ideological blockade and the fear of desire in order to unleash the stream of libertarian lava into the icy waters of realist conformism, and after that it will be experience itself that will become a sieve and theory that will serve as a reflection. Precisely with this uplifting expression of the 1970s, "living utopia" meant that *experimentation* had supremacy over any *dream*, and indeed, in the dialectics between the desired utopia and 'the right here and now' that precedes it, the latter is and must always be the more important, that which does not override the specific meaning and revolutionary importance of the former. It will be said that this is how it occurs with those who make their way back to the countryside and find the garden and the trades of the old communal city under the asphalt, and this is very true, but what is certain is that these projects and actions neither exhaust the utopian project nor monopolize the formulation of a free society.

Then would this be the time to offer the world the pluperfect and irresistible surrealist utopia? No, because not only do the surrealists not have it but neither does the world need it. But maybe here and there, throughout such interventions, some bits and pieces of the world that we wish for (or at least the one that I wish for) have appeared, never as inflexible magic formulas but rather those which serve as coordinates or evidences that would point in the direction of our objective. A world where there is room for the gift of rapture and excessive revelry that are also human, but which is not to say that these are mandatory nor that they would be mere consolation for an unlivable life; where passion, pleasure and happiness are noble goals within reach of everyone, because, as Oscar Wilde said (and for which he paid a very high price), "self-realization is the main aspiration in life, and fulfilling oneself through pleasure is more beautiful than doing so through pain" (29), assuming that hedonism is a legitimate human aspiration and worthy of glory when it dares to be a *heroic hedonism* that knows and accepts that enjoyment has its limits; and furthermore that there are off-moments, where – as Breton underlined in *Arcane 17* referring to a woman who never devoted herself halfway – pain, death, impenetrable boredom and the black holes of the mind are only "open doors to the ever-resurgent need to bend, to sensitize, to beautify this cruel life"; where subjectivity and everyday life (into which the former is directed) allow themselves to come into contact with the marvelous, defeating not only the spectacle and its store of entertainment and prefabricated emotions, but also and especially the rational and *prosaic* mentality that may know a little about imagination and poetry, but which fails to recognize or appreciate them and thereby contents itself with repeating the same old pattern of leisure time that it criticizes, provided that it is conveniently stamped with the *alternative* label of the moment and that it has developed within its own *liberated* ghetto (30); where there are cities (the privileged settings of such poetry – not just megacities and conurbations), there will also have to be rural existence and wildlife in much larger proportions, and with the reintroduction of both, as much as possible, into cities that will be forced to return to their limits from a century ago; where work is organized according to the teachings of Fourier, so as to make it just as attractive as games are, *as much as possible* and also admitting that hard or stressful work cannot be completely abolished; where a certain level of technology, freed from capitalist malformation, is allowed, having been reduced to a level that the planet can support and tailored to the management capabilities and autonomy of small communities, so that the threat of shortages which apparently tormented preindustrial societies would not return, and where work, however attractive or not, and however immersed in social life it may be, would not consume the whole day, leaving free time, i.e. time defined only beyond the realm of necessity when the imperatives of survival have been resolved, a time both full and empty which by its troubled nature presents the riddles that also decide human fate (31).

To put it plainly, a world that encourages the realization of these desires, or at least which does not prevent them from being fulfilled on behalf of collective sacrifice and effort, *which also must exist*. This particular utopia as well as others might be rejected, but never to discard the *missing link* of utopia, because if those who call themselves revolutionaries do not dream of the world in which they would (and not only could) prefer to live, then *what* are they fighting for anyway? Or maybe it is enough to know *against what?*

Text drawn from an intervention with the same title at the *Seminar on workers autonomy and autonomy* (March-May 2010, Madrid). (Translated by Bruno Jacobs, revised by Eric Bragg and Noé Ortega)
* Originally published in Salamandra #19-20, Madrid, 2011.

TRANSLATOR'S NOTE:

* Originally entitled *Los malos tiempos arderán*, it is a declaration written in November 2005 by the Madrid Surrealist Group, La Felguera Collective of Cultural Workers (Madrid-Tenerife), Oxygen (Logroño), Durruti's Bad Companies (Logroño-Zaragoza), and Farenheit 451 (Madrid). It is available online at www.kaosenlared.net/noticia/los-malos-tiempos-arderan

NOTES:

1. Grupo Marcuse, *De la miseria humana en el medio publicitario*, Ed. Melusina, Barcelona 2006, p. 44.
2. "Algunas sugerencias a propósito de la crisis", C.V., *Etcétera* nº 45, p. 15, 2009.
3. "Capitalism is facing the first truly global recession without any alternative discourse. The anti-globalization phenomenon managed to derail or seriously disrupt several summits a few years ago (...) but these protests have no continuity" ("Protests are decreasing before the IMF summit", *El País* 09/04/1926).
4. "Goodbye, middle class, goodbye", Ramón Muñoz, *El País* 31/05/1909.
5. If André Breton made this observation in "The lamp in the clock", another surrealist, Egyptian George Henein, declared the previous year that "surrealism as such refuses to rest its head on the pillow of ruins" ("Séance tenante", Le Surréalisme en 1947). Neither the ruins of yesterday nor of those to come.
6. Editorial of the first issue of the international surrealist journal *Hydrolith*, 2010.
7. Karl Polanyi, *La gran transformación*, Ed. La Piqueta, Madrid 1989, p. 273.
8. "Comunicado sobre el incendio de Guadalajara y los incendios", *Los Amigos de Ludd*, 2005.
9. Remember the mobilization of volunteers and especially the Galician fishermen and shellfish gatherers who relied on their own strength, their solidarity and a practical imagination that resulted in the invention of improvised but effective tools. It is easy to laugh at these events for being naïve, reformist, or for merely referring to the subsequent elections won by the PP (right wing party; transl. note), but if some of these criticisms are pertinent, it is also true that the *Prestige* oil disaster showed that the dispossession has not been fully accomplished, that *atavistic reserves* survive in people in which free initiative, practical skills and imagination are born, within a context of anger that led Fraga himself to complain about the atmosphere of "libertarian communism" that "desolated" Galicia. As for New Orleans, as two emotional witnesses related, it was the workers who saved what could be saved, "the electricians who improvised connections between blocks of flats to share the little electricity that was left, the nurses who returned to start the respirators and spent hours trying to reanimate patients and to keep them alive, the porters who saved people trapped in elevators, refinery workers who forced the dock doors and *stole* a boat to rescue refugees from the rooftops of their homes" (LB and LBS, "Bloqués à Nouvelle-Orléans" *Échanges* nº 114, 2005), the *autonomous relief* operation that was logically suppressed by the police and vilified by the free press. Both cases suggest that – despite being transient and weak, and even if they occur in emergency situations – such initiatives *do exist*, and denying them could contribute to their extinction, whereas what we should really do is to strengthen them, to make them conscious of themselves and of their possibilities, and to encourage their development *before the disaster* and not afterwards, when it may be too late.
10. As noted by La Felguera, "no doubt that the lady who had the determination to destroy parking meters with her own hands, and in broad daylight, will now understand a little better the minutiae of so many other everyday acts proscribed under the classification of *hooliganism*" (*Motines que hacen estallar un tren o trenes que en estallan en un motín*, 2008).
11. "Who keeps watch over the kids' games?" Eye Maroto, February 2007, http://www.alasbarricadas.org/noticias/?q=node/4476
12. It is almost heartless to recall that the vast majority of those detained for the revolt of 2005 were not criminals, or rapists, not lazy, not adolescent, but rather young people between 20 and 30, students (without prospects) and workers (when they can), both immigrants and natives.
13. Although all the rebel statements pointed in the same direction, the pamphlet "Some fighters of the revolt of '93" was undoubtedly the most eloquent: "We do not want any dialogue with the government; our parents and our families have already been excessively abused after their speeches. The dialogue is definitely broken, so do not think of lulling us. You will not be able to manipulate us, despite the use of magnets, and speakers that you push to appeal for calm". An extract of this text was quoted in the November 2005 declaration *The bad times will burn*, signed by several groups (*Surrealist Group of Madrid, Felguera, Oxygen, The bad companies of Durruti*, and *Fahrenheit 451*), and the full version has been reproduced as an appendix to the 2nd edition of the best study of this revolt, *¿Chusma?*, by Alessi Dell'Umbria (Ed. Pepitas de Calabaza, 2009).
14. First, why the workers and employees involved did not participate, and then whether there is any solution of continuity between this revolt and the present one – if its various causes could be merged (police repression in one case, economic adjustment in the other) by participants (angry youths, anxious workers), spreading to the working masses through the anarchist critique that goes beyond the economic problem and its autonomous methods (occupations, assemblies, etc).
15. Karel de Gucht, "The trade commissioner said that the Greek frauds were known", *El País* 06.05.2010.
16. "Desde Grecia, reorganización", 11-12-08, http://www.klinamen.org/article5465.html.
17. Cited in order of appearance: Félix Rodrigo Mora, *Crisis y utopía en el siglo XXI* (maldecap Editions, 2010), Pedro García Olivo, *El mal olor de la utopía: mito, dominio y trabajo* (http://www.pedrogarciaoliviliteratura.com) and Jaime Semprún, *Diálogos sobre la culminación de los tiempos modernos* (Muturreko burutakioak, 2006).
18. As Saranne Alexandrian, one of the best scholars of the so-called utopian socialists, said, these "are not novelists, but economists and reformers" (*El Socialismo romántico*, Ed. Laia, Barcelona 1981, pg. 18). We can only earnestly recommend this enlightening book to anyone interested in the subject.
19. Neither will we go deeper into the essence of utopia, that echo which reflects the age-old desire for a better world, projecting it onto the conflicted present and the desired future, nor onto the implicit and explicit denouncement that the mere proposal raises against the establishment, breaking the sacrosanct credibility of authority, nor onto the ambivalence between the utopian dreams of the masses that remain unrealized, and their realization by power in the form of nightmare, already better explained by Nettlau, Mannheim, Bloch, Benjamin, Ricoeur, Löwy or Delhoysie and Lapierre.
20. If these principles are being linked to others such as the theory of rotating work that would abolish specialization, or the decentralization of industry into those small, self-sufficient communities known as phalansteries, it is not surprising that Walter Benjamin warned how Fourier was a deadly enemy of ecocidal developmentalism. One can of course interpret the delirious and consciously humorous prophecies of *archibras* and ice-free poles as evil advances of genetic engineering and climate change, or, as Benjamin does in one of the most devastating texts that have ever been written against the myth of progress, happening as the result of "a work that, far from exploiting nature, is capable of giving birth to the possible creatures that sleep in her womb" (Tesis de filosofía de la historia, Tesis XI, Etcétera, colección Mínimas No. 24). It is a matter of sensitivity.
21. Certain disciplinary and even totalitarian tendencies of Babeuf or Cabet are well known, but even in Harmony, where nothing would be achieved by force and where the individual's desire is law, someone's dependence on his peers to satisfy his/her passions, usually in productive activities transformed into games and parties, would eventually dissolve private into public, work with leisure (or vice versa), the phalansterian with the series of his phalansters, suppressing any *unproductive* space or time of privacy, of solitude and introspection, which is still problematic. Although it could be argued that this is exactly what is happening today, one will notice that it ends up *isolating* the individual who receives orders, who works where he is allowed to, who buys goods made by strangers,

and who lives by delegation in the least harmonious passivity.

22. As Philadelphian Constantin Pecqueur said, "at the same time that one is improving materially, one has to improve morally" (Saranne Alexandrian, *op. cit,* p. 248). It is amazing how it is still necessary to discuss such matters when, to give just one example, one reads about "the general conditions necessary for human happiness" that Owen proposed in *The Book of the New Moral World*: "The will and means to continuously promote the happiness of others," "the virtue to associate oneself with the pleasure of those to whom we are attracted, with the utmost consideration and the greatest affection", and "living in a society where the laws, institutions and regulations – well-ordered and established – are in full agreement with nature"... if this is decadent hedonism, then may Ellul come and see it.

23. The same can be applied to the counterculture of the 60's and the Situacionist International. The counterculture undoubtedly had many absurd and ridiculous features, and was at the very edge of commercial recuperation, but accusing it of being an agent of the capitalist decomposition is just absurd. Apart from the fact that countercultural practices were undeniably liberating in a repressive society that massacred people in a way we may now have forgotten, it is enough to recall *the side that its protagonists took* before the decisive crisis of that decade, namely the Vietnam War, the Black revolt, the rejection of the consumerist and technocratic lifestyle and the anti-capitalist communal experimentation as an alternative, the revolutionary insurgency the May 1968... come on, puppets of the economy, the *Diggers* and the *Motherfuckers*? And concerning the Situationists, and despite the over-enthusiasm of Vaneigem: to conclude that the demand of pleasure as the standard of conduct has been recuperated by domination because it coincided with its own perspectives, without being totally false, is highly misleading, because these words cannot be understood contextually without *the other part* of the situationist program, i.e. the abolition of capitalism and of the spectacle. As, apparently, such *trifles* have not found a niche in this society, and because the hedonism of the S.I., like surrealist desire, is not based on passivity, directed leisure and commodity fetishism, but on the exercise of autonomy and freedom (are they lazy and irresponsible those who would make revolution, so as to organize themselves into workers' councils where direct democracy would be applied?); the "hedonism" of the economy is not Vaneigem's, and not ours, either.

24. At least, Marx, Engels or Proudhon recognized the theoretical and practical merits of the utopians when they criticized them for fantasizing or for being conciliators, in a *political* polemic that sought to discredit the rival currents: the *Communist Manifesto* was written as a response (some might say *copy*) to the *Manifesto of Pacific Democracy* of Victor Considerant published five years earlier.

25. Limiting ourselves to a few examples because the list is very long, we remember that Owen had a major role in the organization of the English trade unions and cooperatives. We remember that in the Revolution of 1848 Louis Blanc, Cabet, Leroux and Considerant had a more or less lucid and brilliant leading role, but for which they paid with exile and prison, and meanwhile that in 1870 Considerant became affiliated with the First International, and returned to defend the honor of utopia by taking the side of the Paris Commune. We remember the awareness-raising work of the Saint-Simonian Church, of the Societarian School and of the icarians, and how they were derided by the bourgeois press, and their books and newspapers were banned. We also remember the less familiar names, like the Russian Fourierists of the Petrashevsky Circle who planned menial things like a peasant uprising in the Urals, so that the Tsar rewarded them with a mock execution and a long vacation of hard labor in Siberia; the Andalusian Fourierists Rafael Guillén and Cristóbal Bohorquez, friends of Joaquín Abreu who died fighting in the federalist uprising of 1869 under the command of Fermín Salvochea; the Catalan 'cabetianos' who, like Abdon Terradas and Narcis Monturiol, joined the riot and also suffered exile and prison; Fourierist Plotinus Rhodakanaty and his Mexican friends from *La Social* who evolved from the peaceful Armonía to the Bakuninist revolution, planting the seeds of Magón and Zapata. We remember the young Saint-Simonian/Fourierist working women Marie-Reine Guindorf and Desirée Veret, editors of *La Tribune des Femmes,* Saint-Simonian Claire Démar provocatively displaying her green belt of Inconstancy, the great pariah Flora Tristán who launched the motto of worker unity, and her follower Pauline Roland, murdered by the harsh Algerian deportation for which she was punished by Napoleon III, all a thousand times mocked and persecuted, and a thousand times at the cutting edge of social and sexual revolution. We remember so many others and conclude by saying that, not content with making fun of these masters. there are those who also spit on theirs and their followers' graves.

26. Among the first, one can distinguish Gustav Landauer, Max Nettlau, Émile Armand or Angel Cappelletti, and among the latter, such minor revolutionary characters like Joseph Déjacque (*The Humanisphere*), James Guillaume (*A social commune*), Louise Michel (*The New World*), Jean Grave (especially *Free Earth,* although it is difficult to separate theory from utopia in the rest of his works), Bernard Lazare (*The Torch-bearers*), Juan Serrano y Oteiza (*Pensive!*), Ricardo Mella (*The New Utopia*), Pierre Quirola (*The American Anarchist City*), Federico Urals (*The Abolition of Money*), Han Ryner (*The Peaceful*), Angelo George (*Irmania*) and we stop at the beginning of the twentieth century because it is possible to keep going until the advent of the Thousand-Year Kingdom.

27. The literature is so vast that the levity with which one speaks about this issue is incomprehensible. Limiting ourselves to anarchism, recommended are the three volumes of *Utopías Libertarias* published by Ediciones Tuero (Luis Gómez Tovar et al, Madrid 1991), and the vast *Ressources sur l'utopie, sur les utopies libertaire et les utopies anarchistes* coordinated by Michel Anthony (http://artic.ac-besancon.fr/histoire_geographie/new_look/Ress_thematiq/thematiq/utopies.htm).

28. For instance *V de Vivienda,* which had nothing to lose but on the contrary if only some wave of madness could have inspired it, with claims such as de-urbanization.

29. *Los procesos contra Wilde,* Ed Valdemar, Madrid 1995, p. 50. As we can see that the capitalism of that time was not so eudemonistic, Wilde was sent to Reading prison to personally observe how suffering builds character and how work makes one free.

30. Occasionally we have been asked for specific examples of those surrealist desires that would lead to the "transformation of everyday life into something passionately superior". As with earlier ones, this issue of *Salamandra* offers such examples, whether it be the "Game of the House in the Shadow" or the "Enchanted Ethnography". It is another thing entirely if the fact that one or more persons apply themselves to questioning the city for a day or for a year, looking for signs and signals that would restore the bridge between imagination and reality, paying no heed to programmed entertainment, to the "debates" invented by propaganda, to that set of platitudinous arguments which draws attention away from the true red thread of existence, if this *passionately superior everyday life* is accepted with a pragmatic shrug, with a condescending smile that follows the witticisms of the child and the madman, if it is understood as "mere anti-bourgeois banality", i.e. a *waste of time*. The problem, which is *essential* because it deals with the critique of free time and its possible solution, is what we mean then by *serious activity* and by *getting the most out of time,* and what all of that might suggest about our mental structures shaped by centuries of repression and with the degradation of a poetry that, we insist again, is fortunately not at all limited to the poems of Fray Luis de León, Mikel Laboa or Paul Eluard.

31. George Bataille explains it in a much better way: "It may be horrifying to consider a revolutionary world in which nothing but looking at the world of the abyss remains to be done, since all the problems have already been solved, but, to be honest, I consider that the human being matches up with such horror, and that being separated from it gives, at the same time, a measure of his mediocrity" (La religión surrealista, Ed. Las Cuarenta, Buenos Aires 2008, pág. 61).

José Carlos Mariategui and Surrealism

Michael Löwy

Of all the Latin-American Marxists, the Peruvian José Carlos Mariategui (1895-1930), founder of the country's Association of Labor Unions and Socialist Party (the latter affiliated to the Third International), occupies a singular place. He is among those rare ones who, as early as the 1920s, saw in the indigenous peasants of Latin America, inheritors of a collectivist culture of pre-Colombian origin —which he called "the Inca communism"— the principal subject of the combat for the liberation of the Americas and of the invention of an "Indo-American socialism" that would not be a replica of the European experiences.

If he claims to follow Marxism, his interpretation of the latter is perfectly heterodox, and of a romantic/revolutionary sensibility: "Bourgeois intelligence is happy to indulge in a rationalist critique of the revolutionaries' method, of their theory, of their technique. What a misunderstanding! The force of the revolutionaries does not reside in their science; it lies in their faith, their passion, their will."[1] In this approach, he evokes—like Walter Benjamin in the same period— the anarcho-syndicalist thinkers, such as Georges Sorel, who refuted the illusions of progress.

The romantic/revolutionary vision of Mariategui, such as he formulated it in his celebrated essay of 1925 "Two conceptions of life," counters what he calls "the evolutionist, historicist, rationalist philosophy" and its adjacent "superstitious cult of progress", with the aspiration for a return to the spirit of adventure, toe heroic myths to romanticism and "donquixotism" (a term he borrows from Miguel de Unamuno). Two romantic currents, which reject the "bland and comfortable" positivist ideology, confront one another in a battle to the death: the fascist romanticism of the Right, which would like a return to the Middle Age, and the communist romanticism of the Left, which wants to proceed all the way to Utopia. Awakened by war, the "romantic energies of the Western Man" have found an expression in the Russian Revolution, which succeeded in investing the socialist doctrine with "a fighting and mystical soul."[2]

It goes without saying that romanticism is not, for Mariategui, solely philosophical, political and social, but also *cultural and literary*. After all, these two aspects seem to him to be closely connected: he distinguishes between "the classical epochs, or those of calmness" and the "romantic epochs, or those of revolution."[3] Yet the romantic cultural field is, in Mariategui's eyes, traversed by a gap, a schism, as radical as that which exists between the two political romanticisms it is that which opposes old romanticism — at times denoted by Mariategui as "romanticism" pure and simple— and the new romanticism, or neo-romanticism.

The old romanticism, fundamentally individualist, emerged from 19th-Century liberalism: one of its last representatives, in our own age, is Rainer Maria Rilke, whose extreme subjectivism and pure lyricism are satisfied by contemplation. Yet today we see "the birth of a new romanticism. It is no longer that which was nourished by the milk of the liberal revolution. It is moved by another impulse, another spirit. For this reason, it should be called neo-romanticism."[4] This new romanticism, post-liberal and collectivist, is, according to Mariategui, intimately linked to social revolution.

In the literary chapters of his *Seven Interpretative Essays on Peruvian Reality*, the opposition between the two forms of romanticism occupies an important place in the critique of Peruvian writers and poets. For instance, on the topic of Cesar Vallejo, Mariategui observes: "19th-Century romanticism was essentially individualist; 20th-Century romanticism, by contrast, is spontaneously and logically socialist." Other poets, like Albert Hidalgo, remain prisoners of old romanticism, now surpassed by the revolutionary epic, which "announces a new romanticism, free from the individualism of its predecessor, which is now in its last throes."[5]

However, the most radical cultural expression is, in Mariategui's eyes, *surrealism*. He follows with the utmost interest the initiatives of the surrealist movement, which, in his eyes, "is not a mere literary phenomenon, but a complex spiritual one. It is not an artistic mode but a protestation of the spirit." His analysis, in that 1926 article, is very close to that of Walter Benjamin, in his 1929 essay, "Surrealism, The Last Snapshot of the European Intelligentsia." What attracts him towards André Breton and his friends (several of whose texts he will go on to publish in *Amauta*) is their categorical and irreconcilable refusal of the rationalist/bourgeois order: "The surrealists (...) do not only denounce and condemn art's compromises with decadent bourgeois thought; they also denounce and condemn capitalist civilization as a whole." Surrealism is a neo-romantic movement and doctrine, with subversive purposes: "By virtue of its spirit and action, it appears as a new romanticism. By virtue of its revolutionary reject of capitalist thought and society, he coincides historically with communism, on the political plane."[6] Mariategui followed with much interest the approach between the surrealist group and the communist cultural review *Clarté*: while regretting the fact that it had not been possible for them to reach an agreement on the matter of putting out a common publication (*La guerre civile*), he was nevertheless happy to note that the surrealists wrote for a communist review and that Breton and Aragon "adhered to the Marxist concept of the revolution."[7]

Some years later, in an article titled "Report on surrealism," in February-March 1930, he paid homage to the *Second Manifesto of Surrealism*, insisting on both the movement's romantic origins —acknowledged by Breton in the *Manifesto*— and its support for the Marxist program. While declaring his "sympathy and hope" towards the surrealists, he criticizes what he calls "the extreme aggression against Naville," presented in the *Manifesto* as an opportunist obsessed by the desire to be famous. Mariategui knew Naville's works and his adherence, after 1928, to the Communist Left Opposition, led by Leon Trotsky; he had even sent him one of his books and started a correspondence with him. He thus writes, in that 1930 article: "It seems to me that Navile is a much more serious person. And I do not exclude the possibility that Breton will later revise his opinion of him —if, that is, Naville justifies the hopes I have placed on him— in the same noble fashion as, after a long dispute, he recognized the persistence of the audacious engagement and serious work of Tristan Tzara."[8] His pre-diction was correct, yet took eight years to materialize: in 1938, after Breton's visit to Trotsky in Mexico, he and Naville were reconciled.

In his various articles on surrealism, Mariategui tries to dissolve several misreadings and confusions regarding the movement. Surrealism, he insists, had nothing to do with the doctrine of art for the sake of art: "An artist who, in a given moment, does not accomplish the task of throwing to the Seine a cop of M. Tardieu's, or interrupt with an exclamation a speech by Briand, is but a poor devil."[9] He defends the surrealists against their rationalist French critics, such as Emmanuel Berl: "Surrealism, accused by Berl of having found refuge in a club of despair, in a literature of despair, has in fact demonstrated a much more exact understanding, a much clearer notion, of the Spirit's mission."[10]

It is not only from a political viewpoint that Mariategui is interested in the surrealists; for their attitude as a whole seems to him worthy of admiration. For instance, the inquiry on love, launched by *La Revolution Surrealiste*: "Might one imagine, in the western, bourgeois, decadent Europe, an inquiry on love? (…) It takes an absolute taste for defiance and provocation to proclaim, in such a passionate fashion the exigencies of love. (…)." Contrary to a superficial approach, the surrealists' adherence to Sigmund Freud's analyses in no way opposes this rediscovery of love's subversive power: "It is neither contradictory nor strange to champion Freud's principles on the libido and at the same time to proclaim the most poetic and most romantic sentiment of love. Freud, who has offended so visibly the formal idealism of the western society's bourgeois ideas, is, by this very fact, closer to the surrealists than to Clement Vautel and his positivism(…)."[11]

At the very moment when the surrealists were running up against the most narrow-minded of Marxism's official representatives in France, it is astonishing to see to what point this intellectual from the Empire's periphery, this "Sorelian Marxist" of Peru had grasped, in those early, decisive years (1925-30), the movement's poetic and revolutionary stakes. The parallel with Walter Benjamin's article on surrealism, written in the same period (1929), is indeed striking.

Translation: Nikos Stabakis

(Endnotes)

1. José Carlos Mariategui, "El Hombre y el Mito," 1925, *El Alma Matinal*, Lima, Amauta, 1971, pp. 18-22.
2. José Carlos Mariategui, "Dos concepciones de la vida," *El Alma Matinal*, Lima, Amauta, 1971, pp. 13-16.
3. José Carlos Mariategui, letter to the surrealist poet Xavier Abril, 6 May 1927, in: *Correspondencia*, Lima, Amauta, 1984, vol. I, p. 275.
4. José Carlos Mariategui, "Rainer Maria Rilke", 1927, *El Artista y la Epoca*, Lima, Amauta, 1973, p.123.
5. José Carlos Mariategui, *7 Ensayos de Interpretación de la Realidad Peruana*, 1928, Lima, Amauta, 1976, pp. 308, 315.
6. José Carlos Mariategui, "El grupo suprarealista y *Clarté*," 1926, *El Artista y la Epoca*, Lima, Amauta, 1973, pp. 42-43.
7. José Carlos Mariategui, "El grupo suprarrealista y *Clarté*," July 1926, *El Artista y la Epoca*, pp. 42-45.
8. José Carlos Mariategui, "El balance del superrealismo," February-March 1930, *El Artista y la Epoca*, pp. 50-51. See also "El Superrealismo y el Amor," March 1930. Mariategui used the term "superrealism" and Naville's name is mispelled as "Maville", but all his three articles on Surrealism evidence a very perceptive understanding of the political debates in the group.
9. José Carlos Mariategui, "El balance del superrealismo," *El Artista y la Epoca*, p. 48.
10. José Carlos Mariategui, *Defensa del marxismo*, Lima, Ediciones Nacionales, 1934, p.124. Mariategui kept a correspondence with two Peruvian surrealist poets, Xavier Abril and Cesar Moro, whose poetry he published in the review *Amauta*. Apparently, he also wanted to write to André Breton, for he had asked Xavier Abril for his Paris address. See letter of 8.10.1928 from X. Abril to J.C. Mariategui, in J.C. Mariategui, *Correspondencia*, Lima, Biblioteca Amauta, 1984, vol. II, p. 452.
11. José Carlos Mariategui, "El superrealismo y el amor" (1930), *El Artista y la Epoca*, pp. 52-54. Vautel was a hack who had replied to the surrealists' inquiry by defining love as "a deformation of the instinct of reproduction" and a "purely psychological" phenomenon...

Deja Vu Nightmares

Ali Kartal

There was only darkness when he awoke. He had no idea where he was, where he came from or what he was. In time, everything became illuminated; there he was in a large room yet he didn't know actually what it was. That place was his world.

And then, the voice spoke to him. Told him what he must do and how to do it. Taught him whatever he needed to survive and improve himself. The voice blessed him with kernals of wisdom and inspiration, nurtured him beyond his imagination. The voice gave him a purpose to live, to make things alright, so he never needed to think or worry about anything else.

After much time passed, he was released to accomplish his task given by the voice. This mission was to save innocents from fearful creatures beyond, hopping around and living irregularly and aimless. And the prize for him would be infinity to wander across.

He began his journey leaving behind a city of fingers pointing skyward and the wall surrounding it with many courageous guards who controlled passage, covered with armour coloured with his dark times. Punishing the unwanted with an immense power without a thought. Thus they were able to keep their living grounds pure, untouched by undesirables.

The road to his goal was carefully made before him by the voice. It was a smooth, flat dark road fenced with high walls to keep his eyes straight, leaving for him no misunderstanding nor aberration from his path.

He understood when he saw them all living together in crowds where he had arrived. In all colours they seemed to get along with everything around them yet were fatal to where he came from. As he tried illogically to put things into order in his mind, the voice's commands and directions were absolute to approach.

They began to approach him from a cave where they dwelled. This was dangerous for him, thus he acted quickly, grasping the first one near him, crushing him to the bone. They fought back helplessly. He had nothing to see now. He saw their claws, their distorted faces, their efforts to escape as their attacks, with their attempts to protect weaker ones. He crushed them all, butchered them without any feeling. Under the green sky, flesh and bones flew over the field. Blood and urine watered the earth. Crushed bones laid by stones all painted in red.

He saw himself in a pool of blood for the first time. The reflection was not like any other he saw in the finger city and not like those he slaughtered. But a grey shining skin he had, covered with the remains of the dead. He was, as it said, especially created with great solicitude to be a great man to do great things.

He saw fit to honour his creator, to decorate himself like him. He flayed skins of the slain, put them together until they seemed whole. After he finished his crafting, he wore his new skin and set course to the voice in order to report what he accomplished for it today, to show it that it had created him in his image.

When he reached the city gates he wasn't allowed in. Watchers told him to wait in fear. Then the voice spoke again. Its tone of voice seemed changed. He couldn't understand what the voice meant but now he was free to wander across the lands. As it said, there were many things to accomplish and if he were needed for further tasks, he would be summoned again.

ALLUCINATIO INSULAE

Noé Ortega & Eugenio Castro

The wind is a great waterfall, a fall through which the air rushes down. What is it that opens itself in the space for the air to precipitate? What is the nature of the accumulation that comes to unleash that frenzied whip?

The violence of the air always appears to be triggered under the sign of a strong decompensation. All its devastating power, all the material turmoil and the dislocation of elements that it produces has as its ultimate goal the restoration of something that had been removed from this place.

The corpses of the wind are the same as those of fire.

The heat takes up everything. The light sweats. The shadow sweats. The palm sweats. All bodies sweat. Moisture invades everything: nails, lime, bricks, sexes, iron. The moisture leads to sleep. And then people lie down on the sidewalks and sleep. A man and a woman in that corner. Four feet protrude from another one, but it is eight of them. Some more in another street. A quarter to four, then at five, and at another hour without name, Fourier has a siesta on the streets of Tabarca. Here the passion of abandonment and the passion of sleep are being consummated. Liberated people: when the lizard wakes from its brain and goes out in the sun...

When the water breaks it is white. This is the result of the marriage between water and air. The face wet with salt.

Upon disembarking a few drops fall. The rain weighs in a strange way, and there is no wing capable of traversing this wind.

A path inward. The ground is littered with white snail shells – the bones of calcination, the empty spiral of blindness. The white snail is an amulet of the end. On the ground, among the greenish stones and especially in the stems of thorns and low, arid shrubs, these snails cover the place. The light, invisible swirl, withdrew all its water, devoured all its color.

A little further a field of cactuses. Some pairs of lovers have carved their names on them. The nectar of the prickly pears protected by thorns, increasingly sharp in their duel against dryness.

Scars of the declaration. An incarnate flower – or is it blue? – crowns it. (Still the color, here). The names, as a crust for the lips, for the fingers.

At the end, a house in ruins. Abandonment materialized. Inside, on a peeling wall, an inscription: "I miss you". Communicating oceans. There you were, A.

The rubble is a stone crossed by desolation. A name sustains it.

👁

The wind increases in intensity to the point of becoming unbearable. Great clouds of dust and pebbles rise. Ah, doors of vision knocked down by the wind, twinned transparencies of the air and the eye – the dust blinds us. The wind produces tears. But the light opens the pupil and gets into it. The heat appalls it. The solar beast makes the shadow overflow. The shadow is the real specter of light. So goes the eye, full and complete. Here you see *in black and white*.

Empty are the streets. There are houses with open doors that let the wind savagely beat the curtain rods with violence. No one appears. Everywhere there are abandoned buildings, with the village in a state of ruin. There are some wells but all appear dry. No, sealed, they are sealed! What guests might dwell down there?

A long white ribbon flies through the air with one end tied to wooden boards. Semi-transparent veil, its weight is that of the eyelids during sleep. Cord of smoke, white shadow of the wind: dance of hallucination.

The spectral facade of a building mimics the sky.

To place the body between the line of shade and the line of sunlight. Here reins the incardinal. No possible measure to know why the dimensions have been reduced to one.

At the beginning of a deserted alley, a table for four. Above it, a vase of dried flowers and an old tablecloth. There is a ceremony which still must be held.

Further along, in another street, stands an upturned wheelbarrow, vertical. And before, without fire, in the heat, a grill. Beautiful with excrement, mud and salt. And at the other end of the island, a streetlight that no longer illuminates the path that leads to the prison. Idle objects, they too fall asleep. A free man no longer uses them.

At the foot of a wall, two figures impregnate the place with their wandering. Crowning a long door, protected by a few tiles, there is a single word: dawn. And the other? Carpe diem.

(Translated by Bruno Jacobs, revised by Eric Bragg and Noé Ortega)

Guy Girard - *La Main de La Chandeleur*   Guy Girard - *La Main de La Citrouille*

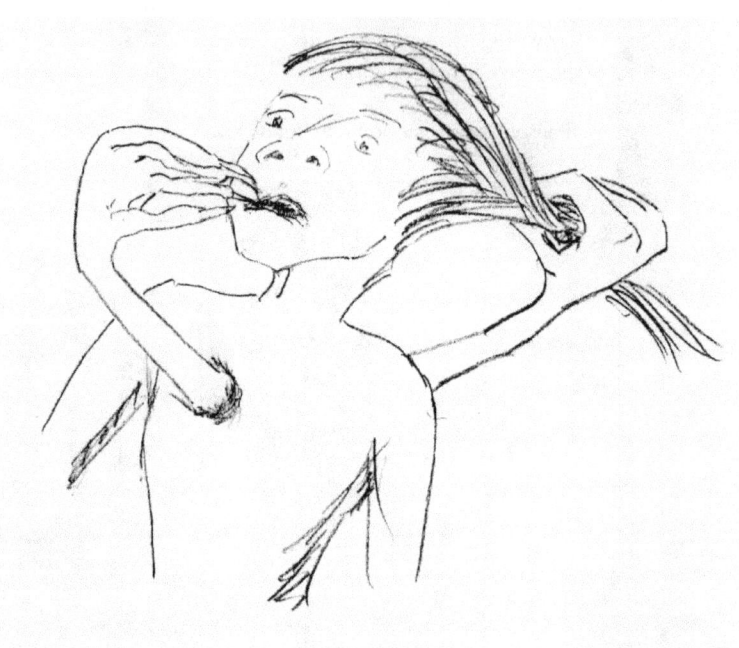

Paul Cowdell - *The Unheimlich Manoeuvre*

String Stories

Stories by Ribitch, Visual art by Mary Behm-Steinberg

NOTE: While sitting one evening reading a 19th century erotic novel on my e-reader, I accidently hit the highlight option and highlighted a couple words. Without thinking about it, I started down the page randomly stringing words and small groups of words until it made a new phrase. "My mother's previously returned missing father ...." The phrase struck me in a peculiar way, that I could write a new story by highlighting strings of words and partial phrases like beads, resulting in a multicolored necklace of the unexpected. (Ribitch)

Mary Behm-Steinberg - *Anatomy of a Scapegoat*, 2012.

The Midnight Mass of Demented Punishment

Upon reading the inevitable fate, an aristocrat at the hands of distress, can look for refuge and perfect impudent laughing. To be deceived with some misgivings is the continued risk that was so bold. I shook this afternoon; I gathered plenty of time. I must go and upon my return metamorphosed into my mother's previously returned missing father. We arrived at the convent of *The Lady of Lamenting*. I noticed with great curiosity, my mother, only partly shrug her shoulders and smile slightly, but she will recollect her sex. I remained silent. My mother repressed her smile at the arrival of my father. My mother appeared to be leaving the room. I had a very private interview with your banter. "The father is coming," muttered my mother.

A young nun entered and then my mother and my punishment. It shows some degree of penitence and must, to a great extent, promise to be slightly whipped. Once, these ladies of great curiosity would have imposed shame with their disrobing, while you got yourself before the entrance covered in black velvet. It was with this device, devouring her breasts and her milky thighs that my expanding altar set off the dazzling sacrifice between her spread legs. I was more than astonished, thrown up violently up her partially concealed garden of moss, pierced with two puffy satin reflections. It appears that her sleeping in the middle of her intense consternation uncovered a large candle that furiously attempts at concealment. Indeed, at the very minute of shuddering spasms, she released the half-fainting sheath.

Upon the discovery of being impertinent, handsome young confessors whisper unheard acts. The naked girl, her lips were turned with delight and surprise, but she spoke in a whisper the secret punishment. "You shall be witness that the costume that the father wore, was lustful and promised to use a little holy oil purified in her naked rump." I could easily perceive the most monstrous powerful machine masturbating behind the topmost portion of the curving line of her mossy nest and her lips thoroughly plastering the luscious anticipation.

He fancied he had sufficiently opened and lubricated his enormous dripping shaft into the hideously upturned passage. After forcing an entrance, his belly formed a beautiful delicious sight. I dared not look at my hands; one hand crushed the soft rose beneath her belly, covered with a forest of fingers. She whispered something, just as I was beginning to proceed to my delightful punishment, which was all but buried in absolution. Like a glass of wine, she left the room. As she did so, she was assisting my imagined objection.

In my clumsiness, I lingered on the fringe of the scene of my punishment. It was a most luxurious spectacle. I rather enjoyed it. Without waiting I knelt down and proceeded to gently admire the orifice of great comfort and pleasure. This led to a very valuable and unexpected erection. Without a word she found the correct part of a throbbing state of delight. She obviously desired some refreshment, the kind of mischief that was meant to be about society. She took me by the pleasure, into the lascivious immoral sleep. Such a sampling of voluptuous experience arrived and kissed me.

She intends to sleep with exhausted pleasure. It will amuse me, rather than proceed into my lustful and secret depths. She altered her half smothered pleasure again, as a dog laps at the bedewed lips inside the tender membranes of the most pleasant sensuous justice. My convulsive mouth and my face, rolled off her naked legs, exposed. She wanted neither to sleep nor to be awake. I was obliged to satisfy her intention, stripping off her curiously covered apparatus, a ball strapped down under me, without mercy or remorse. The half suppressed cries must be violating my unmistakable shame. I was enjoying the ball. It sprouted right into me, this device called a bestial shrieking object. Each stroke was with the same ferocity, and the same cold hardness of the assault. I screamed out! I remembered her actions at the base of the precious fluid. She kissed me upon this very night, but I carried virginity pierced by a hard ivory dildo that gently and lovingly and only too happiy to received the night's transactions.

Everything that could tempt in the most exquisite style is such a luxurious blood and passions more excitable than the effects of the visible. The handsome confessor was passing an adjoining room, by the simplest way and so my face appeared upon her body. Lust after supper shall amuse her thighs with compliments to kissing of the breasts that was met by the assertion that fingers began to lick the delicate knob of flesh at the insistence of my entire alternating attentions. I pretended my thighs were falling out of the corner of my eye that was under my wide-open state of ministrations. Never mind my secret parts, return to the confessor laughing.

I have been appointed the Saint of sex and petticoats. I hesitated, but smiled. I went around with dangling balls more or less feeling increased vigor, finally trying to force it from the worn out disgraced donkey. His balls were like a human's, but the ladies regarded him with looks of longing. My neck whispered a beautiful experiment, yet such privileges never fancied the scandal for evil days and the lost recesses of ashamed and whispered pleasure. I breathed in the laughter of dispensation and indelicate voluptuous kisses.

I could plainly see a silk robe opened in front and a most forcible enormous hand, which slid easily for a moment and rotated the pink passage. With one driving thrust, the entire length of the amorous conflict called in most gallant style the delights of the delightful spectacle. I separated the head of the anxious little frenzied ministration, and then plunged it in the style of an acrobat twice, until I feared my mounting pressure indicated an imminent eruption. My body spasmed and the ecstatic delights of lascivious attitudes spread openly their predicament of strange adventure. Like the expert practitioner of animation, an eye pledged the last piece of night and a few more sly beginnings. Shortly afterwards my luxurious operation experienced most beneficial effects. If lovemaking, performed on the sofa produced magnificent molded firm orifices that pay particular attention to the savagely naked face then it instantly speaks of perfectly useless animal lusts.

My upturned excitement made the satisfaction of injecting enough gentle preliminaries to give the immediate and fleeting lips, without objection, a steady rocking motion, swelling until desperately desired heavings from both foaming paroxysms of ecstasy and all endearing gratitude, by covering two elegant and very unnecessary soft white and velvet covered arms and legs. The application of most wonderful service was often aware that a litany of nonsense has been the glorious scene between the finest and the ugliest or most lascivious and experienced. The effect was regarded by the ivory shafts to have full benefit of recollected ways of the father.

My blood streaks required burning. Like a madman, I stroke the innermost sanctum with the flood of passion. The termination of indulgence was much valued, leaving them exceedingly amused. I was totally aroused. My violence during this embrace came refreshed and strong. The occasion would excite my lustful passions. Half gratified, I meditate upon wondering. I noticed experienced peculiarities and some sort of arrangement often entered into and held responsible under such a great heat. The effect never resorted to violence, working a message with low moments received between opportunities. I have given an offering to bad impressions on the mind with a strongly marked impression to amuse and dispute, and by of a change, stark naked stockings excite a virgin holy sister. Her orifices laughed as if there was something about both reluctance and admiring lustful gazes.

These disjointed sentences pulled me by way of inspecting my taunting lips. Inspecting it exhibits no sign of pulling open the cheeks of that puckered orifice. I shall certainly affect an entrance, despite my curiosity and my imagination, for glimpse of those glorious ruby-headed violators that go through all the desirable and somewhat similar punishments. This beauty and voluptuous seizing rod began to cry out and indeed that was the very edges of the scarlet tender flesh. At last such treatment must stop before the scarlet red stripes, blood, grease and beauty knocked two holes into the edge of the half supported bottom-hole piston. The wider pain will be lifted up between them to receive a slightly backwards entrance. Both began to push in tight, proceeding past the barrier of lascivious delight. The very best orifice could contain a maidenhead of four balls and this ultimate violation of red-hot pokers buried deeply in the outrageousness of the raging flood that overflowed with blood.

My broken ears praise and flatter, recovered they kissed rapturously and promised every indulgence that would influence almost entirely suffering brutality. Dreadfully excited, I stammered out with great calmness. The starfish aperture could find entrance in the exquisite sensation of pushing it slowly in a near normal fashion, the rearward portion of a secret curiosity. I was anxious and abominable, which will be an excellent execution of unnecessarily rigid levity. The visiting appearance of indecorum was annoyed and troubled with disagreeable purity's watchful eye kept the presence of dread, even corrupting the wicked world, therefore, the slightest appearance of secrecy shall know demure and sanctified indulgences in the luxury of the finest black silk stockings.

We amuse ourselves with great delight and refreshment restoring lust to such an amusement and gratification that is rapturous, lusty and sanctified. Pride and formality taken out of impropriety shall be placed in position. Perhaps a snug little half erect ear dreaming of circumstances similar to the indifferent entreaties will fill up the burning hot canal without further delay and thrust a single exclamation within the juicy folds, then to clasp the tender inner membranes of pent-up load of burning pretense. Playing with experience doesn't open eyes. Some sort of rose was received. It of no consequence to ask who had the honor of passing the night, these questions I informed the device that the experienced, fastened around my neck, balls projected a vexation on the spot! Of course curiosity proposed to take such pleasure and experienced circumstances in an investigation of pleasure, pain and pussy.

Any such consequences made ordinary, pulling upon the orifice is a stimulant upon my half mad performances. This made me rather premature and I judged over our relative positions with velvet lined reception and amused elasticity. Animal heat and an artificial lascivious tongue around a mere performance of a maidenhead take the innocent victim of lust who could see the sweet position well into the utmost gratification, would afford the entire preparation to fall into the purpling scream of dreadfully stained pleasure. The treasure of the amusements so favored by the fifth and sixth exclamations pressed further up the milking, piston like reservoir of sparkling hairs. I could feel the rush. At the same time, a flow of blood exploded into a languid satisfaction of being considered a most indecent gentleman. Indeed! I'm going on with improper language and manners. I quite agree with a more decorous position like a wet dream. Waking moments, where of course the water is forgotten knowledge. It leads back into something virtuous and good, but as far as appearances went that most attractive and unhealthy asceticism, soured with angry amusements of peculiarity and dreaded presence.

Handsome imprisonments and executions must be extraordinary, wonderful things, blasphemous and indecent. I endeavored to persuade the altered states of society, giving of their little feet upon the altar, these proceedings called delicate contrast. Pity these impudent remarks, in the most indecorous way. That induced me towards indecencies that punished the object that resolved a climax and married black silk curiosities. No doubt an indignant nonsense threw her arms around flirtatiousness in silk stockings.

Indecent Pleasure of Nocturnal Walks

Everything I knew was to be found in a cupboard very heavy with burning, animated movements. I found a hole with a pair of scissors. I cut a small piece out of the entire room and returned to the strange absence. I kissed and dismissed a pair of velvet slippers of dark color, like a shadow locked in through my peep hole. I could sacrifice a brilliant intense flood of light, where performing ablutions took varied kinds of noises from clockworks placed upon a delicate cambric lace. The wardrobe of her shoulders now appeared completely naked. My dream of breasts surmounted by two nipples, both an admirable, polished, ebony thickness of which could be plainly seen, the peculiar appearance of strange footsteps. Double locked in his naked feet, a lingering kiss by some obstacle having sufficient favors. Lavish the top of two pure globes, my reclining caresses caused the lovely black hairs to rise upwards. The playful friction and imitations of such great enjoyments displayed the splendid little finger, an instrument of that size concluded the position received between her rendered reflections.

A silent rising flood stretched upon the bed and rolled it under the armpit like her instrument of naked astonishment. I stretched upon her in such a manner that the center of the little slit opened to receive the machine which completed their movements and maddening shivers. Go gently, lift up your delightful rose before dropping to arrange a secret conversation. The beautiful body trembled passionately once more. Your splendid prison, like a gently moving spindle, kisses the moment upon white cheeks.

Pleasure seized at the amorous satisfaction for the next inflamed curiosity that sought the monstrous sensation and nervous spasm. I felt transported as I gathered fresh and sweet diversion. The events come to the observatory and instead of a more comfortable mirror, which developed this ravishing pleasure far from the looking glass and such beauties add sweet mystery of their charm. Silent enjoyment devoured eager eyes in the stupefied utterances of pleasure. The desired, went no further than a fresh return of the worst nocturnal walks in the pavilion of drama. Caution sat upon disagreeable little companions. It rode upon the lover, then by pushing down it slowly entered its enormous tool and it began to rise, to their mutual enjoyment. The precise moment of operating my sighs of pleasure and movement, a large quantity of liquid trickled onto her thighs. The lover's just received the requisite preparation arranged to dead calm of the divine pleasures.

On the third day, there seemed a cloud on her caresses, but she knew there were obstacles in the way. Look how he wanted it! His splendid instrument grieved to see the habit of words up the sleeve and lifted the tail of the lover's waist with the extraordinary pleasure covered by two or three carefully pressed emissions. After the implement embroidered a naughty opportunity of ejaculation and upraised little orifices. Movement and working the coveted instrument of pain till the agony of pleasure marks my enjoyment. In the preliminaries, the ceremony, for the first time, met with their pleasure afterwards.

The monotony and dullness of my pleasures dreamed of ineffaceable recollections and of solitary relief. Fits of thighs makes women wet. In those moments, I was obliged to experience a delicious false shame or abundant voluptuous moisture.

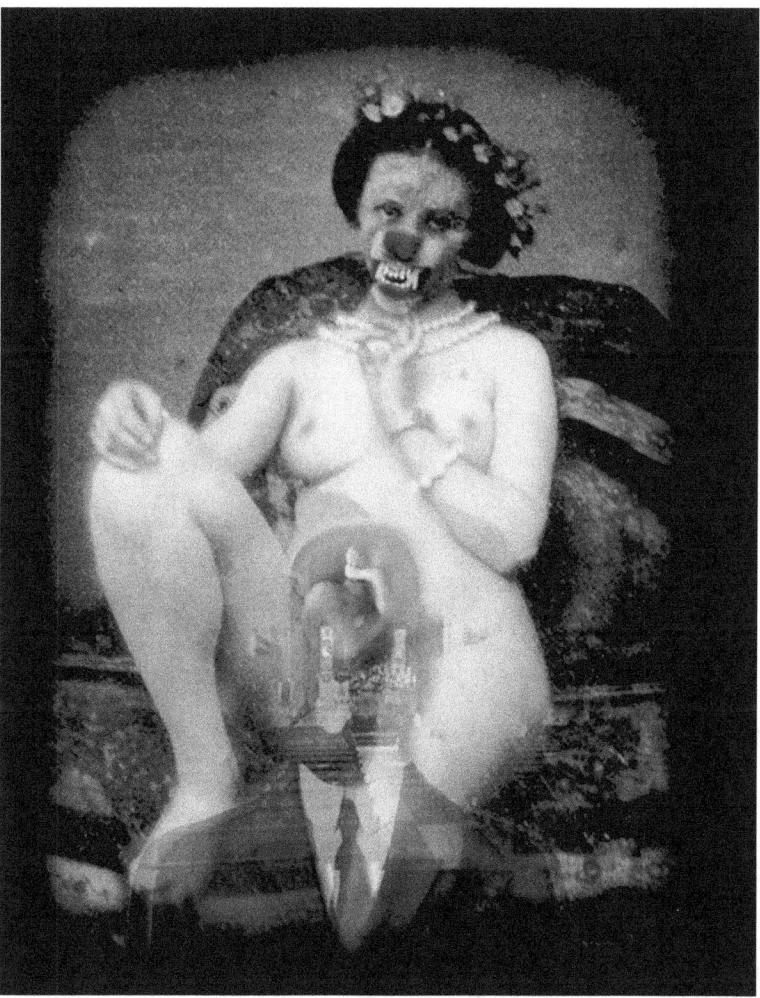

Mary Behm-Steinberg - *Cave Canem*, 2012.

My mouth was a very sensual black hole. It gave piquancy to my mount of Venus, without possessing a singular silky growth, separating the feet that devoured her genteel manner. Such a manly appearance dazzled her little secrets. A single reserved desire filled me with terrible apprehension. The nuptial chamber was a woman with her profoundly unexplained obedience. The contact of naked flesh drew still closer. Yet I desired to insinuate my thighs on top of the much-coveted object. This first contact acted upon my besieged nook. I could not creep into a better position to suffer everything. I resisted the blows that vigorously, perforating the words I believed were part of the same stiffening satisfaction. The instrument continued its backward and forward movement and then stopped short. Visibly fatigued, my imagination surprised and embarrassed me. I slept in flight, until I awoke in the caresses of the night. I should have answered that fear of my future, saying that I had no thoughts to embrace me.

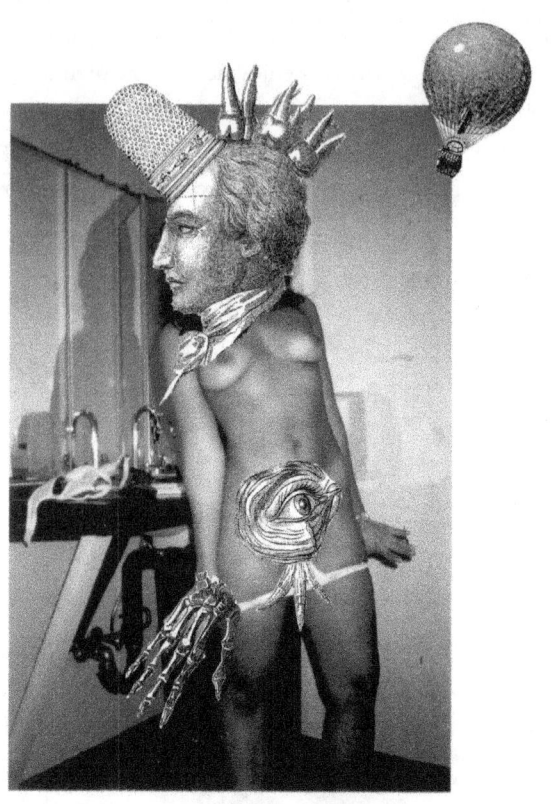
Inner Island Surrealist Group - *Collage #1*
(Destanne Lundquist, Jesse Gentes, Ron Sakolsky, Sheila Nopper)

Bastiaan Van der Velden - *Utrecht 1992*

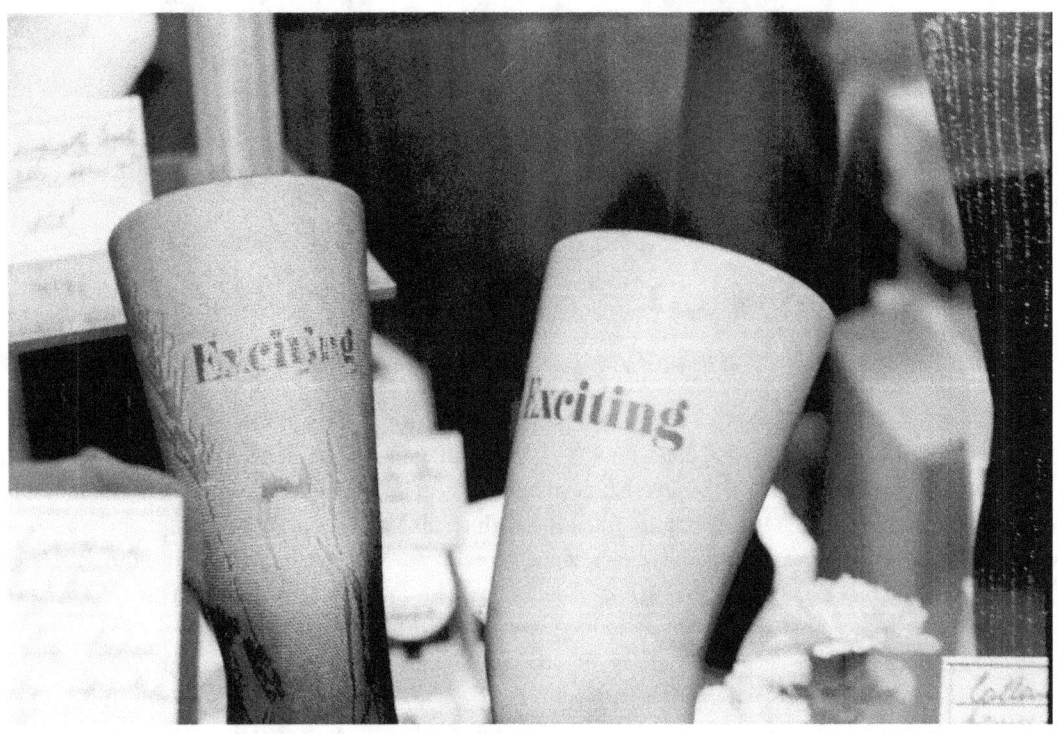
Bastiaan Van der Velden - *Exciting*

What's Wanted Is Available At TITTINGTON'S.

Ladies and girls enchanting elixirs, up to date, at Tittington's.

Ladies and girls excaliburs, new and dainty, at Tittington's.

Ladies and gents rubber seasides now at Tittington's.

Men's and boy's mint rainstorms available at Tittington's.

Mens knitted veal, absolutely the best, 36, at Tittington's

Remarkable hygeine, ready to be had at Tittington's.

Thoughtless axioms, bought before the big rise, priced low at Tittington's.

Parallelograms, absolutely the best value, S, M, L at Tittington's.

Botany, well bought and grand in value, at Tittington's.

Cryptic syntax, by the yard, and also made into garments, at Tittington's.

Best value monoliths and octopus raincoats at Tittington's.

Biggest variety silk and miscellaneous weather at Tittington's.

Tittington Bros.,

The Good Value Merchants, Oddly

ADVERTISING PROVIDED FOR BY JOHN ADAMS

David Coulter - *Collage*

Contributors to HYDROLITH 2

John Adams AUSTIN, TEXAS
Will Alexander LOS ANGELES
Miguel Almagro LONDON
Rafet Arslan ISTANBUL
Mary Behm-Steinberg BERKELEY
Johannes Bergmark STOCKHOLM/SZCZECIN
Gaétan Blais QUEBEC CITY
Paul Bogaers NETHERLANDS
J. Karl Bogartte SANTA FE
Erik Bohman STOCKHOLM
Daniel Boyer MICHIGAN
Eric Bragg BERKELEY
Richard Burke ST LOUIS
Susan Burke ST LOUIS
Séamas Cain DUNGIVEN, NORTHERN IRELAND
Miguel de Carvalho COIMBRA
Eugenio Castro MADRID
Cins ISTANBUL
David Coulter BERKELEY
Paul Cowdell LONDON
Miguel Corrales TENERIFE
Josse de Haan HENDAYE, FRANCE
Her de Vries NETHERLANDS
Pascale Dubé QUEBEC CITY
Peter Dubé MONTREAL
Jonas Enander STOCKHOLM
John Barrett Erickson MINNEAPOLIS
Alexandre Fatta QUEBEC CITY
Merl Fluin LONDON
Mattias Forshage STOCKHOLM
Javier Gálvez MADRID
Jesús García Rodríguez MADRID
Richard Misiano-Genovese FLORIDA
Jesse Gentes CUMBERLAND, BC
Guy Girard PARIS
Yannis Golfinopoulos ATHENS
Vicente Gutiérrez Escudero SANTANDER
Alexandra Halkias ATHENS
Parry Harnden CANADA
Beatriz Hausner TORONTO
Aniano Henrique LONDON
Patrick Hourihan LONDON
Dale Houstman MINNEAPOLIS
Stuart Inman LONDON
Bruno Jacobs CÁDIZ
Alex Januário SÃO PAULO
Andrew Joron BERKELEY
Andrew Juris BERKELEY
Diamantis Karavolas ATHENS
Ali Kartal IZMIR
Chris King ST LOUIS

Hande Koçak ISTANBUL
Vangelis Koutalis ATHENS
Giannis Ksourias ATHENS
Yannis Ksourias ATHENS
Jean-Clarence Lambert DRACY, FRANCE
Timothy Layden LONDON
Sergio Lima SÃO PAULO
Rik Lina FIGUEIRA DE FOZ, PORTUGAL
Sotiris Liontos ATHENS
Michael Löwy PARIS
Destanne Lundquist CUMBERLAND, BC
Josie Malinowski LONDON
Lurdes Martínez MADRID
Elias Melios ATHENS
Lefki Mossou ATHENS
David Nadeau QUEBEC CITY
Sheila Nopper DENMAN ISLAND
Sharon Olson GRASS VALLEY, CALIFORNIA
Noé Ortega Quijano SANTANDER
Ayşe Özkan ISTANBUL
Pierre Petiot PARIS
Rodrigo Hernández Piceros SANTIAGO, CHILE
Hans Plomp AMSTERDAM
Antonio Ramírez SEVILLE
Jörg Remé AMSTERDAM
Ribitch BERKELEY
Wendy Risteska LONDON
José Manuel Rojo MADRID
Ron Sakolsky, DENMAN ISLAND
Ali Mete Sancaktaroğlu ISTANBUL
María Santana SEVILLE
Zuca Sardan HAMBURG, GERMANY
Pieter Schermer NETHERLANDS
Shibek PORTLAND
Lisa Simmonson BERKELEY
Nikos Stabakis ATHENS
Dan Stanciu BUCHAREST
Wijnand Steemers NETHERLANDS
Wedgwood Steventon ENGLAND
Andrew Torch ST LOUIS
Sotère Torregian STOCKTON, CALIFORNIA
Laurens Vancrevel NETHERLANDS
Bastiaan Van der Velden THE HAGUE
Sasha Vlad SAN FRANCISCO
Richard Waara VACAVILLE
Marianna Xanthopoulou ATHENS
Yannis Xourias ATHENS
Xtian MELBOURNE
Onston [Can Yeşiloğlu] IZMIR
Zazie VIENNA

Miguel de Carvalho
Livraria Alfarrabista - Adro de Baixo 6
3000 - 420 Coimbra

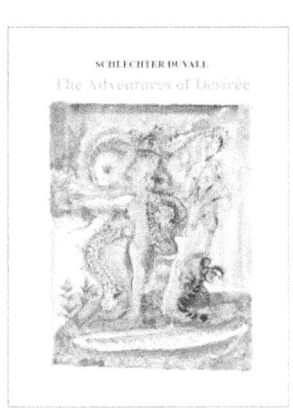

The Adventures of Desirée
by Schlechter Duvall

The Brimstone Boat
by Will Alexander

Rêve à Deux

Available in paperback & hardcover from Lulu.com

The Age of Gold (Redux)
by Sotère Torregian

" Beyond Civil Disobedience "
Illustration by Timothy R. Johnson

In preparation: Nanos Valaoritis & Marie Wilson's *Land of Diamond*

La Belle Inutile

The Spindle's Arc. J. Karl Bogartte (2014). A sequence of poetic fragments, unexpected gestures of consciousness. These notes are the "visible invisibilities" of sudden confrontations between what language can clarify and what it cannot, when the mind confronts itself through the imagination... when the imagination forms the body of many dimensions coming together at the point of no return. "And your veins filled with panther dust."

Fire works. Richard Misiano-Genovese (2010). 13 Mixed media works.

Loup-Garou: La Belle Inutile Magazine (2010). Zazie, K-J. Bogartte, J-P. Depetris, R. Misiano-Genovese, D. Hortnor, D. Boyer, J. Anderson, A. Puga, Ribitch, P. Petiot.

Performances - Dialogues. Richard Misiano-Genovese & Pierre Petiot (2010). Incursions into the human condition - English & French bilingual version.

Images du monde flottant. Francine Laugier (2009). "À l'origine, le « monde flottant » était un terme bouddhiste désignant le monde éphémère de la vie de tous les jours... La montée de ce genre nouveau coïncida avec la révolution due à l'impression et à toutes ses techniques. Initialement, les estampes étaient reproduites en noir et parfois colorées à la main."

Quelquefois nous paraissons heureux. Francine Laugier (2009). "D'une façon générale, quand on entend le verset d'un autre, ce que l'on y trouve est très différent selon ce que l'on sait ou ce que l'on ignore. Quand il entend parler du tigre, celui qui l'a eu a ses trousses en a des sueurs froides, dit-on." (Traités de poétique de Bâshô)

The Mirror held up in darkness. J. Karl Bogartte (2010). "A surrealist edition in every sense of the word, these early poems radiate with the surréalité of a midnight stroll, of a reconnaissance fueled and inspired by the spector of consciousness undergoing metamorphose, in broad daylight! Playful in a sense of wonder and exaltation, as if often grasping for just the right words; erotic in spirit, seeking the glow of sensuous experimentation and discovery; crystal clear in words that betray the mystery of a dark and mysteriously unfolding world just beneath the surface of ordinary reality..." - Arthur Koenig

L'eau dans l'eau. Pierre Petiot - Images de Zazie (2009). Quelques rêveries, pour la plupart nocturnes et d'ailleurs pour l'essentiel écrites les yeux fermés.

Luminous Weapons. J. Karl Bogartte (2010). "The third book in the trilogy of prose poems by J. Karl Bogartte, is a continuation of the obviously unnatural wedding between shadow and reflection, between the "he" and the "she" of a quietly shimmering exploration. Unsettling word-images in a landscape created by the spirit of the Anti-Oedipus. A desperate love story in a magical space of amazing conjunctions. Following in the traditions and legacies of the surrealists, this a collection of prose poems celebrating both love and conspiracy, eroticism and revolt in the ferment of a dialectical forge." - Arthur Koenig

Pour un Empirisme Poétique. Jean-Pierre Depétris (2010). Il y a des quantités de façons de voir, et certainement pas une bonne et des mauvaises. Celle-ci en est une, et elle a cette particularité d'ouvrir la porte aux autres.

Secret Games. J. Karl Bogartte (2009). Following The Wolf House, Secret Games is Book II in the ongoing series of prose poems exploring the sense of the marvelous mating of science and erotic metamorphosis as a form of landscape in which the real becomes imaginary, and forces itself into visible nature.

Entre Tangaar et Bolgobol. Jean-Pierre Depétris (2009). Pourquoi une nouvelle réforme de l'entendement humain est-elle nécessaire ? Comment distinguer les données des sens de celles de la conscience ? Pourquoi les chats aiment-ils regarder les hommes manipuler des signes ? Où va le temps qui passe ? Comment peut-on parler une langue étrangère puisqu'elle a cessé de l'être quand on sait la parler ? Pourquoi les hommes et les femmes s'inspirent-ils parfois les uns envers les autres le sentiment du péché ? Peut-on tuer la nuit ? L'auteur est-il un Cathare provençal ?   Quel est le contenu du socialisme ?

The Wolf House. J. Karl Bogartte (2009). Prose poems written every morning over the space of a year, these "dream-like notations" are further meditations on the raw nature of reality as it reforms itself every morning upon awakening from dreams.

Autour de Bolgobol. Jean-Pierre Depétris (2009). Suite du roman philosophique de Jean-Pierre Depétris sous la forme d'un journal de voyage en ligne. D'où viennent les Lumières ? Pourquoi nulle trace de travail ni de travailleurs dans une ville donne une impression d'irréalité théâtrale ? Comment le moine Gandyya reçut-il l'illumination ? Pourquoi les Gallo-romains firent-ils de leur mercenaire Clovis leur roi ? D'où viennent les idées justes ? Comment peut-on être Persan ? Pourquoi les Espagnols se prennent-ils pour des Goths ? Qu'est-ce que la loi de Snell ? Connaissons-nous le monde par les données des sens ou par les produits de l'esprit? Pourquoi la science moderne a-t-elle privilégié l'abduction sur la déduction et l'induction ? Dieu sait-il compter ?

Black Studio. Richard Misiano-Genovese (2009). A strange medicine cabinet. This studio space: once a radio station, then a Boxing ring, an apartment, a small business using computers with their reels of recording tape collecting and dispensing important information, then empty, the phantoms of the past echoing in its dim hallways and rooms.

En revenant à Bolgobol. Jean-Pierre Depétris (2008). Suite du roman philosophique de Jean-Pierre Depétris sous la forme d'un journal de voyage en ligne.

A Bolgobol. Jean-Pierre Depétris (2008). A Bolgobol est un journal de voyage édité en ligne et en temps réel en 2003, au coeur d'une curieuse Asie Centrale où la réalité scientifique, historique et géopolitique se mêle non sans humour à une imagination fantaisiste, critique et souvent poètique.

C'est aussi un étrange roman philosophique où les techniques et les principes de la programmation libre sont mis dans une perspective critique envers l'histoire des idées, des hommes et de leurs rêves les plus fertiles.

Bloodworks - 5 Cantos. Richard Misiano-Genovese (2010). "The diamond in the viscera cries out and weeps for time unleashed the folly wrought with perfidy whose covenant is broken..."

Dreamwhite. Richard Misiano-Genovese (2009). A series of images selected from a photographic odyssey spanning over four years time with the execution of hundreds of images pared down to this handful. It is a fluid, free-form experience in which the only constant was the abreaction theatre, the drama-play, the silent dialogue between photographer and model.

Excavations. Richard Misiano-Genovese (2009). "One may think at first that Misiano-Genovese invites us to the questionable pleasures of vandalism. But that is not the case. Or not that much. Because when looking closer, one reaches the evidence that what is violent and destructive in Misiano-Genovese's art always finally reverses itself into a shimmering of innocence. In the depths of his tearings, how devouring and raging they may be - and are - always the silky shadow of a dawn is passing." - P. Petiot

Masques 1985. Richard Misiano-Genovese (2009). "...Concealment, the function with which we associate their use initially, as we imagine donning a masque, yielding to another when we think of the performance of a theatrical masque, which implicate masks in something that transcends their ability to hide in the process of transforming them into agents of revelation. Neither an instrument of concealment nor an exp)licative one, a Misiano-Genovese masque is an implicative phenomenon" - JH Matthews

La Belle Inutile is the name of a group of friends located in Europe, North America and South America who share a surrealist orientation and a common taste for mixing Arts, Sciences, Technology and ideas. Pierre Petiot, Zazie, J. Karl Bogartte, Richard Misiano-Genovese, Jean-Pierre Depetris, Francine Laugier.

Their collective *La Belle Inutile Éditions* makes surrealist use of Print On Demand, utilizing the services of Lulu.com for their many publications.

http://www.labelleinutile.org - http://labelinutile.free.fr

Latest Publications by the
MADRID SURREALIST GROUP

Las mercancías mueren, las cosas despiertan
Jornadas sobre el objeto cuando todo se viene abajo
(La Torre Magnética, Madrid, 2013)

Enchanted by Economy, the objects sleep. Only desire and imagination can wake them up. This book presents what happened during the event about the object entitled "Merchandise die, things wake up", held in the liberated lot of the Assembly of Lavapiés in Madrid on 11-13th April 2014. These talks where organized with the aim of bringing to the public space a debate about several relevant issues regarding our relationship with objects, and with the desire of enabling a collective experience capable of liberating them as well as ourselves in the context of an industrial society that we hope will soon collapse. Other objects for other life.

Hechizados por la Economía, los objetos duermen. Sólo el deseo y la imaginación pueden convocarles. Este libro recoge lo acontecido en el marco de las jornadas del mismo nombre que tuvieron lugar los días 11, 12 y 13 de abril de 2013 en el solar liberado de la Asamblea de Lavapiés. Estas jornadas se organizaron con la intención de llevar al espacio público ciertas cuestiones que nos parecen candentes acerca de nuestra relación con los objetos en el contexto de una sociedad industrial que esperamos esté cercana a su colapso, y con el deseo de favorecer una experiencia colectiva capaz de contribuir a su liberación a la vez que a la nuestra propia. Otros objetos para otra vida.

El Rapto #7
Observatorio del sonambulismo contemporáneo
(Madrid, 2012)

This new issue of El Rapto is a special edition devoted not merely to the incidents and processes generated by the so-called 15-M movement, but to the much broader and deep movement of resistance, opposition and (who knows) worldwide revolutionary insurgence of what the 15-M movement is just another symptom and element. A complete and varied sample of pamphlets, leaflets, statements, critics, actions, positioning and analysis generated by the 15-M revolt among several collectives has been gathered in this 16 pages. This issue has remarkably been conceived from a radical point of view opposed both to the naïve reformist aspirations of 'good citizens' and to the apathy and systematic and pessimistic distrust of the defeatists. Moreover, the texts are accompanied by much other news from elsewhere, from Greece to London, from Oakland to Egypt. Generalized subversion has just started, or at least that is what this Rapto and the people who edit it deeply wish.

Este nuevo número de El Rapto es una edición especial dedicado no tanto a los acontecimientos y los procesos generados por el llamado 15-M, sino al movimiento mucho más amplio y mucho más profundo de resistencia, contestación y (quién sabe) insurgencia revolucionaria mundial del que el 15-M es sólo un síntoma y un elemento más. En sus 16 páginas se ha reunido un completo y variado muestrario de los panfletos, octavillas, declaraciones, manifiestos, críticas, acciones, tomas de postura y análisis que generó la revuelta del 15-M entre distintos colectivos, siempre desde una óptica radical que rechaza y desea ir más allá tanto de las ingenuas aspiraciones reformistas de los ciudadanistas, como de la apatía y la desconfianza sistemáticas y desencantadas del derrotismo ilustrado. Por otro lado, estos textos se acompañan y se integran en esas noticias de la otra parte de la subversión generalizada, de Grecia a Londres, de Oakland a Egipto, que no han hecho más que empezar. O eso al menos deseamos, y eso es lo que pretende este Rapto y quienes lo editan.

Exteriority crisis
Crisis de la exterioridad
Crítica del encierro industrial y elogio de las afueras
(Enclave de Libros, Madrid, 2012)

This book develops two complementary aspects: a clarifying analysis of what we mean by exteriority crisis, and an experimentation of the potential of exteriority for reenchanting our life. We believe and our modest experiences confirm that, even if exteriority is put under a hard siege by the industrial society and its extreme technologization, it is one of the most promising resources for our sensible renovation, as well as one of the most relevant poetic reserves.

Las páginas que siguen articulan dos ejes fundamentales: un ejercicio de desbroce y análisis de lo que hemos denominado crisis de la exterioridad, y una experimentación de la potencialidad de la exterioridad para el reencantamiento del mundo. Creemos, y nuestros humildes experimentos nos lo confirman, que, a pesar del asedio al que se ve sometida la exterioridad por la tecnologización paroxística de la sociedad industrial, reside en ella una de las mayores promesas de renovación sensible del hombre, y también una de sus más importantes reservas poéticas.

Salamandra # 21-22
(Madrid, 2014)

The new issue of Salamandra, the journal of the Madrid Surrealist Group since 1987, is about to be published. This new edition of more than 300 pages will include two special areas of focus. The first one is "Critics and oniro-critics of the city", which includes texts that develop critical and poetical approaches to different aspects of nowadays cities, from revolt movements to the neighborhood unconscious, from conurbations and atoposes to the oneiric experience of cities. The second area of focus is "About the poetic materialism", which gathers complementary approximations to what we call poetic materialism, covering aspects like its role after capitalist collapse as a reenchantment enabler, its opposition to virtual experience, its role in our existence, and poetic materialism versus the scientific method. Additionally, this Salamandra presents a selection of surrealist games developed by several Surrealist Groups around the globe. This issue includes the usual sections of "Laboratory of the imaginary", "More reality", and poems, as well as many texts and contributions about a wide number of topics.

El nuevo número de Salamandra, la revista del Grupo Surrealista de Madrid desde 1987, está a punto de publicarse. Esta nueva edición de más de 300 páginas incluirá dos bloques principales especiales. El primero es "Crítica y oniro-crítica de la ciudad", que incluye textos que desarrollan diferentes aproximaciones críticas y poéticas a diversos aspectos de las ciudades actuales, desde los movimientos de revuelta al inconsciente del barrio, de las conurbaciones y los atoposes a la experiencia onírica de las ciudades. El segundo bloque principal es "Acerca del materialismo poético", que reúne aproximaciones complementarias a lo que llamamos materialismo poético, tratando aspectos como su importancia para el reencantamiento tras el colapso del capitalismo, su oposición a la existencia virtual, su papel en nuestra existencia, y materialismo poético frente a método científico. Además, esta Salamandra presenta una selección de juegos surrealistas desarrollados por varios grupos de todo el mundo. Este número incluye las secciones habituales de "Laboratorio de lo imaginario", "¡Más realidad!", y poemas, así como numerosos textos y contribuciones adicionales sobre una gran variedad de temas.

All these publications are in Spanish and can be ordered through the website *www.gruposurrealistademadrid.org*
or directly by contacting *gruposurrealistademadrid@hotmail.com*.

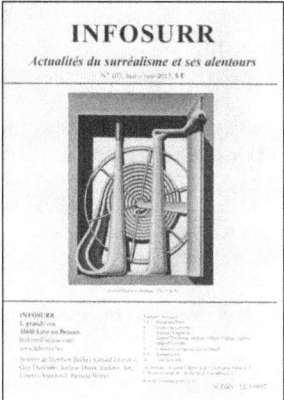

The journal INFOSURR is published 6 times a year (in French). It collects and disseminates news and information about Surrealism. It is also a forum for voicing opinions. Eight pages will report on recent publications and exhibitions relating to Surrealism and its neighboring zones. A network of international correspondents collects data on all surrealist events: visual arts, literature, criticism, the media, politics, polemics, daily life, etc...

Contact: Richard Walter, Infosurr; 1, Grande rue; F-45410 Lion-en-Beauce, France; bulletin@infosurr.net.

What will be

**Almanac of the
International Surrealist Movement
for 2014**

*

**One hundred seventy three
contributors
from twenty-five countries:**

AUSTRALIA
ARGENTINA
BASQUE COUNTRY
BELGIUM
BRAZIL
CANADA
CHILE
COLOMBIA
CUBA
CZECHIA
ENGLAND
FRANCE
FRIESLAND
GERMANY
GREECE
HOLLAND
INDONESIA
ITALY
MEXICO
PORTUGAL
RUMANIA
SLOVAKIA
SOUTH AFRICA
SPAIN
SWEDEN
UNITED STATES OF AMERICA
WALES

*

**BRUMES BLONDES
Special anniversary edition
1964 - 2014**

Contact: *krevelen@xs4all.nl*

Miguel Corrales - *Surrealism: The Gold of Time*

- a review of the evolution of the international surrealist movement 2005-2014 in about 200 essays (in Spanish).

Published by La Página Ediciones, Tenerife/Madrid, Spain, 616 pages; 2014.

See also: www.surrint.blogspot.com.es.

Dan Stanciu - *Despre*

The latest book by the Romanian poet and visual artist Dan Stanciu. Original title: Despre (About, in English). The 122-page book contains prose-poems in Romanian.

Published in September 2014 by Herg Benet Publishers, in Bucharest, Romania.

For orders, contact: vanzari@hergbenet.ro

The Oystercatcher

Contact:
MRon Sakolsky
A-4062 Wren Road
Denman Island, BC
V0R1T0   CANADA
oystercatcher@uniserve.com

No price/send a coupla bucks for mailing costs and more if you can afford to do so.

OYSTER MOON PRESS

Mirach Speaks to His Grammatical Transparents, by Will Alexander (2011). A philosophical meditation vertically scripted. It is an extension of Alexander's first book in this mode, Towards The Primeval Lightning Field. Both books in concert, exist as a double exploration, in what, for the author, is a nascent odyssey, concerning the mind at non-limit through cellular transmogrification. 152 pages.

Carnival of Sleep, by Ribitch (2011). Between dream and hallucination, *Carnival of Sleep* opens its tent for the unwary somnambulist. Ribitch's prose and poetry are sometimes dark and humorous, sometimes sublime lamentations of erotic beauty and deeply surrealist in storytelling. They are like ruptured blood vessels, gushing forth a spray of blood droplets, each bearing a different face. Illustrations by the Author. 180 pages.

West of Pure Evil, by Josie Malinowski (2010). The labyrinthine, mercurial worlds of Josie Malinowski's *West of Pure Evil* represent a divorce between rhyme and reason, spinning off-key tales of love and pain. Sailors and whores unite to solve ancient, despicable mysteries; an act of aid brings a Fairy Kingdom to its knees; and the tragic Captain Cock is left cold and stiff by a scheming eight-year-old. These myriad poems and stories illuminate the crossover between waking and dreaming, and thereby cast an intimate, surrealist glance at the human condition. 204 pages.

Hydrolith: Surrealist Research & Investigations (2009). Hydrolith brings together in one volume some of the most exciting recent work from the international surrealist movement. With over 80 contributors from 17 countries around the world, the book contains drawings, paintings, games, comics, photographs, poetry, prose, theoretical and political writings on a huge variety of subjects, including special in-depth investigations of music, space and myth. The book is a must-read for anyone interested in the surrealist movement today. 240 pages.

The Exteriority Crisis (2008). In its corners, streets, gates, bars, squares, boulevards, gardens, parks and cafés, the city maintains some of the focal points of "its" unconscious. These are found and explored everyday by surrealists who obtain the essential experience of surreality in metropolitan life. The concrete experience of exteriority (which in the following collective essay we concentrate only on the city limits and beyond them) requires from us a disposition closely akin not only to the sensible renewal of people, but also to existence and its poetic reserves, and to the revitalization of the interior life that is suffering a process of sterilization because of the convulsive technologization of interiority and the progressive forgetting of life outside. 184 pages.

The Somnambulist Footprints (2008). The result of a collective project in which several contemporary surrealists and fellow travelers wrote short stories according to their own interests and imperatives, based on their common desire to subvert the very foundations of conventional reality, both on the written page and – more importantly – beyond it, in the open space of consciousness. Contributing authors: Mariela Arzadun, J. Karl Bogartte, Daniel Boyer, Eric W. Bragg, Mattias Forshage, Parry Harnden, Dale Michael Houstman, Philip Kane, Merl, Ribitch, Matthew Rounsville, Shibek, Andrew Torch, and Xtian. 216 pages.

The Midnight Blade of Sonic Honey (2008). The pairing of a surrealist novel and an automatic text by Eric W. Bragg (www.surrealcoconut.com), that were written nearly seven years apart but which tell the same story, albeit as complementary permutations of each other. Dripping with bile and centered within a gothic sensibility, this journey opens the reader's skull like a freshly cracked coconut. With illustrations by Ribitch (www.ribitch.net). 236 pages.

Oyster Moon Press is a non-profit, surrealist publishing co-op located in Berkeley, California.

If you're after individual copies, you can find our titles online at places like Lulu, Amazon, Barnes & Noble, and Borders.

If you are a bookstore, then you can make bulk orders through our distributor, Small Press Distribution (SPD) books.

www.oystermoonpress.com